BETTER BETTING
WITH A DECENT FELLER

To Dad and Grandad Chinn who laid 'em, and to Grandad Perry and Grandad Wood who backed 'em.

BETTER BETTING WITH A DECENT FELLER

A SOCIAL HISTORY OF BOOKMAKING

CARL CHINN

AURUM PRESS

This revised and enlarged edition first published in Great Britain 2004 by
Aurum Press Ltd, 25 Bedford Avenue, London WC1B 3AT

Originally published in Great Britain 1991 by Harvester Wheatsheaf, a division of Simon & Schuster International Group

A catalogue record for this book is available from the British Library.

ISBN 1 84513 009 X

10 9 8 7 6 5 4 3 2 1
2008 2007 2006 2005 2004

Designed and typeset in Sabon and Gill Sans by M Rules
Printed and bound in Great Britain by MPG Books Ltd, Bodmin

CONTENTS

LIST OF ILLUSTRATIONS

PAGE 1

Top left: An illustration from the *Betting Post* in the late 1700s by Rowlandson, showing the Prince Regent on the left and the blackleg Colonel O'Kelly on the right; from Ralph Neville, *Light Come, Light Go* (London: Macmillan & Co., 1909).

Centre left: An etching from 1863, entitled *Victoria Street, E. C. – Betting-Men Making Up Their Books for the St. Leger*. Victoria Street later became Farringdon Street. Thanks to Islington Libraries, Finsbury.

Top right: George Langham, a leading member of the Derby Sabini gang, but also a highly respected figure on England's racecourses, aged about thirty, just after the First World War. Born in 1888, George was also a top boxer who fought Charles Le Deux in France for the European Flyweight Championship. Thanks to Dave Langham.

Bottom left: Mr Guy, counting his money in the centre, and his children Percy and Gertie at Birmingham Racecourse in 1923. Thanks to the Guy family.

Bottom right: A race-ticket belonging to Sydney Lewis, a Jewish racecourse bookie whose family suffered from the bullying of the Brummagem Boys.

PAGE 2

Top: Alfie Bottrell, known as Bottle, betting as 'Joe White, The Silver King', on an English racecourse *c*. 1924. Like many racecourse bookies after the First World War, Alf dressed up in uniform – in his case in a midshipman's uniform. Alf made his first book when he was seventeen at Wolverhampton Racecourse in 1902 and was still laying them into his eighties. Wounded on active service in the First World War, he raised thousands of pounds for hospitals and other good causes and in the 1970s was named Bookmaker of the Year. Thanks to Horace Bottrell.

Bottom left: Rose Pickering took bets at her fish and chip shop at 28 Darwin Street, Highgate, Birmingham, in the late 1930s. Next door at number 29 (left) was Ingram's the butcher, who put double doors (on the right of the photo) at the entry to their shared yard. Rose's runner took bets through a door in the gates. Thanks to Sylvia Leigh.

Bottom right: The bookie's rulebook of Dick Seymour (1930s). Thanks to the Seymour and Story Group.

PAGE 3

Top left & right: Cartoons published in *Punch* and the *Daily Mail* in the 1920s, depicting bookmakers as greedy and grasping. *Left*: © Punch, Ltd. *Right*: © Tom Webster, courtesy Solo Syndication/Centre for the Study of Cartoons and Caricature, University of Kent.

Bottom left & right: *Banyan* was the publication of the National Association of Bookmakers. In the 1930s it included a number of hard-hitting and powerful cartoons in defence of racecourse and street bookmakers. Thanks to the National Association of Bookmakers.

PAGE 4

Top: A coach trip for the youngsters of Footdee, Aberdeen, in the late 1930s, paid for by the local bookie, Jim Forbes. Thanks to Ronald Forbes.

Centre: A trip from the Old Horseshoe pub in Mexborough, South Yorkshire, to Scarborough in 1937, paid for by the local bookie, Mr C. Woodhead (*second row, second from right*). Thanks to Vinny Grant (*front row, right*).

Bottom left: A receipt for a fine for street betting incurred by George Brown of Sunderland, 13 June 1935. Thanks to George Brown.

Bottom right: A National Anti-Gambling League poster from the 1930s.

PAGE 5

Top left: Horace Bottrell, in the bowler hat, taking bets on an English racecourse after the Second World War. Bert Kirby is seated on the right. Bert and his brothers were from a very tough family in Summer Lane and were noted as boxers. Jim Davis, who was to become a well-known Birmingham racecourse bookmaker, is wearing a mac, to the left of Horace. Thanks to Horace Bottrell.

Top right: Bert Harris setting up his stall on race day. Thanks to his wife, Cecelia Harris.

Bottom: A jump meeting in the 1950s: a wonderful action shot which also shows the lines of bookmakers beneath the embankment. Thanks to Cecelia Harris.

PAGE 6

Top left: Billy Newbold (*back row, second from left*), the bookie in Hick Street, Birmingham, at a local boys' football club outing he paid for in the early 1950s. Thanks to the late Trevor Newbold.

Top right: Henry Ford checking the bets at his Leicester home, *c*. 1953–55. Thanks to the Ford and Kimberley families.

Bottom: Matt O'Malley (*centre*) writing out a line (bet) in the back court off a Glasgow street, where he took bets as an illegal bookie in the early 1950s. Behind Matt, copies of the *Sporting Chronicle* for the use of punters are stuck behind the drainpipe, and a punter wearing a flat cap is on the left. Thanks to Matt O'Malley.

PAGE 7

Top: The illegal betting shop of Bert Jenkins (*second row, sixth from right*) in Fallin, Stirling, *c*. 1958. Thanks to Bert Jenkins.

Centre: The summons for my Dad, Alfred Chinn, to appear before the magistrates for operating a betting office on 28, 29 and 31 July 1958, contrary to the Betting Act of 1853.

Bottom: The exterior of my Grandad's illegal betting shop in Sparkbrook, Birmingham, just before legalization. The business was in the name of my Grandad, Alf, and his younger brother, Wal, but Alf was also my Dad's proper name and his older brother was another Wal. This was an illegal betting shop, but like so many similar operations, it advertised a phone number to give the illusion that it only took phone bets, which it was legal to do. These premises had formerly been an off-licence.

PAGE 8

Top left & right: Pat Wilson's betting shop in Bright Street, Birmingham, in the late 1950s (*left*) and in 1962 (*right*), before and after legalization. The man outside in the left-hand picture is probably Bill Wilkes, Pat's runner, who would take bets on the front doorstep. He always wore a camel coat, a buttonhole and a flat cap. Pat was recalled by Ken Probyn as a man who was 'always very generous to the kids, particularly at the time of the 1935 Jubilee and the 1937 Coronation'. Like so many betting shops, this was simply the front room of a house.

Centre: The betting-office licence for James Jennings of 92 Stoney Lane, Sparkbrook, 22 March 1961. My Dad later bought this shop and I worked there on and off for many years from when I was about fourteen. Of course, it was against the law to work in a betting shop until you were twenty-one, but no one took any notice. Upstairs there was a flat, while downstairs the old front room was the betting shop. It included a toilet and on the left-hand wall was pinned up the sheet of runners. The old back room was divided from the betting shop by a partition, just above waist height, and behind which was the counter across which we took the bets. There was a door on the right through which you went into the office part of the premises. Behind the counter was a table where the manager settled the bets. Alongside the counter were pigeonholes into which winning bets were placed and another set of pigeonholes where the losing bets were placed. We used to put the bets in alphabetical order according to the *nom-de-plume* of the punter. The toilet for the counter clerks and the settler was in the backyard.

Bottom: A cartoon by Archie Exton of Smethwick, depicting the 1960 case in which local magistrate Arthur Smith refused to sit in judgement against street bookmakers because on the previous day he had betted on the Derby with an illegal bookie. Thanks to Archie Exton and the Smethwick Local History Society.

ACKNOWLEDGEMENTS

I could not have written this book if I had not been a bookmaker, so thanks are due to my Grandad Chinn and to my Dad, Buck Chinn, for following an occupation which has provided me with so fertile a field to study. However, I would not have written this book if academic friends had not encouraged me to do so. In particular, I should like to thank Dorothy Thompson, who was a constant source of encouragement to me in the 1980s, years in which I struggled to become a historian; Harvey Kaye of the University of Wisconsin-Green Bay, who pestered and cajoled me until I began my research into the social history of bookmaking; and John Bourne, who read and commented on various drafts of the book before it was first published in 1991. They may disagree with some of my arguments, but they have the consolation of knowing that without their support we would have had nothing to disagree about.

When writing a book, an author incurs many debts – some tangible but many intangible. In my case, the latter are owed to my family. When I researched and wrote this book it was very difficult for younger historians to follow their calling, and without the help and loyalty of my family I would have abandoned my chosen career. I am grateful to all of them, especially to my wife Kay, and to our children, Richard, Tara, Catríona and Rochelle; they have all inspired me and waited patiently till I got a 'proper job'; to my Mom and Dad, who always have backed me; and to 'our kid', Darryl, whose small stationery business subsidized my writing when I was out of work or in part-time employment.

My tangible debts range more widely. This book is based firmly on primary material and literally hundreds of people have assisted me in assembling it. If I were to list so many names here, then their individual contributions to this book would be obscured. Instead, their invaluable help will become apparent when readers examine my references. However, collectively I would like to place on record my gratitude to the following: the 161 local studies librarians, reference librarians and archivists throughout Great Britain and Ireland who scoured their holdings and sent me so much information which I could never have found myself; the thirty-eight librarians who searched their records but who discovered no material relevant to my study; and, for processing so many requests so cheerfully and promptly, the staff of inter-library loans at the University of Birmingham and the British Library.

I wish also to place on record my gratitude to the editors of the forty-two local newspapers from Aberdeen to Exeter who published my letter appealing for their readers to write to me about illegal betting, and the 400-odd people who replied to that letter, thus providing me with a priceless source. In the notes after each chapter 'Chinn Letters' refers to the written material of these people. If a person wrote more than one letter to me, then this is indicated in the notes. Additionally, my thanks are due to the 120 people who allowed me to interview them and to record their memories, thereby giving me so much marvellous material. These interviews were carried out by me between 1987 and 1989. The interviewees were varied in backgrounds: many were bookies; some were ex-runners; and others were punters or former policemen. They were chosen via my contacts in bookmaking and through my appeal for information about illegal betting. In the notes after each chapter, 'Chinn Interviews' denotes this oral evidence. Both my oral and letter evidence is deposited in the Heslop Room, the Main Library, the University of Birmingham. Here it is available for the research of other scholars, who should write to the Librarian for access to it. The interviews and letters are to be indexed, as they not only include much material about illegal betting, but also a good deal of information about working-class life in general.

I must also acknowledge the financial support of the Twenty-Seven Foundation, whose grant paid my travelling costs to the British Library; the National Association of Bookmakers, without whose generous support I would not have been able to go to Scotland and the North of England so as to interview people; and the Nuffield Foundation, whose welcome grant facilitated the transcription of my oral evidence. Indeed, perhaps my biggest debt is owed to Barbara Bourne and Sandra Chinn, who carried out this painstaking task. I extend my deepest appreciation to them, to everyone who has helped me, and to all those who showed me courtesy and hospitality on my travels.

Last but no means least, I would like to thank Aurum Press for republishing this book and allowing me to write a new final chapter to bring matters up to date. In particular I appreciate the interest and support of Karen Ings, the Commissioning Editor, who was one of my first students when I began teaching in the Department of Modern History at the University of Birmingham in the early 1990s. *Better Betting* took up a large part of my life, and that of my family, between 1989 and 1991 and it is a thrill for me to have it in print once again.

FOREWORD

My mother wasn't best pleased when, straight from school and at the expense of what she had hoped would be a productive spell at university, I took up journalism. A few years later, she was even more miffed when I began working for a bookmaker. 'From disreputable hack to unscrupulous bookie' was the gist of her complaint. 'All you need to do now is become an estate agent and you've completed the unholy trinity.'

Having now both bought and sold properties, I know that the last leg of my Mum's nightmare career treble will remain incomplete. But I am proud to retain the tag 'journalist' on my passport and to still work for a bookie – the same one; well, the same name anyway – thirty years and more down the line. Mum's still disappointed that I wasted my talents, but my role in bookmaking has become sufficiently high-profile over the decades to enable me to disappoint many more people along the way, mostly for not permitting them to get away with blackening the name of bookies in general and William Hill in particular – and also, oddly, for not being Ginger McCain.

The latter incident occurred in June 2004, when I was prevailed upon by the National Horseracing Museum in Newmarket to perform the official opening of their exhibitions about Red Rum and betting. McCain, the trainer of the triple Grand National winner, was of course the original choice to do the honours, but he was jocked off at the last moment for some reason and I was called in at short notice with a hugely flattering appeal from museum bigwig Hilary Bracegirdle: 'You're the only person coming with any profile at all in racing or betting, so will you do it?' I was honoured to be asked and duly obliged, particularly as the exhibition marked, to my eyes at least, a significant step forward in the ongoing campaign to secure for the bookmaking business the seldom-granted respect to which it is entitled.

Despite what some of the thoroughbred snobs of the racing world may believe, bookmaking and racing are indubitably and inextricably twinned, and together reportedly rate as one of Britain's six largest industries. I have invested what little reputation I have ever had and pretty much my whole working life in an effort to remove the stigma which for so long, and so undeservedly, has hung over betting and bookmaking like a glowering, storm-filled cloud. And the change in attitudes between 1971, when I began the task, and today is startling. Betting shops had only been legal for a decade back then and only the most thick-skinned of individuals would be happy to be seen crossing the threshold of one. And when he – almost invariably in those days it was he, unless a 'she' was working in the shop – did, it was to encounter the most spartan of environments, courtesy of the rigid laws of the day.

Fortunately, we live in more enlightened times now, when betting shops are fit to measure themselves against any other well-established component of the high street; when they boast some of the most technologically advanced websites on the internet; when they still offer efficient, speedy, state-of-the-art telephone betting facilities and have finally moved their racecourse presence – possibly in some cases kicking and screaming – into a suitably twenty-first-century incarnation, while retaining echoes of their proud(ish) eighteenth-century origins.

No longer is there a stigma attached to having a bet – whether it be on the 2.30 at Sandown, the FA Cup final, Wimbledon – or the outcome of the latest *Big Brother* or *I'm A Celebrity Get Me Out Of Here* reality TV show.

There have been few allies in evidence along the way as I have battled to persuade the media, and thereby public opinion, that bookies are decent chaps – but one of them has been Carl Chinn, a man for whom the battle on behalf of bookies has been personal. Because he is from a three-generation family of bookmakers and has therefore experienced what it means to be a bookie literally at the sharp, vulnerable, business end. I am only too pleased to be able to endorse this latest edition of what is a most comprehensive, readable and downright entertaining study and story of the social role of bookmaking over the course of four different centuries, taking in along the way its history and influence on society.

Carl Chinn will go down in bookmaking lore as a figure as significant as William Ogden, frequently dubbed the first true bookie; John Banks, who associated betting shops with the phrase 'a licence to print money'; Barry 'Bismarck' Dennis, who is the most recognizable contemporary layer in the land; and, yes, John 'Big Mac' McCririck, guardian of the bookmaker's own, endangered, sign language, tic-tac, and a self-confessed failure as a bookie.

These and many other characters populate the hugely colourful, intriguing and unique back pages of a business which for too many years was a closed book to all but its exponents, but now, thanks to the resourceful and indefatigable efforts of Professor Chinn, is accessible to everyone who has ever fancied a flutter, or, like me, disappointed his – or, increasingly these days, her – mum.

Graham Sharpe, Media Relations Director, William Hill
August 2004

PREFACE

In 1922, my Grandad Chinn knowingly defied the law by becoming a street bookmaker in Studley Street, Sparkbrook, in Birmingham. He continued to flout Parliament's edicts until the early 1950s, by which time my Dad was running the outlawed business. Our family felt no shame at its involvement in an activity which the state had decreed was unlawful but which millions of working-class people felt was legitimate. Indeed, while it is a family joke that Dad cannot emigrate to Australia because he is an undesirable – having been convicted in 1958 of running an illegal betting house – we would be insulted if outsiders accused us of past involvement in criminal activity. It is true that Grandad and Dad had broken the law, but in our eyes they were not lawbreakers. This thinking might seem paradoxical to some, but to us and many others it was self-evident. Unfortunately for us, it was not so obvious to everyone; some people actually thought that Dad and Grandad had been criminals.

My first awareness of this fundamental difference of opinion came when I was a child of eight or nine, just three or four years after the legalization of betting shops – and my Dad's business – in 1961. I was exchanging light-hearted banter with a girl in the school playground but, as so often happens, our gentle mockery degenerated into hurling barbs at each other. Unkind remarks drew blood on both sides, but for me the most wounding comment occurred when the girl slandered my Dad as a thief. I remember looking at her, scandalized, and then asking her what she meant. She replied that her father had said that my Dad was a bookie and that bookies took other people's money. In her childhood innocence, by using the word thief, she had given voice to her father's true estimation of my Dad's job. I remember my outrage at her reasoning, and I recall that in my anger I pushed her hard. In the longer term, I believe the event was one of a number which made me aware of my class loyalty. The girl's father was a middle-class professional, and while economically and residentially we too might have been regarded as middle-class, in fact we were not. Culturally and occupationally we were working-class, and I soon realized that Mom and Dad were proud to be so.

Since that childhood wrangle, I have realized that it symbolized a clash of views between two opposing interpretations of life. On the one hand was a basically working-class attitude which tended to judge people in a down-to-earth way: what kind of person were they; in what ways did they contribute to their community; were they good fun; were they thoughtful and generous; were they good pals and neighbours? On the other hand was a largely middle-class explanation which often categorized people in a more materialistic sense. According to this code, a person's morality and respectability – or lack of them – could be deduced from his or her job or residence. This discordance between two conflicting value systems, between two divergent attitudes to life, is at the heart of this book. In it I seek to examine the importance of betting to the British working class; the way betting was carried on; the position and significance of bookmakers, especially street bookies, within working-class life; and finally, how these topics related to the law and to the opinions of many upper- and middle-class people. In the process, I hope to show the independent nature of working-class communities in industrial Britain, their vitality, and their strength of communal feeling.

I have written the book with passion. After all, I am the son and grandson of bookmakers and I was a bookmaker myself. I would be a fraudster if I pretended that my background had not influenced the writing of this study. Of course it has. However, I am not an apologist for bookmakers; like any other section of the community they have their good and bad points and I have indicated both. What I have tried to do in this book is to explore and explain that deep-rooted dissension between two lifestyles. I have sought to understand why so many working-class people protected bookmakers and regarded them as integral members of their communities. At the same time I have striven to recognize why other working-class people and most of the middle class abhorred them. I see no purpose in attempting to reconcile these contrary outlooks; they are irreconcilable. The same bookmaker who was respected by many was loathed by others, and it would be blatant partisanship if I attempted to prove that only the former were right. They were both correct according to their cultural loyalty. I believe it more significant to discover why this should be so, although, of course, my personal sympathy is with those who see bookmakers in a more positive light.

While this study is a social history of bookmaking, I believe that it relevant to life today. Betting shops have been legal for over forty years and they are familiar sights in high streets across Britain. All the big bookmaking businesses are part of huge public companies and betting takes place on most events – from horse-racing to general elections, from dog-racing to the likelihood of snow falling on Christmas Day. Yet old prejudices die hard and slowly. A stigma attaches itself still to bookmaking, and for many people bookmakers remain a faintly disreputable and slightly shady lot.

The media have played an important role in maintaining these attitudes. In particular, writers for television have emphasized the negative stance towards bookmakers, often ignoring any alternative sentiment. Regularly bookmakers are depicted as seedy, unsavoury characters whose sole interest is in taking money from other people. This point was illustrated and given credence in 1984 by the miserly, miserable and scruffy bookmaker in the popular series *Big Deal*. Still, while frowzy and tight-fisted, he was honest, a trait seen as lacking in many other screen bookies.[1] In an episode of *Wings* in 1988 an objectionable character was described as 'having the morality of a bookie's runner', while in *Bergerac* in 1990 viewers were alerted to the dishonest nature of a racecourse bookmaker by his name: Eddie Neptune. Sure enough, he was crooked, paying out winning clients with dud five-pound notes.[2]

Not only are bookmakers usually portrayed as grubby and dishonest, they are often shown as villainous and violent. In *The Paradise Club* in 1989 a gangster-like Liverpool bookie demonstrated his vileness by threatening the priest who owed him money; and in *Chancer* in 1990 a father was ruined physically, emotionally and morally by a blood-sucking female bookmaker who employed heavies to enforce payment from punters who had lost everything.[3] More recently, in 2003 and 2004, in both *EastEnders* and *Coronation Street* the local off-course bookmakers have been represented as the most repugnant of personalities. In the northern soap, Peter Barlow was an unfaithful, deceitful and lying man. He had to sell his betting shop when he was forced to flee the street after betraying his partner, Shelley, and his general treachery became public knowledge. In *EastEnders*, the bookie, Andy, is an even more repulsive person. A ruthless gangster, he has no compunction at blackmailing his neighbours and is swift to authorize thuggery against those who have crossed him. Sharply dressed, as was Peter Barlow, still he is malicious, perfidious, cruel and unforgiving.

So often are bookies portrayed as low, despicable and rascally that it is unsurprising that such judgements on them have become popular and accepted as truthful. At the core of these anti-bookmaker feelings lies the conviction that bookmakers are callous and hard-hearted. This impression was epitomized in 1987 by the succinct comment of Kieran Prenderville when describing to Radio 4 listeners a photograph of a group of Dr Barnardo's children. He proclaimed the condition of the orphans as so heartwrenching that 'it would melt the heart of a bookie'.[4] The belief that bookmakers are odious has a long lineage, but so too does the assertion that they are honourable and generous. However, this opinion has made but little impact on the media, which seems to prefer the deprecatory figure of the bookmaker to one that is more praiseworthy. Scottish Television's *Bookie* (1988) has been perhaps the only series that successfully drew on the positive aspects of bookmakers. In it, a back-street Glaswegian bookie was represented as a local boy made good. Though a little flash and a bit of a Jack-the-Lad, he was popular with his punters; and while he was comfortably off, he remained loyal to working-class values.[5]

The tension remains taut between those who decry bookmakers and those who accept them. While it would be futile to expect either side to accept the viewpoint of the other, I hope that this book will indicate to both the roots of their disagreement. For while the two traditions of thought towards bookmakers can be traced deep into the nineteenth century, they embody emotions which remain strong today and which reflect class divisions still powerful in modern Britain.

This vital issue of class looms large in two major works on gambling written since *Better Betting* was first published. In 1992 Mark Clapson brought out *A Bit of a flutter. Popular gambling and English society* c. *1823–1961*. His work covers street betting between 1906 and 1961 and horse-racing and on-course betting between *circa* 1839 and 1960, but additionally it examines aspects of gambling not addressed fully in *Better Betting*. These include gambling on birds, bowls, cards and coursing, while Clapson also looks in detail at football-coupon betting, dog-racing, lotteries and the premium bonds. The whole work is embedded within the contexts of gambling, culture and economy in England, and the social evolution of the English working class. Clapson argues successfully that for the great majority of punters, gambling was 'a moderate, economistic and expressive form of recreation' that could be perceived and used as a form of self-help. In an unequal society 'most people had a good idea of the odds facing them, and of how the dice were loaded, and they spent their time and money as best they could'. For such people, their regular and moderate betting was part of a continually evolving culture in which leisure and economy were fundamental to their lives.[6] Consequently, this general moderation in betting and gambling slowly but surely undermined attempts to marginalize popular gambling and meant that the authorities came to accept it as having a legitimate place in the family and national economy.

Five years after Clapson's wide-ranging work came Roger Munting's *An economic and social history of gambling in Britain and the USA* (1996). A much-needed and thoughtful comparative history of gambling in the two countries over a two-hundred-year period up to the mid-1990s, it does attend to betting and bookmakers, but it has two main thrusts. First, to analyse the changes in the social and economic positions of gambling activities and businesses – from an environment of hostility in the nineteenth century to overt expansion in modern times. And second, to consider the development of gambling media in the economy of both Britain and the USA. In itself, this latter approach leads to an investigation of government and lotteries, the Tote and *pari-mutuel*, gaming, the taxation of gambling, the volume of gambling, and social problems associated with gambling. Importantly, Munting makes it plain that over the last thirty years or so, there has been an upsurge in public tolerance and exploitation of gambling. This means that gambling 'has become a regular and well-publicized recreation, provided by big business organizations, taxed by governments'.[7]

My own family moved out of bookmaking in August 1984, at a time when many of the old-established back-street bookies like us were disappearing under the pressure of taxation, social change, recession, and competition from big firms. As someone who is not a punter, since then I have only stepped into a betting shop on two or three occasions. In particular, it has been a salutary and interesting experience to walk into a modern betting shop as part of my research for a new concluding chapter, which concentrates on the changes highlighted by Munting. I am struck most by two things: the physical transformation in betting shops; and the positive spin now put on the language of betting and gambling because of rapidly changing official attitudes. When we were bookmakers, betting-shop windows had to be covered in some way so that non-betting folk could not look inside and be tempted to bet. Inside, betting shops were unattractive, dark and enveloped in clouds of smoke from cigarettes, despite the fans. Bookies were not allowed to make their premises bright and breezy for fear that punters would stay inside them and bet all day long.

Now betting shops have see-through windows emblazoned with advertising urging people to enter and bet, while bookmakers are allowed to sell tea and coffee, thereby encouraging punters to remain within their premises and spend more money. And if that were not enough, bookies are able to provide gaming machines, which have become a major source of profit. At the same time, because of the government's promotion of the National Lottery, gambling is now pushed as a game not as a gamble, while gamblers are no more – instead, they have become players. The use of popular and positive words like game and player represents a remarkable and powerful shift away from negative governmental attitudes towards betting and gambling. No more are they evils to be actively discouraged, fought against and eradicated; instead they have become something that all citizens should take part in because gambling fills the coffers of grant-giving bodies that can distribute some of the money to worthy causes. Coupled with cheery and colourful advertising calling upon us to do our bit for the nation by having a go on the Lottery, this makeover in terminology now means that the government is overtly inducing people to gamble.

There are many people who feel uncomfortable at the changes wrought by the relentless and unquenchable desire for increased state income. A third-generation bookie as I was, I abhor both the enticement to gamble and bet and the ease with which punters and gamblers can now lose all their incomes on the Lottery, scratch cards and in betting shops. I was brought up by a father who operated his business within the moral economy of working-class life. Dad wanted the punter's pocket money but not his or her housekeeping. I have watched Dad refuse to take bets from a man he thought had spent enough and who was in danger of throwing away the funds necessary to feed, clothe and house his family. Scottish bookie David McAllister did the same. In an article in the *Daily Record* prompted by the series *Bookie*, he stressed: 'I've seen me pulling aside a guy who's a mate, to tell him he's going a bit strong. So what happens? He cools it with me because he knows I mean well and he piles it on just as heavy with another bookie.'[8] Such a moral code has been battered and all but destroyed by the unfettered capitalism of big business and government. They justify their lack of responsibility towards their 'customers' on the grounds of free will, asserting that punters are adults who should be allowed to spend their money as they see fit and implying that they should not be protected either by old-fashioned paternalism or traditional working-class values.

This lack of concern for bettors and gamblers and the insatiable desire to make money is predicated upon untrammelled laissez-faire capitalism and has been exacerbated by the decline of traditional working-class neighbourhoods. Physical redevelopment as much as social change has swept away the old working-class localities of big towns and cities such as Birmingham, Salford, Glasgow and Swansea. Their disappearance has been accompanied by the marked decline in the concept of neighbourliness, which was vital to the existence of the delicate framework of profit-making and mutuality according to which the old street bookies operated. Perhaps in their own running of gambling operations, the lesson governments may learn from the illegal street bookies of the past is this: if you are to take something out then you have to put something back in.

Interestingly, as the old back-street bookmakers have fallen away, so too has the puritanical opposition to bookmaking. No longer is there a National Anti-Gambling League, and in place of the vitriolic comments of the likes of Canon Peter Green, there arose the thoughtful and sensitive words of the Reverend Moody. In 1958, he became secretary of the Churches' Council on Gambling, and he went out to meet and to talk to street bookies. He found that he respected them. The Reverend Moody gained a high reputation among bookmakers. They may have disagreed with some of his comments, but none doubted his sincerity and knowledge. Nor should it be forgotten that he devoted his life to helping compulsive gamblers and that it was his initiative that led to the founding of Gamblers' Anonymous.

Reverend Moody understood the ethics of bookmaking. Though derided and decried for generations, most street bookmakers felt a responsibility both to their punters and the neighbourhoods in which they took bets and often lived. As the Glaswegian bookie Norman Miller put it, 'people were going to bet anyway, so it was better betting with a decent feller'. As in any occupation, street bookmaking had its bad 'uns, but there were plenty of decent fellers. Punters preferred to bet with them and not with the state-operated Tote. I have no shame that my Dad was convicted as an illegal bookie. I am proud to be associated with his kind, people like the Glaswegian Laurie Ventners, at whose funeral the poor turned out in their thousands to pay their respects to a man who was renowned for his generosity; people like the highly regarded Boltonian Bella Thomasson, who carried on a successful illegal betting business for decades; and people like the Salfordian Billy Brady, a deeply religious bookie who gave back to his own and who was regarded in the highest esteem by his working-class fellows. I am proud to be the son and grandson of street bookies.

INTRODUCTION: WHAT IS BOOKMAKING?

Middle-class moralists had little doubt about the nature of bookmakers, disparaging them as non-producers. Shamefully, while they neither toiled nor spun, they succeeded in living off the fat of the land, spending largely and leaving great fortunes to their descendants.[1] This denunciation of bookmakers as idle and parasitic lies at the heart of the arguments against them. Yet, if they did not toil, how then did they earn their livings? Once again, this puzzle highlights that deep fracture between a mostly working-class position towards life and an essentially middle-class conception of living. For, of course, bookmakers did work, but the 'respectable' members of society sneered at their job as immoral, offensive and unfitting for self-respecting citizens. In their opinion, bookmaking was indecent and because it was dishonourable it could not be dignified as work. What then is bookmaking, and what is it about the occupation that should make it so repugnant to some people?

In essence, bookmakers are professional bettors, and it is the fact that they make their living from betting that causes certain persons to regard them as odious. A bet is 'something to be staked or won on the result of a doubtful issue', and all bettors hope that the result of their bet will be resolved in their favour and so give them a remuneration.[2] In this sense, there is no difference between bettors and bookmakers; what separates them is the crucial distinction that most bettors are amateurs because they do not rely on betting for their income. If they are successful, they have a reward, usually monetary; but for bookmakers, their trade is betting and a win gives them their profit and their livelihood.

To earn their money, bookmakers offer odds against the likelihood of something taking place and then accept bets from others who disagree with them and who think that it will happen. The bet might be on the chances of a certain horse or dog to win a particular race; it might be on which football team will win the English or Scottish Premier League in a given season; or it might even be on which black pudding will win the annual World Black Pudding Championships.[3] Whatever the type of bet and whichever the event, bookmakers hope that their judgement will be proven correct and that the 'fancy' (choice) of their 'punter' (customer) will be wrong. If it is, they will keep the money that has been 'laid' (placed) with them by the punter; if it is not, then they will have to pay out to a winning client his or her stake money multiplied by the odds offered by the bookie against the occurrence.[4]

Some bettors devote their lives to betting and become professional punters, but there are two crucial differences between them and bookmakers.[5] First, although bookies might 'back' (bet on) a horse if it is to their advantage, they are in the business of taking bets and not placing them.[6] They hold themselves open to accept bets from all comers, not just from another individual. This means that while the punter bets with the bookie on a one-to-one basis, the bookmaker bets with a number of punters who make a variety of bets. The second distinctive feature of bookmakers is that they offer to lay bets on all the participants in an event. Whereas a punter chooses a fancy and makes a bet accordingly, the trade of a bookmaker is to take that bet and those of other punters on other fancies in the same contest. Of course, bookmakers can refuse to accept a bet or else they can decline to take the bets of a certain punter. Like other businesspeople, they reserve the right to turn down trade that they believe to be on disadvantageous terms. However, once a bookmaker becomes habitual in rejecting bets on a particular competition, or on specific entrants to it, then he or she ceases to be a bookie. In effect, by picking and choosing the type of bets they will accept, they have become punters.

If bookmakers generally take bets on all the contenders in a contest, and one of them must win, how then do they make a profit? It is the manner of achieving this feat that forms their final trait. True, they are professional bettors who accept bets from all comers on a variety of issues whose outcome is doubtful; and they also take bets on different competitors within that competition, but if they do not make a profit they will lose money and go out of business. It is this reality that makes so important the formulation of the odds about the contestants in a betting event.

In a horse-race of four runners, each has a possibility of winning. Theoretically, that chance is one in four, meaning that the odds of every horse should be 3 to 1 against winning the race. If a bookmaker takes a £10 bet on each runner, then he or she will have £40 in stake money. However, one of the horses must win the race, and so the bookie will have to pay out to the successful punter the £10 staked on the bet multiplied by the odds of 3 to 1. This will give the winning client £40, exactly the sum taken by the bookmaker on the race, meaning that he or she will break even on the whole transaction – neither winning nor losing. But if bookmakers are to make a profit they cannot afford to break even continually, nor can they lose too often; they need to win on most of the events on which they take bets. Consequently, bookies adjust the theoretical odds against a runner so as to try and make a profit on a race whichever horse wins it. For example, in the four-horse contest, they will offer a price (odds) of 'shorter' (less) than 3 to 1 against the runner which they think is the 'favourite' (most likely) to win; while they will offer odds of 'longer' (more) than 3 to 1 against those which they believe are 'outsiders' (least likely to win).[7]

It is difficult for a bookmaker to determine what price to offer on which horse and often the decision is made on both objective and subjective information. So, while reference is made to the 'form' (record) of a runner, account is taken, also, of the 'feel' of the course, the punters and the day. In the words of Len Boden, a leading Midlands racecourse bookie:

> Oh yes, that's where you've got to know the ability of the horses which you're betting on. That's where your form man comes in. He's not always right, 'cos there's some information you haven't got. Some horses are better on some ground, some horses run better for some other reasons. Perhaps they weren't doing their best the last time they raced. Perhaps they weren't quite fit enough. So all those things have to be taken into consideration and that's what you have to guess from the market. It's a great thing in the market to have a feel for the market. As a bookie you've got to learn and you don't learn this by reading a book but from experience. From the feel of the market you can tell if something's not quite right. One horse doesn't seem to be in battle, nobody fancies it at all. The feel of the market – unless you've got it, it's a little bit more difficult for you making a book. You've got to be able to feel the market, you know. I can't quite explain it, but otherwise without that you're in trouble.[8]

Once a bookmaker has assessed the race according to these various criteria, he or she puts up a price on each runner and offers these odds to the punters. If the punters think that the price is 'good' and that it reflects well the chances of the horse winning the race, then they may take it; if it is regarded as 'bad', then the bookmaker will take no bets and the odds on that runner will have to be improved. Equally, if the price is too generous – if punters think it good value – then the bookie will take too many bets on one horse and its odds will have to be shortened.

It is after they have begun to lay bets that bookmakers are able to have another 'feel' of the market. This time the testing is based more firmly on empirical data – how much money has been taken on each horse, and what amount will the bookmaker have to pay out on each if it wins the race. Even though the mystic mist that envelops bookmaking is not dispelled fully, the crucial factor in making the odds is now the 'weight' (amount) of money laid on each runner. If bookmakers take a lot of money on one horse it means that they will have a losing race if it wins, and so they counter this possibility by 'attracting' (taking) more money to the others. This is done by shortening the price of the runner that is most heavily backed, so as to make it less appealing to punters. They are put off backing the horse because the lowering of the odds means that they will win less money for the same stake than if they had backed it when its price had been higher. At the same time as the bookmakers shorten the odds of the horse made favourite by the punters, they lengthen those of the other horses in the race so as to make a bet on them more enticing.

Obviously, it is crucial that either the bookmaker or an assistant has a good head for figures. By reacting swiftly and correctly to the weight and flow of bets on a race, and by a clever and successful manipulation of the odds, the aim is to ensure a profit whatever the result. Of course, this is not always possible. No matter how adroit a bookmaker is with figures, and no matter how adept he or she is at the job, it would be incredible if all races were profitable for 'layers' (bookies). They are not; but patently, there would be no bookmakers if many of them did not win most of the time. The fact that they do is thanks to both their skill at 'reckoning up' and to the in-built profit margin provided by the odds they offer. The task of compiling, rectifying and balancing the odds is the fulcrum of bookmaking, and it is only from a coherent arrangement of the bets laid that bookmakers can assess their liabilities (their chance of winning or losing) on a race, and so rejig their prices. It is from this arrangement of the bets in a book that both the term 'making a book' on an event and that of bookmaker itself are derived.[9]

In modern bookmaking, it is mostly on-course bookmakers who make a book in the true sense of the phrase, and off-course bookmakers rely on them to enable betting to take place on horse- and dog-racing away from the racecourse. This is achieved by a transmission, from the race meeting to betting shops, which gives the average odds offered on each runner in a race. Prices on other sporting contests are usually formed by large off-course betting businesses such as William Hill and Ladbrokes. Today, bookmakers accept bets on events as disparate as the naming of a royal baby and who will win *Big Brother*, but their main business is concerned with sport. In particular, they are associated with horse-racing, and it was on the racecourses of Britain that their forerunners made their first appearance, in the later part of the eighteenth century.

1

BEFORE BOOKMAKING: GAMBLERS, ADVENTURERS AND SHARPSTERS

MATCH BETTING

Racing horses had been known in Britain and Ireland for centuries before the arrival of bookmakers. In Irish tradition, the sport was instituted as an important feature of assemblies by the artistic and athletic god Lugh; and among the *fiana* (professional warriors) of Ireland, orders of merit were established according to a fighter's prowess at horse-racing and chariot-racing.[1] Still, little is mentioned of the sport during the Middle Ages, although folklore dates to 1160 the running of the first of the Lanark Races in Scotland.[2] Whether or not this is correct, there is not much other evidence of horse-racing before the sixteenth century, when it began to attract the notice of chroniclers. In 1504, James IV of Scotland attended races run on the sands at Leith; the Chester Cup was competed for first in 1512, making it the oldest extant thoroughbred race in the world; and the earliest recorded reference to horse-racing at Ayr concerns a contest in 1576 which was the occasion of a fight between the feuding Crawfords and Kennedys.[3] Within the next fifty years, an increasing number of races began to be held regularly, so providing the beginnings of established race-meetings: the Paisley Silver Bell dates from 1620; the earliest shield on the Lanark Silver Bell is from 1626; and silver bells were also run for in England during this period: at Chester, Gatherley, Croydon and Theobald's.[4]

It is obvious that horse-racing was gaining in popularity by the early seventeenth century, and it is as apparent that betting was associated intimately with it. Though owners raced their horses for small prizes, they staked large sums on their chances of winning, as a Scottish Act of 1621 made clear. It was entitled 'Anent playing at Cardes and Dyce and Horse-Racing' and it decreed that gamblers and bettors had to give to the poor any winnings over the sum of 100 marks.[5] The incidence of heavy betting on horse-races is made clear by a scene from Shirley's play *Hide Park*, performed at Drury Lane in 1637.

> *Confused noise of betting within, after that a shoute*
> MISTRESS CAROLL: They are started.
> *Enter Bonvile, Rider, Bonavent, Tryer, Fairefield*
> RIDER: Twenty pounds to fifteene.
> LORD BONVILE: Done, done. Ile take all oddes.
> TRYER: My Lord, I hold as much.
> LORD BONVILE: Not so.
> TRYER: Forty pounds to twenty.
> LORD BONVILE: Done, done.
> MISTRESS BONAVENT: You ha lost all, my Lord, and it were a Million.
> LORD BONVILE: In your imagination, who can helpe it?
> MISTRESS BONAVENT: Venture hath the start and keepes it.
> LORD BONVILE: Gentlemen, you have a fine time to triumph,
> 'Tis not your odds that makes you win.
> *Within*. Venture! Venture![6]

As this extract indicates, in the early seventeenth century, betting on horses was conducted in an amateur way without recourse to bookmakers. At a race-meeting, individuals might have a strong fancy for a certain horse and so would indicate to others that they were willing to back their judgement with money. If another person felt forcefully that this opinion was misplaced, then a bet might be struck between them. This did not mean that either of them were bookies; they were betting with each other on a one-to-one basis and although they might offer each other odds against their choice, they were not open to all comers and they did not make their living from betting. Crucially, this match betting, as it was called, was induced by the form of horse-racing then prevalent. Most races were run between two horses, matched against each other by their owners, and it was the predominance of two-horse races which militated against bookmaking.[7] It is not impossible to make a book on an event with two contestants, but it is difficult; and while bookmakers today offer odds on such competitions, they are not common. Successful bookmaking relies on contests with several entrants. Quite simply, this is because events with a variety of possible outcomes enable bookmakers to take different bets, allowing them to adjust the odds more effectively, and hence permitting them to make a better book.

While match racing remained pre-eminent, conditions remained unfavourable to the start of bookmaking.

During the time of Cromwell, horse-race meetings were suppressed as dangerous assemblies, but with the Restoration the fortunes of the sport revived. Charles II gave it royal patronage; Newmarket came to be its centre; and wealthy aristocrats began to import and breed from Arabian, Turkish and Barbary stallions which were famed for their speed.[8] By the eighteenth century, horse-racing was becoming increasingly organized and popular. Constant records of races were kept from 1709; from its formation in about 1752, the Newmarket-based Jockey Club soon came to be the most influential body in British racing, formulating rules and laying down procedures; and race-meetings began to be held on a more regular basis.[9] This uncontrolled expansion of horse-racing worried the government, so much so that an Act of 1739 included a provision 'to restrain and prevent the excessive Increase of Horse Races'.[10] Although it was ineffective, it was probably prompted by two factors. First, race-meetings were occasions which attracted large and potentially disorderly crowds. Second, because of their popularity, they attracted working-class people to them and so induced them to miss work and to become idle – a heinous sin for the poor, but not the rich.

Horse-racing was not the only popular diversion which exhibited these two traits, fearful to many of the elite and to the middle class. As the meticulous research of Robert W. Malcolmson has shown, blood sports, wakes and fairs all had 'a general tendency to undermine social discipline'.[11] Those who campaigned against them were prompted not merely by religious and moral objections, but also by a concern to maintain their privileged position within society. These mixed motives, overlapping and vying with each other for prominence, are evident in a pamphlet from 1823. Though from a later date, it exemplifies well the hostile attitude to popular pastimes prominent in the mid- and later eighteenth century. In it, the author fulminated against racecourses, theatres, gaming tables, feasts and fairs. He denounced them as the strongholds of Satan in which he and his followers planned and devised schemes against Christ Jesus and his humble followers. Not only were such events hotbeds of lewdness, sensuality and blasphemy, but they also encouraged the idle, the licentious and the profligate to join together and waste money. More than this, they were dangerous assemblies which the wealthy attended and allowed to continue and flourish at their peril.

Let parents and masters, who frequent the Racecourse, Theatre and such places, chastise their children, rebuke their servants, and inflict

> pains and penalties on lawless and incorrigible offenders, will they not say '*Physician heal thyself*?'
>
> If the higher powers wish to preserve their property from thieves and robbers, and their lives from the bloody hand of murderers, surely it is not the most prudent or likely way to obtain their wish, so long as they associate with these characters. While this is the case, no one need wonder at the increase of those horrid and atrocious crimes which are perpetuated day and night amongst us.[12]

The pamphleteer indicated another characteristic of race-meetings which made them unacceptable to the puritanically minded. He declared that they were 'intended to draw money from the pockets of the unwary'; and, indeed, they did provide an excellent opportunity for the exchange of cash by way of betting and gambling on a large scale.[13] The increase of race-meetings had led to more races on which people could bet; in fact the dominance of match racing meant that this trend was exacerbated. Often, several horses were entered for the same race, and in these circumstances they were paired into heats. Each runner might compete several times before a winner was found, with the result that bettors had increased possibilities on which to stake their money.[14] Betting rose in proportion to the growing appeal of horse-racing, and in most matches in the early and mid-1700s the two owners staked upwards of 100 sovereigns on the outcome.[15] Significantly, the 1739 Act sought to stop the proliferation of race-meetings and to facilitate 'the more effectual Preventing of excessive and deceitful Gaming'.[16] Although this latter provision was aimed specifically at gambling with dice and not at betting on horse-racing, it does reveal that the authorities were concerned enough about the extent of wagering that they sought to curtail it. How widespread, then, was gambling in the eighteenth century, and why was the activity perceived as a threat to the public good?

THE EXTENT OF GAMBLING

The 1700s were years in which members of the British ruling class sought the answer to a conundrum that bedevilled them. How were they to while away the endless hours of leisure with which their wealth had provided them? In their seminal study of the country's elite, L. and J. Stone explained how the privileged found a solution to this pressing problem by indulging in numerous pleasurable activities. They gave endless parties and flitted from house to house paying visits; they hunted and they played cards; and they escaped from the rigours of managing their estates 'to do' the season in London and Bath.[17] More than this, to add spice to lives jaded by the wearisome burden of enjoyment, they lost fortunes through gambling.

As W. E. H. Lecky wrote, the passion for gambling had long been prevalent among the upper classes, but it reached an unprecedented height under the first two King Georges.[18] It was a climax maintained for the rest of the eighteenth century. Horace Walpole reported that the young Lord Stavordale lost £11,000 in one day's gambling, but recovered it all by one 'great hand at hazard'; while Charles James Fox, the leading Whig politician and a famed and inveterate gambler, had lost £140,000 to his obsession by the time he was twenty-one.[19] Gambling dominated his life and was detrimental to his duties as an MP. Walpole recorded that the gifted young politician did not shine in a parliamentary debate of 6 February 1772. It was unsurprising. Fox had sat playing the dice game of hazard from the evening of the fourth until five in the afternoon on the fifth, losing £11,000 in the process. On the sixth he spoke in the debate; dined at eleven-thirty that night; went to White's club where he drank until seven the next morning; and then proceeded to Almack's club where he gambled and won £6,000. Finally, on the afternoon of the seventh, he made his way to Newmarket, presumably to bet on horse-racing.[20]

Fox was not alone in his passion for gambling; large numbers of the upper class were as engrossed by it as he.[21] So were other sections of society, as is indicated by an entry in the diary of William Bulkely of Brynddu, Anglesey.

> JUNE 4 . . . I went to the cock fight at Llandyrydog about ten, which was for eight silver spoons, the real value of the spoons was 14/– a piece. Each engager laid down 15/6 and whoever got a battle was entitled to a spoon, for two battles two spoons (that is, a spoon each battle), a third battle was to have two spoons more. I got the first battle and consequently a spoon, and William Hughes the parson of Llantrisant, having got another battle, we agreed to share the spoil and he getting the prize had three spoons to divide betwix him and me, so that I got two spoons and seven shillings for my share . . . I brought home two spoons at the expense of eight shillings, having won six or seven shillings by betting . . .[22]

The prevalence of gambling among some of the middle class is emphasized by the diary of Thomas Turner, a shopkeeper and general dealer in East Hoathly, Sussex. In November 1759, he noted that he and four friends played the card game of 'bragg in the even; and, though we plaid as low a game as possible, it was my unhappy lot to loose 3s'. He was stricken by remorse that the money could have been spent better by giving it 'to some necessitous and industrious poor, than fooled away in this manner'; but two months later, he and his wife lost jointly the sum of 3s 7d at another game of brag.[23] Turner continued to record incidents of his gambling, the last of which was a game of cricket played in June 1763 for half-a-crown's worth of punch.[24] More research is needed into the subject of middle-class gambling, but evidence such as that of Turner and Bulkely indicates that it existed. It suggests, also, that there were members of that class whose lifestyle does not slot easily into any blanket definitions as to its cultural characteristics.[25] In contrast to these cautious statements, it is possible to make bolder ones about working-class gambling and its extent in the eighteenth century. It not only existed, but was wide-ranging.

During the later 1800s, puritanical Christians were aghast at what they perceived as the novel phenomenon of betting among the working class. Its ubiquity staggered them and its expenditure appalled them.[26] Desperately searching for a cause of the 'evil', as they perceived it, they found it in the 'bad' example of the landed elite. They ignored the fact that men like John Northbrooke had used the same arguments in the sixteenth century, and glibly they pronounced that the vile habit of gambling had become 'less aristocratic, and much more democratic than it was'.[27] This explanation became almost a tenet of faith and it was unquestioned that the nineteenth century was the period when 'the gambling habit showed itself amongst all classes of society'.[28] In many respects, the upper class was an obvious scapegoat for the appearance of a social problem which was apparently new to the working class. The landed elite had a long, well-documented and highly publicized association with gambling – all of which linked it inextricably to the 'curse'. It was a connection highlighted by a working class which, before the 1800s, was seemingly untarnished by the wicked pastime. Obviously, then, the aristocracy were responsible for its dissemination.

This choice of culprit fitted well with the social profile of many involved in the struggle against gambling. Its fiercest critics were often middle-class clergymen, drawn especially from the Presbyterian and Methodist denominations and from the low-church party of the Anglicans.[29] Spiritually and socially, they were the lineal descendants of the seventeenth-century puritans who had garnered much strong support among sections of the bourgeoisie.[30] The puritanical tradition of extreme strictness in religion and morals remained strong among their successors in the late nineteenth and early twentieth centuries. On to it had been grafted, in the early 1800s, an antipathy to the aristocracy and a loyalty to what were regarded as middle-class values: individualism, self-help, hard work, utilitarianism and an attachment to 'respectable' and sober behaviour. These codes of conduct contrasted sharply with the lifestyle of most of the upper class, and in the first half of the nineteenth century elements of the bourgeoisie launched a fierce attack upon the elite. They were emboldened by the economic power gained from industrialization, and they were fortified by an ideology which exalted them into 'both the most wise and the most virtuous members of the community'.[31] In the words of Harold Perkin, the entrepreneur was 'a puritan pilgrim seeking both earthly success and heavenly bliss through work'.[32] On the other hand, the aristocracy were idle, parasitic and useless; they were dissolute and immoral, and they spent their time worthlessly in 'gaming and debauchery'.[33]

By the late nineteenth century, much of the venom had been drawn from the middle-class tirade against the landowners. After all, both classes were propertied and they needed to unite to protect their possessions against the threats of organized labour and socialism.[34] Still, middle-class puritans retained both their hostility to the aristocracy and a revulsion at their way of life, and they found an outlet for their spleen in the anti-gambling crusade of the 1880s onwards. Ironically, both their argument that the problem was a recent one, and their contention that it was an infection which was spread downwards to the working class, were welcomed readily by the movement which many of them feared: socialism. Most socialists believed that betting was a pernicious habit that diverted the attention of workers away from involvement in the struggle to change society. They felt that its rise to popularity in the 1880s had come at a time when there had occurred a 'loss in the democratic fervour which characterised the people during about three-quarters of the nineteenth century'.[35] To the socialists, this seemed no coincidence. A betting mania had made the working class apathetic about politics. Unlike their forebears, who had thronged to join Chartism and who had demanded political and social reform, now they clamoured merely for the racing results. The sources of this unhappy transformation in the working class seemed obvious. According to J. Ramsay MacDonald, later leader of the Labour Party:

> Gambling is a disease which spreads downwards to the industrious poor from the idle rich. In its most common form, betting on horse-racing, it is the only way in which the outcast plebeians can be joined with their betters in a bond of freemasonry. An elevating knowledge of distinguished jockeys and an exhilarating

> acquaintance with the pedigree of horses raise the poor parasite to the level of the rich one and make them both men and brothers.[36]

This conviction that gambling had percolated from the rich to the poor gained wide acceptance, and early labour historians tended to agree that the problem 'was scarcely known' among the working class before the late nineteenth century.[37] Guy Chapman thought that up to the 1840s, 'betting appears to have been entirely the vice of the wealthy and their parasites'; while G. D. H. Cole and Raymond Postgate believed that eighteenth-century London was 'given to gin in its poorer parts and to gambling and wine drinking among the rich'.[38] However, the evidence supports neither the impression that gambling was a habit peculiar to the landowning class before the later 1800s, nor the assertion that aristocratic bad example corrupted the working class with the 'evil'. Certainly, by the 1880s, betting among workers excited much interest and aroused great concern, and Ross McKibbin and Gareth Stedman Jones were right to emphasize that this was so. But both historians made the necessary point that working-class gambling was evident before the late-Victorian period.[39]

McKibbin stated forcefully that 'wagering in some form or other had been endemic among the lower classes since time immemorial'.[40] He would appear to be justified in his assertion. In *The Iliad*, Homer described how the knuckle bones of sheep and other animals were used as dicing implements; the ancient *Rig Veda* of India contains a poem on the tragedy of a gambler's life; and St Mark wrote that the soldiers who crucified Jesus 'parted his garments, casting lots upon them, what every man should take'.[41] It would seem that gambling was as widespread in Britain during the later Middle Ages as it was in the ancient world. The letter books of the Corporation of the City of London indicate that, in 1311, one Elmer Multone was indicted 'for being a common night walker; and, in the day, is wont to entice strangers and persons unknown, to a tavern, and there deceive them by using false dice'; and Nottingham Borough Records for 1482–3 contain details of men who were sued for gambling with dice, and of 'householders who were prosecuted for keeping gaming houses by night for serving men'.[42] By 1541, all 'manner of artificer or craftsman of any handicraft or occupation, husbandman, apprentice, labourer . . . or any serving man' were so keen at playing and gambling at dice and cards that it was proving a counter-attraction to serious pastimes; so much so that an Act was passed 'for the Mayntenance of Artyllarie and debarring of unlawful games'.[43] It failed in its objective. In an age when there was no police force, legislation could be enforced only if the local gentry were prepared to do so. Unsurprisingly, given their predilection for gambling, many showed a marked reluctance to act against working-class people who transgressed the gaming laws. As the puritanical John Northbrooke explained in 1577, these were

> . . . good lawes in dede; but I feare it may be aunswered, as one aunswered the Athenians (who bragged of their lawes) that they had good lawes in dede, but few or none duly executed: for I see that a great many of our rulers and magistrates doe not only neglect the execution of the lawes herein upon diceplayers, but are content to receive into their houses, very worthily, such loytering diceplayers and mummers; yea, rather than they should depart without play, they joyne fellowship with them, and play at dice themselves, whereby they do great hurt to the people whom they rule over . . . they doe more hurt by their example of lewde life, than by the sin itself.[44]

During the Commonwealth, the strictures of Northbrooke and other puritans who abhorred gambling were heeded.[45] Along with other activities which they loathed as frivolous, irreligious and immoral, dicing and card-playing were suppressed vigorously and sternly.[46] This hiatus in the popularity of gambling was short-lived, and like horse-racing, it gained a new vigour with the Restoration of Charles II. Indeed, many members of the working class seemed as willing to gamble inordinately as did large numbers of the elite. In 1663 Samuel Pepys recorded his wonder at seeing working people losing as much as ten or twenty pounds on bear-baiting and cock-fighting; and in 1668, writing about the high stakes gambled for in games of dice, he was amazed at how 'persons of best quality do here sit down, and play with people of any, though meaner'.[47] By the eighteenth century, there is further evidence to corroborate his observation that there was working-class wagering on a wide variety of sporting contests, as well as on dice and cards and other games.[48]

One such was the tossing of coins. In the 1800s, this game was inwrought in the working-class districts of Britain and Ireland, and in the early part of the twentieth century it achieved notoriety because of its association with gang warfare. There is little mention of it in the 1700s, probably because it was a predominantly working-class form of gambling at a time when most attention was concentrated on the wagering of the upper class. Still, it is an age-old pastime, which was called cross and pile by Joseph Strutt in 1833. This comprehensive chronicler of English recreations named two other coin games: chuck farthing and pitch and hustle – later known as pitch and toss – which he described as 'commonly played in the fields by the lowest classes of the people'.[49] It would seem safe to assume that gambling at these coin games was widespread in the eighteenth century. Certainly, this is implied in a brief notice in the *Gentleman's Magazine* of 1763. In it, the term 'toss up' is used without any explanation, suggesting that readers would be familiar with it; while the tone of the communication alludes to the popularity of the game: 'An old notorious gambler, who has infested *Moorfields* for many years corrupting youth by gaming, being tied to a tree near the place where they toss up, received fifty-six lashes on his bare back, pursuant to his sentence last sessions at *Hick's Hall.* He is to undergo the same punishment twice.'[50] This 'old notorious gambler' would not have been a bookmaker. Like match bettors on horses, gamblers in tossing wager on 'two runners': whether the two coins tossed will come down heads or tails. It is probable that the 'notorious gambler' was the equivalent of a toller – that is, he organized the tossing ring and took a cut from the winnings of successful gamblers.

Similarly, bookmakers were absent from all other forms of gambling, working-class or otherwise – either because the event involved matches, or else because it was a game of chance or a 'one-off'. Indeed, unusual and grotesque wagers abounded among all classes in the eighteenth century: two lords once staked their money on whose grandmother would live the longer; and another two betted on which of two noblewomen would give birth first.[51] Often, bets were made on how much a person might eat or drink in a given time, or how far they might run or walk; and in 1736, a Nottinghamshire framework-knitter wagered that he could walk upon the hand-rails between two bridges over the River Trent when it was in flood.[52] Despite their frequency, contests such as these could never become organized into a coherent sport, nor could they become regular competitions, since they were mostly unrepeatable. Consequently, they were unable to compete with the well-established blood sports, either in popularity or in the amount of money betted on their outcome.

As Pepys indicated, working-class people placed bets on bear-baiting, and it is likely that betting occurred at dog-fights, ratting pits and at other occasions when animals were made sport of cruelly. Betting was definitely a pronounced feature of cock-fighting. This was one of the most popular activities in the eighteenth century, and as such it was a foremost type of betting event. As the diary entries of Thomas Turner and William Bulkely disclosed, it had a cross-class appeal, and Malcolmson concluded 'that the common people were by no means uninvolved in the sport'.[53] Its attraction to the working class was regarded as great enough to warrant the attention of the prominent Evangelical Hannah More, who issued against it one of her Cheap Repository Tracts. In particular, the pamphlet was directed at colliers, among whom the matching of cocks was 'a favourite diversion' on a Sunday. Accordingly, their sins were four-fold: they betted, they promoted blood sports, they defiled the Sabbath, and they blasphemed.[54]

The cock-fights mentioned in the tract were single-class affairs; yet a marked feature of the sport was not just that it transcended class barriers, but that regularly members of the different classes were brought together in the same place and for a shared occasion. *The Cockpit*, the celebrated 1759 engraving by William Hogarth, illustrated well the mixing of people from different social groups at cock-fights; and in 1710, a German traveller described the same phenomenon and detailed how betting on the contests was carried on.

> The people, gentle and simple (they sit with no distinction of place) act like madmen, and go on raising the odds to twenty guineas and more. As soon as one of the bidders calls 'done' . . . the other is pledged to keep his bargain . . . As soon as the cocks appear, the shouting grows even louder and the betting is continued . . . those who put their money on the losing cock have to pay up immediately, so that an hostler in his apron often wins several guineas from a Lord. If a man has made a bet and is unable to pay, for a punishment he is made to sit in a basket fastened to the ceiling, and is drawn up in it amidst peals of laughter.[55]

This account by von Uffenbach stressed that wagering on cock-fights was not a light matter, and one eighteenth-century authority on the sport urged that no one should go to 'the pit' without money in their 'breeches'. He cautioned potential bettors that '"Done and done" is cockpit law, and if you venture beyond your pocket you must look to it or you may lose an eye in the battle'.[56] Most fights were simply matches between two cocks, although in a Welsh Main a larger number were matched in a murderous knockout competition until only two remained to fight for victory. Wagering was heavy on both kinds of event, as it was on pugilism, another match-betting sport.

Originally, bare-fisted boxing had been a means of settling a dispute between two working men, as was noted by the French traveller, César de Saussure, in 1727. After two rivals had agreed to fight each other, they would

> retire into some quiet place and strip from their waists upwards. Everyone who sees them preparing for a fight surrounds them, not

> in order to separate them, but on the contrary to enjoy the fight, for it is a great sport for the lookers-on, and they judge the blows and also help to enforce certain rules in force for this model of warfare. The spectators sometimes get so interested that they lay bets on the combatants and form a big circle. The two champions shake hands before commencing, and then attack each other courageously with their fists, and sometimes also with their heads, which they use like rams. Should one of the men fall, his opponent may, according to the rules, give him a blow with his fist, but those who have laid their bets on the fallen man generally encourage him to continue till one of the combatants is quite knocked up and says he has had enough.[57]

From the mid-1700s, fights such as this developed into the organized sport of pugilism.[58] Fighters were matched against each other for a sum of money which was put up either by themselves or a 'backer', often a member of the gentry or the aristocracy if the pugilist was famous.[59] At a contest in Norwich in 1772, Sylas Neville was amazed at 'what a concourse of people of all ranks there was to see this fight and what gambling'.[60] His comment could have been applied as readily to cock-fights and to horse-races as to prize fights.[61] By the late eighteenth century, these constituted a pre-eminent trinity of popular sports which were linked inextricably to betting and to each other.

As the number of meetings increased, and as horse-racing became a favourite pastime for the working class as well as for the upper class, so too did racecourses become the venues for cock-fighting, bare-fisted boxing and other diversions. Indeed, the magnetism of racecourses was strengthened by this confluence of sports and activities at one site and on one date. Crowds of working-class people flocked to their local races, drawn in by their fair-like atmosphere, their numerous attractions, the plentiful supplies of drink, and the chance of winning money.[62] Thomas Holcroft's father was an itinerant shoemaker, and he so enthused his son with descriptions of the hurly-burly of the races that the boy itched to visit those at Nottingham in 1757.

> My father was a great lover of horses . . . and from his discourse, as well as the little I had seen of these animals, I was eager to become better acquainted with them. My father recapitulated the different places at which he had seen horses run, recounted the names of the famous winners he had known, and filled up the picture with the accidents common on such occasions, the amazing cunning of sharpers, the punishments inflicted on some of their detected rogueries, the cries of the betting chair, the tumult of the crowd when the horses were running, the danger of being too near to the

> course, with the difficulty of keeping it clear, the multitude of gaming and drinking booths, and all the variety of delightful commotion which was calculated to gratify my boyish fancy. The whole scene was like enchantment; and all my wishes were now centred on it being realised.[63]

Holcroft went on to describe how the main race at Nottingham was a match between two runners: Careless and Atlas. As the local horse, the former was 'the decided favourite of every man in Nottingham, gentle or simple'; and after it was beaten 'there was many an empty purse on that night, and many a sorrowful heart'.[64]

For most of the 1700s, there were no facilities at all for betting off-course; consequently, for working-class people, betting on horse-races was limited to when a meeting was held locally. Yet it would be unwise to underestimate the amount of money staked by them on these occasions. As Holcroft indicated, it could be heavy, and he produced further evidence of this elsewhere in his autobiography. He became a stable-boy at Newmarket, and he recounted that when a race-meeting took place there, he heard 'nothing but cards, dice, cock-fighting, and gambling to an enormous extent'. Other stable-boys told him 'of the sudden rise of gamblers, their reverses, desperate fortunes, empty pockets at night and hats full of guineas in the morning'. Seduced by this talk, and in a 'state of puerile avarice', he made a series of match bets with his fellow workers on a number of races to be run in the same week. He staked crowns and half-crowns, and ended up losing about a guinea-and-a-half, more than half of his wages for one year.[65] Thomas Turner, too, remarked on the betting of grooms, noting that in 1757 a number of them laid £100 on Careless to beat Newcastle Jack at Lewes Races, which he did.[66] Of course, men and boys employed by race-horse owners had plenty of opportunity to bet, and they were more likely to do so regularly than were other members of their class. Still, the evidence suggests that working-class wagering was extensive in the eighteenth century, even though it was associated with a diversity of games, sports and events. This popular activity was carried on without bookmakers, and they must therefore be seen as the product of mass gambling and not as its creators.[67]

ADVENTURERS AND ANTI-GAMBLING LEGISLATION

The authorities were not unaware of the prevalence of wagering in the eighteenth century, especially among the upper and working classes; and the Gaming Act of 1739 exemplified their concern to curb it. This official reaction was separate from the constant battle waged by puritanical sections of the middle class against popular diversions and their concomitant: gambling. Their moral and social objections to 'Dicing, Dauncing, Vaine playes, or Enterludes, with other idle pastimes' were rooted deep in the sixteenth century, and despite the post-Restoration reaction against puritanism, their aversion to disreputable customs stayed steadfast.[68] Writing in 1738, after a visit to a race-meeting, the non-conformist Richard Kay exhorted the Lord to keep him 'in good and sober Company and ever give Grace and Strength to watch and guard against mad Frolicks, foolish sports, unreasonable and dishonourable Diversions, and wicked and sinful Irregularities'.[69] His insistence would have been shared by many more who were attracted by notions of 'reticence, sobriety and thrift, punctuality, self-discipline and industry, chastity, prudery and piety', as Malcolmson put it, and who were repelled by the hedonism which seemed to characterize both the upper and working classes.[70]

But, in the first half of the eighteenth century, this puritan doctrine competed and clashed with a revived Tory traditionalism. Gambling was associated with a host of activities redolent of the spirit of 'Old England'; and as Malcolmson has shown, many members of the gentry were unwilling to 'meddle with the people's affairs on the grounds of religion or morality'.[71] That is not to say that Tory traditionalists gave a free hand to the working class to act howsoever they wished. There were limits to their tolerance, but in so far as it did not affect public order, gambling lay within those bounds. This toleration was made easier by the nature of wagering among the common people. Though widespread, it was dispersed over various activities; much of it was 'hidden' among themselves, in their alehouses or in their districts; and, for the main part, it was carried on without professional gamblers. More than this, it was felt that gambling and other popular activities kept the people happy and ensured their satisfaction with the status quo.[72] As Northbrooke had pointed out in the later 1500s, while working-class gambling was regarded leniently by the gentry, moralists could do little but inveigh against it. If this was the case, why was an attempt made to curb wagering in the Gaming Act, 1739; and why was it preceded and succeeded by similar legislation?

In short, this provision was directed at restraining the gambling of the upper class and not that of the working class. According to the famous jurisprudent, Sir William Blackstone – writing in 1755 – 'at present, it is the gaming in high life that demands the attention of the

Magistrate, the offence of gaming comes after the offence of luxury . . .'[73] Apparently, the sober and prudish among the middle class were not alone in their concern at the monomania for gambling which had affected the upper class. In 1751, a correspondent to the *Gentleman's Magazine* held forth against the three great evils that were afflicting Britain, and that he feared were so widespread that they would be fatal to the nation's survival. He named them as '*lewdness, gaming and gin-drinking*'; and while he gave the latter as the curse of the 'small' in society, it was gaming which was the vice of the 'great vulgar'.[74] Neither his concern, nor that of Blackstone, was altruistic. Their preoccupation with upper-class gambling was propelled not by religious or moral motives, but by a desire to protect the interests of their class and to secure its well-being. As Blackstone put it, 'gaming was an offence of the most alarming nature . . . frequently attended with the sudden ruin and desolation of ancient families . . .'[75]

In a scholarly and effective study of gaming, David Miers has observed that the gambling of the elite in post-Restoration Britain was distinguished not by its novelty, but by its intensity.[76] Unsurprisingly, fortune-seekers flocked to cash in on the predilection of the rich to gamble and to lose heavily. They found their 'pigeons' (dupes) waiting eagerly to be 'plucked' (fleeced) in the gaming houses of London, Bath and other places in which the upper class congregated.[77] Although places for gambling with dice and cards had been present in Britain since the Middle Ages, they proliferated in the new atmosphere of 'deep gaming'.[78] Some were run by the wealthy for the wealthy, but many were owned and patronized by 'common people', professional gamblers who eagerly stripped the rich of their cash, and whatever else of value they could.[79] As Miers has emphasized, the resultant 'uncontrolled exchanges of mortgages, bonds, conveyances and other securities' was an unwelcome development. Attempts were made to check it and so reduce 'the economic impact' of upper-class wagering.[80]

An Act of 1664 – the first passed against gambling specifically and not games – made void all securities over £100 which related to gaming debts and which were incurred at any one time or meeting.[81] Forty years later, the rage was so great for 'the playing of Cards and Dice' in Edinburgh – the focus of the Scottish upper class – that it had caused profound social problems. In particular, it had 'ruined the Estates of many, and redacted them and their families to Poverty'. In consequence, an Act was passed which forbade these games to be played 'in any Coffee-house, Tavern or other publick or common Houses within this City'. Gaming-house keepers were to be fined £40 for a first offence, and they were to be imprisoned for a second.[82]

Neither piece of legislation prevented excessive gambling. In 1710, another attempt was made to do so by way of a national act which declared void all notes, bills and securities given over while wagering.[83] Again, it was ineffective in causing 'little interruption in the depth of gaming' and in reducing huge monetary losses, but it did hinder 'the wholesale transfer of real property'.[84]

By 1738, the custodians of the good of the landowning class had realized the futility of dissuading affluent gamblers from the folly of losing money to those outside their privileged circle. Their attention turned to the crux of the gambling problem: those commoners who were lightening the load of wealth carried by the rich. An act was passed that was directed at stymying the activities of professional gamblers, or 'adventurers' as the law termed them. It made it an offence to 'set up, maintain or keep the said games of the ace of hearts, pharaoh, bassett and hazard'; and it provided a fine of £50 for lawbreakers.[85] The next year it was amended to include more games of dice; and six years later a further amendment embraced roulette-type games.[86]

This gaming legislation failed blatantly to diminish aristocratic losses to adventurers. Its lack of success was due to the continued passion for gambling among the upper class, and to lethargic magistrates who did not implement the law. There were exceptions. In February 1751, Justice Fielding and a strong group of guards seized forty-five gamesters at a rendezvous in the Strand; thirty-nine of them were committed to the gatehouse and the remaining six were bailed.[87] Three months later, Justice Lediard, accompanied by 'some constables, and a party of guards', raided the long room in James Street, Westminster. Seventeen gamblers were arrested, among them the proprietors of the gaming tables. All had been charged before and so they forfeited their recognizances.[88] However, such deeds were infrequent and their fitfulness ensured that they were no deterrent to professional gamblers.

The ineffectiveness of the law inspired another effort to reduce the movement of upper-class wealth to adventurers. This time it focused on alerting the privileged to the dangers they faced in gambling with professionals. The first issue of the *Gentleman's Magazine* (1731) detailed the snares of a gaming house, and in 1750 one John Brown preached a powerful sermon which warned the landowning class of the dire consequences of its proclivity for gambling.[89] It was called *On the Pursuit of FALSE PLEASURE, and the Mischiefs of IMMODERATE GAMING*; significantly, it was given in Bath, a key centre of the British ruling class.

> Do we not see *Men* passing their best Hours, and their Prime of Life, in these Scenes of *Folly*, whose Rank, Fortunes, and Natural Abilities might entitle them to the highest Offices in the Common-Wealth? Degrading themselves to the low Level of professed Gamesters, and herding with these, as their chief Intimates, their bosom Friends: Blind to every Kind of Merit, but that of the learned Artist, whose boasted Qualification is, that he is both able and willing to ease them of the *useless Burthen* of an *Estate*. Yet, fond as they are of this mad Extravagance in Theory, the practice of it is attended with the most consummate Misery . . . their false Pursuits too generally conclude with cursing themselves, and blaspheming Providence. Here then behold the *Wretch compleated*! Surrounded by a Train of inextricable Miseries! His Fortunes vanished, beyond Redemption! *He cannot Work; and to beg he is ashamed*: He hath disgraced his Ancestors and ruined his Posterity . . .[90]

Six years later, Justice John Fielding wrote *The History of Gambling* to alert the public to the ease with which adventurers took money from dupes.[91] This admonition, like that of Brown, was as much unheeded as the law was ignored. Still, reproofs continued to be aimed at the landed elite. In 1778, Philip Thicknesse felt the need to caution visitors to Bath against '*ingenious Men*, who live by their *great Talents* for *Play*'; and in 1799, Thomas Rennell preached a sermon in Winchester Cathedral entitled *The Consequences of the Vice of Gambling*.[92]

SHARPSTERS

The diatribes against eighteenth-century adventurers have much in common with the invectives against nineteenth- and twentieth-century bookmakers. In both, two strands can be discerned. First, a puritanical contempt for those whom middle-class moralists regarded as un-Christian, unpatriotic and criminal parasites involved in a loathsome and useless occupation. Second, an aristocratic disdain for common people who wagered not for fun but in deadly earnest, and who were abhorred as leeches feeding off games and sports. As Rennell put it at the end of the 1700s, his sermon censured 'those atrocious practices by which the *formed Gamester* deals havock and ruin around him'; it did not condemn 'innocent recreations' which terminated merely in pleasant diversions. He strove to distinguish the '*amusement* of cards from the *vice of Gaming*', the better to make distinct the player of games for pleasure from the gamester – the person who played for money. Once the two were separated, he was able to damn the professional gambler as a 'lover of lucre', as a fraudster, and as a person with the 'most ungovernable FEROCITY OF DISPOSITION' who was full of impudence.[93] Adventurers were outcasts, existing beyond the pale of acceptable and respectable behaviour.

> . . . the misery which an habitual Gamester suffers, hazards, and occasions, must render him completely and systematically callous. Without a single sentiment of remorse or compassion, he coolly and designedly inflicts utter and irretrievable mischief on the greater part of those with whom he is conversant. What though everyday he lives he wrings the heart of many a fond wife, many an helpless orphan, many an aged parent, by effecting the rapid and instantaneous ruin of those to whom they looked up for support and comfort: what though the wretched Suicide, unable to bear the complicated agonies of those whose affections nature has wound closest round his heart, leaves them to deplore his loss in this world, and his DESPERATE STATE in that which he precipitated himself; what though of all such horrors HE is the witness, the cause, and the accomplice; what though he is the patron and the legislator of the system which diffuses them; yet, with all this, HE remains calm, easy and collected.[94]

The hypocrisy inherent in sophistry such as this is glaring. Professional gamblers were cursed because they won money from the landed elite, the very class who themselves were idle and who gained their income from the sweat and misery of working-class people. The law conspired in this special pleading. As D. M. Downes and his co-authors underline in their study on gambling, work and leisure, the anti-gambling legislation of the eighteenth century 'was chiefly aimed at the threat posed to large fortunes'.[95] Little account was taken of the small sums of money gambled in the 'copper hells' and gaming booths at race-meetings that catered for the common people. The officers of the law, too, engaged in this class-based quibbling and, apart from the brothers Fielding, tended to act – when they did act – against the 'gold and silver hells' (gaming houses) in which the wealthy lost their cash.[96] This is not to uphold all professional gamblers as paragons of virtue. Many were dishonourable in their dealings, base in their objectives and reprehensible in their conduct. They were sharpsters who would countenance any form of trickery in their pursuit of profit.

Cheating at cards and dice was prevalent in the Middle Ages, but with the heavy gambling of the post-Restoration period it plumbed new depths. An effort to fetter it had been made in the Gaming Act of 1664, whereby the victim of swindling was enabled to recover from the cheat three times the sum that had been lost; and in 1710, this clause was increased to five times the amount won unfairly. These provisions were unsuccessful in deterring 'fiddlers'. In his raid on a meeting of professional gamblers in the Strand in 1751, Justice Fielding seized three gaming tables which cost nearly £60 each. Underneath them were found two iron rollers and two private springs by which 'those in the secret could touch, and stop the turning whenever they had any youngsters to deal with, and so cheat them of their money'.[97] If the gaming rendezvous was not controlled by sharpsters, then intricate machinery designed for cheating was replaced by a dexterity skilled at palming a card or cogging a die.[98] Of course, while the pickings were richer at the gaming tables of the wealthy, the sharpsters were as willing to fleece the poor. One of John Wesley's standard sermons provided evidence both of their activities among the common people and of a reaction to them by his society's members.

> In clearing the streets, fields and ale-houses of Sabbath-breakers, they fell upon another sort of offenders, as mischievous to society as any; namely gamesters of various kinds. Some of these were the lowest and vilest class, commonly called 'gamblers'; who make a trade of setting on young and inexperienced men, and tricking them out of all their money; and after they have beggared them, they frequently teach them the same mystery of iniquity. Several nests of these they have rooted out, and constrained not a few of them to earn their bread by the sweat of their brow, and the labour of their hands.[99]

Sharpsters were despicable, but it is as necessary to differentiate them from adventurers as it is to separate charlatans from those who are knowledgeable. It is a distinction that evaded most contemporaries.[100] Both were involved in gambling; whether adventurers were fair in their dealings mattered not a jot, they were tainted by the way in which they made their living. For the puritanical, an honest gamester was a contradiction in terms. This conflation of twisters with honourable gamblers had implications for later attitudes towards bookmakers. They, too, were guilty simply through their involvement in wagering; they were debased further by its historic connection with the double-dealing of sharpsters.

BETTING AND GAMBLING DEFINITIONS

The hostility towards bookmakers and the hatred of eighteenth-century adventurers were inextricably linked, but the two occupations were not the same. Bookmakers are professional bettors; they are not professional gamblers. This setting apart of the two groups is a crucial, although arguable, distinction; but it is one that is based on both authoritative and popular interpretations of the words 'bet' and 'gamble'. In the opinion of C. F. Shoolbred, an expert on the law of betting and gaming:

> The term 'betting' is now more usually restricted to wagers on events in connection with sports or games, whilst gaming is associated with the staking of money or money's worth on the result of pure chance, or mixed chance or skill, and 'wagering' is now applied to any person who hazards money on a contingency without having any interest in the risk other than the amount of his stake. It is nevertheless apparent from the above definition that betting, gaming and wagering, are so closely allied that in dealing with any one of these three subjects it is advisable to include the other two.[101]

This final caveat needs to be borne in mind, but it does not reduce the significance of the essential distinction between the two forms of wagering. Implicit in betting is the recognition that the activity is reliant not only on chance but on skill, too. Thus, in a sporting event, a bettor assesses the form of the contestants and takes account of the 'going' (conditions) before deciding on which competitor to stake his or her money. Of course, the result is not predetermined and it can be affected by luck. However, to gamble is to play a game of chance for money, and while the game might involve an element of expertise, on balance its resolution is dependent on luck.[102] In particular, dice and card games which are occasions of gambling are devoid of skill and it is impossible to make a book properly on their outcome. For these reasons, adventurers were not bookmakers. Yet they were involved in a related activity, and it is likely that some of the first bookies were drawn from their ranks.

2

BETTORS ROUND, BLACKLEGS AND BOOKMAKERS

BETTORS ROUND

Adventurers and sharpsters abounded on racecourses in the late eighteenth and early nineteenth centuries. They were pulled there by the same magnet that drew them to the hells, or gaming rooms: the opportunity for plucking pigeons, of which there were plenty. Before the 1830s, travel may have been restricted to walking and riding, but attendance at the races could be large, even at small, local meetings. At the great fixtures, the crowds could be enormous. Spectators flocked to meetings at Doncaster, Epsom, Manchester and Nottingham from all over their respective regions; and on 28 June 1791, it was estimated that at least 40,000 people watched the running of the Oatland Stakes at Ascot – 'numbers of them coming from remote parts of the kingdom'.[1] Among others, Hannah More recognized that race-goers were attracted as much by the chance of winning money as they were by the sport itself. In 1795, she issued another of her Cheap Repository Tracts, entitled *The Horse Race; or the Pleasures of the Course.* Written as a poem, it warned all manner of folk against misusing their money at the races. Gentlemen, the wives and daughters of farmers, apprentices and old women were all urged not to drink and not to game.[2] This kind of caution was ignored. Betting was feverish on the racecourse, and it was calculated that on the day of the Oatland Stakes, the huge sum of £100,000 was lost and won.[3]

Much of this money was spent in gambling and not in betting on horse-racing itself. Adventurers leased gaming booths from the race-committees that organized a particular meeting, and these itinerant hells were so profitable that at Ascot in 1792 a weekly rent of 100 guineas each was charged for the ten marquees allotted to EO, a fashionable game similar to roulette.[4] In 1828, the interiors of these 'club houses' were described as 'set off by rich gilding and the gayest of colours'.[5] At the great northern meeting of Doncaster, the gambling went on in private houses and shops which were illuminated at night, but in 1826 its focus shifted to the infamous Betting Rooms which were opened in the High Street.[6] These were built in the classical style: at the front of the building, the Ionic columns and pilasters imitated the temple on the Ilissus at Athens; and there was a spacious loggia which led to the principal room for gambling.[7] Here, adventurers paid a considerable rent for the lease of individual gaming tables, and 'large sums of money changed hands during the "small hours" when courage often got the best of discretion'.[8]

One thousand people were members of these rooms, which operated during race-week, and they each paid an annual subscription of one guinea. Like the patrons of the marquees at Ascot, most of them were upper-class and the adventurers who catered for them were likely to be 'respectable men in their calling'.[9] This could not be said of many of the other professional gamblers who worked the racecourse. They were sharpsters who aimed at 'conning' their customers, and they preferred to operate outside a booth because they could disappear into the crowd if they were discovered and upbraided.[10] The games they favoured were prick-the-garter, hustling in the hat (hussle cap) and thimble-rig.[11] This latter was the forerunner of the three-card trick, and its operators were rife wherever crowds gathered. Their manner of working was explained in 1825, during a court case that related to an offence committed at Ascot races.

A gang of seven or eight men would set up a table, after which they would appear as strangers to each other. Only one of them would show any connection with the game, and he was the 'master of ceremonies'. After putting three thimbles on to the table, he would place a pepper-corn below one or two of them and then offer bets as to which thimble was empty underneath. His associates would take up his offer, and they would win.

> He pays the losings freely, and the other members of this joint-stock company affect a laugh at him, as what they call a good 'flat' (fool). When they have thus drawn the attention, and probably excited the cupidity of a stranger who appears to have money, they suffer him to win a stake or two, and get him to increase his bets. When he seems thoroughly in the humour, the master of the table lifts a thimble under which is a pepper-corn, and turning his head aside to speak to some one, he suffers the corn to roll off, and seeming to be unconscious of this he replaces the thimble, and offers bets to any

> amount that there is a corn under that particular thimble. The stranger having seen the corn roll off with his own eyes, as the phrase is, chuckles to himself, and eagerly takes the bet. The thimble is removed and behold! there is a pepper-corn under it still, the fellow having dexterously slipped another under it when the first rolled off the table.[12]

Wealthy punters could lose as much as twenty or thirty pounds before they realized that they had been duped, but most thimble-riggers preyed on gullible members of their own class who betted sums of tuppence and upwards.[13] Some of these bettors became aware of the con and attempted to retrieve their losses through threatening the master of ceremonies. When this happened, his cronies would leap to his defence and beat up the objector.[14]

The pickings were rich on racecourses for adventurers and sharpsters, but they made their profits from gambling and not through backing horses. Because it did not afford them the opportunity of adjusting the odds in their favour, match betting held no allure for them. They may have staked money on certain contests, but it was difficult to guarantee a profit on a two-horse race. The lack of interest of professional gamblers in the turf was not to last. By the later 1750s, their attention was grabbed by the appearance of the sweepstake race. This is a competition in which a number of horses are entered and for which the owner of each puts up a sum of money – a stake – to be pooled as a prize for the winner. Obviously, this increased with the number of runners, and it is likely that the impetus to sweepstake racing came from owners of race-horses who wanted greater monetary rewards from their involvement in the sport.

Most historians would agree with F. M. L. Thompson that 'the commercialization of popular entertainment and leisure was a prominent feature' of the second half of the nineteenth century.[15] The acknowledgement of this process should not obscure the fact that a businesslike spirit had infused the provision of leisure for many years prior to that period. As J. M. Golby and A. W. Purdue pointed out, it is mistaken to sustain 'the notion of a sharp break between a world of pre-commercial leisure and a more exploitative commercial one'.[16] In particular, horse-racing had been associated with financial considerations from at least the early 1600s. Owners had sought to make a profit from the sport through betting, but by the middle years of the eighteenth century this was becoming more difficult to achieve. An increasing number of matches were 'certainties'; that is, one of the horses was so superior to the other that it was unlikely to lose. In these circumstances, the owner of the favourite was unable to find anyone who would lay a bet; while the owner of the outsider thought that it would be foolish to waste any money on backing it.[17] These sterile contests were not good for business, and a demand arose for more exciting, less certain and more profitable races. It was met by the sweepstake, which boasted two clear advantages over matches: owners could put up less money for the chance of a greater return; and it widened their betting opportunities, as was made clear by the stable-boy Holcroft.

> In addition to matches, plates and other modes of adventure, that of a sweepstakes had come into vogue; and the opportunity it gave to deep calculators to secure themselves from loss by *hedging* their bets, greatly multiplied the bettors, and gave uncommon animation to the sweepstakes mode. In one of these Captain Vernon had entered a colt or a filly, and as the prize to be obtained was great, the whole stable was on the alert. It was prophesised that the race would be a severe one; for though the horses had none of them run before, they were all of the highest breed . . . As was foreseen, the contest was indeed a severe one, for it could not be decided, – it was a dead heat; but our colt was by no means among the first. Yet so adroit was Captain Vernon at hedging his bets, that if one of the two colts that made it a dead heat had beaten, our master would, on that occasion, have won ten thousand pounds; as it was, he lost nothing, nor would he in any case have lost anything. In the language of the turf, he stood ten thousand pounds to nothing.[18]

Like other owners, Captain Vernon realized that by backing against his horse winning a sweepstake, he could 'cover' (insure) himself against it losing the prize.[19] This system of 'hedging bets' was adopted as enthusiastically by other turfites.[20] 'Cute' (ingenious) punters comprehended that because of the larger fields (runners) in sweeps, they could make a series of bets in the same race and secure themselves from loss whatever the result.[21] Their aim was 'to get round' in their betting by buying cheaply and by selling dearly; in other words, they sought to back their fancy at a high price while they laid it at a lower one.[22] For example, if a punter had backed his favourite for £10 at 3 to 1, he would seek to lay it for £10 at 2 to 1. If the horse won, he would make a profit of £30 on his first bet, and a loss of £20 on the second, giving him a gain overall of £10; if it lost, he would break even, as his own bet was covered by that which he had laid.[23]

If a punter was to get round, it was essential that other bettors were available with whom to do business. Holcroft indicated that in the 1750s they gathered at a betting chair. His description of the one at Newmarket suggested that it was a wooden stand of some type; and a letter from 1802 indicated that at Brentford Races, betting took place in the grandstand itself.[24] By the 1820s, many big meetings had a stand which had been built specifically to accommodate 'betting men'. At Ascot, it was situated next to the gambling marquees; it was two storeys high and it was capable of holding 'an immense number of persons who were admitted at 3/– each'.[25] In the eighteenth century, it is improbable that even regional centres of racing boasted a structure which was as grandiose as this; while at small-scale and infrequent meetings, it would not have been feasible to erect any permanent building. Instead, punters congregated at the betting post, as Thomas Rowlandson showed so evocatively in a drawing in about 1789. He depicted an unruly scene, in which bettors on horseback shouted the odds at each other in a manner reminiscent of the wagering at cock-pits. This is not surprising. Often, dedicated race-goers were regular attenders at cock-fights, and both groups shared the same betting terminology. According to *The Sporting Dictionary* in 1803:

> Persons taking bets should, if the odds in fighting come to 2 or 3 to 1 in favour of the cock they have backed, immediately take such odds, which is called 'hedging' (alluding to a fence for the bet), and the party then stands the chance of winning a certain number of pounds to the losing of nothing! This is the only mode by which money can be made in the cock-pit, and what the professional amateurs are always prompted to do by prudence.[26]

As this writer pointed out, match contests were not prohibitive to hedging, but not always did they make it practicable: the competition might have been a 'sure thing' for one entrant; or else there was uniformity in the odds available about the contestants. By contrast, sweepstakes provided punters with a variety of possible outcomes, a selection of prices on offer about the runners, and a means of betting to figures in a sophisticated manner. In 1850, an informed writer on the turf noted that bookmaking did not begin 'till money might be had for the making – scientifically – on the racecourse'.[27] He was correct, but even though bookmakers themselves did not emerge before the dawn of the 1800s, their appearance was facilitated by the evolution of mathematical and systematical betting in the eighteenth century. Bookies did not burst unannounced on to the historical stage; their coming was heralded by betting round, and its terminology remains in use in modern bookmaking.[28] In particular, the phrase 'over-round' refers to a situation in which the bookmaker is guaranteed a profit on a race whatever the result: 'for instance, if the largest take-out on a horse is say 600 quid, and you've taken £630 on the whole of the horses then you're £30 over-round. I mean the least thing that you can win is £30.' The opposite to this occurrence is under-round, that is when a bookie bets over-broke to no profit in an event.[29]

Bookmaking resulted from the development of hedging into a methodical procedure, but essentially bettors round remained backers. They hedged because they wanted to cover their betting and they did not offer prices to all comers. However, as their pattern of backing horses developed, so too did some of them come to resemble layers rather than punters. A vital stage in this process was the onset of ante-post betting – that is backing a horse before post betting began on the racecourse. The betting chair and the betting post were crucial facilities for those who wanted to hedge their bets, but they could make more formidable the task of getting round. If all the punters were assembled in one place, each would be aware of the prices on offer about a certain horse. As a consequence, it would be harder for a bettor to lay a horse at a price that was shorter than that at which he had placed his bet. This difficulty could be overcome if the punter could back a horse at high odds well before a race, and then lay it at a lower price on the day of the event. In 1852, Nimrod explained how this procedure worked.

> Let us, then, suppose A beginning to make his Derby book at the commencement of the new year. B bets him (about the usual odds) 20 to 1 against an outsider, which A takes in hundreds, viz., 2000 to 100. The outsider improves; he comes out in the spring, and wins a race, and the odds drop to 10 to 1. A bets 1000 to 100 *against* him. He is now on velvet; he cannot lose, and may win 1000. In fact, he has one thousand pounds in hand to play with, which the alteration of the odds has given him. But mark, he is only playing with it; he may never pocket it: so he acts thus. The outsider – we will call him *Repealer* – comes out again, wins another race, and the odds are only 5 to 1 against him. A bets 500 to 100 more against him; and let us now see how he stands:
>
> If Repealer wins, A receives from B £2000
> He pays to C £1000
> Ditto to D £500 = £1500
> Balance in A's favour by Repealer *winning* £500
>
> If Repealer loses, A receives from C £100
> Ditto from D £100 = £200
> A pays B £100 – Deduct £100
> Balance in A's favour by Repealer *losing* £100[30]

As Nimrod's exposition implied, ante-post betting was dependent on three factors: races on which punters wanted to bet in advance of the event; information about the entrants for those contests; and a place or places where bets could be struck away from the course. The first of these criteria was met by the great sweepstakes introduced in the later eighteenth century: the St Leger in 1776; the Oaks in 1779; and the Derby in 1780. With the One Thousand and Two Thousand Guineas – inaugurated in 1814 and 1809 respectively – these competitions became established quickly as the 'classics' of British racing.[31] From the outset, they attracted tremendous public interest by reason of their explosive nature. Most matches were boring to spectators because they were run slowly by older horses racing over long distances – usually four miles – but the classics were fast races for three-year-olds. They ran over a shorter course – two miles or less – and they were decided in a single contest and not by heats.[32] This meant that each race had a large field, and it made the classics pre-eminent as betting events. They gave plenty of options for punters to hedge and were recognized by Admiral Rous as the stimulus for the emergence of bookmaking from the chrysalis of betting round.[33]

In particular, the classics prompted ante-post betting because horses were put in for them as yearlings. Not all of them would run in the race itself, but this early system of subscription ensured that punters could follow the prospects of the various entrants over a period of about eighteen months. Despite the absence of mass media, racing information was disseminated by word of mouth from those who travelled the country to the leading meetings. It was among these *cognoscenti* that betting in advance of an event became popular, and from 1789 Tattersall's gave them an acknowledged meeting-place at which they could discuss and bet on future races. Situated at Hyde Park Corner, this horse-dealer's had been set up by Richard Tattersall in 1773. It was described as a place 'where men of honour might congregate, free from the smell of the stable and enjoy a view of the most beautiful horses without being perpetually in contact with the jockey or the horse-dealer'.[34] Quickly, Tattersall's became a rendezvous for racing men, and in 1789 the owner opened a subscription room where his patrons 'could transact their Turf financial business' in comfort.[35] The subscribers were a select group of aristocrats who were prominent figures in horse-racing, and the prices which they offered and laid among themselves in 'The Room' became the market leaders in ante-post betting.

Until the later nineteenth century, Tattersall's remained unrivalled as the principal British centre of betting transactions, but much business was done elsewhere. In 1845, Benjamin Disraeli detailed how members of the upper class betted with each other in their exclusive London clubs.

> 'I'll take the odds against Caravan.'
>
> 'In ponies [twenty-fives]?'
>
> 'Done.'
>
> And Lord Milford, a young noble, entered in his book the bet which he had just made with Mr Latour, a grey-headed member of the Jockey Club.
>
> It was the eve of the Derby in 1837. In a vast and golden saloon . . . were assembled many whose hearts beat at the thought of the morrow, and whose brains still laboured to control its fortunes to their advantage.
>
> 'They say that Caravan looks puffy,' lisped, in a low voice, a young man, lounging on the edge of a buhl table . . . and dangling a rich cane with affected indifference, in order to conceal his anxiety from all, except the person whom he addressed.
>
> 'They are taking seven to two against him freely over the way,' was the reply. 'I believe it's all right.'[36]

Even though Milford and his companions entered their bets in a book, they were not bookmakers. They were amateur hedgers, and on the day of the Derby they tried to get round at the course itself by backing with bookies.[37] As Disraeli intimated, the 1820s and the 1830s were decades in which amateur and professional bettors co-existed because of their involvement in betting round; but by the 1840s, this system was in eclipse to the rising star of bookmaking. By the late nineteenth century it was obsolescent, and betting on racecourses was dominated by working-class layers who made their living from their occupation.[38]

BLACKLEGS

People from all classes attended, took part in and betted on horse-racing, but it was felt strongly that the sport 'belonged' to the upper class. In many respects it did. The local gentry organized and controlled race-meetings; the aristocratic Jockey Club was the chief arbiter and authority on racing matters on the flat; and most of the best horses were owned by members of the landed elite. Sweepstake racing threatened this ownership. It would be an exaggeration to suggest that it 'democratized' the turf, but its advent did make it more difficult to keep races as single-class affairs. In a celebrated court case in 1791, the clerk of the course at York was sued for withholding the prize of £123 for a sweepstake won by the horse of one Thomas Burdon. The clerk justified his action on the grounds that the terms of the race stated that all the riders had to be gentlemen, and Mr Rowntree, the winning jockey, could not be described as such. Not one witness for the defence could impeach his character, nor deny his standing as a prosperous farmer; but he was 'degraded as the scum of the earth, as the indignant object of contempt and contumely, as deserving to be kicked off the floor of society, for daring to lay claim' to the rank of gentleman.[39] The defence declared that this term was sacrosanct to those who fulfilled three criteria: possession of a hereditary estate; an enjoyment of the sports of the field; and a freedom from any business or profession.[40] This aristocratic arrogance incensed the populace and there was great rejoicing when the jury found for Burdon. A reporter commented tartly that had he taken his case before 'a jury of men of the turf, before the jockey-club, the pretensions of such a man would not have been a moment discussed, they would have been instantly rejected with derision'.[41]

If upper-class turfites were disturbed at the 'opening up' of racing because of sweepstakes, many were as agitated by the egalitarian effect these races had on betting. Members of the landed elite may have betted with commoners on occasion in the cock-pit and at prize-fights, but for the most part, match contests induced wagering between social and financial equals. As a consequence, match betting was deemed respectable. In the opinion of Robert Black, a historian of the Jockey Club, as long as it was between nobles it was a comparatively harmless pastime; but he felt that it was 'sordid' for an aristocrat to bet with a commoner.[42] This 'abhorrent practice' became a frequent occurrence with the advent of sweepstakes and betting to figures. Because it rewarded the alert and the quick-witted, betting round appealed to adventurers and to '"horsey" persons of low extraction' and some of them became professional bettors.[43] Up to the 1790s, there were too few sweepstakes to allow them to make their livings from horse-racing alone. Like the well-known Dennis O'Kelly, they varied their activities between the betting post and the gaming table.

At one time, this Irishman had worked as a sedan-chair man, but 'his elegant legs and fine figure took a lady's fancy, and she started him in life' as a gentleman.[44] Through gambling and betting mathematically, he became a wealthy man and he achieved fame through his ownership of the immortal race-horse Eclipse; but he never escaped the stigma of his origins.[45] He was unable to gain election to either the Jockey Club or to any of the London clubs which were patronized by the landed elite, and it was believed that 'there was a strong smack of the blackguard about him'.[46] Probably there was, but it would appear that he was blackballed by 'society' chiefly because he was a working-class Irishman who regarded betting as a serious matter. He and other professional bettors round were useful to their upper-class counterparts because they expanded the group of people who were prepared to lay and back horses; but they were not respected. As Curzon perceived, 'my lord felt no scruples in betting with a man in Tattersall's, or on the racecourse, on whom he would have scowled had he sought admission to his house, even by the area-gate'.[47] Like the adventurers of the early eighteenth century, men like O'Kelly were regarded with odium and they were lumped together under the abusive epithet of blacklegs: turf swindlers.

This pejorative term dates to the 1770s, and it is presumed that it arose from the black boots which were worn by professional bettors; or else, it is derived from the noun 'rook', which signified a sharpster, rooks having black legs.[48] Whatever its etymology, the word was loaded with class prejudice and snobbery against those who betted for profit and not for pleasure. As the sagacious J. Fairfax-Blakeborough sensed, it was 'certainly meant to connote an inferior order, men whose honesty was not to be trusted, and men who preyed on their fellows as unscrupulous opportunists'.[49] It cannot be denied that many working-class bettors round were unattractive characters, and the respected turf writer Thormanby went so far as to say that these 'fathers' of bookmaking were 'sharpers pure and simple'.[50] He mentioned that one, Dick England, was 'one of the most unmitigated ruffians ever connected with the English Turf'.[51]

Like O'Kelly, England was a working-class Irishman and he had been a journeyman cabinet-maker in Dublin before turning pugilist. After moving to London in the 1770s, he was employed as a 'bully' – a prostitute's protector – after which he became a successful gambler and bettor round.[52] As with many other immigrants who were prevented by prejudice from finding well-paid, secure and respectable jobs, he found that professional betting was an open occupation. It had no apprenticeship regulations and neither did it exclude the poor nor discriminate against foreigners. The sole qualification for entry into the business was a sharpness of wit combined with a head for figures, and England possessed these in abundance. Contemporaries recognized him as having

> a proficiency in the science of betting, and the profitable arrangement of his account, equal to that of any *professional sportsman* of his time; he moreover, by dint of sedulous observation, attained considerable knowledge of the racehorse, and the practical

> business of the course; branches with which mere betters seldom concerned themselves, holding the opinion, generally, that in a race, far more depends on the state of the proprietor's betting account, than on the qualities of the horse.[53]

England's career exemplified the trend towards bookmaking and away from betting round which was evident among professional bettors at the dusk of the 1700s. Even though he remained a gambler, he realized that money could be made 'scientifically' on the racecourse, and in deciding his bets he took as much notice of the form of horses as a modern bookmaker would in arranging his or her prices. For a number of years, he was acknowledged as 'nearly at the head of his profession of *aventurier*, gambler, or black-leg'. More than that, it was assented that 'he was the architect of his own fortune', and it cannot be doubted that it was this characteristic which grated with those who had inherited their wealth.[54] That is not to say that England was an exemplary person; he was not. In many respects he was an unpleasant man who was as willing to pluck a 'raw Irishman' as he was a member of the gentry, and he would stoop to trickery to do so. He was not alone. His companions were 'the most noted black legs' and included Jack Tetherington, Bob Warr, Tom Hull and, of course, Dennis O'Kelly. All of them were men who gambled with the odds stacked in their favour, and each of them was a man of 'turf repute'. In the early 1780s, they met at Jack Munday's coffee-house in the Strand, and here they laid ante-post bets several years before The Room was opened.[55]

These men were the most well-known professional bettors of the time, and their ill repute ensured that when it emerged bookmaking would be sullied as a deceitful occupation. Without exonerating England and his ilk, it should be emphasized that there were also plenty of upper-class turfites who were defrauders. In 1820, Pierce Egan related a number of the swindles they perpetrated against other members of their own class. He denounced these aristocratic sharpsters in no uncertain manner.

> I have no terms of contempt sufficiently strong to reprobate such conduct. If gentlemen can league together for the purposes of dishonesty and of plunder, what can be expected from the lower orders? With such examples, can we wonder at fraudulent bankruptcies, at swindling tricks, or even at open robbery in the inferior ranks of life? Or may we not suspect that HONOUR . . . has deserted the higher classes, and has quitted the gilded palace to sojourn and to pine in the straw-covered and wretched cabin.[56]

Curzon believed that there was no more humiliating spectacle than that furnished by a 'noble' sportsman 'doing' his friend over a race.[57] Yet, so long as a man boasted a title or an inheritance, then he was a gentleman, and he remained so no matter how duplicitous he was in his conduct. An upper-class fraudster was never decried as a blackleg; that distinction was reserved for working-class professional bettors, whether or not they were honest.

BOOKMAKERS

It would seem that England, O'Kelly, Tetherington and their associates confined their double-dealing to the gaming table, a view substantiated by a leading London magistrate, Patrick Colquhoun. In his *Treatise on the Police of the Metropolis* he listed blacklegs among the criminal groups of London, and he defined them as those 'proselytised to the passion of Gaming, or pursuing it as a trade, who are in constant habit of frequenting houses opened for the express purposes of play'. He gave their number as 2,000, but he made no mention of their connection with deception in betting on horse-races.[58] With reluctance, even their detractors admitted that professional bettors were scrupulous in paying out when they had lost. Nimrod concurred with another writer that they were 'the most unprincipled and abandoned set of thieves and harpies that ever disgraced civilised society'; but he conceded that 'pecuniary obligations are commonly discharged by them with as much integrity and despatch as by the most respectable persons in the commercial world'.[59] This reputation for probity was belittled and ignored because it was as likely to be based on self-interest as it was on an upright character.[60] Of course, full-time bettors round would gain more custom if it was well-known that they paid their losses promptly and without quibble, but the recognition of this ulterior motive should not diminish the significance of their actions. Drily, Rice contrasted them favourably to 'the gentlemen' who had lost money to their friends and who took time 'before handing over the guineas and the bank notes'.[61]

The dualistic attitude towards bookmakers is tied closely to the contradictory opinions held of the professional punters of the 1770s onwards. On the one side, they were jeered at as lower-class rogues; on the other, their rectitude was acknowledged, albeit in a grudging fashion. The maintenance of this positive attribute owed much to the existence of a group of regular backers and layers whose fair dealings made it difficult for them to be impugned. They were quick-witted, swift to take advantage of a situation and alert to the chance of making money; but although they were sharp, they were not sharpsters.[62] The Druid was an expert on horse-racing and he named these men as Ogden, Davis, Holland, Dearden, Kettle, Bickam and Watts. He judged that they ruled the 'Turf 'Change' (racecourse betting) in the days of 'powder and periwigs', and he stated that Ogden's standing was so high that he was the only betting man ever to be admitted to the Jockey Club Room at Newmarket.[63]

With confidence, one authority declared that 'records clearly prove' that this Lancashire man 'fathered' bookmaking in 1790, when he offered to all comers different prices about the horses in a certain race.[64] More cautiously, another informed commentator wrote that as early as 1793, he was 'laying the foundations of the modern science of bookmaking'.[65] In fact, that basis had been built in the 1750s and 1760s by men like Captain Vernon; and it had been extended by O'Kelly, England and their type in the 1770s and 1780s. William Ogden's significance is not that he was the first bookie, but that he and the others named by The Druid were the architects of the final stage in the development of professional betting into bookmaking. They were practitioners of 'betting one with the field'; that is, they would lay a horse in a race and offer one price for the rest of the runners collectively.[66] Unlike bookmakers, they did not offer individual odds about each horse; but in contrast to bettors round, they were prepared to lay bets on all of the runners.

If a punter backed the field, he had several horses going for him; consequently, layers could offer only a shortish price if they were to get round on their betting with the favourite. Backers were prepared to accept this so long as the fields were small – three or four horses – but as sweepstakes increased, so too did the number of runners. As Charles Sidney has made clear, in these circumstances a bettor was likely to be laid at an unfavourably low price if his fancy was offered in the field.[67] Punters became dissatisfied with this, and a demand arose for individual prices about each runner in a race. By 1815, it was obvious that it had been met by men who had abandoned betting one with the field and who had adopted bookmaking in its stead. With precision, the redoubtable Admiral Rous gave 1804 as the year in which the new system 'came into vogue'. He probably settled on this date because it was the year in which Henry Raikes noted that shoals of bettors had arrived at Brighton to do business at Lewes races. Among them was Jerry Cloves, the former gentleman's gentleman, who was acknowledged as one of the earliest bookies.[68]

Curzon disagreed with Rous's exactness, emphasizing that no data existed which showed when the first bookmakers came upon the scene. He was correct, but it is likely that they appeared in the first few years of the nineteenth century, as proposed by the knowledgeable correspondent to the *Illustrated London News*.[69] By that period, sweepstake racing had achieved superiority over match racing. The figures provided by Wray Vamplew show that in 1807, 263 sweeps were run compared to 189 matches.[70] This type of race had spawned professional betting, and it cannot be doubted that the emergence of bookmaking was associated with its rise to dominance on the racecourse. Perceptively, Black commented that 'the betting ring' (bookmakers) struggled into existence between 1760 and 1820, and he identified Tattersall's as the place where it attained for the first time a 'corporate existence'.[71]

At the turn of the nineteenth century, professional bettors had begun to congregate at this horse-dealer's, attracted there by the chance of laying bets and of picking up information. Because they were scorned as blacklegs, they were unable to gain admission to the rarefied atmosphere of The Room, and as a consequence they walked about the yard 'picking up a stray "pony" [a bet of £25]' whenever they could.[72] By 1818, their presence had become so significant that it was decided to open a small room for their accommodation. This ensured that Tattersall's would give

> a *tone* to the *sporting* world, in the same way that the transactions on the ROYAL EXCHANGE influence the mercantile part of society. It has likewise its '*settling days*' after the great races at *Newmarket*, *Doncaster*, *Epsom*, *Ascot*, &c. I do not know about the *bulls* and the *bears*; but it has no *lame ducks* to *waddle* out, it has sometimes Levanters [defaulters] that will not *show* for a time, and others that will *brush off* altogether. But this does not happen very often; and Tattersall's has its '*good* MEN' as well as the '*Change* [racecourse]; and whose '*word*' will be taken for any amount.[73]

Betting at Tattersall's was with credit, and as Pierce Egan mentioned, after each big competition, a day was set aside for the settling of accounts. As the number of attractive 'betting' races increased, so it became necessary to settle up on a weekly basis, and bookmakers achieved a reputation as 'good payers' on the settling day of Monday.[74] Despite this – or because of it – their presence was detested by those who wished that Tattersall's and the turf would be rendered free of them, 'becoming the presence and patronage of gentlemen'.[75] Nimrod called bookmaking an 'accursed system', and he thought it quite unworthy for an English gentleman to be connected with it. He was scathing about upper-class bettors who compared their books with that of 'a low-bred fellow who ought to be considered the very antipodes of themselves', and he considered that they 'abandoned their caste' as a result.[76] Like others of his class, he loathed bookmakers as interlopers, and Black went so far as to associate the emergence of bookmaking with 'the descent upon our racecourses of the foreigner, represented by Philippe Egalité'.[77] Those who viewed bookies as aliens expressed their disdain for them by calling them 'legs', meaning swindlers, an abbreviation of the derogatory term of blackleg.[78] It was a name which lent itself to propaganda against professional bettors, and 'gentlemen' put it about that legs were 'so called because they run away when they lose and can't or won't pay'.[79] This slur was unjustified. Egan mentioned that Tattersall's had 'its good men' whose word was their bond; and the leading bookmakers could not have enjoyed their long careers if they had not paid out to winning clients.

Among these men could be included: 'Crutch' Robinson, 'Facetious' Jemmy Bland, Jerry Cloves, Myers, Richards, Mat Milton, Tommy Swan of Bedale and John Justice.[80] All of them were from working-class backgrounds. Myers had been a butler; Richards had worked as a stockinger in his native Leicestershire; and it was thought that Bland and his brother, Joe, had started out as post-boys, becoming bookmakers after a time as livery-stable keepers. 'Facetious' Jemmy could neither read nor write, and The Druid mentioned that he was made a man of mark by his long nose, his white flabby cheeks and his 'acute rough expressions, such as "*niver coomed a-nigh*"'.[81] Illiteracy and a broad accent were features of most of the early bookies, but neither of these traits handicapped them against doing 'their "sooms" in their heads with wonderful readiness and accuracy'. Rice was awestruck at some of their feats of mental arithmetic, and he was astounded at how their memories of odds and bets were as 'retentive as a vice'.[82] Curzon agreed that they were 'not particularly bright' so far as education and manners were concerned, but he believed that 'these defects' were overlooked because of their prompt payment when they lost.[83] He was wrong.

Not only were bookmakers stigmatized because they were professionals, but they were also loathed because they were successful. To the consternation of those who had never worked for their income, Jem Bland boasted a 'noble house in Piccadilly, and drove his phaeton'.[84] Like John Justice, he was not fearful to lay a bet of £1,000 which might cost him ten times that sum if it won, and it was reputed that he paid out £80,000 when Shillelagh won the Derby in 1836.[85] The wealth of Bland and other bookmakers could buy them property, but never could it purchase for them status. They remained cast out from those among whom they lived, and their neighbours sneered at them as ignorant lower-class upstarts. Sylvanus made clear their contempt with his unflattering description of 'Crutch' Robinson, the former stable-boy from Cheshire who vied with Bland and Cloves for the title of leader of the first generation of bookmakers.[86]

> A more domineering, uncouth being than this sporting cripple could not be encountered . . . and to see an old man, disabled from the use of his limbs, and blanched by time, shouting out his odds, and dealing in the lowest bitter sarcasm and racing slang, either mounted on a four-legged brute as rough as himself, or leaning on his trusty crutch in the midst of the crushing throng, was an irreverent and disgusting sight, even in the motley scene wherein he figured. In a dialect of true Tim Bobbinish accent, the halting old 'leg' added a sneer and a surly importance of manner peculiarly his own.[87]

Robinson had much in common with 'Hump' Chippendale, the bookmaker drawn so well by Disraeli in *Sybil*. Both had a physical disability – the one a severe limp, the other a hunchback – and each was 'a democratic leg, who loved to fleece a noble, and thought all men were born equal'.[88]

The sensibilities of the 'cultured' were offended by the coarseness of bookies like these. More than this, the oligarchic tendencies of 'gentlemen' bettors were subverted by the egalitarianism of legs, and their pockets were hit hard by the success of their working-class rivals. It was these 'jealous minds' who accused bookmakers of profiting through dishonest means, and who branded them as rogues who prevented well-backed horses from winning their races. Fairfax-Blakeborough had little doubt that the baiting of bookies was motivated by haughtiness. He was certain that it was based on the bigoted view that 'because a man was a bookmaker he must therefore be without honour, without scruple, without any true sportmanship and willing to adopt any means to make money'.[89] Yet, the 'fixing' (arranging) of contests had been an unwelcome concomitant of horseracing from its earliest days; and by the early eighteenth century, 'crimping' (foul play) was rife, even though bookmakers did not exist. Often, owners would arrange for their horses to be 'pulled' (held back), or for 'ringers' (substitutes) to be run in their place. If an owner wanted to win a race, then he would use a ringer that was superior to his horse; but if his success in betting depended upon his entrant losing, then he would use an inferior substitute.[90]

Titled turfites were not averse to stooping to these and other ruses if it served their cause. In the reign of Queen Anne, a visitor to the races at Newmarket deplored the bad conduct of a 'great concourse of the nobility and gentry'. He regretted the eagerness with which they abandoned faith, honour and good manners in favour of the 'sharping part of the sport', and he bewailed the alacrity with which they tried to pick each other's pockets.[91] Dennis O'Kelly observed sardonically that the real 'blacklegged fraternity' was composed of the Dukes of Cleveland and Grafton, Lords Abingdon, Foley and Derby, and other members of the aristocracy.[92] Their connection with foul play did not seem to prevent their entry into the Jockey Club, nor has it blemished their reputations. It is no coincidence that their involvement in shady practices has become overlooked, while that of bookmakers has become exaggerated. In his history of horse-racing, Roger Longrigg dealt with bookies under the heading of 'The Problems and Scandals of the Turf'; and he conflated them with blacklegs, the more easily to tarnish them as villains. He alleged that in 1843, 'a new phenomenon appeared: the big bookmaker who was honest'. Before then, he supposed that bookies had 'stopped' horses from winning races whenever they were faced with a heavy pay-out.[93] Longrigg ignored the fact that in the same contest, various bookmakers might each have had a different 'bogey' (a horse which, if it won, would have given them a losing book).[94] If his sweeping conjecture is to be believed, then it would have meant that in every sweepstake, numbers of runners would have been 'nobbled' (tampered with) by bookies with opposing liabilities (possibilities of paying out).[95] It is a ludicrous scenario, but he justified it by reference to a single, notorious affair: that of Daniel Dawson.[96]

In 1811, four horses were poisoned by arsenic at Newmarket, a crime for which Dawson was charged. He was a tout; that is, he spied on horses while they were in training and he sold his information on their condition to those who were interested. In his case, his paymasters were bookmakers, but other touts sold racing news to owners and punters as well. It is apparent that he thought that he would profit from those who might have gained from the withdrawal of the poisoned horses from specific races; but Rice pointed out that there was no insinuation that any bookies 'had actively instigated' his crime.[97] Longrigg disregarded this caveat. He presented Dawson as a 'quiet, red-faced little chum . . . always so sociable over his pipe and pot in the evening'.[98] So he was. He was well-liked and jovial; but he was, too, 'rascally' and 'a profound hypocrite'.[99] This failing was ignored by Longrigg, who contrasted the simple, friendly Dawson with those who were behind him in the crime: 'the sinister Bland brothers'.[100] To the historian's chagrin, they were not bothered, while the gullible tout was hanged. Unfortunately, Longrigg omitted to relate that Dawson was acquitted on the charge which connected him so tenuously to the Blands, and that he was executed for another case of poisoning.[101]

It is impossible to determine whether or not these bookmaking brothers were implicated in the Dawson affair; although most nineteenth-century turf writers thought that the circumstantial evidence indicated that they were.[102] As with O'Kelly and England, it would be wrong to make the Blands paragons of virtue, and it would be difficult to deny that some of the early bookmakers may have been responsible for nobbling horses on occasion; but it would be unwise not to recognize that roguery on the racecourse had taken place before their coming. Longrigg attempted to do this and he declared that the first notorious examples of the stopping of horses occurred in 1809–11. But he himself mentioned that in 1772, the fancied horse, Rosebud, was poisoned; while in 1778, another favourite, Miss Nightingale, was found dead with two pounds of duck-shot in her stomach.[103] Even after the appearance of bookmakers, it should not be presumed that villainy on the racecourse was their preserve. It was not. Crimping and sharp practice were widespread among all types of turfites, and Admiral Rous recounted a 'big ramp' (racecourse swindle) by an aristocratic owner who intended to fleece 'the ring' through his chicanery.

> In 1812 a circumstance occurred at Newmarket which ought to have opened the eyes of the Jockey Club to the fact that . . . the ring could not protect itself against the trickery of owners . . . Two horses belonging to a noble lord – Cwrw and a colt by Remembrancer – were in the Two Thousand Guineas. The latter was backed to win £20,000. He was ridden past the ring with Chifney on his back and a stable lad on Cwrw. At the starting post Chifney changed his mount and Cwrw became first favourite and won an immense stake. The Remembrancer colt did not start, by which the ring lost a great portion of their field money . . .[105]

Lord Darlington had bred Cwrw as a 'dark horse' (an animal whose form was unknown to bookies and to other backers).[106] Because of this its price was high, and by putting a stable-boy on it until the starting post, Darlington encouraged further the offering of long odds about its chances by the bookies. Of course, they realized that they had been duped when Chifney, the Lester Piggott of the era, swopped mounts. Alongside this 'wangle', Darlington had connived to enter for the race the Remembrancer colt, even though he had no intention of running it. By doing this, he hoped that it would lead to a better price about Cwrw, with the bookmakers not becoming aware of the ramp until after the withdrawal of his other horse, just ten minutes before the off.[107] Turf scandals of this and other kinds were widespread, and one infamous case concerned Lord George Bentinck, a leading member of the Jockey Club. In 1844, he had two horses entered for the Chester Cup: Red Deer and Bramble. This latter was the heavy favourite, but Bentinck laid against him while backing Red Deer to win £100,000, which it did. 'The dictator of the turf' opened himself to charges of foul play because he was the starter for the race and he ensured that Red Deer was in the second row at the starting post, behind Bramble and Best Bower. Their jockeys were instructed to act as 'caretakers' for Bentinck's fancy and to allow it to pass between them as soon as the flag fell, thus giving it a better chance of victory.[108]

In the early nineteenth century, horse-racing was rife with trickery and sharp practice, but it is bookmakers who have become slandered and libelled as the sole culprits responsible for 'dirty tricks'. In particular, condemnation has focused on the activities of two leviathans of the betting ring: William Crockford and John Gully.[109] 'Crocky' was an old-fashioned adventurer who had started work as a fishmonger in the 1780s before becoming a professional gambler. So successful was he at his chosen occupation that in 1827 he opened what became swiftly the foremost gaming house in London. It was in St James's Street, and the 1,200 members paid £25 a year to belong to 'this gorgeous temple'.[110] In it they could game to high stakes while drinking the best wines and eating sumptuous meals prepared by the celebrated chef, Ude, whom Crocky paid an annual salary of over £1,200. It is reputed that the former fishmonger won £300,000 from the aristocracy in the first two years in which his club was open. Pithily, Ashton commented that 'as is often the case at Lord's cricket ground, the great match of the gentlemen of England against the professional players was won by the latter'.[111] His victory was resented. He was reviled as 'the father of hazard and hell – ye fiends! what a title! yet truly his own by infernal right'.[112] Still, even his enemies allowed that gaming was conducted fairly in his house. Demonstrating a realistic outlook, one nobleman commented that if his sons were 'so foolish as to risk their money on the die, they are less likely to be cheated at Crockford's than at any other place'.[113]

Unable to traduce Crocky as a sharpster in gambling, his detractors assailed his standing as a bookmaker. Like O'Kelly and England before him, he was attracted to the racecourse and soon he established himself as 'conspicuous above his associates'.[114] In common with other bookies, he was 'possessed of a marvellous memory', and it was he who popularized the system of laying multiple bets; that is, he quoted odds against backers finding the winners of two, three, four or even five events.

> Old Crocky loved to coax the tyro with an offer of a 'thousand pounds' to some of the youth's pocket money against his naming the winner of the great events, viz. Derby, Oaks and Leger. Many a thousand he picked up in this way, leaving the simple taker of the odds to gloat over the four grand figures on paper, while the astute layer invariably pocketed the 'reality'.[115]

Patently, it is more difficult for a punter to be successful in multiple betting – although their rewards are greater if they win – and by laying this kind of bet, Crockford increased his profits enormously. This prosaic account of his prosperity as a bookmaker failed to appeal to Longrigg. He preferred to defame Crocky as 'the second most evil man on the 19th-century turf', basing his detraction on the Mameluke affair of 1827. This Derby winner was well-fancied to win the St Leger, and without citing any sources, Longrigg proposed that its chances of victory were ruined by a number of false starts, all of which were engineered by the starter because he was bribed by Crockford.[116] It is probable that this was so, yet this chicanery did not make the bookie any worse a person than scions of the nobility such as Darlington and Bentinck.[117] But it would seem that in Longrigg's opinion, iniquity was the preserve of working-class layers and not upper-class turfites. Ironically, Crockford's death was brought about by the nobbling of his horse, Ratan, the hot favourite for the Derby of 1844. It was 'got at' the night before the race, in which it ran last, and the shock of the result killed the bookmaker, who was in any case seriously ill.[118]

Crockford's unattractive appearance exacerbated the abhorrence felt for him, and Longrigg drew attention to this. One contemporary described the bookmaker as tall and corpulent, and looking like a country farmer, but the historian preferred to rely on a more derogatory description. Instead, he dwelt on the bookmaker's white and flabby cheeks, his apparently knuckleless hands – which were as 'soft as raw veal', as 'white as paper' – and his 'large, flexible mouth' which was stuffed with false teeth. Bernard Darwin agreed that there was 'about the creature something obscene', and he mentioned that like Crutch Robinson, Crocky was paralysed in some way, having a crippled gait.[119]

Whatever other insults were hurled at his friend and rival, John Gully, he could not be taunted for loathsome looks. Originally a butcher from Gloucestershire, Gully was over six feet tall and he was possessed of an imposing physique. He led a chequered and exciting life: debtor imprisoned at Fleet; bare-fisted boxing champion of England; publican; bookmaker and race-horse owner; MP for Pontefract; and wealthy colliery proprietor. Thormanby styled him 'the most remarkable man the sporting world' had seen in the nineteenth century, but others saw him in a less favourable light.[120] William Day condemned him as a man with 'a tyrannical and overbearing disposition, extremely avaricious, and, like men of his class, not over-scrupulously nice in the acquirement of wealth'.[121] Longrigg concurred with this denunciation. He shrank from Gully as the most evil man to be involved in horse-racing in the 1800s, and he convicted him of winning money through methods which were 'as crooked as they could be', his 'principal technique being to bribe jockeys'.[122]

Gully was both a bookie and a punter, and with his associate, Harry Hill, he was a prominent engineer of 'coups' (successful betting moves). Their practice was to lay and back against 'dead 'uns', horses which they knew would not run in a race, which were unfit or which would be pulled.[123] Obviously, if a coup was to work, then the confederates needed information from jockeys or trainers, but Hill and Gully were not the creators of this system by which the result of a race might be predetermined by those who were 'inside' (in the know). The renowned jockey Samuel Chifney revealed that on one occasion in the eighteenth century, he had backed against his mount winning because he knew it was not fit enough to gain victory.[124] To keep the public 'outside' the secret, jockeys like him gave their stakes to commissioners who placed their bets for them without arousing suspicion. The same was true of trainers who betted against the horses which were in their charge, some of whom were not averse to stacking the odds even further in their favour. They did this by giving their runners an opiate ball on the night before the race; this would not prevent them from competing but it would slow them down.[125] Indeed, Day himself nobbled Gully's horse, Old England, which was entered for the Derby of 1845 and which was trained by the poisoner's father![126]

Hill and Gully did not need to pay for their information. Both of them were commissioners as well as backers and layers, and it was this role which kept them inside.[127] By the standards of horse-racing in the twentieth century, their methods of ensuring a profit were dubious and underhand. But as Darwin pointed out, they operated in a dishonest age in which otherwise 'respectable' men felt that cheating at sport was acceptable.[128] In the words of the racing commentator Newmarket, the ex-butcher was no hero, but he was a sporting representative of his day who had an 'honest and substantial shrewdness'.[129] These praiseworthy characteristics have been obscured by the arrogant assessments of posterity, and it is apparent that Gully's blameworthy traits have been stressed by those who wish to demean bookmaking as a system and who want to portray bookmakers as unwholesome.

In a familiar pattern, it is impossible to separate this scorn from a dislike of the working class. When Gully was elected to Parliament in

1832, he stood as a Radical; his defeated opponent was the son of Lord Mexborough, who regarded the seat of Pontefract as a sinecure. Charles Greville lamented Gully's victory, bracketing it with that of William Cobbett and other 'very bad characters' who believed in democracy; and he derided Gully's wife as 'a coarse, vulgar woman'.[130] A former boot-black and thimble-rigger, Gully's associate Hill, too, was looked down on for his vulgarity. His conversation was dismissed as licentious, his dress was mocked as slovenly, and his lack of education and dense ignorance were ridiculed.[131] Hills's status was 'exquisitely plebeian', and it was proclaimed that the class to which he belonged was 'one of the worst in any moral or social scale'. Of course, it was not, but just as working-class people were shunned as 'coarse, boorish' and offensive, so too were bookmakers eschewed as low-born louts who had an unfortunate propensity for making money from the landed elite.[132] One of the most successful of them was William Davies, and it was because of his outstanding moral rectitude that it became difficult for bookie-baiters to carry home their attacks.

In the early 1840s, this carpenter had begun to take half-a-crown bets from his workmates while they repaired the Jockey Club Rooms at Newmarket; by 1850, he was laying £50,000 to £1,000 against Lord Exeter's horse winning the Derby. Contemporaries acclaimed him as:

> the sole unaided and unassisted architect of his own fortune; gifted with a clear head and quick perception, calculating mind, and most retentive memory, he has undoubtedly turned those natural endowments to the very best advantage, and he now shines forth in the sporting hemisphere as a 'star' of no common magnitude; his unassuming deportment and unwavering probity of conduct during his career on the turf . . . have earned for him 'golden opinions' in every sense of the word.[133]

Davies established his righteousness early in his career when he lost over £10,000 on the result of a handicap at Newmarket. To the consternation of those who believed that bookies were 'knockers' (defaulters), he paid his losses with alacrity and in thousand-pound notes which were 'sparkling, crisp . . . and as big as your portmanteau'.[134] The Druid compared his reliance on ready cash to that of Dennis O'Kelly at his zenith. He recounted that on one occasion the Irishman had laid a heavy bet and he had been asked where his estates lay. In reply, he told his interrogator that he had 'the map o' them about me' and he proceeded to show off a perfect roll of banknotes.[135] Unlike O'Kelly, the honesty of Davies was unimpeachable – even Longrigg acknowledged it as such – and this characteristic enabled him to make an innovation to bookmaking which was of great significance. He differed from his colleagues in that he did not 'exchange parole undertakings' (credit) with his customers. Instead, when he laid them a bet, he took their cash and he promised to pay them out if they won. This he did. Like other bookmakers, he prospered when the outsiders were successful and he lost when the 'cracks' (race-horses of excellence) were victorious, but his clients were assured of their winnings whatever the result.[136] It was this uprightness, and that of other professional bettors, that sounded the death knell for the abusive epithets of blackleg and leg and which announced their replacement by the more descriptive term of 'The Ring'.

By the early 1800s, betting posts had begun to disappear, and bookmakers were gathered to do business in a part of the main stand of a racecourse. In 1839, one of the stewards at Doncaster, Lord Kelburne, argued that this arrangement 'caused annoyance to the ladies' and so the town council agreed to place bookies and punters in a railed-off lawn, or ring as it became known.[137] Other committees followed suit, and in 1850 a contemporary described the hurly-burly of the betting ring at Epsom at the time of the Derby.

> The million are in Surrey; they strew the greensward at Banstead as the leaves clothe Vallambrosa. Behold, the din of myriads rising fast and furious around – while above all, like Koenig's horn in Jullien's concerts, there is heard one pair of human lungs repeating the cabalistic call 'I'll lay *four* to one against Bowlinbrook; I'll bet 5 to 1 against *Milljew*; I'll lay 5 to 1 against *Pittsfurd*; I'll bet 7 to 1 against Niggur. I'll lay &c., &c., &c., &c., against Voltigur, Nutsell, Ghillie Callum, Cariboo, oo, OO, &c., &c., &c., &c.' That's Mr Davies, with a dapper little satin tie around his vocal culverin and a hat with the tiniest of brims covering his Californian *caput*. He never tires, calling unceasingly the prices he is prepared to pay – that is to say, offer – passing perpetually inside the rails of the ring, as doth the lion at the Zoological Gardens behind the bars of his cage. In his grip a bookling and a morsel of a pencil . . .[138]

On a modern racecourse, bookmakers are excluded still from the more exclusive members' enclosure and they stand at the rails which cordon it off, shouting the odds across this barrier. They are placed in Tattersall's Ring, so named because in the later 1800s, most of the bookmakers who operated there were subscribers to The Room. By contrast, the medium-sized layers gathered in the silver ring – to which it was cheaper to gain entry and in which the bets laid were lower –

while the small bookies would have betted outside, that is, in those parts of a racecourse to which entrance was free.[139]

As a phrase, 'The Ring' achieved prominence during the 1850s, by which time its members were acknowledged as practitioners of 'bookmaking'.[140] This term was mentioned as early as 1824 in the *Sporting Magazine* and it was derived from the practice adopted by bettors of pencilling their transactions in a book.[141] By the 1830s, it was obvious that the word was restricted to the actions of full-time layers, but there is no evidence of the use of the noun 'bookmaker', although the Druid wrote that 'about two hundred men may be said to have had books in 1856'.[142] Ten years later, the term bookmaker was in common currency, and soon it was joined by the word 'penciller'.[143] Both were neutral in their connotations, describing an occupation without giving loaded judgements on its practitioners. Their appearance owed much to the integrity of men like William Davies, a characteristic which not only effected a change in language, but also facilitated the expansion of bookmaking away from the racecourse and into the towns and cities of Britain.

3

POPULAR RECREATION, LOTTERIES AND BETTING HOUSES

POPULAR RECREATION

After the Napoleonic Wars, the decline of matches became inexorable, so that by 1843, only eighty-six contests of this type were run compared with 897 sweepstakes. This latter figure was a 350 per cent increase on that for 1807, and it reflected the burgeoning popularity of horse-racing.[1] New meetings proliferated, and even a small fixture like that at Horsham could attract 12,000 people in 1837, while Aberdeen drew a crowd of 30,000 in 1843.[2] Five years later, there were 130 racecourses in Britain compared with ninety-five in 1823, and this growth was accompanied by a rise in betting and the advancement of bookmaking.[3] All three processes were regarded with alarm by a reinvigorated puritanical movement.

Perkin described how the Industrial Revolution was entangled with a 'moral revolution' which profoundly changed the English national character. He proposed that between 1780 and 1850, England ceased to be a country notorious as one of the world's 'most aggressive, brutal, rowdy, outspoken, riotous, cruel and bloodthirsty'. Instead, it became a nation which was famed as 'inhibited, polite, orderly, tender-minded, prudish and hypocritical'. In his opinion, this transformation was effected by an imposition on both upper and lower ranks of the traditional puritanism of the English middle orders – as remoulded by the campaigning of the Evangelicals, the Dissenters and the Benthamites.[4] His argument is important and relevant, but it does underestimate the vitality of autonomous working-class efforts to reform their class.

Many workers disliked gambling and heavy drinking, not because they subscribed to bourgeois values, but because both activities could impose an unbearable strain on a family's inadequate income. As Dorothy Thompson has shown, most Chartist women were strong in their desire to 'remove the Charter from the Pothouse', and temperance was a key element of the movement.[5] Likewise, while the local curate resented the Horsham race-meeting because it attracted 'undesirable characters', the fixture was avoided by some working people because of its attendant evils of betting, drinking and swindling, all associated with a foolish expenditure of money.[6] It is essential to recognize that working-class respectability was not imposed from above, and that it was often connected to a desire to break out of the poverty trap. At the same time, there should be no exaggeration of the conversion of the English – or the Irish, Scottish and Welsh – into a 'respectable' people during the Industrial Revolution.

It cannot be disputed that many aspects of British society were deeply affected by industrialization and by the development of the factory system. In particular, E. P. Thompson has made it clear that factory masters rearranged the pattern of work and leisure for those whom they employed. They strove to enforce a time and work discipline on their 'hands', through which they sought to make them more amenable workers.[7] Employers disdained leisure as a period which encouraged idleness and wastefulness, and their desire to reduce its length dovetailed neatly with the contemporaneous moral crusade of the Evangelicals. These aimed to eliminate bloody and immoral pastimes and to exorcize the working class of 'roughness'. Consequently, there was a two-pronged assault on popular amusements which appeared to be successful. Legislation outlawed many abhorrent sports, local opposition brought to an end numerous wakes and fairs, and employers squeezed their workers into a straitjacket which drastically diminished their free time.[8] Long-established pastimes seemed to go into decline, and historians like the Hammonds and Chapman believed that this trend was accelerated by urbanization, a phenomenon which swallowed up open spaces and which thus allowed the workers nowhere to play.[9] They felt that the early decades of the nineteenth century were a 'dark age' for popular culture in Britain's towns and cities, and Malcolmson agreed with them that this period remained a recreational vacuum until new pastimes emerged after 1850.[10]

Historians like Peter Bailey have confirmed the view that a 'new leisure world' was created in Victorian Britain, but they have disputed that there was a hiatus between older and novel forms of recreation.[11] In particular, Hugh Cunningham has stressed the vitality of traditional amusements and their survival in urban areas.[12] Perceptively, he observed that much of working-class leisure remained privatized 'in the sense of being class-bound and invisible to those outside the culture'.[13] Protected by the impenetrability of their neighbourhoods, working-class supporters and promoters of illegal sports were hidden from the prying eyes of reformers. From the 1820s, cock-fighting and pugilism may have been bereft of most of their upper-class patrons, but both maintained their popularity into the second half of the nineteenth century.[14] So too did other blood sports. In the Potteries of the 1850s, Thomas Hawley thought that the condition of the masses 'was on a very low plane'. Dog-fighting, cock-fighting, rabbit-coursing and pigeon-shooting were weekly occurrences, and they led to a lot of gambling, Hawley recalling that a fireman once staked as much as £10 on a rabbit-coursing match.[15] In horrible detail, Henry Mayhew recounted how ratting was carried on in London in the 1850s, and in the same decade, Hugh Shimmin commented on the vigour of the 'canine fancy' in Liverpool.[16] He described graphically a dog-fight and the betting which accompanied it.

> The growling of the brutes at each other – the cursing of the men at each other and at the dogs – the shouts of delight when the dog which an enthusiastic looker-on is backing obtains an advantage – the crushing to the edge of the pit – the heat of the close room – the sound of money changing hands – the demoniacal expression of the men in the pit, and the terrible excitement of all around, carry the mind far away from happy England in the nineteenth century, and we look in vain for any scene amongst the degrading exhibitions or pastimes of savage nations, at all to compare with what surrounds us, and what takes place in Liverpool almost every day . . . and again the dogs run at each other, and growling, gnawing, twisting, tearing, biting, writhing and wrestling, they go through another round.[17]

The survival of traditional recreations should not detract from the potency of the campaign against them. It was well thought out; it boasted powerful supporters; and it was comprehensive in its coverage. Among its targets was horse-racing. From the 1820s, a sustained offensive was made on the sport as an activity which encouraged time-wasting and engendered immorality. Like the eighteenth-century drive to eradicate gaming, it focused on places where the 'evil' was prominent, and it was led by local clergymen. In Cheltenham, the Reverend F. Close viewed with apprehension and disgust the approach of the town's annual races in 1827. In common with other moralists, he condemned theatres and racecourses as places of evil where a multitude of sins were rampant: 'adultery, fornication, uncleanness, lasciviousness – hatred, variance, emulations, wrath, strife – envying, drunkenness, *revellings*, and SUCH LIKE'. It was his belief that race-week drew to Cheltenham large numbers of the most worthless members of society, and he thundered that these reprobates blasphemed, drank, engaged in the lowest profligacy and increased the crime rate.

> But the master sin of the week, the most frightful demon of this moral storm, remains to be noticed; the foul spirit of gaming! a spirit without which the race course would offer no charm to the greater number of those who frequent it. Gambling is the very essence of the amusement; a vice which appears to be growing in our land; though it be a vice which is more pre-eminently destructive both of body and soul, than any other which Satan ever devised for the ruin of mankind. Every vile passion of our corrupt nature is excited and inflamed by it; envy, malice, revenge, the lust of money, pride, contention, cruelty, and as we have on one occasion known, murder! And who can deny that a taste for gambling is easily acquired upon the race course?[18]

Like other puritanical clerics, Close bemoaned the impoverishment of wealthy houses as a result of gambling, and he bewailed the spreading of the vice to the lower orders of society.[19] But his tirade did not go unchallenged. Popular Toryism was by no means a spent force, and in the *Gentleman's Magazine*, a correspondent rebutted with vigour the clergyman's censure of horse-racing. He was accused of spouting 'dangerous ultra-piety' that menaced Cheltenham and towns like it with ruin. It was pointed out that horse-racing had brought prosperity to the place, and that it would go into economic decline if the races were ended. Close's critic accused him of 'hypercalvinism', emphasizing that the principle of his sermon was hostility to all public amusements. The Tory writer agreed that these could be accompanied by licentiousness and gambling, but he claimed that their benefits outweighed these abuses. It was his firm belief that popular activities gave employment and increased trade, and he stated that if they were suppressed, then many people would be thrown out of work and would commit 'more and greater crimes than those which now attend theatres, concerts, races, and pleasure gardens'. Close's antagonist believed that the social order was threatened by the pronouncements of 'ultras', and he declared that the party of religious enthusiasts was composed chiefly of Radicals and Evangelical London tradesmen who were 'hostile to the sovereign'.[20]

Cheltenham races were a major event in the sporting calendar, and the attempt to end them was frustrated by the forceful opposition to Close's invective. But if Tory traditionalists succeeded in this battle, then they faced a sterner conflict elsewhere in the country. In south-east Lancashire, there was an eruption of wakes-time race-meetings between the 1820s and the 1840s, some organized by publicans.

Robert Poole has emphasized that their promoters were aware of the reservoir of spectators in the expanding populations of nearby cotton towns, a fact of which they were quick to take advantage. These sporting men were supported by 'beleaguered upper-class Tories' who were attempting 'to appeal over the heads of reformers to popular hedonism'.[21] They felt that their patronage of 'manly sports' would buy off working-class support for the Charter, and their stronghold was Rochdale. Here, the gentry backed the races run at Bagslate, where at the same time they actively encouraged the continuance of the 'nudger sports' – old English sports and pastimes.

Locally, they were vehemently opposed by writers in the Rochdale *Spectator*. These disapprovers were an eclectic group, and as elsewhere in Great Britain, they included, in the opinion of Golby and Purdue, 'middle-class reformers, working-class radicals and non-conformists alike'.[22] These groups were united by their disdain for amusements such as wrestling, climbing the greasy pole for a prize of an ox's heart and five shillings, and diving for silver in flour with the hands of the entrants tied behind their backs. It was believed that such activities so degraded their competitors that they were unable to appreciate either morals or political power.[23] The antagonism to these kind of games was summed up by a Radical who made an appeal in dialect to fellow members of the working class:

> Ol just ax thoose on yo us went to Bagslut rases wat yo larnt we gooin? Yo noan vert weel us ther wur naut gooin on theer but lyin, un swarin, un gammin un sich lik wark, un o sworts o raskuls un rapskallions wur theer o purpose ur to chet un steyle. Un just unbethink yo wat mak o wark wu gooin on oppo th' rase greawnd o Rushbarin Sundy, waw mony o hunderth nu theawsunds o foke went theer o sted o gooin to th' church ur elze to o chappel, un lots on um went whoam ut neet, Sundy us it wur, us drunken us pigs. Neaw, ol ust ax yo whoo it is us brings o this wark o beawt? Waw its o lot o chaps us koes thersels gentelmen, un sum landlorts us expektud fur to get howd o yore brass we sellin drink . . .[24]

A major target of this tirade against the races were bookmakers, who upset 'respectable' working-class people because of their calling and because of their habit of loudly shouting out the odds.[25] Not for the last time were bookies to be associated with popular Toryism, but this particular attack on nudger sports was unsuccessful. That did not deter their opponents, but with the decline of Chartism after 1848, their political motivation became reduced. At the same time, moral and religious objections to 'manly' amusements became prominent. In 1850, the campaigners felt that their prayers for divine intervention had been answered when the Rochdale races were ruined by a week of heavy rain, and following this disaster they were discontinued until 1884.[26]

The efforts to quell horse-racing in Rochdale were mirrored elsewhere in Great Britain. At Horsham, the curate succeeded in closing down the meeting in 1840, after its seventh fixture; and in Paisley, a strident pamphlet was issued against the sport in 1836, prior to the town's race-week. Like others of its type, it emphasized the uselessness of racing horses and stressed that hostility to the activity was rooted in its link to gambling. This 'most fatal and pernicious of vices' was bonded as closely to other popular recreations and activities, and so the agitation against them focused increasingly on this connection.[27] Obvious targets for the reformers were pitch and toss and tossing. These were games the entire purpose of which was gambling and, unlike horse-racing, they could not be defended as a sport that enhanced the breeding of its competitors. More than this, they were feared because they attracted large and potentially riotous crowds of working-class men and youths. This was a serious threat at a time when huge numbers of workers were disaffected, and it also posed a problem for the work discipline of factory owners and other employers. In 1824, an indignant writer to the *Bolton Express* summarized the various objections to the pastime of throwing coins for money.

> I would lay before the public, and in particular, before those who have it in their power to suppress illegal proceedings, that abominable practice of gaming, vulgarly called *pitch and toss*, which prevails in this town to an alarming degree. The swearing and blasphemy which are belched forth at some of these diabolical gaming convocations, are truly horrific, for when the gamesters have been remonstrated with upon their wicked course of life, the following expressions have burst forth from some of their impious lips: 'That there was no Hell;' 'That God Almighty had nothing to do with their actions &c.' . . . I hope that this matter will be taken up by those who have power and love good order . . .[28]

The 'problem' of pitch and toss was nationwide, and in 1826, a vestry meeting at Bexley in Kent noted that the village's constable was unable to abate the nuisance of men and boys gambling on the heath on Sundays.[29] It was this desecration of the Sabbath which provided moralists with their best opportunity to try and suppress this and other pastimes. Unsurprisingly, working-class games were played most on the one day which officially was given over to rest, but respectable members of the middle class disliked the way in which Sunday was regarded as 'free time'. They strove to make orderly, moral and reputable all activities on that day, and they employed the forces of authority to implement their wishes. In Scotland, their actions were co-ordinated by groups like the Society for Promoting the Sanctification of the Sabbath, and in Paisley, for example, people were prosecuted in 1826 for fishing and bathing in the canal on a Sunday.[30] Over the border in England, the Society for the Reformation of Manners performed a similar function, attempting to enforce the Sunday Observance Act of 1625 – which had forbidden people to meet outside their own parishes on the Lord's Day for 'any sports or pastimes whatever'.[31]

In the context of early-nineteenth-century Britain, a new relevance was given to this kind of legislation and to puritanical movements. Across the country, they were marshalled to impose a time and work discipline on the working class, and one of their main targets was gambling on a Sunday. In 1834, Abraham Driver, the Deputy Constable of Broughton near Salford, was asked by 'some gentlemen' to take into custody a group of gamblers. After a severe struggle, he captured two men – who were committed for trial for assault upon him – and in the same year he arrested other gamblers on Kersal Moor.[32] At Warrington, the police commissioners observed that in 1839, 'a great number of persons have been convicted for gambling and drunkenness, particularly on the Sabbath Day'; and by 1853, the *Burnley Advertiser* was reporting that 'we can scarcely take up a provincial paper, but we find convictions for Sunday Gambling'.[33] Pitch and toss was not the only working-class game which was prohibited. In 1825, an anonymous writer appealed to Brecon magistrates to act against publicans who permitted the 'nefarious' practice of gambling with cards in their houses; and in 1842 at Wakefield, magistrates told five young men that they were 'very disreputable' to play the athletic game of knurr and spell on the Sabbath. They were fined one shilling each, and with unconscious hypocrisy, the bench declared that England was a land of liberty where all might worship as they pleased, even if it did not only mean going to a church.[34]

In an attempt to increase the cost to those found guilty of the 'offence' of pitch and toss, towns like Lancaster passed byelaws against it which provided for the imposition of a 'heavy penalty'. Even then, 'gangs of idle lads' continued to play the game, and in 1853, it was estimated that at Burnley, around one thousand youths and men 'are regularly engaged every Sunday in gambling, pigeon flying and water-rat hunting'.[35] The might of the ruling classes, however, was unable to quell these pastimes. Their suppression was made impossible by their popularity and by the determination of male workers to defy class-biased laws. This victory has remained unrecognized, but it is no less significant for that.[36] Nevertheless, if the law could not squash irregular forms of gambling intrinsic to working-class communities, then they were able to crush more regular wagering via lotteries and gaming houses.

LOTTERIES AND GAMING HOUSES

The earliest English lottery had been projected in 1566 and was drawn three years later. It had included 400,000 lots with prizes in plate, tapestry and money, and its profits had been used to strengthen the 'Realme, and towards other such publique good workes'. Over the next one hundred years, this motive provided the *raison d'être* for many semi-official promotions, until in 1694, Parliament sanctioned the first English state lottery, the profits of which directly benefited the Exchequer. These official promotions paid for the building of Westminster Bridge (1739) and for the beginnings of the British Library (1753), and from 1776 lotteries became a regular institution authorized annually by Parliament. They were supported by those who advocated voluntary taxation and state levies on luxury expenditure, and they were justified because of their remuneration. In 1802, the Exchequer benefited by £340,458 from that year's promotion, and the government ensured such large rewards by 'farming out': if shares in a lottery were worth·£10 each, then they were sold to leading stockbrokers for £15; and these men then recouped their outlay by selling them to the public at a further inflated price.[37]

This process attracted opportunists who placed themselves as middlemen between the lottery farmers and the purchasers of tickets. Patrick Colquhoun described them as 'a class of Swindlers, Cheats, and low Gamblers, composed of idle and dissolute characters, who have abandoned every honest pursuit, and who live chiefly by fraudulent transactions'.[38] By 1808, their depredations had become so notorious that a Select Committee was established to enquire into the 'Evils attending Lotteries'. It declared that they were abused by sharpsters, but it also pronounced against their ill effects on the working class. Lotteries were condemned as the cause of idleness, dissipation, poverty, crime, madness and suicide, and they were eschewed as a proper form of raising money for the state.[39] This disapprobation was not new. In 1699, private lotteries had been outlawed, and in 1707, the Irish Parliament had denounced them as 'mischievous and unlawful games which evil disposed persons had for years set up and thereby fraudulently got to themselves great sums of money from children, servants and other unwary persons'.[40]

Henry Fielding, too, had disapproved of lotteries, chiding their subscribers as fools, but his and other eighteenth-century objections to the continuance of state promotions foundered against the rock of profitability.[41] It was this imperative which scuppered the 1808 committee's avowal against lotteries, yet once the Napoleonic Wars were over, resistance against them again increased. In 1817, Samuel Roberts issued a virulent pamphlet against the legislature's encouragement of 'the wheel of fortune', arguing that 'for a little present profit', the state lured people into crime.[42]

> That fiend comes forth like Aetna's flame,
> The SPIRIT OF GAMBLING, call his name,
> So flush'd and terrible in power,
> The priests themselves he would devour,
> But straight by Acts of Parliament,
> Loose through the land his plagues are sent.[43]

Led in Parliament by Wilberforce and Lyttelton, the anti-lottery campaigners stressed that the people's industriousness was weakened by 'the spirit of gambling'. They emphasized that this would have an adverse effect on other sources of government revenue and these arguments convinced MPs to end state promotions after the scheme for 1823.[44]

Flushed with success, the opponents of gambling turned their attention to gaming. Despite the fierce campaign waged against it in the 1700s, the activity flourished, to the chagrin of many. In 1828, an association was set up in Doncaster for the 'Suppression of Gambling Houses and Gaming Tables'. Its members objected to the 'notorious and shameless' manner in which these facilities were used during race-week; they abhorred the 'profligate and debased characters which such a practice draws together from all parts of the Kingdom'; and they loathed the 'consequent plunder of the unwary and gross violation of the laws'.[45] Like their upper-class predecessors, these bourgeois enemies of gambling were motivated partly by a concern for the well-being of people of their own class. They realized that gaming was a pastime that appealed to raffish members of the middle class, and they were aware that this attraction could lead to the dissipation of a family's wealth and to its loss of status. During the 1820s, these fears were apparently validated by the doom of David Hoggart. A man from a 'respectable' middle-class background, his character was ruined by a fondness for 'raffles, cards and dancing' and by the company of 'loose females'. Eventually, he was imprisoned in Dumfries gaol, and while there he killed a turnkey, a crime for which he was hanged.[46]

Hoggart's descent into the mire of self-destruction became a prototype for other cautionary tales against the sin of gaming.[47] These stories were useful as propaganda, and they formed part of the wider anti-gambling campaign which became pronounced during the 1830s.[48] In 1833, *Fraser's Magazine* published a lengthy, well-researched and strident attack on the hells of London; and four years later, it was followed up by Nimrod's renowned denunciation, 'The Anatomy of Gaming'.[49] By 1844, the clamour against gambling had become irresistible, and a Select Committee of the House of Lords was set up to inquire into the laws which governed it. Upon its advice, an Act was passed in 1845 which strengthened police powers against hells, and which nullified and made unenforceable in law all contracts or agreements which related to gaming and wagering.[50] This brought English legislation into line with that of Scotland, and shrewdly, Mark Clapson has observed that the new law restated the principles which had led to the abolition of state lotteries. He concurred with E. C. Devereux that gambling was shunned by the authorities because its rewards were dependent upon chance and not upon hard work and effort. In consequence, it 'exposed the raw nerve of the profit motive' and as the 'unacceptable face of capitalism' it had to be attacked.[51]

Significantly, the legislation against gambling did not extend to betting on horse-races. Despite the pronounced hostility to the sport, its aristocratic supporters proclaimed that it was advantageous to society. They vaunted its success in stimulating the blood stock of horses; they bragged that it brought together peacefully 'vast bodies of people all over the country'; and they boasted that it promoted intercourse between the different classes.[52] The Select Committee agreed with them, and although it condemned excessive betting, it did not outlaw the activity itself. This is not surprising: the members of the inquiry were lords and horse-racing was regarded as an aristocratic recreation. Indeed, when called to give evidence, Admiral Rous warned the committee that if they were to legislate against betting, then they would make 'this country not fit for a gentleman to live in'; and as late as 1861, Lord Palmerston proposed successfully that Parliament be adjourned until after the day of the Derby.[53]

BETTING HOUSES

By the later 1840s, gaming houses were in decline, a development which Miers attributed as much to an increase in new opportunities for leisure and gambling as to the effects of the law.[54] In particular, off-course betting on horses had become popular, as Charles Dickens explained in 1852.

> Presto! Betting-shops spring up in every street! There is a demand at all the brokers' shops for old, fly-blown, coloured prints of race-horses, and for any odd folio volumes that have the appearance of Ledgers. Two such prints in any shop-window and one such book on any shop-counter, will make a complete Betting-office, bank, and all.
>
> The Betting-shop may be a Tobacconist's, thus suddenly transformed; or it may be nothing but a Betting-shop. It may be got up cheaply . . . by the removal of the legitimate counter, and the erection of an official partition and desk in one corner; or it may be wealthy in mahogany fittings, French polish and office furniture.[55]

It is ironic that the emergence of these betting shops was facilitated by the authorities, who had unwittingly created a gambling vacuum; not only did they act against gaming houses, but also against sweepstakes. These popular lotteries on horse-races had appeared in the early 1840s, and rightly, David Itzkowitz has seen them as a transitional form of gambling.[56] Before their emergence, it is improbable that there had been any mass betting on horses away from racecourses, and it was the suppression of sweepstakes which led to off-course bookmaking as it is familiar today. In 1845, they were made illegal by a number of court decisions, and three years later the Attorney General decided to prosecute the proprietors of newspapers that printed advertisements for them.[57] Although not stifled, sweepstakes were hindered. The demand of punters for off-course betting, however, was not, and so men to cater for it were called into existence.

As G. H. Stutfield observed in 1901, 'it is the backer who creates the want of the bookmaker, and then the bookmaker springs up', and it was a demand for their services which led to the appearance of list bookies towards the end of the 1840s.[58] A combination of factors enabled them to fill the gap which had been left by the demise of sweepstakes, one of which was the legality of their operations. Equally significant was the provision of the Act of 1845, which had forbidden the legal recovery of gaming debts. This inevitably discouraged credit transactions and as an incentive to cash betting its timing was fortuitous, precisely because this form of business was better suited to the dealings of bookmakers with a mass clientele.[59] Layers like Leviathan Davies realized this and they also appreciated that the new procedure of wagering allowed them to gather in large sums of ready money before an event. Indeed, in 1850, it was estimated that at Davies's two betting shops in London, £300,000 was staked each year in small bets alone.[60] With this cash in hand, he and others like him were able both to finance their on-course operations and to make better books.

In fact, it was widely accepted that it was Davies who was

responsible for the extension of bookmaking away from racecourses.[61] Rice stated that numerous customers pestered him for odds about future events, and so he decided to cater for them by advertising his prices in London, at the Durham Arms in Serle Street and at Barr's in Long Acre. Here, he hung up lists of runners for forthcoming events and beside the name of each horse he quoted a price about its chances. When bets were laid, Davies or one of his clerks would enter them into a large banker's ledger, and in exchange for their cash punters were given a ticket which recorded the transaction. Successful clients were paid out the day after a race was run, and such was the certainty that claims on him would be paid on demand, that a winning ticket of his was as negotiable as a banknote.[62]

Not everyone agreed that list betting was the invention of the Leviathan. The Druid stated that Messrs Drummond and Greville began the system in 1847; Itzkowitz concurred with the year, but declared that it was William Turpin who 'was a man ahead of his time'; while Charles Sidney wrote that the lists appeared first between 1815 and 1820, when they were displayed in homes, clubs, shops, warehouses and inns.[63] Unfortunately, he gave no sources to support this assertion, and given that on-course bookmaking was in its infancy until the early 1840s, it is unlikely that there was any sophisticated form of off-course betting until later in that decade. This view would seem to be validated by the lack of mention of lists in the deliberations of the Select Committee of 1844, and their appearance must therefore be attributed both to on-course layers and to sweepstakes promoters who adjusted to new circumstances produced by state interference.[64] Still, whoever devised them, their popularity could not be denied, as was acknowledged in 1852 by a contributor to *Chambers's Edinburgh Journal.*

> But the betting lists are the attraction – these are the dice of the betting man; a section of one of the side-walls within the office is devoted to them. They consist of long strips of paper – each race having its own strip – on which are stated the odds against the horse. Hasty and anxious are the glances which the speculator casts at the betting-lists; he there sees which are favourites; whether those he has backed are advancing or retrograding; and he endeavours to discover, by all kinds of movements and dodges, the knowing one's opinion. He will drop fishing words to other gazers, will try to overhear whispered remarks, will sidle towards jockey-legged or mercurial-costumed individuals, and aim especially at getting in to the good graces of the betting-house keeper; who, when his business is slack, comes forth from behind the partition and from the duties of the pigeon-hole to stretch his legs and hold turf-converse. The betting-house keeper is his divinity.[65]

Such a scene would be familiar in a modern betting shop. As a portrayal in the mid-nineteenth century, it disproves the suggestion that it was the Betting and Gaming Act of 1960 which gave birth to the new industry of betting offices.[66] Indeed, in 1852, George Cruikshank 'ascertained that there are nearly three hundred Betting-shops in the metropolis, independent of sporting public-houses and beer-shops'.[67] Despite the disapproval of the licensing magistrates, these latter premises thrived, and they were as evident in Bolton as they were in the capital.[68] Betting shops, too, were present elsewhere in the country. In 1851, it was reported that 'in one of the most public thoroughfares in Hull, a public Betting-Office is actually opened'; and two years later, the Attorney General stated that there were a considerable number of them in the larger towns of the provinces.[69] Their ubiquity was assisted by technological progress. As early as 1840, Paisley racecourse had announced a plan whereby the results of races at the meeting would be transmitted to list-house keepers via the new telegraph system, and its idea was 'followed up with satisfaction in some of the most distinguished racecourses in the south'.[70] Obviously, this means of communication was far superior to that of sending out the results with pigeons, and after 1850, private contractors began to extend telegraph lines to racecourses. This vital development came as racing was expanding because of the advent of railways, and it meant that results could be known nationwide by the day after an event.[71] The importance of this process was recognized by the executive of Doncaster racecourse; from 1853, it provided accommodation for members of the press in its new stand.[72]

Avidly, the betting public called for racing news, and it was supplied by a number of publications, chief of which was *Bell's Life in London*. This weekly newspaper came out on Sundays, and when it started in 1822, it covered a wide range of topics. However, after 1824, it concentrated increasingly on sport, and twenty years later, its editor was receiving a weekly total of 1,500–1,600 sporting communications.[73] Even though it cost sevenpence, its readership was extensive, ranging from the aristocracy to the working class, whose members read it in public houses which advertised that they took it in.[74] By the early 1850s, it was joined by a number of other publications, as described by George Cruikshank. 'These worthy people [the bettors] encourage literature! But it is a literature exclusively their own. Why, here are four "turf newspapers" in the field already; supported entirely by this vagabond class of betting people! "The Turf", "The Racing Post", "The Racing Telegraph", and the "Racing Times".'[75] These four 'racing papers' were supplemented by the *Sporting Weekly*, the *Old Sporting*, the *New Sporting Magazine*, *The Sportsman*, and the *Sporting Review*.[76] To a greater or lesser degree, all these publications included information, reports and results about horse-racing and they gave the tips (predictions) of their own tipsters, much of whose knowledge was supplied by touts.[77] Despite the dubiousness of their advice, these 'sporting prophets' were popular, and newspapers also employed them. Even so, the supply of other tipsters was plentiful and many of them sold their fancies through advertisements in sporting papers, or else hawked them at racecourses.[78]

The increase in racing circulars was dependent upon a public that wanted to bet on horses, yet the popularity of off-course bookmaking was regarded as an unwelcome development by the 'respectable' of the middle class. Their antagonism to the practice was summed up by an editorial in the *Hull Advertiser*. All classes of the town's inhabitants were solemnly warned

> of the corrupting influence of a practice which we understand is greatly on the increase in Hull and Beverley – we allude to that of betting on horse-races, and staking money in chance speculations of all description. Betting on the part of shopkeepers and working men is the high road to ruin – the macadamized path to the Prison and the Workhouse. It saps the foundations of all honesty and of all morality . . . Betting among the upper classes is a terrible evil – a social leprosy which creates more corruption of blood than ever high treason did; but it is only when it reaches the trading and the working classes that it threatens the total subversion of society.

As with lotteries, it was feared that the intoxication of betting would lead to clerks stealing from their employers, to tradesmen becoming insolvent, and to workmen acquiring 'a distaste for the slow progress of honest industry'.[79] Other writers agreed that the social order was endangered by the activity, and it was emphasized that bookies were the cause of this menace. With horror, a correspondent to *Chambers's Edinburgh Journal* exclaimed that, 'the insane are shut up – the desperate transported – the dead buried – the deserted families carried to the workhouse; and the betting-office goes on as before'.[80] Cruikshank perceived that 'these places' held out a great temptation to the ignorant and to the needy, realizing that 'poor creatures' dreamt of changing their destiny through the outlay of a sum as little as a shilling. However, he believed this to be a false hope, and he felt that its existence was the strongest argument for the suppression of betting houses. It was a call taken up readily by others.[81]

Throughout 1852, the movement against betting shops gathered momentum and it was aided by the influx of levanters into the ranks of off-course bookmakers. In *Household Words*, Dickens recounted how he placed a bet with a Mr Cheerful, the proprietor of a new betting shop in the vicinity of Drury Lane Theatre. His fancy won, but when he went to collect his winnings, he found that the proprietor had absconded and that the betting office was filled with a confused crowd of boys, 'mostly greasy, dirty and dissipated'. Dickens himself was against legislation to put down off-course betting, and bookmakers who conducted their 'business on honest and honourable principles' strove to defuse the tension against them.[82] It was to no avail. The scandal of defaulters climaxed when a cheat called Dwyer fled with £25,000, and the government became convinced that list bookies promoted theft and disorder.[83]

In 1853, a bill was presented to Parliament which aimed at quashing betting houses. The Attorney General, Sir Alexander Cockburn, stressed the evils to which they gave rise and he reiterated the objections that had been made by the editor of the *Hull Advertiser*. He discounted the suggestion that betting shops should be licensed, stressing that the government believed that such an action would increase the mischief associated with them. Without discussion, the bill was enacted and betting offices were outlawed and declared a public nuisance. Those who were found guilty of keeping them were subject to a penalty which could not exceed £100, or else they might be imprisoned for six months; the advertisement of them was prohibited; and if a place was thought to be in contravention of the law, then it could be broken into and its inmates arrested; any documents which related to racing and betting could be seized.[84]

ILLEGAL LIST BETTING

When the government had come to frame its bill against betting houses, it had been faced with the difficulty posed by its disinclination to deal with the kind of transactions which went on at Tattersall's. In its view, while off-course betting with professional bookmakers needed to be prohibited, amateur wagering between individuals was legitimate and ought to be allowed.[85] There can be little dispute that this reasoning was dictated by a desire to allow the betting of the gentry and the aristocracy to continue, and it would have been scorned by men like Cruikshank who affirmed that there was small difference between 'The Exchange' and a 'common Betting-shop'.[86] Of course, such an egalitarian opinion was dismissed by upper-class turfites and their apologists, as it was by moralists who opposed popular betting because supposedly it destroyed habits of thrift and perseverance among the 'lower classes'. Like Sylvanus, this group, too, believed in the partiality of government action and they justified it on the grounds that the empire needed to be safeguarded from a dangerous vice: 'A good government is not merely a diplomatic conclave, or a higher assize court; it should be paternal, watchful, and directing; yea, correcting with rod in hand, and stern looks occasionally, whenever the public welfare in morals and domestic exchequer is threatened.'[87]

It was generally accepted that the authorities showed bias when they interfered with the amusements of the people, and that they agreed with 'puritanical saints and tyrants' only when they advocated action against the pleasures of 'tradesmen, mechanics and artizans'.[88] The Betting Act exacerbated such feelings, showing that selfish upper-class legislation overlapped with the aim of the 'respectable' of the middle class to enforce their discipline and morality on the rest of society. Betting shops remained outlawed for over a hundred years, but historians are mistaken to accept that they disappeared after 1853 and that they were immediately replaced by the street as the focus of off-course bookmaking, particularly for working-class punters.[89] For a number of years, the law against betting houses was unenforced or ignored in many parts of the country, and this led to local patterns of betting away from the racecourse.

In 1856, Shimmin recited how betting offices thrived in Liverpool. The city's largest was located in a public house. It was about eighty square yards in size and it contained one hundred volumes of the Turf Register, portraits of race-horses and celebrated jockeys, and a board covered with green baize. On this were pinned the most recent telegraphic messages and the latest state of the odds, the proprietor deciding his own prices, as did other list bookies.[90] There were many other betting offices in Liverpool, and Clapson and Itzkowitz have revealed how they flourished, also, in Manchester and London during the 1860s.[91] However, in some parts of the capital, the authorities did act against their existence, with the result that many list-house keepers were driven to operate on the street. Here, betting was thought to be permissible because the 1853 Act applied only to offices and not to public spaces. In 1865, Thomas Archer mentioned that Bride Passage, Fleet Street, was the 'old station' of outdoor bookmakers, but that they were moved on from there and congregated now at 'the ruins' in Farringdon Street.[92] George Sims recalled that several well-known ready-money bookies stood here daily and exhibited their lists; and he mentioned that there was another public betting place at the corner of Oxford Street and Tottenham Court Road, while at the coffee-house in Foubert's Place, bookies sat in boxes with their lists in front of them.[93]

During the 1850s and 1860s, a feature of off-course bookmaking was its appeal to a wide range of clients. In Liverpool, some illegal betting shops catered for either working-class punters or for 'calico coves' (drapers and general shopkeepers' assistants); but at the city's leading list house, clerks and men of 'superior education and attainments' mixed with 'vulgar' fellows.[94] It was the same at the Ruins, where Sims noted that the youth of the City 'flocked to put their money on' and joined a motley crowd disparaged by Archer as 'seedy, buttoned-up, greasy, napless, flushed, beshawled, hard-hatted; plain mechanic-looking; flashy, butchery, bakery, cornchandlery, and knavish, but never jovial'.[95] These variegated punters were united by their keenness on betting and by their belief that 'laws were only made for slaves – they are free-born Englishmen'.[96] It is important to be aware that whatever their class, all of these punters resented the Betting Act as an unwarranted restriction on a 'habit and custom of a free people'.[97] Their collective response needs to be emphasized, because it has been implied that illegal betting in the mid-nineteenth century was a working-class preserve. It was not. Certainly, it is correct to stress that the 1853 Act was regarded as an aspect of class warfare, but as such it affected lower-middle-class punters as well as those of the working class.[98]

In many respects, then, the inculcation of respectability was as much a product of vertical fractures within the classes as it was of horizontal divisions between them.[99] Consequently, outdoor betting attracted attention not only because it was regarded as an offensive nuisance, but also because it brought together 'disreputable' people of all types who could contaminate the young. Ironically, this gathering was encouraged by a conflict within capitalism. As Downes and his co-writers pointed out, at the same time as attempts were made to control popular leisure, entrepreneurs were catering for it and feeding it.[100] This paradox was explained by James Greenwood in 1869.

> It may not be generally known that the proprietors of the *Sunday Times*, *Bell's Life*, and other journals of a sporting tendency, in their zeal to outdo each other in presenting the earliest possible information to the public, are at the trouble and expense of securing the earliest possible telegram of the result of a horserace, and exhibiting it enlarged on a broad-sheet in their shop-windows . . . Three o'clock is about the time the great race is run at Epsom [the Derby], and at that time the Fleet-street crowd begins to gather. It streams in from the north, from the east, from the south.[101]

Of course, the posting of racing news made backing with street bookies more popular, and it is not surprising that their major haunt at Farringdon Street was close to Fleet Street. Indeed, in another article on betting, Greenwood stated that on one occasion, he counted sixty-three list bookies doing business in an alley there. Each of them stood in front of boards on which were marked their prices, and the scene was reminiscent of the racecourse – with the vital difference that there was 'no roaring and bawling out of the extraordinary odds that the self-sacrificing professional is prepared to lay; no bewildering Babel of the names of the whole stampede of horses cried at the same time'. These Fleet Lane bookies were quieter because their business was steadier and more settled than that of their on-course fellows.[102] However, as much as 'the best and biggest men in the Ring', most of these list bookmakers were of the 'highest respectability, and discharged their obligations'.[103] This characteristic made little impression on Greenwood. He detested off-course bookies as 'vermin' and he castigated them as rogues and blacklegs who desecrated even the infamous site on which they stood and below which flowed the filthy Fleet ditch.[104] His opinion held sway among the respectable and their disgust at street betting led to the passing of Section 23 of the Metropolitan Streets Act in 1867. Accordingly, it became an offence of obstruction for three or more people to meet for the purpose of betting on a street in the capital, and the magistrates were enabled to fine miscreants not more than £5.[105]

Following the passage of the 1853 Act, anti-gamblers had become less strident in their campaigning. They had made good use of the notorious case of William Palmer, a middle-class man whose betting debts had led him to murder his wife, his brother and his best friend; and in Paisley, especially, determined opposition to horse-racing continued unabated.[106] But for many people, legislation appeared to have stymied off-course betting, and it took the publicity associated with the passage of the Metropolitan Streets Act to disabuse them of that belief. Once again, interest was aroused in bookmakers, and in addition to Greenwood, other writers commented on them. In 1868, articles on racecourse bookmaking appeared in *All the Year Round* and in *Chambers's Journal*, both of which impressed their readers with the honesty of most layers.[107] The latter praised the majority of professional bettors as 'civil, sober and certainly persevering', even though they were 'not too refined, not too well educated, not too patrician in appearance'. Likewise, in 1873, a writer in the *Contemporary Review* affirmed their lowly origins, but contrarily, the correspondent did so to demean them and to associate them with the frauds and the chicaneries of the turf. For this person, there was no such thing as a respectable bookie, all of them were 'ignorant roughs' who were pronounced guilty as criminals by dint of physiognomy.[108]

This was a potent weapon in the hands of the anti-gamblers. For many years, anti-Irish prejudice had been fuelled and justified by vicious cartoons which stigmatized Irish people as apelike and less than human.[109] By stressing that bookies were stamped with criminality, and by affirming that they were insect-like 'swarms of harpies', it was made clear that they were inferior in a similar way.[110] Despite the rebuttal of this view by informed commentators, the anti-gambling movement was informed by the firm opinion that bookmakers were inferior beings and that, for social and moral reasons, they had to be eradicated. As Thomas Houston put it, as early as 1853, gamblers personified man's fallen nature, and they 'should be regarded as less men than demons in human shape'.[111] Twenty years later, an increasing number of people held that view, as they beheld with loathing the continued existence of bookmaking in spite of legislation. In the words of William Skerry, bookies were a 'nuisance to their friends, and a disgrace to every community'. He agreed with a writer in *Le Figaro* that betting was the English road to ruin.

> There are three classes connected with the turf. The votaries who spend their money freely in the sport. The villains who live by betting, paying when it pays them to pay, and welching when it pays them to cheat the fools who trust them. The victims and their families, and the employers who are robbed by their betting *employés*, constitute the third class.
>
> Probably, two-thirds of stolen bank notes pass through the hands of the bookmakers.[112]

Strictures such as this did not discriminate between on-course and off-course betting, and increasingly horse-racing was censured because it was regarded as the sport which stimulated gambling the most. For the respectable, the turf was as immoral a place as it ever had been, but its ill effects were more pronounced as a result of its heightened popularity. Betting could be suppressed only if racing horses was purged of its incitement to bet, or if the sport was extinguished.[113] Once again, the supporters of the turf mustered their forces to protect from assault what was still deemed a gentlemanly pleasure. In 1868, *The Times* thundered against extremist English moralists who could not see a middle course and who were blind to the important fact that half of English life and over half of the nation's trade was little more than gambling.[114] This was a popular theme, and as Clapson has shown, it was emphasized in Liverpool in *The Porcupine*, a satirical weekly whose writers mocked a society that banned betting but encouraged capitalists to gain wealth by gambling on the Stock Exchange.[115] *The Times* went even further. It declared that betting had a useful side because 'it makes people give their attention, think what they are about, form the soundest opinion they can, sift the counter-statements, weigh their own words, prepare for events, and realise them when they come'.[116]

Supporters of horse-racing agreed that it was betting to excess which brought stigma on the turf, and they concurred that the simplicity of the activity was deteriorated by 'London roughs and legs and the lower forms of the ring'. However, as in the past, they stressed that the sport led to the intermingling of the classes 'on the happiest terms', and they emphasized its wholesome features – 'a day in the fresh air, holiday from work, the meeting of friends, and honest pleasure'.[117] These arguments were successful in defending horse-racing from the outrage of the anti-gamblers, and their notice was deflected back towards off-course betting.

Itzkovitz revealed that, in 1869, the police raided several well-known betting houses in London. Their operators argued that they were not covered by the law because they were commission agents, that is, they charged a fee to place bets for clients who could not go to racecourses. The honesty of these men was acknowledged in court, but it was ruled that they were off-course bookmakers and as such, their dealings were illegal.[118] This purge on outlawed list bookies was evident, too, in Manchester. On 18 May 1869, fines of £75 with 8s costs were imposed on John Franklin and Thomas Finch for running betting houses – at 8 John Street and 50 Back Turner Street respectively; on Thomas Capstick and Charles Marshall, for operating betting offices in two yards in Tib Street; and on James Burns, for using as a list house a room at the Napier Inn, a beerhouse in Thomas Street.[119] Publicans elsewhere sought to increase their trade by acting as bookies, while others did the same by promoting illegal lotteries or by allowing gaming in their premises.[120] Consequently, moralists targeted them as important proponents of the vice of gambling and in 1872, the Licensing Act was passed to stop their promotion of it. A fine of £10 was provided for first offenders, while second and subsequent contraventions of the law were subject to a penalty of up to £20.[121]

This law signalled a spate of legislation against betting and gambling. In 1873, the Vagrancy Act was amended to include as rogues and vagabonds those who gambled with coins and cards in public spaces; and the next year, the attention of the anti-gamblers became focused on tightening up the 1853 Act.[122] For an unknown reason, this law applied neither to the Channel Islands nor to Scotland, and many bookmakers took advantage of this legal loophole to set up business in Glasgow. They advertised their prices in certain English newspapers, and they did a considerable ready-cash trade by post.[123] Patently, this system of betting was open to abuse, and it attracted opportunists who had no intention of paying out if their clients won. Still, honest bookmakers must have been conspicuous because punters continued to send their money eagerly until 1874, when another bill to curb betting was introduced. Its sponsor was George Anderson, an MP for Glasgow, who fulminated that Scotland presented a more demoralized arena of dishonest betting than any other part of the empire. His opinions were supported vehemently by a writer in the *Dublin University Magazine*.

> It is unfortunate that the noble and useful sport of horse-racing cannot exist and be enjoyed without giving birth to, as a class, the most unmitigated scoundrels that are to be found in the world. The fraudulent 'list-keeper', and the welcher of all grades and degrees, represent a seething mass of cunning, audacity, roguery, and crime that is to be found in connection with no other national amusement except horse-racing.[124]

Not only did Anderson propose to extend the 1853 Act to Scotland, but he also sought to prohibit in the United Kingdom the advertisement of a betting business as defined by that law, even if it was situated abroad. This provision threatened a lucrative source of revenue for the sporting press, and it led this interest to object stridently to the bill.[125] Anderson defended his measure by stating that it did not interfere with horse-racing at all; indeed he felt that the status of the sport would be enhanced by the removal from its reputation of the 'blot' of off-course bookies. In reply to the charge that he intended to introduce a piece of class legislation, the Glaswegian representative stormed that he did not wish to interfere with anyone's right to bet, but he wanted to act against the poor man's privilege of being robbed and to prevent unfair inducements which made him bet.[126] Rapidly, the bill was passed and the new law allowed a maximum fine of £30 or two months' imprisonment for those who ignored its sections which forbade advertisements connected with betting.[127]

Initially, the Act appeared to be successful in its objectives. Betting shops were closed in Scotland, and in England illegal list houses seemed to disappear. But as had been discerned in 1868, 'the demand for betting agents created the supply . . . everybody who in these days wishes to bet, looks out for a "bookmaker"'; and the period after 1874 proved no different.[128] Legislation failed to stifle the demand for off-course bookmaking by working-class and lower-middle-class punters. In these circumstances, bookies did not disappear; instead, they avoided and evaded the law and they were able to do so because they had the active and passive support of large numbers of people. Indeed, the authorities encouraged this, for their laws against betting served only to push many off-course bookies deeper into the communities which sustained them.

4

BETTING CLUBS AND STREET BETTING

BETTING CLUBS

Anderson's bill was not an isolated attempt to control off-course betting on horse-racing. It had been preceded by two proposals which Parliament had failed to enact, and its passage was the fruition of several years' agitation aimed at quashing, or 'at any rate of so crippling the ready-money betting business as to render it unprofitable, and consequently not worth following'. Within months of becoming law, a percipient writer asserted that this wish would remain unfulfilled because the Act was fatally flawed. Even though it tightened up the restrictions against cash betting, it maintained the legality of credit transactions and this partiality made it unworthy of the British Legislature. Sardonically, the commentator wondered at how the Glaswegian representative could have introduced a law against speculation; after all, was he not a former chairman of a notorious mining company and had he himself not engaged in speculative undertakings?[1]

No better example was needed of the hypocrisy inherent in the conjugation 'I invest, you bet, he gambles', and once again, legislation on betting exposed the double standards of the British ruling classes.[2] *Laissez-faire* (the economic doctrine of non-interference) and free trade were their lodestars, but both were ignored when the social order was threatened. Ready-cash betting was an activity indulged in by members of the working and lower middle classes and because it rewarded luck and not hard work it set a bad example to the 'lower orders'. As such, it had to be acted against. Moreover, the law had to disclaim off-course bookmakers as entrepreneurs for two reasons. First, their profits could not be justified by the puritan work ethic; and second, like that of the eighteenth-century adventurers, their success meant an unwelcome circulation of money over which the propertied classes had no control. In 1895, the fear of this led Harry Sargent to proclaim that ready-money betting with bookies was 'about the greatest ally the communist possesses'.[3] In spite of its melodramatic tone, his suggestion reflected a widespread belief that off-course bookmaking had no place within capitalism. As with the antagonistic attitudes towards Dennis O'Kelly and his kind in the 1780s, it is clear that this idea was founded on the view that 'lower class' 'wheelers and dealers' were unacceptable because of their origins, no matter how successful they might be.

For most Members of Parliament, the theory of betting revolved around the idea that amateur wagering between two 'gentlemen' was respectable, 'but that a bookmaker who lays the odds to all and sundry is as nearly as possible a blackguard'. The correspondent to *Fraser's Magazine* carried his destruction of this class-biased reasoning to its logical conclusion: that there was no difference between any of the parties involved in betting. Credit punters were as much motivated by a desire to win money as were bookmakers, and their wagering was neither more nor less moral than was betting with money. Indeed, this latter system recommended itself because it limited the stakes of bettors to the supply of ready cash, and so it made them more temperate in their transactions. The writer concluded that Anderson's Act would be ineffectual unless the law outlawed the breeding and owning of race-horses and until it acted against punters as well as layers. Given the unlikelihood of this happening, then off-course betting would continue to flourish.[4] He was correct.

Some of the larger bookies fled Glasgow and Edinburgh and relocated their businesses in Calais and Boulogne, towns closer to London than the Scottish cities. This move to the Continent proved a wise one, as most letter bets emanated from the capital. From France, layers maintained a considerable trade with bigger punters and they continued to advertise in British newspapers, for many of which sport was now a major source of information and of revenue.[5] In 1870, the three morning dailies in Manchester had tried to resist this trend towards giving betting news, but because of financial losses, only the *Guardian* did so for any length of time.[6] The public's desire for racing knowledge was too great to be ignored and it encouraged the expansion of the sporting press. In 1859, the *Sporting Life* was founded and it was joined in the 1860s by the *Sporting Gazette*, the *Sporting Opinion*, the *Sportsman* and the *Sporting Times* (the 'Pink 'Un'), and in 1872 by the *Sporting Clipper*, all based in London.[7] In Ireland, they competed with the *Irish Sporting Times* and the *Irish Sportsman*, but their major rival was the Manchester-based *Sporting Chronicle*, which had first appeared in 1871.[8]

These publications were not only useful to bookies abroad, but they were also vital to those who remained in Britain and who catered for the majority of off-course backers. Because of the clampdown on list houses and before Anderson's Act, many of them had switched their operations into so-called clubs, and this measure only speeded up this process.[9] Ostensibly, these betting clubs were able to flout the law because they were 'private' associations formed for a social purpose other than betting.[10] This fiction was maintained by an elected committee, which supposedly restricted the membership of each club. In reality, they were controlled by former list bookies who facilitated entry to them.[11] Rice recalled that one of the most successful was at a roofed-in yard in Whitefriars Street, where prospective members were proposed, seconded and elected within three minutes.[12] In fact, betting clubs were list houses in all but name, and they catered for punters who were willing to bet in cash for sums of one shilling upwards.[13] Consequently, they should not be confused with the Victoria Club, which had started in 1860 and which had replaced Tattersall's as the chief meeting-place for credit betting and for the settling of accounts.

The Victoria Club itself was the meeting-place of turf accountants such as Alfred H. Good, who had more upper-class connotations. Good began his bookmaking career in the late nineteenth century, taking bets for friends and acquaintances. Gradually his business developed, because of his reputation for honesty, cheerfulness and hard work. At one time, Washington Singer, one of the brothers famous for the Singer sewing-machine company, paid Good £500 a year to collect his winnings and pay his debts. After starting out in Catherine Street, Good moved to Arundel Street and then the Victoria Club in Wellington Street, where he had offices on the first floor. Here he worked with a clerk and his younger brother Edward. His business closed down in 1940 after his death, but its profits had made wealthy both his family and that of his brother.[14]

By contrast, betting clubs occupied a dubious position within the law – despite their private nature – and in some places their existence was made possible only by the bribing of police officers.[15] Elsewhere, they were subjected to occasional raids, like that on the Beaufort Club in London, or else they were the target of well-planned purges, such as those of 1885 in Lancashire.[16] Here, vigorous police action quashed the Astley Club and others in Burnley, while in Manchester, bookmakers from twenty-three betting clubs were arrested on 20 May. The exercise which captured them was welcomed by a writer in the *Manchester Evening News*, sending him into a paroxysm of militaristic language: 'Raids have been recently made in London and elsewhere, but never before have operations been conducted on so large a scale as in Manchester yesterday. The attack was not the result of some sudden whim. It was projected long ago, the details were carefully planned, and its execution was a clever piece of strategy.'[17] Nearly fifty men and boys were prosecuted in connection with this action, but betting clubs were extirpated neither by this raid nor by those in other parts of the country.[18] They continued to thrive and, as with the betting houses before them, their popularity was enhanced by technological progress.

Before the 1870s, telegraphic messages were reliant upon operators who could transmit and understand information given in Morse code. However, from that decade, the Exchange Telegraph Company (Extel) began to instal tape machines in the offices of its subscribers. These printed out messages on to a thin strip of paper threaded through each machine. At first, 'the Tape' was limited to transmitting news about the Stock Exchange, but soon Extel set up a racing service. At every meeting, it had a representative who sent back to head office the runners and result of each race, information that was passed on quickly to those who rented a 'ticker tape' machine.[19] Betting-club proprietors were swift to realize the advantages of this system of transmission. It meant that they had access to results before they were printed in the newspapers the next day and it thus guaranteed the excited interest of their punters. In 1897, this attraction was explained by a writer who visited a 'typical London betting club'.

> So the wagering briskly proceeds for four or five minutes, only two of the nine horses competing being supported to any extent. Then, as the 'tape' gives a few warning clicks, the clerk shouts out: 'They're off! Any more bets, gentlemen?' A few backers, who until now have not been able to make up their minds, rush hurriedly to the table and support their 'fancies'; and scarcely has the last shilling been booked when the 'tape' recommences clicking. All conversation is hushed as Mr — leans forward and glances at the slowly uncoiling strip. 'Negress has won, gentlemen,' he unconcernedly remarks; and I notice the countenances of several members droop visibly, while a few others give vent to exclamations of disgust. For Negress, it appears, is an unreliable animal, whose recent performances in public have not warranted 'students of form' in supporting her today for a single sixpence.[20]

For a punter, the great advantage of the tape was that its swift dissemination of news facilitated race-by-race as opposed to multiple betting. Obviously, it is easier to find one winner than it is to pick several, and betting-club owners garnered much custom because they accepted single bets. In 1889, the Reverend Chorley guessed that there were 300 betting clubs in London alone, but as an anti-gambler he had a vested interest in exaggerating their number.[21] A more plausible figure was provided by the knowledgeable Curzon, who estimated that there were between six and twenty of them in the capital, as there were in Manchester, Liverpool, Bradford, Leeds and Birmingham.[22] Of those in Hackney and the East End of London, Charles Booth stated that some were 'respectable' and were frequented by bookmakers of good repute, while others were a disreputable combination of 'gambling hell with the lowest type of dancing saloon'. Whatever their status, all of them were jealous of their privacy and police raids made them short-lived, although it is likely that they sprang up again in new premises.[23] Certainly, their existence continued elsewhere in Britain and in 1895, a court judgement exemplified the 'grey area' that they occupied in law. It ruled that members of a social club did not contravene the 1853 Act so long as they betted among themselves and on the premises. However, if it were shown that facilities had been provided for a bookmaker to take bets, then a conviction would result, even if the bookie claimed membership.[24] This decision was upheld in 1904, but betting clubs continued in spite of it, and in 1914, the Blackburn Chamber of Commerce complained that the Post Office charged less for the transmission of racing news than it did for commercial messages.[25]

After the First World War in some industrial parts of the country, quasi-social clubs remained a major medium for backing horses off-course, as was indicated in 1932 by the Royal Commission on Lotteries and Betting.[26] Indeed, in Bradford, the scene in the Lonsdale Club was reminiscent of that described in *Chambers's Journal* in 1897. Mr Cooper recalled that its entrance was by way of a padlocked door, on which there was an alarm button which would be pressed if the police were spied through a peephole. In the betting room, two clerks sat at a table, taking bets, reading the tape and paying out any winnings once the result was known. Most of the club members were businessmen and shopkeepers and they could play billiards and cards and drink as well as bet on horses.[27] The situation was similar in the private members' clubs operated by Walter King during the 1930s in Grimsby, and after 1945, this town and Hull became notorious for the ubiquity and popularity of their betting clubs.[28]

During the 1950s, both of these ports were magnets for trawler skippers, and they enjoyed an economic boom because of the free-spending ways of many fishermen, who had two days' onshore leave after three weeks at sea.[29] In particular, these workers spent heavily on drinking and betting, and clubs therefore proliferated at which they could do both. Gordon Roper recalled:

> In Hull in the good old days, when the fishing industry was at its peak, there were many working men's clubs and gambling went on [on] a very large scale. Most of these clubs were raided by the police at one time or another and I was in one of those clubs, the St Andrew's Club down West Dock Avenue in Hull, when it was raided. Dozens of police suddenly burst in and told everyone present to sit where they were. Then they took photographs of the table where bets were being placed and of the marker board where the names of the runners and riders and the current betting odds were being displayed, then they stuck labels on everybody's beer glass. One or two people received a fine, mainly the bookies, and some of the clubs were closed down for a while, only to reopen shortly after with the prefix NEW in front of their old name.[30]

Over a three-year period, thirty clubs were struck off the register in Hull, but as is indicated by this evidence, they continued business so long as their names were changed slightly and their owners paid a five-shilling registration fee.[31] In 1954, disgusted at this blatant contravention of the spirit of the law, local magistrates warned that they would close down thirty-two clubs and imprison the bookies who ran them.[32] These threats were ignored. Simply, the profits from betting clubs were sufficiently large as to encourage bookmakers to risk imprisonment, and at the same time some of them had 'understandings' with the police. Roper remembered that the Hessle Ex-Serviceman's Club was just across the town boundary and that it was never raided; while as a police constable in Hull, L. E. Armitage believed that although some senior officers were sticklers for the enforcement of the betting laws, others turned a blind eye towards those who contravened them. Indeed, he mentioned that a serving police sergeant was captured in one raid, and that he retired from the force for reasons of health, just three weeks later.[33]

The same disrespect for the law was evident in Grimsby, despite the imposition of fines totalling £350 on six men and two women who were convicted of betting offences at the Ambassador Club in 1957.[34] In the same year, the famous Leeds bookie Jim Windsor was fined £50 for operating a betting room above the Commercial Club in Vicar Lane. Here, part of a bar had been converted into a kiosk with a pigeonhole through which bets were passed to an agent of Windsor. He in turn sent them upstairs via a pneumatic tube, while the stakes were placed in a till. As for the club, it had been set up by the bookmaker in 1936, and its secretary was his son-in-law, who was fined £50 for aiding and abetting. The prosecution sought for the club to be struck off the local register, claiming that it had no volition of its own and that it was run in pursuance of Windsor's wishes, even though he was not involved in it as an officer. Opposing this move, the defence stressed that women made up 40 per cent of the club's membership, which also included police officers. Moreover, former chief constables had attended social functions there. It is probable that these revelations were as responsible for it retaining its licence as was Windsor's undertaking that betting would cease at the place.[35]

STREET BETTING IN THE 1860S AND 1870S

Betting clubs were never snuffed out by repressive laws, but they did decline markedly after 1961 when cash betting was legalized.[36] Historically, their importance is three-fold: first, they indicate the ingenuity of bookmakers in finding ways to circumvent anti-betting legislation; second, they show that these laws were unsuccessful where punters demanded that bookies catered for their wishes; and third, they provide a connection both with illegal betting in the nineteenth century, and with the lawful list houses of the later 1840s. Yet betting clubs were 'private' in nature and they were restricted to a number of towns and cities. Consequently, their proprietors were not subjected to the spleen of the anti-gamblers as much as were the ubiquitous and public street bookies.

These, too, had emerged in the 1860s and 1870s, following the clampdown on unlawful betting offices in London and elsewhere, and in some places they thrived with the connivance of the authorities. During the race-week of 1875, Doncaster Corporation was accused of renting a small plot of ground for £800, the leasee of which sub-let it to list bookies at a cost of £15 per lineal yard. Moreover, it was maintained that the Race Committee had instructed the police not to interfere with their business, even though this body was 'almost identical in its composition' to the Watch Committee and was chaired by a JP![37] Two years later, it was the turn of officers of the law in Liverpool to be the victims of probings about their attitudes towards illegal betting. A writer in the *Porcupine* was scathing about the way in which lists were displayed blatantly in the city, and with sarcasm, he asked:

> Who has authorised the men on duty to permit the daily crowds to gather and hang about in Williamson-square? When we consider that energetic action can render the mere existence of the greater number of bookmakers difficult and precarious in the extreme, we feel that these are questions which, being neither unfair nor unreasonable, should be very easily answered; and we base our right to ask them

> upon the fact that this betting nuisance is one of the crying sins of our town, and that, being allowedly such, it is nevertheless permitted to exist in quiet comfort, under the very wing of the law.[38]

In Manchester street bookmaking was similarly prevalent and in 1875 the council passed a byelaw to try and suppress it. Like the Metropolitan Streets Act of 1867, it made it an offence of obstruction for three or more people to gather in the street 'for the purpose of betting'. Culprits could be arrested without a warrant so long as they committed their offence in front of a police officer, and they could be fined not more than £5.[39] Except in the case of betting clubs, it seems that often magistrates used this penalty as a norm, even for those who were charged under the 1853 Act. For example, in 1877, Christopher Wood was fined £5 plus 10s 6d costs for taking bets in his beer shop in City Road, while Samuel Whitaker was levied the same amount with £4 7s costs for using a house in Liverpool Road for a similar purpose.[40]

It is apparent that in the later 1870s the official response to illegal betting was varied and localized in its nature, despite the existence of national codes which governed the issue. In some places, outlawed bookmakers were tolerated because of their relevance to a district's economy or because it was accepted that they could not be put down. Sporadic raids may have been made against them in response to local pressure, but many policemen were lax in their implementation of the anti-gambling laws. This leniency was only one of numerous anomalies demonstrated by the policing of working-class people. As David Jones has indicated, police officers had to balance their task of enforcing class-biased legislation with their need to obtain community support.[41] Middle-class moralists, however, were faced with no such dilemma, and they continued to berate those who betted and to condemn those who laid bets. In 1877, the Leicester Sunday School Union published a cautionary tale about the dire effects of gambling, and in the same year, Charles Kingsley warned young men about its anti-social implications:

> . . . betting and gambling of every kind, is in itself wrong and immoral. I do not say that every man who bets is an immoral man. Far from it: many really honest men bet; but that is because they have not considered what they are doing. Betting is wrong: because it is wrong to take your neighbour's money without giving him anything in return. Earn from him what you will, and as much as you can. All labour, even the lowest drudgery is honourable; but betting is not labouring nor earning; it is getting money without earning it, and more, it is getting money, or trying to get it, out of your neighbour's ignorance.[42]

RACECOURSE BOOKMAKERS

Kingsley's denunciation of professional bettors as idle thieves was given added force by his status as a well-known clergyman, and his invective provided a moral justification for the snobbish disdain of bookies. He emphasized that those who lived by betting were the most selfish of men and that they were given up to distrust, cunning, treachery and falsehood. Indeed, he declaimed gambling as almost the only thing in the world in which the bad man was the stronger by very virtue of his badness. Morally, the pastime was unchivalrous and un-Christian; more than that, it was an intrinsically savage habit which 'has been the peace excitement of the lowest brutes in human form for ages past'.[43] The cleric was not alone in connecting bookmakers with barbarians and in 1879, a writer on the turf bemoaned the 'fall' of the racecourse to an irruption of Goths and Vandals, smaller bookies who were branded the dregs of racing society and who had routed the 'knights of the pencil'.[44]

Although full of hyperbole, this lamentation indicated that some upper-class turfites had accorded many of the larger on-course bookmakers a degree of social acceptability, if not respectability. Like Davies before them, these layers were honest and prompt in their payment of winnings and their position on the turf was compared to that of brokers on the Stock Exchange.[45] For the most part, their origins lay still among the 'lower classes', but by the 1880s, they were regarded as more responsible and better-mannered than their 'noisy, blustering, pugilistic, hard-swearing' predecessors.[46] This gradual adjustment in attitudes towards the leviathans was not universal, and some continued to regard them as instigators of racecourse chicanery, even though the existence of 'gentlemen blacklegs' was acknowledged.[47] Still, the favourable trend towards the bigger bookies was noticeable and it was aided by a slight yet conspicuous movement into their ranks of 'men of education and good family', of whom Thomas Henry Dey was the prototype.[48] But if their status had become enhanced, then that of the majority of racecourse bookmakers remained dismally low.

Their numbers had increased as the popularity of horse-racing had grown, and at one fixture at Doncaster it was reported that there were present over 700 'industrious pencillers'.[49] Most of these catered for the cash bets of working-class and lower-middle-class punters, and their presence was disdained by those who sought to preserve an aristocratic aura around the turf. These bookies were slandered as 'a wretched crew', and just as all adventurers had been slurred as sharpsters, so too were they stigmatized as welchers.[50] There can be no denying that some of them merited this charge; Dey explained how they tricked their clients.

> . . . the *modus operandi* of a gang of welchers, who operate on a big scale, is for one of them to stand up and make the 'Book', taking the money for the bets from the public and to hand the cash at intervals to a confederate, so that when the bookmaker is ready to vamoose, he has practically no money on him, and, in consequence, is more or less in a position to plead mistaken identity if caught. The money is subsequently divided between the confederates.
>
> There is another way of welching which is described as 'ringing the Book' . . . and consists simply of booking any big wagers to a horse different from the one really backed. If the horse that is backed is a loser, naturally the backer makes no claim, but if it wins, the written entry by the clerk is shown there is generally a confederate to substantiate the bookmaker's word – and even if the assistance of a policeman, or an official of the Ring is sought, he is practically helpless.[51]

Usually, welchers operated where there was little or no supervision of bookmakers by racecourse officials, setting themselves up outside the enclosures – which had began to appear at racecourses from 1875 – or else at badly organized flapping meetings.[52] Of course, their actions were despised and Greenwood recounted the story of one of them who was caught and beaten up so badly by an irate mob that he died of his injuries.[53] Like the thimbleriggers before them, defaulters sought to protect themselves from this kind of violent reaction to their swindling, and they tended to go about 'mob-handed'. On one notorious occasion at York in 1881, nearly forty of them armed themselves with cudgels and with impunity they marched away from the course with their ill-gotten gains.[54] The Birmingham bookmaker Dyke Wilkinson was a knowledgeable observer who differentiated these gangsters from the old school of welchers, most of whom were characterized by him as 'rather elderly men, with a dejected, seedy and out-of-elbows look about them'.[55] He dated their demise to about 1872, and although it is likely that he diminished the extent of organized ruffianism before then, it would seem that this phenomenon became more pronounced as horse-racing expanded. [56]

Significantly, Wilkinson emphasized that gangs of non-payers were not *bona fide* bookmakers and that they were thieves who were as willing to fleece layers as they were backers.[57] Indeed, the Birmingham bookie himself was maimed for life after he was kicked mercilessly by a pack of defrauders to which he had given offence.[58] Curzon agreed with Wilkinson's argument. He stressed that the majority of small bookies were as honest as their more prosperous fellows, and he pointed out that they stuck to their local circuit of racecourses, not only because of the difficulties of travel but also of the need to be known as good payers. A layer from this period made clear the significance of these two factors.[59]

> Bookmakers had their own following in a certain area, and in the days when travel was not so easy England was divided up into at least four racing sections to which the racing public therein confined their race-going. It wasn't much use a bookmaker going outside the area in which he was known, as he would get little betting . . . I well recall being persuaded to attend some little jumping meeting in the West Country and scarcely taking a bet because I was a stranger and possibly thought not to be trusted.[60]

This 'clannishness' among punters accorded with the wish of some layers to work close to home and to avoid the expense of paying for overnight accommodation, necessary if they attended a distant fixture.[61] Frequently, such men could not make a living from their bookmaking alone and so they combined it with another occupation.[62]

At the same time, all on-course bookies had begun to employ clerks, men who wrote down in a ledger the bets that their 'gaffer' (boss) had laid and who alerted him as to his liabilities.[63] The bookmaker himself would shout out the odds and would put the money staked with him into a large satchel, hung around his neck. Both members of the team operated from 'judies' – wooden 'joints' or stalls – which often were decorated gaily with baize and banners. Sometimes, these were the property of the layer, while on other occasions they were rented from men who travelled to meetings with large supplies of them.[64] As the enclosure of racecourses progressed, the joints of the larger bookies were pitched in the more expensive Tattersall's Ring, adjoining the socially select Members' Enclosure from which bookies were excluded; while the smaller men placed themselves in the Silver Ring, with the least prosperous of their number positioned outside.[65]

Like most occupations, bookmaking manifested a hierarchy of status and income, and even within the ranks of its lesser operators, a similar structure existed. Still, whatever their standing and however fair in their dealings they may have been, as a body, the men of the ring remained a focus of dislike for some upper-class aficionados of the turf. In 1885, one of these inveighed against bookmakers as a 'roaring mob' who made 'the face of the day hideous, screaming like vultures flocking to the prey', and he sorrowed at the gains that they had made from aristocrats such as the Marquis of Hastings.[66] James Runciman shared his grief, but neither writer mentioned that bookmakers 'came up smiling' when they had to pay what they owed to credit punters. Nor did they recite that 'when *gentlemen* have to receive, they are the first on the scene; when they have to pay, they are the last to be seen'.[67] 'Blue-blooded' defaulters were numerous, but these welchers did not attract disgust and condemnation as did their working-class counterparts. Neither was attention paid to the fate of the bookmaker Jim Buxton – driven to commit suicide by bad debts – nor to the way in which 'knockers' had led the 'genial and straightforward' J. B. Morris to abandon bookmaking in Britain.[68] The double standards of the landed elite were glaring and they were mocked in a popular song of the later nineteenth century:

I went towards the Members' Stand, my patrons to be near;
The keeper at the gate, says he, 'We want no Bookies here';
The swells a-passing through they grinned and sniggered fit to die,
I paid the sum for Tattersall's, and to myself sez I:

'O, it's Bookey this, and Bookey that, and Bookey, go away;
We're far too swell to have you near, so by the railings stay.
Behind the railings is your place, so please behind them stay,
And when we want you we will come.' So there I had to stay.

I looked above the iron rails, as patient as could be,
I saw they'd room for titled rogues, though they had none for me;
We are not fit to mix with them – our calling's much too low –
But if we stopped away, I guess, they'd find it pretty slow.

Chorus

Yes, making mock of those you use, and for your pleasure keep,
Is cheaper far than honour – and with some that's deuced cheap;
And betting with a Bookey, on a certain tip you've got,
Is safer far than it would be with some of your own lot.

Chorus[69]

As in the eighteenth century, middle-class moralists agreed with those members of the upper class who despised full-time bettors. In 1890, the Reverend Alfred Rowland calumnied them as 'the dregs of city scoundreldom – idle, worthless, dishonest men'; and fifteen years later, John Hawke, the secretary of the National Anti-Gambling League, denounced the 'ruffianism of the professional betting men and their hangers-on'.[70] Still, from the close of the 1880s, much of the puritanical venom against layers was directed not at those on-course, but at their fellows who plied their trade in the streets of the towns and cities of Britain.

STREET BETTING: THE SIGNIFICANCE OF THE 1880S

With great exactness, R. H. Gretton gave 1889 as the year in which the national concern about off-course betting 'expressed itself so largely'.[71] In fact, this preoccupation became prominent in the previous year, when the Reverend S. Reynolds Hole delivered an address on 'Gambling and Betting' to the Church Congress at Manchester. In tone, it differed little from earlier attacks against the twin 'evils'. Like John Ruskin in 1865, the Dean of Rochester stressed the wastefulness of the pastimes, and like Kingsley, he emphasized that they were un-Christian.[72] But in the general discussion which ensued, the contributors seemed to be animated by a new feeling of panic about their extent. As a writer in the *Spectator* explained:

> Many clerical speakers recounted in the language of alarm how the passion for gambling is spreading among the working classes, especially in the North of England. That gambling is seriously on the increase among the working classes, and that its effects are even more disastrous amongst artisans and colliers than upon the rich, there seems no possibility of doubting. It would seem as if the moral disease of gambling which, though always capable of affecting individuals, is generally kept under restraint, were apt occasionally, and during certain stages of human development, to break out in the form of an epidemic.[73]

Over the next two years, other publications seemed to substantiate the belief that off-course betting was burgeoning throughout the nation. According to a report which was delivered to the Convocation of York in 1890, the only areas which were free of the 'contagion' were the Isle of Man, a few quiet towns and some country districts; and it stated that the localities which were affected worst by the 'disease' were those of a mining and manufacturing nature.[74] Runciman concurred that the 'problem' was spreading, but like the editor of the *Hull Advertiser* in the early 1850s, he feared most that the fever was raging among the lower middle class – 'which used to be the main element of our national strength'. A contributor to the *Spectator* stressed this point, holding that members of the petit bourgeoisie were affected as much by the vice of gambling as were the poor.[75] Whether or not they were, anti-gamblers were depressed and anxious about what they perceived as the spread of the evil from the upper class. In the apocalyptic words of the Reverend Alfred Rowland, 'those who have the welfare of the English people most at heart' were sounding their warnings from 'the pulpits of the land, in magazine articles, and at diocesan conferences'.[76]

Apart from Itzkowitz, historians have accepted this contemporary emphasis on the last quarter of the nineteenth century as the time in which betting on horses rose, especially among the working class.[77] In particular, McKibbin has focused on the 1880s, regarding that decade as crucial for three reasons. First, it was then that mass gambling was made possible by the completion of the electric telegraph system, which allowed the press to publish speedily results and starting-price odds. Second, it was not until these years that 'a large enough part of the working classes had sufficient disposable income to bet even on the small scale that they did'. Finally, from this period onwards older forms of gambling were joined and largely replaced by an organized betting which had no precedent in its scale or character.[78]

STREET GAMBLING

It is difficult to support McKibbin's last assertion, given the longevity of illegal list houses and the vitality and prevalence of the outlawed betting clubs and street betting during the 1860s and 1870s. Moreover, older forms of gambling remained vigorous, especially those using 'coppers': pennies and halfpennies. Their supporters had succumbed neither to the protestations of the moralists, nor to the attacks of the forces of law and order, and a variety of coin games continued to thrive throughout Britain and Ireland.[79] Often, their names differed according to the locality in which they were played, but their rules were similar to those extant in Salford in the inter-war years. In the game of 'Nudgers', one player acted as a 'banker' (dealer). Individually, he tossed five coins into the air – catching them with his free hand – and after they were all collected, he would take bets on how many of them had come up heads or tails. Like a bookie, he would offer odds against certain possibilities, such as 2 to 1 against three or four heads, or 10 to 1 against all heads or all tails. With 'Nearest the Mottie', competitors stood about three yards away from a coin or a small piece of crockery, at which they threw their coppers; the person who came closest to the mark won the money 'chucked' by the other gamblers. A similar game was 'Pitch and Toss', in which he who threw best at the target then tossed all the coins in the air, keeping those which landed heads up. If any coppers were left, they were thrown by the person who had come next, and this process continued until all the money had been won.[80]

Nationally, pitch and toss was the most popular and widespread of these three coin games, and before 1914, convictions against its supporters are recorded in areas as diverse in their nature as rural Essex and industrial Sheffield.[81] As elsewhere, the police in this

Yorkshire city fought a losing battle against the eradication of the pastime, as is indicated by police archives.[82] Regularly, gamblers were prosecuted, but it would seem that the risk of capture was not great enough to act as a deterrent; indeed, the evasion of the police was facilitated by the simplicity of the game itself. No equipment was needed and it could take place whenever and wherever it took the fancy of an informal group of men and youths. This might be outside a public house after it had closed, or on a street corner; it could be in the courtyard of a terrace of back-to-back houses, in the back close of a Glaswegian tenement, or in a Hunslett 'ginnel' (narrow alleyway); or it might be underneath the arches of a railway or along the canal bank. Many of these spots were hidden away from the police who patrolled the streets, while those which were more open to view were guarded by unofficial watchers.[83]

In some parts of the country, pitch and toss was regarded as the game of teenagers, and it was tossing – the famous 'two-up' of Australia and New Zealand – which was fancied by adult males who were fond of gambling with coins.[84] Again, the rules of this game varied according to the locality, but in essence it consisted of a group of men who gathered in a ring with a largish space in the middle. Into this would step a man who was prepared to act as a banker, and who would offer to bet that he could toss two pennies which would land heads upwards. If they came down tails he would lose, while if they showed one head and one tail there would be another toss. The banker himself might stake any sum, depending upon the size of the school, and this could be covered by one person from the crowd or by a number; at the same time, side bets would be staked among the spectators. As C. J. Morgan recalled of the tossing schools of Liverpool:

> The bank and the stakes were always kept in full view of everybody on a cloth, but mostly in a flat cap in the event of a raid by the law. When everybody had laid their bets, the two coins would be tossed they could be two pennies or two halfpennies . . . The coins would be examined by one who had a bet, to make sure there were no 2-headed coins used or weighted ones, the coins had to rest on two fingers, the index finger and the second finger, tails up. Some toss schools depending what district you lived in would use a piece of wood, just the size to rest two coins on, which was held by the finger and thumb.
>
> The coins would be thrown in the air and they must be turning all the time at a reasonable height. If there was any doubt about the throw a punter must shout out (bar that toss) before the coins touch the ground, and the throw would start again.[85]

If the banker was successful in his first toss, then he was entitled to another spin of the coins, so long as he doubled his stake; while if his luck continued, he could toss for a third time, once more doubling his stake.[86] Bets were paid out at even money, with the consequence that if the first gamble had been for £5, then a thrice-winning tosser could make £35, or odds of 7 to 1 for his original layout. Such large sums were not unusual, even before the First World War. In 1891, Lancashire police picked up £50 in one raid on a tossing school at Widdup, while Jack Lawson – later a Labour MP – regretted that 'from twelve to twenty years I would gamble my shirt'. Indeed, he remembered that in the 1890s, when he was barely sixteen, he plunged 'until ten pounds have been lost or won by me on one toss of the pennies'.[87] By the early 1920s, the amount of money gambled on tossing had increased, despite the economic depression. This fact disgusted a writer on the *Nelson Leader*. In a report on a police raid on a well-known rendezvous of 'scholars', he exclaimed that:

> Coldwell has long been notorious in East Lancashire as a gambling school which has earned Nelson an unenviable name, lying just over three miles from Nelson Centre in a half developed area Quarry on the Moors which flank the easterly side of the town it has for 40 years boasted a reputation far and wide as a gambling School where big and little monied men would find accommodation for satisfying their particular kind of pastime. Practically every day of the week, the year through, there is an average attendance of about a hundred youths and men, gathered from all parts of the district. Many make the journey on foot, in clogs and weekday attire, but these men will produce notes in such abundance that one wonders if unemployment and relief queues are but a Myth.

Gallingly, it was revealed that parties of men ordered cars to take them to the ring, while a 'bus was run by a driver who has a regular clientele'; and rubbing salt into the wounds, it was disclosed that the punters could even purchase pies, cakes, cigarettes and hot tea while they were gambling![88]

Like that at Widdup, the tossing school at Coldwell had been set up because of the repression of the game within the nearby towns of Nelson and Colne. Here, the police had harried and captured gamblers, while the magistrates had imposed harsh fines on them. Indeed, in 1880, twenty-one offenders had been fined 20s each plus costs, a considerable sum when it is considered that an unskilled man would not earn that much money for a week's work.[89] Isolated rings similar to Coldwell existed elsewhere in the country. Near to Burnley, Hambledon Hill was a long-standing 'public gambling resort'; close to Bradford, Queensferry was regarded as the leading school in West Yorkshire; at Tinsley Park Wood was one of Sheffield's largest tossing rings, while Tudhoe Wood was acknowledged as a chief centre of 'hoying' (spinning) in the North East. There were also numerous 'burling' schools along the Clyde and in the woods and on the pit banks of Lanarkshire; while the gamblers of Swansea met on the beach or in the local quarries.[90] Even though tossing was a dominantly working-class game, these district schools attracted a wide range of punters, from weavers and miners to prosperous tradesmen; and at some, there were copper, silver and gold rings to cater for the differing levels of affluence among them.[91] Yet, whatever their status, all were protected from the police by 'crows' (sentries). Indeed, at Coldwell, the lookouts were provided with field glasses with which to search for signs of hostile activity![92]

These watchers were paid 10s a day for their trouble by tollers who controlled most of the large district rings. These were local 'tough nuts' who made a living from levying a fee of around 2s 6d in the pound from winning punters.[93] The 'masters' of the ring were men like 'Two Ton Titley' of Cannock, whose activities at the local school were detailed by Arthur Hopcraft, a child of a respectable and chapel-going working-class family.

> Two Ton did not appear to be throwing anything. He was holding money in large quantity. He was the pivot around which the other men conducted themselves. They brought him coins and notes, and sometimes he gave them some back. He kept up an encouraging, belching banter, his puce face prickly with pinheads of sweat nestling in its creases. 'C'mon lads, yer luck's in. Doa be frit. The wife woa know.' He had money in his hands, in his pockets and often between his teeth and tucked between his trousers-top and his swelling midriff. 'That's the way lads. Naow we can see ooz married to the moonishun wairkers . . .'
>
> He was a picture of godlessness, rampant with beer and blatant in his love of money – of the feel of it, of its corrupting desirability. He was immodesty personified. He was wicked . . . Two Ton looked gigantic and unassailable in this setting. He was at work, selling sin with a grand flair.[94]

Tossing was a game at which a man could readily lose a week's pay, and because of this, it aroused the condemnation of many working-class people who were neither religious nor 'killjoys'.[95] As it was put by Abe Moffat, a leader of the Scottish miners, such gambling meant that 'if you won it was at the expense of your fellow workers, and it was bad enough to be robbed by your employers, but it was worse to be robbing one another'.[96] Still, it would be wrong to see the practitioners of tossing as reprobates. The game itself was regarded by many people as intrinsic to working-class life in numerous localities, and although Lawson came to abhor it, still he admitted that among its players were fine men. He proclaimed them to be characters 'who commanded respect, as straight and true as steel, and selfless as a saint when a man was in danger deep below'; and to the amazement of Hopcraft, even Two Ton Titley was loved and 'tenderly regarded' by his wife.[97] In Lanarkshire, tossing promoters like this Black Country giant were known as 'babbers', while in County Durham, a 'bebber' was a professional hoyer: a man who threw the coins for all the bankers and who was paid from their winnings.[98] Differing from tollers, bebbers did not have to be hard men, but like them, they justified their payment on the grounds that they ensured fair play. They brought to the school a supply of 'jubes' – Queen Victoria pennies – which were neither weighted nor double-headed, and when they threw them, they avoided 'flamming': spinning the coins in such a fashion as to ensure that they went in the air heads up and remained that way.[99]

Most of the best-known and well-organized tossing rings were to be found in the countryside, yet, though the game had been driven from the streets of many towns and cities, in certain places it survived strongly, until the 1950s at least. In Gateshead, informal schools developed after the pubs closed on a Sunday afternoon – although an organized ring existed at Wreckenton.[100] A similar pattern of small ad hoc meetings prevailed in Birmingham and in parts of London; while in Leicester, Manchester and Coventry, men gathered each Sunday at well-known sites, but without the presence of tollers.[101] In Liverpool, these weekly meetings flourished 'on waste ground right out in the open and everybody could see', but here they were controlled.[102] Their 'masters' were called belt men and their job was to keep the circle clear . . . with the aid of the leather belt'.[103] As evoked by Máirín Johnston, these men were similar to the 'boxmen' of Dublin.

> Sartini was one of the two boxmen who ran the toss-up school in the Greenhills, beyond Griffith Bridge. Like a ringmaster in a circus he stormed about the centre of the toss-school circle wielding a short-handled dray driver's whip. The lash of the whip was about three feet long, and Sartini would use it mercilessly to enlarge the circle so as to enable the other boxman to get the bets down for the tosser, who would then throw up the two 'makes' (coins) off the 'feck' (stick).[104]

The domination of a tossing ring was a lucrative proposition, and in 1922, it was claimed that the promoters of the Coldwell school each made upwards of £10 a day.[105] Such profits could attract jealous attentions, and at one stage, the infamous Animal Gang of Dublin's north side challenged Sartini for the supremacy of his circle. Although he fought them off successfully, similar power struggles took place at other rings, particularly those of a 'city' nature.[106] The most notorious of these was that which resulted in the so-called and exaggerated Sheffield Gang Wars of the early 1920s.[107] In this steel city, there was a pronounced hierarchy among its gambling schools, ranging from the many irregular meetings, through to established and controlled local pitches, and to the large city-wide rings of Tinsley Park Wood and Sky Edge, which appealed to punters from across South Yorkshire and North Derbyshire. After the First World War, this latter was controlled by the Mooney Gang – a collection of racecourse hangers-on and 'bruisers' – but they were challenged for its domination by the Park Brigade. Led by Sam Garvin – another habitué of the turf – this gang was successful in their objective, after which they turned their attention to gaining the protection of the city's local schools. In their attempt to do this at Norfolk Bridge, one man was killed and two brothers were hanged for his murder.[108]

This fight for the ownership of Sky Edge was unusual in both its intensity and its length, and most tollers gave up the control of their rings either as younger or harder men came along, or else in a straight fight.[109] As in Australia, which boasted renowned two-up schools in its cities, the game itself went into decline after the Second World War, although it is rumoured that rings still exist in Dublin, Fifeshire, Liverpool and at the horse fair in Appleby.[110] Certainly, it was not eclipsed by street bookmaking in the 1880s, and in Glasgow during the inter-war years, E. McGuinness believed that 'it was as big as the bookmaking, along with banker'.[111] Like pitch and toss, this card game could be played anywhere among small groups of men and boys.

> *Banker*, you placed a number of lots on the ground and the punters backed all the lots except one, they put their coppers on top of the cards on the ground and the banker would then turn his lot over and he would then start to turn the other lots over all that beat his lot he paid out to, losers he kept, this was another game where you kept a sharp eye on the banker, he could mark certain cards whilst shuffling them before dealing, and very often two or more deuces would appear enabling him to keep the bank going.[112]

As described by a Liverpudlian, banker was a purely gambling game 'with no skill or brain power required'. Simply, it was a means 'of losing one's pocket money, or winning someone else's very quickly depending on one's luck'. Its monotony did not diminish its popularity, for it could be played at a factory during the dinner break, or in the street, or in a backyard.[113] In Birmingham, open-air card games were protected by 'karsters' ('dog-outs') who watched for the police; while in Gateshead, these people were called 'tooters', and for their services they were paid 'odd coppers according to how the dealers were performing'.[114]

Pontoon, three-card brag, six-card rummy, nap and solo were also played widely, and along with tossing and pitch and toss, card games were a feature of many gambling schools.[115] Unlike the former, they were not associated solely with industrial areas and convictions against card players were recorded in agricultural parts of Essex and in the rural adjuncts of Sheffield.[116] Indeed, in Warmley in the West Country, in the 1930s 'it was common for a group of men to hold a card school in a field', as it was in the border village of Bronygarth in Shropshire.[117] As with street bookmaking, contemporaries regarded the 1880s as the decade in which gambling such as this became a problem. In 1889, it was reported in the *Dudley Herald*:

> According to Police Inspector's Gasson's statement at Tipton Police Court on Monday, gambling, especially juvenile gambling, and more particularly on a Sunday, is on the increase, but unfortunately this complaint is not confined to Tipton alone. Only a week or two ago we were told by a correspondent that the Wren's Nest had become a popular resort of all the lowest characters of the town on a Sunday for the purpose of gambling, and of this fact we have ourselves been an eye witness. Whilst however, we are not prepared to echo the common cant about the wholesale wickedness of playing cards for stakes or betting, which is equally as bad as gambling . . . feeling as we do that no amount of persuasion, or legislation either, would ever put down these insidious infatuations, yet we are bound to say that we heartily condemn Sunday gambling, especially in our public thoroughfares, and also its alarming growth among the juvenile portion of the community.

This writer recommended 'a little wholeseome severity' to cure pitch and tossers and other young gamblers of their 'infatuation'.[118]

Although I have no evidence of magistrates taking up his suggestion of birching offenders, there is plenty to indicate that many heeded urges for harsh penalties, even fifty years later. In 1940, eleven men from

Aberfan were fined a total of £76 for playing pontoon in a house, and Merthyr magistrates told one of them that he was 'a very bad man'; while in the same year, these 'justices' sentenced three cardsters to three months' hard labour, exclaiming that their offence 'saps the very foundations of the youth of this country'. Repression such as this led the mother of one young 'culprit' to declare that the arresting police officer was 'worse than the — Germans, and it was a pity that Hitler did not come here'.[119] The forces of law and order in Merthyr were not unusual in their severe response to gambling, and in 1943, two men from Lancaster were fined £2 each for playing cards on a public footpath. It mattered little that one of them was in the armed forces, for it seemed that even the exigencies of war could not dampen the ardour of those who were determined to stamp out the 'evil' of gambling.[120]

For all their determination, these 'puritans' were engaged in a battle they could not win. Street gambling abounded in Britain and it was characterized more by its variety than by its diminution. In inter-war Burnley, men and youths wagered on 'buck and stick' – a type of knurr and spell which was played still on the moors near Halifax; in some mining districts, they continued to stake money on quoits; in the North East, bets were laid and paid on handball matches; in Swansea and most industrial areas, boys gambled for cigarette cards and marbles; and in Aberdeen, Luton, Southampton, parts of Stockport, and the villages around Peterborough, the board game of crown and anchor reigned supreme, having ousted pitch and toss and tossing in the favours of local gamblers.[121] Throughout industrial Britain, street gambling in all its forms coalesced to become an unquenchable and vital element of working-class culture. Resilient and lively, it was drawn vividly by Bill Naughton, in his perceptive description of the back-street gamblers of Bolton in the 1920s.

> These youths and men are not playing marbles for the love of the game but for ready cash. Having gone to work in the mill at the age of twelve for ten shillings a week seems to have made them set a value on every activity, so that even a game of football is usually played for a 'tanner a man'.
>
> The marble players are spread out along the length of the backstreet, with three or four separate games going on, about four players in each group, divided according to skill and the size of stakes, and at a penny and twopence a hit there is much handing of money. Nor are they using the common stone marbles, which they would consider childish, but each player has his own iron bobber. Aside from the marble players there is a game of pitch-and-toss going on, with money won and lost at every toss of the two pennies

> in the air, then up against our midden door is a banker school – 'Peter pays Paul,' calls Tommy Burton as he turns up the cards and switches the stakes from a losing to a winning card, 'an' the banker gets sod all.' There is even a little crown-and-anchor game, 'The more you put down the more you pick up', comes the invitation, '– you come in rags an' go away in motor-cars.'
>
> If our backstreet isn't exactly the hub of the world, I feel it cannot be far from it, with all that money changing hands. It makes you feel hoarse in the throat from excitement.[122]

With retrospect, one Salfordian wondered that 'it's unbelievable the games they would gamble on in the old days', and this passion for gambling was not peculiar to the British and Irish working classes.[123] It was as noticeable among the Arab and West Indian immigrants of Tiger Bay in Cardiff – where cards, dice and domino games were wagered on – and in particular, it was apparent among the Chinese workers of Limehouse in London's East End.[124] Here, the lottery-style game of puk-a-pu was so prevalent that local magistrates feared 'that it would spread all over the district among the native population'.[125] It would seem that while indigenous forms of gambling were reprehensible and abominable, foreign types were even more insidious to the well-being of the nation.

SPENDING AND THE SPORTING PRESS

Far from largely disappearing in the 1880s, street gambling did not begin to weaken until the 1950s, when its decline was induced by social changes and urban redevelopment. If it is difficult to argue otherwise, it is as problematical to make assertions about working-class expenditure with street bookies in the last two decades of the nineteenth century. It may be accepted that there was a general improvement in the incomes of some members of that class during that period, and it can be presumed that there was an increase in the amount of money betted; but it would be unwise to draw too definite a comparison with the outlay of punters before then.[126] Nonetheless, Gareth Stedman Jones made a decisive attempt to do so. Citing only the impressionistic evidence of anti-gamblers, he declared that betting and gambling increased enormously in the second half of the 1800s, and that this trend was apparent at the end of the 1860s.[127] In fact, the growth in off-course betting began in the mid-1840s, with the emergence of list houses, but it is impossible to determine whether or not the sums laid out then were substantially less than those wagered from the 1870s onwards.

The inability to draw such a conclusion is enforced by a lack of statistics for the earlier period and by their paucity for the later years. Indeed, those cited by McKibbin all relate to the time between 1913 and 1939, and not to the 1880s and 1890s.[128] However, some figures are available for those decades and for the early 1900s, but they are unreliable because they are the exaggerated estimates of those who were opposed to betting. In 1890, the Convocation of York was told that some idea of the business done by prominent bookmakers could be gathered from 'facts' about their wealth. For example, it was stated that at his death, the estate of one member of the fraternity was £152,000; while that of another – formerly a 'common sailor' and pugilist – was £54,000.[129] Certainly, on-course leviathans did gain massive wealth, but this was obtained from the bets of the rich, and it would be ludicrous to presume that any street bookie made a fortune on anything like the scale of their bigger racecourse fellows.[130] This reality did not deter anti-gamblers from continuing to quote unsubstantiated amounts of money betted illegally, and in 1905, the editor of the *Chiswick Times* expostulated that 'we have in this country something like 20,000 bookmakers turning over upwards of £50,000,000 annually'.[131]

All this is not to argue that street bookies did not take significant sums of cash. In 1902, it was stated that one of them in Glasgow had £800 on him when he was arrested; it must be remembered, however, that such a figure reflected turnover and not profit, and that it might have included monies owed to winning punters from previous days' betting.[132] Nevertheless, the fines paid by outlawed bookmakers would indicate that their winnings could be substantial. In 1900, it was reported that five bookies from Smethwick were levied a total of £27, and that 'each defendant had the money ready, and this greatly facilitated the business'; while in 1902, the Chief Constable of Glasgow told of a man called Miller who had been fined £10 on five separate occasions.[133] Yet from such snippets of evidence it would be foolish to extrapolate any firm statistics about either the income of illegal bookies or the spending of working-class people with them before 1914. Indeed, it would be sounder to bear in mind the caveat of that dedicated anti-gambler, B. Seebohm Rowntree. In his celebrated study of poverty in York in 1901, he stated that with regard to betting and gambling, 'it is obviously not possible to obtain even approximate statistics regarding the extent to which the habit prevails amongst the working classes'.[134]

In some respects, then, caution is needed in assessing the importance of the 1880s to the history of both betting and gambling; it should also be borne in mind that legislation against them was introduced well before that decade. That is not to ignore the plethora of publications that suggested a new problem was erupting; nor is it to dismiss the nervous excitement that attended debate about the matter. In 1889, this excitement was illustrated by the storm that followed the calm pronouncements of the Bishop of Peterborough. He had stated that while he regarded all gambling as wrong, he 'could not say that "*all*" betting was, under all circumstances, sinful'. For his insufficiency of zeal, he was excoriated and told that if his words were not actually wicked, they were rash and mischievous.[135]

British anti-gamblers seemed swept along by a wave of hysteria, but this was not an insular phenomenon. It was part of a surging tide of puritanical feeling throughout many parts of the English-speaking world. In Melbourne, the gambling mania was blamed for the land boom and the bank crash of 1893, which so distressed the local Council of Churches that it declared a Day of National Humiliation; and from 1900, in New South Wales especially, middle-class Protestant 'wowsers' targeted the pastime as an evil which had to be eradicated.[136] Across the Pacific, in the United States of America, an article appeared in 1892 which discussed 'The Increase in Gambling and Its Forms'. In it, W. B. Curtis asserted that it was safe to say that 'there never was a time in the history of the world' when the activity was so rife among all classes of people as at present; and three years later, Newman Smyth railed against the American rage for betting on athletic games, gambling on the numbers, and laying money on horse-races.[137]

This outpouring of venom against betting was distinguished not by its novelty, but by its scale and intensity, and a temperate writer for the *Spectator* discerned a reason for this obsession. He noted the 'lugubrious' estimates which indicated that Britain was degenerating rapidly into 'a society given up to gambling', but he argued that to believe them would be

> as great a mistake as it would be to assert that, because the newspapers were full for some weeks of the Kentish Town murder, and for other weeks of a great Liverpool poisoning case, the lower and upper strata of the middle class are rapidly sinking into habits of deliberate murder. It is always the most difficult thing in the world to compare the prevalence of any kind of evil or crime in such a century as ours, with the prevalence of the same evil or crime in a comparatively undeveloped period, if only because we hear so much more of it in days of cheap newspapers and cheap telegrams than we could possibly have heard in days when newspapers were few and telegrams had not even been conceived.

As this correspondent made clear, every scandal was reflected back and magnified from the narrative of scores of journalists and not a few informal interviewers, and he stressed that the awareness of social ills was inflated in the same manner.[138] In this light, credence may be given to Robin Miller's claim that there was 'some element of fashion' to the post-1889 upswing in books and pamphlets about the gambling problem. He argued that as a focus of condemnation, it exemplified the 'transitory nature of late Victorian bourgeois morality', which targeted for attack various sins at different times.[139] There is much evidence to support this assertion. It cannot be disputed that, from the 1880s, betting and gambling joined intemperance and impurity as 'one of the partners in that great Trinity of Evils'; nor can it be denied that by the turn of the century, they were feared as 'a worse evil and a more serious cause of poverty than drink'.[140] In 1902, this shift in attention was exemplified by the Reverend R. F. L. Blunt, when he praised the marvellous success with which public opinion had been 'aroused, instructed and elevated' about the 'sister' sin of drunkenness. At the same time, he appealed for this process to happen with regard to betting and gambling.[141]

Not only did articles and reports in the press indicate that these activities were increasing, so too did the dominance of racing news on its back pages. In Australia, John O'Hara noted that extensive 'coverage of racing information, including pre-post markets, predictions, detailed race descriptions and post-race analyses' was provided by the most conventional of the dailies, such as the *Sydney Morning Herald*. This attentiveness was matched by weekly publications and by specialist sporting magazines like Sydney's *Referee* and Melbourne's *Sportsman*.[142] In America, Curtis observed that a few years previously, no more than four or five journals of this kind had existed, and they had been published weekly or monthly. Now, there were forty of them each week and one daily, while the ordinary morning papers gave out betting news and published the predictions of their tipsters. He emphasized that a similar spectacular growth was evident in England, and he was correct.[143]

By the 1880s, horse-racing, like association football, had begun to take on the form that it presents today: a big business run professionally, albeit with amateurish trappings. Rowdy suburban meetings were closing down and the enclosure of the better-run courses proceeded apace. As Vamplew has pointed out, this latter phenomenon brought significant changes to British racing. By charging gate money, race-committees were forced to become attentive to the wishes of their spectators – 'especially the working man' – and what they wanted to see were exciting events such as sprints, handicaps and the races of two-year-olds.[144] Similarly, this kind of explosive contest appealed to off-course punters; indeed, until recent years bookies suffered a pronounced loss in trade when the 'Flat' ended and the 'Jumps' (steeplechase and hurdle racing) began.[145] As with football, a host of publications hurried to supply a public eager for news about their fancies.

The variety of these organs of information was wide. Some were like the *Musselburgh Chronicle* of 1889, a short-lived racing sheet which provided the form for a plate to be run at the Lothian fixture; others were longer-lasting and more substantial, such as Birmingham's *Sporting Star*, brought out in the late 1890s by George Pearce, a publican and racecourse bookie; and still more were similar to the same city's *Racing Analysis*, in 1882, just one of a number of tipsters' publications which arose and disappeared with bewildering rapidity.[146] At the stable end of the market were the well-established sporting papers of a national relevance, the chief of which was probably the *Sporting Life*. This had become a daily in 1883, and three years later its prestige was enhanced by its incorporation of the famous *Bell's Life*. Its main rivals remained the *Sportsman* and, in the North of England and Scotland, the *Sporting Chronicle*, selling 30,000 copies a day in 1883. In addition to giving out racing news, these dailies employed tipsters who wrote under *noms-de-plume* such as 'Kettledrum'.[147] Rapidly, this practice was adopted in the 1880s by the racing journalists of daily newspapers, one of the first of whom was 'Captain Coe' of the *Star*.[148]

With justification, Tony Mason has pointed out that 'the development of sport and the expansion of sporting news obviously fed off each other', and he could, with justification, have added betting to that symbiotic relationship.[149] Astutely, Gretton recognized the cohesion holding this triad together. He commented that, by the 1880s, England had begun to be a newspaper-reading nation, thanks both to the abolition of stamp duty on such publications and to compulsory education. In one respect, this phenomenon was evinced by the influence of the newspaper agitation in sending Gordon to Sudan; and in another, 'it disturbed the minds of the respectable by its obvious fruitfulness in new forms of gambling', like newspaper competitions. Moreover, the cheap press was the cause of an expansion in popular interest in horse-races, while the sporting dailies were responsible for the 'starting price' idea, 'the real secret of the spread of betting' on the sport.[150] The publication of this price by the press in general – as well as its speedy transmission of results – gave McKibbin his primary reason for focusing on the 1880s as significant to the history of betting. The evidence justifies his perception.[151]

5

STREET BOOKIES

STARTING-PRICE BETTING

The starting price (SP) of a horse is the average odds offered about its chances by racecourse layers at the time of 'the off', and it is this that modern off-course bookmakers use to determine the payout to winning clients. As a means of settling cash bets by post, it is likely that it was employed in the later 1870s by layers who were based on the Continent; Charles Sidney attributed its first use to one of their number, Valentine and Wright, a firm established in the late 1860s.[1] However, it is probable that it was not until 1884 that it was adopted by ready-cash bookies in Britain. In that year, Frank Harris established the London *Evening News* as the first 'national paper to publish the starting prices'; within three months, his move had trebled its circulation.[2] This innovation was followed by newspapers across the country and two years later, *Bell's Life* announced that starting-price betting had 'assumed immense importance'.[3]

Indeed, the impact of its advent cannot be over-estimated. It allowed off-course bookies to dispense with displaying bulky and conspicuous lists, and it induced them to do away with making their own prices. The significance of this latter change was made clear by Henry Butly-Smith, the managing director of the *Sportsman*. In 1902, he informed the Select Committee on Betting that in the past, punters had lacked information about the runners in a race. This had put them at a disadvantage to listmen who could draw in money on horses which they knew to be unsound or unprepared, and who could offer whatever odds they wished about the competitors in any contest. Now, bettors were provided with racing news each day, while the ascendancy of the starting price meant that similar odds were laid nationally.[4]

John Hawke, Secretary of the National Anti-Gambling League, agreed that this development was a guarantee of good faith between the working man and the street bookmaker, and he believed that this trust had led to the recent enormous increase in betting.[5] Whether or not his claim was justified, it is likely that people were more inclined to bet because they were assured a fair return. At the same time, it is probable that the simplicity of the SP system encouraged a rise in the number of small bookies, as the *Bulletin*, the publication of the National Anti-Gambling League, had suggested in 1894.[6] Again, it is impossible to determine if this led to a proportionate rise in the total amount of money staked off-course, or whether the same expenditure was simply spread out between more layers.

The SPs themselves were determined on the course by representatives of the *Sporting Life* and the *Sportsman*, and they were transmitted to their offices via the electric telegraph system. On the following day they were published, and bookies made it known to their punters that they would settle their bets according to the returns given in the sporting paper of their choice; in the North it is likely that many followed the SPs given in the *Sporting Chronicle*, while in London some favoured the *Evening Standard*, because this meant that they could pay out on the evening of a fixture.[7] Of course, there could be differences between the various returned prices, but in 1924, the *Sportsman* was swallowed up by the *Sporting Life*. Two years later, the management of the latter came to an arrangement with that of its northern competitor. Each of them agreed that at every meeting they should have an agent whose joint responsibility was to compile one SP that would be accepted universally.[8]

From the later 1880s and in many parts of the country, local evening newspapers pre-empted the publication of the odds by their originators.[9] Throughout the afternoon they would print various editions; in fact, as was the practice on the *Lancashire Evening Telegraph* and the Sheffield *Star*, it was usual for these editions to differ only in the inclusion of the latest result(s) in the stop press.[10] The importance of this practice was emphasized by Thomas Buckley, once a paper-boy in Stockport.

> Going back nearly sixty years, the wireless hadn't come on the scene, and one of the greatest unknown assistants to the street bookie was the newspaper lads of those days, and I was one of them. To be successful and earn your coppers one had to be strong, to carry five or six dozen under one's arm, have a good voice, and also to be a top-class runner, because we had the winners as they came out, and ours was the first news, so the faster we ran to the

> pubs and along the main roads and anywhere where there were people, football matches etc., we sold the news.[11]

Despite the availability of ticker-tape machines, in some districts, illegal bookmakers continued to rely on the press for their information until well after the end of the Second World War. My Dad recalled that as a boy in the 1940s, he would go to a local newspaper vendor to fetch the 3.30 edition of the Birmingham *Evening Mail* or the *Evening Despatch*. These would have the early racing results, enabling my Grandad to start settling the day's bets. Then Dad would go to town, to the offices of the *Mail* in Cannon Street, to buy several copies of the later editions of that paper. He would deliver these to my Grandad and to the five nearest bookies to him in Sparkbrook. At the end of the week, each would give him between 6d and 1s for his trouble.[12]

The onset of starting-price bookmaking in Britain was paralleled by developments in the structure of off-course betting elsewhere in the English-speaking world. In the United States, pool rooms became the main venue for the activity, and in 1892, it was claimed that there were between fifty and sixty of them in New York City alone. Each was connected to the electric telegraph and telephone systems and they operated in a similar way to the *pari-mutuel*.[13] This method of betting had been devised in 1872 by a Frenchman, Pierre Oller. His main concern had been to supplant bookies on the racecourses of France and his system worked on the principle of pooling the stakes of the punters on a particular race, after which an amount would be deducted to cover expenses and to allow a profit for the promoter. The remainder was divided up among winning clients and from the later 1870s, their dividend was calculated by a totalizator, a machine devised in New Zealand.[14]

As in the United States, so too in Australia did some enterprising off-course bookies adopt pool-betting, and in 1893, John Wren founded the Collingwood Tote, which Keith Dunstan dubbed aptly 'the most notorious illegal betting institution the country has seen'.[15] In France, too, 'secret agencies' of the *pari-mutuel* became common, but it was not until the 1920s that similar premises emerged in Britain.[16] At first, they operated on credit, but after a favourable judgement by the House of Lords, it appeared that it was legal to open cash clubs for members, the first of which appeared in 1932. Like others, it was run by a syndicate and not by bookies, and its parent company was Pool Clubs Limited. Within a few months, this firm had opened thirty-two totes. Overall, they had a membership of 40,000; and it was reported that the club at Baker Street was filled on occasions with as many as 2,000 people.

For a short time, it seemed that tote betting might succeed in driving street bookies out of existence, a feat which the full rigour of the law had failed to accomplish. However, an appeal court found that under the 1853 Act, it was an offence to operate a totalizator outside a racecourse, where its use had been legalized in 1928. Because of their large size, their static position and their prominence, the now outlawed tote clubs were quashed rapidly and this 'menace to bookmaking' thus disappeared as quickly as it had arisen.[17] Their suppression ensured that starting-price betting would remain supreme among illegal bookies; at the same time, it meant that the pattern of their operations adhered to the mosaic that was formed in the later nineteenth century.

Except in Manchester and London, street betting was not banned by local authorities. Consequently, many of the first SP cash bookmakers tended to gather in one location in a particular town or city, as had the listmen of Williamson Square, Liverpool and those of Farringdon Street, London. At these standing markets, it was observed with dismay that 'betting transactions are conducted as unblushingly as are business transactions in the neighbouring exchange', and the Midden at Leeds was given as a notorious example.[18] Charles Winter was a bookie who had stood at this open space, and he stated that he and other layers had commenced to use it in 1886; four years later, it was reported that it was frequented by as many as two or three thousand people at a time, some of whom gambled with dice in addition to betting on horses.[19]

As well-attended and as notorious as the Midden were the Jarrow Pit Heap and the Middlesbrough Bank – nicknamed the town's Monte Carlo – which was visited in 1889 by a Special Commissioner of the *North-Eastern Daily Gazette*. He wrote that he saw twenty or thirty bookmakers standing on boxes 'clearly visible above the crowd, and above the hum of conversation rise their stentorian cries, as they announce their willingness to relieve the by-stander of their superfluous cash'.[20] In a few parts of Britain, public betting grounds like this continued to exist into the twentieth century. One such was at the Market Place in Chesterfield, where large numbers of men gathered on racing days in the mid-1930s; another was the Paddock in Springburn, Glasgow, a well-named piece of ground which was a rendezvous for about eight to ten lifters (bookie's street takers) each Saturday in the inter-war years; and one other was the 'Wag Back' in Blackburn – situated in Calendar Street, near to the town's brewery and the office of the *Lancashire Evening Telegraph* – where a runner (lifter) took bets throughout the afternoon, surrounded by a well-attended gambling school which survived until the later 1950s.[21]

THE PATTERN OF STREET BOOKMAKING: SHOPS

Places such as the Wag Back (so named because it was at the back of the *Wag*, the local newspaper) were vestigial, and most standing markets had disappeared in the 1890s, as a result of a spate of byelaws aimed against street betting.[22] These measures were passed either under the guise of the Municipal Corporations Act of 1882, or under that of a local Act, and they fell into two groups.[23] First, there were those of the 1880s, which treated street betting as an obstruction and which made it an offence for three (in Scotland, two) or more people to assemble for the purpose of betting. The usual punishment was a fine of £5, although in some places it was £2, the same as the Scottish penalty which was laid down by the Burgh Police Act (1892).[24] In England and Wales, these byelaws were ineffective because they allowed street betting between two people. Consequently, in the 1890s, many local authorities adopted the second type of byelaw, that which made it illegal to frequent and use any street 'for the purpose of bookmaking or betting'.[25] Once again, the usual punishment was £5, but faced with the continuing defiance of bookies, a wave of councils followed the example set by Blackpool in 1901. Under its Improvement Act, this borough was enabled to fine second- and third-time offenders a sum of £10, while it levied £50 on those who were convicted of more offences than these.[26]

Such anti-bookmaking measures did not eliminate starting-price betting for cash; instead, in many areas, they shifted its focus away from the street, as happened in St Helens. In 1902, an editorial in the local newspaper noted:

> The next danger is, of course, that the betting evil when driven from the highways and byways will seek a local habitation in out of the way houses and shops. That it already has taken a step in this direction is common knowledge. Premises occupied by not very reputable barbers and tobacconists, which are to some extent places of public resort, are the natural hiding places of the gambler who preys on his fellows.[27]

By 1924, it was believed 'that our industrial areas are permeated with these secret and illegal betting houses', and until 1961, many small shopkeepers continued to 'double up' as starting-price bookmakers.[28] Indeed, several famous firms were founded as a result. In London, David Cope took bets in his barber's, and by the inter-war years, his family had become established as leading credit bookmakers as well as football pools promoters; during the 1950s, Joe Ward Hill (the younger brother of William) laid punters in his hairdresser's in Stevenage, presaging a flourishing business after legalization; and in the late nineteenth century, the Layfields used similar premises in London as a front for bookmaking, so laying the foundations of a thriving credit concern.[29]

Of course, such success stories were unusual, but for many small shopkeepers it was true that bookmaking enhanced their standards of living. By making it known that they accepted cash bets, they attracted customers to their 'open' businesses and they hoped that this would increase their profitability. At the same time, the nature of their 'real' occupations covered their 'hidden' activities. Consequently, it was difficult for the police to take action against them, and this was especially the case with those who relied on purchasers 'popping in and out'.[30] It was for this reason that barbers, tobacconists, confectioners and newspaper sellers were identified by the authorities as centres of illegal betting. The testimony of working-class people would support this contemporary observation.[31] In the Meadows district of Nottingham, the local newsagent became a bookie because punters gathered in his shop to wait for the half-hour delivery of the *Nottingham Evening Post*, in which would be the latest results. Across that city, in Basford, one barber's had a trigger bell, and Albert Hardy recalled that 'this would be continually ringing, and not for haircuts'. Throughout the 1930s, Mr Riddall – a tobacconist – took bets as a commission agent in Brighton; and at Edward Wright's confectioner's in Bradford, customers 'would often buy a loaf of bread and a few buns and leave the "slips" [bets] on the counter'.[32]

However, illegal bookmaking was not confined to the four types of shops highlighted by the Select Committee on the Betting Duty (1923). A. McIntyre wrote that in Bingley, 'most of the bookies usually ran small businesses', and he remembered that one such was a cobbler's; while in Birmingham, Lew Reeves would take the bets of his Mom and Dad to

> a gentleman by the name of W. who owned a greengrocer's shop at Dogpool. The procedure was to eye up the outside of the shop, looking to see if any uniformed police were about, or strangers – we knew all the locals in those days; when it was 'all clear' we walked into the shop – if it was clear of customers we walked straight through to a shed in the back-yard where we handed in the coppers, wrapped in our betting slip.[33]

Likewise, Albert Stanton – one of the oldest-established bookmakers in Coventry – operated behind the façade of a greengrocery business, as did a female bookie in Brighton; while in Warrington and Carrington in Nottingham, two leading layers used their butchers' shops as their headquarters.[34] 'Secret' bookies were to be found among other small traders, such as the Shipley pea and pie shop owner for whom Samuel Fulwood was a works' agent, and their numbers included general-store keepers, wet-fishmongers and coal merchants.[35] However, some of the most prominent of them were based in fish-and-chip shops and Rose Pickering was typical of them. A popular bookie in Birmingham, she

> got the fish shop in the front and the little house at the back, the little room at the back where she used to take the bets . . . Well, it was in a yard and there was four of us in the yard. There was the butcher's, there was us the fish shop and next door there was Elliot the barber's and then next door to that was Ingram's the butcher's and we was all in this one yard, and being a butcher he had a fridge in the yard. So he had two great big doors put on the yard so that it was all private and there was a little door cut in the big door and of course they used to put their bets in there and of course you used to have a man on the door because of the police, it wasn't legal then and that's how they used to just give the man the bets behind the door and he used to put them in a bag and we used to bring them in the house and Mom and Dad used to do 'em in the house.[36]

Reg Betts recalled that Newport's best fried fish was sold in a shop in the Caerleon Road area, and that its proprietors were also bookies. In his opinion, the betting business was a bonus to them. Nevertheless, the illegal activity benefited sales of take-aways, for numerous punters placed bets at the shop itself, and they had to buy food if they were to deceive the police.[37]

In fact, in many cases, bookmaker/shopkeepers took more money illegitimately than they did legally and for some, their shopkeeping status became a fiction.[38] Just before the Second World War, Mass Observation noticed that in a main street in the centre of Worktown (Bolton) there was a large cigarette shop that did not sell any cigarettes. There were dummies in the window, but the counter inside was used only for passing bets. It was pointed out that everybody knew about this situation – including the police – since anybody could walk into the premises.[39] This tobacconist's was in Great Moor Street and it was run by Bella Thomasson, a woman highly respected in Bolton who had been convicted of her first betting offence in 1905.[40] At that time, her premises had been used as a fruiterer's, but by the 1930s, that business had faded away; twenty years later, so too had the pretence that the place was selling cigarettes. By then she had taken a partner called Albert Hampson, and their undertaking had become the most well-known illegal betting shop in the town.[41]

When discussing the variegated design of illegal bookmaking, it is essential to use the term street betting. It was the phrase adopted universally by anti-gamblers, newspaper writers, government inquirers, punters and bookies themselves, and it would be fruitless to dispense with it. The words themselves have a power to evoke the phenomenon that they represent but they should not obscure the fact that much illegal betting was carried on away from the street. Certainly, street takers were employed by many shopkeepers who acted as bookies, yet their operations were not based in that public space. Neither were those of publican/bookies.

THE PATTERN OF STREET BOOKMAKING: PUBS

Licensed premises had been a focus of outlawed wagering since the mid-1840s. Because it was less blatant than list betting, the coming of starting-price bookmaking was a boon for landlords who acted as layers, as it was for those who ran 'old-fashioned' pubs. In 1889, it was the opinion of a public-house valuer in the Midlands that such places 'can't be made to pay now-a-days', and he suggested that if he had one, 'I should go in for a bit of betting, and I could retire in ten years'.[42] Such hopes were recognized by George Moore when he wrote *Esther Waters* (1894), and they were expressed by him through the character of William Latch. A betting man who aspired to be a bookie, he took over the King's Head, 'a humble place' which 'was not an up-to-date public house, quite the reverse'. Even though he served the best liquor in the neighbourhood, Latch found that his business was 'cruel' and to improve it, he arranged a betting room and began to lay the fancies of his multiplying number of customers.[43]

The strength of this anti-gambling novel lay as much in its reality as it did in its message, and this distinguished it from others of its genre.[44] In particular, Latch himself was a convincing portrait, not only of a publican-cum-starting-price-bookie, but also of a licensee who was a part-time bookmaker on the course. In this respect, he had much in common with Jim Shaylor, of the Carpenters' Arms in Birmingham, and with the entrepreneurial George Pearce – another Brummie and publisher of the *Sporting Star*, landlord of the Golden Cross and flamboyant layer of the odds at race-meetings. Betting under the slogan of 'The Same Old Smile', Pearce promoted himself with a leaflet headed 'What's in a Name?'

What's in a name? Well a good name's a lot,
And it's not every man who a good name has got.
But I'll mention the name of a good man and sound,
And whose motto is 'CASH – twenty Bob in the Pound'
That's GEORGE PEARCE of Brum, who at home or abroad,
Wears '*The same old Smile*' ready for Peasant or Lord;
On the Racecourse or off it, he's always the same,
And the world well respects both the man and the name.
There's this in a name – if with GEORGE PEARCE you bet,
You know if you win that your money you'll get.
No haggling or quibbling, but all fair and square –
The name and the man, and the money are there.
With 'the same old Smile' GEORGE PEARCE the odds freely lays,
With 'the same old Smile' freely his losses he pays,
If you'd bet with a 'Bookie' who plays a straight game,
Put your coin on with PEARCE of 'The same old Smile' fame.

Unlike his fictitious counterpart, Pearce ran a busy city-centre pub and it is not known whether or not he laid SP bets. However, he advertised his business as a place where customers could obtain 'special tips free', and it would not be surprising if he had engaged in off-course bookmaking.[45] Certainly, the law relating to gaming and betting was 'illogical and confused' and this legal fog seemed especially to hinder the stamping out of these activities on licensed premises.[46] A publican/bookie could be convicted of an offence only if it were proven that he himself had made bets with his customers; while if a bookmaker operated in a pub, the licensee could not be acted against unless it were shown that he had 'knowingly allowed' the layer to ply his trade.[47] These provisos presented the police with great difficulties, as was illustrated by the prosecution of Thomas Patterson, publican of the Church Inn, Bolton. In 1891, he was charged with using his house for betting purposes, but the case was dismissed because 'he was not in the room where the proved bets were made, another man acting as bookmaker'. Forestalled in this instance, the police took out a fresh summons against Patterson and he was fined £1 for allowing a bookie to take bets in his pub.[48]

Moralists believed that, in many instances, bookmaking on licensed premises was countenanced by brewers who owned tied houses, and in 1884, there were exclamations against their conduct in St Helens. The editor of the local newspaper deplored the policy whereby tenants were told that they would be discharged if they were '*caught*' betting. He argued that the stress was on the word caught and that it was understood that tenants could do what they liked, 'so that they but bring grist to the mill'.[49] Yet, as elsewhere in the country, the police kept up the pressure on publicans who acted as bookies – despite the problems of gathering evidence and of securing convictions – and by 1902, it was reported that in the Merseyside town, 'most of the licensed houses may now be considered fairly clean'.[50] Eight years later, the issue was taken up nationally and a law was passed which provided a summary fine for licensees who operated in contravention of the 1853 Act, or who allowed their premises to be so used.[51] Coupled with the threat of a lost licence, this code served to eliminate most men of Latch's type, although a few of them continued to ignore the law. In the 1930s, John Cooke kept the Shakespeare in Newcastle-under-Lyme, and 'also did a spot of Book-Making'; and twenty years later, so too did Jack Scotney, first in the village of Farcet and then in nearby Peterborough.[52]

Still, if men like this were distinguished by their rarity, then the authorities were undecided as to the extent of 'the use of licensed premises for betting'. The members of the Royal Commission on Lotteries and Betting (1932–3) failed to come up with any conclusive evidence as to its prevalence. With exasperation, they noted that some witnesses thought that it was negligible, while others believed it to be considerable. There can be no doubt that the latter were correct.[53] Legally, there was no complete prohibition of the use of a public house for the receipt of bets, while it remained lawful to pay out there.[54] This meant that many licensees were prepared to turn a blind eye to bookmaking on their premises, as did the landlord of the Park Hotel in Ince-Wigan.[55] Others actively encouraged and protected it, like Charles Gleed's father who ran a pub near to the docks in Ipswich before 1914. He let a bookie use the back of his premises, and he positioned his son at the bar – facing the door – so as to keep a watch for the police coming in.[56] Similarly, Jean Davies remembered that a Scunthorpe landlady secreted her father's betting slips when detectives sought to catch him.[57] The reason for such assistance was simple: bookmakers spent freely and they attracted custom. As one licensee put it, 'betting is forbidden by most pubs, but the pubs that do the best trade are those that have a means for that entertainment; a good bookie is a great asset to a pub'.[58]

In some houses, the activity went on surreptitiously, as in the George at Cannock, where Mr A. Griffiths recalled that the bets were handed over in the toilet; in others, it was carried on openly but quietly, as in the Railway at Selston, where John Ward received his customers while sitting in the bar.[59] The scene here was reminiscent of that described in 1947 by an observer for Mass Observation. A newcomer enters a pub and

> receives nods of recognition from all the people in the room and seats himself on a chair close to the domino table. He is of medium height, sandy-haired, round-faced, fresh-complexioned. He wears a single-breasted blue suit with a neat pin stripe, a white shirt and collar, blue tie, and brown shoes well polished. His hands are clean, the nails carefully trimmed, in contrast to the blackened work-stained hands of the other men in the vault.
>
> As soon as he seats himself, 70D with the long nose produces a slip of paper, rises with difficulty and walks lumpingly across to him. He hands over the paper slip, counts the coins . . . The other pair each push a slip and money across the table . . . the thick-necked 50D turns in his chair and gives him a slip and a 10s 0d note and then returns to his game of cribbage . . . Not a word has been uttered concerning his business.[60]

Blatant betting of this kind was common in working-men's clubs as far apart as Yorkshire, Port Talbot, Swindon and Higham Ferrers; it was regular in Conservative clubs in towns that were as diverse in their nature as Oldham, Nuneaton and Colwyn Bay; and it was as apparent in billiard halls in a variety of places including Rotherham, Bristol and Norwich.[61] Indeed, bookmaking on licensed premises was characterized by its ubiquity and not by its particularity. Certainly, in a town like Chesterfield, it was the dominant form of illegal betting, but prosecutions against the activity were recorded for publicans who worked in Cirencester, Derby, Lanark, Patricroft and Neath, and the evidence of working-class people substantiates the belief that it was rife in a multitude of towns and cities: from Bristol in the west, across to Bedworth in the midlands, and to Ipswich in the east; and from Southend in the South East, across to the Medway towns and to Exeter in the South West.[62] Still, in most urban districts, pub betting was one strand in the pattern of cash bookmaking, unlike in rural Britain where it was preponderant.

By 1901, it was noted that 'the betting system' had spread to the countryside and that it was confined no longer to towns and populous districts.[63] Even though it would seem that agricultural labourers betted infrequently – because of their low wages, their bi-annual payment (in some localities) and their diffusion in the fields – there were plenty of other punters to be found in the countryside. Among them were farmers, shopkeepers, miners, quarrymen, postmen, brickyard workers and railwaymen. Bookies found that in areas where the population was scattered, then the most efficient way of taking bets was via the pub.[64] The chief layer in the Oswestry region was a farmer, and he stationed takers in the licensed premises of the town's hinterland, giving a collector the use of a motor car to fetch the bets that had been staked; while in the villages around Norwich, landlords gathered the fancies of their regulars and then telephoned them in to a city-based bookmaker, who settled his accounts on a weekly basis.[65]

THE PATTERN OF STREET BOOKMAKING: WORKS

Occasionally, a large number of workers were gathered in one location in a rural district, and then it became feasible to place bets away from a pub, as Roy Whitehead explained.

> My father, Charles Whitehead, acted as a bookie's runner during the middle thirties. Our home was on the outskirts of Whittlesey in Cambridgeshire (a small market town in the Fens, pop. *c.* 8,000 in those days). He worked for the Whittlesea Central Brick Company at one of their works at King's Dyke . . . as a yard clerk or checker. The important thing for any runner in rural areas was easy access to a phone in the days when few people had a private phone. The office in which he worked, shared only by the yard foreman . . . had an outside line . . . No doubt he phoned through the bets to a bookmaker in Peterborough (so far as I know there was no bookmaker in Whittlesey at the time) and every Saturday afternoon/evening went into Peterborough (about seven miles distant) to settle up and receive any winnings due to his clients. In this job he had daily contact with perhaps well in excess of a hundred brickyard workers . . . together with many lorry drivers and railway staff.[66]

In fact, betting at a place of employment was endemic throughout Britain – even among the Brummie workers of the Quaker Cadbury's – and by 1923, it was stated wearily that 'there is scarcely a works in the country employing more than 20 workmen where one is not a bookmaker's agent'.[67]

There can be little doubt that this was true, and numerous working-class people remembered the popularity of betting with a factory taker. During the 1930s, at a shoe works in Raunds (Northants) this person was the daughter of a local bookie, but usually it was someone who was unrelated to the layer.[68] Often they were young workers like Robert Hird, whose unofficial job was to gather the 'lines' (bets) from other employees in his Dundee jute mill; or else they were people who had access to various departments within a large manufactory, as had Jean Hall in the Cleckheaton mill in which she worked.[69] This latter practice was widespread, and even on a building site someone could be found to collect the bets of his fellow workers.[70] Nor was the phenomenon restricted to those who were employed in traditional industries. Nora Hog acted as an agent in a big telephone maker's in Liverpool; and in the early 1950s, Norman Backhouse trained as a male nurse in a large general hospital in Bradford, where he recalled vividly

> the activities of the hospital barber (an ex-porter). He was ideally placed for activity as a runner – he never had to advertise his service, as established patients told new patients the drill! After he had shaved a patient or trimmed someone's hair, the 'tip' – money and a scrap of paper – was surreptitiously passed. The same 'sleight of hand' was used for paying out winnings – he was always kept busy changing money or patients! The activities were carried out with such care that close observation would have been needed to have caught him . . .
>
> I don't know whether Ward Sisters, Matrons and administrators knew what went on, but certainly many members of staff used his services as well.[71]

In the shoe factories of Northamptonshire, the rule was instant dismissal for anyone who was caught betting at work. But in the opinion of Mrs Davis, 'looking back we feel quite sure the management knew or even placed bets themselves but turned a blind eye'.[72] It was obvious that this was the general attitude of managers in whatever place of employment; Mass Observation recorded that in one hospital, the doctors betted with its furtive bookie.[73] Employers found that 'it was impossible' to quash betting on their premises, as did the police.[74] Usually, they needed permission to enter a works and even if this was given, they had little chance of catching illegal bettors or runners. Mr G. Squires served as a policeman in Liverpool during the 1950s. He remembered that a 'great number' of street bookies operated on the city's docks, and their most popular venues were the canteens. These were open throughout the day and they were ideal 'pitches' (bookmakers' sites) for two reasons. First, they were indoors and protected the bookies from bad weather; and second, they enabled bets to be taken in 'comparative security – as a police officer would be quickly identified by the dockers' upon his arrival.[75]

Given the safety of betting at work, it is not surprising that some employees began to operate as bookies in their own right, like Sid Whitby, who took at Willmot Breedon's in Birmingham, between 1949 and 1966; or like James Heald, a weaver at a mill in Blackburn.[76] In early 1920, he became 'fed up with working for a pittance' and to supplement his earnings, he started taking small bets of 2d or 3d. By 1923, he had left his employment and had gone 'on the streets from pub to pub, picking up bets'.[77] His route was followed by other works' bookies, and some of them set up successful businesses – as did 'Big' Horace Foster. In 1910, this foreman-toolmaker began laying the fancies of his fellow workers at the Birmingham brass-founders of Samuel Heath; by 1926 he was a full-time bookie in nearby Kyrwicks Lane.[78] Across the city, close to the famed working-class neighbourhood of Summer Lane, Arthur Overton began bookmaking in similar circumstances in the early 1920s. He 'started taking a few bets in a foundry', leaving his employment to be a street bookie after 'a pot burst over his foot . . . and it filled one boot with molten metal and even to the day he died he was picking bits of metal . . . out of his foot'.[79]

After 1945, the tradition of these layers was continued by men like Jim Farrar in Halifax and R. Elliot in Paisley. Still, works' bookies were never predominant over the hosts of agents who took bets for the payment of 'a drink' or for a commission of between 10d and 2s 6d in the pound.[80] Some were like Nora Hog, whose agency made 'work more enjoyable', and which added 15s a week to her wages; many were similar to Bernard Ryan's father, a skilled worker and 'a sporting man *par excellence*' who did 'fairly well' as a taker; or else they resembled Mrs Baines's Dad, a badly paid mill-worker in Bolton who earned just 17s a week in 1919, 'so with the money he got from the Bookie he brought 12 children up'.[81] As agents, these people received their commission whether or not their bookie won or lost, and this was an incentive for them to remain as collectors and not to set up in business themselves. Indeed, the biggest problem faced by most works' takers was that of placing their bets with their bookmaker. Usually, it was difficult to do this by telephone and in most instances the handover was accomplished on the street.

As early as 1890, it was noticed that bookies or their 'middlemen' tended to 'loiter about the large workshops that they may collect bets and push business', and seventy years later this practice remained prevalent.[82] In Norwich, runners waited for workers 'in the street and alleys, especially in the vicinities of the Boot and Shoe Factories and of the local breweries'; while in New Mills near Stockport, Mildred Jennings went to 'pubs, clubs, factories, quarries, shops etc', putting into a shopping basket the bets gathered by her father's agents.[83] Other bookmakers were more mobile in their manner of collection. In Nottingham, Lewis Marsden cycled to fetch his bets, while in the inter-war years in Birmingham, Ernie N. used his car to 'do the round' of his nine takers.[84] But after the Second World War, even this more sophisticated set-up paled in comparison to that of Ernie Lester. In order to fetch the bets from over two hundred agents whom he employed in Coventry, this enterprising bookmaker used three full-time collectors with vans.[85] Sid Brooks explained how he achieved the same task for a Wolverhampton layer.

> I used to hire a scooter with a sort of a mud guard . . . I used to wear a big mac, with big pockets, and I used to go round . . . it was governed by what the dinner hours were in the factories, and in the pubs . . . and then I'd go round and I'd have these calling places. I'd probably do, oh, twelve or fifteen about, say, an hour. I used to dash to one, dash to the other, in a radius. I'd cover twenty miles sort of thing . . . Factory gates, collect them, pubs. Some blokes used set spots like on a canal bridge, and all this sort of thing, caper, like. Meet them at a set time within a couple of minutes, and then come back . . .[86]

THE PATTERN OF STREET BOOKMAKING: HOUSES

In Hyde, Cheshire, George Kemp was a leading bookmaker who took from factories; Bernard Ryan's father was his agent. As a boy in the 1930s, he would meet his Dad as he alighted from the tram which brought him from work and together they would go to the Kemps' family home. Here they would join with takers from other large factories, and while they sat in the living room, their commissioner would settle up their accounts.[87] This procedure was not unusual in the town, as James Sefton recalled. His father had taken bets first as a metal polisher at Jones sewing-machine factory, and then as a full-time bookie who operated from his house. Like George Kemp, he 'had a lot of agents in works', whom he had acquired in 'the usual way'. That is, 'when one of the punters came with a few bets you gave them a shilling or two; then as they brought more bets you put them on commission ranging from a shilling to 1/6 in the pound'.[88]

William Hall operated a similar system in Bradford, while in South Hempsall (South Yorkshire), Mrs Edwards received her runners in a shed behind the 'camouflage' of her sweet shop.[89] But in other parts of Britain, dwellings were used not only as a place in which to gather bets from agents, but also as somewhere for the placing of the fancies of punters in general. Dick Lord was a well-known runner in Audley Range, Blackburn, and his daughter remembers:

> We lived in a small terraced house, and people and neighbours from all around used to be at our house all Saturday morning, with their

> various bets; they were written on scraps of paper, and some were just a few coppers they were betting on a horse. The local milkman also came to our house to place his bets and the grocer where my mother did her shopping. The night before a big race our house was like an open house with people coming. If anyone knocked at the door my mother used to put all the papers and money either in her apron pocket or under the table cover.

As well as his wife taking bets in their home, Dick Lord was an agent in a mill and he acted as a runner in a pub on weekends.[90] Likewise, in Barton Hill, Bristol, the local bookie allowed punters to come to his house, while he commissioned takers in nearby factories.

This man was raided twice by the police and it is unsurprising that their attention was drawn to his activities by a constant flow of bettors to his home, no matter how discreet they were.[91] Elsewhere, 'house' bookmakers and agents adopted various procedures in the hope of reducing their visibility. At the age of eight or nine – in a working-class neighbourhood of Plymouth – Mrs L. R. Kelley remembered 'putting notes with a sixpenny piece through a letter-box and being warned not to let anyone see me, especially a policeman'; and in Colwyn Bay, Mr W. S. Davies repeated this procedure.[92] Throughout the country, working-class children grew up with an awareness that cash betting had to be done in secret. Rita Coe took her mother's fancies to a bookie who lived on the same council estate in Brighton, and 'we were told to hide this little package and, if anyone strange was around to bring it back home – in those days everyone knew everyone else'.[93]

Similar memories were shared by people from London's East End, Bradford and Featherstone, but although illegal betting was, as Mrs G. Strachan emphasized, 'like a secret gang going on in the street', the danger of arrest remained real.[94] At the same time, if their home was raided more than once, then a bookie increased his or her chances of suffering a higher fine, and possible imprisonment. In these circumstances, many of them rented alternative accommodation for their businesses, as was indicated in 1936 by a prosecution against Mrs Lily Simpson. She was fined £20 for using a house in Patricroft for the purpose of betting on horse-racing; while Isaac Kershaw was ordered to pay £4 for permitting his dwelling to be so used; his wife, Edith, was punished in the sum of £3 for having the care of their home at the time of the offence; and eight other persons each had to pay between 15s and £4 10s for aiding and abetting.[95]

Like factory agents, householders such as the Kershaws were encouraged to assist bookies because it increased their earnings, as was made clear by the case of Edward and Florrie Cuddy of Eccles.

After their arrest in 1932, their solicitor told the court that they were the parents of six young children, the oldest of whom was ten. The father was a labourer earning £3 a week and this sum was added to by the 8s to 10s they received from a bookie for the use of their house.[96] Barbara Harsant's parents were in a similar situation. Their home was used as a collection point for a large number of agents who worked for a big bookie in Poplar. The family was 'very poor' and 'the fee paid the rent, which in those "good old days" was nearly 50 per cent of my father's very hard earned wages' of £2 10s a week.[97] As late as the 1950s, this kind of financial reward remained a powerful incentive to householders to allow bookies to use their homes. Evelyn Gregory was a young married woman and she lived with her husband and baby daughter at a cheaply rented dwelling in Burleigh Road, Portsmouth.

> The house had been rented to us by a very generous man, Mr Bertie W., an ex-Marine Sergeant from the First World War; housing was nearly impossible to obtain owing to the devastation in the Portsmouth area due to the bombing in the 1939 war. Mr W. allowed us to move into his empty house on the understanding that his business as a bookie was carried on . . .
>
> My duties were to answer the door and accept any bets on his behalf; these were collected and were taken to . . . a house with a long passage to the back . . . where a panelled partition barred the way; on knocking, a small opening appeared, followed by a large red nose and hand which took the bets and money and promptly disappeared. As the passing of bets was illegal I took the money safely installed in the basket of my daughter's pushchair underneath a fluffy toy.[98]

Unlike the Cuddys and Gregorys, other house-based agents were without a proper income and so their payments from a bookie were essential to their survival. In Leicester, Maureen Newton's Dad was a victim of tuberculosis, adding to his sick pay with his 'running', as did June Bailey's grandfather, a semi-invalid who 'took' in Smethwick.[99] After his death, his wife carried on his job, joining other widows like Mrs G. A. Mason who worked from her Birmingham back-to-back.[100] Throughout Britain, the ranks of agents were swelled by people like these and they were joined by those such as Mr Haworth – a Blackburnian who was forced to leave his job because of an industrial disease – and by unemployed men like James Tilsley.[101] In common with most house-agents, this Boltonian gathered bets in pubs as well as in his home, and as with many, he was a veteran of the First World

War.[102] So too was Fred Proctor's Dad. He was subject to seizures because of a serious wound he had received at Gallipoli. Unable to work, he became a runner 'like thousands more of Englishmen etc, he had to have a bit of something extra apart from his pension to make a go of it with my mother who was a cotton weaver but not earning much money'.[103]

It should not be presumed that house-betting was restricted to the older, industrial areas of Britain. In the market town of Towcester and in Lutterworth, the local bookies received at their back doors both their punters and their factory agents; and in the rural town of Thetford, Fred Cross recalled that

> As a schoolboy I used to take father's bets, written on notepaper with the money wrapped inside; only a shilling or two, as you could have a 6d place bet. I would go to a room at the back of the bookie's house where there was a table with a chalk line down the middle, put the bet on the right-hand side of the line. If there were any winnings from the previous day they would be on the other side of the chalk line wrapped in the original betting slip with the name on. If there were any queries you rang a hand-bell to get the housekeeper, who would refer it back to the bookmaker.
>
> Such was the honesty of people in those days, I never once heard of money being stolen. Bets had to be on the table before the first race time as the door was locked by his housekeeper to ensure that no bets were made after the result of the first race.[104]

Numerous prosecutions are recorded against house bookies and their prevalence was acknowledged by the members of the Royal Commission (1932–3).[105] As they pointed out, the use of a dwelling as a headquarters was the normal organization of what could be dealt with most conveniently 'under the heading of *Street Betting*'. They noted also that many bookmakers operated from 'an office kept ostensibly for credit betting', and that this was a ruse which was adopted to disguise their involvement in illegal activities.[106]

THE PATTERN OF STREET BETTING: OFFICES

From the 1880s, continental layers like Dey had returned to Britain and they had opened up SP offices for credit customers, who were overwhelmingly upper- and middle-class punters.[107] These credit turf accountants, as they preferred to be called, were joined by some racecourse bookies such as Dick Seymour – 'the silver king of

Manchester' – who had started laying bets in 1868, and whose descendants run Britain's oldest firm of bookmakers.[108] While cash betting remained illegal, these businesses thrived, receiving the bets of upper- and middle-class punters as well as those of other SP layers who wished to cover (protect) themselves from a potentially 'bad' result.[109] The number of credit firms increased rapidly, and after 1919, some of the most highly successful of the illegal bookies abandoned their cash undertakings and became legitimate. Among these men were the Copes and Layfields, and they were joined by the celebrated William Hill. In the inter-war years, Hill had been an unsuccessful factory bookmaker in Birmingham, but after he moved to London in 1929, he became the 'biggest bookmaker in the world'. He started off taking bets in the cheap rings at the dogs, at the pony racing at Northolt Park and Portsmouth Park, and at the Pelican Club, where he acted as an illegal bookie. Here he had a blackboard showing the runners and riders and upon which the results were chalked up after they became known via the ticker tape. After a year, this pitch was raided and closed down and Hill focused on his racecourse bookmaking. In 1934 he moved into credit betting and within fifteen years he was regarded as the number-one bookmaker in England. Throughout the 1950s, his business prospered and in 1962, it was reported that he had a 'personal fortune bordering on the £10,000,000 mark'.[110]

In Scotland, Hill was rivalled by the redoubtable James McLean and by Harry Miller, a man whose rise to wealth had begun when he had been a lifter for a Glaswegian bookie.[111]

> Actually how ma father built his tank up he was very, very clever with figures . . . And what happened was the betting slips got out into envelopes and the runner took them into the head office, and the head office did the processing, they made them up. And they were put on sheets and there was a copy sheet, and they all had *noms-de-plume*. Willie 2 Z three sixes, so and so and so and so. Now ma father would be given a sheet the next day t' pay out the punters. And the punters'd come up to him and say t' him, 'Harry, is there anything on the sheet f' Willie 3?' And Dad would say, 'What did ye back?' 'Oh, I had a half-a-crown double, 2 t' 1 and 5 t' 4.' So Dad would know right away, seven and sixpence, that's fifteen bob, that's sixteen and ten pence. He'd look at the sheets and it'd be twenty-two bob. So Dad would pay them the correct amount, and the rest was his.[112]

Building up his reserves in this way, Harry Miller ventured out as an independent bookie. By the 1950s, he was a well-known racecourse layer and he operated a credit business. But unlike Hill, he maintained a close connection with illegal betting, controlling at least a hundred street pitches and receiving the bets from numerous works' takers.[113]

The Glaswegian was not alone in hiding an illegal undertaking behind a façade of legitimacy. Bill Chandler was also on the racecourse and his family became a respected credit firm, but for many years he was the biggest street bookie in Hoxton, as well as the best-loved.[114] His pitches were taken over by Joe Coral, a Polish Jew who had been an office-boy taker and then a pub bookie in Stoke Newington. By the 1930s, Coral boasted an open credit office in the West End of London, but the core of his business was based on a band of seventy to eighty agents who brought in cash bets. This entrepreneur recollected that he would go out every morning with the aim of increasing this number. As he put it, 'Where they took the bets wasn't my business.'[115] Forty years later, he was the head of a huge leisure empire.

Like Coral, the renowned firm of Guntrips mixed their credit business with 'lucrative' cash bets, in common with the Moists of Birmingham. Both businesses had been founded in the late nineteenth century as illegal operations: Tom Guntrip was a farmer who laid punters from the early 1880s, both on his delivery rounds and in the Park Hotel, Catford; and William Henry Moist was a tailor from Newton Abbot who became a street bookie in 1894, standing in Cambridge Street.[116] Well before legalization, their successors severed their connections with outlawed betting and their firms are prime examples of the process of legitimization which was undertaken by some ready-cash bookmakers. But it is important to be aware that while there was no reverse flow of credit layers becoming illegal bookies, many of the former were heavily involved in forbidden forms of betting. Dey himself had employed two runners in the 1880s, and like later office bookmakers, the impulse to do so was provided by profit.[117]

My Dad reckoned that the problem with account customers was that bookies had to beat them twice: first by having a good result and second by securing the money that was owed to them. There can be little doubt that credit businesses had to 'write off' a significant proportion of their winnings – in the 1950s, Ken Overton of Birmingham had debts 'amounting to thirty-odd grand' – and a good way of offsetting these losses was by taking cash bets.[118] Indeed, in many instances, this side of the undertakings became 'the main revenue', as it was in the Dundee credit office in which Squadron Leader Blacklaw worked in the late 1930s.[119]

Office bookmakers who engaged runners had the same difficulty faced by bookies whose businesses were based in factories and pubs:

that of gathering the bets before the first race. This was essential if frauds by punters or takers were to be avoided, and before the 1920s, it is likely that three methods of collection were adopted: first, a layer could emulate Harry Miller's gaffer and employ a runner to visit his lifters; second, they might ask their takers to bring their bets into the office; and third, they could instruct their agents to post their bets to them, as did the house-based bookie for whom G. W. Yendell's parents took.[120]

> In 1923 my father took bets off his workmates at Griff Pit where he worked as a shunter. Every day when I came out of school I used to run to the pit about one and a half miles and collect the bets off my Dad. My Mum used to sit in the ladies' room at the Conservative Club which was in the same street. She used to stay from twelve noon till one o'clock and the customers in the bar gave her the bets. The steward also had a bet. She collected bets off the neighbours as well. Then all the bets were put in a large envelope. The bookmaker . . . lived about two miles away and so my mother had to post the bets. There was a post box at the top of the street and she had to post them before 2 p.m. Letters were time stamped then so she had to get the two o'clock postmark as the first race was two o'clock. The letter was delivered at Mr B.'s home by 4.30 p.m same day . . . His son used to cycle round in the evening bringing any winnings.[121]

It should be noted that in Glasgow, the firms of McLauchlan and McLean had businesses which flourished on the cash postal bets of punters in general. Their operations were illegal, but it seems that letter betting had emerged in that city and in Edinburgh because of the tardiness of applying the 1853 Act to Scotland.[122] This led to an apparently anomalous position, as was explained by B. Bagley who became a settler in 1947:

> My first job was in Cardiff with a national firm of bookmakers, Shermans, who together with William Hill, Ladbroke, Coral, McLaughlin and Copes advertised daily in the *Sporting Life* and *Sporting Chronicle* offering a bet by post service. All these firms had accommodation addresses in Glasgow as cash bets by post in England and Wales were illegal. The adverts did not bluntly point out that it was cash with bet, but were worded on the following lines.
>
> 'Bets are accepted on plain paper, write down your selection(s) and inserting your stake post to – —.' The bet was acknowledged win or lose with a supply of betting slips and business reply envelopes but with a London or Cardiff address.[123]

As the 1920s progressed, cash bookmakers in general sought means whereby they could enable their runners to take bets throughout the afternoon, thus increasing their turnover. George Bailey recollected that his Potteries bookie achieved this by giving a number of envelopes to his street takers. These were sufficient to cover the times of the day's races and bets for each would be sealed at the official off.[124] Obviously, this system was open to fraud and soon it was made redundant by the telephone and by clock bags. Squadron Leader Blacklaw's employer encouraged his runners to use the former. This means of communication alerted him to the bets which they received after his collector had gathered the 'morning' bets (those taken before the first race); but it was clock bags that had the more profound effect on the organization of illegal betting.[125]

Simply, these were leather pouches into which a taker would place his or her bets. At the time of the first race, their operator would stop the clock attached to the bags, and at the same time this would activate two steel pins. These would go through two eyeholes at the top of the pouch, preventing the inclusion of further bets. The bookmaker would be the only person with a key to open the bags and this meant that some of them dispensed with collections from their takers. Instead they allowed them to bring their bets to their houses or offices after the day's racing. So as to encourage betting throughout the day, some agents were given a number of pouches, and after the Second World War, this procedure was simplified by the widespread use of six-clock bags.[126]

One result of their use was that layers were betting blind: that is, they did not know what kind of bets they had taken nor whether they could cost them a lot of money. Consequently, as had most street bookies from the 1880s, they protected themselves against high payouts. They did this by imposing limits on the amount that could be won on a certain kind of bet, particularly multiple betting. For example, a double is a wager in which two horses must win for the punter to obtain a return. If they do, the odds of the runners are multiplied, so that if the stake is £1 and the first horse wins at 3 to 1, then the backer has £4 going on to his or her next choice; and if this wins at 2 to 1 also, then the client has a return of £12, or 11 to 1 to the original stake. In 1905, Dick Seymour's rules limited the winnings on doubles to 25 to 1 and on trebles to 50 to 1.[127] Over the years, these ceilings were raised by bookmakers in an individual fashion, and in 1948, my Grandad's limit on doubles was 300 to 1, while those for trebles and accumulators (four or more horses) were 400 to 1. Eleven years later, he had no limit on doubles, a maximum of 400 to 1 on trebles, and a limit of 500 to 1 on accumulators.[128]

Of course, the chief function of limits was to restrict winnings to an amount a bookie was able to pay out. Protected by this strategy, cash bookmakers eagerly made use of clock bags, and in 1939, a York solicitor declared that 'the real method of betting was by means of leather bags distributed at factories'.[129] However, these devices were not restricted to works' takers. They were given out to house agents, pub collectors and to runners and lifters in the street. Their emergence encouraged certain credit layers to increase or initiate their involvement in street betting. For them, clock bags had two advantages other than as a protection against fiddling. First, their diffusion 'has enabled commission agents to increase their business many-fold', and there is no doubt that they allowed many bookmakers to engage a large number of takers; and second, they were beneficial because it seemed that their use allowed credit firms to argue that they did not take cash bets.[130]

In 1949, an important case appeared to validate this belief. Woolf Sherman and Percival Way had been fined heavily because they allowed their office to be used as a place of deposit for the clock bags of a number of runners. However, on appeal, their conviction was quashed because the magistrate had not made the appropriate committal order. Although this was a technicality, the judge made the point that the runners were the people who made the bets with the punters, and that these illegal transactions took place outside the office. This meant that the agents resorted to these premises not to bet, but to give an account of their dealings. Second, he noted that in cases such as this, the prosecution had to prove that the runners had taken ready-money bets as distinct from bets on credit.[131]

Both Sherman and Way worked for Harry Sherman Ltd, a firm which exemplified those of its type which were involved in every aspect of betting, legal and illegal. The business was one of the leading football-pools promoters in Britain; it operated a credit office; it advertised for postal betting; and it employed street runners.[132] In fact, with the firm of John Charles, Shermans was remembered by Mr Hantman – one of their former employees – as receiving much of the cash betting in South Wales; while most of the rest was garnered by smaller credit concerns, such as the Port Talbot office that employed as a runner the father of Elizabeth Evans.[133] A similar situation was evident elsewhere in Britain. In Plymouth, Barbara Gynne worked for Charles C., the city's leading credit bookmaker and commissioner of a large number of runners; in nearby Devonport, Iris Holden's employer was of the same mould; and in Hove, Harold B. had premises with twelve telephones, while he controlled the same number of runners.[134] The value of their takings was immense, as Terry Murphy emphasized. During the 1950s, he worked in the office of the

Sussex bookmaker, and he estimated that some of his agents had an average turnover of £400 to £500 per week.[135]

There were many bookmaking businesses which were not as large as Shermans, Corals and the like, but which resembled that of Harold B. These medium-sized firms were town-based and they had the facility of ticker-tape machines which gave them betting information and which allowed them to settle up with their runners after a day's racing had finished.[136] As early as 1919, Elizabeth Dawson's mother had operated this system in her Hackney office, which she had established after she had realized that her commission as an agent was more than the profits from her newsagent's shop.[137] However, it was not until the 1930s that this set-up became general, and when it did, it proved advantageous to office-based layers. Unlike some of their smaller competitors, they did not have to wait until results were printed in local evening newspapers. This meant that, if they wished, their runners could pay out quickly. In itself, this feature attracted custom, but from the later 1920s, it had an added significance in districts in which evening greyhound-racing was popular.[138] Simply, if successful punters received their profits early enough, they were likely to 'lay-out' (bet) on the local 'dogs' (greyhound meetings).[139]

It is apparent that in many parts of Britain, bookies were remote from their punters, as Cyril Lofts explained in relation to pre-war betting in Ilford.

> Of the three factions involved, the bookie, the runner and the punter, the runner was the link man. He knew the bookie and he knew all the punters, whereas the other two were mostly unknown to each other. The bookie would have a number of close acquaintances who knew him intimately. These would consist of people he met socially at a club he belonged to, or in his local pub. Through these sources he would undoubtedly pick up business, usually whereby an account could be arranged and the potential investor could place his investments by telephone. There would be no need or occasion arise for the bookie to become known to the small punter who gave his bet to his runner, and by the same token, whilst the punter obviously knew the bookmaker's name, the probability was that they were hardly likely to meet in person.[140]

This type of distance was not limited to relationships between 'credit' bookmakers and their 'illegal' clients. Necessarily, it was as apparent among some bookies whose businesses focused on cash betting, but who worked via a large number of works' and pub agents. During the 1950s, Ray Fear built up a thriving concern in the Potteries, but he knew few of his punters as he had commissioned sixty takers; in Leicester, Frank Ford came from a working-class background, but by the same period, he was living in a 'top-class' area and he was employing twenty people to take his bets, among them, members of his family; and Sid Brooks and Syd Farrow recalled similar bookmakers in Wolverhampton and Chesterfield.[141]

THE PATTERN OF STREET BOOKMAKING: TRAVELLERS

The runners employed by Fear and others had a tendency to move from place to place for the collection of their bets, a practice which was noticed in 1890, when such men were called 'travellers'.[142] This procedure remained common until legalization, and its practitioners were of two types: full-time runners and part-time agents. As Victor Baker recalled, in Brighton, the former 'had their Rounds, calling at pubs, clubs, markets, factories etc. and were nice men'; while in the Potteries, the father of Mr A. Williams added to this list by visiting 'grocers, butchers, cobblers shops, the barbers, even the pawnbrokers'.[143] He favoured this means of collection because he did not want to 'encourage people to come to our little terraced house too much as it was illegal'. It is obvious that 'travelling' runners were more difficult for the police to catch.[144]

Moreover, some bookies specialized in 'house-to-house canvassing' – as it was called by the authorities.[145] In 1923, this was noted as a recent phenomenon, and it was popular because it ensured that the runner could not be charged with frequenting the street for the purpose of betting.[146] Of course, he or she might be prosecuted for using a house for that reason, but because the dwelling was not a bookie's headquarters, the betting transaction took place only between two people within a private home. Consequently, it was hard for the police to prove that an offence had been committed.[147] As J. Fisher of Swansea remembered, doors were left open for the entry of the local runner, and if a policeman was sighted, then the agent was hidden in the house on which he was calling.[148]

This door-to-door collection of bets was suited to some part-time takers, in particular those whose jobs involved them in deliveries. Ellen Smith lived in a poor part of Portsmouth, and she remembered that bets were put on with her milkman as he stood pouring milk from his churn into the family's jug; and it was officially recognized that roundsmen were notable figures in illegal betting.[149] So too were tradesmen, such as Jack Proudfoot of Walthamstow.[150] He was a window-cleaner, and after he had placed his ladder against the fence of a home, he would ask the housewife to fill his bucket with water – 'and she'd take it in and fill it up with bets, not water, put the cloth over the top'.[151] Similarly, other part-time agents were protected partly by their calling: Peter Softley's father had a fish barrow in Eastney, which he stopped outside the pubs he took from; while William Leatham sold bacon and eggs from a stall in London's East End, and in 1951 he was fined for taking bets as well.[152]

However, 'travelling' was not restricted to runners. In a working-class neighbourhood of Plymouth, Patsy Dunstan took credit bets over the two telephones he had in his house; he received cash punters at his back door; he had takers in pubs and works; and his two daughters 'went around the district calling at houses to receive their bets'.[153] So too did Alan Needham's Dad, a small bookie who operated in the North Midlands. At midday, he would

> walk to the most distant of the village public houses, having picked up betting slips en route from various domestic locations. The pick-up points (domestic) would probably have already collected betting slips and cash from near neighbours . . . On arrival at the most distant public house the bookmaker would pick up bets from the clientele, usually miners, and accept bets from the landlord. The bets would have been accepted by the landlord from miners having already left on the afternoon shift.
>
> Having satisfied himself that all bets had been placed, the bookmaker then walked to his next public house call where collection was repeated. Previous days' settlements and any queries were dealt with on these calls.
>
> Betting slips were also collected:
>
> From and by the bookmaker's eldest son at the local mine. The bookmaker's youngest son at the local brickworks.
>
> 1. runner in the next village.
> 2. runner in a local smelting works.
> 3. Home address by bookmaker's wife.[154]

THE PATTERN OF STREET BOOKMAKING: THE STREET

Both Patsy Dunstan and Mr Needham embraced a variety of strands in their patterns of bookmaking, and they exemplify how difficult and unwise it is to place pre-legalization bookmakers into exclusive categories. Certainly, both men were street bookies, but they were other types of bookie, too, and they were not alone in their wide-ranging operations. Still, the term 'street bookie' has a specific meaning in the popular imagination and in the memory of many working-class people. That is, it represents a man who took bets while standing in one place in a particular street. This site was isolated from others of its type, and it was not part of a standing market; indeed, pitch bookmaking had arisen as a result of the byelaws that had successfully suppressed such gatherings.

Fearful of arrest if they met in large and conspicuous groups, cash bookies fled not only into the safety of shops and pubs, but also into the security of working-class neighbourhoods. In those that were poorer and situated in the larger urban areas and in mining districts, some of them decided to remain in public and to operate from a set position. Naturally, they sought places that gave them a certain protection from the police, and a popular rendezvous was described in 1926 by the Liverpool Council of Voluntary Aid.

> The backer who wants to make a bet can either wait for the tout (runner) to call on his house in the morning or else he can go to a certain street corner where he can count on meeting a particular tout. He will then hand his stakes to the tout, and the stakes are usually wrapped in what is known as a betting slip, i.e. a scrap of paper on which is written the name of the horse or horses backed, the amount of bet on each horse and the assumed name of the backer. Occasionally the bookmakers issue more elaborate printed slips giving the names of all the horses with a column for indicating those chosen, but the former method is more usual. Presuming that the backer's horse wins and he wishes to collect what is owing to him, he can either go and meet the tout at a certain street corner at a fixed hour, or he can go round to the bookmaker's office.[155]

Corner pitches were not peculiar to Liverpool. They were as apparent in the Sandfields area of Swansea, while they were the focus of most of the street betting which went on in the East End of Aberdeen and in much of London.[156] Their appeal was simple. First, as Bill Gleghorn stressed, in Easington Colliery, 'each block of streets had a *corner end bookie* which meant he *always* stood at a certain street end so as the punters could find him easy'.[157] Second, this position gave the taker an opportunity to flee in the opposite direction to that from which the police were approaching; and it also facilitated the positioning of lookouts. During the 1930s, J. Hobbs lived in a poor part of Chelsea and he explained that two 'touts' (watchers) would take up vantagepoints at the triangle formed by the joining of Norman Street and College Place. From these positions, they could scan both roads and alert the taker to any danger.[158] At the same time, this man connived with the punters to make as surreptitious as possible the passing-over of bets. Kit Brown came from the colliery village of Witton Park, near to Bishop Auckland, and he evoked the stealth of this handover.

> The bets and money were collected by the runner in devious ways, e.g. a handshake, or 'Gis a touch' whereby the punter leaned forward 'fag' in his mouth and touched his cigarette end to the one held out (alight) by the runner and when the runner withdrew his hand the 'slip' was in it, or 'Lend's your paper' and when the paper was handed back the bet was transferred with it. Naturally ploys were only resorted to if the street around was not clear.[159]

The secrecy of the affair was enhanced by the way in which bettors signed their bets or lines with *noms-de-plume*. This served a dual purpose. It maintained their anonymity if and when the taker was captured, and thus ensured that they could not be arrested; and second, it identified winning clients to the runner for the purposes of the payout.[160]

Despite their advantages, corner pitches were noticeable because of their openness, and as such, they were susceptible to police raids. For this reason, they ceased to be prevalent in Liverpool, and by the 1950s, its pitches were distinguished by their concealment, as described by G. Squires, a former policeman who dealt with street betting in the city in 1956–7. He recalled that the most popular hiding places for runners were 'back entries in working-class neighbourhoods and in the passageways and staircases of tenement blocks whilst in the more affluent areas where their presence on the street would be too obvious they were more likely to be found in public houses'. Of course, while these refuges were safer, they remained accessible and well-used by the public, and bets were taken between midday and 2 p.m.[161]

The same times of business were adhered to by bookies in the East End of London; similarly, they favoured more secluded spots for the placing of their pitches. In 1932, the deputy commissioner of the Metropolitan Police acknowledged that there were many of these to choose from and his observation is supported by the memories of East Enders.[162] L. Caket recalled that his Shoreditch bookie worked from a narrow passage; in Bethnal Green, a favoured location was a court of houses which was situated off the main thoroughfare; and Robert Barltrop explained the attractions of Florfield Road in Hackney.[163] Known as 'the bookies' turning', it was 'a kind of double cul-de-sac, a short L joined to a short T and backed against the railway line', near to which gathered the taker and his punters. They were guarded by an older resident of the road who sat on his doorstep, pretending to read a newspaper. If he sighted 'any unknown person', he would give a signal – 'possibly holding the paper, or putting out his cigarette' – at which, the street would be cleared in seconds.[164]

Elsewhere in industrial Britain, pitch bookies were as keen on hideouts as were their associates in London's East End or in Liverpool. It is apparent that two factors affected the position of their static sites: first, the nature of the housing in a district; and second, the layout of that area. Nowhere were these determinants more crucial than in the North East, as Mr J. Clark explained:

> I was born in Gateshead, County Durham. When I was about 10 yrs of age, I used to take bets to those bookies, that was in 1928. The main road was called Askew Road and it ran parallel to the River Tyne.
>
> From the road ran streets of terraced houses which had a front and back door leading into a back lane. If I remember right there was about seven or eight such streets. There was an alleyway which ran the full length of these streets at the bottom.
>
> The bookie used to stand in one of the back yards taking bets.[165]

Back lanes were away from the streets and main roads, yet they were well used and approachable. Consequently, they were renowned centres of pitch bookmaking throughout Tyneside and Wearside. John Hodgson brought to mind his bookie in Byker, Newcastle, whose yard was protected by two lookouts positioned at either end of Parker Street back lane; Lilian Crawford's uncle adopted the same procedure in Johnson Street, Sunderland; and Lorna Morton noted that in South Shields, 'it was a regular sight to see a crowd in the back lane', all of them punters.[166]

In some districts, takers eschewed the safety of a yard for the freedom of the alleyway itself, as Alex Meldrum recollected. His family lived in the East End of Sunderland and his mother 'wore a large pouch type apron with two deep pockets', into which she placed the bets which she collected as she patrolled the back lanes of Cousin and Wear Streets.[167] Alleys like these were as attractive to corner takers as much as they were to Mr Meldrum's mother. In Monkwearmouth, Jim Addison recalled that one bookie stood at the top of Barrington Street back lane, while another was positioned at the bottom. Both were guarded by groups of unemployed men who gathered near to them, and like others of their type, they were able to 'duck' into the alleyway once the alarm was given.[168] Indeed, many Geordie takers were nicknamed ducker after this action.[169]

The ubiquity of back-lane pitches did not mean that other forms of street betting were absent from the North East. Patricia Bell's bookmaking family lived in Heaton, 'in a street of back-to-back flats exactly the same as everyone else'. Punters would place their bets in an old shed in her grandfather's backyard, which was equipped with 'the daily racing papers and plenty of scrap paper and pencils'. But this was only one side of the business; and it was supplemented by the takings of runners 'who worked in the local shipyards and collected there and in the working men's clubs and pubs'.[170] Indeed, Bill Evans described the shipbuilding area of Southwick as 'the haunt of many illegal bookies and their runners', and this comment was as applicable to the localities of other works.[171] Not far from Sunderland lies the town of Hetton. During the inter-war years it boasted a population of 26,000, which relied for its employment on three pits, brickworks, a brewery and sawmills. Mr Armstrong noted that each of these had its own agents; that three or four takers operated in each of the town's four working-men's clubs; that there were corner-end runners; and that bets were taken at the homes of bookies such as himself.[172]

Across the Pennines, in the cotton district of Lancashire and Cheshire, a similar wide range of betting practices was evident, but as on Tyneside and Wearside, pitches formed the core of the local structure of illegal bookmaking. Anne Spence brought to life how they manifested themselves.

> Now nearly sixty years ago, I grew up in a very poor district of Manchester, called Harpurhey. I suppose I would be about ten years old when I first became aware of the network of illegal betting in the neighbourhood, and indeed, for a year or two in my teens, I was drawn into it by the fascination it held for almost all working-class people. The daily bet was a way of life, and appealed to women as well as men. The back-to-back terraced houses of those days had a small, flagstoned backyard opening on to an 'entry' or passage which ran between two rows of houses. The bookie would rent the back room of one of these houses from the tenant. The clientele walked through the yard and handed in the betting slips and stake money at the kitchen door. I think there was only about three of these operating in Harpurhey, it was after all an illegal transaction.[173]

Pitches such as these had much in common with the house betting that was obvious in nearby Eccles and Patricroft and that had not been quashed by police raids. Rather, such pressure had led to its adaptation. As Anne Spence indicated, in her area, punters did not enter the dwelling; instead they remained in public while the bet was passed over. Moreover, in many districts of Manchester and Salford, this transaction was pushed on to the street itself – so as to reduce further the risks of arrest for the layer and the householder. Mr C. Percy recalled that during the 1920s in Knott Mill, bookmaking was run from 'back street alley ways' and that 'the bookies would have their stand out men, and the punters would give him their bets'; twenty years later in Openshaw, Bill Whitely wrote that the 'the runner would stand behind or near the back door'; and D. Homer recollected that in Ardwick, the takers were protected by three lookouts, one at each end of the entry, and one outside the yard itself.[174]

Bookies' yards were as prominent in Stockport – where a number of them achieved fame locally – and they were present in force in nearby Hazel Grove.[175] This Cheshire village had a population of just 5,000, but Eric Thornley Downs – an ex-runner – counted eleven pitches there.

> The bookies' runner plied his trade from his main point (the bookies' yard) to covering most pubs and any position where he could accept bets. Outside the local mills, laundry, engineering works he would be seen. Generally wearing a flat cap and scarf, with a jacket fitted with a 'poachers' pocket on the left-hand side to take his customers' bets. Bets would be taken unopened, just the cash wrapped in paper like toffees and slid into his 'pocket' . . . No bets were taken by the runner from half an hour before racing, that being his time to return to the yard. Having garnered all his cash and slips the runner would actually start the second phase of his job. His pocketful of bets would be emptied on to a table with a thick cloth (so no sound was made by coins rattling on wood). The bookie would then take over the financial side, then opening the slips, flattening them into a pile and putting the cash on one side. The runner would then make a detour of the house and yard to make sure the coast was clear from any gentlemen in blue (police).[176]

Bob Crewe noted a similar process in 'the twin cities' of Manchester and Salford, as did Ken Wadsworth, who worked as a settler for a number of bigger bookies; and the use of a pitch as a headquarters as well as a betting location was as marked in Birmingham.[177]

In 1932, Sir Charles Haughton Rafter, the city's Chief Constable, gave evidence to the Royal Commission on Lotteries and Betting. In agreement with his counterpart in Manchester, he believed that 'practically the whole' of pitch betting was 'carried on in the working class districts and industrial areas'; and he observed that its location was 'usually an entry', the narrow passageway which connected the street with a courtyard of back-to-back houses.[178] Once again, the memory of working-class people substantiates the observation of contemporary policemen. Mrs Peak's cousin took bets in an entry in Small Heath; the father of Mr E. Evenson was a labourer who collected the fancies of his fellows at Mitchell and Butler's Brewery, Cape Hill, and he placed them with a runner who stood near an alley which was opposite Tudor Street; and Joseph Hillshead recalled that his local bookie was 'a round-faced, florid-complexion man' who took bets in an entry opposite his yard in the Gooch Street neighbourhood.[179]

Such a site was favoured by my Grandad in 1922, when he began to take bets in his own right (before the First World War he had been an agent in a factory); but this system was not restricted to Birmingham.[180] It was as obvious in other places where back-to-back housing was widespread, and its popularity was explained by Joseph Riley. His uncle operated in Temple Street, 'a tough area' of Bilston, and his

> pitch was in the entry with one eye open for the police. He was often tipped off by the people in the street when their was a stranger about who might be a copper in disguise. Many a time he has been chased up the entry by a copper dressed up as a coalman with a face disguised in coaldust. Sometimes he escaped up the entry into the maze of Brewhouses [communal wash-houses] and yards. And it was very exciting when the cry went up in the street: 'They've got Jim'.[181]

Throughout the West Midlands, back-to-back houses had been thrown up pell-mell by jerrybuilders during the Industrial Revolution. As Harry Vokes noted of Aston, this meant that 'our neighbourhood gave a rabbit warren impression of entries, yards, back alleys, all getaway runs for the bookies touts, takers, runners and punters'.[182] These advantages were enhanced by communal buildings such as 'miskins': outhouses which were built for the deposit of rubbish and which went across two yards. Consequently, if the police were sighted, a taker could flee into them and escape into the next court. Other shared facilities were as useful and Jean Burton recalled that in her district of Walsall, the bookie moved away from the entry and took bets hidden behind the door of the brewhouse.[183] Moreover, many poverty-stricken neighbourhoods were intersected by 'double knacks'. These were entries which turned at a right angle and which led out into another street, thus making them invaluable to a taker who was fleeing from capture.[184]

Often, Brummie and Black Country bookies were local people and it was helpful to them that they lived in the area of their pitches. Miss Thexton made the point that in Blakenhall her bookmaker was able to take bets in his house because it was hidden down the entry and up the yard; and Albert Clamp's daughter was mindful of how important her home was to the family business in Birmingham.[185]

> When my father was demobbed from the 1914 war he started this bookmaking business at the house where we lived which was no. 50 Darwin Street, only one room downstairs with scullery, one bedroom, and one attic . . . The business flourished and we moved to a larger house across the street, no. 165 . . . We had some very hectic times there. The regular man would stand at the entrance to the entry and another two men would stand on street corners one above and one below. As soon as one or other of them saw a policeman they would signal down to Dave (the taker) and he would run up into the house. Once inside a very thick plank of wood was placed in two iron brackets across the door.[186]

Entry betting was as obvious in Sheffield – another city in which back-to-backs predominated – and as late as the 1950s, Jim Stock would stand in a yard to do his business. It was situated in Grimesthorpe, and after he had taken a few bets, he would place them in an envelope. This done, he would enter a 'safe house' and put his takings in a 'little holdall', repeating this procedure until he stopped work at 2 p.m.[187] However, by the same period, many pitches in Birmingham had come off the street, and this process had started in the inter-war years. Horace Foster remembered that his Dad rented the front room of a dwelling in Kyrwicks Lane, and that their taker stood on the front step, bringing the bets inside once the local factory workers had finished their dinner hours; and in Aston, Arthur Overton's employee took the slips while he was sat within the 'office'.[188] My Grandad's *modus operandi* exemplified this trend away from the street, as my Dad made clear.

> We were still taking them in the street but what we did, they was putting them through the letter-box and virtually this is what started to happen at the back end of the war. You had your shop (front room) and what they started to do instead of putting the man on the door you let them put them through the letter-box . . . From when I was a kid it was one of my jobs to sit behind the door and take the

> bets, so what we used to do was have a chain on the door, this is now going about 1945, just after the war, '44/'45, and the situation was then that Dad used to always stand across the road. If he then got his handkerchief out and blew his nose I'd then gorra close the door as the policeman was about.[189]

My Grandad was a local bookie. He took bets in the street in which he was brought up and in which he lived. His type was also noticeable in Glasgow, another city in which pitches were the fulcrum of illegal betting.

As in the rest of Scotland, many Glaswegian street bookmakers operated in closes, the common entrances to tenement buildings. They did so for the familiar reason of a need to work from a site which was secluded yet well used and easily approached by punters. Moreover, while the Burgh Police Act had stamped out standing markets, the case of Vallance v. Campbell indicated that its provisions did not extend to closes. This loophole was closed in 1906, when the Betting Act forbade cash betting on the street, defining this place as 'any highway and any public bridge, road, lane, square, court, or passage, whether a thoroughfare or not'. Furthermore, a passage was declared to embrace 'any close or common stair or passage leading thereto'.[190] Still, betting in closes remained advantageous to bookies and this national act failed conspicuously to eradicate it, as Joe Gray emphasized. He grew up in Kinning Park, south of the River Clyde, and he recalled:

> My first encounter with a bookie is when I was sent by my mother with a line in approx 1936. He was to be found in a tenament close at the rear because the rear led on to the back court and other closes were available in case he had to make a quick getaway if the police were near at hand and that included the punters. At the front of the close there was always the lookouts ready to inform him of any danger.[191]

North of the Clyde, in Maryhill, Walter Littlejohn observed that steep steps raised his close from the level of the street, thus creating an 'obstacle for raiding police' and so making the place 'a good one' for bookmaking'; while Robert Reid explained that his Maryhill bookie stationed himself halfway down their close, because he 'could run in either direction during a raid'.[192] He was alerted to danger by three watchers: one stood at the front entrance to the tenement; 'another was at the nearest corner, so he could see up and down and along the streets'; and the third 'was posted in the back-court so he could spot any police coming through the other closes, or over the "dykes" (walls) to pounce from the back'.[193] Similarly, Norma Brodie mentioned that in the Plantation district, the local bookie 'always had at least one man on look-out', but differently, he 'collected his bets on the half-stair landing which overlooked the back court'.[194]

This system was favoured by other bookmakers such as the one from Maryhill who was described by Mr E. McGuiness, but by the 1940s, many of them had moved away from the staircases and closes and into the back courts (back greens) themselves.[195] Their reason for doing this was explained by Henry McQuade, who lived in the Gorbals.

> In the street where I lived which was a little over half a mile long there were about six illegal bookies who plied their business usually in the back courts of the tenements each with their own clientele who used to congregate around a paper called the *Noon Record* which was solely devoted to all the horse and dog meetings in the UK; this paper was pinned often on a door which was nearly always the communal toilet, and the punters studied the lists of runners and their form before making their bets.[196]

In Parkhead, Maurice McMahon noted that the *Noon Record* was fixed to a 'concrete covered structure containing three or four bins for the use of tenants to deposit rubbish'; while Ernest Kyle mentioned that in Lawmoor Street, it was pinned to a board which was hung from a nail on a wall.[197] Wherever it was placed, its presence attracted punters, and this meant that the bookie or lifter needed to operate in a space that was bigger than that which was provided by a close.

The opportunity of exhibiting the *Noon Record* was not available to the many corner bookies and takers in Glasgow, and it is likely that this factor contributed to their decline after 1945. Nevertheless, before that date, they were a familiar sight, and an observer for Mass Observation reported that certain corners were the focus points for groups of men. These would be reading the sporting papers, and although the informant 'failed to notice anywhere the actual passing of betting slips', he or she perceived that 'the way in which men are continually entering and leaving these groups leaves no doubt in my mind of their purpose'.[198] This supposition was given firm support by Wilson Ditty of Parkhead.

> Of course you must understand that in those days, that is the 1920s and 1930s there was the depression – mass unemployment, those fortunately with jobs suffered low wages and worked long hours, the unemployed finding it hopeless to get work stood in groups at

> street corners and were constantly harassed by the police for loitering, if caught they were fined five or ten shillings at court.
>
> To avoid this happening to him the bookie usually stood with just one or two friends well apart from groups and also easily accessible to punters placing their bets with him; when he had a bundle of lines collected he would slip a rubber band round them to hold them together then place them in the gutter under scraps of rubbish – a purely precautionary measure should the police catch him with the lines on his person.[199]

In 1937, a reporter for the *Evening News* wrote that 'at almost every street corner in every working-class district in Glasgow stands a group of men . . . openly carrying on an illegal business – street-bookmaking – for which very severe monetary penalties are imposed'.[200] Similar scenes were evident in other areas in which pitches were widespread, and moralists and the authorities feared that 'the greatest volume of street betting is conducted in the poorer localities of the large towns'.[201] The evidence from working-class people has indicated that it is likely that contemporaries underestimated the amount of betting that went on outside these places, simply because so much of it was well hidden in pubs, works, shops and houses. In contrast, although many pitches were concealed, they remained part of the public sphere. For this reason, they attracted the attention of anti-gamblers who were affronted by the temerity of street bookies in flaunting their success at defying the law. Determined to eradicate the 'evil' of betting, they attacked street bookies with every weapon at their disposal, seeking to sweep them out of the towns and cities and into oblivion. Their repression was singular in its failure. Pitch bookies could not be defeated because their pitches belonged to the street.

6

BOOKMAKING: REACTIONS

BETTING: A SOCIAL PROBLEM

There can be little doubt that the burgeoning number of starting-price bookmakers contributed to the late-nineteenth-century explosion of interest in their occupation. Among the 'respectable' of the middle class, this awareness excited disgust and disdain for bookies and punters, and it led to a sustained and severe attack on betting as the root of a foul relationship. As the Reverend E. C. Chorley discerned, 'if there were no "backers" there would be no books'.[1] Consequently, it was essential to understand the conditions which gave rise to both groups, and to identify a reason for their existence. An answer was found readily: the culprit was modern town life.

As early as 1890, the Convocation of the Province of York was told that the spread of the gambling spirit was due largely to the love of excitement. This was a characteristic feature of the age and it could be attributed to a sense of monotony that afflicted both the leisured and artisan classes. However, while the former gambled to find 'a relief from ennui', the latter did so because it was an escape from 'the intense sameness which the introduction of machinery, and the division of labour have brought about in their occupations'.[2] This theme was picked up by a wide range of commentators, from R. F. L. Blunt, the Bishop of Hull, in 1902, to the members of the Select Committee on the Betting Duty in 1923. Indeed, thirty years later, a refined version of it was proposed by Ferdynand Zweig.[3] He declared that workers were not satisfied with their present conditions and so they sought an escape from reality in 'a world of dreams', which was to be found in 'religion, socialism or gambling'.[4]

Other social observers, such as Walter A. Raleigh in 1903, stressed that while gambling was a result of the 'economic civilisation', this phenomenon was linked inextricably to 'city communities'.[5] 'New Liberals' like J. A. Hobson agreed with this analysis, and it gained wide currency because of a growing intellectual revulsion with industrialization and urbanization.[6] For many middle-class thinkers, the town was a distasteful place. They believed that its lack of light, fresh air and open spaces had created a physically inefficient urban working class, and they felt that its members exhibited a commensurate moral, intellectual and emotional degeneration. Neither of these concepts was new. In the 1840s, Friedrich Engels had struggled with them, and twenty-odd years later, John Edward Morgan had warned of *The Danger of Deterioration of Race from the Too Rapid Increase of Great Cities*.[7] However, from the 1880s, both beliefs gained a greater potency because Britain was no longer the world's supreme power, either economically or industrially. This loss of status induced a crisis of confidence among the nation's rulers, and they fastened on the unfitness of the 'town race' as the reason for British decline. A surfeit of books was published on this subject, and in common with Dr Milner Fothergill in 1889, most writers deplored the way in which industrial workers had abandoned active pursuits for sedentary and non-participatory pastimes, betting among them.[8]

With justification, Clapson asserted that this 'problem' of betting was frowned upon partly because it was 'a symptom of the sickening "condition of England"' in the later 1800s.[9] Yet, if betting was a sign of Britain's loss of supremacy, by the 1920s, it had come to be regarded as a factor which had contributed to that process – and which was continuing to have an adverse effect on the industrial well-being of the nation. Echoing the fears of the editor of the *Hull Advertiser* in the 1850s, this argument was given a deeper significance as a result of the Depression of the inter-war years, as was indicated by the vigour with which it was propounded by Arthur Shadwell: 'Whatever interest and attention are left over from games and theatres are devoted to betting, and it has a much more injurious influence upon industrial efficiency than they, because the delusive prospect of making money without earning it, which is kept in view by occasional wins, gradually destroys all tastes and appetites for work.'[10]

Shadwell was supported in his opinions by economists like Sir Leo Chiozza Money and by prominent anti-gamblers – among them the Reverend J. Glass and Isaac Foot MP – as well as by those who were less well known, such as the Reverend J. Glyn Davies in Wales. Indeed, Chiozza Money's argument was propounded by the Reverend J. Clark Gibson as late as 1956.[11] Significantly, these men were impelled by the opinion that betting was harmful not only to notions of hard work, but also to financial good sense.

If the anti-gambling literature of the later nineteenth century is characterized by the idea that betting was a new social problem, then that of the 1920s and 1930s is distinguished by the belief that there was an appreciable increase in expenditure on the activity. The Select Committee (1923) suggested that the annual turnover on horse-racing was £200,000,000, and Glass agreed that this amount 'may be safely assumed'; six years later, the Racecourse Betting Control Board put the figure at a probable £230,000,000; and in 1936, a contributor to *The Economist* gave a 'conservative' estimate of £250 to £300 millions.[12] Wisely, members of the Royal Commission of 1932–3 avoided giving a definite amount. Instead, they preferred to 'reach the conclusion that the total turnover on gambling to-day is probably at least as great as at any recent date and much greater than it was at the beginning of the century or earlier'.[13]

Their cautious judgement would seem to be justified, for as McKibbin pointed out, 'as a measurement of gambling, total turnover is confusing and probably only useful in assessing changes in the popularity of certain sports'.[14] Total turnover is problematical for several reasons: first, before 1961, it is impossible to approximate it because of the illegality of cash betting off-course; second, turnover includes the money reinvested by winning punters as well as the stakes of those who have lost; third, it does not give any indication of the sums that were laid out by clients of different classes; and last, it fails to make clear how many bettors there were, and thus, whether or not exorbitant sums were staked by a few punters, or if small amounts were laid out by many. Indeed, if the assessments of contemporaries are to be believed, it is likely that the latter is correct, as was indicated by the members of a Royal Commission (1932–3). They believed that there were now more bettors than there had been before 1914.[15]

In 1919, the Reverend Ernest Benson Perkins, a redoubtable opponent of gambling, wrote that the First World War had been responsible for the growth of the betting 'evil' among munitions workers and soldiers. He attributed this last phenomenon to 'the operation of professional bookmakers' and to the 'greater leisure' which forces' personnel had, an observation which was backed up strongly by an ex-serviceman.[16]

> You won't mind if I speak plainly? Gambling in any form is *the game of a fool*. I should have come to that conclusion in the army, if I had not formed it years before. It has to be admitted that the army allowed the thing to grow during the war. As in certain other

> matters, discipline was often relaxed just where it was most needed. I wonder if you went out to France. I shall never forget as long as I live the surprise I had when I arrived at the Base and saw how gambling was tolerated, almost encouraged in the great camp. It was practically an organised recreation – which recreated nobody, but started a good many youngsters on the road to ruin.

This former soldier described how 'House' (bingo) and crown and anchor were widespread among British servicemen, and his comments are corroborated by the evidence of working-class people.[17] Steve Nicholls recalled that his soldiering Dad was a 'barker' (frontman who attracted attention) for crown and anchor, while Ellis McCormick remembered that his father 'got most of his money' in the same way.[18] Indeed, in the early 1920s, the popularity of crown and anchor in many areas must be attributed to veterans of war like Jack Scotney's brother, who brought his board back with him from the fields of Flanders to those around Farcet.[19] But this dice game was not the only popular form of gambling in France, as Jack Pearce indicated. His cousin was an expert 'flammer' who practised his skills in games of 'two-up' with Australian soldiers; and O'Hara noted how 'tossing' became accepted as a form of national sport because of its appeal to Anzacs during the First World War.[20]

THE EXPANSION OF STREET BOOKIES

Circumstantially, there is much material to bolster the argument that gambling increased because of social conditions engendered by conflict, among them the higher wages which were enjoyed by war workers. At the same time, similar evidence would suggest that an influx of demobilized soldiers was responsible for an increase in the number of street bookies. G. W. Cutts emphasized this point, explaining that in Nottingham many ex-servicemen set up as bookmakers with their gratuities.[21] Others did so with their profits from running crown-and-anchor boards, as did Mr Nicholls in Barn Street, Birmingham, and Mr McCormick in Salford; while still more turned to bookmaking after a short time spent working in another occupation, in common with James Duke of Plymouth.[22]

> At the age of around 17–18 years old he fought with the 1st and 2nd Devons in South African Boer War and was with the force in the relief of Ladysmith after that work as a plate layer for GWR (Great Western Railway) in Millbay Docks Plymouth on the

> outbreak of the 1914 war rejoined the Devon to fight in France on demob in 1918 worked again at the docks for maybe a year then started to take bets and found out to be a full time job.[23]

This was the path followed by my Grandad. In 1912 he had been a works' agent, and after losing his job, he joined the Coldstream Guards. Upon the outbreak of war, he became one of the Old Contemptibles who ignored the Kaiser's slur and defied him, holding back the might of his army. Grandad was wounded in the process, and while he was at convalescence, 'he took a few bets'. After the war, he set up a small business with his gratuity, and when that began to struggle, he became a bookie in the tough street in which he had grown up.[24] It is impossible to determine how many other street bookmakers were ex-servicemen, but that they were conspicuous was intimated by Walter Greenwood in *Love on the Dole*, his evocative novel of working-class life in Salford in the 1920s. In it, the local bookie is represented by Sam Grundy, a man who had 'got his tank' (bank of money) by running a crown-and-anchor board while he was serving in France.[25]

Bookmaking was an egalitarian occupation in that it demanded no entry qualifications. Still, it is obvious that bookies need certain funds if they are to be able to pay out winning punters during a losing run – and they do have such periods. Essentially, the First World War provided opportunities for many men to build up the cash reserves which were necessary for them to enter 'the game' (business).[26] I would argue that this development coincided with a move by some established works' agents to set up on their own, perhaps prompted by a wartime increase in their takings and commissions. These processes meant that cash bookmaking off-course was opened up to those who were neither penny capitalists or credit layers – and they facilitated the appearance of local pitch bookies such as Grundy. Indeed, there can be no doubt that it was during the 1920s that the map of pitch bookmaking was drawn in the twin cities of Manchester and Salford, Birmingham, the Black Country, Glasgow and the North East.

In 1900, a writer in the *Hampshire Times* had noticed that Portsmouth was 'divided between the 25 bookmakers who are carrying on operations in the town, so that each bookmaker has his own district, and his own circle of "clients"'.[27] It is likely that this territoriality and paucity of bookies were replicated elsewhere in the country, even in those districts in which pitches were emerging. This form of bookmaking was in its infancy, having arisen in response to the spate of byelaws that were passed in the later 1890s, and its minor status is indicated by the rarity of families who can claim that their pitches were established before 1914. For example, in Birmingham, the Moists took in Cambridge Street in the 1890s, while the credit firm of Mealings had a taker in Severn Street, in addition to their large number of factory agents. Both these pitches were close to the centre of the city, but before the 1910s, the only other evidence of their type is in Vere Garratt's autobiography, relating mostly to the Holloway Head area.[28]

It appears that much of the city's illegal betting was carried on in pubs – as was indicated by a letter in the *Birmingham Argus* in 1894 – and in works.[29] Indeed, the oldest Brummie bookmaking firm was founded by George Shepherd, a railway clerk who began to take bets in the 1880s at Monument Lane Station. However, it was not until 1916 that his coal-merchant son started to set up pitches locally, using a general stores as a collection point and as 'a blind for the betting'.[30] Obviously, this move was made possible by the financial security which had been provided by his original business, and the same was true of Harold Reynolds's Dad. His family owned a building firm and about 1911, he bought a house in Conybere Street, using it as a base for a pitch which he opened up in nearby Hick Street.[31] Within the next fifteen years, his position ceased to be solitary and he was joined by a large number of other pitch bookies who set up in the same Gooch Street neighbourhood.

Just after the First World War, the ex-serviceman Sid Clamp began bookmaking in Darwin Street, and in 1926 he was joined by Rose Pickering, the owner of the local fish-and-chip shop; on the corner of Emily Street and Vaughton Street, Harry Hudson 'stood up' from 1920; in Moseley Street, Mrs Eyres used her greengrocery shop as a front for her bookmaking; and in Highgate Street, Harold Reynolds employed Georgie Morgan's father as a full-time taker.[32] A similar increase in pitch bookies took place in the adjacent working-class district of Sparkbrook. Alf Chinn started up on the Ladypool Road in 1922, later taking over the Studley Street pitch vacated by 'Nack' Carey. He was another wounded veteran from the First World War, but unlike my Grandad he was employed to take the bets by 'Jocky' Powell, from 1919 a man who ran a thriving factory-focused business from his pitch in nearby Stoney Lane.[33] Two or three years later, Horace Foster ceased to be a works' bookie, moving into the game full-time from a house in Kyrwicks Lane. In addition, he employed a fruiterer as an agent in Colville Road, while my Grandad had a street taker in Oldfield Road.[34] The ranks of the 'established' bookies of the area were completed in the mid-1920s, when the Wilsons began business in Mole Street.[35]

This upsurge in pitch bookies was as noticeable in the Summer Lane district, where the ex-serviceman, Ernie Cashmore, established himself in Clifford Street, while the ex-factory bookie, Arthur Overton, moved into public in Geach Street.[36] Moreover, it was not restricted to Birmingham, as J. A. Croll stressed. He was a street bookmaker who worked in the Plantation area of Glasgow, and after he was given immunity from prosecution, he gave evidence to the members of the Select Committee (1923). They were told that he had set up his pitch in 1913, at the same time as one other bookie. Ten years later, their territory of four streets had become the scene of twelve pitches controlled by six bookmakers and their lifters.[37]

Men like these could find their sites in one of three ways. First, they could buy a pitch, but this procedure tended to be favoured by existing bookmakers who wished to expand their 'patch' (area). The Moists did this in the mid-1920s, when they paid about £50 for the rights to take the bets in Bell Barn Road; and so did my Dad in 1959, when, for £2,000, he bought Ernie Cashmore's branch in Oldfield Road.[38] Obviously, most aspiring bookies were discouraged from making a purchase because the cost would make a deep dent into their tanks. Consequently, some of them pursued the second route into the game: they took over a vacant pitch, as did Matt O'Malley and his brother in the Calton in Glasgow.

> Oh what would it be, 1943 – during the war years, yeah, yeah. It was a pitch, a good pitch, a street pitch like and the feller who had the pitch was called up and first off a guy went in and bumped (failed and welched) another guy went in and bumped after a short time, so my oldest brother he went in and it built up and it built up and built up.[39]

The third way into pitch bookmaking was simpler even than this process: entrants set up new pitches.

A recurring theme among street bookmakers is that they frowned upon 'poaching': taking bets on someone else's pitch.[40] However, this static site was different from the fluctuating and amorphous notion of territory; generally, it was accepted that newcomers could open up on that area so long as it was not in the same tenement or street as the established bookie.[41] For example, from the mid-1920s, my Grandad's pitch was in Studley Street, while he had takers in nearby Oldfield Road and at the Red Lion pub in Brunswick Road, thus extending his territory into much of the Ladypool Road area of Sparkbrook. In the 1950s, this space shrank because new bookies opened up in each of his 'agency' roads, but this development was acceptable because no one infringed on his proper pitch.[42] Indeed, because of working-class notions of ownership and belonging, poaching was infrequent, although Frankie Goodwin recollected that in The Buildings in Scotstoun, there was 'about 8 or 9 that tried to lift in opposition to my mother' over a number of years.[43]

The idea that a pitch was inviolable was linked to the presence of unseen but powerful pitch boundaries. These were delineated by bookies and the communities to which they belonged, as Ernie Cashmore made clear. In the 1950s, George Davies of Summer Lane informed him that he had declined the chance of buying out a bookie who operated between them. His decision was based on the fact that the pitch was nearer to that of the Cashmores' and so he believed that his 'rival' should have first refusal on the business that was for sale.[44] In fact, during the early 1920s, neither long-standing or new bookmakers had any worry about poaching, for there were plenty of sites available to be used as pitches.

STAKES AND PUNTERS

It is difficult to determine whether the increase in pitch bookmakers led to a rise in the number of people who staked money on horse-races. The Reverend Benson Perkins indicated that this was not so, stating that in 1927 about 80 per cent of the working class betted more or less regularly, the same proportion as in 1914.[45] It is impossible to validate this claim, although four years before, the National Sporting League gave a figure of four million regular bettors on the horses.[46] This number coincided with that put forward by Kemsley and Ginsburg in 1950, but understandably, McKibbin thought that it was not 'unfair' to give it credence.[47] However, he noted that the figure needed to be doubled if less frequent punters were taken into account.[48] Based on the impressionistic evidence of working-class people, I am inclined to agree with McKibbin, with the proviso that there were probably more irregular bettors than he allowed for. This last claim would seem to be borne out by a survey in 1951, which revealed that 51 per cent of men and 38 per cent of women betted on major horse-races.[49]

In any case, it would seem that pitch bookmakers drew their punters from the existing pool of punters and not from new sources. As Horace Foster remembered, after his Dad left Samuel Heath's, his clientele remained based on working men and women.

> They'd all knock off at one o'clock and they'd always come up Kyrwicks Lane from all the factories. Heath's, Leopold Street,

> Bradford Street. They'd all come up for their dinner. It was only ten minutes' walk. Fifteen minutes to home, fifteen minutes back. Half an hour to have their dinner and they was back again. They always come past our place – that's what made our place. You see, they came from all over the place. Out of Highgate Square and all down Stratford Road, there was little factories down there, where the garage is now, there was a couple of little factories down there, and they always come past our place, especially up to the local pubs.[50]

If it is unlikely that pitch bookmaking led to a growth in the numbers of punters, it is as improbable that they caused a soaring in stakes.

In 1912, the police arrested James Pattman, a large cash bookmaker based in Poplar. At the premises that he used as a centre, they found 3,109 betting slips, relating to the previous week's racing and football matches, and £200 in gold and silver as well as some postal orders. It was not reported how much these totalled, nor was any indication given as to how much of the cash was 'payout' and not takings. Consequently, it is impossible to gain any real impression as to the amount of money that was laid out on each bet.[51] In fact, what this case illustrates is the problem of doing this with regard to any bookmaker before 1914. This means that our best estimates of stakes are based on those of informed commentators, such as the one who wrote in *Tit Bits* in 1897. He observed that 'the poorer classes cannot afford to wager more than a few pence at a time, or at the most a shilling or two'; and he noted that regularly punters 'clubbed' their money in order to raise the 6d that was the minimum stake accepted by some bookies. Interestingly, he found that other bookmakers catered specifically for the smaller 'penny' punters, and seven years earlier it was observed, in Middlesbrough, that 'two telegraph' boys had become penny bookies.[52]

Justifiably, moralists deplored the betting of children and young teenagers, yet it is difficult to assess the prevalence of this practice. Still, in 1892 it was believed necessary to pass the Betting and Loans (Infants) Act so as 'to render Penal the inciting of Infants to Betting or Wagering or to borrowing money'.[53] Forty years later, the Reverend Perkins felt that the measure was unsuccessful and he decried the way in which 'some bookmakers are all too ready to encourage the children to use their own pennies in making bets'. It may be argued that these were unlikely to be local bookies sensitive to the mores of their communities as well as to their own moral codes, and some of Perkins's exaggerated claims can be regarded askance. For example, in support of his case that disastrous consequences resulted from gambling in childhood, he cited an enquiry made by the Salvation

Army. It aimed to find out the period at which betting had commenced for 'certain selected groups of men and women', all of whom were sheltering in the organization's homes in London and nine of the largest provincial cities. Roughly one-third of them were unable to remember, but of the remaining two-thirds, 20 per cent had begun betting before school age and nearly 50 per cent had commenced during the years of adolescence. Perkins concluded that this survey gave 'a fair indication of the general situation regarding men and women who had become social derelicts'.[54]

The defects in such reasoning are glaring, but they should not invalidate the clergyman's general point about the existence of children who betted. In Shropshire, Tom Davies recalled that 'during the dinner hour I would go to my aunt's house which was near the school and study the racing in the *Daily Herald*', after which he would place a 6d each-way bet 'on Billy Nevetts' mounts who was the leading jockey up north in those days'; a Glaswegian, Albert Mitchell, regretted that he was 'a gambling addict at 10 yrs of age'; while in the 1930s, Maurice McMahon remembered that disreputable 'Penny Bookies' collected bets outside Parkhead's secondary and high schools.[55]

However, most anti-gamblers were outraged not so much by occurrences like this as by the wide-ranging involvement of youngsters in street bookmaking. At the one level were those like Peter McCusker, a Glaswegian who worked for a bookmaking uncle in the early 1920s. His job was to go 'into town after school hours and pick up what we called a "Tishy" which was simply a thin copy paper with the day's results and this was the official results from which returns were made to the punters'.[56] Another layer of participation was indicated by those children such as Mr A. T. Richardson of Cattel Road, Small Heath. In the early 1930s, this Brummie joined 'with a couple of my school pals on Saturdays and School Holidays' and 'we used to be "lookouts" for bookies' runners who used to give us a 3d bit or even 6d sometimes'.[57] Finally, there were those hosts of children whose parents used them as messengers to put on their fancies, or, as in the case of L. S. Davis of Ashted in Birmingham, sent them to pick up their winnings.[58] Their large numbers were emphasized in 1935, when the Birkenhead Vigilance Society reported that over an eleven-year period, 'no fewer than 3,743' children acted in this manner, in respect of just twenty-eight betting raids.[59] Twelve years later, the *Gateshead Times* noted that 'police kept watch on a house in Brussels Street' and over three days, they observed '117 men, 159 women and 105 children, the latter between the ages of five and 14, enter the building and re-appear a few minutes later'.[60]

In 1923 and 1924, scenes such as these led the *Glasgow Herald* to run a series of articles on the 'evil' of child 'runners' for bookmakers. Locally, the practice was causing so much concern that the city's Education Authority had urged scholars to sign a pledge card which warned them against the habit of betting and gambling. At the same time, parents had been sent letters which informed them of the wrongness of using their children as go-betweens, and the resultant furore led to the passage of The Betting (Juvenile Messengers) (Scotland) Act, 1928.[61] This prohibited 'the use of young persons in the conveyance or delivery of messages or information relating to betting', and it enabled magistrates to fine and/or imprison bookies who dealt with those who were under sixteen years of age.[62] It was a failure; the memory of Brian McQuade reveals its ineffectiveness.

> Our backstreet bookie in Govan, where I still live, was known to all the punters simply as 'Steve the Bookie'. I used to 'Run The Cutter' for him, as we called it, i.e., collect the bets, put them on and hand over any winnings. I did this in the late 50s from the age of eight. This may surprise you, but shouldn't, as the police never suspected me, myself being so young. My method of working was thus: I would go round the tenement buildings, where I stayed, chapping the doors of the known gamblers (I had a list anyway) and ask if they wanted a bet on that day. Usually they did and had it written out . . . These bets I collected during my dinner-break from school (if I went!) returning the winnings, if any, at tea-time.[63]

Such procedures were not restricted to Glasgow. In Birmingham, in the 1920s, G. W. Langham was paid 2s a week to collect bets in Wright Street, Small Heath; during the same period in Keighley, a similar task was performed by Mary K., for which she received 3d a day 'with which I used to get 3d worth of damaged bananas a bag full that I took home for all our teas in between two slices of bread'; and in Ashley Downs, Bristol, Mrs P. Buckell took to the credit bookmaker the bets that were collected by her runner father, as did John Bosworth in Smethwick.[64] Children such as these were keenly aware that subterfuge was essential if they were to fool the police and Mrs L. Osborne explained how she evaded capture. Her family lived in Winson Green, Birmingham, and when she fetched the bets for their mother who was a runner, 'the coins were put in a pocket in my underwear, the paper slip in my shoe'.[65]

If anti-gamblers were unsuccessful in eliminating children from involvement in street betting, their disappointment was as great in severing the connection to the activity of working-class women. Many of them had a keen interest in horse-racing, and in 1926 the Liverpool survey stated that in one poor district '50 per cent of the women have the betting habit' compared to 50 per cent to 75 per cent of the men.[66] These statistics were impressionistic, but they emphasize that off-course betting was not a gender-specific activity, as were games such as tossing, pitch and toss, and cards. Moreover, the participation of women in betting on horses was not a phenomenon of the twentieth century. It had been noticed in the 1850s at the time of the first betting houses – and it was made clear in 1890, when a Leeds vicar described the scene that he had witnessed at The Midden.

> Young girls fresh from the work-room, and flushed with excitement, are to be seen carrying on hurried conversation with those who are only too ready to act as decoys to lead on the unwary. Motherly-looking persons mingle with the crowd, waiting for an opportunity to back their favourite horse. It is no uncommon thing for a shrewd clever woman to act for a number of others who have clubbed together to bet on some race.[67]

This evidence intimates that many women betted on a small scale, and such an interpretation is substantiated by the comments of the writer for *Tit Bits*. He noted that when he was in Nottingham, the 'system of penny wagering was in great vogue among the young women in the lace factories', and he added that a similar state of things existed in works in Northampton, Manchester and Leeds. In his opinion, although it ought to have been discouraged, this kind of betting was 'harmless enough if kept to the pence'.[68] This realistic assessment found little favour with other observers.

The Special Commissioner of the *North-Eastern Daily Gazette* proclaimed that female punters were 'slatternly and unkempt, telling of household duties undone and family duties undischarged'; while a Lancashire clergyman exclaimed that the gambling of mothers led to 'furniture pawned, homes desolated, children starved'.[69] There was to be no abatement in this theme that female betting destroyed family life. In 1902, it was propounded by Robert Knight, General Secretary of the Boilermakers' Society; two years later, John Hogge stressed it with a heartwrenching tale, as did C. E. B. Russell in 1913; and in 1922, Isabel Parlane amplified it when she declared that while betting was a curse for men, it was 'a positive degradation for women'.[70] In fact, the pressure against women having a 'flutter' (bet) continued until the 1950s, when it was superseded by the notion that 'children are kept without food and clothing by mothers with the housey-housey [bingo] craze'.[71]

It would be wrong to deny that betting could lead some women into financial difficulties. Dorothy Johnson remembered that during the Second World War, one of her friends 'was a real gambler' and 'when she had no money she asked who had any bottles with a pence or twopence on them and she would take them back for the money'.[72] Similarly, Alice Linton wrote that in Shoreditch, women often 'put a precious sixpence on a horse and if it lost it meant no dinner because you could buy a pound of mutton for 4½d and a pound of mixed potherbs for 1½d'; while Evelyn Gregory and Nellie Stamer pointed out that in both Portsmouth and Manchester, housewives would wash and pawn their clothes on a Monday, placing some of the cash raised on a horse. Still, the sums involved were usually small, and this was true of most of the women who backed their fancies.[73] In Swansea, Doris Magness's mother and friend 'loved a gamble on the horses', laying out 3d wins or 3d each-ways. This latter bet meant that they had a return on their money if their horse lost but came second or third, depending on the number of runners in the race. To make their limited funds go even further, they marked their slips 'any to come' – as did Mildred Kershaw's mother in the Old Kent Road – and below this statement they named more horses. If their first selection won, this instruction meant that they had another bet at the same stakes.[74]

Such careful betting was in evidence throughout Britain. Mr Riddall remembered that one of his father's female punters would back two horses 3d each way up and down, this command telling the bookie that if one horse was successful, part of the returns would go to supplement the bet on the other.[75] Likewise, other women tried to maximize their possible winnings from as small an outlay as possible. In Birmingham, Mr C. Brice recalled that his gran 'used to back the "Whip's Three"', the selections made by the tipster in the *Sporting Buff*; while in Scotland, Mr J. Forbes pointed out that the same fancy was called 'Scotia's Three', after the racing correspondent of the *Scottish Daily Express*.[76] The usual outlay on these choices was three 3d doubles and a 3d treble, meaning that if only one horse won, the punter would have no return. However, if two or more of the mounts were successful, then the odds on them would be multiplied and the bettor would have higher winnings than if she had backed the horses singly.[77]

The dominance of small outlays was as noticeable among male bettors. Andrew Walls mentioned that before 1945, 6d to 2s were the usual stakes in Aberdeen; Mr J. M. Blevins explained that in Edinburgh, 'the most popular betting in 1937' was backing three doubles and an each-way treble for a cost of one shilling; and Mr J. W. Davies of Dudley noted that 'most of the bets that Dad took were for 1 shilling or 1 shilling and sixpence', consisting of 'two Fourpenny Wins and Fourpenny Double or two Sixpenny Wins and a Sixpenny Double'.[78] The general lowness of stakes was emphasized by Mr J. Aslin, a former works' agent in Nottingham. He stated that he took '3d doubles 3d roll-ups 2d E. W. [each way] 3d Yankees [eleven bets on four horses] and 2d & 3d Doubles'. Indeed, he drew attention to the fact that 'it was very rare for me to take a 6d or a 1s bet; if it was a 6d bet it was from our Local Bobby'.[79]

His memories are given added force by the fact that in the inter-war years, the minimum stake of most bookies was 3d, as in the case of Maurice McMahon's employer in Maryhill.[80] Consequently, this sum became entwined with some perceptions of working-class betting and 'the thrupenny flutter' was a phrase which was bandied about by those lawyers who defended bookies and their runners.[81] In fact, in some places, 2d was the lowest unit that was accepted by bookmakers – as with Dick Riley and Jim Knight in Bilston.[82]

BETTING AND GAMBLING: AN EVIL OR A PLEASURE?

The lowness of stakes was made clear by police officers, but this defence found little favour with moralists.[83] Instead, they accepted the unsubstantiated claims of unnamed economists who pronounced that in 1937, Britain's 'annual social waste bill' was £600,000,000, of which a third was squandered on drink and gambling. The real social cost of this prodigality was proclaimed by William Lovedee, a member of the Friends' Committee Against the Gambling Evil. Decisively, he pronounced that '£100,000,000 spent on productive consumption per annum would find work for 2,000,000 people'. At a stroke, such useful expenditure would slay the dragon of unemployment, for 'the problem would then be not to find work for the unemployed, but men for work waiting to be done'.[84] The same reasoning was employed by Isaac Foot and other leading anti-gamblers, and almost twenty years later it was expressed still by the Reverend J. Clark Gibson. He declared that at a time when 'the nation's survival depends upon maximum production', some £750,000,000 was diverted from productive to non-productive uses.[85]

It was impossible to dispel the belief that betting was ruinous, and in 1933, to those who disagreed with it, D. R. Grenfell asked if they realized 'the number of homes that are wrecked by the gambler – children underfed, rent in arrears, clothes in rags?'[86] Nor was this notion restricted to the middle class. As Arthur Hopcraft pointed out, in Cannock:

> The supreme sins in my chapel-goers' world were drinking and betting. Drinking was the more 'low', because of the carelessness it encouraged in matters of public conduct such as speech, dress and control of bodily gases; but betting was the deeper wickedness, because it broke up homes, sending the furniture to the pawnbroker and the wife to the canal, and made children's bones rot for lack of regular meals.[87]

Once again, it would be incorrect to diminish the ill effects that could be produced by excessive betting. In his sad and moving autobiography, Vere Garratt told how his Brummie Dad was an 'inveterate gambler' whose 'one absorbing interest in life was to risk money' on racing. This ensured that 'he dreamed horses, ate with them, studied their daily form, gave them control over his thought, his money and his home and his children', until his whole aim in life was to 'hazard his wages on the turf'. As Garratt recalled with sorrow, there was little laughter or happiness in his home, for his father's moods were governed by his fortunes on the racecourse.[88] By contrast, Raymond A. and his Swansea family 'adored' his Dad, who was reputed to be lucky in backing horses. He was a man who dressed immaculately, 'everything matching', and he worked hard until he retired at the age of sixty-five. Yet, he 'never went on holiday, or owned a car, drank and smoked hardly at all'. In fact, he begrudged spending, except on betting, after a lifetime of which, 'he had nothing to show for it'.[89]

Still, the economic and emotional well-being of his family was not affected adversely by his passion; the same could not be said, however, of Alex Granger's father. His compulsion to bet led to a scarcity of food in his house, and he was not alone in allowing his children to suffer because of his misspending.[90] Based on the awareness which he gained as a runner in a mining village, John Ward's father recalled that 'he had known men put their last "tanner" on a horse when there was not a crust of bread in the house'; while the severe losses of George M.'s Dad led his son to state that he 'med up me mind as a kid that I'd never live that kind of life'.[91] It was this fear of poverty caused by betting that gave rise to the dictum of Joseph Armitage's father: 'if you 'oss race, gamble, borrow money or go to pop shops [pawnbrokers' shops], you'll never have money in yer pocket'; and it was the same fright that led Friendly Societies to rule that sick members would lose their relief if they were found gambling.[92] Indeed, it is likely that each community could point to families and individuals demoralized by the activity, and it is not surprising that many working-class people viewed any form of betting as disreputable, as did Eva M. She used to place the bets for her father in Salford, but even now 'I do not like to think that I did it'; and likewise, Maureen Marsh of Hull 'dreaded my lunch time at home to hear the familiar words – "on your way back to school Maureen I want you to take a bet to the bookie"'.[93]

For most middle-class anti-gamblers, there was no distinction between those bettors who were compulsive and those who were moderate. Many of them disregarded environmental reasons for the activity, and instead they fastened on the notion that it was an illness. In the words of Harry Payne in 1907, it was a 'positive mania', 'slow, insidious, but deadly sure';[94] his certainty was shared by a commentator in the *Manchester Guardian*.[95] Writing in 1924, he asserted that gambling was an 'endemic disease that was eating into the vitals of the English people as the murrain eats into the life of the cattle of Cheshire'. It was a purposeless activity which destroyed the fineness of every faculty, which caused flaccidity and which made its victims 'incapable of enthusiasm, or even of fixed attention – negligent employers, slack workmen, careless parents, worthless citizens'.[96]

Thus was connected the downfall of the individual with the doom of the nation. Gambling was unpatriotic, as had been stressed by the ex-serviceman who had fulminated against its ill effects on his fellow soldiers; and if proof was needed of its possible destruction of the nation, then it was provided by the Japanese defeat of Russia in 1905. For as the *Bulletin* of the National Anti-Gambling League thundered in Old Testament fashion, had not 'the untarnished sword' of the former 'struck to the ground the Russian gamester's half-palsied arm'?[97] Moreover, as it cautioned its readers in 1915, while Britain was free from direct blame for the war with Germany, perhaps it had to accept guilt indirectly. Had not the prevalence of the evils of gambling and drinking contributed to strengthen the opinion 'as to ours being a decadent people, unworthy to hold any longer the leading position which we have for so many ages enjoyed in the world'?[98]

After 1919, anti-gamblers forsook such fatalistic judgements, but like F. S. Preston, they maintained a steadfast determination to view 'The Gambling Spirit as a National Problem'; and in common with Professor Murphy, they manifested a willingness to incorporate its 'causes' into the developing science of psychology. The latter was the headmaster of Malvern College and in 1933, he diagnosed a punter as a 'patient who suffered from a gradual weakening of the nerve centres and power of volition'. The symptoms of the illness were those which had been established in the nineteenth century: 'lack of concentration, a craving for excitement and extreme restlessness'. Similarly with the effects: 'a dislike for other people (betting is the most selfish vice in the world)'; while the last stage of the disease 'might be a condition of complete anaesthesia to all higher considerations or pursuits, even in extreme cases to duty and honesty'. Murphy's comments were bolstered by those of H. Crichton Miller, founder and Honorary Senior Physician to the Institute of Medical Psychology. He had no doubt but that the national problem represented by the gambling spirit was broader than the mere dilemma of the activity itself. In fact, 'it belongs to the universal and permanent problem of immaturity in a competitive and acquisitive society'.[99]

Two years later, in *The New Survey of London Life and Labour*, John Martin went a stage further than Miller when he classified gamblers into three groups: the instinctive; the environmental; and the social.[100] Since then, gambling and betting have been the subject of many sophisticated psychological and sociological enquiries, but one of the most profound insights into their appeal to numerous working-class people was provided by William McIlvanney.[101] In *Docherty*, his intuitive portrayal of life in a fictitious Scottish mining village, he sought a reason for a fight between two men.

> Their satisfaction in this pointless contest had the same ancestry as their love of gambling, drinking, fighting. It wasn't only, as the socially conscious were inclined to say, the pathetic desire to escape from their condition. They were, much more profoundly, the expression of their condition. They gambled to gamble, they drank to drink, they fought to fight.[102]

In this penetrating statement, McIlvanney recognized the reality of working-class betting. No matter how good the win, it would not – except in the rarest of cases – change the long-term lifestyle of the successful punter. This understanding was made apparent by the story of Victor Andrews's father. A keen student of form who read only the racing page of a newspaper, he recorded his 'greatest achievement as a selector of winning horses' one week in 1907. His run of luck began when a 2s double came up and it continued 'until his final Saturday bet of sixty-four shillings netted him a fortune of nearly two hundred pounds – the equal of two years' wages as a metal polisher'. With this sum he moved to Redditch, 'intent on living the life of a country gentleman', but this proved an impossible dream. Soon, his tank dwindled as it was dented by the expense of living; a year later he was back in Birmingham, working at his trade in the BSA.[103]

Walter Greenwood's character Harry Hardcastle was another punter who belonged to the select band of those who could boast fantastic wins. For a 3d outlay he gained £22, but this amount disappeared rapidly following handouts to family and friends and a holiday of five days in Blackpool for himself and his girlfriend.[104] Betting could not change his life for the better in the long term, nor could it that of any working-class punter, but it could improve life, if only fleetingly. In the late 1930s, Christy Rees was unemployed in Swansea and after doing a 'foreigner' (a job which he did not declare to the authorities) he staked 6d up and down, winning 15s as a result. He spent 12s 6d of this on a hat for his wife: 'and she was happy, see, I was happy'.[105] Both this purchase and his bet would have been condemned as wasteful by many middle-class moralists, but they failed to perceive the nature of poverty. If spent in a more utilitarian fashion, the small stakes laid on horses could not have meant an escape from poverty's clutches, but such stakes did give a chance of parole, as did the 'pictures' (cinema). In the words of Jim Ross, from the mining village of Burnopfield in the North East:

> I remember my father furnished the house when he won the Autumn double with Niantic and Nevermore. Up till then he had *made* our furniture as he made our shoes. Six kids of us too. He was a cobbler and carpenter (yet could only get labouring – if he was lucky) . . . Morality was very high in the villages. Chapel had a big influence. There was a lot of John Wesley in our Socialism. A big win might get you a new pair of boots. To be well shod was something to thank God for. The poorer people were more religious than the rich. My mam once won a cake at the Labour Women's section meeting: 'Eldorado'.[106]

Even smaller wins could give a short-lived freedom from want, for as Jessica Martin stressed, 'imagine winning one and sixpence in old money; it was a fortune: one could have a good night out for two people on that amount'.[107]

Sensitive middle-class observers struggled to acknowledge such hopes. C. E. B. Russell deplored betting, but although he subscribed to the notion that the activity gave excitement to those who worked in monotonous jobs, yet he recognized that its initial attraction lay in the grimness of life for the poor in northern England. It provided them with the glimmer of a little betterment in their dire economic condition, and his interpretation was shared by Lady Bell – who investigated the ironworkers of Middlesbrough in 1905 – as well as by E. Wight Bakke, who made a social study of unemployed men in 1933.[108]

Five years afterwards, a similar enquiry was carried out by the Pilgrim Trust. In their report, the team of investigators made several perceptive observations about the generally depressed condition of those who were out of work: first, a winning punter acquired 'a definite social standing, and his views on very different matters are heard with respect'; second, to those who had despaired of finding a job, betting was an activity in which 'they stand as good a chance as anybody else'; and finally, it was 'the only possibility of making a decision, of a choice between alternatives, in a life otherwise prescribed in every detail by poverty and necessity, and always the object of other people's decisions'.[109]

In agreeing with J. A. Hobson, B. Seebohm Rowntree and G. R. Lavers contended that 'the essential ethical harm of gambling lies in the implicit abandonment of reasoning'.[110] The report from the Pilgrim Trust indicated that this was erroneous, and with a perspicacious argument, McKibbin emphasized the rationality of much working-class betting. It was 'fairly regular, prudent, usually considered', and punters manifested their reasoning by not staking 'everything in one go'.[111] Moreover, as Jerry White made clear in his study of Campbell Bunk in North London, for the poor a gamble 'was scarcely less certain than the daily roulette of economic enterprise; it became just one more way of earning a crust'. As such, it was 'a perfectly rational response to the daily struggle for subsistence'.[112]

The reasoned betting of moderate punters was indicated further by their reliance on skill in picking winners, for as Richard Hoggart noticed in Hunslett, respect was accorded to the man who had a system 'for playing the "pools" or horses'.[113] Perhaps with exaggeration, but certainly without falsehood, Robert Roberts declared that 'many a man made the breakthrough to literacy by studying the pages of the *One o'Clock*'; while Joe Kay stated with pride that his Dad 'could reckon up bets that would have made Albert Einstein scratch his head and ponder'.[114] This kind of alertness had led A. G. Markham to tell the 1902 Select Committee that gamblers were sharper and keener than drunkards, and it induced McKibbin to comment that an intellectualized betting provided mental stimulation to a class that was denied this activation in other forms.[115] Yet a scientific or studious attitude towards choosing fancies was not restricted to males. Before making their 3d bets, Mary Barras recalled that women in Hull would scour the *Pink* – the Yorkshire racing paper – while John Blake gave further evidence that the study of form was not confined to large punters.[116] In his household in Poplar

> Dad would tell Mum, that he had 'sorted out a horse', after intense perusal of the 'Midday Star'. He had weighed the past form of the horse, the thorough preparation of the training, and the fact that a top jockey had the mount. He had a summit meeting with his

> partner, and after lengthy discussion they arrived at a decision as to the horse they were going to squander their great wager on. Mum got a little nervous and asked Dad if he thought he had done a wise deed. He calmed her fears and said if ever there was a racing cert [certainty], this was it, and so the wager was laid; sixpence win and sixpence place [6d each way].

The Blakes' bet lost, but as their son discerned, this did not disallow the fact that it gave them happiness to have a little flutter now and then.[117] From his St Helens background, Eric Fairclough came to the same conclusion about the betting of his own parents, and he urged his readers not to decry them for finding fun in this harmless pastime.[118] Both men made a crucial and telling point. For if historians such as myself can defend most working-class betting as rational, then many members of that class justified it because it was pleasurable. On this level, it mattered little if punters were 'form merchants' or if they picked their horses with a pin like Betty Simonite's mother – or because of a dream, as with Ruth Johnson's uncle.[119] In the words of Rose McHugh, betting was a poor person's access to a form of leisure, it provided excitement, and it offered a thread of hope. More than that, it was a way of life.[120]

Anne Spence's husband represented just how much so. He recalled that up to dinner (lunch) time, the standard greeting between two men was, 'What are you on today?'; while of an evening it became, 'Backed anything today?'[121] In his insightful account of life in Sunderland's poverty-stricken Johnson Street, Patrick McLoughlin gave further evidence of how much backing horses was embedded in working-class culture. Regretfully, he noted: 'Oh the betting . . . and the way they worked at it in The Street', while he mentioned that his father was nicknamed the Horseman, because of his love of following his fancies.[122]

BOOKMAKERS: BLOODSUCKERS OR FINE GENTLEMEN?

For Elizabeth Goodhead, working-class interest in betting was dispiriting, and she observed that in the poor West End of Derby, 'the most depressing sight of all was to see the men on the street corner gather round one newspaper and argue loudly among themselves as to which horse would win the next race'.[123] Her belief that betting demoralized the working class was shared by many people in the labour movement, amongst them J. Ramsay MacDonald. In 1904, he wrote an article called 'Gambling and Citizenship' in which he exclaimed:

> To hope . . . that a Labour party can be built up in a population quivering from an indulgence in games of hazard is pure folly. Such a population cannot be organised for sustained political effort, cannot be depended upon for legal support to its political champions, cannot respond to appeals to its rational imagination. Its hazards absorb so much of its leisure; they lead it away from thoughts of social righteousness; they destroy in it the sense of social service; they create in it a state of mind which believes in fate, luck, the irrational, the erratic; they dazzle its eyes with flashy hopes; they make it absolutely incapable of taking an interest in the methods and the aims of reforming politicians. They lay it open to the seduction of demagogues, to the blandishments of the hail-fellow-well-met type of candidate, to the inducements of the common briber, to the flashy clap-trap of the vulgar and ignorant charlatan.[124]

As James D. Young has shown, MacDonald's fears were articulated first by Karl Kautsky in 1892, and on the part of some socialists, they exemplified a lack of tolerance 'of the English workers' culture and way of life'. In particular, Young argued that this attitude was evident in 'the elitism and socialism-from-above orientation' of the Social Democratic Foundation.[125] Still, MacDonald's fears were shared by working-class MPs like Will Crooks and John Burns, both of whom stressed that workers had a responsibility to elevate themselves above drinking and betting; and they were held strongly by members of the more proletarian-based Independent Labour Party.[126] Moreover, they dovetailed nicely with the non-conformist beliefs of many Labour activists. For men like Arthur Henderson, drinking and gambling were vices as well as habits which weakened the working-class movement, and in the 1920s this dual disavowal of betting was proclaimed with vigour by Scottish clerics like the Reverend James Barr and the Reverend A. N. Boyle.[127]

Their bilaterism was not new, having been propounded before 1914 by a few Anglicans such as the Reverend Arthur Price of Bury. He had emphasized that betting was individualistic and thus the antithesis of collectivism, and his argument gave a political edge to the religious notions that the activity was selfish and anti-social.[128] Central to this theme was the contention that full-time bettors were hawks who fed on their more foolish fellows, and many socialists took up this idea with alacrity. In 1906, a writer in the *Commonwealth* castigated bookmakers as 'bloodsuckers', exclaiming that the law had to be enforced sternly and rigorously 'with a view to killing out this social pest'; and almost twenty years later, John Brown put forward the same opinion in a similarly strident fashion.[129] With some friends he had gone to a back-lane bookie in the North East, and he announced that he felt 'disgusted at the sight of these harpies who preyed on the workers by holding out to them the promise of big gains'.[130]

Brown's repugnance was shared by Kathleen Woodward. In her despondent quasi-autobiography of life in South London, she observed solemnly that if one person 'had the least advantage in brains, initiative, or thrift, he soon turned this advantage to battening on neighbours as a moneylender or a bookmaker'. She avowed that 'then were the poor the worst enemies of the poor' and her affirmation was popularized by Walter Greenwood.[131] In his novel, the socialist hero, Larry Meath, is a lonely figure, separated from his fellow workers by his love of books and by his determined political beliefs. By contrast, Grundy, the reprehensible backyard bookie, is gregarious and popular and after Meath's death, he gains the socialist's girlfriend, Sal Hardcastle. In portraying this triumph of harsh reality over conviction, Greenwood used all his powerful literary skills to bring to the fore his abomination of bookmakers.[132]

> The back door opened; an unprecedented occurrence. A small, upturned box was to be seen ready as for the reception of an orator. A buzz of murmured conversation arose from the crowd accompanied by much neck straining as a small fat man, broad set, with beady eyes, an apoplectic complexion, came out of the house, crossed the tiny backyard and stood upon the upturned box, thumbs in waistcoat armholes. Preposterous-sized diamonds ornamented his thick fingers and a cable-like gold guard, further enhanced by a collection of gold pendants, spade guineas and Masonic emblems, hung heavily across his prominent stomach. He chewed a match stalk; his billycock [bowler hat] rested on the back of his head; he wore spats. Self-confidence and gross prosperity oozed from him. The notorious Sam Grundy himself.[133]

Love on the Dole was set in Hanky Park, and Greenwood represented its people as not only the quarry for Grundy, but also for Ezekiah Grumpole – the money-lending proprietor of the Good Samaritan Clothing Club – and for Price, the pawnbroker.[134] This area was the home of the author, and in his autobiography he showed that Grumpole and Price were based on people whom he had known.[135] He made no mention of any street bookmakers, but evidence suggests that he drew Grundy partly from the character of Nobby Clarke. This childhood acquaintance was from a poverty-stricken family, but he was streetwise, a card sharper and a man who became successful in business, thanks to the profits he had made from running a crown-and-anchor board while he was a soldier in the First World War.[136] In creating the composite figure of Grundy, it is likely that Greenwood grafted these personal features from Clarke on to those of street bookies who were well known in Salford; and again there are hints to his sources. When Harry Hardcastle won his £22 for a stake of 3d, Grundy boasted that while other bookies had limits which would have lowered the punter's returns, with him, the 'sky's the limit'.[137] Significantly, James Cush remembered that in Salford, Billy Brady 'had a large notice painted on the end of his house and pitch(s) proclaiming "world-record pay out"; an old lady had gone down the card with a 6d accumulator and won several hundred pounds'.

Brady was born in 1881 in Yorkshire Street, Salford and after leaving Salford Cathedral Boy's School (St John's), he worked at Glover's Cables, Trafford Park. A good rugby league player for the works team, he later played for Salford. Brady and his brothers took bets at Glover's for their father, but were sacked about 1902 for their activities – after which Brady started up as a back-street bookie close to Yorkshire Street. In the First World War, Brady was a sergeant and was involved in the Battle of the Somme. Invalided out of the army, he returned to bookmaking, basing himself at his family home in Yorkshire Street itself. Cush emphasized that this bookie 'achieved great status in the community; Billy Brady was a "king"', and his comments give support to Young's belief that some socialists were insensitive to working-class culture.[138]

In particular, this opinion is applicable to Greenwood and his mother. While this woman was not unfriendly, she disliked behaviour which seemed 'low bred' and 'undignified'; and her disapproval of 'standing with groups of neighbours exchanging tittle-tattle in the street' was reminiscent of Meath's distance from his fellow workers. Moreover, her father had been a well-read member of the International Labour Party and as a young woman she had attended their meetings and had sold copies of Robert Blatchford's *Merrie England*.[139] She despaired of the Tory working man and mentioned that her parent had earned three times as much as those who had rejected his appeals for them to change their politics. Mrs Greenwood was a sensitive and intelligent woman, but her disdain of the poor was as much a reflection of her upper-working-class status as it was of her views.[140] It was this background that made her son so critical of popular working-class culture and that engendered his hostility towards street bookmakers – a hostility that contrasted with the positive attitude shared by many other working-class people, typified by John W.

> Regarding your latest letter: are all bookies like the one Walter Greenwood wrote about? The answer is a very big 'NO'. I never met one like that. In my mind the bookies close to me were good, kind, fine gentlemen and I mean gentlemen . . . Jack Doyle, a very fine boxer . . . one of the kindest, nicest gentlemen I have ever encountered, this man when he knew anyone was ill or in hospital . . . sent fruit or flowers. On Saturdays the little ones in our Back all got matinee money . . . and at Christmas got sixpence and an apple, orange and toffee. He was one of the best. Billy Brady a good churchman and family man who never missed church was on the Church Council and helped them tremendously, another gentleman. Mick Mcarthy as Billy, a strong churchman and family man who helped many people in hard times . . . There were many others too numerous to mention, and I never, and I mean never, met one who didn't respect the people in the area he worked. They were all gentlemen in my eyes.[141]

The careful research of Andrew Davies in both his thesis and his investigation of leisure, gender and poverty in Salford and Manchester has indicated that many Salfordians disagreed with Greenwood's interpretation of life in their city; but as Stephen Constantine has made clear, the novelist had an ulterior motive in representing it as 'a society preoccupied with mean economies, exploited by bookies and pawnbrokers, bullied by petty officials, sliding hopelessly towards the horrors of the Means Test'.[142] For this grim picture was intended to shock his mostly middle-class readers and thus galvanize them into demanding social reform.[143] In order to do this, he had to include points of reference with which his audience was familiar, and that of the gross, flashy and greedy bookmaker was the one which served his purpose best.

As early as 1856, Shimmin had described the leading Liverpudlian bookie as 'a thick-set, corpulent fellow, the *beau ideal* of a John Bull in appearance', and he had noted that other betting men in the city were decorated with jewellery, massive breast pins and Albert chains, while they smoked cigars.[144] Likewise, James Greenwood portrayed the list men of Farringdon Street as jauntily dressed. They boasted 'sportsmanlike pins' in flashy neckscarves and they exhibited watch chains which were 'not to be weighed in the puny scales of a gold smith'.[145] Moreover, a sketch in Finsbury Library shows them as obese fellows who were bursting out of their waistcoats and their check trousers.[146] Forty years later, a writer in the *Bulletin* shrank from the figure of Bill Burke – an ex-prizefighter turned bookie in the East End of London – and his depiction bore an uncanny resemblance to

Greenwood's portrait of Grundy. His metropolitan counterpart was broad-shouldered and red-faced, dressed in a loud check suit, 'has rings on his fingers, and a large diamond pin in his tie, and a heavy gold chain stretched across his waistcoat'. Burke had his hat placed showily at the back of his head, and altogether he was deemed a coarse, repulsive-looking person. Indeed, his detractor wondered at how he was the focus of a circle of admirers, despite his odious appearance.[147]

This image of bookmakers became ingrained in the public consciousness. In the later nineteenth century it was reinforced by cartoons in *Punch*, and in the inter-war years it was popularized by Tom Webster, the prolific sports cartoonist.[148] As a schoolmaster put it in 1953: 'The uninitiated public are prone, largely owing to the efforts of the cartoonist, to regard bookmakers as a loud-voiced, uncultured, overbearing, stout, florid, bowler-hatted, cigar-smoking gang, intent on lining their satchels with other people's hard-earned money – no matter at what cost to the punter.'[149] However, the gaudy bookie was not just a figment of the imagination of sober, middle-class anti-gamblers. In the late nineteenth century, many racecourse layers were flamboyant, and Fairfax-Blakeborough described how some wore 'the loudest checks and the most brilliantly coloured waistcoats', vying with each other to dress the most outrageously.[150] This showmanship continued into the twentieth century. Sam Dell recalled that when his uncles settled on their pitch at a meeting, they would put up a huge black streamer with their betting name scrolled on it in white; while Horace Bottrell recollected that before 1914, his father wore a top hat and grey coat.[151] After the First World War, he abandoned this gear and adopted military-style clothes, as did many other layers.[152]

There were sound business reasons for on-course bookmakers to be ostentatious. First, they had to inspire punters with the confidence that they could pay out winning bets: they had to look wealthy. Secondly, they needed to attract custom in a market in which they might not be known, and this could be achieved best by the projection of a loud image, as in the case of the exuberant Ted Lewis.[153] This latter imperative did not apply to street bookies – especially not to those who had pitches – and while their dress had to indicate their prosperity, it was important for it not to be too pretentious. In trying to reconcile these pressures, their responses resembled those of the post-war illegal neighbourhood bookmakers of the United States. As Robert Perrucci explained, these men were people of prestige locally, and they had to behave in a manner that was consistent with their high position, thus ensuring that they validated their success with the usual symbols. However, while doing this, they had to be 'careful not to overdo it'.[154]

Like the fictitious Arthur Ross in *No Mean City*, most British street bookies were 'well put on'.[155] B. Bagley recalled that some of them 'had a navy blue milton overcoat fitted with inside pockets designed to take clock bags', while Bill Caldow remembered that in Dumfries, 'Big Dod' Urqhuart sported a crombie and a huge fedora hat.[156] But, in general, as John Hawke told the Select Committee in 1902, 'they wear nothing to show that they are bookmakers as they sometimes do in the ring'.[157] Indeed, their clothing was distinguished by its variety and not by its uniformity. Mr H. Dabbs pointed out that in Wednesbury, Bert Middlebrook 'was the very epitome of what a bookie should look like, slightly rotund and well built', while Harry Earp dressed 'in keeping with most of the people he dealt with i.e. cloth cap, waistcoat and jacket'.[158] Similarly, in Stockport, Mr Knowles mentioned that Harry Clarke 'never dressed' up, preferring to wear a little red silk scarf, clogs and a cap; while in nearby Hazel Grove, Frank Smith was another bookie who was not noticeable because of his clothing.[159] By contrast, in the same village, Eric Thornley Downs described Jack Tudge as a man who 'wore bowler, black pinstripes, wing collar, gold-hunter strung across his voluminous stomach, set off with grey spats and black shoes', and Bill Hallworth resembled him.[160]

As with all the most effective of caricatures, Grundy was well drawn and had some resemblance to some street bookmakers. But as an exaggerated image, its power lay not just in its representation of bookies as gaudy and vulgar but in its depiction of them as immoral and grasping. For Greenwood's character was also a pimp who lived no longer by his pitch, having moved to a prosperous area.[161] Significantly, in the *Pub and the People*, Grundy's type were discussed under the heading 'Singers and Pianists: Bookies and Prostitutes', and it is obvious that the conflation of these two 'vice-ridden' occupations had an immediate effect on middle-class readers.[162] They feared the movement of wicked bookmakers into their own districts, and by implication, Greenwood emphasized that this could be stopped only if society rooted out the dreadful conditions which gave rise to betting.

However, there is no evidence to suggest that street bookies were engaged in the organization of prostitution, and within Salford, at least, such a suggestion is ludicrous given the strongly held Catholic views of the city's leading backyard bookmakers.[163] Furthermore, as has been shown by the painstaking research of Elizabeth Roberts, working-class people manifested strong codes of conduct with regard to sexuality, contrary to the lurid and voyeuristic imagination of many of the bourgeoisie.[164] Pitch bookies needed the support of their communities if they were to survive in their illegality. Even if some of them had wished to become pimps, common sense would have prevented them from offending their constituency in this way. But more than this pragmatism, they were the children of their neighbourhoods and they were imbued as much with working-class notions of honour as were their neighbours. The great majority of them would have abhorred becoming men who lived off the bodies of women, as an indignant Mrs Overton stressed. After her husband died she became an illegal bookie in her own right, and her son remembered that she 'was greatly upset' when 'Lady Astor equated the activities of bookmaking . . . with the activities of prostitutes'. She was so irate at this slur that she swore at the peeress.[165]

In contradiction to Greenwood's portrait of Grundy, Wilson Ditty drew attention to the esteem in which many Glaswegian bookmakers were held.

> The Bookie and the pawnbroker were respected members of our community – on par with the local priest as they could bring comfort, hope and help to those in dire need in those days of poverty; no such things as social security existed then, just the 'parish' (poor relief) and the workhouse, the people were a mixed bunch from Ireland or the Highlands living in slum conditions in homes built during the Napoleonic Wars consisting of one room and kitchen or single ends, no bath or hot water and an outside toilet shared by several families, and families were large in number then, perhaps ten or twelve persons in each house.[166]

From the Cheshire village of Scholar Green, Jim Taylor agreed with this interpretation as to the high standing of illegal bookies. He praised Bill Ward as a man who was renowned for his 'civility and service, honesty and integrity', while he accorded his runner a similar dignified status. In his opinion, the villagers regarded the position of 'Cocker' Wakefield 'as part tradesman, part public servant, in much the same way as old Peter Jones, the gravedigger, or Mrs Pugh, the accepted authority on laying out the dead, or Mrs Bowyer the Church organist'.[167] It is as difficult to identify Grundy with men like this as it is to relate him to Patricia Bell's back-lane bookmaking family in Heaton. She recollected that its members were 'very respectable, my Mother and Aunt would never dream of going into a pub or club, neither did they drink', while 'we children were quite strictly brought up, we attended Sunday School and Church regularly'.[168] Yet, if it is likely that Grundy's sexual immorality was grounded in fantasy and not reality, then his upward residential mobility was not.

BOOKMAKERS: SUCCESSES AND FAILURES

When my Dad was born in 1932, my grandparents were living in a three-roomed back-to-back which had communal facilities. A year later, they had moved within the same street to a front-and-back house: a dwelling which boasted two rooms downstairs and its own outside toilet; and by 1939, they had taken over the tenancy of a larger building with four bedrooms. This was located in Alfred Street, which adjoined their original home of Studley Street, and their migration within the same neighbourhood was replicated by other Brummie bookmakers.[169] Harry Hudson improved his residence by exchanging the tenancy of number 5, back of 130 Vaughton Street, for that of number 30, a house which fronted the same street; and Albert Clamp imitated this process in Darwin Street.[170] Unlike these families, the Fosters, Overtons and Cashmores moved to modern houses in middle-class areas of Birmingham, joining credit operators like the Moists, agency-based bookmakers such as Ernie Nichols, and racecourse layers like the Bodens and Bottrells.[171] In fact, this late-1930s trend towards the suburbs was a national phenomenon: in Manchester, both James Cush and Mr Whitely noted that bookies 'used to live in a "nice" part of the town'; while L. Caket recalled that his East End bookmaker resided at Southend.[172]

Generally, this suburbanization was not welcomed. Horace Bottrell bought his semi-detached house in Bearwood in 1937, paying £750 for it, and he remembered that his next-door neighbour made disparaging remarks about his occupation. In reply he told him, 'Don't you say anything about me being a bookie because it's open to you or another fellow to try, but you're safely in your job and you'll be safe at the end, I don't know how I'm going to finish up.'[173] Similarly, Rosemary Whitaker was deeply offended by the snobbish disdain shown towards bookmakers. Her father had a flourishing business in Blackburn and he used some of its profits to buy greyhounds, often racing them in Dublin. On these occasions, he would fly himself and his family to luxurious weekends at the Gresham Hotel. Yet his wealth did not bring with it social acceptability among the middle class, as his daughter recalled. In 1940, she was seven years of age and she overheard her teachers saying that she could not be chosen as May Queen because her Dad was a bookie.[174] Mr E. W. Burkinshaw concurred:

> There was always a stigma attached to bookmaking, I think it must have been originated by what was called middle-class morality and probably started in Victoria's reign. To emphasise this I well remember an incident in the hot summer of 1921 when I was 10 years old. A great aunt and uncle stayed with my family. It so happened that earlier that year one of their daughters was married. The wedding group photograph was brought for us to see, in it was a picture of a man of about 40 standing next to the other daughter to whom he was engaged. The remark made by my great aunt has remained in my memory all these years and I quote. 'Would that he could be removed from that photograph.' It transpired that he was a 'bookie' quite unsuitable to marry into the great aunt's family. She made these remarks in the like of Edith Evans as Lady Bracknell. So it seems that people of that generation and my parents regarded bookmaking quite beyond the pale.
>
> The strange thing is that when I go into a Betting Shop in these days I feel that deep down I should not be there. One looks both ways when coming out in case the vicar might be passing, it is ridiculous really but the old standards remain.[175]

Of course, it was profit that paid for the rising residential status of bookies. During the inter-war years, Ken Overton explained that most of them did not take any notice of margins – 'if they got something in their pocket at the end of the day, that was good enough' – and Horace Foster agreed with him.[176] Neither he nor his father 'worked to percentages, you just took what was coming along and we made a living out of it, you know'.[177] This unbusinesslike attitude seemed to be prevalent among street bookmakers, and Mrs J. Davies stressed that it was a feature of those in Scunthorpe.[178] Nevertheless, it would seem reasonable to assume that their incomes were derived from a figure of 15 per cent gross profit on their turnovers. Certainly, my Grandad reckoned that so long as he could keep 3s in the pound then 'he's OK'.[179] This figure was higher than the 10–12 per cent gross that was estimated by a writer in *The Economist*, and which was the same percentage as that which was skimmed off by the tote from its pool.[180] However, it is validated by reference to the commissions that were paid by a few bookmakers. By the 1940s, some agents were receiving 2s 6d in the pound on their takings; consequently, if their commissioners were not making more than 12½ per cent, then they could not gain a profit.[181]

During the 1920s, Peter Cuthbert had several pitches in Halchesontown, Glasgow. His nephew estimated that each would take '£30 to £40 a day rising to £100 on a big race day, the worst maybe only £5 to £10'.[182] This latter figure was more than the £3–£6 daily that was gathered by 'Little' Dickie Jones, a 'tekker' in Sloane Street, Birmingham, but the larger amount appears to be representative of the turnover of the better pitches.[183] In Nottingham, James Jepson recalled that in the very poor district of Hyson Green, 'there was not much money about and we only took £20 to £30 a day except big race day when it would be £100'; from the early 1920s, my Grandad increased his turnover from about £40–£50 weekly to around £300–£400 per week; while Horace Foster recalled that usually his father took 'about £70' on a Saturday, the busiest day of all.[184] Of course, these sums included those taken by factory agents and pub runners and they are applicable only to the flat-racing season; indeed, the quietness of the winter months was the inducement that, from the 1890s, had led some bookmakers to adopt fixed-odds betting on football matches.[185]

It is likely that there was little change in this kind of turnover as the 1930s progressed: Ken Overton's father averaged about £300 a week in 1938; while in the same year, Mr S. Murphy lifted about £80 weekly at the pitch he worked in Cedar Street, Maryhill.[186] He guessed that his boss had a wage bill of £4 for this site, and in 1937, a writer in the *Glasgow Evening News* accepted this figure as normal for the city.[187] This correspondent mentioned that he talked to one street bookie who lifted his own bets and who reckoned to clear £7 to £8 a week on takings of about £20 per day.[188] His income indicated that he was working to a net gain of around 6 per cent. Of course, this figure is problematical and it does not take into account hidden expenses such as the payment of police officers. Nevertheless, after allowing for these difficulties, it would suggest a significant disparity with the 'rough approximation' of a 1 per cent net profit that was suggested for credit layers in 1923.[189] Partly this difference can be accounted for by the uncertainty of this latter percentage, but mostly it is explained away by the higher expenses of legal bookmakers. For example, an office was costly to rent; it required telephones and a ticker-tape machine; it needed a full-time staff commensurate with its business; and the proprietor had to include in his accounts an amount which 'wrote off' unpaid debts.

In the light of this discussion, it is not unreasonable to accept the claim of the Glaswegian investigator that his informant had ambitions 'to make about £20 a week, as some of his colleagues "at the game" do!'[190] For example, if my Grandad and Arthur Overton had netted 6 per cent of a turnover of £300, then each of them would have had an income of £18 a week. In the 1930s, this compared to an average industrial wage of £3, or of £4 for skilled workers.[191] Again, it must be stressed that this sum was not a week-by-week norm. It was likely to be much lower in the winter, when a reduced turnover on the jumps was aggravated by bad weather that could cancel a day's racing. Moreover, bookies like my Grandad did not take fixed odds on the football. Still, it would be safe to presume that if a street bookie had one pitch, then he or she had an income that was between two and five times that of a well-paid working man. It was figures like these that enabled Arthur Overton to purchase a detached house for £1,800 in 1938; while they allowed the ex-weaver James Heald to have 'a very good standard of living'.[192]

However, it should be borne in mind that bookmaking was a precarious occupation and that it had its casualties as well as its successes. W. J. Campbell remembered that in Lutterworth, 'the D. family was never on an even keel financially'. Their roller-coaster existence was typified by the purchase of three new bicycles for their children, all sold a couple of months later.[193] Similarly, in Liverpool, Trevor Morris brought to mind a one-legged veteran from the Great War. He 'eked out a meagre existence from the turn-over' of a surreptitious betting business in Sidlow Road, Stanley.

> One day our family noticed three men (possibly four) coming down the middle of the street: one was singing and the others playing instruments (one was a violin). This was normal practice in those days when ex-world war I soldiers (who were so badly done by after the end of the war) sang in the streets for money (several were Welshmen). On the day I refer to, one of the three men gave a betting slip to a boy to deliver to a house. They were, of course, detectives disguised as musicians and it was their way of gaining entrance to make a raid and search. The lady of the house told my mother that they made a very thorough search, even under the mattresses, for betting slips. Her husband, who ran the betting business, was duly prosecuted and convicted under the then existing betting laws, and the upset of it all ruined their lives. They felt they were in disgrace but the local people deeply sympathised with them. It goes to show that what is illegal and possibly immoral in one age is acceptable and pleasurable in another.[194]

Twenty-five years later, it was similar police action that was responsible for ending the career of 'Big' Bill Beesley.

In 1949, Bill Beesley was a full-time taker working outside the dockyard gates in South London, and he achieved fame when he gave evidence to the Royal Commission on Betting, Gaming and Lotteries.[195] As the *Daily Mirror* described it, he was 'sick and tired of always being just on the wrong side of the law' and he urged that street betting should be legalized so that the working man could have his fun.[196] Unfortunately, the local police and magistrates did not appreciate his act of going public. In twenty-five years of taking bets, he had on average been fined once or twice annually, but 'now the slings and arrows of outrageous fortune fell thickly about his ears'. On 4 November, three weeks after he had submitted his memorandum to the commissioners, he was arrested and fined £30 for street betting; and on 28 November he received an income-tax demand for £117. Not surprisingly, this annoyed him. As he pointed out, the government would not allow him to do his work, yet they taxed him for it.

Four months later, he was apprehended and fined £30 again, as he was on 20 March and 1 April. His wife 'said that honest Bill Beesley, the man who never welched, the man who was "not frightened and scared to make a statement" left the court looking an old man, white and terribly upset'. Broken by repressive acts which seemed unbelievable in 'democratic' Britain, Big Bill disappeared. Pertinently and sardonically, John Bingham drew attention to the class bias that was inherent in the nation. Bill Beesley was a law-breaker, but in the reporter's opinion, he was a man of courage, 'a man who had earned for himself a reputation for honesty in his own world'.[197] Sadly, many in authority were not ready to accept working-class values as valid, but by vanishing, Bill Beesley highlighted an iniquitous law and perhaps hastened its end. His case led people to write letters to *The Times*, it encouraged MPs to ask questions in Parliament, and it made good copy for the newspapers, one of which paid his fines when he reappeared after twenty-one days.[198]

If they wished, the police were able to waste many man-hours in standing on a pitch in order to drive a bookie out of business. This was most unusual, and its rarity speaks volumes about the attitude of many officers towards a law that they agreed was blatant in its class discrimination. Consequently, it was bad results that were to blame for the failure of most bookmakers. In Plymouth, Ginger Duke rose from the position of a works' bookie to that of a man who owned one of the city's first cars – driven by a chauffeur – but his mistake was to offer fixed-odds betting on football results. One 'black' Saturday of results left him reeling from his losses and 'every penny we had was pay-out'. His son believed that this disaster 'killed him in the end at 56 years', but with pride, he remembered that he did not welch and he declared that 'if I am half as good as he was I would thank God'.[199] Indeed, Tom Golding wrote that, in Birmingham, one coal merchant-cum-bookmaker committed suicide when he could not meet all his obligations to his punters.[200]

The path of bookmaking was strewn with those whose ventures had failed. Before 1914, Charles Gleed's nascent career 'came to an abrupt end' in Ipswich when White Bull won the Lincoln at 66 to 1; in Whitehouse Street, Birmingham, the longer-established Bill Thomason went bust in the mid-1930s; while T. W. Allen recalled that in Ferryhill, Aberdeen, the local bookie was 'a nice man and was respected'.[201] But in 1946, he took a 'fair loss' when Airborne won the Derby, and he 'never really recovered to carry on his book'.[202] His demise as a bookmaker replicated that of James Jepson's father. Formerly the manager of a butcher's shop, 'he did of what we called a back street Bookie up to about 1928'. His son recalled that 'he had not got much money and his status was not much different to any working man's'. In the end, 'he went broke over a horse called Yellow Underwing which I seem to remember won at 9 to 2; the very next day he was raided by the police'.[203]

BOOKMAKERS AND POLITICS

Large numbers of the working class were as much aware of the pitfalls of bookmaking as they were cognizant of its benefits.[204] It is impossible to know whether or not this realization affected the attitudes of many labour activists, but as Stephen Jones made clear in his stimulating thesis, a vehement disapproval of betting never held sway within the Labour Party as a whole. First, because of the importance of the libertarian socialist tradition, which supported the democratic right of the proletariat to spend their money as they wished; and second, because of a wariness against losing electoral support.[205] Given the huge amount of working-class punters, this latter was a powerful factor and it is unsurprising that the leadership of the Labour Party felt it prudent to avoid policy statements on betting. Instead, it preferred to leave the issue to the conscience of individual members, a strategy highlighted in 1959 when Labour MPs were given a free vote on the bill proposing to legalize cash transactions off-course.[206]

But there were two other reasons why the Labour Party found it difficult to place itself firmly in the camp of the anti-gamblers. Related to the arguments of the libertarian socialists was the firm conviction that legislation against cash betting was class-biased; while there was an increasing involvement in the labour movement of people from traditions that were different from those of Henderson and Barr. Before 1914, the most prominent of these was A. G. Markham. In addition to his post as secretary of the Racing Correspondents'

Association, he was founder and General Secretary of the Tram and Bus Workers' Union, while he was actively involved as a Labour representative in Poor Law matters.[207] With the decline of influence of non-conformity on the Labour Party, Markham's type became more common from the inter-war years onwards. Joe Gormley – a former leader of the National Union of Miners – made no secret of his love for gambling, which he believed he inherited from his father; while former MP Jack Ashley has written that small flutters enlivened Wellington Street, his childhood home in Widnes.[208]

Men like these were joined by others who had a more direct involvement in illegal betting, as Jim Farrar explained.

> From being demobbed up to the 1961 Betting and Gaming Act I worked in Engineering and also did a bit of illegal bookmaking along with being Secretary of the Halifax and District Trades Council and very active in the local Labour Party, my bookmaking activities providing financial help to the party who as now were always hard up, some of this help and payments being as you are quite aware being well out of order at Election times so imagine my horror when one of the local Aldermen decides to nominate me for the Magistrate bench and which I declined very quickly. The 1961 Act, well not only did it make ready-money betting legal (betting being legal before if you had the required banker's references to open an account but most of the working class having little more than a few bob in the post office didn't qualify so they were breaking the law every time they passed a bet in ready money) but we changed our status in name from engineers, joiners, market traders etc to become Turf Accountants, didn't we?[209]

The exploits of Jim Farrar were matched in Aberdeen by those of Ronald 'Mac' Davidson, a larger-than-life character who came from the town's tough East End. Like others who had experienced poverty, he sought to escape its straitjacket by becoming a street bookie, but at the same time, his hatred of hard times led him to join the Communist Party. He felt no conflict between his two roles. As a bookie he was providing a service that a class law sought to deny to the working class, while much of his profits were used to subsidize his local party. Indeed, his financial contribution was substantial, especially after he opened an illegal betting shop in the centre of Aberdeen, in a building that is now home to the town's Trades Council.[210]

In Leicester, Cyril Ford's father was a socialist who had helped to organize local support for the Jarrow marchers, but unlike Mac

Davidson, his family's political allegiance shifted slowly as its members became more involved in bookmaking.[211] Given their entrepreneurial activities, it is no surprise that many illegal bookies were Conservatives, as Jim Sefton noted in Hyde. His father was Tory mayor of the town in 1946–7, while George Kemp was another bookie who shared his political beliefs and who became a local councillor.[212] But just as Jim Farrar and Mac Davidson were distinguished by their unusualness, so too were these men. For while credit layers were remote from their punters, most street bookmakers were not and they could not afford to antagonize clients through well-publicized political views.[213] Indeed, it is likely that the politics of many of them reflected the dominant opinions of their communities. Certainly, in pre-1914 Salford and Birmingham, working-class Conservatism was a powerful force – particularly among the poor – and it is probable that this tradition influenced the views of Harry Hudson, Rose Pickering, Ellis McCormick and my Grandad.[214] Furthermore, army backgrounds reinforced the attitudes of these latter two men. Grandad had left school illegally at the age of eleven – barefoot and ragged-arsed, as working-class people described those who were poor – and he had 'took on' his politics from his father, a badly paid labourer who had been in the Coldstream Guards.[215]

Patriotism was as prominent an influence in the political allegiance of James Beasley of Scunthorpe, another bookie who had suffered 'an extremely poor childhood', but the popular Toryism of such men sat uneasily with that of upper-class turfites.[216] In 1905, Sir T. A. Cook expostulated that starting-price bookmakers were fraudsters who preyed on those who 'never saw the horse they backed', and Colonel Fluder, the Chairman of Tattersall's, reiterated this theme.[217] In his opinion, street betting was pernicious and it ought to have been suppressed, thus leaving the racecourse as the proper place for wagering.[218] Generally, the landed elite regretted that industrialization had increased wealth and facilitated social mobility, for this had caused an invasion of the gambling field by 'upstarts with no morals', or so Henry Durant believed in 1938.[219] But behind this hauteur towards those who sullied their hands by betting to make money there lurked as greedy a desire for lucre as ever was evinced by the most grasping illegal bookie.

In a vicious attack on such men, the Duke of Portland denigrated them as 'uncleanly parasites' who dishonoured the turf with their 'nauseous abuses', but his righteous indignation was laid bare by his statement that the money lost to them 'does not go into the pockets of people who support the Turf in any shape or form'.[220] This comment made it abundantly clear that he and his ilk were not averse to the working class losing their cash, so long as they received it and not bookies. They may have couched their desire in the argument that profits from betting should go to support horse-racing and -breeding, but no honeyed words could obscure the reality that from ordinary punters they sought subsidies for the hobby of rich men.[221] Their means of achieving this was to be via the quashing of bookmaking and the adoption of totalizators, part of the income of which should 'help' racing.[222]

Unabashedly, the nobbler William Day had advocated the introduction of these machines in 1889, but it was not until 1928 that an Act of Parliament allowed their use on racecourses.[223] Two years later, Sir Clement Hindley proclaimed that the machine was the 'democrat of the turf', and in 1933 the Aga Khan, the immensely wealthy race-horse owner, appealed for an extension of the tote off-course.[224] Interestingly, this religious leader was a sponsor and shareholder in Tote Investments Ltd, one of the large concerns which opened up Tote Clubs in the early 1930s, before they were deemed illegal.[225] His contention that bookmakers should be abolished was supported by another hugely rich man, Sir Abe Bailey.[226] In 1937, he declared that 'the owners of race-horses do not receive as much consideration as they should', and he called for 'a concerted effort' to close down SP betting.[227]

These assaults on bookmaking did not go unchallenged. In 1921, a Bookmakers Protection Association (BPA) had been formed in the south of England, and over the next few years it was imitated in other parts of Britain. Mostly, their memberships were racecourse layers, but they felt themselves responsible for protecting bookies of all types. In 1932, faced with the growing threat of the tote, these various organizations bonded themselves into a confederation and they created the National BPA.[228] Chaired by the formidable George Picken, this body launched into a vehement defence of bookies. It thundered that they were opposed by vested interests which were 'united, powerful and crafty' and which aimed 'to give legal sanction to the operations of *their own* betting interests, to the exclusion of bookmakers'.[229] Repeatedly, it issued calls to arms to all layers – irrespective of their status – and it engaged in withering attacks against upper-class tote monopolists.[230]

These enemies of bookmaking were damned as 'needy Nobles, grasping Generals and Majors on the Make'; allegations were made that their brainchild – the tote – employed 'sweated labour'; and their undemocratic tendencies were trumpeted loudly and longly.[231] In June 1934, it was intimated that a well-known owner had been informed that his horses ought not to be trained at Newmarket because he was connected with bookmaking; and the following month, under the heading 'Life and Death Legislation', a bold notice appeared in *Banyan* – the journal of the NBPA. 'During the recent debate in the House of Lords on the Unemployment Bill (which provides 2s. a week for the upkeep of a child), we are told that the benches were almost empty. During the previous week, when the Betting Bill was being discussed, noble lords appeared in full strength and worked till midnight.'[232] Among other things, this Bill aimed to allow the establishment of totalizators at greyhound tracks, at which there would be a 2s unit.[233] Obviously, this figure was the same as that which provided benefit for the children of the unemployed; this coincidence enabled *Banyan* to include a scathing cartoon against the aristocracy.[234]

At the same time as the selfishness of the upper class was stressed, so too were emphasized their bad manners and their wastefulness; in April 1934, bookies were presented with a perfect opportunity to parade these failings. Writing in the *Sunday Dispatch*, Lord Donegall described how great precautions were taken to prevent gate-crashing at the 'After-the-National' Dinner and Dance held at the Adelphi Hotel, Liverpool. He reported that 'bookmakers particularly were kept out', with the exceptions of the aristocratic Tommy Graves, Helen Vernett and Archie Scott.[235] Cleverly, a contributor to *Banyan* made use of the content of this article to ridicule real 'ladies' and 'gentlemen'.

> We are also told that during the evening these 'nice people' – not bookmakers – indulged in some ladylike and gentlemanly horse-play.
>
> First of all, the handpicked gentry pushed chairs across the ballroom floor, but this was mild compared with the unseemly conduct that followed.
>
> 'Glasses began to leave the tables and fly through the air – propelled by hand, of course – and finger bowls, wrapped in serviettes, soon followed. A very popular and old-fashioned diversion, this.
>
> 'A cupboard filled with condiment containers gave an excellent scope for the more exuberant members of the party.'
>
> If this had been the conduct of the chosen ones who claim to be ladies and gentlemen, we are glad that bookmakers were barred. Responsible people naturally would not feel at home in such an atmosphere of hooliganism.[236]

Not all prosperous turfites regarded bookies as anathema, and in 1939, Lord Harewood averred that he 'would very much dislike to see racing carried on without this extremely honest and extremely fair fraternity'.[237] He acknowledged that many on-course layers were suffering because of the introduction of the tote and his views found favour with a wide range of racing correspondents.[238] Generally, their successors in the popular newspapers continued to support the existence of bookmaking, and polls indicated that they had the backing of the majority of punters.[239] Still, tote monopolists such as Ivor Herbert persisted in their endeavours, and in 1955, this commentator made a vitriolic attack on bookies that would have been worthy of the Duke of Portland. He slammed the 'stay-at-home punter' as someone who did not support racing, and he accused them of 'doing no more than increase the wealth of a tribe who are little more than parasites'.[240]

Fortified by his vociferous support and that of 'Hotspur' in the *Daily Telegraph*, the next year, the Racehorse Owners' Association proposed that all betting should be carried on through the tote.[241] Eleven years later, its president, Sir Robin McAlpine, rallied members with the battle cry 'Out with the bookmaker'; and in 1970, his successor threatened the possibility of strike action by owners if bookies did not pay more towards the upkeep of race-horses.[242] It is interesting to note that in the former year, the following were directors of his association: a lieutenant, major and brigadier general; a lieutenant colonel, a major and a captain; three knights; one 'gentleman'; six other people, all of whom had extensive interests in business; and a member of the London Stock Exchange.[243] Indeed, it might have been asked of this person, whether he believed that his institution should have been nationalized, and if not, did he think that he should have paid a levy towards those firms in whose shares he dealt? Not surprisingly, similar questions rose to the lips of layers. George Lodge, Chairman of the National Association of Bookmakers, found it 'quite extraordinary that the Council of the Owners' Association, many of them directors of large companies, who have benefited from private enterprise in a competitive world, should even talk of a Tote Monopoly, which is after all another word for nationalisation'.[244]

Bookmaking remained outcast from the world of capitalism and its pariah status led to some strange political bedfellows. Consistent with its principles, the Labour Party has included large numbers of MPs who wished for the control of betting by the state, and in 1967 an article by William Keegan appeared in the *New Statesman* which called for the industry to be nationalized.[245] However, socialists have not been alone in looking for this development. Two years before Keegan's proposal, a Tory suggested that betting was a sign that people had too much money, and he argued that if they were going to waste it in this way, then the government should receive the profit; while in 1966 Norman St John Stevas, a fellow Conservative, exclaimed that betting brought suffering and misery to many homes.[246] He desired an end to this state of affairs, but he did not suggest that betting should be quashed. Instead, with unconscious irony, he favoured 'the abolition of betting in the form we know it today and the establishment of a tote monopoly'.[247] Presumably, unhappiness was acceptable so long as the state caused it and not bookmakers.

The most prominent and strident of the Tory tote monopolists were Sir John Astor, MP, and his brother, Viscount Astor. In 1956 the latter told the House of Lords:

> The Tote has no temptation to corrupt jockeys into giving information about what is happening in the stables and employees of the Tote Board do not engage in gang warfare. Any Chief Constable would tell you that the bookmaker was the main cause of corruption of the police. Bookmakers tended to associate with people engaged in crime because a large amount of money passed through their hands and they could afford to finance other forms of crime as well, although there were many fine, respectable and honest bookmakers. Here was a border land between betting and crime. The police, and all interested in law and order, would be delighted to see it finished by establishment of a Tote Monopoly, which had proved successful in other countries. If there had been all these gang troubles at the time the Royal Commission sat, the view might have been taken that a tote monopoly would be a fine thing for sport and morale in the enforcement of law and order.[248]

Many of Astor's declamations against bookmaking were white with age. Since the 1850s, off-course bookies had been blamed for forcing punters into breaking the law so as to pay for their losses, and the *Bulletin* had contained a regular feature on 'Suicides, Crimes etc'; while from the later 1700s, a hardy perennial had been the corrupting influence of layers on the morality of jockeys, trainers and stable-boys.[249] But to this list of iniquities of bookmaking, Astor added the powerful item that the occupation was inherently criminal.

This claim exemplified the chasm that divided Britain into two nations. For as Horace Foster expressed it, street bookies 'were doing wrong, but we were not criminals'.[250] But the wrong which they were doing had been interpreted by members of the upper and middle classes and Matt O'Malley gave voice to those millions who disagreed

An illustration from the *Betting Post* in the late 1700s by Rowlandson, showing the Prince Regent on the left and the blackleg Colonel O'Kelly on the right.

George Langham, a leading member of the Derby Sabini gang but also a highly respected figure on England's race-courses, aged about thirty, just after the First World War.

Victoria Street, E. C. – Betting-Men Making Up Their Books for the St. Leger (1863). Victoria Street later became Farringdon Street.

Mr Guy, counting his money in the centre, and his children Percy and Gertie at Birmingham Racecourse in 1923.

A race-ticket belonging to Sydney Lewis, a Jewish racecourse bookie whose family suffered from the bullying of the Brummagem Boys.

Alfie Bottrell, known as Bottle, taking bets as 'Joe White, The Silver King', on an English racecourse *c.* 1924.

Rose Pickering took bets at her fish and chip shop at 28 Darwin Street, Highgate, Birmingham, in the late 1930s.

Established 1870.

January 1st, 1905.

Dick Seymour

(SILVER KING),

23a, Bridge Street,

MANCHESTER.

Telegraphic Address:
"ISINGLASS," MANCHESTER.
Telephone Nos.: **5776—4516.**

Bankers—UNION BANK OF MANCHESTER,
York Street.

ALL OTHER RULES VOID.

The bookie's rulebook of Dick Seymour (193

CASH BUSINESS AS USUAL.

RKING MAN. "WHAT'S ALL THIS ABOUT THE HOUSE O' LORDS INTERFERING WITH 'G?"
K-STREET BOOKIE. "OH, THAT WON'T AFFECT US, MY BOY. YOU CAN GO ON LOSING WAGES TO ME THE SAME AS EVER."

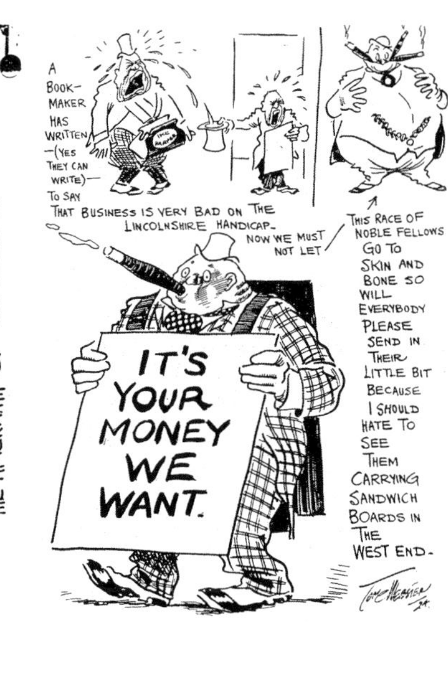

THE AFTERMATH OF THE DERBY.
A BOOK-MAKER HAS WRITTEN —(YES THEY CAN WRITE)— TO SAY THAT BUSINESS IS VERY BAD ON THE LINCOLNSHIRE HANDICAP.
NOW WE MUST NOT LET
THIS RACE OF NOBLE FELLOWS GO TO SKIN AND BONE SO WILL EVERYBODY PLEASE SEND IN THEIR LITTLE BIT BECAUSE I SHOULD HATE TO SEE THEM CARRYING SANDWICH BOARDS IN THE WEST END.
IT'S YOUR MONEY WE WANT.

Cartoons published in *Punch* and the *Daily Mail* in the 1920s, depicting bookmakers as greedy and grasping.

The Chief of Police and Members of the Force formulating plans to arrest a Street Bookmaker.

"AS FOREMAN HERE I'D LIKE TO KNOW IF YOU ARE GOING TO DO ANYTHING TO-DAY?"
"CAN'T, THERE'S NO RACING."

m was the publication of the National Association of Bookmakers. In the 1930s it included a number of hard-hitting owerful cartoons in defence of racecourse and street bookmakers.

A coach trip for the youngsters of Footdee, Aberdeen, in the late 1930s, paid for by the local bookie, Jim Forbes.

A trip from the Old Horseshoe pub in Mexborough, South Yorkshire, to Scarborough in 1937, paid for by the local bookie, Mr C. Woodhead (*second row, second from right*).

Telephone 2222.

Sunderland Borough Police. Z 159

13th June 1935.

Received from George Edward Brown

the sum of Nine Pounds, twelve shillings

and pence for fine on commitment

Street Betting 27th June 1935

£ 9 : 12 : -

Wm Kitley

Asst. Warrant Officer

A receipt for a fine for street betting incurred by George Brown of Sunderland, 13 June 1935.

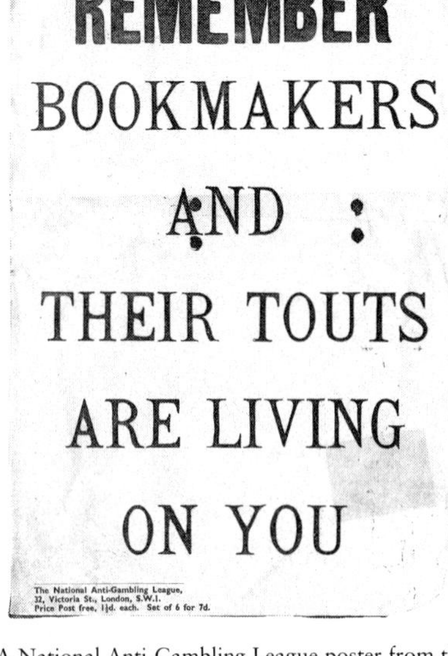

IF YOU GAMBLE
REMEMBER
BOOKMAKERS
AND :
THEIR TOUTS
ARE LIVING
ON YOU
The National Anti-Gambling League,
32, Victoria St., London, S.W.1.
Price Post free, 1½d. each. Set of 6 for 7d.

A National Anti-Gambling League poster from the 1930s.

lorace Bottrell, in the bowler hat, taking bets on an English race-
ourse after the Second World War.

Bert Harris setting up his stall on race day.

jump meeting in the 1950s: a wonderful action shot that also shows the lines of bookmakers beneath the embankment.

Billy Newbold (*back row, second from left*), the bookie in Hick Street, Birmingham, at a local boys' football club outing he paid for in the early 1950s.

Henry Ford checking the bets at his Leicester home, *c.* 1953–55.

Matt O'Malley (centre) writing out a line in the back court off a Glasgow street, where he took bets as an illegal bookie in the early 1950s.

'he illegal betting shop of Bert Jenkins (*second row, sixth from right*) in Fallin, Stirling, *c.* 1958.

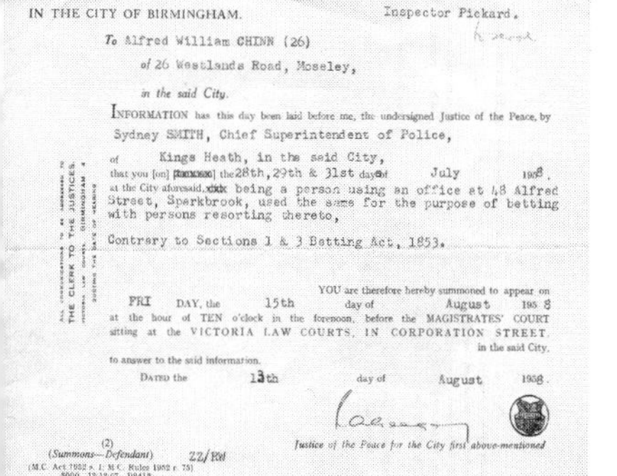

IN THE CITY OF BIRMINGHAM. Inspector Pickard.

To Alfred William CHINN (26)

of 26 Westlands Road, Moseley,

in the said City.

INFORMATION has this day been laid before me, the undersigned Justice of the Peace, by Sydney SMITH, Chief Superintendent of Police,

of Kings Heath, in the said City,

that you [on] [xxxxxx] the 28th, 29th & 31st days of July 1958, at the City aforesaid, xxx being a person using an office at 48 Alfred Street, Sparkbrook, used the same for the purpose of betting with persons resorting thereto,

Contrary to Sections 1 & 3 Betting Act, 1853.

ALL COMMUNICATIONS TO BE ADDRESSED TO THE CLERK TO THE JUSTICES, VICTORIA LAW COURTS, BIRMINGHAM 4 QUOTING THE DATE OF HEARING

YOU are therefore hereby summoned to appear on FRI DAY, the 15th day of August 1958 at the hour of TEN o'clock in the forenoon, before the MAGISTRATES' COURT sitting at the VICTORIA LAW COURTS, IN CORPORATION STREET, in the said City, to answer to the said information.

DATED the 13th day of August 1958.

Justice of the Peace for the City first above-mentioned

(2)
(Summons—Defendant) 22/RH
(M.C. Act 1952 s. 1; M.C. Rules 1952 r. 75)
8000 13.12.57 D8413

The summons for my Dad, Alfred Chinn, to appear before the magistrates for operating an illegal betting shop in 1958.

.e exterior of my Grandad's illegal betting shop in Sparkbrook, Birmingham, just before legalization.

Pat Wilson's betting shop in Bright Street, Birmingham, in the late 1950s (*left*) and in 1962 (*right*), before and after legalization. Like so many betting shops, this was simply the front room of a house.

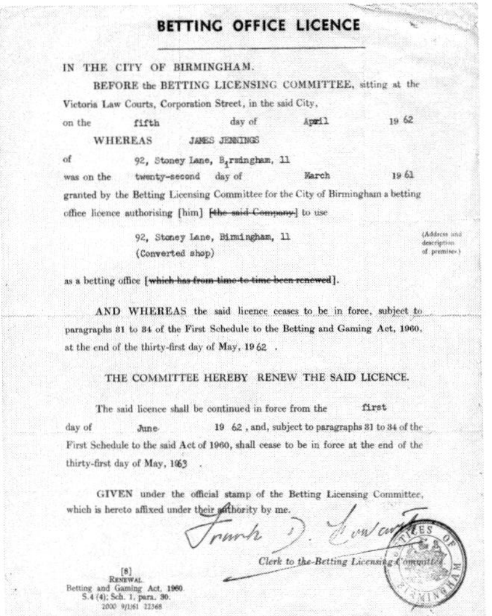

BETTING OFFICE LICENCE

IN THE CITY OF BIRMINGHAM.

BEFORE the BETTING LICENSING COMMITTEE, sitting at the Victoria Law Courts, Corporation Street, in the said City, on the fifth day of April 19 62

WHEREAS JAMES JENNINGS of 92, Stoney Lane, B,rmingham, 11 was on the twenty-second day of March 19 61 granted by the Betting Licensing Committee for the City of Birmingham a betting office licence authorising [him] ~~[the said Company]~~ to use

92, Stoney Lane, Birmingham, 11 (Converted shop) (Address and description of premises)

as a betting office ~~[which has from time to time been renewed]~~.

AND WHEREAS the said licence ceases to be in force, subject to paragraphs 31 to 34 of the First Schedule to the Betting and Gaming Act, 1960, at the end of the thirty-first day of May, 19 62 .

THE COMMITTEE HEREBY RENEW THE SAID LICENCE.

The said licence shall be continued in force from the first day of June 19 62 , and, subject to paragraphs 31 to 34 of the First Schedule to the said Act of 1960, shall cease to be in force at the end of the thirty-first day of May, 1963 .

GIVEN under the official stamp of the Betting Licensing Committee, which is hereto affixed under their authority by me.

Frank D. Howcroft

Clerk to the Betting Licensing Committee

[8]
RENEWAL
Betting and Gaming Act, 1960.
S. 4 (4); Sch. 1, para. 30.
2000 9/1/61 22368

The betting-office licence for James Jennings of 92 Stoney Lane, Sparkbrook, 22 March 1961. My Dad later bought this shop and I worked there on and off for many years.

In June 1960 Smethwick magistrate Arthur Smith refused to sit in judgement against street bookmakers because on the previous day he had betted on the Derby with an illegal bookie.

with their definitions. It was his firm opinion that 'these people who were Progressive or Tory minded, y' know, you were a criminal in their eyes but not to the ordinary working people you weren't a criminal, I mean after all, where would they go in for a bet if you weren't there?'[251] This assertion is supported by the overwhelming evidence from the working class, and it is corroborated by the statements of police officers. In 1932, the Chief Constable of Manchester commented that 'unlike most offences against the law, street and ready-money betting enjoys the sympathy of the major portion of the public, consequently the police are never assisted by the public as in other offences'; and seventeen years later, the Police Federation of England and Wales noted that the betting laws were 'held in undisguised contempt' by most of the population.[252]

In fact, this attitude was shared by many policemen themselves. Edmund King was in the Metropolitan Police from 1929 – retiring as a superintendent in 1962 – and he stated that neither he nor his colleagues looked on bookmakers or their runners as criminals. Generally, they felt that the law was unfair, and he mentioned the hypocrisy of one magistrate who 'was never easy with street bookmakers', but who would tell his clerk of his lunch-time betting transactions at his club.[253] However, some justices refused to be party to such duplicity, as Arthur Smith of Smethwick made plain.

> I think it was in June of 1960, the day following Derby day. And I'd never seen so many bookmakers lined up before me. There was seven of them lined up . . . And I'd had a bet on the Derby. I only ever had one bet a year, that was on the Derby. But I told him [the clerk of the court] that in these circumstances I didn't feel I could adjudicate. And he said, 'I'm really quite annoyed Mr Smith, state your reasons.' And you'd just sit apart. So I said in court that as one who like many more had a bet on the Derby yesterday, I don't feel that I can adjudicate in this case, and I sat apart. And the cases went on. There was not a reporter in the court the whole time, and I was astounded, when I went out, the whole host of reporters there and the television cameras were there to take an interview.[254]

This factory-worker JP was not alone in his views, for in 1950, the Chief Constables' (Scotland) Association had noted that often, the bench showed its disapproval of betting legislation by inflicting derisory penalties against offenders.[255] Nevertheless, for those who were distant from the working class, bookmakers remained criminals, even though men like the Lord Chancellor stressed their honesty in dealing with their punters.[256]

RACE GANGS AND ON-COURSE BOOKMAKERS

In convincing their detractors of their integrity, street bookies faced two major problems, both alluded to by Astor. First, they were regarded as prone to breaking the law in areas other than betting. This was an unfair insinuation, for just as they could not have prospered if their communities had regarded them as immoral, neither could they have flourished if their neighbours had deemed them criminal according to their own codes of conduct. As early as 1903, the wrongness of this slur was indicated by Martin Cobbett when he observed that 'the artful professional criminal seeks for mitigation of his proper penalty by bringing in "betting" as an excuse for his wrong-doing'.[257] Forty years later, a contributor to *Banyan* drew attention to the increasing number of cases 'where so-called "Bookmakers" have been involved in charges of petty larceny, etc'. He condemned these people as spineless scoundrels who were using bookmaking as a subterfuge, and in 1956, the NAB wrote to *The Times* to complain of the prevalence of this tactic.[258] The police agreed with its contention, and in the same year, Sir John Nott-Bower made it clear that gangsters 'are apt to describe themselves as bookmakers (generally using some foolish periphrasis for the term)'.[259] His comments highlighted Astor's second implication, that layers were involved actively in gangsterism.

Since the eighteenth century, thimbleriggers, prick-the-garter merchants and other fraudsters had haunted Britain's racecourses, as they did any place where large numbers of pigeons appeared ripe for the plucking. Indeed, in 1839, the Constabulary Commissioners outlined two main routes taken by the travelling criminals who lived in this way: the Midland Beat, which consisted mostly of race fixtures; and the Nottinghamshire–Lincolnshire beat, which related mainly to fairs.[260] Over fifty years later, Jerome Caminada, the Manchester detective, indicated that little had changed. He noted that the principal meetings were attended by a large class of thieves. Some were pickpockets, whilst others were three-card tricksters, or welchers who pretended that they were *bona fide* bookmakers, and he mentioned that, as a rule, they worked in gangs.[261] Their activities continued into the inter-war years and Sam Dell brought to mind those of the Aldgate mob.

> They were all pickpockets, they used to walk around, a gang of pickpockets. They were led by a face amongst them called D. Right villain and he was the leader and they used to operate mostly on Bank Holidays and High Days and Holidays and they'd be twenty-handed and this new thing that goes on called steaming – when they

> rush in and knock you – well they did that sixty years ago. They, what they would do, they would lift a guy in the air, someone would take his money, and I've seen 'em come up to your joint and as you see their hands, Bank Holiday Monday, you'd see their hands coming out to give you a, you know their stake, somebody'd take 'em.[262]

Similarly, the three-card trick remained popular with cheats. Les Lewis recollected that one 'megging mob' came from Walsall, but the most notorious gang was from Mexborough in South Yorkshire.[263] In 1921, three of its members were arrested for carrying out their chicanery on a train. It was revealed that between them, they had a total of forty-one convictions – thirteen of them for gaming – and each was sentenced to three months' hard labour.[264] However, their imprisonment did not deter them from continuing their fraudulent practices, and Albert Henson recalled that throughout the 1930s, they continued to live 'by their wits', often travelling to racecourses in southern England where the pickings were richer.[265] Still, many of the larger northern meetings were profitable occasions for their kind – and for those who operated spinning jennies – as is indicated by the race-week books of Doncaster police.[266] In fact, as late as 1933, the *Police Review* included an article which sought to explain the various frauds that went on at meetings.[267] These tended to peter out after the Second World War, although Jim Davis, Patsy Collins and Mr Price recalled the activities of a remnant of con-men.[268]

Most of the gangs of defrauders included members who were 'hard' and who could deal with those people who were aggrieved at losing their money through cheating; but their violence was a last resort and it did not compare to that of those mobs who flourished on intimidation. In 1848, a writer for the *Renfrewshire Advertiser* had noticed that a crowd of the 'Glasgow Fancy' had attended the Paisley races, and that they had used brute force to obtain a levy from the owners of stalls at the meeting.[269] By the early twentieth century, their successors were known as 'The Redskins' – because their faces were scarred with razor slashes – and they roamed the Scottish racecourses in much the same way as the 'Newcastle Boys' did those of the North East.[270] One bookmaker remembered a favourite dodge of these gangs. They would 'go round with a bogus subscription list for "Pore old Bill", "Dear old Charlie", or some fatherless family said to be at the brink of starvation'. Those who refused to pay up were marked men 'and often had a bad time of it in the afternoon'.[271] Another ruse adopted by mob members was to shout out a bet to a bookie; if it lost, they did not pay, but if it won, they expected to collect their profit.[272]

Fairfax-Blakeborough was of the opinion that the Geordie crew 'had many good points, at any rate, as compared with the even more notorious, more violent and often really inhuman gangs from Birmingham and Glasgow', and C. R. Acton agreed that the Birmingham mob were the 'toughest of the tough'.[273] In order to convey their bloodthirstiness, he dwelt on their involvement in dog-fighting, bare-fisted battles and the killing of rats with their own teeth.[274] No doubt there was a good deal of journalistic exaggeration in these descriptions, but the 'Brums' were feared as 'roughs of the lowest type possible', as they were slammed in 1898, when there was an outcry in the press about 'ruffianism on the turf'.[275] Certainly, their extortionate practices had led to the closure of many small meetings in the Midlands, just as in 1878, hooliganism had led to the banning of suburban fixtures around London; and the fearsome reputation of the 'Brums' owed much to a well-organized 'raid' on the principal enclosure at Scarborough in 1893.[276] At a signal, they and their allies from Leeds rushed the turnstiles, robbing all the money that had been taken up to then. This action diverted the attention of the few policemen who were on duty, thereby allowing dozens of gangsters to climb over the rails dividing the course from the paddock. A layer who suffered at their hands evoked the pandemonium which ensued: 'bookmakers were "held up" where they stood ready to commence operations on the first race, watches and money were stolen on all sides, and for some minutes the utmost lawlessness prevailed'.[277]

Edward Spencer pointed out that 'the boys' was 'the generic term for the felonious ruffians who were the curse of bookmakers', and he made it clear that the authorities seemed unable or unwilling to squash them.[278] So as to protect themselves from intimidation, many layers employed 'minders', as Alex Scott explained:

> The first definite breakaway from this astounding state of affairs was the hiring of professional pugilists by the bookmakers to protect their persons from violence and their pockets from the tribute demanded by 'the boys'. Paradoxical though it may seem nowadays, it was the straight men among the ready-money bookmakers of the 'seventies, 'eighties, and 'nineties who had well-known boxers standing beside them while they transacted their business. Popular imagination, of course, always credited the bookmaker's escort with being there to silence dissatisfied punters instead of protecting his employer from 'the boys'. George Gurney, one of the big ready-money men in the 'seventies and 'eighties, employed Bob Travers, the negro fighter, and afterwards Nunc Wallace, to act as protectors. Jack Edge, another big ready-money

> man, also employed a well-known pugilist whose name I now forget. Edge told me it cost him £5 to £10 a week, plus expenses, for his services, but they were well worth it.[279]

Unfortunately for the good reputation of bookmaking, Scott was correct to identify a negative response to the employment of minders. In 1905, an article in the *Birmingham Mail* stated that if a man's character was to be known by the company he keeps, 'then the bookmaker stands condemned at once'. The writer declared that 'a more villainous-looking horde than the "bookie's" retinue would be hard to find'. They were vulgar in their attire, cunning – 'in many cases criminal' – in features, loud-mouthed, and filthy. Many of them were 'discredited prize-fighters' who came in useful when their bosses wanted to take over a favoured pitch, or else, if they wished to 'pacify' an obstreperous client. This image of 'Jack Thick Ear' haunted racecourse layers and street bookies alike, particularly after 1919, when gang warfare broke out at many of the meetings in Britain.[280]

Following the First World War, attendances at fixtures boomed, particularly at the numerous racecourses in the south of England, and it seems that the Birmingham gangs tried to make their grip as strong in this region as it was in the Midlands.[281] They coalesced into a firmer grouping which was known as the Brummagem Boys, under the aegis of which a number of rackets were operated. First, there was the system of dots and dashes. As Dave Langham described it, this was a simple operation whereby a race-card was marked with these symbols in order to alert bookies to the form of the runners. In fact, this service told the layer nothing more than he knew already, and it was merely a means to obtain money from him.[282] Connected to this scheme was another, that of calling out the numbers of the horses in a particular event, while bookmakers were 'encouraged' also to pay for 'tools of the trade'. Included among these were lists of runners; stools on which to stand; pieces of chalk with which to mark up the prices on their boards; and water with which to rub them out.[283]

Huge sums have been bandied about concerning the income gleaned from these 'services'. Chief Inspector Dan Gooch, from the Flying Squad, estimated that the 'annual tribute' paid by bookies to the gangs was more than £1,000,000; while Norman Lucas put the daily figure at a minimum of £25.[284] But in reality it did not reach this total. Layers paid 2s 6d for each 'facility' with which they were provided, but as Jim Cooper made plain, 'considering there could be, at meetings like York, all up to sixty bookmakers, 60 half crowns, well a wage for a week, for £50, it were a lot of money then'.[285] Indeed, in the 1930s, the son of a leading gang member recalled that his Dad would come home from the races with bags full of silver. So much was there that the coins were poured into the bath, whence they would be shared out with his associates.[286]

Whatever the amounts involved, they were certainly substantial, and in the immediate post-war period, most of the 'services' to bookmakers were overseen by Billy Kimber and Andrew Towie. The former described himself as a bookmaker and a punter from Bordesley in Birmingham, while the latter was remembered as 'a tremendous gambler'.[287] In reality, Kimber was not a layer, but he and his partner would control the five or six best pitches on a course, putting their own men on them on a 'ten bob in the pound' basis.[288] Most of the Southern bookies accepted their presence philosophically and given the chaos which had pervaded racecourses before 1914, it is likely that they brought some order to the dearer rings at certain meetings. Moreover, unlike the depredators of the pre-war period, they were regarded as obtaining a living in a legitimate manner and Sam Dell praised them as men who were greatly respected.[289] Another Londoner, Charlie Maskey, worked for Billy Chandler and he recalled Towie as 'a good man', while Horace Bottrell went out of his way to make clear the integrity of his fellow Brummie.[290] These positive views were shared by Tom Divall, a former chief inspector at Scotland Yard. In his opinion, Kimber was 'one of the best'.[291]

However, not all of the Brummagem Boys were held in such esteem, for while Kimber and Towie were the 'guv'nors', their grip was not total, and they were unable to stop the violent actions of a small number of Brummies who favoured brutal intimidation. By 1916, the directors of racecourses had employed Divall to supervise and keep order at various fixtures, and he noted that the cheap rings were visited by 'three low blackguards, always more or less full of liquor'. Known as the 'Lunies', they terrified and blackmailed a number of small East End bookmakers, most of whom were Jewish.[292] Simmy L. corroborated this version, explaining that his brother was one of those who was beaten up. In desperation, he and his fellow victims turned for help to the Sabini boys, and it became 'us against them, the North against the South'.[293]

The Sabinis came from Saffron Hill, London's Little Italy, but as Arthur Harding recalled, they included a number of Jewish fighters.[294] Their intrusion on the racecourse was resented and on 25 March 1921, their leader, Derby, was attacked by some Brummies at Greenford Trotting Park. He saved himself from a severe beating by brandishing a revolver.[295] A few days later, Kimber himself was shot when he went to the Italian's flat to try and dampen down the trouble. He refused to 'grass' on his assailant, although a Jewish bookmaker told the police that he had shot the Brummie by accident.[296] This did not end hostilities, and on 4 April, the newspapers reported on a fight at Alexandra Park racecourse, noting that 'there appears to be a feud between a Midland gang and another set of men'.[297] Several weeks later, a large group of the Brummagem Boys 'mauled the East End Jews' who were taking bets in the silver ring at Bath. Some of them fled to Divall for assistance and he in turn asked Billy Kimber 'and a few of his leaders' to help quell the trouble.[298] Over the next few months the violence escalated, but the cause of the Sabinis was helped enormously on 2 June when twenty-eight men from the Birmingham district were arrested after they had attacked a coach-load of bookies from Leeds.[299] This was a mistake on two counts. First, the Yorkshiremen were allies of the Brummies, and second, the foolish assault led to the imprisonment of twenty-three of their number.[300]

Unastonishingly, Southern layers remained fearful of what the *Glasgow Herald* called the 'gangs of men who visited race meetings and terrorised bookmakers by any means which occurred to them'.[301] Consequently, on 21 August 1921, a number of them joined with some punters to form the Racecourse Bookmakers and Backers Protection Association.[302] As Ron Whytock observed, 'of necessity it was a question of fighting fire with fire in the early stages, and "strong-arm" men were recruited to defend the members of the new Association'.[303] A month after its founding, it appointed eight stewards, at the high wage of £6 a week. Among them were Derby Sabini and Philip Emmanuel, a relative of Edward Emmanuel, the association's vice-president.[304] This latter man was a punter not a bookmaker and Arthur Harding described him as the boss of 'the whole Jewish underworld'.[305] It seems that at this time, the Sabinis were under his command, and he saw the gang war as a chance to wrest from Kimber and Towie their control of the 'services' given to bookies. Certainly, he became involved in printing the lists and he later set up a company which provided layers with tickets for their punters.[306]

However, the Sabinis tired of Emmanuel's control and they began to act in a manner which gave grave concern to the association. On 15 May 1922, an allegation was received that stewards had demanded a royalty of a shilling on every set of lists that they sold; a month later, further complaints were dealt with; and on 4 September, the general committee agreed unanimously to dispense with their services.[307] This move came at about the time that the Sabinis and the Brummagem Boys had agreed to divide the country into spheres of control, and it meant that the members of the BPA were undefended.[308] Harold Hodgson explained that their secretary needed 'almost permanent police protection', while their president, Mr Yeadon, was attacked brutally; and from Birmingham, Sam Froggat recalled this period as a time when might was right.[309] A leading layer from that city, Teddy Sturmer, concurred that bookmakers had to be able to stand up for themselves, and it was true that often they had to fight for their pitches against those gangsters who wished to control them or to take them over.[310]

Because of this, minders remained common. Sam Dell recalled that a renowned bookie from Birmingham was accompanied by Owen Moran, the famed boxer from that city; while Joe Martin remembered that his Dad was the protector for another top layer.[311] Gradually, the organized gangs that had waged war against each other ceased to be the main fear of men like this. From 1923, both groups were gaining their incomes from 'servicing' the bookmakers in their regions, and just as Kimber and Towie were respected, so were the leaders of the Londoners. Warren Hill described Harry Boy Sabini as 'handsome, suave, and brilliantly intelligent', a man with such tremendous powers of command that 'a quiet word from him was sufficient to settle any situation however explosive it might be'; while Georgie Langham, a number caller, was looked up to as a person who was hard yet 'nice'.[312] Racecourses were almost unsupervised at this time, and in this atmosphere, the activities of such men were accepted as necessary. Moreover, they provided protection against the depredations of smaller, less scrupulous gangs, and even Divall recalled separate occasions when Kimber and Derby Sabini saved him from violence.[313]

The threat of this was real, as was manifested by the murder of Dai Lewis, a popular 'chalk and water' man in Wales. In 1927, he 'muscled in on the territory of the Rowlands brothers', a Cardiff-based race gang. For his temerity, he was attacked and his throat was slashed in a wound seven-and-a-quarter inches long and one-and-a-quarter inches deep; as he lay dying on the pavement, 'prostitutes rushed to his aid, ripping off their petticoats in a desperate effort to staunch the flow of blood'.[314] This terrible murder came at the end of another period of gang hostilities, although it would seem that they had little to do with racecourses. In London, they were related to rivalries between district-based mobs; in Sheffield, they centred on the tossing rings; and in Glasgow, they focused on claims to the title of 'hardest' gang.[315] Indeed, as Chief Inspector Greeno pointed out, there were even reports of a mythical battle in Petticoat Lane in which fifty mobsters 'fought with razors, stopping the traffic and terrifying the citizens'.[316] This 'event' prompted the Home Secretary to exclaim that he would 'smash gangdom', and convinced that every mob was a race-gang, he ordered the Flying Squad to make racecourses safe.[317]

Even though violence had declined at meetings, intimidation remained a problem for bookmakers and so their organizations welcomed this move. Led by the formidable Nutty Sharpe, the Squad targeted meetings where trouble was likely, and as Sam Dell explained it, when he 'walked on a racecourse they ran for their lives, every, all the villains ran'.[318] His presence was appreciated also by the Jockey Club. Stung by the determination of layers to stamp out gangsterism, in 1924, this body had set up a department to supervise the rings. It engaged a number of inspectors whose duties were threefold: first, they were to watch the entrance gates and keep out undesirables; second, they were to patrol the rings to spy out welchers and 'known bad characters'; and third, they were to look out for suspicious cases of disputed bets.[319]

The senior supervisor of these men was a former soldier, W. Bebbington, and he made it clear that before the later 1920s, 'the lot of a bookmaker was certainly a very unhappy one'.[320] However, by the end of that decade matters had improved enormously because of the combined action of the Flying Squad, the Jockey Club and the bookmakers' associations in the South, the Midlands and the North.[321] These latter had made a vital contribution to the rehabilitation of racing. First, they had manifested the seriousness of the problem of gangsterism; and second, they had initiated prosecutions against those who had attacked men like Mr Yeadon. His bravery cannot be diminished, for not only did he fight back against his assailants, but also 'undeterred by threats he determinedly gave up time and business to secure a conviction'.[322] Third, members of the bookmakers' organizations advertised their honesty with badges which proclaimed their affiliation. They defended their integrity strenuously by prosecuting welchers who used their sign and by alerting the public to 'mushroom bookies': fraudsters who appeared at big meetings and who fled with their takings.[323] Finally, the various BPAs formed Pitch Committees 'to protect and safeguard racecourse bookmakers' rights'.[324]

These could work only with the co-operation of the Jockey Club and from 1929 this was secured.[325] With a few modifications over the years, this meant that:

> The bookmakers' pitches on any course under the jurisdiction of the ruling body for flat racing or for National Hunt racing are allocated only by the Racecourse Personnel acting in liaison with the Bookmakers' Protection Association for the district.
>
> The Racecourse Personnel are appointed by the Jockey Club and the National Hunt Committee, and anyone who wishes to act as

> bookmakers on a recognised racecourse must apply to them and be in a position to have two already established bookmakers willing to act as guarantors for him.
>
> On every racecourse in Britain bookmakers' pitches are allocated on the seniority of the layers and only in the case of a bookmaker giving up business or withdrawing from his pitch can a newcomer be considered for a vacancy. Even then he would be considered only for the last place – and the least favourable pitch.

In one fell swoop, this system ended fights over pitches and it brought to an end the overseeing of the best of them by gangsters. To make certain of these results, the BPAs made it clear in their rules that a pitch was allotted for personal occupation, thus ensuring that no one other than the bookie appointed could stand up on it; while the 'buying, selling, lending, exchanging or otherwise disposing of any pitch' was prohibited.[326] So successful was this system of administering pitches that in 1958, the Jockey Club and the National Hunt Committee handed over complete responsibility for its control to the NAB.[327]

By the later 1930s, in the Southern BPA's region, only two places remained where Pitch Rules could not be applied. These were the Downs at Epsom and Brighton; their exclusion was because neither area could be effectively enclosed.[328] Consequently, there was some gang involvement at both meetings and it is not surprising that Graham Greene's novel of the underworld was set in the Sussex town.[329] The idea for *Brighton Rock* had come to Greene after he had read of an attack on a bookmaker and his clerk at nearby Lewes races.[330] As it was, this assault had nothing to do with pitches. Quite simply, in 1936, the Hoxton mob had gone 'tooled up' to 'sort out' the Sabini gang, a member of which had slashed one of the East Londoners at Liverpool Street station. They were unable to find their quarry, but because they were connected to the Italians the unfortunate layer and his workman were beaten up by the Hoxton team.[331] This occurrence led the *Daily Mirror* to proclaim '500 Gangsters Threaten New Race Track War', vying with a previous announcement by the *Daily Express* that the racecourse gangs were 'as well organised and nearly as ruthless as the racketeers of Chicago'.[332] Indeed, it seems apparent that in the so-called race gangs, the media sought a comparison with the mobsters of the United States of America; in 1938 the *Daily Sketch* proclaimed, 'The Gang Terror Here Now, Mobs Led by U.S. Criminals'.[333]

Greene avoided such hysteria. His characters were well drawn and not hyped-up examples of media fantasy. As he stated, 'In those days

I used to go frequently to Brighton and once spent an evening with a member of a gang who introduced me to a certain amount of slang in use and took me to one of the meeting places of his fellow gangsters.'[334] However, as Norman Sherry noted, the strangest aspect of Greene's novel was 'the development of the religious theme, which changed it from a story about gang warfare into a struggle between good and evil'.[335] Unhappily, this observation was lost on some reporters. In 1953, an article on purported race gangs included a bloody extract from *Brighton Rock*: 'One of them leant forward to cut his cheek and when he put up his hand to shield himself they slashed his knuckles again. He began to weep, as the four-thirty went by in a drumbeat of hoofs from the rail.' Delighted with his erudition, the writer pointed out that the novel had been 'a box-office' hit, and he exclaimed that at some meetings, the scenes were 'just like in the films'.[336]

Such comments were devoid of reality. There may have been some intimidation at unofficial and unsupervised point-to-points, but by the 1950s, race gangs as such had become extinct.[337] Indeed, their disappearance had been commented on by Nutty Sharpe in 1938, when he had noted that the BPA was a reputable society which had 'done much to clean up the sport of kings'.[338] This fact failed to impress the Canon Peter Green, a man whom few could match in his loathing of bookmakers. In 1913, he had denigrated them as predators, comparing them to the 'gunmen of New York or the Apaches of Paris', and twelve years later, in *Betting and Gambling*, he exceeded himself in hyperbole.[339] He exclaimed that the BPA had hired gangs of ruffians with 'browning pistols', and that 'bloodthirsty fighting took place in a score of big towns'. In 1935, his book was reprinted, upon which the BPA issued a writ for libel. The publishers were the Student Christian Movement Press, and they agreed to delete the offending passages and to ensure that unsold copies of the work were returned and exchanged for the revised edition. Also, they signed a document which explained that they had not intended to make any allegations against the BPA, regretting it if the book's readers made any such inference, and they paid the costs of the action.[340]

As it was, Sharpe's confidence in the decline of the race gangs was well placed. By the later 1930s, both the Sabinis and the remnants of the Brummagem Boys were ageing men and while their services were accepted on the racecourses, no longer was there any hint that they threatened bookmakers to accept them. This was emphasized in 1940, when the Northern BPA announced that it was 'entirely optional' to pay for dots and dashes and number-calling. Moreover, it made it plain that after the death of Andrew Towie, both operations would cease in its region.[341] He and his fellows continued to make a living from racing, but their profits were nowhere near as substantial as they had been fifteen years before.

The Sabinis had recognized this change and to counter the decline in their income, they had moved into 'protection' in the West End of London. Upon the outbreak of the Second World War, they were interned as aliens, but this area remained the focus of attention for the new gangs that succeeded them. As Edward Smithies emphasized, clubs provided the main source of profit for the gang leader Billy Hill, and this gangster himself stressed that he had no connection with racing or alleged race gangs.[342] For him and his rival Jack Spot, racecourses remained important only because the Sabinis had established them as places where leading gangsters flaunted their power by wandering around in a 'kingly' fashion. Certainly, both men were known to some bookmakers, but this did not make those layers into gangsters.[343] Moreover, outside the free course at Brighton, it was blatantly untrue that either of them controlled pitches, as it was alleged in 1955–6, when an orgy of journalistic exaggeration relating to Spot sought to raise the spectre of the race gangs.[344]

This interest in Spot had been precipitated by a razor fight between him and Albert Dimes, an associate of Hill. In court, both protagonists claimed to be bookies, as had previous gang members, in this way hoping to account for the large sums of cash that they possessed. It was these assertions which gave Lord Astor the opportunity to attack bookmakers.[345] In doing so, he showed that he was oblivious to the changes which had shifted the power base of the London gangs, but more than this, he manifested a crass ignorance of the history of bookmaking. The occupation was not nor ever had it been gangsterism writ small. It was layers who had suffered most at the hands of gang violence and intimidation and it was they who had led the way in cleaning up racing. As the NAB stated indignantly:

> Their lordships would have been more helpful if they had paid more attention to facts and had thrown less 'mud'.
>
> The deplorable attempt to associate bookmakers with the stories of gang warfare prevailing in the newspapers at the present time was really a gigantic red herring produced deliberately to obscure the true purpose of the debate.
>
> It is obvious that it was hoped by the introduction of the stories of gang warfare to prejudice the Government and the public against bookmakers.
>
> A further object was to press the interests of the minority who favour a totalisator monopoly.

> To damn the bookmaking profession because the gangsters often choose to describe themselves as bookmakers is rather like condemning all women who follow the respectable occupations of actress or model because the 'call girl' elects to describe herself as an actress or model when she is in the witness box.

The NAB added that they and the Jockey Club controlled rigidly course layers, and 'those whose conduct is in any sense open to question are immediately called to account'.[346]

Like their fellows, street bookies were not immune to false accusations of involvement in gangsterism. In the opinion of John Martin, the lower strata of them were liable especially to acquire delinquent habits, 'owing to their being in permanent touch with the criminal classes'. Indeed, they ran a particular risk of becoming enemies of the state, 'on account of their unceasing fight against the Police'.[347] Unfortunately, this habit of making sweeping generalizations from unsupported assertions has spread to scholars. Philip Jenkins and Gary W. Potter stated categorically that 'English race gangs operated as off-track bookmakers', and they added that 'taxes would be levied on legal bookmakers both on the course and on the street'. Moreover, they explained that within urban working-class areas, 'bookies associated with race gangs were a major force in the community'. As with Martin, they gave no evidence to support their case, and it stands on the flimsiest of supports.[348]

First, there is nothing to suggest that street bookmakers belonged to race gangs or were connected intimately with them. Moreover, these mobs came from two specific places, and this fact in itself invalidates the suggestion that every working-class neighbourhood had associations with them. Second, neither the Brummagem Boys nor the Sabinis ran street pitches, although it is true that Arthur Harding mentioned that in the East End of London the latter received rent from many of the street bookies.[349] But there is no indication that this practice was standard elsewhere in the country. There was no other gang in Britain that could compare with the Italians for their cohesion, organization and longevity. Unlike them, their Midland rivals were not based in one area – they were drawn from all over Birmingham – while other local gangs were short-lived and were concerned with showing their hardness.[350] Bill McGhee summed up the attitude of Glaswegian gangsters. He observed that 'the majority of the most notorious and hardened of them in the pre-war years made scarcely a penny out of their crimes', and he added that the normal charge against them was for breaches of the peace.[351]

Occasionally, some of Glasgow's gangs did try to intimidate street bookmakers, as in the case of the Burnistons. In 1934, these two brothers were arrested for a breach of the peace when they had stood up to the 'Cheeky Forty'; and Norman Miller recalled how his father dealt with a similar threat.[352]

> Ma father had a Jewish chap working called Sojer . . . and two tough nuts took a liberty with him and ma father got t' know about it. So ma father said to Sojer, 'Right we can't stand fer that. If we stand fer that we'll be, we'll be out of business.' So he said, he got Sojer and another feller, there were three of them, and they were walking up main street, Gorbals, and who's walking down Main Street, Gorbals, but these two hard knocks, with the real hard man. He was with them. And ma Dad walked straight up t' 'em and he says, and he didn't know this, he didn't know this Sojer was scared, so because he was scared he stuck a hammer in his pocket, in his back pocket . . . So ma Da says t' the two geezers, 'I want t' speak t' you!' And the hard nut in the middle, numero uno, he says, 'Miller, be careful what ye're doin'! They're with me!' And before he could say anymore the feller with the hammer had brought it out and crushed in his skull. Dad, he says, we never had any more trouble.[353]

This event was outstanding because of its rarity and it was made so by three factors.

In 1973, Ken Coates and Richard Silburn dashed the expectations of 'those who wish to view slum life as a cut-price bacchanalia'; equally, they could have warned against seeing poor districts as a jungle in which violent acts took place continually.[354] The reality was not so vivid, as a host of working-class autobiographies and a plethora of oral evidence suggests. As prosaic an interpretation applies to street bookies and protection. In most cases, they did not have to pay it, simply because they were never asked for it. Second, like Harry Miller, many of these men could 'handle themselves'. Mr Gilliver recollected that 'the three Chinns were a tough mob' and while my Grandad and his brothers were not trouble-makers, neither would 'they stand no nonsense'.[355] My Dad brought to mind one occasion when two henchmen of the Tyseley Terror – a local tough – claimed that they'd had 'a dollar [five shillings] on a non-runner from the day before'. Of course, the bet was fictitious, and Grandad refused to pay them. A few days later, he met the Terror who told him that 'he'd had the bet somewhere else'.[356] Many other street bookies were respected for their hardness, and as Frankie Goodwin pointed out, it was 'quite a common thing, boxers going into bookmaking'. He himself had been in both games – as were all my Dad's family – and his uncle, Scotty Adair, had been well known as 'a really good fighter'.[357]

Like the Tyseley Terror, if 'tough nuts tried it on', they were looking for small amounts of money – another observation made by Bill McGhee – but in agreeing with this, Robert Reid provided the third reason why intimidation was unusual.[358] He came from Maryhill, Glasgow, and he remembered:

> Our bookie was never mugged and no hard men ever tried anything on, because as I've said, the bookie was well-liked and had plenty of 'helpers' who would have retaliated. Some of the 'individual' bookies had a hard time occasionally, e.g. one of the tough locals (and usually he was a regular punter) would get drunk and would go to the evening pay-out and demand payment for a fictitious winning bet. The bookie, who had all his silver laid out on the table in front of him (but notes in pocket), naturally didn't want to see the table go up in the air, so he would pay out to keep the peace. This didn't seem to happen regularly or on any organised basis.[359]

Ernest Kyle emphasized this point. He stated that in the 1950s, 'contrary to popular mythology, Glasgow street bookies did not, as far as I'm aware, ever have to pay protection money'; while Matt O'Malley stressed that as a local bookmaker, he was part of the community.[360] He felt that he was protected by his neighbours because he was 'one of the boys, you mixed with 'em, you stood at the corner with 'em, you went and played football with 'em . . . you'd go to the match with 'em, y' know, this was the sort of thing'.[361] Jack McGhee agreed with this opinion. He lifted bets on the street in the Gorbals, and he felt that if a bookie was 'well liked', then his punters would tell extortioners 'to take a walk, you know'.[362] In common with many other Glaswegians who were active in illegal betting, both of these men were Roman Catholics of Irish descent, and as with all else to do with layers, their religion and their ethnicity were used against them by their detractors.

BOOKMAKERS: RELIGION AND ETHNICITY

Like their predecessors, the anti-gamblers of the late nineteenth century were concerned that betting was an un-Christian activity which 'was undermining the religious life of the nation'.[363] In 1890, this belief was expressed succinctly by the Reverend John Roberts. Writing in Welsh, he declared that because gamblers relied on chance, they did away with God.[364] At the centre of this selfish mislocation were bookmakers and once it was established that their occupation was irreligious, then puritanical clerics could compete with each other to find the most powerful indictment of the pariah group which they despised. The Reverend C. W. L. Christien expostulated that the betting ring was unrivalled as a place that was 'debased, immoral and godless'; J. M. Hogge equated layers to thieves, because they were engaged in 'a contract to steal'; while the Reverend J. Malet shrank from them as wolves.[365] This latter condemnation of them was insufficiently damning for a contributor to the journal of the Barnsley and District Sunday School Union. To ensure his readers had no doubt about the diabolical nature of professional bettors, he proclaimed that 'if you want to see the face of a devil going about seeking whom he may devour, look at a "bookmaker"'.[366]

Such fulminations were not new, and they drew on well-established attitudes which compared bookies to predators as well as to parasites. However, a new edge was given to them in the gloomy and despondent atmosphere of late-nineteenth-century Britain. Stedman Jones has made it plain that in this period 'Victorian civilisation felt itself increasingly threatened by "Outcast London"', and from the 1880s, an explosion of social explorers visited this foreign land.[367] They brought back tales about the inefficiency of the 'street people', as Jack London termed them; like Arnold White, many of them stressed that the unfitness of the 'residuum' was dangerous to Britain's imperial grandeur; and most of these travellers emphasized that the 'town race' was un-English – that is, according to bourgeois notions of Englishness.[368]

William Booth explained that just as there was a 'Darkest Africa', so too was there a 'Darkest England' – which needed to be civilized and Christianized by missionaries – and it is not surprising that the language of ethnicity imbued defamations of bookmakers.[369] In 1896, Reuben Manton stunned his readers with revelations about 'Darkest Grimsby. Gambling. The Town Saturated with the Vice'; while Charles Booth placed working-class bookies in Class A: the barbarous and dangerous very poor.[370] Nearly thirty years later, the Reverend Benson Perkins agreed with this identification. He denounced gambling as the vice of the savage, thundering that 'true civilisation ought to have outgrown it as it has outgrown tattooing and cannibalism'.[371] In 1934, his vituperation was matched by Frank Lenwood, when he decried Derby week because it brought with it 'something fierce, foul, rotten and mean; it brought the bookie, the tout, the thief, the blackmailer; it brought cruelty, hatred, lust'.[372]

Bookmakers were uncivilized: in the opinion of Archdeacon

Madden, they were 'hell's tatterdemalions', examples of 'man at his lowest'.[373] Consequently, they were symptoms of Britain's decline but also they were causes of its fall. As late as 1937, E. Rosslyn Mitchell declared that a gambler was an obstacle to the attainment of a perfect nation, while the men who enticed him 'to gamble and then thrive on his weakness I regard as enemies of the ideal State'. It was her decided opinion that punters had minds which were excitable, feverish and neurotically unstable, thus making them poor material for administering the affairs of a great Empire.[374] Her arguments followed a well-worn path. In 1890, the Reverend Alfred Rowland had stormed that a vast army of touts and blacklegs was battening on the folly of bettors. The result was terrible. English games were corrupted and degraded by the vice of gambling, 'like a filthy fungus which grows and swells in the dank shade till the beautiful tree falls through sheer rottenness'.[375]

The next year, George Ridding, Bishop of Southwell, extended this contention by proclaiming that betting was unmanly, and in 1894, Seton Churchill agreed with him.[376] He was frightened that racial deterioration would follow the popularity of such an effeminate activity.[377] Indeed, at the turn of the century, some anti-gamblers blamed betting for Britain's reversals in the Boer War. Rightly, David Dixon has observed that such people exhibited a 'melange of prejudice, self-persuasion and proto-medical phraseology'. As he explained, they saw themselves as part of a 'crusade to save England from economic and social disaster, to maintain political stability, to preserve the Empire, even to halt the degeneration of the English race and so to defend civilisation'.[378] In this Holy War, not only were bookmakers unpatriotic – as the *Bulletin* strove to prove during Britain's conflict with the Kaiser – but also they were infidels, as the Reverend Arthur Prince had intimated.[379]

This was made clear during 1938, when the *Luton News* asked the question, 'Can a bookmaker be a Christian, or can a Christian be a bookmaker?' A 'friendly' Methodist was adamant that the answer was in the negative, while another contributor stated that 'according to ordinary ideas of Christianity a bookmaker cannot be a Christian, but there is no reason why he cannot be the next best thing, which is a Jew, and most of them are Jews in some way'.[380] This comment reflected that made by Nimrod a century before, when he had announced his abhorrence of the owners of the Athenaeum gaming club. These were Messrs Bond, 'who a few years ago were what are called dealing Jew-boys in the streets, [and] are now worth about 60,000l'.[381] His loathing of the brothers arose from his blatant elitism as well as from his obvious xenophobia: they were lower-class; they were successful; and they were Jewish. Such outrageous racism was avoided by Nimrod's anti-gambling successors, but there can be little doubt that behind their denunciation of bookmakers as un-English and un-Christian there lurked the shadow of racial and religious prejudice, as well as class bias.

Certainly, by the 1920s, Jewish layers were prominent on British racecourses. Like Simmy L., some of them betted under an English name because they feared that they 'wouldn't take a penny' if they did otherwise, but the majority were more anglicized in their way of life than they were in their patronymics.[382] The Mendozas were Sephardi Jews whose famous ancestor, Daniel, had been a bare-fisted boxing champion, and they were intermarried with the renowned Gentile bookies, the Chandlers and the Thompsons; likewise, the Da Costas were related to the Harrises, an Ashkenazi-Irish bookmaking family; while Lou Prince was another layer whose relations spanned religious and racial divides.[383]

In his account of life in inter-war Aldgate, Ralph Finn highlighted the cultural split between the cockneyfied Choots – Dutch Jews – and the Yiddish-speaking Polacks, who came from Eastern Europe. He felt that it was from the ranks of the latter that 'most of the musicians, doctors and lawyers' were drawn, while the former 'became bookmakers and grew rich'.[384] There is much to justify Finn's observation, but he ignored the existence of Ashkenazis who imitated the Choots in their adoption of English ways and for whom bookmaking provided a chance of escape from the ghetto. As early as the 1860s, Leonard Himstein's father was taking bets in Whitechapel, and by 1902, his type were notable in this heartland of Russian- and Polish-born Jews.[385] Twenty years later, Mr S. Moses recalled that Jewish bookies dominated street betting in this part of London's East End; while Mr P. J. Ryan noted their influence in Bethnal Green, where Lou Laski, a barber, employed several takers.[386]

Moreover, Jewish bookies were not restricted to the capital. Mrs V. Connors remembered Izzy Myers, 'a small dapper man' whose pitch was in Hurst Street, Birmingham, the middle part of which 'was mostly shopkeepers of Jewish Origin'; in Liverpool, Mr C. J. Morgan's uncle was a runner for a 'Jewish gentleman and he was well dressed with lovely big overcoat and trilby'; while in Dundee, Mr N.'s parents came from Minsk, and they had no objection when he became connected to 'the betting business' at the age of fifteen.[387] Elsewhere in Scotland, a number of Jewish bookmakers were to be found in the Gorbals, a centre of Ashkenazi immigration which was described sensitively and intuitively in Ralph Glasser's memoir.[388] In this East End district of Glasgow, the leading layer was A. B. Tich, for whom

Jack McGhee lifted in the later 1930s. This bookie was recalled with affection as a well-liked and 'a very, very kind person', and it was brought to mind that he was nicknamed the 'gambling Jew', an adjective affixed to the Jewish people as a whole.[389]

Like the communist Joe Jacobs, many commentators noted that while Jews were moderate drinkers, a large number of them 'gambled very heavily', and in 1968, three High Court judges upheld a decision to allow bookmaker Danny Quastel to open a new betting shop because 'nobody likes a flutter better than the Jews'.[390] This supposed keenness for gambling has been put forward as a reason for the large number of Jewish bookies, but Lou Rose gave an alternative explanation for this phenomenon. A Glaswegian racecourse layer, he believed that Jewish parents had high aspirations for their children, and often the well-being of their younger offspring was secured by the money which was provided by a bookmaking older brother.[391]

Ashkenazis were not the only people from Eastern Europe who were active in street betting. Jack McGhee recalled a Polish lifter in the Gorbals, while during the 1950s in Bellshill, Sam Dunleavy worked for Peter Julius, a Lithuanian bookie who had been a miner in the Lanarkshire coalfields.[392] He was a Roman Catholic, and in much of this county illegal bookmaking was the domain of his co-religionists who were from an Irish background. Significantly, while the Scottish Black Country was ridden with sectarianism, betting was the one activity that seemed to transcend religious barriers. As Sam Dunleavy expressed it, 'in the social sense everybody wanted to get together with their own kind', but 'gambling was purely everybody against the bookie . . . so everybody was united in that'.[393]

In particular, his comments were applicable to New Stevenson, a place which exemplified the full depth of the barriers between Catholics and Protestants. Physically, the village was split by a burn: on one bank lived families of Irish descent, while on the other dwelt indigenous Scots. Both sectors had their own pubs and shops, and on 'Paddy's Day' and 12 July, it was likely that the fighting men of each group would meet in battle on the bridge which connected them, as they sought to invade the territory of their opponents. The Laffertys were renowned hard men for the Catholic cause, but also, on their side of the stream, they were the lifters at the village's only pitch. In a remarkable exception to the religious bigotry which plagued the area, Protestants would come to bet at this site, with no fear of violence breaking out.[394] Similarly, in Bellshill, Peter Julius employed a Lithuanian lifter who took in a pub that was 'blue'; while in Glasgow, Matt O'Malley had an agent in licensed premises in Bridgetown, the stronghold of Orangeism in Glasgow.[395]

Lou Rose was correct to stress that 'in the gambling everybody mixed', and it seems that most punters did not discriminate against bookies on the grounds of religion.[396] Still, there was a general belief that religious affiliation was important in bookmaking, as was made clear by Vince McGlennan.

> In the West of Scotland, particularly Glasgow, bookmakers, like public house owners, came disproportionately from among the first or second generation Irish Catholic immigrants. Since the Irish Catholic did not enjoy the respect of the native and Protestant Establishment anyway, the added slight opprobrium which might have accompanied the trade of bookie or publican scarcely mattered and the extra money, sometimes considerable wealth, was a consolation. In his own community, while the respect he was accorded did not approach that given to immigrant-stock teachers or lawyers, the generosity which his relative wealth allowed him to exercise gave him some standing. It also enabled him to buy a better and more respectable future for his children, who often attended the more prestigious fee-paying schools such as Saint Aloysius, run by the Jesuits. Professional people in Glasgow with clearly identifiable Irish names in many cases owe their middle-class respectability to bookmaking fathers or grandfathers (and frequently do not wish to be reminded of the fact!)[397]

Mr R. Elliot was a Paisley bookie who agreed with this interpretation. He felt that 'the Catholics got all the menial jobs, so a Catholic had to do something, to start something of his own'. Consequently, he estimated that in Clydeside, 60 per cent of bookmakers were his co-religionists, when their proportion of the overall population should have meant a lower ratio of one in five.[398]

It is difficult to assess the validity of these impressions. Certainly, Catholicism was the religion of leading credit bookmakers like Flynn, Trainer and McLean and there is abundant evidence of the number of street bookies who shared their adherence.[399] In Rolland Street, Maryhill, E. McGuinness mentioned that both pitches were run by Catholics, while Henry McQuade recalled that this was the faith of most of the bookies in the Gorbals.[400] However, in neither district were Protestant bookmakers absent. In the former, Walter Littlejohn praised Alex Scott as a local benefactor who 'ran a sort of benevolent fund for 1) families of impoverished punters! 2) "worthy causes" at the behest of local priest (despite Alex being a Presbyterian!)'; while in the latter area, Ernest Kyle was sceptical about assertions as to the generally Catholic persuasion of its bookmakers.[401]

> Glasgow is something like 1/3 Catholic and 2/3 Protestant. The Gorbals was more evenly divided – probably 50/50. So perhaps it is safe to assume if the claim were true anywhere it would be true in the Gorbals. I've tried to sort out Protestants from Catholics among the bookies I knew. With surprise I find that even among the bookies I knew personally, save for one or two, I'm not sure if they were Catholic or Protestant. Except, that is, for those whose kids either went to school with me or with my Protestant friends. (I have not been a practising Catholic since age 13.) It worked out at the same ratio as the population of the neighbourhood as a whole. This is too small a sample for the Gorbals, let alone for the city as a whole, I admit, still, if it did hold true throughout the Gorbals, then I doubt if there would be any significant disproportion, to say the least, for the city as a whole.[402]

Ernest Kyle's caution needs to be borne in mind, as does the observation made by Perrucci that the American neighbourhood bookie 'shares the ethnicity of the dominant group in the area'.[403] If this view is applied to the west of Scotland, it is not surprising that Catholic bookmakers were prominent in those districts which boasted a large number of their co-religionists. In Wishaw in Lanarkshire, 'Craigneuk was known as a tough area of the town, about 80 per cent were Irish Catholic', and John Rourke stated that the locality's two leading layers were members of this group.[404] So too were most of the lifters, as Peter Plunkett noted.[405] Similarly, in Govan, Wilson Ditty's uncle was a Northern Irish Protestant, his beliefs reflecting the allegiance of most of his punters, as did those of the Goodwins in Scotstoun.[406]

Mr G. Squires concurred with Perrucci's assessment, maintaining that in Liverpool, 'by and large the street runners lived in the area in which they operated and followed the religious pattern'. Still, he felt that among the actual bookmakers, there was a preponderance of Catholics.[407] Despite the reservations against this interpretation, I would tend to agree with it, and I would argue that Catholics were over-represented among the bookmakers not only of Merseyside and Clydeside, but also of Northern Ireland and south-east Lancashire.[408] In Salford, Tommy Carroll recalled that Billy Brady 'was No. 1, a man whose family stood for Catholic principles and were seen as a model of honesty and good faith'. Along with Jack Doyle and Tommy Riley, he participated in the annual Whitsuntide processions of witness, where all three bookies 'were given a special cheer from the onlookers'.[409] Likewise in Blakely, near Chadderton, Ken Wadsworth recollected that Johnny Foy 'was a staunch Catholic, 'cos he gave well to the church so he was respected throughout'.[410] However, not all Catholic bookmakers were Irish or descended from Irish immigrants. Nellie Nicholas remembered that her bookie was George Guiseppe, 'a real character born of a Lancashire mother and Italian father'; and in the South of England, families like the Tianos were able to leave London's Italian quarter of Saffron Hill because of the profits that they had made on the racecourse.[411]

The egalitarianism of bookmaking was at its most obvious in the appeal of the occupation to minorities. Nevertheless, its attraction was enhanced by rabbinical attitudes and those of Catholic moralists. The former tended to be critical of gambling, yet they accepted the activity if it was moderate and engaged in for relaxation and not for the gain of 'substantial unearned profits'; similarly, the latter did not believe that gambling was inherently immoral, instead arguing that the danger of the pastime lay in its excess.[412] Obviously, this liberal view was an influential factor when the government of the Irish Republic legalized betting shops in 1926, as it was when the Irish Sweepstake was instituted; and it led many Catholic clergymen to seek an income for their parishes via raffles and other forms of gambling, as the *New Statesman* pointed out in 1950.[413]

> It is reported that many Roman Catholic churches are running football pools, some of them bringing in £1,000 a week; the church takes perhaps 25 per cent for its building fund and the rest, after expenses are met, goes to the 'punters'. As befits the courage and broadmindedness of the Catholic church, this goes far beyond the daring with which, at church bazaars under other denominations, competitors have been invited to guess the weight of a cake or (worse) accept the arbitration of a brantub. Those citizens who have the hardihood to observe this new crisis impartially may feel it to be no bad thing that some of the wealth now sucked in by the 'pools' promoters should go instead to churches, especially if they are likely to use it in social services.[414]

It cannot be doubted that this kind of enterprise was enhanced by the working-class background of many priests, and as Doris Hall remembered, some of them betted with her father-in-law, a bookie in St Anne's parish, Bradford.[415] In fact, men such as William Hall were regarded sympathetically by the Catholic Church as a whole. As it was put in 1950, 'in the opinion of the Catholic moralist there is nothing essentially wrong in a man earning his livelihood as a gamester or as a bookmaker'.[416] Moreover, it was felt that large numbers of racecourse layers were 'quite honest men and do not appear to make excessive profits', while it was acknowledged that 'it seems intolerable that the humbler citizen cannot place a bet because he cannot afford to have credit with a bookmaker'.[417] Of course, these opinions were in tune with the largely working-class membership of the Roman Catholic Church in Britain, and this meant that bookmakers could acquire status among this community by way of their generosity. As Matt O'Malley put it, 'we always felt that if you were gonna give to charity, the church was first'. In his case, this meant that he sponsored the boys' guild football team, although he stressed that 'you can get into the boys' club, a feller, who doesn't care if you were black, white, Jew, Protestant, you were gonna play football, right you can play'. At the same time, as with other Catholic bookmakers, much of his support for his parish was not publicized, remaining confidential between him and his priest.[418]

This kind of connection to the 'evil' of gambling caused grave offence to puritanical Protestants. In 1884, the *St Helens Newspaper* had given voice to those who had hinted that 'the local Blue Ticket swindle is in the hands of Catholics only, some half-dozen men, who are regular chapel-goers, and are said to stand high in the confidence of their priests; in fact it has been said, no doubt as a passport to favour, that occasionally some of the prizes have found their way to the church'.[419] Seventy years later, this theme was reiterated when the Reverend Benson Perkins chastized the 'Roman Church' for its promotion of 'gambling practices such as lotteries and football pools'.[420] However, the ire of anti-gamblers was not aimed solely in this direction. In 1934, Northampton Methodists condemned the Anglican Church for the encouragement of gambling, and it was true that Episcopalians tended to hold a midway position in attitudes towards the activity.[421] Some of its members opposed it 'root and branch, but most consider that it can be, within strict limits, a harmless recreation'.[422]

Consequently, in areas where there was a split between Church and Chapel, it is likely that bookies and runners were drawn disproportionately from adherents of the Church of England. In particular, this observation would seem relevant to South Wales, as Ivor Edwards explained. His cousin took bets in the small village of Felinfoel near to Llanelli and he recalled:

> The attitude of the local ministers, well they regarded betting in any form a big SIN, and as most of the village had to attend a Church, Chapel or Mission, each minister were of the same opinion, yet I had to smile to myself when I used to hear my vicar Mr J. voice the same opinion on gambling, as an evil sent by the Devil, yet his

> weekly bet, if he won would go to the Church funds, so his wife used to say to me. I knew he had some good wins at times, and I'm sure he was well informed from someone. Maybe the Lord himself . . . the Methodist preachers or lay preachers were far stricter than the vicars of our church. They were very anti-gambling, and cursed the bookmakers as evil men, causing hardship to families in every village and town. They even reckon no bookmaker would reach the gates of heaven, and as for runners like my cousin, who would attend church regular as a ritual, would simply laugh at such comments.[423]

Whatever their personal morality, men like this runner were condemned in the same fashion as the chapel-goers of Cannock decried Two Ton Titley, a brazen figure who 'lorded the streets on Satan's behalf with massive jocosity'.[424] Unastonishingly, the movement to eradicate them drew its strength from Evangelical Anglicans, Methodists, Presbyterians, the Society of Friends and the Free Churches.[425]

7

STREET BOOKIES: REPRESSION AND RESISTANCE

THE NATIONAL ANTI-GAMBLING LEAGUE

The later 1880s had witnessed an avalanche of publications about the threat of gambling, and in the last year of that decade, there arose the stirrings of a move to co-ordinate and direct the energies of anti-gamblers throughout Britain. It was initiated by Mr F. A. Atkins, editor of *Home Words*, and in response to his ideas, a National Anti-Gambling League was founded in 1890.[1] Simply, it aimed to offer a 'strenuous and uncompromising opposition to every form of Betting and Gambling'; while it pursued the objective of promoting 'reform by Legislation and the effective administration of existing laws and byelaws'.[2] Led by the indefatigable J. M. Hogge and John Hawke (honorary secretaries) and by the tireless John Gulland (organizing secretary), committee members travelled the nation in their evangelistic quest to establish local branches and to arouse public opinion against the 'evil' which they were pledged to battle.[3]

They were confident in their puritanism and they were impelled by the firm belief that their cause was just. Unsurprisingly, then, many of their meetings had a revivalist feel, none more so than those open-air gatherings of the 'vigorous campaign' of 1906–7. Reported under headlines describing a betting or anti-gambling 'crusade', they featured the 'confessions' of a reformed tipster, 'Dock' Sharpe, as well as the dire warnings of clergymen and the fearful pronouncements of local dignitaries.[4] In another comparison to the Temperance Movement, the league issued a stream of leaflets which indicated the folly of betting and which urged working-class punters to repent of their wrongdoing. These publications gloried in titles like 'Betting. A Boy to the Bishop' and 'Shall I Bet?', and they included attempts to speak to the poor in what moralists felt was their own language. The supreme example of these was the crushingly didactic and overwhelmingly patronizing, 'On Losing m' Last 'Arf-Crown'.

> What a fule I've been! I wonder how much good money I've chucked away the last ten yur on hoss racin'?
>
> No wonder them bookies can do the flash, allus wear good togs, keep them fast trotters, spend money freely, and never do a stroke of work, except p'raps boss a pub and lay traps for such as we!
>
> . . . But I reckon 'taint the money loss does the most damage, it's the vexation at losin' and 'opin' to win, that puts you off your work and causes trouble; you can think o' nothin' else, and talk o' nothin' else. Why, all the talk in our shop is about racin'!
>
> You somehow have no care for politics, for wife and kids; and as for religion, why, I've never been inside a place of worship since I took up wi' bettin'.
>
> . . . I know lots of chaps that have been in quod and lost their chances in life through bein' tempted to try a dead cert wi' money that wer'n't their'n to play wi'.
>
> So I've taken me solemn davy to be sport for no more bookies, to chuck the bloomin' lot, and see what Adult School can do for me and mine.
>
> Lately I've had my eyes open' at what it's done for many a bloke I knows that goes reg'lar and has put a bit o' money in th' savin's bank . . . so I've made up my mind to joining next Sunday and stick to it.[5]

Unwilling to trust that pamphlets such as these would stop working-class betting, the leadership of the NAGL supported policies which would remove the preconditions for its prevalence. Thus, Rowntree proposed that the 'monotony of life' could be 'cured' by encouraging interest in 'some great religious, political or social movement', as well as by providing counter-attractions to betting; and he argued that the decrease of the 'evil' would be facilitated further by 'the provision of better housing'.[6] Still, these were long-term measures, and men like John Hawke believed that they needed to be accompanied by an immediate campaign of repression. First on their list of targets was ready-cash transactions on the racecourse, the source of the SP, which was acknowledged as the reason of the recent upsurge in betting.[7] In 1897, these appeared to be outlawed when in Hawke v. Dunn, the High Court ruled that a betting ring was a place within the meaning of the Act of 1853. However, as the NAGL termed it, 'the Jockey Club and the bookmakers immediately trumped up a collusive court case', and the original decision was reversed.[8]

This defeat gave added urgency to the League's aim to suppress the publication of betting odds. Rightly, its leaders identified this factor as a major element in the growth of off-course bookmaking, although its true significance was not manifested until 1955. In that year, a strike closed the three London evening newspapers, and without the dissemination of racing information, metropolitan bookies found that their trade dropped drastically, by up to 75 per cent in some cases.[9] Such statistics were unavailable to the anti-gamblers of the late nineteenth century, but their impressionistic evidence was strong enough to lead them to similar conclusions about the importance of betting material and thus into battle against newspaper proprietors who profited from its inclusion. In 1893, John Hawke denigrated them as 'pests of society', while twenty-five years later, Perkins exclaimed that they were fattening on a wasting national disease, 'like the worms that live upon the worthless dog whom they help to reduce to emaciation'.[10] Going on to mix his metaphors, he compared them to those who traded munitions with the enemy at the time of war.[11] The loathing of this cupidity was exhibited by a verse in the *Bulletin*.

He saw a ragged-breek'd urchin run
A-shrieking out 'All the winners!!!'
And the Devil smiled, and he sniggered, 'What fun!'
What a bait for the greed-fired sinners!
Whilst the gambling-demon is awake,
Half my imps may be idle snoosers.
But wouldn't it sell if I published – from Hell –
My records of 'All the Losers!'
Of all Primrose paths 'tis the Betting trade
Leads straightest down to perdition,
And the losses each day (of their souls) I should say
Would fill a big 'Speshul Edition'!![12]

Despite its 'fire and brimstone' feel, this rhyme stressed correctly the popularity of racing information. Joe Savage recalled that in 1930s Salford, 'the paper boys would be running down the street shouting, "One o'clock", and although it was called the "One o'Clock News" it was on sale much earlier'; while in Sheffield, Mr J. Smith remembered that 'about 11.00 a.m. they used to come round selling a racing paper called *The Early Bird*, and then the serious business used to start studying form'.[13] In Birmingham, the equivalent publication was the *Sporting Buff*, as was noted by James Whelan and by James Bromley, who mentioned that it included 'up to date information and a list of runners, plus pickings of possible winners selected by all national newspapers'.[14] Mrs G. Strachan stated that in Bradford, this service was provided by the 'Tishy or Tissure'.[15] Its correct name was the *Sporting Pink*, and Mr McIntyre recollected that it cost just 1d.[16]

These local racing sheets were joined by national and regional newspapers, which published betting information to a greater or lesser degree. In Manchester, the *Evening News* avoided giving tips, but like its rival, the *Evening Chronicle*, it printed the SP and reports of races. One of its owners was Russell Allen, a non-conformist, and in 1902, he had made it clear that his competitor garnered a large readership by providing a full racing service.[17] In fact, twenty-one years later, Canon Green estimated that if it were not for their betting editions, half of the Northern evening papers would have to close down.[18] It was this financial imperative which stymied the hopes of the NAGL that their owners would cease to pass on such matter. As Claud Cockburn found when he introduced greyhound tips and results to the *Daily Worker*, the need for creditable circulation figures overrode principles.[19]

Indeed, this necessity affected even members of the vehemently anti-gambling Society of Friends, as was indicated by Sir Edward Fry. In 1911, he circulated a pamphlet severely criticizing those Quakers who were connected to newspapers which were well known for their inclusion of betting information. Notably, he showed that the Rowntrees and Cadburys were involved deeply in the *Northern Echo*, the *Sheffield Daily Independent*, the *Morning Leader* and the *Star*.[20] Their defence was summed up ironically by Lord Sands: 'We detest betting, we spend large sums in the anti-gambling movement but we publish betting tips because we cannot sell our newspapers without them.'[21]

Patently, it was useless to wait for a voluntary cessation to the printing of the starting prices, and in 1902, the prohibition of this feature was urged by the Select Committee.[22] This proposal was never carried out, but this failure did not prevent the NAGL from welcoming other forms of censorship. In 1891–2, Leicester Libraries had blotted out the racing news from the daily papers which they displayed, and three years later, the *Bulletin* reported gladly that this procedure had been adopted in Aston and Worcester.[23] During 1898, there was a fierce debate in Longton over whether or not the town should follow these precedents, and although the council rescinded its original decision to do so, other boroughs were more consistent in their resolution to obliterate racing matter.[24] As in St Helens, this policy was welcomed by local puritans, and in 1905, Wigan and District Temperance Council sought its implementation locally.[25] In response to their request, the town's librarian was instructed to inquire into attitudes elsewhere, and 138 places replied to him. Twenty-four of them favoured blocking out, and of these, six had based their decision on moral grounds, while a further eleven had been influenced by this factor.[26]

Over the next twenty years, there was a rise in the number of libraries practising censorship. But increasingly, the impetus to this move was utilitarian rather than idealistic, as the Ulster novelist Michael McLaverty explained in *The Three Brothers*.

> He took wide steps across the damp floor, hung up his coat in the staff room, and came to help the janitor to black-out with inked roller the sporting columns in the morning's papers prior to screwing them into their jackets in the public newsroom.
>
> It mystified him, at first, this black mourning that was plastered on the newspapers, and on the day he had asked the janitor the reason for it, the tiny little man smiled at him somewhat patronisingly: 'Mr Caffrey, my lad, you don't know the meanness of the public the way I do. If the racing columns were exposed to all and sundry that newsroom would be like a bookmaker's office and instead of a parquet floor we'd have to strew it with sawdust like a butcher's shop on a wet day. There'd be no silence; the police would be in to keep order; they'd scribble horses' names on the walls, and some of the early birds would cut out the racing column with a razor blade . . .'[27]

McLaverty emphasized the nuisance of readers whose only concern was racing, and his comments were supported by the findings of a survey made by Huddersfield Libraries in 1930. Out of two hundred places that replied to their inquiry about blacking-out, fifty-three were in favour of this practice. Of those which gave a reason for their censorship, only Accrington's librarian mentioned that it was 'moral, presumably'. The other thirty-six agreed with the reply from Birmingham, that 'persons interested in betting news were monopolising newspapers' and thus they were preventing 'legitimate' readers from gaining access to the material that they required.[28]

Throughout the 1930s, libraries continued to adopt censorship because of the annoyance caused by punters, and blacking-out continued in Wolverhampton until 1956.[29] Nevertheless, as was remembered by a former librarian, Eric Jenkins, at the town's central library, the newsroom was 'constantly haunted by shady characters placing and taking bets'. It was popular for this purpose because it was 'remote from the busy counter of the lending library, and not staffed', while it had external and internal doors which made it 'unlikely that the punter and bookie's agent would be caught unawares'.[30] A similar situation was recalled by Ronald Garnett. In the 1930s, he worked at Manningham Branch Library, which

> had a large reading room where newspapers were displayed on wooden slopes and fastened with brass rods. Bradford was an authority which did not advocate the 'blacking out' of racing information. Consequently, we had a daily visitation from the local betting fraternity who compared their own fancies with those of the Newspaper Tipsters. Around 1.30 am the 'bookies' runner' used to appear and collect the betting slips and the cash from the punters. Any winnings would be returned the following day when bets were collected. The staff knew what was going on but it was difficult to prove it without a physical confrontation. I imagine that the library caretaker (an ex-policeman) worked hand-in-glove with the 'runner'.[31]

Such scenes were noted as early as 1813, when gaming was stated as a problem in the circulating libraries at Worthing.[32] Fifty-three years later, it was deemed necessary to forbid betting in the Oxford Public Library Rules and Regulations, and by 1898, the activity was banned in all public libraries by the Libraries Offences Act.[33] Obviously, this law failed, a fate that was to be experienced more spectacularly by the next and more comprehensive piece of anti-betting legislation.

THE BATTLE AGAINST STREET BOOKMAKERS

In an article in which he discussed the principles and programme of the NAGL, John Hawke declared that the organization did not wish to meddle with personal liberty. Unconscious of his hypocrisy, he added that 'we would still call upon the strong arm of the law to stretch its utmost length to punish *mercenary temptations and inducements to the vice*' of betting. It was his opinion that bookmakers 'should be placed in the dock', and in 1902, he recommended the outlawing of their occupation.[34] As Dixon has shown, this desire to eradicate bookies was but one plank in the platform of the NAGL. In general, its middle-class leadership was as keen on quashing the bad example of upper-class gamblers as it was on the elimination of working-class betting.[35] But for almost twenty years, it was this latter phenomenon that had been highlighted as a problem by myriad commentators, and given the aristocratic contempt for stay-at-home bettors and those who serviced them, it is little wonder that only street betting and street bookies became the targets for repressive legislation.

This class bias was blatant in the deliberations of the Select Committee on the Betting Duty (1901–2). It had been set up 'to inquire into the increase of public betting of all classes', but its recommendations were class-specific.[36] This became obvious in 1906, when the Street Betting Act sought to trample out the activities of 'any person frequenting or loitering in streets or public places, on behalf either of himself or of any person for the purpose of bookmaking, or betting, or wagering, or agreeing to bet or wager, or paying or receiving or settling bets'. First offenders could be fined up to £10; this amount doubled for those who were convicted twice; and for third or subsequent contraventions, law-breakers either could be levied a maximum of £50, or else they could be imprisoned for no more than six months, with or without hard labour. Furthermore, the police were empowered to confiscate any articles which related to betting and which were found on those whom they arrested. Finally, in a crushing denial of the rights of individuals and in an abrogation of the much-vaunted principle of British freedom, officers of the law were empowered 'to take into custody without warrant any person found committing an offence under this Act'.[37]

Huntley Jenkins and his co-authors pointed out that it was the first piece of anti-betting legislation in which bookmaking was mentioned, and Dixon emphasized that its provisions criminalized the occupation. But as he added, it 'struck not only at the commercial exploiter, but also at the punter', while it exempted credit betting and that on racecourses.[38] As a result, many MPs viewed it with distaste as creating 'one law for the rich and another for the poor'.[39] It was this feature which did so much to compromise the position of the Labour Party towards betting and bookmakers. Indeed, as John Givens made clear, in Scotland, it meant that it was 'noticeable that the fines imposed by Labour Magistrates were much more lenient than those imposed by their Tory counterparts', and Matt O'Malley agreed with him vehemently.[40] But Labour activists were not alone in expressing disgust at the Street Betting Act. In the radical weekly *Truth*, the Englishness of street bookies was stressed, as was their battle against an unjust law.

> The man of means can back his fancy with a starting-price office if he is unable to get to the racecourse, but Alf the Tried and Trusted,

> the bookie of the streets, is harried by the Police. It is a survival of the old Puritan hatred of gambling (and, indeed, pleasure) in any form. But whereas the Puritan could stop the poor man from backing his fancy, he was impotent against the rich man who wanted to do the same.[41]

This alternative vision of illegal bookies harked back to notions of the free-born Englishman that were voiced by Liverpudlian punters in the 1850s, and the 1906 Act served only to strengthen them. Writing in 1921, Samuel Hardman gave the opinion that the sporting instinct was strong in the British 'and they will not willingly be restrained by laws which make legal what is done in certain stated places by the rich, or well-to-do, and an offence, visited by heavy fines and imprisonment, to those who have no access to such places'.[42] Thirty years later, Peter Donnelly made clear this working-class contempt for class-prejudiced legislation.

> If you should ever be in Barrow and want to place a small bet you will not lack the opportunity, for though the local Directory may give the names of only two or three commission agents, that is no measure of our interest in horse-racing. There is a 'bookie-man' on every corner. God bless them, they are scarcely a municipal institution, but they are certainly a public service. By a strange twist of the English mind they are made a secret service, and, like all things secret, they are much abused by righteous, unimaginative people who do not understand them. They are, perhaps, the only completely honourable law-breakers, for they break nothing but statute law (which is often fit for nothing but breaking), nor rob anyone nor anything, not even the revenue. They are innocent gamblers.[43]

Such a view was held widely, and behind the class bias of the law, working-class people espied not only the authoritarian paternalism of the upper class, but also the insensitivity of puritanical Protestant clergymen.[44] In the words of W. H. Norris in 1894, 'these pious gentlemen have arrived at such a state of arrogance that they claim the right to dominate the pleasures of other people'. More than this, they wished to force their doctrines 'down your throat and no name is bad enough for you if you question their soundness or unsoundness'. In his *Hint to the Clergy and Anti-Gambling Crusades*, this bookmaker and backer declared that he looked upon the parson and his spy 'as the most contemptible worms that crawl on the face of the earth'. His diatribe called their congregations 'dupes' who thought that they were going to enjoy eternal bliss as a reward for a few prayers and some thrupenny pieces, and it slammed the church as a body of 'snivelling hypocrites' which had robbed the poor and given their rights to the children of the richest families in the land.[45]

Few people would have concurred with the violence of this rhetoric, but in the inter-war years, many members of the working class would have agreed with the underlying sentiments. For as John Givens explained of the Presbyterian ministers in Lanarkshire, they 'all tended to be regarded as tories, after all they lived in big houses and were always well dressed, and no matter how socialist their preaching might be they were always regarded with suspicion'. Furthermore, they were 'very much anti-drink', while they were totally opposed to gambling in any form, and these beliefs 'did not endear them to the working classes'.[46] But while puritanical clerics were unsympathetic to working-class culture, and while they attempted to 'reform' it by supporting measures like the Street Betting Act, it was not they who had to try and enforce such detested legislation.

In 1902, the Chief Constable of Manchester told the Select Committee that it would be possible to work out a law which made bookmaking 'illegal altogether', and six years later, this positive attitude was reiterated by the Royal Commission on the Duties of the Metropolitan Police.[47] Its members found that corruption was evident in relation to the enforcement of the 1906 Act, but they noted that, in general, its stringent provisions 'have made it impossible for bookmakers in future to carry on their business'.[48] Given the inability of the police to quash illegal betting during the second half of the nineteenth century, Dixon expressed surprise at such confidence. However, he made a number of pertinent observations that sought to explain it. First, he pointed out that police morale was high, and he noted that this factor was allied to the impression that serious crime had declined considerably in recent years. Second, he showed that the Metropolitan Police Commissioner, Sir Edward Henry, 'had strong informal links with the NAGL and seems to have accepted their programme and their conversion to belief in the possibility of suppression'. Finally, he maintained that the willingness of the police to tackle street betting had to be embedded within the context of the development of the late-Victorian state, whereby efforts were made to extend police power into working-class areas and to control space there.[49]

In fact, as Bailey has shown, 'the battle of the streets' had begun in mid-century – if not before – but Dixon was correct to identify the 1906 Act as a major offensive within that war.[50] Moreover, at the time of its passage, he was justified to stress the importance of the attitudes of senior police officers. They regarded street betting and bookmaking as social evils, and like Chief Inspector John Monk of the Metropolitan force, they saw action against them as part of a 'cleaning-up' campaign in working-class neighbourhoods. Yet Monk came to recognize the futility of his efforts. As he stated, it was 'a hopeless task endeavouring to suppress this type of crime; one could only try and control it'.[51] By 1919, his loss of confidence was widespread and in this sense, Dixon was right to regard the First World War as a watershed for police attitudes towards the Street Betting Act.[52] However, it was not until the 1920s that officers came to realize fully that the measure was unworkable. That they did so was a result of the conspicuous failure of innumerable local actions against the explosion of pitch bookies and runners.

About 1890, Monk mentioned that 'an order was made instructing each sub-division to employ two plain clothes men with the sole object of suppressing street betting'.[53] As John Solway recalled, in the central Metropolitan divisions this practice continued into the 1950s. Usually, those concerned were from the uniformed branch of the force, while they were used on 'another sub-division, and changed often'; and former sergeant Cliff French remembered that in East Ham, their spell of duty lasted a maximum of ninety days.[54] However, according to Edmund King, this latter policy was an innovation of the later 1930s, as before then, 'employment to deal with betting was confined to a very few officers, and some of them performed no other duties'.[55] This procedure was replicated across Britain, and in the years immediately after 1919, some of these plain-clothes men fulfilled the expectations of the NAGL that they would wage war against 'a great army of bookmakers'.[56]

In Gateshead, Bob Sinclair emphasized that 'relations with the Police in the early days were bad; harassment and arrests were normal'; while Bill Smith recalled a rhyme about the two officers who 'were a source of trouble': 'Ashes to Ashes, Dust to Dust, If Corrigan doesn't catch you, Drummond must.'[57] Similarly, in nearby Sunderland, Jos Harding recollected that two officers 'were the scourge of the back street bookies'.[58] James Lee agreed with him, naming the men as Sneddon and Ginger Taylor, and he pointed out that 'the latter of the two had a reputation of a bit of a runner over short distances'.[59] Obviously, this was a great advantage in his job, but it was more than offset by another factor which was made clear by Jimmy Addison. He brought to mind how the pair of officers tried 'all ways' to catch the two bookies who stood at either end of Barrington Street Back Lane.

> The men standing at the corners always got word through that they were on their way. The bookies used to disappear for a while until the

> all clear. I used to deal with Tommy Elliott and sometimes when the Tecs got close to him and gave chase he used to run up the back lane to our house and run through the yard along the passage and out the front door. The doors were never closed. I remember one such time when the Tecs were chasing him, he dashed into the yard while my father was getting a bucket of coal from the coal house. My father said, 'In here, Tommy', pointing to the coal house. Tommy Elliott ran into the coal house and my father put the lock on and when the Tecs came into the yard they were completely baffled.[60]

In Wolverhampton, the noted 'bookie snatcher' was a man called Darnley, and like his Geordie colleagues he was often frustrated by communal antagonism to his efforts, as was remembered by the niece of a crippled bookie. On one occasion 'time was short for the getaway', and as the officer went down the narrow entry into the courtyard, he was confronted by my 'grandmother [who] was very fat'. This woman refused to move in any direction except forwards, and at the same time, local housewives locked themselves in 'each of the lavatories and the "decs" were convinced my uncle was in one of them so until the "all clear" signal was given, they would not come out, thereby giving him the extra time to get away'.[61] Likewise, in 1937, when Liverpudlian police tried to arrest an illegal bookie, it was reported that they were 'exposed to a very considerable danger of being seriously hurt by a large and hostile crowd', mostly composed of women; while in the same year, a similar action provoked the 'utmost resistance' from another angry gathering in Camden Town.[62]

There can be no doubt that if the anti-gamblers felt themselves engaged in combat against street bookmakers, then many members of the working class were in the opposite camp. In the words of Terry Monaghan, during the 'hungry twenties', the Arthur Hill area of Newcastle was the scene of 'a constant war between the police, the bookie and his runners, but the great advantage the "runners" had over the police was the very ready help by ALL the householders'.[63] The same support was obvious in Glasgow. Wilson Ditty stressed that 'in our little community almost everyone was an unpaid "police watcher" so if any man, woman or child saw anything suspicious which looked like the law then the warning cry of "Edge Up" rang out and everyone would scatter off'; and in Maryhill, 'Wee' Jimmy McLaughlin 'had the families all on his side as when the police raided he could go into any of the houses to hide'.[64]

Of course, there were working-class people who objected to the presence of street bookmaking. Catherine Wilson mentioned that in her Springburn tenement, some of the residents were offended by the 'undesirable characters' who were attracted by the bookie in the back close; while in Bury, Mr H. McLennan thought that men such as this 'were hated by many housewives whose husband had lost most of his dole money with them'.[65] As May Anderson put it, 'bookies were nice guys if you had money back but not so nice if not'; and in Nottinghamshire, Tom Sprowell loathed his Dad's occupation, because 'I had it rammed down my throat every day of the week from my early days'.[66] These negative views should not be dismissed nor should they be diminished; nevertheless, the evidence suggests that in industrial Britain, the majority of the working class sustained bookies, as the police themselves acknowledged.

Even before the First World War, the Chief Constable of St Helens was exasperated by the many persons who 'would go out of their way to shield or give warning to offenders', and by 1923, the unanimous verdict of the police was that 'the sympathy and active assistance of the general public is with the bettor, whether bookmaker or backer'.[67] Nine years later, John Maxwell, Chief Constable of Manchester, supported this contention, as did Sir Charles Haughton Rafter, his counterpart in Birmingham.[68] They identified a general support for street bookies which was based greatly on an abhorrence of a class law, but which was entwined also with the feeling that was expressed by K. Wolfenden of Preston. He observed that on the whole, these 'lawbreakers' 'brought a lot of pleasure to people and not having much money they didn't lose much, also there was a spice of adventure in it as you could get caught for doing it'.[69] Indeed, in the village of Brigham, near to Workington, Mr J. Stephens remembered with relish the time when the local runner was chased across the countryside by the 'bobby' – 'you can imagine the excitement . . . rumours were flying about like chaff'.[70] Robert Roberts concurred with these sentiments. Holding a personal dislike of gambling and raised by a shopkeeping mother who was keen on self-improvement, he felt that runners were at the bottom of the social scale in working-class Salford – a view contrary to the opinions of many other working-class people. Still, he recognized that bookies themselves held an ambivalent social position.

> Through their known affluence bookmakers held positions of importance among us, though many among our upper classes treated them with reserve. We secretly enjoyed their picaresque calling, the feeling of suppressed excitement on big race days and the hope among youngsters of still another police raid; but their 'morals', flash suits and bedecked wives (*they* never wore shawls and clogs) usually put them beyond the pale of proper respectability.[71]

The sociologist Otto Newman recognized that the esteem of illegal bookmakers was enhanced by their 'ability to triumphantly defy the law', but at the same time, the backing for them was bolstered by what Davies termed their 'considerable economic power'. In particular, he proposed that they were able to adopt the position of a benevolent employer because they could 'dispense occasional work to the unemployed'.[72] He was correct in his assumption. Street bookies were engaged in an unlawful occupation and their success in resisting the authorities was ensured partly by a necessary reinvestment of some of their profits within their territory. As Robert Reid remembered, his father had a crippled arm – the result of an accident at his former job – and so he 'couldn't do normal work, and he had to rely on "Parish Relief" to exist'. This meagre sum was supplemented by the 30s a week that he earned by acting as a watcher for a bookie in Maryhill, while in the same district, Anna Campbell's grandfather received half that sum for collecting the lines from a lifter and taking them to the bookie.[73]

But it was not only those who were out of work who benefited from participation in illegal bookmaking. Samuel Watts pointed out that in Springburn, his bookmaker took in the close of his tenement and he paid the rents of the other tenants so as to ensure their co-operation; similarly, in Clapton Park, Alf Holdsworth recalled that the bookie was stationed 'in a nice little flat or room', and he remunerated the residents for his position; while in a mining area of Salford, James Cowie explained that 'for one period about a year one bookie paid my rent for the use of my back yard'.[74] Over the same time, this man worked underground in a mine for 7s 9d a shift, 'and for one spell of night work I stood out for the bookie for 5/– per day – this only lasted six weeks as the Salford Police made round-ups of all runners every six weeks'.[75]

If bookies were the generals in the war against a class law, then men like James Cowie were the foot soldiers. However, in any discussion of the significance of runners, it is important to be aware that this colloquial term has its limitations descriptively. Ron Barnes remembered that his father took bets in Poyser Street, Bethnal Green, and he noted that although 'they used to call the pitchman a bookie's runner', actually this name ought to have been applied to those 'who did the running from the pitchman to the bookie himself'.[76] From Birkenhead, Gerry Beck agreed with him – as did Arthur Rollason of Smethwick – while Mr S. Murphy noted that in some parts of Glasgow, it was usual for four people at least to be involved in a pitch: the 'employer banker'; the runner; the watcher; and the lifter, who was the taker of the bets.[77] Obviously, these numbers were reduced if the bookie was local and if he lifted the bets himself – as did Matt

O'Malley and Frankie Goodwin – but it is essential that these important observations are considered. Still, in the popular imagination, the runner was the person who was regarded as the lynchpin of illegal bookmaking and people believed that he or she was the one to whom cash bets were given.

In 1934, Isaac Foot claimed that if £400,000,000 were spent on productive consumption, then it would provide work for 8,000,000 people, but he maintained that because this sum was squandered on gambling, it 'finds occupation for less than 30,000 bookmakers and the hundreds of thousands of runners who illegally collect bets in the street'.[78] These latter figures were wild exaggerations, and more plausible estimates were given by a writer in *The Economist*. In 1936, he thought that there were about 66,000 persons 'directly dependent upon bookmaking', although this amount could be swollen by the inclusion of works' and other agents.[79] Fifteen years later, the Royal Commission increased this number to about 80,000, but whatever the true figure, most members of the working class rejected the specious theorizing of Isaac Foot and they viewed with disgust attempts to put bookies and runners out of work.[80] According to their thinking, the state was trying to deny these people their inalienable right to make a living in an acceptable manner, for as Mr L. Piper expressed it, 'the bookie was regarded, not as a law breaker, but more or less as a legitimate tradesman'.[81] Moreover, many of those who worked for street bookies were unemployable in any other way, as Ernest Kyle indicated.

> (Runners – a misnomer if ever I heard one!)
>
> The great majority, I would say, were victims of one or more physical disability – heart disease, tuberculosis, chronic bronchitis, game legs and what have you . . . and were therefore unfit for more regular types of occupation. I knew three, personally, in our street alone who died in their late twenties or early thirties. (Old women would insist it was from standing huddled in those cold draughty closes that had carried them off to an early grave.) Anyway, while in the fifties there was full employment, there was no proper provision regarding State Benefits for the disabled and long-term sick . . . There was a great deal of ill health in working-class areas like the Gorbals (most of my mates failed their National Service medicals) and there was, therefore, a plentiful supply of would-be runners longing for the opportunity to occupy their days and supplement their meagre incomes. The main attraction to becoming a runner was, purely and simply, necessity, or, if you like, bread for your children's mouths.[82]

In the bleaker inter-war years, this imperative to put bread in your children's mouths was even more pressing. Consequently, just as credit layers found their house and pub agents in an abundant supply of widows, ex-soldiers and the disabled, so too did pitch bookies tend to take their runners from a similar pool of people. However, probably because their job was in public, it was usual for these persons to be male, even though Anna Campbell mentioned that 'a woman called Deana Reader used to stand in the back close of a tenement in Hugo Street collecting lines'.[83] Certainly, many runners were victims of the Depression. Mrs Smith's father had worked as 'a multi-grinder for Maddocks in Manchester, and in 1933 he came out of work like everybody else', so he began taking bets in Ancoats; while F. Thompson observed that in Motherwell, most of the lifters were laid-off miners.[84] The same phenomenon was noted by Frank Harrison in Wolverhampton and by Paul Clavering in Sunderland, but of course, running on 'the side' was illegal in two senses, as Nicky Marshall remembered.[85] In 1930, his Glaswegian father was convicted for illegal betting, 'fined £2 then as he left the Court he was rearrested for Doing the Labour Exchange (the Means Test) out of two weeks' money and Sentenced to fourteen days' imprisonment'.[86]

During these hard times, religious differences mattered little to lifters: in the words of Mr A. Roseman, a Presbyterian, 'the man we worked for went to Lourdes in France every year for his holidays, but I did not mind, whether he was R. C., Coloured or Orange, as long as we got our wages'.[87] In most cases, these were quite high. Throughout the 1920s, 'Little' Dickie Jones was paid '50 bob a week' to be a 'tekker' in Birmingham, while another Brummie, Cyril Beesley, stressed that 'I got good wages, I got more than I should've got in a factory', as did John Bullivant's father.[88] In Sheffield, during the 1930s, he worked for 'Bob C. who paid Dad £5 per week and provided two Burton's suits a year'. Along with many runners, Mr Bullivant increased his earnings by holding on to bets which he thought would lose.[89] Of course, this action was risky and some runners came unstuck, striking bets that they could not afford to pay out, as Mrs G. Shaw recalled of her pitchman in Holloway.[90] Nevertheless, in general, most runners enjoyed the kind of standard of living that was described by Ron Barnes. His Bethnal Green father was 'out of work for a good while' and he seemed to have little interest in anything. Then he 'struck lucky': he secured a job as a runner.

> We were fairly well-off now, for Dad was working the pitch in Poyser Street then. I can remember at that time I had a summer suit bought me, as well as a navy blue one . . . But the thing was that

> these suits, shirts, socks were brand-new, in a shop, not on a stall down Cheshire Street.
>
> Oh yes, at that time we was well-off. Dad's pocket was full of bees and honey [money], as you might say if you were in a pub . . .
>
> I had a new three-wheeler bicycle bought for me, and a cowboy suit. We were certainly in the money then.[91]

Not all runners were on 'a standing wage'; some were paid commission, and in these cases, their earnings could be substantial. Bill Smith recollected that 'Dole money at the time 1930 + was 17/– for a single man and £1 6s a married man with 2/– for each child under fourteen years'. Compared to these sums, he guessed that in Gateshead, his local runner – a bachelor – received about £1 2s 6d a day, related to a commission of 1s 6d in the pound.[92] Of course, just as with the incomes of street bookies themselves, these figures reflect the top earnings of agents during the flat season, as T. Carse emphasized. In 1937, he lifted in Edinburgh, and 'I may get about £20 or more for a good week, good money in those days'; but during the winter 'things could be tough: less people betting on the Jumps and when the weather bad no wages, so a "Sub" from the boss till things improved'.[93] In fact, Ann Watt noted that at this time of year, her local runner 'went to the parish to collect his allowances', while he was helped out by her shopkeeper husband, a friend from childhood.[94]

Often, runners who were paid commission were men who owned their pitch and they chose the bookmaker to whom they would give their bets. Like Alfie Spittle in Wolverhampton, some of them had bought their site, but the majority of them had been independent bookies who had established the pitches themselves.[95] In the North East, Josephine Bolam recalled that Parker Vietch had been a miner who had suffered an accident to one of his arms while down the pit. With his compensation, he set himself up as a bookie, but 'either his punters were very lucky or his compensation was not adequate because it was not long before in Geordie parlance he was "cleened oot"'. Thereafter, he was employed by an official bookmaker as his representative, and out of his commission he paid for his own watchers.[96] Similarly, in Southwick, Mr Brown's father had been a shipyard worker before becoming a bookie. However, in the 1920s, a tipster on the *Sporting Man* had such a good run of winning selections that the punters backed his fancies in large numbers, and these losing results 'finished me Dad altogether'. Consequently, he began to take for an office-based layer in Sunderland, and as his son recalled, 'he was better off being a commission agent rather than being a bookie'.[97]

There were those who reversed this trend. 'Tot' Bagley was another man who was a former miner in the Wear Valley and at the age of twenty-eight he declared that 'he would not go down the pit again'. Instead, he became a runner for the local bookmaker, and after a while 'using his head for more than "keeping his ears apart" took an avid interest and decided having been left a small legacy from his father to start off on his own'. Soon, he had runners in the surrounding villages, as well as agents in the local factories, and his example was emulated by Tom Archibald in Lanarkshire.[98] Like so many other lifters, he had been incapacitated for work by an industrial injury, and so he began to take bets in Jewel Cottages. His commissioner was Dan Flynn – the big Glaswegian bookmaker and fixed-odds operator – but after some years

> my brother felt confident to break away and start on his own in the village, of course Mr Flynn hired a rival to Tom and he stood on the opposite corner, however there was no enmity between them and Tom through hiring 'runners' managed to increase his clientele to neighbouring villages . . . In the passage of time, my brother purchased the little grocer's shop in the village which, for a cover, he continued to sell goods but also accepted his lines, then moving on he had a phone installed (this was just before legalisation). Thus, he was well prepared when the betting laws were changed and he employed a fully fledged accountant as a 'settler'. Tom then went from strength to strength buying similar little shops in nearby villages and converting them into betting shops . . . Today my late brother has four big betting 'emporiums' in the city of Edinburgh . . . When I went into one recently and saw the banks of television sets relaying horse races, dog races etc., I couldn't help thinking back to the thirties when my brother stood outside a humble miners' row collecting bets in all weathers.[99]

Tom Archibald was exceptional, and his type became more so after the Second World War, when the movement of small-scale bookies into agency became marked.

In 1959, Wilf Sherman claimed to 'employ about 400 street bookmakers', making him the largest operator of pitches in the country.[100] His region of control was South Wales, which never had been noted for its independent bookies, but even in those areas in which they were common, they were facing stiff competition from big bookmaking concerns such as Sherman's. In Glasgow, by the early 1950s, Harry Miller was standing the bets from over one hundred pitches; while in the North East, Albert Donkin was employed by a credit layer who 'had about 40 Agents, 15 of whom operated in Sunderland and the others were situated in the coal-mining villages in the vicinity'.[101] Simply, these men were attracted into their agencies by a high rate of commission – 2s in the pound – and in the post-war spending boom, this percentage ensured them huge earnings. The Geordie settler recalled that he knew a couple of agents who cleared £70 a week, and it was this kind of guaranteed income which induced Jim Jordan to abandon his independence.[102]

> the Leith bookmakers formed their own Leith Bookmakers Protection Association and limits were applied and maintained until 1950 when a new bookmaker W. R. Harrower, formerly managing director of W. S. Murphy's Pools, began to take over the local bookmakers with an enticement of 50 per cent of all profits following all expenses paid plus £20 per week wages, net, and betting no limit with the exception of £1,000 per day per bet.[103]

However, for his punters, Jim Jordan remained the key figure, and as J. Forbes of Aberdeen noted, 'as for the local people and Licensed Bookies, most of them didn't even know about them'.[104] T. McGunigle agreed with him, pointing out that the town's runners were called the bookies, as was the case with 'Manny' Steel, Ned Cooper and the well-known Jim Forbes.[105] For thirty-eight years this man took on the corner of St Clements Street in the working-class area of Footdee, and to its people he was their bookmaker, whether or not he kept their bets or 'gave them away'. Moreover, he was a local man who was unfit for other work because of Parkinson's disease.[106] Similarly, many independent bookies were victims of some illness or injury. In Widnes, Jack Ashley wrote that 'our bookmaker' had a wooden leg, as had the Smethwick layer who was recalled by John Dolman; in her district of Walsall, Jeanne Burton stated that their bookie 'suffered with asthma, very badly'; while in Ashby, R. Wallis-Clarke noted that the man who took the bets had a club foot.[107]

Furthermore, these men shared another vital trait with the Aberdonian agent, Jim Forbes: they belonged to the areas in which they operated. More than anything else, it was this factor which ensured the faithfulness of their neighbours, as Mrs M. Harvey made clear:

> I still feel loyal to my bookie but I shouldn't think I will be giving away any displeasure to him as I expect he may be dead now. I'd hate to discredit him in any way as I told you before he was very well liked and respected; actually the name of my street was Maidstone Street Shoreditch East 2. Yes our bookie lived in my street . . .[108]

BOOKMAKERS: PUTTING SOMETHING BACK

Of course, neighbourhood bookmakers had to earn approbation – just as other residents did – but with that achieved, communal support for them was the stronger because they 'came out of the street'.[109] Two elements were essential in this process of acquiring a good reputation: a firm belief in the reliability of the bookie and an acknowledgement of his or her generosity. Mr J. Kelly stressed that between the punter and the layer, 'trust was the name of the game'.[110] Indeed, this quality was necessary in dealing with any kind of bookmaker, for while it was acceptable for punters 'to try and get one over the layer', it was a heinous sin for the latter 'to do' the client. That is not to say that no street bookmaker ever welched. James Cowie brought to mind one evening when a queue of punters awaited their winnings outside the bookie's yard. Instead of collecting their money, they found a notice which read, 'When the fields are white with daisies', a line from a old ballad which finished with the words, 'I'll return'.[111] Likewise, Walter Littlejohn recollected how he saw a gang of middle-aged men 'surround a stranger in the street one day and punch and kick him senseless'. Later, he found out that the man was an ex-bookmaker who had absconded with the Derby Day takings, and his mother told him that this was the first time that he had returned to the street in twenty years.[112]

Such memories are rare and while newspapers praised the probity of 'Honest Joe' – the runner – even those people who disliked illegal bookmakers acknowledged their trustworthiness.[113] This characteristic was highlighted by Teddy Dean, a Boltonian who had a bet with Bella Thomasson in 1945.

> I was in the merchant navy at the time, and I had to leave sudden the same night, I was away for two years and when I got back she said, I haven't seen you for a few weeks, where have you been, I told her it was two years and not a few weeks, I also told her I had a winning bet, she asked me did I know the day of the bet, which was easy because it was in my M. N. Discharge Book, she told her clerk which book to get from upstairs and the bet was there . . .[114]

Likewise, Lew Reeves observed of his bookie in Birmingham, 'every punter knew that his bet would be settled honestly, what he was due – he would get, "Old George" was never ever doubted safe as the Bank of England'.[115]

Obviously, independent bookmakers and bookie/agents had a vested interest in acquiring the reputation of 'straightness', as it was good for business. Clapson has pointed out that this observation applies equally to their small generosities, which he believed 'were an attempt to legitimise' their economic superiority, by minimizing tensions that might have existed between them and their punters.[116] It would be unwise to ignore this interpretation, and certainly, it cannot be denied that bookies and runners were the best customers in the pub, buying drinks all round, as S. H. Woodier mentioned of those in Salford.[117] This kind of bonhomie was essential in pleasing clients and in establishing the wealth of the giver, and as Trevor Newbold recalled, his father even organized outings for local people because 'it drawed punters'.[118] However, in the poorer neighbourhoods of industrial Britain, the generosity of many street bookies was neither little, nor was it based on self-interest.

In 1979, Peter Keenan wrote that 'every tenement had its bookmaker and our Scotty Adair was a great bloke'. He added that anybody with money worries ran to this Scotstoun layer, and the same could be said of some of his fellows in Warrington, as Charles Dearden recollected, or in Rotherham, as was mentioned by John Shaw.[119] Further south, in Birmingham, Mrs A. Dean stated that my Grandad 'must have given pounds to the poor; my uncle Fred Copson Queen Street, used to say "go and see old Chinn he'll help"'; similarly, Joe Gray declared that 'the working class of Glasgow treated the Bookies with respect because they would help people in need'; while William Later stressed that 'one bookie that was very generous with his money was Wally Wilson. he gave to *many* and helped them in *need* as he knew poverty as there was plenty in them days, he was brought up in a poor area of Bury'.[120] William Later made a vital point. Often, street bookmakers who were renowned for their consistent and unstinting open-handedness were men or women who had themselves experienced hard times.

This factor was highlighted by Les Kane. He praised Curly Howarth of Collyhurst for never forgetting his punters from the back streets – whence he came – and for 'giving thousands to many worthy causes', while he extolled the 'Foy Bros who will never be forgotten; they too ploughed a great deal of cash to build a Catholic Hospice which took all Terminal Cases irrespective of Denomination, a Godsend to Manchester inner-city area'.[121] Likewise, 'Little' Johnny Somerset was born of a poor family in Sheffield, and he 'had a bad fall as a child which left him with a deformed spine'. At the age of twelve, he was selling papers to support his parents 'but was eventually given a job boot repairing by the Cripples Aid'. By the 1920s, he was established as an illegal bookie and 'when he became well enough off he was very generous to charities and good causes', starting with the organization that had helped him in the past.[122] Mrs E. Heaton recalled that Alf Craven of Bingley was another man who was of this type. He had begun as a penny bookie, but as he prospered 'he used to take so many children off for the day to the seaside', as did Billy Newbold of Hick Street, Birmingham.[123]

In fact, children were favoured recipients of the generosity of illegal bookmakers, and Henry McQuade remembered that in Lawmoor Street, Glasgow,

> the Scotts were looked up to by the inhabitants of the district as they were good at helping people out, particularly the old age pensioners and it was not uncommon for them to supply coal and food to many of them and even paying the rents for some of them, they also used to give a penny to most of the children in the district on a Saturday and I have seen almost a hundred kids all queued up myself included to get the money, they also laid on a Xmas party for all his punters' children when the younger Scott dressed up as Santa and handed out presents and I was fortunate to have been at most of them, so all in all they were a compassionate family and had the respect of the whole community . . .[124]

Joe Savage had similar positive memories of Mr Jennings, his local bookmaker in Lower Broughton, while Peter Plunkett commented that in Craigneuk, everybody had a favourite bookie, depending upon how good they were to children, and whether or not they were 'stingy when the hat came round to bury somebody who had no insurance'.[125]

Still, it could be maintained that selfishness motivated all these examples of philanthropy, but it must be remembered that large numbers of working-class people were keen to bet, whether or not their layer put anything back into the community. Consequently, there was no need for many street bookies to be as giving as they were, and in these circumstances, the only reason for their helpful actions was an ingrained belief that they owed loyalty to their own people. Moreover, much of their assistance was given without the aim of attracting attention, as James Young made plain. He wrote that the Jenkinses were the main working-class bookies in his locality, and he mentioned that they often displayed real generosity, coming to the rescue when working people were threatened with a pauper's grave or the poor house. Pertinently, he added that they did so 'without any ceremony or ostentation'.[126] This telling point was highlighted by Mass Observation in its survey on gambling, when it included a newspaper description of the funeral of the Glaswegian bookmaker, Lawrie Ventners.

> I came upon the scene unexpectedly. I found the crowd so great, lining the whole length of the street on both sides six to eight deep, that special police had to take control. Every window, too, was crammed with spectators.
>
> I soon learned that this wasn't just a gathering of Lawrie's clients. It turned out to be the massed tribute of his friends, the humble folk of Garscube Road and the congested area around.
>
> Wedged in the mass, I heard people speak of Lawrie. It seems he was one man who could not say 'No' to any appeal of the heart. Unsolicited, men and women began to give me examples of his goodness.
>
> Many a family, threatened with eviction, had had their homes secured.
>
> Every week without fail a cripple received an envelope with enough in it to keep a roof over his head.
>
> When families were in difficulties, or there was some illness, food and dainties would arrive from some mysterious source.
>
> One venerable old woman put all this in a nutshell: 'Ye never needed to be stuck if Lawrie knew about it.'
>
> Yet Lawrie's good deeds were not done ostentatiously.
>
> Only little by little, over a long period of years, did it come to be known it was the bookie who was the good fairy.[127]

Even today, the memory of this good-hearted man is revered among some Glaswegians, but his funeral was not the only one which reflected the popularity of street bookies who remembered their roots.[128] Elsewhere in Glasgow, when 'Wee' Jimmy McLaughlin was buried, 'the street was lined with punters and police as well', while in Sheffield, the same scenes were witnessed at the death of Thomas Tait.[129]

During her lifetime, this kind of respect was accorded to Meg Queen, the sister of the well-known Tony. In her own right, she was looked on 'as a great friend of the people' and such titles were bestowed not only because her kind of bookmaker 'put it back into the street', but also because they did not take out too much.[130] In Smethwick, James Bromley noted that one bookie 'if he heard a neighbour was out of work with a large family and in dire straights would send around a parcel of foodstuff – but never give money saying it would only encourage the man to gamble with it'; and men like Matt O'Malley and my Grandad refused to take bets from punters whom they felt were losing too heavily.[131] Incidents like these could happen only if the bookie knew and was concerned for his or her customers, as was the case with Frank Gardner in Stockport. Mr Knowles brought to mind the occasion when one of this man's customers won just over £50 for a 2s accumulator. He recalled that the bookmaker told his client that he would never take another bet off him unless he gave his mother and father £5 each and bought himself a new suit and a new pair of shoes.[132]

Obviously, it was easier to have this kind of interest in the lives of punters if a bookie lived within the area in which he or she took bets. Nonetheless, men like Ernie Cashmore and Horace Foster may have moved into middle-class districts, but they continued to run their own pitches and to feel part of the surrounding communities. Indeed, into the 1960s, the latter was paying for Christmas parties for those of his punters who were pensioners.[133] As a consequence, both men remained local bookmakers and during the time of their illegal operations, they retained the active support of the people of their territories.

REPRESSION: BOOKIE SNATCHES AND BACKHANDERS

The bookies of Bidder Street, Liverpool, were also noted as belonging to their neighbourhood, so much so that the district was described by Michael Quinn as 'the police's nightmare'. He explained that officers 'had no chance of getting near any of the Bookies because the children's mothers and fathers would sound the alarm off by shouting busies', a cry which spread right round the street.[134] It is apparent that a similar situation existed in most poorer areas, and even in a smaller town like Northampton, Mrs Clark mentioned that 'every one that was about at the time used to keep an eye out' on behalf of bookies, while Mrs Morphew recalled similar communal support in Ipswich.[135] In these circumstances, the inter-war police were forced to adopt one of two main strategies to deal with illegal betting: open toleration or subterfuge.

The former response was suited best to small centres of population, as often these were places where the police were well known to the local bookies. For example, in Towcester, Jack C. was left alone because he was a drinking partner of the town's superintendent, who was a punter as well.[136] According to R. W. Jefferis, so too were the officers of Brislington, while the village policeman in Felinfoel was given a free bet because 'then he would not harass my cousin doing his runner's job'.[137] However, in many localities, the lack of interference with illegal bookmakers was not based on corruption; rather it was related to the attitude illustrated clearly by F. C. Moffatt. As a former detective chief superintendent of the Northumberland force, he stated that bookmaking 'was looked on very tolerantly by the police'. In his opinion, stern action was not taken unless there was a complaint by a member of the public, while the bookies 'looked on it as a natural part of life that they would be "knocked off" now and then'.[138]

This kind of policing was evident both in Portsmouth – as was recalled by Kenneth Batt, a former court clerk – and in Bristol.[139] In this West Country city, Mr H. Hawkes believed that officers 'usually turned a blind eye to the activity', letting the local bookie know when he was to be picked up; and Ernie Wheeler agreed with him.[140] His father was an agent who operated from his home in Bedminster, while he himself took outside a local factory.

> The police knew us all. Pub talk, neighbour talk, they knew just where to put their hands on yer, see. Which they did every so often. And when they come in, I can remember my father was in court, see 'cos they knew him, from boyhood days . . . but they had to do their duty, and they used to come in and say, 'Right, come with us.' So we used to give him the slips, see, otherwise, if you'd made a fuss, they would have searched the whole house, the police would come in there as well, see. So you just had the slips for evidence, see, and of course, they'd let you go after a certain time . . . So then they had the case and you were fined, and you'd go back as if nothing had happened. Then about a few months later, it was so and so's turn . . . see, and that was it unless you got a dissatisfied punter see.[141]

This evidence suggests that tolerant policing was easier where illegal betting was carried on 'hidden away' in homes, factories and pubs. By contrast, police attempts at repression and their use of deception were most common in those urban neighbourhoods in which open pitches were prevalent.

As early as 1902, Samuel Chisolm, Lord Provost of Glasgow, had observed that the 'police have to adopt disguises' to catch runners.[142] His comments were substantiated by John Moir of Hopehill Road, Maryhill. He recalled that his street had three lifters who each had three watchers. These men

> stood at vantage points, like the next corner, or in a back court, to look out for the police or the plainclothes men and they gave signals to the lifter to skip into a house until the all clear was given . . . somebody who lived in the close would keep their door open in case of an emergency. For this they received a couple of shillings each week. They also got a shilling for the extra washing of the close with the tramping of feet by the punters. The plainclothes policemen used to get up to disguises like putting on dungarees, and dirtying

> their faces to look like workmen, and come sauntering up the road. Of course policemen in those days were all about six feet which was tall for a man then, and they were of good build. The watchers would recognise them and there would be shouts of geroff-geroff which means get off for the lifter.[143]

Similarly, in Birmingham, Frank Southall's father would dress up scruffily for special duty to catch 'the illegal bookmaker's touts', while in the same city, Mrs A. M. Zebrzyski recalled the two policemen who caught a bookie because they were dressed as 'strange ladies'; and in the colliery village of Ryhope, Mr A. Burnett mentioned that 'sometimes the police would come up the street dressed as beggars, or clergymen just to catch em'.[144] In fact, as late as the 1950s, J. Abbott and other Lancashire officers had 'to take certain disguises to follow certain "runners" who were known to be very "active"'.[145]

As daughters of such men, both Mary Pearson and Irene Rowe remembered clearly their childhood fears of police raids and their concern that their fathers would be captured.[146] Contrarily, in Glasgow, James Crawford relished the tale of how he was shadowed by a plain-clothes officer, and he made it plain that he was delighted at the manner in which he outwitted his 'tail'.[147] Still, because of communal support and the system of lookouts, it was unusual for lifters or runners to be caught by surprise. Moreover, as Lew Warren recalled, some London bookies had an 'outside man that used to go round to Old Street nick to find out who was out to catch the bookies that week'. This person was praised as 'always right so he came to see all the bookies to tell us [and] we used to give him two or three pounds for the information'.[148] Faced with such severe difficulties impeding the successful implementation of the law, it is not surprising that many police officers gave up the fight to suppress street bookies. Instead, they came to mutually satisfactory arrangements with their 'foes', as A. W. Dance explained:

> I'm going back a few years too, to 1945 onwards when as you know the police nicked the runner and when he got nicked the first time it was a £5 fine, second £10 and so on that's when he would get a stand in . . . the copper would come and tell the Bookie his runner at a certain pitch was due to be nicked and it might be his third or fourth time so the bookie gave someone £5 to stand there and get nicked in his place. I should think the copper who tipped him off got the same. Well I did it on three occasions and this is what happened, the bookie gave me lots of old bets plus a handful of notes and silver to make it look real, well the first time I did it I

> didn't know what to expect, but a rag man with a push barrow came down the road calling out old rags and iron. When he got close to me he came over to me with a bet in his hand but when he came up to me he said are you standing here in place of Teddy B? I said yes then he said, Well I've got to nick you and you mustn't run away 'cos it's all fixed with Ted M. [the bookie].[149]

Of course, in addition to his wages, the bookie gave this West Ham man the amount of his fine.[150]

This procedure benefited bookmakers in three ways: first, it meant that they paid a lower penalty if their stand-in was a first offender; second, it ensured that their regular runner was protected, meaning that they did not have to lay him off for the worry that he would incur a high fine; and third, it did not interfere with business. On the part of the local police, the understanding was satisfactory because it kept up their arrest figures for a known pitch; it did not bring them into conflict with the community; and for those who accepted bribes, it added to their income. Finally, the 'dummy' or 'stooge' was happy because he had received a significant sum for his services, and if, like Fred Calvert, he was unemployed, then the extra income was even more welcome.[151]

Given these advantages, it is obvious why this system was widespread in areas where there were pitch bookies. Both Mr Morfitt and Jack Bullivant noted its ubiquity in Sheffield, as did Jack Brodie in Salford.[152] In this latter city, G. Percy mentioned that the 'stick up' was known as a 'joey' – although John W. named this person as a 'jockey' – and according to W. Flood and G. Steele, the procedure was as prevalent in Collyhurst and Longsight.[153] During the 1920s, in the twin cities of Manchester and Salford, the 'fee' for the 'service' was 'an odd half crown', but in Byker, Newcastle, R. Gallagher recalled that bookies gave a 'standing bet for the polis 2/6 on the first winner'.[154] However, although this form of bribery became commonplace in the inter-war years, it should not be presumed that it was absent before 1914, when senior police officers had been confident of quashing street betting.

In 1904, 'a very influential Deputation' met with Birmingham Watch Committee. It complained that 'there seemed to be an understanding' whereby the 'betting men' knew when they 'would be brought up and fined', and their insinuations are substantiated by the oral evidence of Fred Sutton.[155] At about the same time, in London, Monk noted that his detective inspector kept a bookmaker alerted to police activities, and that he received £3 a week for his information.[156] It is likely that it was cases such as this that led to the deployment of plain-clothes officers to deal with illegal betting, but by the 1930s, some of these men had been in their jobs so long that they had developed close relationships with outlawed bookmakers. In fact, as Edmund King mentioned, the problem of corruption was revealed fully in the infamous case of Sergeant Goddard; it was this exposure which ensured the rotation of duties in relation to street betting.[157]

Yet, if it is right to stress that 'back-handers' had been taken since before the First World War, it is as fair to comment that many policemen refused the offers of 'drinks'. As Hetty Bradbury explained, in Birmingham, her father would 'grease the coppers' hands' for two reasons: so he would know when he was to be raided; and to prevent the local uniformed officer from literally standing on his pitch and putting it out of business. However, she recalled that the system 'did not always work', for on one occasion, the taker was arrested by a plain-clothes man in disguise.[158] Similarly, as 'a young and innocent P.C.', George Fancourt was unaware of the arrangements between bookies and the 'decs', and when he arrested one of the former out of turn, it 'caused somewhat of a stir among the plain clothes regulars'.[159]

Yet, for those officers who eschewed bribery, there remained sound operational reasons why they were content to leave street bookies alone for most of the year, as Cliff French made clear. In the early 1950s, he was a sergeant in the East Ham sub-division, and he believed that:

> Ours was I feel in retrospect a somewhat 'gracious system'. Our method was to make one arrest each day, this may not sound like overwork but it must be remembered that in those days runners were not declared overnight and it was necessary for the punter to buy the mid-day paper for the names of the horses. This was not available till 12 noon and the first race might well be 2.30 p.m. We therefore had to wait until the runner had a few slips before arresting him and then came the problem of transport to the nearest station – mostly we travelled on public transport – either bus or underground train. This may seem strange in this day of cars by the million, but then over the three stations we had . . . a van – the Supt's car and a CID car and that was all!!
>
> . . . Of course it was often alleged that with one arrest a day that the plain clothes boys went around on a rota and the runner knew when he would arrive. This was not true – but I had a list of 45 pitches so you will see that to spread our effort 'fairly' over the 'mob' we had to keep some fairly meticulous records. Arriving back too soon at the same pitches would have caused howls of rage!![160]

Terry Nattrass was a policeman in Goldthorpe, South Yorkshire, and like Cliff French he remembered that raids 'were very docile affairs, very clinically carried out, with a minimum of fuss and inconvenience'. Furthermore, he emphasized that in the 1950s, betting was 'a fact of life' which was very much accepted by the local officers, and he added that some of the bookies were 'pillars of society, and certainly friends of the Police'.[161] This opinion was in marked contrast to that expressed at the turn of the century, but it was one that had considerable support after the Second World War. Indeed, the positive attitude of the police towards street bookmaking was epitomized by Terry Saunders's father, a former inspector who became an illegal bookie.[162] Finally, allied to this feeling that the law was wrong was the belief expressed by John Solway that 'many officers considered the use of Police time to chase bookmakers was wasting resources better used elsewhere'.[163]

Given such reasoning, it would be wrong to assume that there was a coherent and nationwide police policy towards illegal bookmaking. There was not. Instead, the control of the activity was dependent upon local custom and the attitudes of individuals. However, by the 1950s, in many places much of the 'greasing' was on the wane, even though some officers continued to avail themselves of bookies' favours. In Ancoats, Manchester, John Sands recalled that 'the police came round about every two weeks had a cup of tea and also had a "drop", about £1 each', while in Birmingham, my Dad brought to mind the first time he passed money to a bobby.[164]

> Well basically at that particular time I used to feel very embarrassed. I remember the first time I had to go across the road it was to T. and I think at that time it was about 1948–49 and by then we used to give them five shillings, and I'd gorra go across to the bus garage, the doors when they were open, and I would just go and Dad used to tell me to go and shake hands and the first time I did it I was about sixteen and I shook hands with a, I said, 'Oo, 'ello there constable, how are you?' and I shook hands and I, 'cause I always, Dad always made sure we must respect everybody, it was always Mister to anybody or Misses to anybody every time, it was respect to your elders, it was an absolute must with Dad it was, and I'd shake hands and the first time I did it was very very embarrassing.

The sums involved in this case were trifling, although until the later 1940s, Grandad continued to pay £2 a month to each of the two local detectives.[165] However, in the 1950s, there were serious police/bookmaker corruption scandals in Brighton and Leeds, while

Gilbert Kelland made it plain that large-scale bribery was a problem with certain officers in the Metropolitan force.[166] As a former Assistant Commissioner at New Scotland Yard, Kelland pointed out that these difficulties did much to lead to an amalgamation of smaller police forces.[167] At the same time, they quickened the pace towards the legalization of cash betting off-course.

8

BETTING SHOPS

REPRESSION: AN IMPOSSIBLE TASK

Dixon argued that after 1914, the anti-gambling movement lost its force as radical non-conformism declined and as the Labour Party adopted a neutral attitude towards the 'evil'.[1] There is much to justify this proposal, although it needs to include in its equation the acceptance by upper-class turfites of off-course betting, so long as it was via the tote. Still, it should be borne in mind that the NAGL did not lose its vigour suddenly and completely. It was not until 1927 that a similar organization was set up in Scotland, and throughout the inter-war years, both groups maintained a vehement antipathy towards bookmaking.[2] At the same time, newspapers continued to carry reports about the 'never ceasing war against illegal betting', and like one London magistrate, many people remained firm in the belief that bookies made a living at the expense of the poor, 'without working and are practically on the level of receivers and thieves'.[3] In the appeal court in Edinburgh, they were warned that there was no 'kind of prescriptive right' which meant that law-breakers would 'be let off with a fine and never to undergo any risk of imprisonment', and several of them suffered this fate; while some police forces seemed willing to use cinematograph film and 'secret agents' to stamp out their activities.[4]

Still, among most of those who had to enforce the Street Betting Act, there was a significant groundswell against its provisions. An increasing number of magistrates believed that it had set them an 'almost impossible task'; and in 1923, it was proclaimed officially that some policemen betted when they were not at work, while 'to nearly all the duty of hunting street bookmakers is distasteful – indeed, hateful'.[5] By 1932, like the Chief Constable of Birmingham, senior police officers were concerned that 'it is only in street betting that the public shows a decided antagonism to the police'.[6] The Royal Commission on Lotteries and Betting recognized these worries, and its report recommended the registration of bookmakers and the legalization of cash betting by post.[7] Nothing was done, but three years later, action was urged on the government by Salford Council.

As Wilf Murphy remembered, this was the city 'where it was an open boast that the local magistrates imposed more fines per session than any other court'.[8] Indeed, in 1933, it was declared that bookmakers there were 'gradually being fined out of business', the reporter noting that in nine months fifty backyard operators had paid a total of £4,826 in penalties.[9] This purge against them had followed well-publicized claims that local plain-clothes men accepted bribes from bookies. The charge had been laid by the vociferous anti-gambler Canon Peter Green, Rector of St Philip's Church, Salford, and four years after his allegations stunned the city, another furore arose when William Bowen complained of how the well-being of the community was imperilled by street betting and by the arrest of jockeys and not bookies.[10]

In response to his assertions, the Chief Constable, Major Godfrey, pointed out that in 1935, his force had made 414 arrests in relation to illegal bookmaking. By contrast, in Cardiff, which had a similar population as Salford, the corresponding figure was seventy-seven, and in Leeds, 'which includes almost twice as many citizens', only twenty-eight offenders were captured. In agreement with the majority view of the Royal Commission, Godfrey believed that ready-money betting needed to be legalized under strict supervision.[11] So did his watch committee, and in February 1936, it passed a resolution to this effect, sending it to the Home Office in the hope that an official initiative would follow.[12] This action received wide publicity, and in the ensuing debate, even the National Anti-Gambling League accepted the idea that postal cash betting should be made lawful.[13] However, hopes of progress were frustrated, for the government announced that 'there is no prospect of time being found in the near future for legislation to deal with this very controversial question'.[14] In these circumstances, cash bookmaking continued to develop free from the restraint of the law.[15]

BETTING ON INDIVIDUAL RACES

At the same time that Rafter was articulating fears that the 1906 Act harmed relations between the police and the working class, the Chief Constable of Greenock reported that a new form of betting had emerged. He called it 'betting on individual races', and the way it was carried on was explained by Mr Lafferty.[16]

> During the years of the Depression, my brother founded one of the earliest pitches of Shovel betting in the small village of New Stevenson, Lanarkshire.
>
> This consisted of pinning up a copy of the Noon Record or Chronicle which contained the Race meetings each day, with the aid of two or three helpers they would take the small bets from punters which would be noted on a writing pad with Carbonised Copies, the top copy would be placed in a pouch named a Clock Bag and then would be clocked at the approximate time of each race, then I would proceed to the Telephone Box at Holytown and wait for the Phone to ring, someone would then give me the winners of the race, and runner of the next race . . .
>
> I might add that we were able to pay out on the spot as we carried a Float (bank) of £100 from our Bookmaker.[17]

In effect, 'shovels' such as this heralded the era of betting shops.

Betting by telephone had been noted as early as 1907, when a barber in Bridgeton had been prosecuted for using his private line for this purpose.[18] However, its spread was restricted until public telephones became more commonplace, as they had by the 1930s. The growth of this facility meant that agents could communicate swiftly with their distant and credit-based employers, who in turn received a full racing service from the Extel. As Gerald Lucas explained, for punters, the appeal of this development was that 'we got paid instantly after each race'. Equally, the system was attractive to bookmakers because their turnover was increased significantly – for the shovel introduced race-by-race-betting outside the private sphere of clubs; and for agents, their larger take meant that their commission rose appreciably, as James Condron of Mossend made plain.[19]

These benefits ensured that shovel betting spread rapidly and soon it had taken a firm hold in Glasgow, where it manifested itself in back courts.[20] As elsewhere, it put at a disadvantage those street bookies who relied on newspapers for their results. Because they continued to take only during the dinner break and to pay out on an evening, they lost trade. Consequently, the popularity of the shovel facilitated the move of independent bookies into agency for those of their fellows who had ticker-tape machines and telephones.[21] Ron Hanley recalled a similar process in Grimsby, noting that 'passage' bookies like his father could not compete with the local club bookmakers who had no limits and who were offering race-by-race betting.[22]

Generally, in England, shovel betting on the Lanarkshire model was rare. Bill Gleghorn noted that in Easington Colliery, only one corner-end bookie operated in this way, although he 'always had a crowd of men standing around, maybe 60 or more'; while in Liverpool, G. Squires mentioned that in the 1950s, betting 'on the pad' was quite prevalent.[23] He added that the system 'required at least four operators, namely, the main runner, a second runner who is responsible for the money and the paying out, a person to take the sheet to the phone and ring it through and the fourth whose job it was to keep the phone free'. Of course, the number of employees meant that the expenses of the bookmaker rose, but this problem was more than offset by the gathering of punters who were attracted by the service they offered. However, as the former Liverpudlian policeman noted, the size of the betting crowd did lead to complaints – as did the monopolization of the telephone by the runners – and these factors militated against the ubiquity of outdoor shovel betting.[24] Instead, those English bookies who gave a race-by-race service followed the example that was set in Glasgow: they integrated it into existing patterns of illegal bookmaking.

ILLEGAL BETTING SHOPS

In Bolton, Mrs Rylance's husband was an agent for Albert Hampson and she recalled that during the 1930s, her husband was given a sufficient number of clock bags to cover each race. To cater for those punters who wished to bet throughout the afternoon, he covered in the backyard of his house and he put up a board on which he pinned the 'One o'Clock'. Still, he could not pay out until after racing – when his employer had opened up the bags and reckoned up the bets – but by the early 1940s, this problem was solved by the introduction of a ticker-tape machine and a telephone.[25] With either of these facilities, any betting yard could become an illegal betting shop, as Ken Green explained.

> These three bookies were *BOOKIES NOT AGENTS* – They had as their office a house in a street and entrance was by the back door. You could stay in there all afternoon and bet there was no Tannoy or how the betting was going – NO JACKSON WALL LIST – you just had the *Sporting Chronicle* pinned on the wall – the runners were ticked after he had phoned the big bookie in the town centre who he would have an account with he would shout time of race – no more bets and close a small shutter across the hole you put your

> bet thru he would allow average time of running the race and then ring up his bookie and get the result and write on the particular race in the *Chronicle* the result . . .[26]

Elsewhere in the town, Albert Hampson superseded these services. About 1944, as a partner with Bella Thomasson, he installed two loudspeakers in the yard of her shop. Here, up to 150 punters congregated to listen to a full racing service as it appeared on the ticker-tape. It was read out to them on a microphone, and as the Boltonian bookie stressed, 'in no time at all we didn't know where we were, it grew that quick'.[27] Since the 1850s, punters had shown a wish for race-by-race betting, and although this desire had been largely stifled, it did not disappear. From the 1930s, because of better communications, the demand became resurgent, and after 1945, an increasing number of bookmakers contributed to this movement by opening illegal betting shops. They were impelled in their actions by three factors: first, the increased profits that resulted from a higher turnover; second, the post-war spending boom; and third, the Royal Commission of 1949–51, the deliberations of which encouraged the conviction that the legalization of cash betting off-course was imminent.[28]

Barbara Gardiner remembered that in the late 1940s, illegal betting shops were everywhere in Newmarket, and she observed that because the town's economy was dependent upon racing, their owners were quite open about their purpose.[29] Similarly, in 1958, Redcar was described as a 'paradise for punters', while two years later it was revealed that there were between forty and fifty illegal betting shops in York, compared with thirty-five in Doncaster.[30] However, this phenomenon was not restricted to racing towns. G. Ritson recalled that in Keighley, '"Smokey Joe's" was up a flight of stairs adjacent to the Devonshire Arms'; in the mining district of Goldthorpe, T. E. Nattrass counted twenty-seven such premises; while nearby in South Kirkby, John Atkinson recollected two betting huts.[31] In fact, in many colliery areas, this was a common form of structure for illegal betting shops, as Joe Jordan and Hazel Horsley noted for Yorkshire and as Bert Jenkins observed of Stirlingshire.[32]

During the 1950s, there was a widespread assumption that 'so far as the betting habits of the nation go England is not one but two countries and the dividing line, broadly speaking, can be taken as the River Trent'.[33] North of this barrier, it was felt that betting shops were common, while south of the division, it was believed that street betting was in the ascendancy.[34] This was a massive simplification of betting patterns in England. As Mrs Murrell recollected, illegal betting shops were common in Brighton; newspapers reported that they were obvious in Coventry and Leamington; while Gilbert Kelland recalled that they were present in parts of London.[35]

Moreover, they were numerous in Birmingham, and my Dad explained how our family moved gradually and hesitatingly away from the established procedure of taking bets in the dinner-break.

> We still kept to the routine right up to I think about 1950, '51, '52 but it started to get to be that by then, especially of a Saturday, Dad had a very, very good business, he had a very good reputation which he built up all over the years, and of a Saturday he would have literally dozens of people round . . . so we used to employ a chap . . . to have very likely twenty pounds' worth of change, thirty pounds' worth of change in a day, and he used to be in this avenue which was about ten feet wide and it narrowed down to about six feet wide, but it was the length of the shop so that the customers could go up there and write the bets . . . and by then we were putting a box on the door and in the window we used to put the actual time of the race. So gradually, and then it got to be we was giving, then this was 19–, it was coming up to about 1952–53 . . . we was then giving the results because by then we got the ticker-tape in . . . and it was just about this era that then we were trying to give the service to the customer so what we used to do we used to have a little effort in the window and in it we'd have 'the next race is' and we'd put the time 2 o'clock, 2.15 and 2.30 . . . so that we'd take that box off and then we'd stamp each of the bets in that box for the 2.30 race.

By 1958, so many punters were congregating around the pitch that this position had become unsatisfactory and so Dad bought a nearby outdoor (off licence). He transformed it into a proper betting shop and this increased his turnover spectacularly, to £2,000 per week.[36]

Such figures were not unusual by this date, and they had encouraged bookmaking to be flooded with newcomers such as the Currigans and Rogers in Birmingham, the Williamses in Salford and Bill Gallie in Dumfries.[37] In particular, these kind of takings were regular in Glasgow, as Norman Miller made plain. He explained that the city's illegal betting-shop bookmakers paid for a racing service to be transmitted from the four local dog-tracks. The races took place of an evening, and the Glaswegian bookie stated:

> The business was such that you could have a stinkin' lousy, losin' Saturday and you weren't worried, because you knew you were guaranteed to get it back at night if you didn't get the last three

> favourites at Albion, White City and Carntyne. They used to go off about ten o'clock, the pubs used t' close round ten o'clock. Blazes, you couldn't move as they came in. Three doubles and a treble across the card. If you got one of them beat, you could guarantee to get all the afternoon's losses back . . . We had an agent who was taking two thousand pounds a night! An agent!

By 1961, Glasgow's Starting-Price Bookmakers' Association was paying £30,000 to the city's dog-track owners for their service, and Norman Miller estimated that this sum was raised from 300–400 illegal betting shops.[38] In fact, in 1959, the city was dubbed Britain's 'gamblingest' and it was seen as 'Scotland's Las Vegas'.[39] Moreover, its betting shops were spacious, comfortable and provided with up-to-date facilities. A reporter in the *Scotsman* described how each shop had a clerk who sat behind a grille-fronted counter – stamping bets with a time-clock instrument – as well as a 'chalker', a man who recorded the runners and prices on a blackboard. He received this information from the 'blower', a telephone which was 'hooked up' to Extel and which was placed on to a receiver. In turn, this was connected to the shop's loudspeakers, and in this way racing messages were 'blown' to both the bookie and his staff and to the punters.[40] Similar premises were reported in Dundee, Dunfermline and Irvine, while in Aberdeen, the largest of their type was run by Mac Davidson.[41]

As Ernest Kyle pointed out, these betting shops were pleasant and warm to be in during the winter, and they compared favourably to standing huddled together in a draughty close, or a wind- and rain-swept back court.[42] But there was a humorous reason why they were popular with some people. Norma Brodie explained that every so often, the police would raid an illegal betting shop in the Plantation district. Usually, people knew when this was going to happen, as the police station was just in the next street and everyone could see the Black Maria coming. However, if anyone was caught in the shop, they were arrested and fined ten shillings each. So that the bookie would not lose his customers, he would pay all the fines '*and* give the offenders ten shillings each for their trouble'. In the Glaswegian woman's opinion, 'this was a bit of a joke because it was well known that some of the lads who hung about the street corners and were down on their luck with no job or money, would, when they spied the police, come running into the betting shop and get arrested with the betting customers as they knew that after a few hours they would have ten shillings in their pockets courtesy of the bookie'.[43]

As this evidence indicates, during the 1950s, the police response to outlawed betting shops was as patchy, inconsistent and irregular as it had been with regard to street betting. Certainly, there was a widespread belief that legalization was near, and most officers 'eased up' towards illegal betting so long as it did not cause a nuisance. But this attitude did not impress those who were sticklers for the law, and Dad was raided as late as 1958, just three years before betting shops became lawful.

> We then started doing our business, this was about 2, 2.30, Uncle Bill had then come into the office and next bloody thing we knew, we could see what was happening because one or two other bookmakers had been raided, there was two inspectors, an Inspector P. and Inspector F., a sergeant and four constables and all of a sudden they was all on the premises. Next thing Dad was across the road, they claimed they didn't know Ron [Dad's brother] had died. I sez, 'Well, my God, you people take the cake!' I sez, 'Me brother's just died and you raiding us!' The sergeant he was, he was terribly upset, but Inspector P., he in my opinion was a bastard, and to this day I think he was, in my opinion he and Inspector F. both knew Ron had died because it was common knowledge throughout the whole of the Brook [Sparkbrook] but it made no difference to him especially Inspector P., and I believe he finished up as a superintendent with his moral standards. Because no other person, because the integrity of people in them days, would not have raided us that day, they'd have left it till the following week. Well, Dad come on the step with everything that was happening. He was in a terrible state.[44]

My Dad and my Uncle Wal were fined £75 each for contravening the Betting Houses Act of 1853, while because of his age, the police did not charge my Great-Uncle Bill.

In parts of Britain, the police were influential in holding the line against the emergence of illegal betting shops. For example, in Filey, their existence was not tolerated, although in nearby Scarborough they were common; a similar contradiction was manifested between Cardiff and Newport; in Sheffield, in 1960, Jim Stock was taking bets on the street between twelve o'clock and two o'clock, yet in Doncaster, his fellows had shops that were open all day; while in Manchester, John Sands recalled that this dichotomy was evident even between the various police divisions of the city.[45] These absurdities increased the pressure for the legalization of cash betting off-course, a measure which had been recommended by the Royal Commission of 1949–51.[46] In the following years, many commentators seriously considered the ideas of lawful betting by post or on the street.[47] Such notions were becoming redundant and unrealistic. Across Britain, bookies and punters had taken away from the authorities the decision as to the manner of off-course betting when it was to be made legal. What the authorities could do was declare the date when betting shops should become lawful and through legalization impose rigorous controls on how such shops and their bookies should be controlled. This was what they did.

9

LEGALIZATION AND COMMERCIALIZATION

John Bourne has argued that during the First World War, British soldiers manifested remarkable staying power in the face of terrible conditions and a long-drawn-out conflict. Intuitively, he has emphasized that this characteristic was so marked because endurance was the working-class forte.[1] He was right; and working-class doggedness and resilience was shown just as fully in the long battle against the class-biased betting acts of 1853 and 1906. The outlawing of cash betting away from the racecourse was made inoperable by the persistence of working-class punters and bookies in flouting such laws and by their determination to claim the same rights as those enjoyed by the rich. In the end, the authorities had to acknowledge both their failure in suppressing cash betting off-course and the class bias inherent in betting legislation, and on 1 May 1961 licensed betting shops opened for the first time.

Their opening had been anticipated since the Royal Commission of 1949–51. In giving evidence to that body, both the Police Federation for England and Wales, representing rank and file officers, and the Chief Constables of England and Wales had declared their opposition to the existing legislation because it was difficult to enforce and because it brought the forces of law and order into conflict with an otherwise law-abiding population. Both organizations also proposed that cash betting off-course should be legalized by way of betting offices or shops.[2] This recommendation was taken up in the report of the Royal Commission. Interestingly, some illegal bookies were against the introduction of legal betting shops. Concerned at the cost of running a shop, they preferred instead to have their street-betting activities made lawful.

Although redoubtable opponents of betting like Rowntree

continued to inveigh against the activity as a national evil, the pragmatists in favour of legalization were joined by an increasing number of politicians who were abandoning their support for outdated paternalistic attitudes and who recognized that the betting laws, especially, were infused with class discrimination.[3] By 1956, it was apparent that sooner or later some form of cash betting off-course would be made legal. That understanding led Lord Astor to initiate a debate in the House of Lords. He welcomed the government's intention to introduce a comprehensive bill to deal with betting and then went on to push for a tote monopoly and launch a vitriolic attack upon bookmakers (see Chapter 6, 'Bookmakers and Politics'). Astor also identified what he saw as 'a sinister alliance between the Churches Committee on Betting and bookmakers to oppose betting shops and he hoped the Church as represented in the House would not allow itself to play the bookies' game. The betting office was easy to control. In Eire it finished the street and factory bookie.'[4]

In winding up the debate, Lord Mancroft, undersecretary at the Home Office, explained that the Government was satisfied that the best course of action was to legalize betting shops under a comprehensive system of control and regulation. However, he too made plain his prejudices against bookies, stating that although the occupation of bookmaking included a large number of decent, honourable men, there were an increasing number of crooks and thugs. In his opinion, 'of late the government had been a little out of love with bookmakers as a class', while he declared that 'the word "bookie" is strictly Non U'.[5]

The following year, George Wigg introduced an unsuccessful bill to legalize off-course betting. The same fate befell Sir Eric Berrington's similar bill in 1958. By this date, the large credit bookmakers and racecourse layers had organized themselves so as to prevent the imposition of a tote monopoly, an idea which was supported strongly by some members of the Jockey Club, who had been lobbying Conservative MPs. In April 1956 a deputation of bookies led by Alfie Cope had met the stewards of the Jockey Club, following which a Betting Bill Committee was formed to represent all parties interested in racing – including bookmakers. Led by Archie Scott, the National Bookmakers' Protection Association itself also played a key role. Educated at Eton and Cambridge, Scott turned away from a career in the City to embrace a life on the turf. After starting out as a clerk on the course, he joined Dick Fry in their own business. During the Second World War, Scott was commissioned in the Green Howards, serving with distinction in France in 1940 as part of the rearguard protecting the British withdrawal to Dunkirk, and later in the western desert. Regarded as 'a born leader of men', after the war he carried on as a racecourse bookmaker under his own name, but 'it is not unfair to say that in the post war years he devoted more time to committee work on behalf of the bookmaking fraternity than to his own business'.[6]

With his background, upbringing, charm, high reputation and negotiating skills, Scott was vital to the bookmakers. From 1957, he was chairman of the National Bookmakers and Associated Bodies Joint Protection Association and he became the chairman of the organization's 'Inner Cabinet'. As such, he was the bookies' chief spokesman in all negotiations with the Home Office, the Jockey Club, the National Hunt Committee and other organizations concerned with the Betting and Gaming Act of 1960. Indeed, many of those in the game feel strongly that Scott was almost solely responsible for averting a tote monopoly. Under his direction, the Bookmakers' Protection Association, itself made up of various regional associations, joined with the Turf Guardian Society to form the National Association of Bookmakers – although the National Sporting League remained outside this new body. Set up in 1902, the NSL provided members with lists of defaulters and adjudicated on betting disputes.

William Hill was the biggest bookie in the land. He took over the firm of Alfred Cope, which in turn had bought out Archie Scott's business in 1961. Few men were as well qualified to highlight the contribution of Scott as Hill, who paid this tribute to his friend and colleague after his death in 1965.

> To say that Archie Scott will be missed is trite and obvious. To assess how much he will be missed is impossible. What can be said with great certainty is that bookmakers everywhere owe him a great debt of gratitude, and the good things he did upon their behalf will live long after him.
>
> It might even be true that had Archie never lived at all, there might now have been no bookmakers, for without him to plead their cause we might already have had a Tote monopoly imposed upon us to the detriment not only of bookmakers, but the whole racing public.[7]

Hill himself presented an intriguing figure in the lead up to legalization. Hugely wealthy and a noted owner of race-horses, he held strong left-wing views and for many years he was friends with Harry Pollit, the famed communist. Raised in Small Heath, Birmingham, Hill was the third of thirteen children. His father was a highly skilled coach painter and in some regards Hill's opinions on cash betting came close to those of the working-class elite, who regarded the activity with disdain. On 23 March 1956 Hill appeared on a BBC Television discussion called *At Home and Abroad*. He made it plain that although the present betting laws were chaotic and unfair, he forcefully opposed the legalization of betting shops because 'I can visualize lots of people crowding inside and out during racing hours, and I don't think it would be a very nice scene to see at every street corner – a betting shop with all these people hanging about'. Hill went on to say that he had seen many betting shops and 'these "types" hanging about'. Believing that betting shops would lead to irresponsible betting by those on limited incomes, he favoured the legalization of street betting and of cash betting by post.[8]

Hill's position drew unfavourable criticism from many bookies, many of whom felt that he was against betting shops not because of his high principles but because he was scared that they would draw trade away from credit businesses such as his own. In particular, betting-shop bookies and their punters were angered by his comments. Overall, illegal bookies – whether operating on the street or in betting shops – were not well represented in the discussions about the proposed legalization. For all the important work carried on by the National Bookmakers' Protection Association, that body was dominated by racecourse layers and credit bookmakers and it pushed forward the outlook and anxieties of these specific groups.

Despite the deep concerns held by many about legalization, it was obvious that the law would have to be changed. There was growing prosperity and working-class people were increasingly unwilling to continue as second-class citizens. At the end of 1957, the legalization of betting was proposed in the Queen's Speech to Parliament. Soon after, the turning of the tide against the anti-gambling lobby was marked publicly on 23 August 1958 when the BBC began broadcasting the starting prices with its racing news, something it had steadfastly avoided until then – although it had given racing commentaries and results. At last, a year later, the Conservative Government introduced a bill under the aegis of the Home Secretary, R. A. B. Butler. It sought to reconcile the varying interests of the betting and racecourse lobbies, and to keep betting within 'reasonable bounds'.

During the debates on the bill, the Conservative MP William Deedes gave voice to the realization that the betting laws were outdated.

> Much of our former social legislation, now being repaired, reflects a state of mind which saw an obligation to protect the working class from its own excesses and follies. The law that we are replacing is

> typical of that. If one has a telephone one can be entrusted to bet to the limit, if one has to rely on a pub one cannot do so.[9]

On the Labour side, there was a confused response. Some MPs held fast to the belief that betting was against the interests of the working class. Others strongly supported legalization as an egalitarian measure. Among them was Bob Mellish, MP for Bermondsey, who pushed vigorously for the legalization of the existing pattern of bookmakers and runners because it was an integral part of life in working-class neighbourhoods. Mellish believed that agents and runners should become the legal employees of bookies and that the street and public house should be recognized as places both for the taking and paying-out of bets. He also feared that if betting shops were made lawful then large bookmaking businesses would come in and take over cash betting off-course. Indeed, this had already happened in Dublin, where the Kilmartin family had come to own over half of the city's betting shops following legalization in the Irish Free State in 1926.[10]

After overcoming opposition, the bill was enacted, but it did not bring about the wholehearted freeing-up of cash betting off-course that anti-gamblers might have feared. The overarching aim of the government was to restore credibility to the law and to control cash betting off-course without encouraging it. As Butler himself stated, betting was an indulgence and the government did not want do 'anything in the final form of the Statute as it emerges that might encourage continuous betting'.[11] Legalizing street betting would not accomplish these objectives; legalizing betting shops would. At the same time, the legalization of betting shops recognized the reality that illegal betting shops proliferated across much of England, Scotland and Wales. In these circumstances, Mellish's understandable support of street betting was unviable, simply because street betting was already in decline due to competition from betting shops.

The Betting and Gaming Act of 1960 made it lawful to bet with a bookmaker's agent who might be a roundsman, such as a milkman, or with a runner in a workplace, and it also legalized betting at licensed betting offices. Importantly, the Street Betting Act of 1906 remained in force, so that cash betting on the street or in a public house continued to be illegal. Crucially, the fines for street betting were increased substantially: £100 for a first offence; no more than £200 for a second contravention of the law; and for third and subsequent offences, imprisonment for no more than three months, or a fine not exceeding £200, or both. To operate a betting shop a bookmaker had to have a bookmaker's permit and a betting-office licence granted by magistrates in England or the licensing courts in

Scotland. For one year after the passing of the Act, preference in granting betting-office licences was to be given to those persons who carried on as a bookmaker during the whole or substantial part of the year ending 2 November 1959. In this way, illegal bookies were made legal and the existing framework of pitches was sustained.[12]

As part of the conviction that betting itself should not be encouraged and that continuous betting should be made as difficult as possible, the Act made it an offence to take bets from anyone under eighteen and to open on Good Friday, Christmas Day, Sundays and after 6.30 of an evening; while it prescribed restrictions on the exhibiting of written matter or signs other than the betting-office licence and lawful notices. The regulations did allow bookmakers to provide in their betting shops the *Sporting Life*, the *Sporting Chronicle* and sporting pages from daily newspapers, as well as a list of runners. The only sound broadcast allowed was 'one which relates solely to the events on which betting transactions are taking place, i. e. the Blower. This restriction prohibits the use of television or wireless sets brought on to the premises by customers'. It also prevented bookmakers from providing televisions and wirelesses.[13] Police officers had the right to enter betting shops to ascertain whether the rules of conduct were complied with.

Stringent penalties were brought in to enforce these regulations. On summary conviction, those acting as bookmakers in unlicensed premises were to be fined £100 for a first offence. For a second or subsequent offence they could be imprisoned for up to three months or fined £200 – or they could incur both penalties. Upon conviction on indictment the fine was to be no more than £500 and for a second or subsequent contravention the offender faced imprisonment for up to one year and a fine of no more than £700, or both. The same draconian measures applied to those who operated without a bookmaker's permit. If bookmakers broke the rules of conduct for betting offices they could be fined up to £100, while the unlawful advertising of a licensed betting office carried the penalty of a £50 fine for a summary conviction. For second and subsequent offences the bookmaker could be imprisoned for no more than two months or fined no more than £100, or both. Upon conviction on indictment the penalties were even harsher: a fine not exceeding £300, or for a second or subsequent offence imprisonment for not more than six months, or a fine of £500, or both. The taking of bets from a young person incurred the same heavy sentences. There were also severe penalties for not keeping a register of runners, for not furnishing runners with written authority, and for employing runners under twenty-one years of age.[14] Coupled with the cumbersome procedure laid down by the

Act for controlling runners, such measures militated against bookmakers continuing with the system of runners. Moreover, the turnover from individual betting shops was such that runners became unnecessary.

An acclaimed and insightful writer on working-class life, Sid Chaplin lamented both the loss of runners and the sanitizing effect of legalization which meant that gambling 'has become dull and respectable and regulated. We have lost the fire in the belly and turned to the praying wheel of the acquisitive society.' He praised the old way of betting and gambling that he had grown up with in Silsdon in the North East of England.

> In those days gambling was man to man. You grew up with it. From betting marbles, fag-cards or conkers you naturally progressed to the bookie's runner, who welcomed you with open arms. Everbody, including the village slop, knew and respected him. Self-effacing, a walking ready-reckoner, as versed in diplomacy as sleight-of-hand, he was as essential as vicar, doctor, and schoolmaster. He was also honest. You could sharpen his knife on his probity. Where is he know? Lurking behind plastic and beaverboard with the shadow of a wire grill on his face? Not if I know him. He is retired, or the punter who places his bet then walks quickly out into the streets that are always empty and bars which are deadly dull. He cannot resist the old lurch in passing an ex-customer. Habit dies hard . . .
>
> Slipping a piece of paper into the runner's hand you had at least contact with the last link in a vast but human conspiracy; and you broke a law which didn't really count. Now you stand in a queue and get a ticket. Old Jack, the village runner, never forgot your face or your bet, and passed your winnings as smoothly as he had palmed the slip.[15]

For all such misgivings at the passing of a vital part of working-class street life that itself was dying, legalization was broadly welcomed. Yet it did cause some difficulties for the former illegal bookies. Large numbers had to buy or rent new premises and make them fit for their purposes. This led to higher overheads with regard to rents, rates, heating and such like. Despite the outlay, the new betting shops were not attractive. In early May 1961, just a few days after legalization, a reporter from the *Post*, a West London local newspaper, visited a number of betting shops. They were described as looking like small austere post offices, 'complete with bleak wooden shelves and partitions'. The atmosphere was also like that of a post office: 'You simply write your selections on a piece of paper and pass them – and your money – across the desk and behind the grille.' The reporter emphasized the lack of televisions and wirelesses and the fact that there must be no loitering.[16]

The strict trading conditions attached to legalization actually pushed many bookmakers backwards in providing for their punters. My Dad recollected that

> legalization really meant that the first thing they did was that we had to stop the TV. The next big thing was that you closed at six-thirty which was a blessing in one guise but unfortunately it became a drudge in another because you lost your dog turnover . . . the *Sporting Buff* was for dogs, as long as you'd got your *Sporting Buff* you had your customers coming in. They'd come in collect their winnings at six, six-thirty, they then put a bet on, smashing little bet for the dogs so you had two bites of the cherry and we used to close then at quarter to eight in the week and eight o'clock on a Saturday . . . By nineteen fifty-seven, fifty-eight, you was also taking a fortune on night racing you see and you was still taking on the dogs but of course you didn't take as much on the dogs if the night racing was on. But we was open for it then but when legalization come we wasn't open.
>
> Yes the basic of it was that first of all what we tried to do was punters wanted to stay on the premises and it was okay when legalization come when there was no races, no night-racing, but when the night-racing come on it got very, very difficult because punters wanted to stop on and it was a big temptation. We did do it at times where we'd let them stay on for the first race six-thirty and perhaps to quarter to seven, seven o'clock but it was very, very difficult. But what we used to do was let a few stay on of the regular customers because you couldn't turn them out but as time went on it got more difficult 'cos you was scared to death that you're breaking the law and you was worried about your licence but of course it was a big temptation at that time.[17]

Notwithstanding these problems, betting shops boomed. By 1 June 1962, a year after legalization, 13,340 betting-office licences had been issued in England, Scotland and Wales; this was equivalent to 2.6 betting shops per 10,000 of the population. In Wales the density was highest at 4.71, while it was lowest in England at 2.37. Scotland's density was 3.44. However, these global figures did mask significant differences between working-class and middle-class areas. In 1963 Henry Paling and John A. Glendenning carried out a detailed study of off-track betting in England to ascertain whether legalization was a pattern that could be followed by New York City. They showed that within London there were 7.3 betting shops per 10,000 of population in the borough of Stepney. In a number of other mostly working-class boroughs, from Lambeth to Bethnal Green, the figure ranged from 3.1 to 5.2. By contrast, in more middle-class boroughs, the density was no higher than 2.8 in Hampstead and was as low as 1.4 in Chelsea. Outside London it was clear that betting shops were most likely to be found in industrial, mining or railway areas – districts dominated by the working class.[18]

In the first flush of legalization it was as if 'everyone was jumping on the bandwagon' because 'they thought bookmaking was an easy option', and as Paley and Glendenning's report showed there was a noticeable 'tendency of landlords to favor renting premises to betting shop proprietors' because they were prepared to pay higher rents.[19] The number of illegal betting shops had, in fact, begun to increase in the 1950s, stimulated by the belief that legalization was imminent as well as by rising living standards. My Dad recalled how our family's illegal betting shop on the corner of Queen Street and Alfred Street, Sparkbrook, was operating within a shrinking territory by the early 1960s. In the late 1940s, the other main bookies locally were: Chambers on the corner of Highgate Road and Queen Street; Wal Bartlett, just up from Chambers; Wilson's in Mole Street; and Jocky Powell on the Stoney Lane. Within a decade their numbers had been swelled by Willarks, Harry Clarke and Harry Wiliams, in Brunswick Road and Dennis Road; Albert Whittaker, a former postman, at the bottom of Brighton Road; Griffiths in Oldfield Road; the Bates brothers taking bets at their hairdresser's shop at the top of the Ladypool Road; and Collett on the Stoney Lane.[20]

This explosion in the number of bookmakers and betting shops caused established bookies to react in two ways. First, they could object to the granting of a licence, as the law allowed. Any citizen was entitled to object to the granting of a betting-office licence, and clergymen, shopkeepers, civic organizations and others did so – sometimes successfully. By December 1962, 13 per cent of betting-office licences had been refused, but the majority of these were due to the objections of bookies keen on protecting their pitches and turnover and who were following a standard procedure.[21] The second way in which established bookmakers reacted to competition was to buy out their rivals. This is what my Dad did.

> Collett had sold to Jimmy Jennings that's right. Well then I says 'Well basically dad we've got to you know try to do something about it'. Well at this particular time Griffiths sold his pitch to a

> chap called Cash, Ernie Cashmore. His *nom-de-plume* used to be 'When racing is the game Cash is the name'. Now it turned out to be at this time there was a manager up there and that manager betted with us something unbelievable and I mean the bets he had with us was phenomenal. Well at this time you see I'd let word known that if anybody was interested in selling at a pitch, because I could see that we was going to be under pressure with all these betting shops round. It was only our reputation, because they was all around us now we'd had that many shops opened up by nineteen say sixty-one it was just unbelievable and I was on the (B.P.A.) committee and on legalization we thought we'd get some of them closed down but no way it turned out to be that everybody who'd got a pitch was granted a licence . . . and of course it was about this time that I'd also started looking about myself to think we've got to start opening other pitches ourselves. Well anyway it came about that Ernie Cashmore was making no money from this pitch . . . I had rang them to say 'Well if there's any time you do wish to sell your pitch I'd be interested' so that was the first pitch I bought was Ernie Cashmore's pitch.

Dad paid £2,000 for this pitch in Oldfield Road, just a few hundred yards from our pitch on the corners of Queen Street and Alfred Street. Hooking it up with the blower service via the telephone allowed Dad to have the same facilities for race-by-race commentaries as at his main pitch.[22]

The belief that newcomers gained most from legalization was a strongly held one. With an Irish mother and a Jewish father, Ali Harris was a third-generation bookie. His grandfather had started taking bets on the street in Acton Park in the East End of London in the 1880s, while his father carried on the street-betting game until after the First World War – by which time he had moved on to the racecourse. With the coming of legalization, Harris, by now a leading racecourse bookie himself, realized that betting shops would be 'terrific' and he tried to get a local pitch – to no avail. In his opinion, 'it was people from the outside who weren't bookmakers at all came in and got the fruits of it all. When they got their little bit out of it and got quite a bit out of it they sold to Ladbrokes, Hill's and all the various firms. So actually they get the monopoly and they get a bigger monopoly because they would try and buy every shop there is. There's the small man – nothing.'[23]

In the early stages of legalization, the big credit bookmakers mostly shied away from buying betting shops. William Hill, especially, refused steadfastly to become an owner of betting shops. For many years

Howard Hodgson was a distinguished secretary of the National Association of Bookmakers and he knew well the chief figures in the world of bookmaking. He was clear that because of Hill's 'social and political views (certainly not because he may have had any doubts that such a move would have proved highly successful commercially), he declined to have anything whatever to do with the project' of developing a chain betting shops – as his fortune would have allowed him.[24] Interviewed by Paley and Glendenning shortly after legalization, Hill continued to maintain that betting shops enticed working people to bet too much.

> This is what you've got to remember when you talk about a betting shop. People have gone into a betting shop for the first time. They've seen a blackboard. They've seen the runners. They've seen the fluctuations in the betting. Then up comes the winner and the price et cetera. Then they can play the next race.
>
> They have never seen that before in their life and this is a new toy to them, and this will probably last. Previously they might have been encouraged by fancy to bet just spasmodically, but then they wouldn't bother again for months. So they might have been betting just big races. But now they go and see the actual fluctuations on the board. They must like it and they hear it and they get the atmosphere of excitement and the payoff quick.[25]

As it had been before legalization, William Hill's operation – run by himself and Lionel Barber – was the biggest bookmaking firm in England, if not the world. In 1964, John Morgan of the *New Statesman* was staggered at the scope of the firm's operations, which were based at 'the biggest gambling factory in history'. This was Hill House, an eight-storey building off St George's Circus, London. In the basement was an I.C.T. computer costing £150,000 which 'flicks out the punters' bills; it also, with a machine's indifference, rejects the cards of gamblers who have exceeded their limits'. A total of 1,500 men and women worked in the vast enterprise, answering phones, chalking up the odds on blackboards, settling up and much more besides. The incoming bets were handled in one of three sections: trade; large credit customers; and small credit customers.[26] Thence they were looked after by settlers who were alert to any bet that might become a liability.

It was the importance of the trade accounts that led small bookmakers to regard Hill's arguments as specious. Many of those trade clients were betting-shop bookies who laid off with Hill's bets that were too large for them to handle. Indeed, since legalization the turnover in the company's trade department had multiplied fourfold. Over the period 1960–1, weekly turnover had ranged between £75,000 and £390,000. Two years later, takings had increased substantially to between £250,000 and £300,000 a week. These latter figures were all the more remarkable because they covered a period when there was no horse-racing for twelve weeks as a result of a bitterly cold winter which had frozen the snow that had fallen.[27] William Hill may have been against betting shops and paraded lofty morals to justify his opposition, but much of his firm's profits was dependent upon such places. Moreover, it was fanciful thinking on Hill's part to suggest that most punters had betted irregularly before legalization. They had not. Finally, he ignored the reality that before 1961 illegal betting shops had come to dominate betting in much of Britain.

Whatever the case, large concerns soon began to move into cash betting. By 1963, The Hurst Park Syndicate had emerged as a leading chain of betting shops. It was set up in 1961 by Sam Burns, a former employee of Hill's, and the ex-boxer Terry Downes. One of its directors was John T. Chenery, a solicitor who had also worked for Hill's. He made the point that although trade accounts with credit bookmakers had grown, 'the growth in betting shop business was in excess of what Hill's layoff figures suggested'. Since legalization, increased turnover had allowed betting-shop bookies to accumulate more reserves and thus stand bigger risks. This reality was made plain by another leading chain, Mark Lane Turf Accountants Limited, which had twenty betting shops in the West End of London. In the first year of legalization (1961), the firm's pre-tax profits rose from £18,930 to £30,072, despite investment in betting shops.[28]

Obstinately, William Hill refused to be drawn into buying betting shops until the later 1960s. But he was cajoled and pushed by Bill Balshaw, who ran the Glasgow office and later became chairman of Hill's between 1967 and 1972. Finally, Hill gave way and bought out Jack Swift's business when Swift retired. Following legalization, Swift had quickly moved into betting shops, believing that 'there is undoubtedly a number of people betting today who never had a bet before the shops made it easy for them'. While his credit business had dropped by around 10 to 15 per cent since legalization, because of cash betting Swift's overall trade had increased vastly.[29] Ostensibly purchasing a credit business, Hill's also made a decisive shift into betting shops by taking over Swift's. Soon after, Hill's bought out the Hurst Park Syndicate, which had expanded to a total of ninety shops. In 1972, a year after William Hill's death, his company was taken over by Sears Holdings. By then, Hill's had more than 500 shops.

A number of other credit bookmakers saw as great an increase in their ownership of betting shops. By 1962, Coral's had twenty-three shops and over the next decade that number increased dramatically. Similarly, Ladbrokes made itself a powerful presence, so that by 1972 it had 660 betting shops. If anything, the emergence of Ladbrokes was the most spectacular of all, as Ron Pollard stressed. He had started out in 1943 as an office boy at Hill's and moved on to become PR director at Ladbrokes. Pollard had a major impact on bookmaking and is credited for initiating the laying of odds on a multitude of events other than horse- and dog-racing – such as on the results of general elections and the Miss World beauty contest. He was certain that Ladbrokes rise was propelled by the genius of one man – Cyril Stein.

> In 1964, Ladbrokes was just about bust . . . we had lost £2 million on fixed-odds football, had been under orders 'not to lose' on our racing or the firm would go under and we had about fifty full-time employees. Today (1991) Ladbrokes is in the top thirty-five British companies, employs 77,000 people in fifty countries around the world and with a turnover of £3.6 billion made a profit in 1989 of more than £300 million. That is what you call growth. While many have contributed to this amazing success story, one man stands alone as the visionary, the architect and the builder of this enormous empire: Cyril Stein.[30]

Ladbrokes emerged as a bookmaking business in 1902, when Arthur Bendir joined Harry Schwind and a Mr Pennington, who had come together to back horses trained by Schwind at Ladbroke Hall in Warwickshire. Bendir acted as both a bookie and a punter and built up a good business with the help of knowledgeable staff – one of whom was L. P. Joyce, who went on to become managing director of Ladbrokes. Richard Kaye praised Joyce as 'one of the brains behind an astute racing move, without which modern bookmaking could not operate. He was one of the institutors of the "Blower" system.' This was the registered name given to the sending of money from off-course bookmakers to bookies on the course so as to affect the starting price. Thus, if a bookie such as Ladbrokes had a big liability on a horse, it was able to cover part of that bet by contacting the Blower and instructing its agents to put on some of that money at the relevant meeting so as to bring down the price of the horse and lessen the bookmaker's potential losses. By the 1950s, there were two main Blower firms, the Victoria and the London Agency, which was later bought out by the former.[31]

For all of its involvement in this innovation, by the 1950s the turnover of Ladbrokes was declining. It gained the reputation of 'a sleepy credit bookmakers' happy with the tag of 'bookmakers to the gentry'.[32] Its reinvigoration came about after it was taken over by Max Parker in 1956. Parker was Cyril Stein's uncle and he persuaded his nephew to join them in business. The grandson of Russian Jews who had come to London in the later nineteenth century, Stein had grown up in the racing game. His father, known as Harry 'Snouty' Parker, had been an illegal street bookie in Whitechapel before becoming a rails layer on the course in the 1930s. Within a few years he had become 'the man on the rails', a position he had earned partly because of his skills at 'the knock-out'. Deeply knowledgeable about the racing game, Parker was also a punter and when he had information about 'a good thing', he engaged agents to back that horse for him with a variety of illegal bookies at starting price. Then, when betting on that race opened on the course, Parker would offer higher odds against the horse than the punters had anticipated – not that they could get a bet on with him. Parker's roaring out of the odds was for effect, primarily to try and influence the representatives of the *Sporting Life* and *Sporting Chroncile* to return higher odds at starting price for his fancy when it won and thus increase his winnings from his off-course betting. He succeeded often.[33]

However, in 1941, Parker fell from his elevated position when he was 'warned off' by the Jockey Club for allegedly trying to buy information and bribe jockeys. He died four years later. His son, Cyril, was just seventeen. He was to go on to gain a reputation for hard dealing but also one for probity and generosity to charities. So great has been his impact and that of his family that the racing writer Jamie Reid has pronounced that the Steins' 'influence on bookmaking in Britain in the twentieth century has been as far-reaching as that of those other famous incomers Louis B. Mayer and Harry Cohn to the development of the American film industry'.[34] That influence began to make itself felt when Stein took up his uncle's offer to join Ladbrokes. A gambler by nature, but a cute gambler who knew his business and reckoned the odds carefully, he persuaded the board of Ladbrokes to advertise for custom. Trade picked up, also stimulated by Stein's other positive moves: the abolition of the 200 to 1 limit, to bring Ladbrokes in line with other major firms; the introduction of a trade branch and a greyhound racing service; and the taking of bets on events other than horses and dogs.[35] Then Stein decided to go head to head with the mighty Hill's over fixed-odds betting on football.

This form of betting had emerged in the late nineteenth century. Single bets could not be made, and punters were required to make multiple bets. Bookmakers offered a number of lists relating to the English Football League and the First Division of the Scottish League.

The first list offered punters the odds against selecting winning teams; the second against draws; and the third against away teams winning. Companies also offered other lists, which allowed for a variety of selections on certain matches. One of the most popular was the Short List, where punters chose three home teams to win out of eight, at odds of 10 to 1 against.

Hill's had built up a huge fixed-odds business from 1939, when the company took just £6, until 1963, when it brought in £16 million. Stein quickly made Ladbrokes the second-biggest fixed-odds bookmaker in the country and a 'betting war' developed between Hill's and Ladbrokes. This was 'over the fixed-odds betting prices offered on three draws. If Hill's offered 28–1, Cyril would increase the odds to 33–1. Hill's, determined to crush the young pup snapping at their heels, retaliated. It was a war neither side could win.'[36] The cut-throat competition led only to losses and costly court cases, after Ladbrokes was accused of plagiarizing Hill's coupons. As it was, fixed-odds betting was finished off by the Budget of Reginald Maudling in 1964, when the Conservative government introduced a massive 25 per cent tax on fixed-odds stakes. William Hill was certain that such a swingeing measure had been brought in because of the lobbying by the football-pools promoters, whose owners wished to be rid of competition. He pronounced dramatically that 'they will be drinking wine mixed with blood – bookmakers' blood'.[37]

Some small bookmakers blamed Hill for the imposition of the new tax. In a letter to the *Sporting Life*, H. P. Hooper of Plymouth stated that Hill had created the basis for the easy collection of the duty by offering prices over the odds and putting the small man out of business. Like other betting-office bookmakers, Hooper had not forgotten the antagonism shown towards them in the past by Hill.

> He is a clever business man, and is entitled to have made his pile, but I do not think he is doing the bookmaking business a favour when he appears on television and tells people not to bet, but if they must bet to do so with Hill's. Again, he has been an implacable enemy of betting shops, which, surely, are the results of legislation in favour of the working man. Perhaps, as a result of his great success in the credit field, he has advanced so far into the upper strata that he regards betting shops as vulgar, and thinks it better that the lower classes should continue to have their bets furtively and illegally with the milkman, rather than have the facilities that have always been available to their social superiors. It is also, of course, obvious that betting shops must pinch business from Hill's credit set up.[38]

The end of fixed-odds betting (it was to be revived successfully in the 1980s) did not put a halt to Stein's resolve to take on the 'big boys' and become one of them. By 1967, he had so succeeded in increasing business that he was able to take Ladbrokes public, thus joining four other big bookmakers: William Hill's, part of Holders Investment Trust; Coral's; Mark Lane; and the Hurst Park Syndicate. Ladbrokes was valued at about £2 million. Stein owned a third of the business, while the rest belonged to his uncle and an accountant. A remarkable personality, Stein was drawn by Noel Whitcomb in the *Daily Mirror* as a 'quiet, slim, pale, elegantly dressed' man of thirty-eight who 'smokes an occasional cigar, drinks little, works eleven hours a day at administration, [and] devotes week-ends to his wife and three children'. Stein told Whitcomb of the Dickensian scenes when he first walked into Ladbrokes offices. The firm had fifteen telephones, each of which was in a booth. When a client rang, an elderly gentleman would lock himself in the booth and fawningly take the bet from a member of the upper class. Clerks sat on high stools and with long feather pens wrote in ledgers. Now, through his business acumen and flair for pulling in trade, Stein had built up a bookmaking firm that was soon to challenge Hill's.[39]

By 1969, Ladbrokes was vying with Hill's for the accolade of the world's biggest bookmaker. It had over 400 betting shops and in its credit business it boasted 300 telephones. This side of the operations was carried on in a long betting room, at one end of which was a huge blackboard upon which all the details of a particular day's racing were shown. Transactions were recorded so that there could be no disputes. Once taken down, the bets were time stamped and then sorted into alphabetical order by the name of the punter. Big bets were handed to Ron Pollard 'and the men who keep the two clients' Field Books. They sit at a dais at the end of the room facing down towards the blackboard.' Sorted again according to credit limits, the bets were then collected and moved to the Settling Room, where two settlers worked on reckoning up the big bets. These were also phoned down to the Trade Room where 150 telephone operators took between 4,000 and 5,000 bets a day.[40]

The outstanding success of Ladbrokes and other big bookmakers soon gained the attention of larger public companies, some of which saw betting shops as a 'cash cow' that could provide daily injections of ready money. In 1970 Grand Metropolitan bought out the businesses to which the name Mecca Bookmakers was given two years later. Its acquisition was imitated by Bass plc, amother major player in the entertainment sector, which took over Mark Lane and Corals, bringing them together under the latter name. With Hill's owned by

Sears Holdings Limited, that left Ladbrokes as the only one of the Big Four bookmakers that did not belong to another public company.[41]

The inexorable rise of Hill's and Ladbrokes, and that of Coral's, was matched by the beginnings of the decline of small bookmakers. In 1963 there were 14,388 betting shops and almost 12,000 bookmakers with permits, although some of them were on the course. Five years later, betting-shop licences peaked at 15,782, although bookmakers' permits had dropped to 11,069. Thereafter these figures fell drastically, so that by 1983 the number of betting shops had gone down by 30 per cent to 11,237. Similarly, bookmakers' permits had slumped to 7,291 – a drop of 35 per cent.[42] It was always likely that after the first enthusiastic rush to open betting shops that some would have closed down because they were in the wrong position or because they were faced by too much competition. But overall small bookies were facing a number of major problems.

First of all, their overheads had increased noticeably in 1966 when the Labour government introduced a betting tax. This was equivalent to 2½ per cent of turnover, rising to 5 per cent a year later. Eventually it reached 8 per cent. Bookies did pass this on to punters, so that by the time the betting tax reached its maximum amount they were deducting 10 per cent from winnings – or else punters were paying 10 per cent on their stake money to avoid a bigger cut back if they were successful. This deduction was 2 per cent more than the tax, allowing bookies also to claw back their contributions to the Horse Race Betting Levy Board, which helped the racing industry, and a bit more besides. Bookies argued that they needed to round the tax and betting-levy amounts upwards in their favour to take account of the fact that they could not claim back VAT; a further consideration was that when punters paid their tax as part of their stake, bookies were having to pay tax on the tax.

Furthermore, the administration associated with the betting tax was cumbersome and strict. Bookmakers had to ensure that they were in credit to the Customs and Excise, meaning that they had to buy a betting-tax sheet that would cover them for the coming week's turnover. This caused major problems for small firms operating on fine profit margins. The trading conditions of off-course bookmakers are notoriously difficult to predict. Racing fixtures can be cancelled because of bad weather and a bookie could be left having paid too much betting tax for a week when trading was low. Of course this overpayment could be carried over, but it did mean that a small bookmaker may have had to carry an unnecessary and expensive outlay when cash flow was very tight. Then again, a bookie might have taken a lot more in a week than anticipated because of a new punter spending heavily or because of punters on a winning streak. In such cases, they had to go out and buy extra tax sheets at a time when they may have been losing. The Customs and Excise could, if they wished, close down a bookmaker for not operating in credit for betting tax. Most bookies did not dispute that they had to pay this tax, but they would have preferred to pay it retrospectively, after knowing how much they had taken. Of course, bigger companies had the cash flow to ameliorate these problems.

Small neighbourhood bookmakers faced other difficulties, above all the redevelopment of many inner-city working-class neighbourhoods in the 1960s. So-called slum clearance blighted areas by substantially reducing the population and not providing proper compensation to businesses that lost their trade. Like public houses, betting shops were often the last buildings to be knocked down – by which time trade had dwindled almost to nothing. This happened to bookies like Big Horace Foster in Kyrwicks Lane, Sparkbrook, and nearby to my own family at our Highgate Road office. When I was sixteen in 1972, I was running this office by myself for my Dad in the school holidays. We did not open up until an hour or so before racing, as the morning trade had gone, and some days we were lucky to take as little as fifteen or twenty pounds during racing hours. Dad just held on in the hope of getting a better offer of compensation from the council.

The radical changes in bookmaking that made trading so hard for small bookies were stressed by Fred Done. By the end of the twentieth century he had come to own 256 betting shops and was the largest independent bookmaker in Britain. His wealth, and that of his brother Peter, was estimated at £78 million, but he began with little. Interviewed by Graham Rock of the *Observer* in 2001, Fred recalled that he had started in the game in 1959. He was fifteen and worked with his father in the family's bookmaking business.

> He traded in Knott Mill, one of the rougher areas of Manchester, under a tarpaulin in a back yard. He would open the shop from 11 to three and from five to seven for the evening dogs. Bets were written on any scrap of paper, with a nom de plume on the back.
>
> We had runners in all of the factories in Trafford Park, one of the biggest industrial complexes in Europe. We would send a taxi round every day, and the bets would be handed over in clock bags. These were leather bags which, when closed, set the time on a clock, confirming that bets had not been placed after racing had started.
>
> There were no books, there was no income tax, no betting duty. What you had at the end of your day was profit. The only payment you had to make was bribe money to the police, two or three quid

> a week to keep them off your back. If they were going to raid you, they'd let you know. Bookmakers' runners, who earned 10 per cent commission on all the bets they collected, were imprisoned automatically for a third offence; when a raid was imminent, substitutes were employed.
>
> Of course, punters were not as well-informed then . . . Limits on multiple bets protected bookmakers from excessive losses.

After legalization, Done went to work for the Peters chain of betting shops in Salford, rising to become manager of their credit office. He recalled that there was no security camera or till: 'In those days it was so good that you could allow for the fiddling and still make money. But when betting tax came in and we started trimming the odds, it became a business.' The following year, 1967, Done struck out on his own and faced immediate worries: 'Two weeks after we opened our first shop, foot and mouth struck. I had no cash and thought we wouldn't make it through. Most bookmakers closed, but we kept going with the dogs, and the punters came. They wanted to bet.'[43]

Small bookies received little sympathy. Their past high earnings relative to the average working man's wage loomed large in the minds of the public, as did the words of John Banks. A flamboyant self-publicist, he was the owner of a chain of betting shops in Scotland and a major racecourse layer. Banks shouted out to all and sundry that betting shops were 'money factories'.[44] The National Association of Bookmakers knew diffferent. As a new decade beckoned it published a booklet entitled *Into the 1970s with the NAB*, in which it stressed that 'the next few years are going to be crucial for bookmaking. Present conditions are a clear pointer to that. Unless there is a radical improvement, many bookmakers will face the decision whether or not they can stay in business.'[45] It was a downbeat but realistic assessment.

Facing the most difficult operating conditions they had known, small bookies continued to drop away, though large numbers of established bookmaking families did make it through the 1970s. But even harsher trading conditions awaited them with the recession of the early 1980s. This dire economic situation had its worst impact upon manufacturing areas. Factories and mines closed down across the land. It was precisely the workers in industry who had been the mainstay of business for small bookmakers in most towns and cities in the Midlands and North of England, South Wales and Central Scotland. With turnovers falling, or at best not rising in line with inflation, family bookmaking businesses began to sell up in increasing numbers. Our own was among them.

The recession badly affected Birmingham, a pre-eminent manufacturing city. In a few years the city went from a high-wage/low-unemployment economy to a low-wage/high-unemployment economy. As elsewhere in the country, punters understandably cut back on their betting. A general drop in trade was made worse by increased competition from the big bookmakers. They had more money to spend on their premises and were able to offer no-limit or high-limit betting. As a result, small bookies such as ours struggled to compete. During the 1960s and early 1970s, my Dad had realized that if we were to survive in the game we needed not only to expand but also to move out of the back streets and secure more prominent locations in main shopping thoroughfares. With this in mind, he had moved the Oldfield Road shop a few hundred yards away on to the busy Ladypool Road, and he then built up to six shops in and around Sparkbrook. But like other bookies in his situation, he fell between two stools: he was stretched too thin in looking after various betting offices himself, but the business was not big enough to enable him to afford to bring in the necessary skilled and more expensive staff to help him. In effect he needed either to become much bigger or to stay as a one-man band with a single shop. There were times when he could have bought other betting offices and become bigger, but he declined because he felt that the pitch in question was in the patch of another bookie whom he knew. In this way, Dad and other local bookies lost out to the big firms who, for understandable business reasons, were not concerned with neighbourhood loyalties. They would buy out whomsoever they wished regardless of who traded nearby and how long they had done so.

By the early 1980s, we were down to two pitches. Highgate Road had been knocked down; Taunton Road had been sold to a chap who had that as his only pitch; Bristol Road had been bought by Ladbrokes; and the Coventry Road pitch had been cleared for road-widening. Our Stoney Lane pitch was turning over less than £2,000 a week – the same figure that Dad had been taking over twenty-five years previously in his illegal back-street betting shop that had been just yards away. It was barely viable to keep Stoney Lane open, and our main shop on the Ladypool Road was also struggling. Our nearest competitor, Bates Brothers, had relocated from Brunswick Road to the Ladypool Road and was nearer than us to the main pub, the Red Lion. Consequently we lost a lot of trade. Dad reacted by taking over the empty shop on the corner right opposite the pub and we made a comeback – that is, until Ladbrokes bought out the Bates brothers, just twenty yards from us.

There was no way that we could even contemplate trying to

compete with the better facilities or higher limits of Ladbrokes. In these circumstances we did what we knew best: we went back to our roots. Because we had a large number of Irish punters, we began to offer odds on the results of the All Ireland Football and Hurling championships, taking our prices from the big Irish bookie S. P. Graham. Unfortunately, Dublin and Kerry dominated the former competition in the early 1980s and we took few bets on the other counties. Unable to make a proper book, we suffered a loss each year. Still, the offering of such prices gained us attention and we built on that through offering a personal service to our punters. Each Saturday after the dogs finished and before the horses started I would go on a tour of the local pubs. As it was, I drank locally and was known personally in the area as well because of the family name and the bookmaking. My round included the Red Lion, the Clifton, the Railway, the Gate, the Wrexham (properly known as the George) and the Royal Oak. Knowing that I would be along, punters would wait for me and have a drink instead of going to Ladbrokes, or Corals down the other end of the Ladypool Road, or other bookies.

I have taken a £1,000 bet in the toilet of the Clifton and paid out twice that sum, while I also took the small fivepence yankees (eleven bets at five pence) of other punters. I was breaking the law. I knew I was breaking the law. I had become an illegal street bookie like my old man and my Grandad. Like them, I felt no shame and nor did I feel that I was a criminal. I was doing what had to be done to keep our business afloat. Mind you, while the taking of the bets was unlawful, when I got back to the pitch we always put the bets through the till and we always charged the punters tax and paid it to the Customs and Excise. Our street bookmaking was helped greatly because Dad and I knew our punters. Most were English, Irish or Afro-Caribbean and had lived in the neighbourhood since the early 1950s at least. There were also a few South Asians, Palestinians, Somalis and Nigerians who had been settled locally for years. Many of the punters appreciated an old-style bookie who drank with them and fetched their bets from them. One of the best of them was Big Danny, a generous Irishman who loved salmon and duck eggs. Each Saturday I would buy him two or three fresh salmon steaks and a dozen duck eggs. I would also spring for a big round in every pub, and as a result was always welcomed by the gaffers who turned a blind eye to my street bookmaking because of my spending and the custom I brought in.

We had nothing other than ourselves to enable us to compete with the government and the big bookmakers. Our strategy worked in that it increased turnover quite dramatically. Unfortunately there was a small group of big punters who were in 'the know' with a local trainer and who were receiving good information about certain horses. Unable to place bets with the big bookies, who were alert to betting coups, they focused on us and other small bookmakers. Not having been brought up to cover, at first we held on to these bets and took a pasting. We also had a bad run of results generally, and, along with so many shopkeepers, violent crime had become an issue. Back in 1974 when I was just eighteen, we became the first bookmakers in Birmingham to be the victims of an armed robbery when four men came into our Taunton Road pitch. One put a shotgun to my head and another gun was held to the head of the manager. It was a frightening incident, and although three men were charged they were later acquitted.

In the succeeding years we experienced other disturbing incidents. On one occasion a customer who was not a regular insulted my aunt, my Dad's sister, who worked on the counter taking and paying out bets. My first thought was to get the man out of the shop. I managed to do so, but as I ushered him on to the pavement he spat in my face. My aunt rang Dad to tell him and he rushed round to the office. Dad was brought up the old way. If you had trouble you sorted it out man to man in a fair fight and with fists. We had a good reputation for safety in our shops and Dad did not want that jeopardized. He found the customer just up the road in Bates Brothers. The chap went for Dad and the old man laid him out with one punch. Fifteen minutes later, the guy stormed into our shop with a machete.

By this time, we had a small platform on the left of the shop which allowed the marker to reach the board on the wall where we hung the lists of riders for each race. Using felt-tip pens, the boardman or marker wrote down the betting on the board alongside the sheets – wiping it off when that race was over. The betting and the commentary came over loudspeakers via the blower. Around the office were display boards upon which we hung the racing papers and racing pages from the daily papers, and also holders in which were betting slips and fixed-odds coupons. Just beyond the boardman was the punters' toilet and alongside that was a partition. Between the partition and the glass divider above it was a gap through which we took the bets. All bets were put through a special till which registered them with the time and a number. The betting slips had duplicate copies. We kept the top copy, the punter had the duplicate. That day the irate customer kept piercing the partition with his machete; my Dad was shouting at him to drop the weapon and come outside and fight like an Englishman; meanwhile the other punters were putting on their bets, listening to the commentary and carrying on as normal.

Soon after that incident, I was held up as I was about to lock up the shop well after racing had finished. A bloke came in with a gun, which turned out to be a starting pistol according to the police. He placed it at my temple, told me to put my hands up and threatened to shoot me if I did not hand over the money and the keys to the till. I succeeded in bluffing him to accept that I did not have the keys. They were actually in my clenched fist. He took what cash he could find, which was not much, shot at the floor and ran off. After that first armed robbery some years back, we could no longer afford the prohibitive insurance payments, so we had no recompense for what was stolen. These violent events and the losing streak led us to pack up. We did so most reluctantly, dismayed at selling up our family business and leaving Sparkbrook, where my family had either lived or worked for 120 years. However, in August 1984 we sold our Ladypool Road shop to Hill's. Ladbrokes actually offered us more money, but they would not guarantee our manager a job; Hill's did. As part of the deal we also closed down our Stoney Lane pitch.

After sixty-two years trading as bookies in Sparkbrook, we were finished. We did not look for sympathy. As Dad had always stated, bookmaking had made our money and had allowed us to move out of the back houses and to enjoy a very comfortable lifestyle. Still, we were saddened. But we were not on our own. Ron Pollard himself recognized the difficulties facing small bookies. Believing that 'if it moves, you can bet on it', Pollard was a key figure in the rise of Ladbrokes and a close companion of Cyril Stein. His knowledge and understanding of the game were legendary. Encouraged by his awareness of bookmaking, he also ran his own small bookmaking business for three or four years

> But I soon discovered how hard it was to make it pay. In fairness of course I was faced with the additional problem that my work for Ladbrokes meant that I was unable to run the shop myself and I therefore had to have a manager. There are still [in 1991] a large number of bookmakers throughout Britain, mostly one-man small businesses. Properly run, which means the owner running it himself like the corner shop grocer or local shoe repairer, they make a profit. I was trying to make a living for the manager as well as a little something for myself and that simply wasn't on. In the end I was very happy to sell out to Ladbrokes.
>
> I am and always have been a supporter of the smaller man: the bookie in Little Sodbury. I recognise all the difficulties and I do hope they survive because there is a place for them. If you go back to the roots of betting, it was always the local bookie who was the benefactor.[46]

Pollard retired in 1989, although he remained a consultant for and a director of Ladbrokes. By then, off-course betting was becoming more closely drawn into the world of leisure and gaming, thanks in part to a new Betting Act of March 1986. Its provisions allowed bookmakers to provide live television coverage of horse and greyhound racing – as illegal betting shops had done back in the 1950s. The Act also abandoned the pretence that punters should just go into a betting shop, put on their bet and leave, and in so doing it gave bookies the opportunity to make their premises more comfortable and inviting. Thus bookmakers were allowed to have two amusement-with-prizes machines and to provide soft drinks (within a few years, bookies were also allowed to sell hot drinks). Finally, bookies were permitted to open on Sundays.

The racing editor of *Today* was amazed by the changes wrought by the legislation and compared the new facilities with the 'most horrendous privations' that punters had to endure in the illegal days in order to place a bet.

> It never used to be like this. It didn't. Really. Carpets, TVs, drinks, comfortable seats, warm – even plush – surroundings. Ah, it's almost a pleasure to lose your money.
>
> We are discussing, of course, the new-look High Street betting shops which are now going to be veritable oases of creature comforts.
>
> Under new legislation, bookmakers' shops will be allowed to offer facilities undreamed of in 1950, when I first discovered the magical world of betting on the horses.

The place where the racing bug bit Fred Shawcross was actually the famed illegal betting shop of Bella Thomasson in Bolton.[47] Graham Rock also commented on the extraordinary transformation of betting shops from the bleak, early legal premises. The nearest to his school was a short walk away. It 'was a seedy room in the backstreets of Croydon, managed by a formidable middle-aged blonde. When she paid out the winners, her scowl would have petrified a Blackpool landlady.' As Rock pointed out, 'the premises were dingy by government decree; the 1961 Betting & Gaming Act required that licensed betting offices did not encourage loitering. The participants were expected to enter, place a bet, and leave with the alacrity and discretion of a Cabinet Minister visiting a bordello.'[48]

The permission to show televised races was the catalyst for a momentous change. For a number of years, the Big Four had been pushing forward their interests through BOLA, the Betting Office

Licensees Association, and in the late 1980s they came together with other bodies including the Racecourse Association, the Horserace Totalisator Board and Racal Electronics to set up Satellite Information Services (SIS) Their aim was to transmit live coverage of races and racing information to betting shops. This was spectacularly successful. The innovation was adopted with great enthusiasm by the big bookmakers and soon smaller bookies had to follow if, at the least, they were to keep their existing custom. Unfortunately, the coming of SIS led to the ending of Extel, the previous source of betting news and commentaries.

In the wake of the new Act and the emergence of SIS, the Office of Fair Trading made a detailed study of the Big Four bookmakers. This was prompted by a number of anxieties. First, that SIS could be used to bolster the dominance of the leading bookmakers and to squeeze out independents. Second, that the influence of the Big Four on dog-racing was increasing. In a new move, SIS offered live television coverage of afternoon dog-races, and Ladbrokes and Corals each owned two of the tracks that were covered. Under existing legislation, Corals and Ladbrokes were not allowed to make a book on their own courses, but they were allowed to do so in their betting shops. The third main matter of concern was related to computerized betting forecasts. For a number of years, punters had been able to bet on forecasting the first and second in one or more dog- and horse-races. The odds for successful punters were worked out according to a complex payout formula. This incorporated a tax deduction which was multiplied in bets of doubles and trebles. It was argued by some opponents of the Big Four that this procedure meant that punters received less in payouts than they should have, while tax revenue was reduced. The OFT also examined the way in which bookmakers charged customers 10 per cent on stakes or on deductions – depending on the punter's preference – when the betting tax was 8 per cent of turnover and the Horserace Betting Levy Board charge was about 1 per cent on horse bets only.[49]

Little came of these investigations and there was no referral to the Monopolies and Mergers Commission because of the dominance of the Big Four. As Roger Munting has indicated, the concentration of ownership is not peculiar to the gambling industry. Indeed, it is the norm for most productive enterprises in a sophisticated economy. Moreover, this concentration was strengthened by government action via the 1986 Act, simply because it led to more spending on facilities in betting shops. Obviously, as Munting pointed out, the bigger bookies 'could afford the necessary investment more readily than a small independent shop. Similarly the large chains are able to offer substantial maximum pay-out figures, typically £250,000, which no small bookmaker could afford.' And contrary to those who believed otherwise, there was little evidence to suggest that the Big Four exploited their market position to make extraordinary profits.

Ladbrokes' gross profits from racing and related activities were 4.2 per cent of turnover in 1986, although the Royal Commission of 1978 indicated that the Big Four had gross profits of 11 per cent and small bookies of 10 per cent. After all deductions, these left net profits of 2.3 per cent and 2 per cent respectively. Although net profits were reasonable, they were lower than for British industry as a whole; however, returns on investments were good for betting offices. In 1991 the National Association of Bookmakers estimated that large firms made 22–23 per cent on capital and small ones 19–21 per cent, and these returns were higher than those for British industry as a whole. These figures reflected other investigations into bookmakers' profits.[50]

The large bookmakers were also accused of lowering the starting prices of horses that would cost them money if they won. They did this by 'blowing' money back to the course, so that their representatives could place bets with on-course bookmakers and force down the prices offered. Given that 90 per cent of horse-race betting takes place away from the course, it does not seem wrong for bookmakers to lay off some of that money if need be. Obviously, it was difficult for a small bookie to do this, while it was also increasingly tough for newcomers to enter the off-course betting market. Licensing authorities generally were not keen on new betting shops, unless they replaced an existing shop, whereas the big firms had the financial wherewithal to hire expensive lawyers to object to any new applications. Thus, if a company wanted to move into bookmaking or a small bookie wanted to expand, they needed to buy existing premises – and, of course, the big bookmakers could normally outbid their rivals.

Indeed, by 1989 off-course bookmaking was dominated not by the 'Big Four' of Mecca, Coral's, Hill's, and Ladbrokes, but by a 'Big Three'. The previous year the brewing and leisure giant Grand Metropolitan had taken over the William Hill Organization through its purchase of Sears Holdings. This added Hill's betting shops to those of Mecca, which remained a separate trading name for some years until it became part of the Hill's brand. Soon after, both chains were sold to Brent Walker. Coral's, owned by Bass, now included the betting shops of Heathorn and Leisure Bookmakers, and by 1989 it had 906 betting shops. Together Mecca and Hill's had 1,582, while Ladbrokes had 1,814. This meant that the 'Big Four' controlled 41.7 per cent of all betting shops. But their real dominance was made plain by the fact that they accounted for over 60 per cent of turnover. This reached 77 per cent within the next two years. Ladbrokes remained the biggest betting office chain, but Hill's continued to lead in the credit business.[51]

By 1990, the number of bookmakers' permits had fallen sharply to 5,406, down just over 50 per cent since 1968; while there were now 10,081 shops, a fall of a little over a third over the same period. Between the large number of small bookies and the giants of the game lay a few regional betting chains. Stanley Leisure, with its base in Liverpool, was among them. It grew fast in the 1980s so that by 1991 it had 301 shops, mostly in the North of England, and twelve in Northern Ireland.[52] Two years later, the opening of betting shops in the evening was sanctioned by the Home Office. For the first time since the days of illegal betting shops, cash punters could now bet lawfully after 6.30 p.m. The bigger bookmakers benefited from this liberalization of the law, although one-man operations found their working hours increasing substantially. However, all bookies were now buffeted by two new phenomena: the National Lottery and off-shore bookmaking.

Small lotteries had been permitted since the 1963 Betting, Gaming and Lotteries Act, and lotteries for charities and local authorities were given further leeway in 1975 and 1976. Then in 1993, the National Lottery was introduced. This led to a fundamental shift in government attitudes, whereby the state became involved in supporting the advertising of gambling and encouraging the public to gamble. The huge payouts to a very few winners attracted many people to the Lottery, pulling away from bookmakers some smaller punters. However, most serious punters eschewed this game of chance for the seeking of value in bookmaker's odds. In that search, the bigger punters had begun to bet abroad. As Fred Done explained: 'The tax killed off big punters in the shops who wanted to bet the odds-on chances, the man who would have £4,000 to win £1,000. Since offshore betting began, some of my biggest customers have been coming into the shop to see the prices and watch the races, but walk outside to call Victor . . . to bet on their mobile phones.'[53]

'Victor' was Victor Chandler. The grandson of the renowned racecourse bookie, Bill Chandler of Hoxton, and the son of the highly respected layer, Victor senior, the younger Chandler was a bookmaking entrepreneur who took betting back to the Continent in a move reminiscent of that of Valentine and Wright in the 1870s. The owner of a chain of betting shops and a charismatic racecourse bookmaker, Chandler shocked both bookmakers and the government in 1999 when he moved the company's entire accounts operation from London to Gibraltar and introduced tax-free betting for international clients. Within weeks, thousands of account holders with the big bookmakers had transferred their business abroad. According to the Victor Chandler International website:

> From discreet English Gentleman bookmaker, to head of the World's leading independent sports betting and gaming group in just three years. That in essence is the Victor Chandler story so far. And the story is far from over.
>
> It takes a certain kind of man to achieve that. It started when Victor, who was then a credit bookmaker with a small but very select group of wealthy clients, spotted an opportunity to offer tax-free betting from outside the United Kingdom. His vision was to realise that to satisfy the needs of the customers who would come flooding to him, he would have to drive through and deliver the rapidly-emerging new technologies and platforms that are transforming the way we all do business. And the results are there for all to see today. The Victor Chandler name and his ever-growing group of companies have become synonymous with the revolution that is transforming the sports betting and gaming industry.[54]

Victor Chandler's unexpected, bold and winning move had a massive impact, and other bookies followed his lead. With revenue from betting tax falling, illegal betting rising and amid fears that horse-racing in Britain would fall into decline without the investment from off-course bookies, the government acted swiftly. By now, betting tax had been reduced to 6.75 per cent and bookies were deducting 9 per cent from punters, but in March 2001 Chancellor Gordon Brown announced that off-course betting duty would be scrapped from 1 January 2002. Instead, bookmakers would be taxed on their gross profits at a rate of 15 per cent. A spokesperson for Victor Chandler stated that punters would still not have a 'genuine tax-free option', as seen in the offshore industry. He added that 'regrettably, this looks like a hollow victory for the punters, as they will continue to pay – only this time they won't realise it'.[55]

A more optimistic assessment was provided by John Brown, chairman of William Hill. His father having taken illegal bets on commission in his newsagent's shop, Brown himself had worked for Hill's since 1959 and remembered a time when the company boasted 400,000 credit customers. He felt that the abolition of betting tax would destroy illegal betting and invigorate betting shops.

> I think the betting shop will become a mini Las Vegas. Horse racing will flourish, and dog racing. Betting on football will continue to

> grow and I think we will see a new generation of slot machines in which the result is not determined within the machine.
>
> If we are paying the Government 15 per cent of profits, we will be able to put in machines that return 95 per cent of stakes to punters. Numbers games, similar to the Lottery, have proved popular in the last few years. We would like the ability to bet on the Lottery, even if we can't sell the tickets.
>
> The number of shops should increase, but I don't think they will become significantly bigger. You will want one on every street corner. It is still the case that 80 per cent of our customers spend less than 10 minutes in the shop. The British public enjoys betting on horse racing and I think the whole business, horses, dogs, everything, will prosper. In one sense, the high deductions of recent years have protected us. They froze out the skilled punter. The big hitters, the really shrewd punters, will come back, and we are going to have to be proper bookmakers again.[56]

This radical abolition of betting tax was seen by many as 'lending new legitimacy to online gambling', and it was proclaimed by Simon Clare, a spokesman for Coral, as an impetus towards making the United Kingdom 'the hub of the global gambling industry'.[57] In a report for Microsoft's online news service, Mike Brunker declared that Britain would now become the first world power to embrace Internet gambling. British bookmakers were free to accept wagers on sports contests from all over the world and this development was 'expected to put additional pressure on the United States and other nations to either join the rush toward regulation or develop a workable strategy to stop Internet gambling operators from targeting their citizens'. Brunker pointed out that operators who remained abroad in places such as Malta, Gibraltar and Antigua would be banned from advertising their services in the United Kingdom. This would give a competitive advantage to British-based bookmakers, especially the four largest – Coral, Ladbrokes, Stanley Leisure and William Hill. Such an edge was recognized by Andy Clifton, a spokesman for Ladbrokes, Britain's largest bookmaker. He was delighted that punters no longer needed 'to shop around and find the smaller offshore tax-free firms because as far as the customer is concerned they're getting the same deal from the big firms'. [58]

The position with regard to betting in Britain had changed dramatically. Just forty years previously, cash betting off-course had been legalized under the most stringent of regulations that had made many bookies go backwards in their provisions for their punters. Now the British government was making the country 'the premier destination for new and existing online gaming corporations', as indicated by Paul Lavers, chief executive officer of Covers.com, a sports-betting information site. He made it clear that 'not only does the UK offer companies a superior communications infrastructure, but it also offers streamlined access to traditional financial markets and all of the legitimacy attached (to its international reputation)'. Moreover, as highlighted by I. Nelson Rose, a professor at Whittier College in California and a leading expert on gambling and the law, 'Britain's decision to regulate and tax Internet gambling breaks the worldwide pattern that had seen more than 50 smaller jurisdictions — either individual states within a country or small nations — license operators of online games of chance'. He pointed out that 'the bigger governments have been slow to act and when they have, they've tended to say "Hey, let's just wait." For example, the Australian government last year put in place a moratorium stopping its states and territories from issuing licenses while it studied the issue.'[59] In effect, this breaking of the mould had been forced upon the government by the initiative and flair of bookies like Victor Chandler.

Invigorated by the dropping of betting tax, the big bookmakers showed themselves to be dynamic and proactive with regard to another phenomenon – that of spread betting. Hill's had entered this market in 1995, followed by Ladbrokes two years later. Developed in the 1980s by City Index as a sideline to its trading on the financial markets, spread betting emerged from the development of indices for shares, government bonds, commodities and currencies. These indices were used as tools to help clients to manage risk-taking in the City. In effect, spread betting means that odds are neither offered nor taken. Instead the company establishes a performance index in which a different price is quoted for selling and buying. The broker earns a return by way of the spread, the difference, between the buying and selling prices. These prices can be adjusted according to the receipt of new information or the movement of money. Regarded as the betting phenomenon of the 1990s, spread betting has attracted punters over a wide range of sporting events. As indicated by Jacques Black, 'unlike a conventional bookmaker who takes a position on a race or sporting event by laying odds on the outcome, a spread firm does not take a position as such, but rather seeks to make a market between buyers and sellers, and will move its quote up and down in response to the flow of money'.[61]

While spread betting is not exactly bookmaking, still big bookmakers have been able to make their mark on the business. In contrast, the recent emergence of betting exchanges has threatened the concept of bookmaking itself. This development was the brainchild of

Andrew Black, a forthright enemy of bookmakers, who believes that layers are 'financial parasites that build a fat profit into all the odds they offer'. Inspired by the trading of shares on the New York Stock Exchange, Black designed a way to bypass the bookmaker and match both sides of a bet via the internet; that is, he brought together someone who wanted to bet on a horse winning with someone who wished to bet on that horse losing. A software contractor, he was aware that internet technology could bring together such people on a global scale, but that sophisticated software was essential to enable this to happen. As a result he set up a firm called Betfair to act as a broker, taking a commission of between 2 and 5 per cent of the winner's earnings. Launched in 2000 with £1 million, within three years Betfair was employing 290 people and had 80 per cent of the online betting exchange business. The company boasted 30,000 regular customers, each of whom averaged £35 per bet. This was three times the typical wager at a high-street betting shop and indicated that most betting-exchange punters were bigger players who were more attracted to the idea of match betting – one against one.[62]

Unsurprisingly, bookmakers assert that betting exchanges provide unfair competition. In the opinion of David Stevens, a spokesman for Coral Eurobet Ltd, Britain's third-largest bookmaker, 'If I were to go into a pub and take bets from people, I'd be breaking the law, but if I go on the Internet and do the same thing via a betting exchange, it's legal. We think this is a massive discrepancy. We're not trying to get betting exchanges banned. Betting exchanges are here to stay. We just want to see them treated as we are, so there's a level playing field.' Betting exchanges now pay the same taxes as bookmakers, but Stevens argued that some betting-exchange customers were functioning as bookmakers and should also be taxed. Mark Davies of Betfair responded by stating that betting shops should not fear losing customers to the exchanges because 'there are so many people who don't care about value'.[63]

In effect, Betfair, and other betting exchanges such as Betdaq and Sporting Options, offer value to cute and knowledgeable punters who are mathematically inclined – people such as John Exton, racing editor of the *Express and Star* in Wolverhampton and the Black Country. He has been drawn into betting in this way on horses, football, tennis, athletics and a host of other sports because 'I can be the punter and take what I consider a juicy price or play bookmaker and lay one that I think can't win. Betting has never been such fun.' Another attraction is that betting exchanges allow bets during an event. For Exton and other punters who are adept at figures and aware of possibilities, betting exchanges have been empowering 'and best of all you don't have to stand in a smoky shop or battle through the crowds of the betting ring jungle. All you need is a computer and an account.'[64]

For all the exhilaration felt by Exton, there are many punters who offer foolish prices on betting exchanges because they are backing their own feelings and not working to figures. Such people can lose heavily when faced with smart operators. Small bookie Tom Golding stressed another disturbing feature of betting exchanges. The owner of three shops in the Black Country, he acknowledged the ease with which punters can open an account on the internet but warned: 'you don't know who you are betting with and what customer in their right mind would want to back a horse if he was dealing with the owner or trainer or jockey?' Contrary to the assertion that betting exchanges offered a better deal, Dobson contended that because there were just two punters betting with each other on each transaction, 'if it's better for one of them, it must be worse for the other'. Aware that betting exchanges had affected his business, this small bookie still felt that most of his clients would remain loyal. For many of them the betting shop was a place to meet, have a chat and a joke, and 'if they win a few quid they walk out with cash in their pocket. It is the social side of it and you can't have that with a computer screen in front of you.'[65]

Bookmakers are not alone in expressing concern over betting exchanges. Because of their attachment to match betting, these exchanges enable customers not only to bet on horses to win races but also to back them to lose races. This has led to worries that some jockeys and trainers might throw races because they have backed themselves to lose. Amid this growing disquiet, the British Horseracing Board chairman Peter Savill asked the government to form an independent commission of inquiry into betting exchanges. He explained that 'betting exchanges have, for the first time ever, suddenly and immediately enfranchised 30 million-plus people in Britain to make money out of horses losing races. Previously there were only 3,791 people – the number of on- and off-course bookmakers with permits who had passed the "fit and proper person" test – who were so enfranchised.'[66]

Reacting to the anxiety over betting exchanges, Betfair engaged in a memorandum of understanding with the Jockey Club, agreeing to report any suspicious patterns of betting and to pass on information about named individuals. Such an event happened early in 2004 when there was a series of suspicious betting patterns surrounding the horse Ballinger Ridge in a race at Lingfield. The jockey was Kieren Fallon and it was alleged that he had failed to do all he could to win.[67] Since then, Fallon and fifteen other people have been arrested in a police probe into the alleged fixing of horse-races. Jockeys Fergal Lynch and

Darren Williams and trainer Karl Burke were also among those arrested for alleged conspiracy to defraud. The inquiry was headed by Detective Chief Superintendent Steve Wilmott of the City of London Police, who stated that 'we have amassed a large amount of information, including computer records and documentation seized today, and will now start examining it all'. At the time of writing, no charges had followed the arrests.[68]

Betting exchanges have had a powerful impact on both off-course and on-course bookmakers, as Warwick Bartlett outlined when giving evidence in 2004 to the Joint Committee on the Draft Gambling Bill. A racecourse layer, Bartlett was also chairman of of the Association of British Bookmakers. This was a recently formed body, arising out of the coming together of the Betting Office Licensees Association and the British Betting Office Association Limited. This latter body itself had only emerged in 1992 following an advert appealing to independent off-course bookmakers to bond together. This move had been prompted by dissatisfaction with the service and cost of the BAGS (Bookmakers Afternoon Greyhound Service) and SIS, and by a desire to push for the legalization of gaming machines and the Lottery in betting offices. An experienced and articulate bookmaker, Bartlett explained:

> I think the main concern about betting exchanges is that they are, at present, not covered in the 1963 Act. They are, if you like, operating like a dating agency, introducing buyer to seller, if I can put it in simple terms. What concerns us is that the people who are on the exchanges are not licensed and people are making a living out of taking bets and laying bets on the exchanges without paying any tax or levy. What constitutes trading is another matter. It is probably better to ask the advice of the Inland Revenue rather than us but, for example, if a person buys and sells six cars a year, according to the Inland Revenue, he is trading and he is a car trader. So, that might be a useful definition. Since the betting exchanges have existed, margins coming back from the racecourse have gone down; it is affecting the take on the levy. It is very good in the short run for the punters, the punters are doing very well out of it in the short run but, in the long run, it is a question of whether the income going to the levy or to the data charge will be sustainable.[69]

Betting exchanges have also impacted upon on-course bookmakers. Operating in their traditional manner for most of the twentieth century, racecourse layers were buffeted by rapid change as the twenty-first century beckoned. For decades, the betting rings had been dominated by colourful characters and by great bookies who were worthy of standing alongside 'Facetious' Jemmy Bland, John Ogden, Leviathan Davies, 'Red Hot' Fry, and Joseph Pickersgill. Among them was Percy Thompson. At big meetings like Royal Ascot, Percy used to tap his board and shout out boldly to all and any punters, 'Any horse to win five thousand!' That was a huge sum of money in the immediate post-war years. Like Hill, he was a fearless layer and an investor in racecourses, for he had a string of horses. Geoffrey Hamlyn, later the public relations officer for Victor Chandler, recalled Percy as bringing a touch of panache to everything he did and 'if you hadn't known he was a bookmaker, you might have taken him for a big band leader or a particularly stylish impresario in the West End'. When he went to Liverpool for Grand National week, Percy would take on a whole floor at the Midland Hotel in Manchester and he and his entourage would arrive with a fleet of six Daimlers. Unfortunately, in 1951 punters who did not pay their betting debts led to the end of Percy's firm.[70]

William Hill maintained the presence of leviathan bookies on the racecourse. The racing writer, observer and punter Jamie Reid understood why Hill was so popular with the punters. It was because of 'his comprehensive knowledge of racing and the formbook, coupled with his absolute willingness to take a bet, to embrace a risk, to strike a wager. If somebody wanted to back a horse with Hill to win themselves £100,000 in forties money, he would accept the bet – and then proceed to frame his odds on the other runners in a way that would quickly enable him to find enough punters to back them in sufficient proportions to guarantee themselves a profit whatever won.'[71] From the later 1960s, leviathans such as Hill had disappeared from the course. The imposition of the betting tax badly affected the attendance of high-rolling punters at racecourses, and with less money spent on bets at most courses, it became harder for racecourse bookies to take a risk. This problem was exacerbated by the recession of the early 1980s, although on-course bookmakers did make a resurgence after the betting tax was lifted on their bets in 1987. Big layers such as Stephen Little and Victor Chandler made their mark, but as bookie Dave Saphir noted, it remained a fact that 'there are too many books chasing too little money in often contracted rings'.[72]

Some racing people believed that many of the racecourse bookies also had to share some of the blame for the decline of business. This was because they inherited their pitches or gained them through seniority and as such did not want to stick their necks out. This situation led to safe bookmaking, whereby many bookies took only the bets they wanted and refused a take a bet if it did not suit them. To become a bookie on the course it was necessary to be a member of an association affiliated to the NAB, after which a deposit had to be made. This done, the applicant joined the waiting list. Eventually, if a vacancy arose, the budding bookmaker would get a pitch on the boards in the back row – where the least business was done. Movement up to the front and the best pitches might never be achieved in a lifetime.

In 1991, Barry Dennis tried to buy his way into the front line. An established bookie, he had been waiting twenty years to bet in the ring at Sandown and had just been allotted a pitch at Newmarket after a similar lengthy wait. In desperation, he and five other layers offered Lingfield racecourse the sum of £18,000 to let him move up from the back row to the front. Interestingly, not only was his proposition opposed by the NAB, but it was also rejected by the Racecourse Association on the grounds that such a move would lead to chaos. Thus they turned their backs on the free market and stood fast to the principle that bookies paid an entry fee five times that of getting into Tattersall's. In their defence, the NAB, supported by the majority of layers, pointed out that the system that they adhered to had driven out gangsterism and that those who wanted to change a system that worked also had incomes from other businesses – unlike most bookies. Moreover, the NAB approach to the allocation of pitches was enshrined in law, and what was wrong with someone passing on their firm to their family?[73]

There was much to these arguments, but in a society where the Labour Party as much as the Conservative Party was zealously attached to laissez-faire and free trade and thundered against protectionism and closed shops, it was impossible for the old system to survive. In 1998, the National Joint Pitch Council (NJPC) took over responsibility for the administration of betting with bookmakers on Britain's fifty-nine horseracing courses under the National Pitch Rules. The NJPC was created by the Levy Board to administer betting rings following the termination of the Ferguson Agreement, which had been signed in 1958 as a tripartite arrangement between the Racecourse Association, the Jockey Club and the National Association of Bookmakers. At each race-meeting, the NJPC is represented by betting-ring managers who ensure that bookmakers comply with the National Pitch Rules on the day, carry out the allocation of pitches to on-course bookmakers, and help to settle disputes between on-course bookmakers and punters. The Levy Board itself appoints the independent chair of the NJPC Chair and two independent members of the Council, and approves changes to the National Pitch Rules. The sweeping away of seniority and family ties was accompanied by the bringing in of new-style standard joints for bookies to bet from, the computerization of receipts, local joint-pitch councils, the auctioning of list positions and the introduction of boards for rails bookmakers. The NJPC asserts that since its inception betting rings are now more competitive and customer-friendly than before.[74] Many bookies would not agree.

Micky Fletcher is a sharply dressed, sharp-minded and sharp-tongued bookie. Known as 'The Asparagus Kid', he eschews the suits of the old bookmakers and is always immaculately turned out in snazzy, casual clothing set off with a blazer. With the talent, patter and swift reckoning of the odds of a true layer, Fletcher struggled to find pitches in the old system and felt stifled by the damming-out of new blood.[75] The freeing-up of pitches did allow a fresh intake, but as Micky notes, many of the new people who have come in and bought pitches at a big outlay have little notion about how to make a book. Instead, they have been attracted by the fresh air and the flash of being a bookie. At the same time, Betfair has changed how most racecourse bookies operate.

> If you walked on the racecourse now you wouldn't know no one. All they know the old ones was the fresh air. In the old days it was a laugh and a joke. Whether you liked me or not, have a laugh. Whereas nowadays, they bet half hour before the race. It meks me laugh. Do you have your *Racing Post*? Nowadays they're on about how the system's changed, it's different. They all get their prices off Betfair. When I first went Australia about twenty years ago they give em the first show. And there was about twenty bookies or whatever it was all in a line, standing there. And they might as well have been Bubbles, Jackson's monkey, and I thought how horrible. And that's just how it is on our racecourses now. [76]

Fletcher's interpretation was supported by John Stevenson, the chairman of the National Association of Bookmakers, in giving evidence to the Joint Committee on the Draft Gambling Bill. He was in no doubt that there had been a revolution on the racecourse and 'that revolution has been that racecourse bookmakers now are no longer price makers. They were price makers and they used the supply and demand on the racecourse to make their prices. They are now price takers and that is vital. They are taking their prices from the betting exchange.' Initially, as Stevenson explained, this shift was good news to some racecourse bookmakers because there was a significant divergence between the market price on the racecourse and the price on the betting exchange. Bookies who were advanced in their technological thinking were able to take considerable advantage of this divergence by hedging off-course. Now upwards of

50 per cent of racecourse bookmakers were using the betting exchanges 'and the plain truth is that it is uneconomical. It is unviable now for racecourse bookmakers to operate on the racecourse.' This was because on-course layers have enormous expenses, while 'the person in their armchair is unencumbered with expenses of any kind. The margins to which we are betting make racecourse betting unviable. With the passage of time, that 50 per cent will become 75 per cent, 80 per cent and the margins will continue to decline as the statistics quite clearly show.' All racecourse bookies realized that they were 'committing suicide here and that is the hedging side of the coin. On the laying side, the books that are made on betting exchanges are to one or two per cent at the most per race. It beggars belief that anybody can lay bets on the betting exchange and pay their 15 per cent duty, their ten per cent levy, their income tax, their National Insurance, their commission and make a profit. The only people who can make a profit laying horses on the betting exchange are those who know something, those who know that their horse cannot win or the horse will not win.'[77]

The Horserace Betting and Olympic Lottery Bill referred to by Stevenson consists of two parts and is due to be enacted in the summer of 2004. It addresses the government's remaining involvement in the financing of horseracing, allowing for the sale of the Horserace Totalisator Board (the Tote) and the abolition of the Horserace Betting Levy Board (the Levy Board). With no levy, in the future racecourses will have to make themselves commercially viable if they are to survive and thrive. The bill is accompanied by another relating to gaming and casinos. This Gambling Bill will modernize all legislation governing gambling in Great Britain. The proposed changes will provide improved protections for gambling consumers and, in particular, seek to protect children and vulnerable players from exploitation. Additionally, the bills will allow for the establishment of a new regulator, the Gambling Commission. This will transform the existing Gaming Board for Great Britain into a new body with wider functions, greater flexibility to act and stronger enforcement powers.

It is intended for the Gambling Commission to have sweeping powers to investigate and monitor betting office licensees and online betting exchanges. Accordingly, about half of the commission's 200 staff will be investigators charged with monitoring illegal betting activities. These investigators will be able to use reasonable force in pursuit of their job, and will be empowered to issue warrants to search buildings and seize materials if they believe a licence has been breached or if illegal betting is uncovered. Bookmakers will have to provide sight of their books if foul play is suspected. Addressing the worries over race-fixing, the Gambling Bill requires betting operators to provided details on betting patterns and/or individual bets as and when required by the Commission.[78]

Stevenson saw in these bills a considerable downside for racecourse bookmakers: first, because of the proposal to allow racecourses to charge bookmakers whatever they like; and second, because of the potential for higher regulation costs. Moreover, the opening-up of legislation with regard to casinos 'is bound to have an impact. There are only so many leisure pounds available and, if they are going to go into casinos, there will be less for racecourses.'[79]

The problems faced by small on-course bookmakers have been reflected in the lessening of influence of the National Asociation of Bookmakers and its associated organizations. Once the major bookmaking force on the racecourse and a key body for independent off-course bookmakers, it has lost its dominant role in allocating pitches and now is viewed primarily as a forum for bookmakers on the course. This decline in power is reflected in the make-up of the Bookmakers' Committee, which negotiates the amount of the Horserace Betting Levy. The NAB has two seats, compared to four for the newer Association of British Bookmakers. Coral Racing Ltd, Ladbroke Racing Ltd, the William Hill Organization Ltd each have two representatives, while there is also one for the Sporting Exchange Ltd – or Betfair as it is better known.[80]

Christopher Bell, the vice chairman of the Association of British Bookmakers, also asserted that the new legislation was 'at best neutral for us', particularly for off-course bookmakers. He stated that while it may modernize legislation, it was not a deregulatory bill, and he stressed: 'We cannot see anything other than a possible negative for us. We regard it very much as a casino bill. Casinos are going to have betting . . . we do recognise that there will be displacement from our businesses into casinos. Looking across the industry in general – and others can speak for themselves – we see the casino industry as by far the main beneficiaries of this legislation.'[81]

In the increasingly liberalized British betting and gambling market, it seems likely that small off-course bookmakers will continue to find it hard to compete. In these circumstances, big bookmakers will make more gains. As it stands, Stanley Leisure has become the fourth-largest operator of licensed betting offices in the British Isles, with over 600 shops trading under the name of Stanley Racing, and the new Stanleybet brand, which aims to reflect a more broadly based betting business. Meanwhile, Coral's has strengthened its position by joining forces with Eurobet, one of the world's biggest online sports bookmakers. Eurobet offers fixed-odds betting on the world's major sporting events, twenty-four hours a day, 365 days a year. Crucially, the company has customers in over 100 countries, offers a huge range of bets on every major sport, and it makes quick payouts and payments in six major currencies. Coral Eurobet employs over 6,000 people and owns over 800 betting shops throughout the United Kingdom. Its systems handle over 100 million secure transactions worldwide each year. Customer service teams take enquries by e-mail or telephone, offering account services and help and advice in more than ten languages, among which are Greek and Chinese. Bets can even be placed from a WAP phone.

Active as it is in the new world of global betting, William Hill also brings to the fore that it is a long-established firm that with more than sixty-five years' experience of offering betting services and that it is a name to be trusted. Operating nearly 1,500 betting shops in the UK, William Hill boasts 300,000 telephone clients worldwide and its online custom is growing rapidly. In September 2004 it announced that operating profits had soared by 50 per cent to £24.2 million at its interactive division, which allows punters to place their bets on the internet. Hill's sports betting arm, Sportsbrook, also benefited from favourable horse-racing and football results, as did its two other divisions – UK betting shops and telephone betting. In making public its results, Hill's also declared that it was on course for the October 2004 launch of William Hill TV: a twenty-four-hour television channel allowing punters to bet on virtual horse-racing and roulette. Overall, the company's pre-tax profits increased to £118.4 million, up from £85.1 million, while turnover had swelled by 42 per cent to £3.89 billion.[82]

Finally, Ladbrokes UK Ltd remains in pole position in the ownership of betting shops. The betting and gaming division of Hilton Group plc, it has over 2,000 Ladbrokes betting offices and a subsidiary called Ladbrokes Bookmaker.com. Resolved to maintain their position as market leaders, William Hill and Ladbrokes have the verve, expertise, flexibility and will power to grasp the opportunities afforded by the internet and rapidly changing technology. Undoubtedly they will extend their operations further across the globe. After all, there is a big prize at stake – a global market in gambling and big profits.

So different in so many respects from the bookmakers of old, the big bookmaking firms of the early twenty-first century may not be dominated by one man but they do share some attributes with the leviathans of the racecourse in the nineteenth century. They are fast-thinking, adapatable, keen to take advantage of changing technology, alert to the betting public and focused on success. Condemned for 150 years for the job they have chosen, bookmakers now belong to the world of big business. That development and the legitimization of their trade have led to a decline in the old-style neighbourhood bookies – a decline exacerbated by other social and economic changes which have wrought havoc on traditional working-class neighbourhoods. My kind of bookmaker, bookies like Billy Brady, Bella Thomasson, Laurie Ventners and Alf Chinn, bookies who belonged to their neighbourhoods, are dying out. Paradoxically, their falling-off has come about not because of the campaigning of anti-gamblers but because of laissez-faire capitalism, unfettered after liberal legalization from 1961 onwards. It was better betting with a decent feller. Now it's better betting with a mobile phone or a computer.

SELECT BIBLIOGRAPHY

This selection is a list of books, theses and secondary articles. It does not include references to oral evidence, letters, newspapers or contemporary articles and pamphlets. All of these are cited fully in the notes to each chapter.

BOOKS

Acton, C. R., *Silk and Spur* (London: Richards, 1935).

Adelman, P., *The Rise of the Labour Party* (2nd edn, London: Longman, 1986).

Allen, Walter, *All in a Lifetime* (first published 1959. London: The Hogarth Press, 1986).

Allison, William, *Memories of Men and Horses* (London: Grant Richards, 1922).

Archer, Thomas, *The Pauper, the Thief and the Convict* (first published 1865. New York: Garland, 1985).

Arnold, Peter, *The Book of Gambling* (London: Hamlyn, 1974).

Ash, Tom, *Childhood Days. The Docks and Dock Slang* (London: the author, 1982).

Ashley, Jack, *Journey into Silence* (London: The Bodley Head, 1973).

Ashton, John, *The History of Gambling in England* (first published London: 1899. New York: Burt Franklin, 1968).

Ashworth, John, *Strange Tales from Humble Life* (Manchester: Tubbs and Brook, 1867).

Atkinson, Frank, *North-East England. People at Work 1860–1950* (Ashbourne: Moorland Publishing, 1980).

Bailey, Peter, *Leisure and Class in Victorian England. Rational Recreation and the Contest for Control, 1830–1885* (first published 1978. London: Methuen, 1987).

Bakke, E. Wight, *The Unemployed Man. A Social Study* (London: Nisbett & Co., 1933).

Barnes, Ron, *Coronation Cups and Jam Jars. A Portrait of an East End Family Through Three Generations* (London: Centreprise, 1976).

Barnett, Will, *The Life Story of Will Barnett: Better Known as the Ex-jockey. Written by Himself* (Congleton: Spurgeon Memorial Press, *c.* 1911).

Barr, Reverend James, *Lang Syne* (Glasgow: William Maclellan, 1948).

Bean, J. P., *The Sheffield Gang Wars* (Sheffield: D. and D. Publications, 1981).

Bebbington, W., *Rogues Go Racing* (London: Good & Betts, 1947).

Bell, Lady, *At the Works. A Study of a Manufacturing Town* (first published 1907. London: Virago, 1985).

Bellingham, Cathal (ed.), *Confessions of a Turf Crook Told by Himself* (London: P. Allen, 1924).

Benjamin, Harry, *Adventure in Living. The Autobiography of a Myope* (London: Health for All Publishing, 1950).

Benny, Mark, *Low Company: Describing the Evolution of a Burglar* (London: Peter Davies, 1936).

Benson, Ernie, *To Struggle is to Live. (A Working-Class Autobiography in Two Volumes)* vol. 1 (Newcastle-upon-Tyne: People's Publications, 1979).

Benson, John, *The Penny Capitalists. A Study of Nineteenth-Century Working-Class Entrepreneurs* (Dublin: Gill and Macmillan, 1983).

Bent, Superintendent, *Criminal Life. Reminiscences of Forty-Two Years as a Police Officer* (Manchester: John Heywood, 1891).

Berrett, Chief Inspector James, *When I was at Scotland Yard* (London: Sampson, Low & Co., 1932).

Best, Geoffrey, *Mid-Victorian Britain* (London: Fontana, 1971).

Bird, Alex, with Terry Manners, *The Life and Secrets of a Professional Punter. Alex Bird* (London: Queen Anne Press, 1985).

Bird, Thomas Henry, *Admiral Rous and the English Turf* (London: Putnam, 1939).

Birmingham, *Racing Analysis* (Birmingham: 1882).

Black, Robert, *The Jockey Club and Its Founders* (London: Smith Elder & Co., 1891).

——, *Horse Racing in England. A Synoptical Review* (London: R. Bentley & Co., 1893).

Blake, John, *Memories of Old Poplar* (London: Stepney Books Publications, 1977).

Bland, Ernest (ed.), *Flat Racing Since 1900* (London: Andrew Dakers, 1950).

Blyth, Henry, *Hell or Hazard: or, William Crockford versus the Gentlemen of England* (London: Weidenfeld and Nicolson, 1969).

Booth, Charles, *Life and Labour of the People in London. First Series Poverty (1) East, Central, and South London* (London: Macmillan & Co., 1902).

Booth, J. B., *Sporting Times. The 'Pink 'Un' World* (London: T. Werner Laurie, 1938).

Booth, William, *Darkest England and the Way Out* (London: International Headquarters, 1890).

Boyle, Jimmy, *A Sense of Freedom* (London: Pan, 1977).

Brailsford, Denis, *Sport and Society. Elizabeth to Anne* (London: Routledge & Kegan Paul, 1969).

Briggs, Asa, *The Collected Essays of Asa Briggs. Volume I: Words, Numbers, Places, People* (Brighton: Harvester, 1985).

Bristow, E. J., *Vice and Vigilance* (Dublin: Gill and Macmillan, 1977).

Brown, John, *I was a Tramp* (London: Selwyn and Blount, 1934).

Browne, T. H., *A History of the English Turf 1904–1930* vol. 1 (London: Virtue & Co., 1931).

Bull, Phil, *Gambling and the Racing Scene. A Submission to the Royal Commission on Racing* (Halifax: Portway Press, 1977).

—— and a Retired SP Bookmaker, *How to Make a Book* (London: Morrison and Gibb, 1945).

Bulmer, Martin (ed.), *Mining and Social Change in Durham County in the Twentieth Century* (London: Croom Helm, 1978).

Burnett, Al, *Knave of Clubs* (London: Arthur Barker, 1963).

Burnett, John, David Mayall and David Vincent (eds), *The Autobiography of the Working Classes, an Annotated Critical Bibliography* vols 1–3 (Brighton: Harvester, 1984–9).

Burstow, Henry, *Reminiscences of Horsham: Being Recollections of Henry Burstow etc.* (Horsham: Free Christian Church Book Society, 1911).

Cadbury, Edward, M. Cecile Matheson and George Shann, *Women's Work and Wages. A Phase of Life in an Industrial City* (first published 1906. New York: Garland, 1980).

Caine, Hall, *The Christian. A Story* (London: Collier & Co., 1907).

Caminada, Jerome, *Twenty-Five Years of Detective Life* (first published 1895. Warrington: Prism Books, 1983).

Cannon, George, *Betting Men* (Middleton: Jackson & Co., 1901).

Chapman, Guy, *Culture and Survival* (London: Jonathan Cape, 1940).

Charles, R. H., *Gambling and Betting* (first published 1924. Edinburgh: T. & T. Clarke, 1928).

Chesney, Kellow, *The Victorian Underworld* (first published 1970. Harmondsworth: Penguin, 1972).

Chifney, Samuel, *Genius Genuine* (London: 1784).

Chinn, Carl, *They Worked All Their Lives. Women of the Urban Poor in England, 1880–1939* (Manchester: Manchester University Press, 1988).

——, *Homes for People. 100 Years of Council Housing in Birmingham* (Exeter: Birmingham Books, 1991).

Churchill, Seton, *Betting and Gambling* (London: T. Nisbett & Co., 1894).

Clapson, Mark, *A Bit of a Flutter. Popular gambling and English society c.1823–1961* (Manchester: Manchester University Press, 1992).

Clark, Sir George, *The Later Stuarts 1660–1714* (2nd edn, Oxford: Oxford University Press, 1956).

Coates, Ken, and Richard Silburn, *Poverty: The Forgotten Englishmen* (first published 1970. Harmondsworth: Penguin, 1973).

Cobbett, Martin, *Racing Life and Racing Characters* (London: Sands & Co., 1903).

Cockburn, Claud, *I Claud* (Harmondsworth: Penguin, 1967).

Cockerill, A. W., *Sir Percy Sillitoe* (London: W. H. Allen, 1975).

Cole, G. D. H., and Raymond Postgate, *The Common People 1746–1946* (first published 1938. London: Methuen, 1961).

Conway, Michael D., *Half-Timer. A Stockport Mill Boy Remembers* (Stockport: Stockport Metropolitan Borough Recreation and Culture Division, 1983).

Cook, Theodore Andrea, *A History of the English Turf*, 3 volumes (London: Virtue & Co., 1901).

Cope, Alfred (ed.), *Cope's Racegoers Encyclopaedia* (London: Wells Gardner, Darton and Co., 1946).

Cornish, D. B., Home Office Research Study No. 42, *Gambling: A Review of the Literature and Its Implications for Policy and Research* (London: Her Majesty's Stationery Office, 1978).

Cotton, Charles, *The Compleat Gamester* (London: Henry Brome, 1674).

Couchman, Elizabeth (ed.), *Belgrave as I Remember It* (Leicester: Leicestershire Libraries and Information Service, 1984).

Cruikshank, George, *The Betting Book* (London: W & F. G. Cash, 1852).

Cunningham, Hugh, *Leisure in the Industrial Revolution c. 1780–1880* (London: Croom Helm, 1980).

Curtis, L. P., *Apes and Angels. The Irishman in Victorian Caricature* (Newton Abbot: David & Charles, 1971).

Curzon, Louis Henry, *The Blue Ribbon of the Turf* (London: Chatto & Windus, 1890).

——, *A Mirror on the Turf* (London: Chapman Hall, 1892).

Daley, Harry, *This Small Cloud. A Personal Memoir* (London: Weidenfeld and Nicolson, 1986).

Darby, Aubrey S., *A View from the Alley* (Luton: The Borough of Luton Museum and Art Gallery, 1974).

Darwin, Bernard, *John Gully and His Times* (London: Cassell & Co., 1935).

Davies, Andrew, *Leisure, Gender and Poverty. Working-Class Culture in Salford and Manchester 1900–1939* (Milton Keynes: Open University Press, 1992).

Dawson, Elizabeth, *Mother Made a Book* (London: Geoffrey Bles, 1962).

Day, William, *William Day's Reminiscences of the Turf* (London: Richard Bentley & Co., 1886).

Dennis, Norman, Fernando Henriques and Clifford Slaughter, *Coal is Our Life. An Analysis of a Yorkshire Mining Community* (London: Tavistock Publications, 1956).

Dey, Thomas Henry, *Leaves from a Bookmaker's Book* (London: Hutchinson & Co., 1931).

Dilnot, George (ed.), *The Trial of the Detectives* (London: Geoffrey Bleo, 1928).

Disraeli, Benjamin, *Sybil or the Two Nations* (first published 1845. Oxford: Oxford University Press, 1981).

Divall, Tom, *Scoundrels and Scallywags (and Some Honest Men)* (London: Ernest Benn, 1929).

Dixon, David, *From Prohibition to Regulation. Bookmaking, Anti-Gambling, and the Law* (Oxford: Oxford University Press, 1991).

Donnelly, Peter, *The Yellow Rock* (London: Eyre and Spottiswoode, 1950).

Doré, Gustave and Blanchard Jerrold, *London. A Pilgrimage* (first published 1872. New York: Arno Press, 1978).

Dostoyevsky, Fyodor, *The Gambler* (first published 1866. Harmondsworth: Penguin, 1966).

Downes, D. M., B. P. Davies, M. E. David and P. Stone, *Gambling, Work and Leisure: A Study Across Three Areas* (London: Routledge & Kegan Paul, 1976).

Druid, The, *Post and Paddock* (London: Frederick Warne & Co., 1856).

Dunstan, Keith, *Wowsers. Being an Account of the Prudery Exhibited by Certain Outstanding Men and Women in Such Matters as Drinking, Smoking, Prostitution, Censorship and Gambling* (North Melbourne, Australia: Cassell, 1968).

Durant, Henry, *The Problem of Leisure* (London: George Routledge & Sons, 1938).

Eadington, W. R. (ed.), *Gambling and Society. Interdisciplinary Studies on the Subject of Gambling* (Springfield, Illinois: Charles C. Thomas, 1976).

Eddy J. P., and L. L. Loewe, *The New Law of Betting and Gambling* (London: Butterworths, 1961).

Egan, Pierce, *Life in London* (London: 1821).

——, *Pierce Egan's Anecdotes (Original and Selected) of the Turf, the Chase, the Ring and the Stage . . .* (London: 1827).

Engels, Friedrich, *The Condition of the Working Class in England* (first published 1845. Harmondsworth: Penguin, 1987).

Ensor, Sir Robert, *England 1870–1914* (Oxford: Oxford University Press, 1936).

Esquiros, Alphonse, *The English at Home*, 2 volumes (London: 1862).

Fairclough, Eric, *In a Lancashire Street* (St Helens: the author, 1983).

Fairfax-Blakeborough, J., *The Analysis of the Turf* (London: Philip Allan & Co., 1927).

Fawcett, William, *Racing in the Olden Days* (London: Hutchinson & Co., 1933).

Fellows, Alfred, *The Law as to Gaming, Betting and Lotteries* (London: The Solicitors' Law Stationery Society, 1935).

Felstead, Sydney Theodore, *The Underworld of London* (London: John Murray, 1923).

Figgis, E. L., *Focus on Gambling* (London: Arthur Barker, 1951).

Findlay, John M., *The People of Chance. Gambling in American Society from Jamestown to Las Vegas* (New York: Oxford University Press, 1986).

Finn, Ralph, *Grief Forgotten. The Tale of an East End Jewish Boyhood* (first published 1968. London: Macdonald and Co., 1985).

Fishman, William J., *East End 1888. A Year in a London Borough Among the Labouring Poor* (London: Duckworth and Co., 1988).

Fishwick, Nicholas, *English Football and Society 1910–1950* (Manchester: Manchester University Press, 1989).

Foakes, Grace, *My Part of the River* (London: Shephearde and Walwyn, 1974).

Fothergill, John Milner, *The Town Dweller. His Needs and His Wants* (first published 1889. New York: Garland, 1985).

Fowler, Olive, (ed.), *Innings and Outings. Voices from Barnsley* (Yorkshire: Yorkshire Arts Circus, 1988).

Furniss, Ted, *The Walls of Jericho: Slum life in Sheffield between the wars* (Sheffield: Rebel Press, 1979).

Gale, Frederick, *Modern English Sports. Their Use and Abuse* (London: Sampson Low, Marston, Searle & Rivington, 1885).

Garratt, V. W., *A Man in the Street* (London: J. M. Dent, 1939).

Glass, Reverend J., *Gambling and Religion* (London: Longmans, Green and Co., 1924).

Glasser, Ralph, *Growing up in the Gorbals* (first published 1986. London: Pan, 1987).

Golby, J. M., and A. W. Purdue, *The Civilisation of the Crowd. Popular Culture in England 1750–1900* (London: Batsford Academic and Educational, 1984).

Golding, Tom, *96 Years a Brummie* (Stourton: Swinford Press, 1986).

Goodhead, Elsie Elizabeth, *The West End Story. Derby During the Depression. A Social and Personal History* (Matlock: Derbyshire Library Service, 1983).

Gormley, Joe, *Battered Cherub. The Autobiography of Joe Gormley* (London: Hamish Hamilton, 1973).

Granger, Alex, *Life's a Gamble* (Bognor Regis: New Horizon, 1983).

Grant, James, *The Great Metropolis*, vol. 1 (first published 1837. New York: Garland, 1985).

Green, Alfred, *Growing up in Attercliffe. Honey with a Ladle . . . Vinegar with a Teaspoon* (Sheffield: New City, 1981).

Green, Canon Peter, *Betting and Gambling* (London: Student Christian Movement, 1925).

Greene, Graham, *Brighton Rock* (first published 1938. Harmondsworth: Penguin, 1943).

Greeno, ex-Detective Chief Superintendent Edward, *War on the Underworld* (London: John Long, 1960).

Greenwood, James, *The Seven Curses of London* (first published 1869. New York: Garland, 1984).

——, *The Wilds of London* (first published 1874. New York: Garland, 1985).

Greenwood, Walter, *Love on the Dole* (first published 1933. Harmondsworth: Penguin, 1969).

——, *There was a Time* (London: Jonathan Cape, 1967).

Gretton, R. H., *Modern History of the English People, 1880–1922* (London: Martin Secker, 1930).

Hackwood, F. W., *Old English Sports* (London: T. Fisher Unwin, 1907).

Halliday, Jon, and Peter Fuller (eds), *The Psychology of Gambling* (London: Allen Lane, 1974).

Hammond, J. L. and B., *The Skilled Labourer* (London: Longmans & Co., 1919).

——, *The Age of the Chartists 1832–54. A Study of Discontent* (London: Longmans & Co., 1930).

Hanley, Clifford, *Dancing in the Streets* (first published 1958. London: Corgi, 1984).

Hardman, Samuel, *'In the Days of My Youth'. Some Early Reminiscences of Stand Lane, Radcliffe* (Radcliffe: Radcliffe Printing Co., 1921).

Hardy, Frank, *Power without Glory* (East Malvern, Western Australia: Realist Printing and Publishing Co., 1950).

Harris, Constance, *The Use of Leisure in Bethnal Green. A Survey of Conditions in the Borough 1925–6* (London: The Lindsey Press, 1927).

Harrison, Brian, *Drink and the Victorians. The Temperance Question in England, 1815–72* (London: Faber & Faber, 1971).

Hartog, Alexander, *Born to Sing* (London: Dennis Dobson, 1978).

Hawke, John, *A Blot on the Queen's Reign. Betting and Gambling An Appeal to the Prince of Wales* (London: Elliot Stock, 1893).

Heaton, Richard, *Salford. My Home Town* (Swinton: Neil Richardson, 1982).

Hellen, *The Greeks. Being the Jeremiad of an Exiled Greek; A Poem 'Venu de France d'une Mariere Inconnue'; Dedicated to All the Legs* (3rd edn, London: 1817).

Herman, R. D. (ed.), *Gambling* (New York: Harper & Row, 1967).

Hill, Christopher, *Society and Puritanism in Pre-Revolutionary England* (London: Secker & Warburg, 1964).

Hill, Christopher R., *Horse Power. The Politics of the Turf* (Manchester: Manchester University Press, 1988).

Hillocks, James Inches, *My Life and Labours in London, a Step Nearer the Mark* (London: William Freeman, 1865).

Hilton, John, *Rich Man, Poor Man* (London: George Allen & Unwin, 1944).

Hobbs, May, *Born to Struggle* (London: Quartet Books, 1973).
Hobson, J. A., *The Social Problem. Life and Work* (London: J. Nisbet & Co., 1901).
Hoggart, Richard, *The Uses of Literacy. Aspects of Working-class Life with Special Reference to Publications and Entertainment* (first published 1957. Harmondsworth: Penguin, 1958).
Hogge, J. M., *Betting and Gambling* (Edinburgh: R. W. Hunter, 1904).
——, *The Facts of Gambling* (London: Andrew Melrose, 1907).
Holcroft, Thomas, *Memoirs of the Late Thomas Holcroft, Written by Himself and Continued to the Time of His Death from His Diary, Notes and Other Papers* (London: Constable & Co., 1852).
Hollingshead, John, *Ragged London in 1861* (first published 1861. London: J. M. Dent & Sons, 1986).
Hood, Christopher C., *The Limits of Administration* (London: John Wiley & Sons, 1976).
Hopcraft, Arthur, *The Great Apple Raid & Other Encounters of a Tin Chapel Tiro* (London: Heinemann, 1970).
Hore, J. P., *History of Newmarket* (London: A. H. Bailey & Co., 1886).
Horsley, John William, *I Remember. Memories of a 'Sky Pilot' in the Prison and the Slum* (London: Wells Gardner & Co., 1911).
Hughes, Collingwood, *Bets and the Betting Tax* (London: Henry J. Drane, 1927).
Jacobs, Joe, *Out of the Ghetto. My Youth in the East End, Communism and Fascism 1913–1939* (London: Janet Simpson, 1978).
Jenkins, Huntley, F. W. Morley and E. J. Purchase, *The Law Relating to Betting Offences* (London: Stevens & Son, 1912).
Johnson, Ruth, *Old Road. A Lancashire Childhood 1912–1926* (Manchester: E. J. Morten, 1974).
Johnston, Máirín, *Around the Banks of Pimlico* (Dublin: Attic, 1985).
Jones, David, *Crime, Protest and Police in Nineteenth-Century Britain* (London: Routledge and Kegan Paul, 1982).
Jones, Gareth Stedman, *Outcast London. A Study in the Relationship Between Classes in Victorian Society* (first published 1971. Harmondsworth: Penguin, 1984).
Jones, Gareth Stedman, *Languages of Class. Studies in English Working Class History 1832–1982* (Cambridge: Cambridge University Press, 1983).
Judge, Anthony, *A Man Apart. The British Policeman and His Job* (London: Arthur Barker, 1972).
Kay, Joe, *The Chronicles of a Harpurhey Lad* (Swinton: Neil Richardson, 1987).
Kaye, Richard, with Ray Poskett, *The Ladbrokes Story* (London: Pelham Books, 1969).
Keating, Peter J., *Into Unknown England, 1866–1913. Selections from the Social Explorers* (London: Fontana, 1976).
Kelland, Gilbert, *Crime in London* (first published 1986. London: Grafton Books, 1987).
Kelman, James, *A Chancer* (first published 1985. London: Picador, 1987).
Kemsley, W. F., and D. Ginsberg, *Betting in Britain* (London: The Social Survey, Consumer Expenditure Series, Central Office of Information: 1986).
Kingsley, Charles, *The Water Babies* (2nd edn, London: Macaullan & Co., 1864).

——, *Letters to Young Men* (London: 1877).

Lambton, The Hon. George, *Men and Horses I Have Known* (London: Thornton Butterworth, 1924).

Lawson, Jack, *A Man's Life* (London: Hodder & Stoughton, 1932).

Laybourn, Keith and Jack Reynolds, *Liberalism and the Rise of Labour 1890–1918* (London: Croom Helm, 1984).

Lecky, W. E. H., *History of England in the Eighteenth Century*, 7 volumes (first published 1878–90. London: Longmans and Co., 1918–25).

Lee, Alan J., *The Origins of the Popular Press, 1855–1914* (first published 1976. London: Croom Helm, 1981).

Lenwood, Frank, *Gambling – Why Not?* (London: Independent Press, 1934).

Lieck, Albert, *Betting and Lotteries* (London: Butterworth & Co., 1935).

Linton, Alice, *Not Expecting Miracles* (London: Centreprise, 1982).

London, Jack, *The People of the Abyss* (first published 1903. London: Journeyman, 1977).

Longrigg, Roger, *The History of Horse Racing* (London: Macmillan & Co., 1972).

Low, Donald A., *Thieves' Kitchen. The Regency Underworld* (first published 1982. Gloucester: Alan Sutton, 1987).

Lucas, Norman, *Britain's Gangland* (London: W. H. Allen, 1969).

—— and Bernard Scarlett, *The Flying Squad* (London: Arthur Barker, 1968).

Luckman, A. Dick, *Sharps, Flats, Gamblers and Racehorses* (London: Grant Richards, 1914).

MacCanna, Prionsias, *Celtic Mythology* (London: Hamlyn, 1970).

McArthur, A., and H. Kingsley Long, *No Mean City* (first published 1956. London: Corgi, 1957).

McCord, Norman, *North-East England. An Economic and Social History* (London: Batsford Academic, 1979).

McCoy, Alfred W., *Drug Traffic and Organised Crime in Australia* (Sydney: Harper & Row, 1980).

McGhee, Bill, *Cut and Run* (first published 1962. London: Corgi Books, 1963).

McIlvanney, William, *Docherty* (first published 1975. London: Sceptre, 1987).

McLaverty, Michael, *The Three Brothers* (London: Jonathan Cape, 1948).

McLoughlin, Patrick, *The Johnson Street Bullies* (Bognor Regis: New Horizon, 1980).

Malcolmson, Robert W., *Popular Recreations in English Society 1700–1850* (Cambridge: Cambridge University Press, 1973).

Mannheim, Herbert, *Social Aspects of Crime in England between the Wars* (London: George Allen & Unwin, 1940).

Mannion, Pauline and Bernard, *The Summer Lane and Newtown of the Years between the Wars 1918–1938* (Birmingham: the authors, 1985).

Martin, Geoffrey, *Gambling and the Citizen* (London: Student Christian Movement, 1949).

Mason, Tony, *Association Football and English Society, 1863–1915* (Brighton: Harvester, 1981).

Mass Observation, *The Pub and the People. A Worktown Study* (first published 1943. London: The Cresset Library, 1987).

Mayhew, Henry, *The 'Morning Chronicle' Survey of Labour and the Poor in the Metropolitan District* vol. 1, (first published 1851–2. Firle: Caliban Books, 1980).

Mayhew, Henry, *London Labour and the London Poor* (first published 1851–2. Harmondsworth: Penguin, 1985).

Meacham, Standish, *A Life Apart. The English Working Class 1890–1914* (London: Thames and Hudson, 1977).

Meads, Richard James, *Growing up with Southall from 1904* (Southall: the author, 1979).

Mitchell, Jeremy, *Betting* (London: Pelham Books, 1972).

Moffat, Abe, *My Life with the Miners* (London: Lawrence & Wishart, 1965).

Moore, George, *Esther Waters* (first published 1894. Oxford: Oxford University Press, 1983).

Morgan, John Edward, *The Danger of Deterioration of Race from the too Rapid Increase of the Great Cities* (first published 1866. New York: Garland, 1985).

Moriarty, Cecil C. H., *Police Law. An Arrangement of Law and Regulations for the Use of Police Officers* (London: Butterworth & Co., 1931).

Mortimer, Roger, *The Jockey Club* (London: Cassell, 1958).

——, *The Encyclopaedia of Flat Racing* (London: Hale, 1971).

Morton, James, *Gangland. London's Underworld* (London: Warner edn, 1993).

——, *Gangland. Volume 2. The Underworld in Britain and Ireland* (London: Warner edn, 1995).

Muff, Clarence, *Unbelievable but True!* (Bradford: City of Bradford Metropolitan Council, 1984).

Munting, Roger, *An economic and social history of gambling in Britain and the USA* (Manchester and New York: Manchester University Press, 1996).

Murphy, John, *Instinct, Adventure and Gambling* (London: Society for the Promotion of Christian Knowledge, 1934).

Murray, Bill, *The Old Firm. Sectarianism, Sport and Society in Scotland* (Edinburgh: John Donald, 1984).

Naughton, Bill, *A Roof Over Your Head* (London: The Pilot Press, 1945).

——, *Saintly Billy. A Catholic Boyhood* (first published 1988. Oxford: Oxford University Press, 1989).

Neville, Ralph, *Light Come, Light Go* (London: Macmillan & Co., 1909).

Newman, Otto, *Gambling: Hazard and Reward* (London: The Athlone Press, 1972).

Newmarket, *Chapters from Turf History* (London: National Review, 1922).

Newton, Thomas, *Treatise touching Dyce-Play, and Prophane Gaming* (1586).

Nimrod, *The Chace, the Turf and the Road* (first published 1837. London: 1852).

Northbrooke, John, *A Treatise Against Dicing, Dancing, Plays, and Interludes, with Other Idle Pastimes* (first published *c.* 1577. London: Shakespeare Society, 1843).

Ogburn, Frederick Ernest, *The Law Relating to Gaming, Betting and Lotteries* (London: Effingham Wilson, 1910).

O'Hara, John, *A Mug's Game. A History of Gaming and Betting in Australia* (Kensington: New South Wales University Press, 1988).

Oman, Elsie, *Salford Stepping Stones* (Swinton: Neil Richardson, 1983).

Orchard, V., *The Family of Tattersall* (London: Hutchinson, 1953).

Oxford English Dictionary, volume 2 (Oxford: Oxford University Press, 1989).

Paley, Henry D., and John A. Glendinning, *Pattern for New York? A Report on Off-Track Betting in England* (New York: New York State Assembly, 1963).

Partridge, Eric, *The Penguin Dictionary of Historical Slang* (Harmondsworth: Penguin, 1972).

Pateman, T. W. (ed.), *Dunchurch. A Lancashire Background* (London: Museum Press, 1948).

Paterson, Alexander, *Across the Bridges. Life by the South London River-side* (first published 1911. New York: Garland, 1980).

Paterson, Professor W. P., and Dr David Watson (eds), *Social Evils and Social Problems* (Edinburgh: William Blackwood and Sons, 1918).

Paton, John, *Proletarian Pilgrimage. An Autobiography* (London: George Routledge & Sons, 1935).

Perkin, Harold, *Origins of Modern English Society* (first published 1969. London: Ark Paperbacks, 1985).

Perkins, Reverend E. Benson, *The Problem of Gambling* (London: Epworth Press, 1919).

——, *Betting Facts: Being an Account of the Facts of Betting Given in Evidence Before the Select Committee of the House of Commons on a Betting Duty* (London: Student Christian Movement, 1925).

——, *Gambling and Youth* (London: The National Sunday School Union, 1933).

——, *Gambling in English Life* (revised edn, London: The Epworth Press, 1958).

——, *So Appointed. An Autobiography* (London: Epworth Press, 1964).

Peterson, Virgil W., *Gambling Should It be Legalized?* (Springfield, Illinois: Charles C. Thomas, 1951).

Pickering, W. S. F. (ed.), *Anglican-Methodist Relations. Some Institutional Factors* (London: Darton, Longman & Todd, 1961).

Pilgrim Trust, *Men Without Work* (first published 1938. New York: Garland, 1985).

Porter, Roy, *English Society in the Eighteenth Century* (Penguin: Harmondsworth, 1982).

Press Council, *The Press and the People. 13th annual report* (London: The Press Council, 1966).

Procter, Maurice, *Hell is a City* (London: Hutchinson, 1954).

Quennell, Peter (ed.), *London's Underworld. Henry Mayhew* (London: Bracken Books, 1983).

Rees, Alwyn, and Brinley Rees, *Celtic Heritage. Ancient Traditions in Ireland and Wales* (London: Thames and Hudson, 1961).

Reeve, Henry (ed.), *The Greville Memoirs*, 3 volumes (4th edn, London: 1875).

Rice, James, *History of the British Turf From the Earliest Times to the Present Day*, 2 volumes (London: Sampson Low, Marston, Searle and Rivington, 1879).

Richards, Sir Gordon, *My Story* (London: Hodder & Stoughton, 1955).

Rickman, Eric, *On and Off the Racecourse* (London: George Routledge & Sons, 1937).

Roberts, Elizabeth, *A Woman's Place. An Oral History of Working-Class Women 1890–1940* (Oxford: Basil Blackwell, 1984).

Roberts, Robert, *The Classic Slum. Salford Life in the First Quarter of the Century* (first published 1971. Harmondsworth: Penguin, 1973).

Roman, Samuel, and Henry D. Paley, *Off-Track Betting, 1966 Report* (New York: New York State Assembly, 1966).

Rowntree, B. Seebohm, *Poverty. A Study of Town Life* (first published 1901. New York: Garland, 1980).

—— (ed.), *Betting and Gambling. A National Evil* (London: Macmillan and Co., 1905).

——, *Poverty and Progress. A Second Social Survey of York* (London: Longmans, Green & Co., 1941).

—— and G. R. Lavers, *English Life and Leisure. A Social Study* (London: Longmans, Green and Co., 1951).

Rowsell, Herbert W. and Clarence G. Morgan, *A Guide to the Law of Betting, Civil and Criminal* (London: Butterworth & Co., 1911).

Rubner, Alex, *The Economics of Gambling* (London: Macmillan, 1966).

Runyon, Damon, *Damon Runyon on Broadway* (first published 1950. London: Picador, 1977).

——, *Damon Runyon from First to Last* (first published 1954. London: Picador, 1975).

Ruskin, John, *The Crown of Wild Olive* (Kent: Smith, Elder & Co., 1882).

Russell, C. E. B., *Social Problems of the North* (first published 1913. New York: Garland, 1980).

Russell, R. J. (introduced), *The Peril of the Pools* (London: Epworth Press, 1935).

Samuel, Raphael, *East End Underworld. Chapters in the Life of Arthur Harding* (London: Routledge & Kegan Paul, 1981).

Sanders, Peter, *The Simple Annals. The History of an Essex and East End Family* (Gloucester: Alan Sutton, 1989).

Sanger, 'Lord' George, *Seventy Years A Showman* (first published 1910. MacGibbon & Kee, 1966).

Sargent, Harry, *Thoughts Upon Sport* (London: Photoprismatic Publishing Co., 1895).

Sarl, Arthur J., *Horses, Jockeys and Crooks. Reminiscences of Thirty Years' Racing* (London: Hutchinson & Co., 1935).

Scott, Alexander, *Turf Memories of Sixty Years* (London: Hutchinson & Co., 1925).

Scott, J. M., *Extel 100. The Centenary History of the Exchange Telegraph Company* (London: Benn, 1973).

Searle, G. R., *The Quest for National Efficiency: A Study in British Politics and Political Thought 1899–1914* (Oxford: Blackwell, 1971).

Semmel, Bernard, *Imperialism and Social Reform: English Social Imperial Thought* (London: George Allen & Unwin, 1960).

Shadwell, Arthur, *Industrial Efficiency. A Comparative Study of Industrial Life in England, Germany and America* (London: Longmans, Green and Co., 1920).

Sharpe, Graham, *Rare Stakes* (London: Pan, 1986).

Sherry, Norman, *The Life of Graham Greene* vol. 1, 1904–1939, (London: Jonathan Cape, 1989).

Shiman, Lilian, *Crusade Against Drink in Victorian England* (Basingstoke: Macmillan Press, 1988).

Shimmin, Hugh, *Liverpool Life: Its Pleasures, Practices and Pastimes* (first published 1856. New York: Garland, 1985).

Shoolbred, C. F., *The Law of Gaming and Betting* (2nd edn, London: Sir Isaac Pitman & Sons, 1935).

Sidney, Charles, *The Art of Legging* (London: Maxline International, 1976).

Sidney, S., *The Book of the Horse* (first published 1874. London: Cassell and Company, 1893).

Sims, George R., *My Life. Sixty Years' Recollections of Bohemian London* (London: Eveleigh Nash Company, 1917).

Smart, Hawley, *'The Plunger'. A Turf Tragedy of Five and Twenty Years Ago* (3rd edn, London: F. V. White & Co., 1891).

Smith, Sir H. Llewellyn (ed.), *The New Survey of London Life and Labour. Volume IX Life and Leisure* (London: P. S. King and Son, 1935).

Smithies, Edward, *Crime in Wartime. A Social History of Crime in World War II* (London: George Allen & Unwin, 1982).

Smout, T. C., *A Century of the Scottish People 1830–1950* (Glasgow: Fontana, 1987).

Somerville, Alexander, *The Autobiography of a Working Man* (first published 1848. London: Turnstile Press, 1951).

Spanier, David, *Easy Money. Inside the Gambler's Mind* (London: Secker & Warburg, 1987).

Spencer, Edward, *The Great Game and How It is Played etc.* (London, G. Richard, 1903).

Spring, Howard, *Shabby Tiger* (first published 1934. London: Fairwater, 1967).

Stevenson, John, and Chris Cook, *The Slump. Society and Politics During the Depression* (first published 1977. London: Quartet Books, 1979).

Stone, Lawrence, *The Family, Sex and Marriage in England 1500–1800* (London: Weidenfeld and Nicolson, 1977).

Stone, L. and J., *An Open Elite? England 1540–1880* (Oxford: Oxford University Press, 1984).

Strutt, Joseph, *The Sports and Pastimes of the People of England etc.* (London: 1833).

Stutfield, George Herbert, *The Law Relating to Betting, Time-Bargains and Gaming* (London: 1892).

Sugden, E. H. (ed.), *Wesley's Standard Sermons* vol. 2 (London: Epworth Press, 1921).

Swaffer, Percy, *Fleet Street Goes Racing* (London: Hutchinson & Co., 1939).

Sykes, J. B. (ed.), *The Concise Oxford Dictionary of Current English* (7th edn, Oxford: Oxford University Press, 1982).

Sylvanus, *The Bye-Lanes and Downs of England with Turf Scenes and Characters* (London: 1850).

Taine, Hippolyte, *Notes on England* (London: 1873).

Tebbutt, Melanie, *Making Ends Meet. Pawnbroking and Working-Class Credit* (first published 1983. London: Methuen, 1984).

Thomas, ex-Detective Superintendent David, *Seek Out the Guilty* (London: John Long, 1969).

Thomas, Keith, *Religion and the Decline of Magic. Studies in Popular Belief in Sixteenth and Seventeenth-Century England* (first published 1971. Harmondsworth: Penguin 1973).

Thompson, Anthony Hugh, *Censorship in Public Libraries in the United Kingdom during the Twentieth Century* (Epping: Bowker, 1975).

Thompson, Dorothy, *The Chartists. Popular Politics in the Industrial Revolution* (first published 1984. Aldershot: Wildwood House, 1986).

Thompson, F. M. L., *The Rise of Respectable Society. A Social History of Victorian Britain 1830–1900* (London: Fontana, 1988).

Thompson, Paul, *The Edwardians. The Remaking of British Society* (first published 1975. London: Paladin, 1979).

Thormanby, *Men of the Turf. Anecdotes of Their Careers and Notes on Many Famous Races* (London: Bateman & Co., 1887).

Thormanby, *Sporting Stories* (London: Mills and Boon, 1909).

Treble, James H., *Urban Poverty in Britain 1830–1914* (first published 1979. London: Methuen, 1983).

Trescatheric, Brian, *Sport and Leisure in Victorian Barrow* (Barrow: Hougenai Press, 1977).

Trevelyan, G. M., *English Social History. A Survey of Six Centuries. Chaucer to Queen Victoria* (first published 1942. Harmondsworth: Penguin, 1986).

Turner, Thomas, *The Diary of a Georgian Shopkeeper* (first published 1925. Oxford: Oxford University Press, 1979).

Vamplew, Wray, *The Turf. A Social and Economic History of Horse Racing* (London: Allen Lane, 1976).

Veblen, T., *The Theory of the Leisure Class* (New York: Macmillan, 1899).

Victoria History of the Counties of England, *A History of the County of Dorset*, vol. II (London: Oxford University Press, 1908).

Vincent, David, *Bread, Knowledge and Freedom. A Study of Nineteenth-Century Working-Class Autobiography* (London: Europa, 1981).

Watson, Alfred E. T. (ed.), *The Racing World and Its Inhabitants* (London: Macmillan, 1904).

Wensley, Frederick Porter, *Detective Days. The Record of Forty-Two Years' Service in the Criminal Investigation Department* (London: Cassell & Co., 1931).

White, Arnold, *The Problems of a Great City* (first published 1886. New York: Garland, 1985).

White, Jerry, *Rothschilds Buildings. Life in an East End Tenement Block 1887–1920* (London: Routledge & Kegan Paul, 1980).

——, *The Worst Street in North London. Campbell Bunk, Islington, Between the Wars* (London: Routledge & Kegan Paul, 1986).

Wilkinson, Dyke, *Rough Roads. Reminiscences of a Wasted Life* (London: Sampson Low & Co., 1912).

Woodward, Kathleen, *Jipping Street* (first published 1928. London: Virago, 1983).

Wykes, Alan, *Gambling* (London: Alder Books, 1964).

Young, James D., *Making Trouble. Autobiographical Explorations and Socialism* (Glasgow: Clydeside Press, 1989).

——, *Socialism and the English Working Class* (Hemel Hempstead: Harvester Wheatsheaf, 1989).

Zweig, Ferdynand, *The British Worker* (Harmondsworth: Penguin, 1952).

ARTICLES

Chinn, Carl, 'Betting Shops and Race-by-Race Betting Before the Betting and Gaming Act, 1960', *Society for the Study of Gambling Newsletter*, no. 17, July 1990, pp. 10–20.

Clapson, Mark, 'Gambling, "The Fancy", and Poverty in Charles Booth's

"Life and Labour of the People in London"' (paper read to the Charles Booth Conference, 15 April 1989).

Constantine, Stephen, '*Love on the Dole* and Its Reception in the 1930s', *Literature and History*, vol. 8, no. 1 (1982).

——, Eddie Frow and Andrew Davis, 'Walter Greenwood and "Love on the Dole" – A Discussion', *History Workshop 23. Class, Community and Conflict* (3–5 November 1989).

Cunningham, Hugh, 'Leisure', in John Benson (ed.), *The Working Class in England 1875–1914* (London: Croom Helm, 1985), pp. 133–164.

Davies, Andrew, 'The Police and the People: Gambling in Salford, 1900–1939', *Historical Journal*, 34, 1 (1991), pp. 87–115.

Devereux, E. C., 'Gambling in Psychological and Sociological Perspective', *International Encyclopaedia of the Social Sciences*, vol. 6 (1968), pp. 53–62.

Dixon, David, '"Class law": The Street Betting Act of 1906', *International Journal of Sociology of Law*, vol. 8 (1980), pp. 101–28.

——, 'Illegal Gambling and Histories of Policing', *Society for the Study of Gambling Newsletter*, no. 3, April 1983, pp. 1–7.

Fernando, S. J. M., 'Alcoholism and Gambling: the Case of the Jews', *Society for the Study of Gambling*, no. 1, May 1982, pp. 16–21.

Filby, Michael P., and Lee Harvey, 'Recreational Betting: Everyday Activities and Strategies', *Leisure Studies*, vol. 7, 1988, pp. 159–72.

Gourvish, T. R., 'The Government and the Business of Gambling: State Lotteries in Britain, 1750–1826', paper given at the *Institute of Historical Research*, 23 February 1989.

Green, Christopher, 'Birmingham's Politics, 1873–1891: The Local Basis of Change' *Midland History*, vol. 2, no. 2, autumn 1973, pp. 84–98.

Harrison, Brian, 'The Sunday Trading Riots of 1865', *Historical Journal*, vol. 8, no. 2 (1965), p. 219–45.

Itzkowitz, David C., 'Victorian Bookmakers and Their Customers', *Victorian Studies*, vol. 32, no. 1, autumn 1988, pp. 7–30.

Jenkins, Philip, and Gary W. Potter, 'Before the Krays: Organised Crime in London, 1920–1960', *Criminal Justice History. An International Annual* (Westport), vol. 9 (1988), pp. 209–30.

McKibbin, Ross, 'Arthur Henderson as Labour Leader', *International Review of Social History*, vol. 23 (1978) pp. 97–125.

——, 'Working-Class Gambling in Britain 1880–1939', *Past and Present*, no. 82, February 1979, pp. 147–78.

Mason, Tony, 'Sporting News, 1860–1914', in Michael Harris and Alan J. Lee (eds), *The Press in English Society from the Seventeenth to Nineteenth Centuries* (London: Press Group of the Acton Society Trust, 1986), pp. 168–86.

Metcalfe, Alan, 'Organised Sport in the Mining Communities of South Northumberland, 1800–1889', *Victorian Studies*, vol. 25, no. 4, summer 1982, pp. 469–95.

Miers, David, 'A Social and Legal History of Gaming: From the Restoration to the Gaming Act 1845', in T. G. Watkin (ed.), *Legal Record and Historial Reality* (London: The Hambledon Press, 1989), pp. 107–19.

Munting, Roger, 'Betting and Business: The Commercialisation of Gambling in Britain', *Business History*, vol. 31, no. 4, October 1989, pp. 67–85.

Perrucci, Robert, 'The Neighborhood "Bookmaker": Entrepreneur and Mobility Model', in Paul Meadows and Ephraim H. Mizruchi (eds), *Urbanism, Urbanization, and Change: Comparative Perspectives* (Reading, Massachusetts: Addison-Wesley Publishing Co., 1969), pp. 302–11.

Thompson, E. P., 'Time, Work-Discipline and Industrial Capitalism', *Past and Present*, no. 38, December 1967, pp. 50–62.

Webster, Roger, '*Love on the Dole* and the Aesthetic of Contradiction', in Jeremy Hawthorn, (ed.), *The British Working Class Novel in the Twentieth Century* (London: Edward Arnold, 1984), pp. 49–62.

Woods, David, 'Community Violence', in John Benson (ed.), *The Working Class in England 1875–1914* (London: Croom Helm, 1985), pp. 165–205.

Zola, I. K., 'Observations on Gambling in a Lower Class Setting', in Robert D. Herman (ed.) *Gambling* (New York: Harper & Row, 1967), pp. 19–31.

THESES

Benning, Derek Ian, 'The Development of Physical Recreation in the Staffordshire Potteries 1850–1875', University of Liverpool, unpublished MEd thesis (1979).

Chinn, Carl, 'The Anatomy of a Working-Class Neighbourhood: West Sparkbrook, 1871–1914', University of Birmingham, unpublished PhD thesis (1986).

Clapson, Mark, 'Popular Gambling and English Culture, 1845–1961', University of Warwick, unpublished PhD thesis (1989).

Davies, Andrew Mark, 'Leisure and Poverty in Salford and Manchester, 1900–1939', University of Cambridge, unpublished PhD thesis (1980).

Dixon, David, 'Anti-Gambling and the State: Development in the Legal Control of Betting in England and Wales 1890–1929', University of Wales, unpublished PhD thesis (1985).

Eadie, Emma, 'The Racing Career of Lord George Bentinck M.P. 1826–46', University of Birmingham, unpublished BA dissertation (1987).

Harris, George Benjamin, 'Street Betting in the Twentieth Century: Its Social Significance in the Working-Class Community', University of Lancaster, unpublished dissertation (1978).

Jones, Stephen G., 'The British Labour Movement and Working-Class Leisure, 1918–1939', University of Manchester, unpublished PhD thesis (1983).

Miller, Robin, 'Gambling and the British Working Class, 1870–1914', University of Edinburgh, unpublished MA thesis (1974).

Poole, John Rollason, 'Wakes, Holidays and Pleasure Fairs in the Lancashire Cotton District, *c.* 1790–1890', University of Lancaster, unpublished PhD thesis (1985).

Power, James, 'Aspects of Working-Class Leisure During the Depression Years: Bolton in the 1930s', University of Warwick, unpublished MA thesis (1980).

Sponza, L., 'The Italian Poor in Nineteenth Century Britain', University of London, unpublished PhD thesis (1984).

LETTERS

Finally, I should like to thank the following people who sent me information and who are not mentioned in the text or notes: C. Aldridge; Jenny Atherton; Mr J. A. Ayling; Gordon Baird; Mrs J. Bell; K. D. Billam; R. Brown; Mr W. Burr; Mr S. Cantor; S. E. D. Davies; Jim Dawes; Bob Dobson; W. Duggan; Coley Flaherty; Mr S. B. Fox; John Frater; L. H. Furness; Mr Guy; J. Hant; Mrs B. P. Hreet; Mr and Mrs Hunter; Maurice Jacobs; L. R. and E. W. Kelley, Chris Ketchley; M. E. King; Sid Leaker; Mr E. Leaver; W. F. Leggett; Walter Livesey; Mrs M. E. Luck; Jimmy McCafferty; Hugh McCoy; Monty Maxfield; Marian Millington; Wilf Morgan; Mrs R. Murrell; National Oral History Society of New Zealand; W. H. Nevell; G. Oglesby; Mrs M. Oliver; Mrs G. Peters; Mr W. Pirie; F. Rockett; Will Rogers; Margaret Rysen; Dave Scott; Steven P. Scott; J. C. Sharp; Trevor Sidaway; Madge Smith; Joan Stock; South Wales Miners' Library; Joan Taylor; A. W. Teall; Ian Watkins; Mrs E. Whild. My apologies to anyone whom I have omitted.

NOTES

PREFACE

1. BBC Television, *Big Deal* (first episode, 14 October 1984).
2. BBC Television, *Wings* (9 October 1988); BBC Television, *Bergerac* (4 March 1990).
3. BBC Television, *The Paradise Club* (19 September 1989); Central Television, *Chancer* (1 May 1990).
4. BBC Radio 4 (14 October 1987).
5. Scottish Television, *Bookie* (1988).
6. Mark Clapson, *A Bit of a Flutter. Popular gambling and English society c. 1823–1961* (Manchester: Manchester University Press, 1992), p. 210.
7. Roger Munting, *An economic and social history of gambling in Britain and the USA* (Manchester and New York: Manchester University Press, 1996), p. viii.
8. Stanley Shivas, 'Winning way to be tops', *Daily Record*, April 1986.

INTRODUCTION: WHAT IS BOOKMAKING?

1. Rev. A. N. Boyle, 'Sport and Betting. Who Maintains the "Bookies"', in *Forward*, 20 November 1920; source cited in Stephen G. Jones, 'The British Labour Movement and Working-Class Leisure, 1918–1939', University of Manchester, unpublished PhD thesis, 1983.
2. This definition of a bet is that given by Lord Buckmaster in 'A. G. v. Luncheon and Sports Club Ltd' (1929), cited in J. P. Eddy and L. L. Loewe, *The New Law of Betting and Gambling* (London: Butterworths, 1961), p. 3.
3. A collection of unusual and preposterous bets is found in Graham Sharpe, *Rare Stakes* (London: Pan, 1986).
4. In Britain, the colloquial verb 'to fancy' means having a high opinion of yourself, another, or of a thing and it dates from about 1860; the noun, punter, was known by 1874 and it is presumed to have been in use before then; however, to lay a bet or a wager is Standard English – see Eric Partridge, *The Penguin Dictionary of Historical Slang* (Harmondsworth: Penguin, 1972), pp. 305, 734 and 526.
5. The story of probably the most successful professional punter in post-war Britain is in Alex Bird with Terry Manners, *The Life and Secrets of a Professional Punter. Alex Bird* (London: Queen Anne Press, 1985). For professional betting, see also Eric Rickman, *On and Off the Racecourse* (London: George Routledge & Sons, 1937), pp. 219–21.

6. An explanation as to why racecourse bookmakers might make bets as well as lay them is found in Chinn Interviews, George Tiano, pp. 5–6; see also *ibid.*, Len Boden, p. 15, Jim Davis, *passim*; and Patsy Collins, *passim*.
7. The best explanations of the mathematics involved in formulating odds and in making a book are by Phil Bull, 'The Mathematics of Betting', in Phil Bull and A Retired Starting Price Bookmaker, *How to Make a Book* (London: Morrison and Gibb, 1945), pp. 131–54; and Charles Sidney, *The Art of Legging* (London: Maxline International, 1976), pp. 87–104 and pp. 135–95. See also E. L. Figgis, *Focus on Gambling* (London: Arthur Barker, 1951), pp. 99–119; Rickman, *op. cit.*, pp. 211–21; Royal Commission on Gambling, *Final Report*, vol. 1 (London: Her Majesty's Stationery Office, cmnd 7200, 1978), pp. 16–18 and 468–77. For a description of the types of bets available on horse- and dog-racing, see A Retired Starting Price Bookmaker, 'A Starting-Price Office from Within', in Bull and A Retired Starting Price Bookmaker, *op. cit.*, pp. 32–127. A punter's point of view on betting is given by Jeremy Mitchell, *Betting* (London: Pelham Books, 1972).
8. Chinn Interviews, Len Boden, p. 17.
9. For a full description of the betting book and of a racecourse bookmaker's opinion of the mathematics of betting, see Chinn Interviews, Len Boden, pp. 13–18.

1 BEFORE BOOKMAKING: GAMBLERS, ADVENTURERS AND SHARPSTERS

1. Alwyn Rees and Brinley Rees, *Celtic Heritage. Ancient Tradition in Ireland and Wales* (London: Thames and Hudson, 1961), pp. 143 and 171; see also Proinsias MaCanna, *Celtic Mythology* (London: Hamlyn, 1970), p. 119.
2. Dorothy Laird, 'Racing in Scotland', in *Scottish Field*, May 1979, p. 8 (thanks to Kilmarnock and Loudon Libraries). For histories of British horse-racing see: Theodore Andrea Cook, *A History of the English Turf*, 3 volumes (London: Virtue & Co., 1901); Roger Longrigg, *The History of Horse Racing* (London: Macmillan, 1972); James Rice, *History of the British Turf. From the Earliest Times to the Present Day* (London: Sampson Low, Marston, Searle and Rivington, 1879).
3. Laird, *op. cit.*, p. 8; *Paterson's History of the Families of Ayrshire*, vol. 1, p. 81 (thanks to Kilmarnock and Loudon Libraries).
4. Information supplied by Renfrew Libraries, Paisley; A. D. Roberts, *Lanark: The Burgh and Its Councils 1469–1880*, p. 61 (thanks to Clydesdale Libraries, Lanark); cited in John Ashton, *The History of Gambling in England* (first published 1899. New York: Burt Franklin, 1968), pp. 175–6.
5. Cited in Laird, *op. cit.*, p. 8.
6. James Shirley, *Hide Park* (1637) cited in Ashton, *op. cit.*, pp. 176–8.
7. Examples of match racing and betting are given in *ibid.* pp. 179–81; and Cook, *op. cit.*, pp. 104–5, 185–6 and 240–5.
8. Sir George Clark, *The Later Stuarts 1660–1714* (2nd ed., Oxford: Oxford University Press, 1956), p. 408; see also Cook, *op. cit.*, pp. 145–72. The pre-eminence of Newmarket as a centre of horse-racing is

discussed in J. P. Hore, *History of Newmarket* (London: A. H. Bailey & Co., 1886). For sport in general during the time of the later Stuarts, see Dennis Brailsford, *Sport and Society. Elizabeth to Anne* (London: Routledge & Kegan Paul, 1969), pp. 198–216.

9. For a summary of the expansion of horse-racing, see Roy Porter, *English Society in the Eighteenth Century* (Harmondsworth: Penguin, 1982), p. 255. For the Jockey Club see Sir Roger Mortimer, *The Jockey Club* (London: Cassell, 1958); Christopher R. Hill, *Horse Power. The Politics of the Turf* (Manchester: Manchester University Press, 1988), pp. 141–83; Eric Rickman, 'The Jockey Club', in Ernest Bland (ed.), *Flat Racing Since 1900* (London: Andrew Dakers, 1950); and Wray Vamplew, *The Turf. A Social and Economic History of Horse Racing* (London: Allen Lane, 1976), pp. 77–109.
10. The Gaming Act, 1739, 13 Geo. 2, cap. 19, C. F. Shoolbred, *The Law of Gaming and Betting* (2nd ed., London: Sir Isaac Pitman & Sons, 1935), p. 199.
11. Robert W. Malcolmson, *Popular Recreations in English Society 1700–1850* (Cambridge: Cambridge University Press, 1973), p. 138; for a fuller discussion see pp. 89–157.
12. Anonymous, *A Correct Guide to the Frequenters of Races, Theatres, Gaming-Tables, Feasts, &c.* (Rotherham: 1823), pp. 3–5 (thanks to Rotherham Libraries).
13. *Ibid.*, pp. 3–4.
14. Examples of match-racing 'cards' (details of the races to be run at a meeting) are in the Victoria History of the Counties of England, *A History of the County of Dorset*, vol. II (London: Oxford University Press, 1908), p. 316. (thanks to Dorset Libraries, Dorchester). For details of the running of match races see Thomas Turner, *The Diary of a Georgian Shopkeeper* (first published 1925. Oxford: Oxford University Press, 1979), pp. 13, 41, 56, and 68–9. The diary refers to the years 1754 to 1765.
15. *Ibid.*; in 1707, Lord Granby and Mr Young matched their horses for £3,000, and in 1708 the Duke of Bedford and Mr Minchall raced their two horses for a stake of 1,000 guineas, see Ashton, *op. cit.*, p. 180.
16. Shoolbred, *op. cit.*, pp. 199–200.
17. L. and J. Stone, *An Open Elite? England 1540–1880* (Oxford: Oxford University Press, 1986), p. 218. See also Porter, *op. cit.*, pp. 69–83.
18. W. E. H. Lecky, *History of England in the Eighteenth Century* (first published 1878–90. London: Longmans & Co, 1918–25), vol. 2, p. 156.
19. Cited in Porter, *op. cit.*, p. 256.
20. Cited in Ashton, *op. cit.*, p. 75. Gambling at dice games has great antiquity, see Joseph Strutt, *The Sports and Pastimes of the People of England etc.* (London: 1833), pp. 305–8.
21. For more details about upper-class gambling see Ashton, *op. cit.*, pp. 40–172; and David Miers, 'A Social and Legal History of Gaming: From the Restoration to the Gaming Act 1845', in T. G. Watkin (ed.), *Legal Record and Historical Reality* (London: The Hambledon Press, 1989), pp. 107–19.
22. *The Diary of William Bulkely*, *c.* 1720–30 (thanks to Gwynedd

Libraries Caernarfon). The best description of the matching and fighting of cocks is by M. H., 'Cock-Fighting in Newcastle', and Kenneth Dumfries, 'Rules and Regulations of the Cock-Pit', in *Monthly Chronicle*, March 1887, pp. 42–4 (thanks to Gateshead Libraries). See also Malcolmson, *op. cit.*, pp. 49–50.

23. Turner, *op. cit.*, pp. 42 and 44. For a discussion of card playing, its origins, and the various card games, see Strutt, *op. cit.*, pp. 323–38. Turner also indicated the involvement of non-gentry in cock-fighting: 'JUNE 10. Was fought this day, at Jones's, a main of cocks, between the gentlemen of Hothly and Pevensey. *Quere*, Is there a gentleman in either of the places that was consernd?', *op. cit.*, p. 50. It is obvious that often the word gentleman was an elastic term and represented the owners of the cocks rather than their social status; see M. H., *op. cit.*, p. 42.
24. Turner, *op. cit.*, p. 58.
25. I am not suggesting that historians should avoid general definitions of the middle class or else of the middle ranks, whatever term is used to describe them; nor that historians should eschew characterizing their way of life. It is useful and necessary that both these things are done. However, it is important to bear in mind those who did not conform to all the cultural norms of their class, and to recognize their significance. For a discussion of the Georgian middle class, see Porter, *op. cit.*, pp. 83–99; and Harold Perkin, *Origins of Modern English Society* (first published 1969. London: Ark Paperbacks, 1985), pp. 17–38 and 56–62.
26. For a fuller discussion of this issue see Chapters 5 and 6.
27. John Northbroke, *A Treatise Against Dicing, Dancing, Plays, and Interludes, with Other Idle Pastimes* (first published *c.* 1577. London: Shakespeare Society, 1843), pp. 137–8; Ernest Benson Perkins, *The Problem of Gambling* (London: Epworth Press, 1919), p. 10; see also John Hawke, 'The Extent of Gambling', in B. Seebohm Rowntree (ed.), *Betting and Gambling. A National Evil* (London: Macmillan and Co., 1905), pp. 21–4; and 'Is Gambling on the Increase?', *Spectator*, 14 February 1891, pp. 235–7.
28. Rev. J. Glass, *Gambling and Religion* (London: Longmans, Green & Co., 1924), p.4.
29. See Chapters 5 and 6.
30. Of course, there were working-class as well as middle-class puritans, and the inheritors of the tradition were active, also, against gambling in the later 1800s and early 1900s; see Chapter 6. For puritanism, see Christopher Hill, *Society and Puritanism in Pre-Revolutionary England* (London: Secker and Warburg, 1964).
31. James Mill, *An Essay on Government* (1820), pp. 31–2, cited in Asa Briggs, 'The Language of Class', in Asa Briggs, *The Collected Essays of Asa Briggs. Volume I: Words, Numbers, Places, People* (Brighton: Harvester, 1985) p. 10.
32. Perkin, *op. cit.*, p. 277.
33. Patrick Colquhoun, *A Treatise on the Wealth, Power and Resources of the British Empire* (1814), p. 49, cited in Perkin, *op. cit.*, p. 276. For a full discussion of the middle-class attack on the landowning class see Briggs, *op. cit.*, pp. 6–14; and Perkin, *op. cit.*, pp. 176–339.
34. As late as 1883, Joseph Chamberlain denounced vehemently the

landowning class as those who '*toil not neither do they spin*', cited in Sir Robert Ensor, *England 1870–1914* (Oxford: Oxford University Press, 1936), p. 87. In 1886, he and his followers abandoned the Liberals and allied themselves with the Conservatives over the issue of Home Rule for Ireland. Effectively, this signalled a *rapprochement* between middle-class radicals and the upper class. For the emergence of popular socialism, see P. Adelman, *The Rise of the Labour Party* (2nd ed., London: Longman, 1986).

35. J. Ramsey MacDonald, 'Gambling and Citizenship', in Rowntree (ed.), *op. cit.*, p. 134.
36. *Ibid.*, p. 120. For a further discussion of betting and politics see Chapter 6.
37. Guy Chapman, *Culture and Survival* (London: Jonathan Cape, 1940), p. 105.
38. *Ibid.*; G. D. H. Cole and Raymond Postgate, *The Common People 1746–1946* (first published 1938. London: Methuen, 1961), p. 60.
39. Ross McKibbin, 'Working-Class Gambling in Britain 1880–1939', *Past and Present*, no. 82, February 1979, p. 148. Gareth Stedman Jones, 'Working-Class Culture and Working-Class Politics in London, 1870–1900: Notes on the Remaking of a Working Class', in Gareth Stedman Jones, *Languages of Class. Studies in English Working Class History 1832–1982* (Cambridge: Cambridge University Press, 1983), p. 203.
40. McKibbin, *op. cit.*, p. 148.
41. Cited in R. H. Charles, *Gambling and Betting* (first published 1924. Edinburgh: T. & T. Clarke, 1928), p. 4; The Gospel According to Saint Mark, Chapter 15, Verse 24. For a fuller discussion of gambling in history and in various countries see Charles, *op. cit.*, pp. 1–22 and Alan Wykes, *Gambling* (London: Alder Books, 1964) *passim.*
42. Cited in Ashton, *op. cit.*, p. 17; Nottingham Borough, *Records*, ii, pp. 329–31 (thanks to Nottinghamshire Libraries, Nottingham).
43. 33 Hen. 8, cap. 9. The earliest statutory enactment against games was passed in 1388 and it aimed to prevent pastimes from interfering with the practice of archery on the Sabbath. Henry VIII's Gaming Act of 1541 emphasized that the problem was not solved and it made clear the connection between gaming and gambling. It stated that no person 'shall for or their gain, lucre or living, keep, have, hold, occupy, exercise and maintain, any common house, alley, or place of dicing, table or carding . . .'; Shoolbred, *op. cit.*, pp. 2–3 and 193–4.
44. Northbrooke, *op. cit.*, p. 137.
45. Another sixteenth-century work on gambling was by Thomas Newton, *Treatise Touching Dyce-play, and Prophane Gaming* (1586).
46. For example, Dr Marmaduke Moor, Rector of Ordsall, was ejected from his living and had his paternal estates sequestered 'for treason and for the heinous offence of playing at cards, three several times with his own wife'; *White's Directory* (Nottingham: 1844), p. 645 (thanks to Nottinghamshire Libraries, Nottingham).
47. Samuel Pepys, *Diary*, 21 December 1663, cited in Keith Thomas, *Religion and the Decline of Magic. Studies in Popular Belief in Sixteenth and Seventeenth-Century England* (first published 1971. Harmondsworth:

Penguin, 1973), p. 24; and Samuel Pepys, *Diary*, 1 January 1668, cited in Ashton, *op. cit.* pp. 45–6. For gaming in general, see Charles Cotton, *The Compleat Gamester* (London: Henry Brome, 1674).

48. There is further evidence of working-class betting on seventeenth-century cock-fights in Oliver Heywood, *The Rev. Oliver Heywood, B.A., 1630–1702; His Autobiography, Diaries, Anecdotes and Event Books* (1881–5), ii, pp. 271–2, cited in Malcolmson, *op. cit.*, p. 49. He told of a cock-fight in Halifax in 1680 at which betted both 'poor men' and gentlemen.
49. Strutt, *op. cit.*, pp. 276, 337–8 and 386–7. For a fuller discussion of tossing and pitch and toss see Chapter 4. Another popular game with coins was shove ha'penny, which allowed gambling on a small scale; for its origins see John T. Godfrey, *Popular Amusements in Nottingham in the Fifteenth and Sixteenth Centuries* (Nottingham: 1896), pp. 10–11 (thanks to Nottinghamshire Libraries, Nottingham).
50. *Gentleman's Magazine*, vol. 33, September 1763, p. 361.
51. Ashton, *op. cit.*, pp. 155 and 172.
52. *Ibid.*, pp. 152–72; Nottinghamshire County Library, Wagers – Floods.
53. Malcolmson, *op. cit.*, p. 49.
54. Hannah More, Cheap Repository Tracts, *The Cock-Fighter. A True History* (London: 1795), pp. 3–6 (thanks to Avon Libraries, Bristol).
55. Zacharias Conrad von Uffenbach, *London in 1710, From the Travels of Zacharias Conrad von Uffenbach* (1934), pp. 48–9, cited in Malcolmson, *op. cit.*, pp. 49–50.
56. Cited in F. W. Hackwood, *Old English Sports* (London: T. Fisher Unwin, 1907), p. 267.
57. César de Saussure, *A Foreign View of England in the Reigns of George I and George II: The Letters of Monsieur César de Saussure to His Family* (1902), p. 180, cited in Malcolmson, *op. cit.*, p. 42.
58. Grudge matches continued side by side with professional pugilism; see cuttings on pugilism, Islington Central Library (my thanks to). For a short but informed discussion of the origins of the prize-ring, see Geoffrey H. Vines, 'Bare-Knuckled Bruisers', in *Bankway Society Newsletter* (spring 1986), pp. 2–5 (thanks to Hertfordshire Libraries).
59. Matches were made from ten guineas a side, or less, to 300 guineas or more; see 'The Prize Ring', in *Pescott Frost Cuttings Book*, vol. 1, pp. 70–81 (thanks to Hampshire Libraries, Portsmouth); and George Caunt, 'Bare-Fisted Prizefighting in Hertfordshire', in *Hertfordshire Countryside*, vol. 18, no. 70, autumn 1963, pp. 72–3 (thanks to Hertfordshire Libraries).
60. Sylas Neville, *The Diary of Sylas Neville, 1767–1788* (1950), p. 173, cited in Malcolmson, *op. cit.*, p. 43.
61. It is likely that betting also took place on a variety of other sports such as single-stick; kayles and fives; and pedestrianism. See 'Single-stick', in *Pescot Frost Cuttings Book*, vol. 1, pp. 115–16; W. H. Howse, *Radnorshire*, p. 185 (thanks to Hampshire Libraries, Portsmouth, and Powys Libraries); and Walthamstow Libraries, *Pamphlets, Prints etc.*, no. 1401, 1765 (my thanks to).
62. See *Lancaster Gazette*, 5 and 12 June 1813 (thanks to Lancashire

Libraries, Lancaster); and Ralph Neville, *Light Come, Light Go* (London: Macmillan & Co., 1909), p. 200.

63. Thomas Holcroft, *Memoirs of the Late Thomas Holcroft, Written by Himself and Continued to the Time of His Death from His Diary, Notes, and Other Papers* (London: Constable & Co., 1852), pp. 29–30. For this reference and those from some other working-class autobiographies, I am indebted to a marvellous bibliography: John Burnett, David Mayall and David Vincent, *The Autobiography of the Working Classes, an Annotated Critical Bibliography*, 3 vols (Brighton and Hemel Hempstead: Harvester, 1984–9).
64. Holcroft, *op. cit.*, pp. 30–1.
65. *Ibid.*, pp. 62–3. For the fair-like atmosphere of race-courses in the nineteenth century, see 'Lord' George Sanger, *Seventy Years a Showman* (first published 1910. London: Macgibbon & Kee, 1966), pp. 67–72.
66. Turner, *op. cit.*, p. 13.
67. While McKibbin believed that gambling was endemic before the 1880s, he did not think that it could be described as 'mass', *op. cit.*, p. 148.
68. Northbroke, *op. cit.*
69. Richard Kay, *The Diary of Richard Kay, 1716–1751, of Baldingtone near Bury: A Lancashire Doctor* (1968), p. 23, cited in Malcolmson, *op. cit.*, p. 158.
70. Lawrence Stone, *The Family, Sex and Marriage in England 1500–1800* (London: Weidenfeld and Nicolson, 1977), p. 678; see also Christopher Hill, *op. cit.*, *passim.*
71. Malcolmson, *op. cit.*, p. 158; see also J. M. Goldby and A. W. Purdue, *The Civilisation of the Crowd. Popular Culture in England 1750–1900* (London: Batsford Academic and Educational, 1984), pp. 39–62.
72. Malcolmson, op. *cit.*, p. 166.
73. Sir William Blackstone, *Commentaries on the Laws of England* (1755), vol. iv, p. 171, cited in George M'Elry, *Gambling and the Law* (Belfast: address to the Magistrates' Association, 1934), p. 10.
74. Letter from Sunderlandensis, *Gentleman's Magazine*, vol. 21, April 1751, p. 165.
75. Blackstone, *op. cit.*, p. 171.
76. Miers, *op. cit.*, p. 110.
77. The noun 'pigeon' dates from about 1590, Partridge, *op. cit.*, p. 690.
78. Samuel Pepys, cited in Miers, *op. cit.*, p. 110.
79. Descriptions of London gaming houses in the eighteenth century are in Ashton, *op. cit.*, pp. 40–90.
80. Miers, *op. cit.*, p. 111.
81. 16 Cha. 2, cap. 7, Shoolbred, *op. cit.*, p. 3.
82. *Act Against Playing at Cards and Dice, &c.*, Edinburgh, 12 April 1704 (thanks to Edinburgh Libraries).
83. The Gaming Act, 1710, 9 Ann, cap. 19, Shoolbred, *op. cit.*, p. 195.
84. Miers, *op. cit.*, pp. 112–13.
85. The Gaming Act, 1738, 12 Geo. 2, cap. 28, Shoolbred, *op. cit.*, pp. 196–9.
86. The Gaming Act 1739, 13 Geo. 2, cap. 19, and the Gaming Act, 1744, 18 Geo. 2, c. 34, Shoolbred, *op. cit.*, pp. 199–202.
87. *Gentleman's Magazine*, vol. 21, February 1751, p. 87.

88. *Ibid.*, vol. 21, April 1751, p. 184.
89. *Ibid.*, vol. 1, January 1731, p. 25.
90. John Brown, *On the Pursuit of FALSE PLEASURE, and the Mischiefs of IMMODERATE GAMING: A SERMON*, (Bath: 1750), pp. 10–11 (thanks to Avon Libraries, Bristol). Like John Brown, Northbrooke warned of the dangers of losing inheritances through gambling, *op. cit.*, p. 115.
91. John Fielding, 'The History of Gambling', *Gentleman's Magazine*, vol. 26, December 1756, pp. 564–7. Henry Fielding was the London Justice of the Peace who set up the Bow Street Runners; his brother, John, was a JP also; see Malcolmson, *op. cit.*, pp. 156–7.
92. Philip Thicknesse, *The New Prose Bath Guide for the Year 1778 . . .* (Bath: 1778), pp. 82–4; Thomas Rennell, *The Consequences of the Vice of Gaming as They Affect the Welfare of Individuals and the Stability of Civil Government Considered* (Winchester: 1799). For gambling in Bath, see also 'Bath in the Last Century. The Gambling Mania', in *The Bath and County Graphic*, vol. 4, n.s., nos 1–4, May–August 1889, no. 2 (thanks to Avon Libraries, Bath and Bristol).
93. Rennell, *op. cit.*, pp. 2–3, 12–13 and 17. For the view that gambling induced crime, see Henry Fielding, 'An Enquiry into the Cause of the Late Increase of Robbers, &c. with Proposals for Remedy, &c.', *Gentleman's Magazine*, vol. 21, January 1751, p. 4.
94. *Ibid.*, pp. 18–19.
95. D. M. Downes, B. P. Davies, M. E. David and P. Stone, *Gambling, Work and Leisure: A Study Across Three Areas* (London: Routledge & Kegan Paul, 1976), p. 34; see also Miers, *op. cit.*, p. 113.
96. For example, Justice Fielding with Justice Welch raided a gaming house frequented chiefly by 'foreign domestic servants', *Gentleman's Magazine*, vol. 25, December 1755, p. 569.
97. *Ibid.*, vol. 21, February 1751, p. 87.
98. *Ibid.*, vol. 25, May 1755, p. 111.
99. John Wesley, Sermon LII, preached before the Society for the Reformation of Manners at the chapel in West Street, Seven Dials, 30 January 1763; in E. H. Sugden (ed.), Wesley's Standard Sermons, vol. 2 (London: Epworth Press, 1921), p. 487 (thanks to Avon Libraries, Bristol).
100. For a writer who indicated that there was a difference see *Gentleman's Magazine*, vol. 25, May 1755, p. 111.
101. Shoolbred, *op. cit.*, p. 1.
102. For the etymology of gaming and gambling see Ashton, *op. cit.*, pp. 1–2, and M'Elroy, *op. cit.*, p. 5. For agreement on the difference between gambling and betting see Robin Miller, 'Gambling and the British Working Class, 1870–1914', University of Edinburgh, unpublished MA thesis (1974), p. ii.

2 BETTORS ROUND, BLACKLEGS AND BOOKMAKERS

1. James Rice, *op. cit.*, vol. 1, p. 49. For Doncaster race-week, it was stated that 'numerous arrivals' came from York, Sheffield and Leeds, while a steam packet brought 160 people from Hull; 'Sporting Sketch of

Doncaster, 1823', in Pierce Egan, *Pierce Egan's Anecdotes (Original and Selected) of the Turf, the Chase, the Ring and the Stage . . .* (London: 1827), p. 8.

2. Hannah More, *The Horse Race; or, the Pleasures of the Course* (1795) (thanks to Avon Libraries, Bristol).
3. Rice, *op. cit.*, vol. 1, p. 49.
4. *Ibid.*, p. 51; for a description of the game see pp. 46–53; Ashton, *op. cit.*, pp. 199–201.
5. *Bell's Life in London*, 8 June 1828.
6. 'Sporting Sketch of Doncaster, 1823', in Egan, *op. cit.*, p. 9.
7. W. M. Sheardown, *The Betting Club and Gambling Rooms, Doncaster* (Doncaster: 1872), pp. 3–4 (thanks to Doncaster Libraries).
8. John Tomlinson, *Doncaster from the Roman Occupation to the Present Day* (Doncaster: 1887), p. 208 (thanks to Doncaster Libraries).
9. Rice, *op. cit.*, vol. 1, p. 48.
10. The noun 'con' is an abbreviation for confidence trick.
11. Rice, *op. cit.*, vol. 1, pp. 48 and 51; see also *The Gamblers, a Poem* (1777), cited in Ashton, *op. cit.*, p. 199. Well into the twentieth century, prick-the-garter was played on racecourses and elsewhere; while the three-card trick is played still. See Chinn Interviews, Mr Gumley, *passim*. For other con tricks used on the racecourse see Sanger, *op. cit.*, pp. 102–4 and Superintendent Bent, *Criminal Life. Reminiscences of Forty-Two Years as a Police Officer* (Manchester: John Heywood, 1891), pp. 9–18.
12. 'The Thimble Rig', in Egan, *op. cit.*, pp. 72–3; see also 'Life of an Irish Tailor, Written by Himself', *Commonwealth*, 18 April 1857, p. 3; Chinn Letters, Dr Bernard Juby, p. 1; Charles Dickens, *Nicholas Nickleby* (1839), cited in Kellow Chesney, *The Victorian Underworld* (first published 1970. Harmondsworth: Penguin, 1972), pp. 271–2; Peter Quennell (ed.), *London's Underworld, Henry Mayhew* (London: Bracken Books, 1983), pp. 330–4. The noun 'flat' dates from about 1760 and often it was used in conjunction with the noun 'sharp', which means a cheat; Partridge, *op. cit.*, pp. 327 and 823.
13. 'The Thimble Rig', in Egan, *op. cit.*, p. 73; Rice, *op. cit.*, vol. 1, p. 48.
14. See Alexander Somerville, *The Autobiography of a Working Man* (first published 1848. London: Turnstile Press, 1951), pp. 97–100.
15. F. M. L. Thompson, *The Rise of Respectable Society. A Social History of Victorian Britain, 1830–1900* (London: Fontana, 1988), p. 288.
16. Golby and Purdue, *op. cit.*, p. 190.
17. Rice, *op. cit.*, vol. 2, pp. 267–8.
18. Holcroft, *op. cit.*, p. 62.
19. The betting term 'to cover' is derived from the standard English definition of the noun 'cover': 'funds (especially obtained by insurance) to meet liability or to protect against contingent loss'; J. B. Sykes (ed.), *The Concise Oxford Dictionary of Current English* (7th edn, Oxford: Oxford University Press, 1982), p. 219.
20. To hedge is standard English: 'to reduce one's risk of loss on (bet, speculation . . .) by similar transactions on the other side'; *ibid.*, p. 463.
21. The colloquial noun 'cute' dates from about 1730; Partridge, *op. cit.*, p. 237.

22. See Nimrod (Charles James Apperley), *The Chace, the Turf and the Road* (first published 1837. London: 1852), pp. 135–6, and Louis Henry Curzon, *A Mirror on the Turf* (London: Chapman Hall, 1892), p. 205. Partridge dates the term 'to bet round' from about 1820; *op. cit.*, p. 777.
23. There were many female bookies and punters off-course in the nineteenth century, but I have no evidence of women betting on horses in the eighteenth century.
24. Holcroft, *op. cit.*, pp. 29 and 63–4; information supplied by Richmond Libraries.
25. *Bell's Life in London*, 8 June 1828.
26. *The Sporting Dictionary* (London: 1803), cited in J. Fairfax-Blakeborough, 'Memories of Old-Time Bookmakers. Their Turf Terminology', *Banyan*, June 1940, p. 26. *Banyan* was the publication of the National Association of Bookmakers, and as far as I am aware, the only full set of the magazine is held by this organization.
27. 'Epsom Races', *Illustrated London News*, 1 June 1850, pp. 384–5.
28. Curzon, *op. cit.*, p. 205.
29. Chinn Interviews, Len Boden, pp. 15–16; see also Sidney, *op. cit.*, pp. 95–6 and 115.
30. Nimrod, *op. cit.*, pp. 136–7.
31. Eric Rickman, 'The Classic Prospects of 1946', in Alfred Cope (ed.), *Cope's Racegoer's Encylopaedia* (London: Wells Gardner, Darton & Co., 1946) p. 317.
32. For racing in the eighteenth century see Eric Rickman, 'Tests Imposed by Classic Races', in Bland (ed.), *op. cit.*, pp. 119–22; and Vamplew, *op. cit.*, pp. 18–28.
33. Admiral Rous, Letter to *Bell's Life* (1856), cited in Thomas Henry Bird, *Admiral Rous and the English Turf* (London: Putnam, 1939) p. 158; see also Rice, *op. cit.*, vol. 2, pp. 280–2.
34. *Penny Magazine*, vol. 13, cited in Louis Henry Curzon, *The Blue Ribbon of the Turf* (London: Chatto and Windus, 1890), pp. 115–16 (thanks to Surrey Libraries).
35. J. Fairfax-Blakeborough, 'Origin and Evolution of "Tattersall's Ring"', *Banyan*, September 1951, p. 7; see also, V. Orchard, *The Family of Tattersall. Two Hundred Years of Sporting History* (London: Hutchinson, 1953).
36. Benjamin Disraeli, *Sybil, or The Two Nations* (first published 1845. Oxford: Oxford University Press, 1981), p. 1. This scene is set in Crockford's gaming house, see Newmarket (J. S. Saunders), *Chapters from Turf History* (London: National Review, 1922), pp. 105–9. A 'pony' is twenty-five pounds and Partridge dated its use to 1797, *op. cit.*, p. 712.
37. *Ibid.*, pp. 5–9.
38. S. Sidney, *The Book of the Horse* (first published 1874. London: Cassell & Co., 1893), p. 81.
39. A Bystander, *The Famous Turf Cause, of Burdon Against Rhodes . . .* (York: 1791), p. 16 (thanks to York Libraries).
40. *Ibid.*, p. 15.
41. *Ibid.*, p. 21.
42. Robert Black, *The Jockey Club and Its Founders* (London: Smith Elder

& Co., 1891), cited in William Fawcett, *Racing in the Olden Days* (London: Hutchinson, 1933), p. 41; see also Curzon, *A Mirror on the Turf*, pp. 205–6.

43. Rice, *op. cit.*, vol. 2, p. 268.
44. Thormanby (W. Dixon), *Sporting Stories* (London: Mills and Boon, 1909), pp. 20–1.
45. *Ibid.*
46. *Ibid.*, p. 21.
47. Curzon, *The Blue Ribbon of the Turf*, pp. 110–11.
48. Partridge, *op. cit.*, pp. 78 and 773.
49. J. Fairfax-Blakeborough, 'Memories of Old-Time Bookmakers', *Banyan*, June 1940, p. 25.
50. Thormanby, *op. cit.*, p. 20.
51. *Ibid.*, p. 23.
52. Partridge, *op. cit.*, p. 128.
53. 'Portrait of a Professed Gambler', in Egan, *op. cit.*, pp. 347–8.
54. *Ibid.*, p. 346.
55. *Ibid.*, pp. 348–55; see also Thormanby, *op. cit.*, pp. 22–5. For ante-post betting in early-nineteenth-century York, see Sylvanus (Robert Colton), *The Bye-Lanes and Downs of England with Turf Scenes and Characters* (London: 1850), pp. 5–21.
56. 'A Peep at Tattersall's' in Egan, *op. cit.*, pp. 37–42.
57. Curzon, *A Mirror on the Turf*, pp. 202–3.
58. Patrick Colquhoun, *Treatise on the Police of the Metropolis* (5th edn, 1797), cited in Donald A. Low, *Thieves' Kitchen. The Regency Underworld* (first published 1982. Gloucester: Alan Sutton, 1987), p. 26. He included in his list 'A class of Swindlers, Cheats, and low Gamblers, composed of idle and dissolute Characters, who have abandoned every honest pursuit', among whom were gamblers with EO tables.
59. Nimrod, *op. cit.*, p. 126.
60. *Ibid.*
61. Rice, *op. cit.*, vol. 2, p. 270.
62. In betting parlance the noun 'sharp' implies more positive attributes than is allowed in its standard English definition, J. B. Sykes (ed.), *op. cit.*, p. 970. Partridge indicated well the dual meaning of the word, defining it as denoting either a cheat or a sporting expert, *op. cit.*, p. 825.
63. The Druid (H. H. Dixon), *The Post and the Paddock* (London: Frederick Warne & Co., 1856), pp. 46–7.
64. 'Bookmaking Then and Now', *Banyan*, 25 April 1936, p. 78.
65. 'A Retrospect', *Banyan*, July 1934, p. 4.
66. The Druid, *op. cit.*, pp. 46–7.
67. Sidney, *op. cit.*, pp. 34–5.
68. Admiral Rous, Letter to *Bell's Life* (1856), in Bird, *op. cit.*, p. 158; Henry St John Raikes, cited in Bernard Darwin, *John Gully and His Times* (London: Cassell & Co., 1935), p. 64.
69. Curzon, *A Mirror on the Turf*, p. 205. 'Epsom Races', in *Illustrated London News*, 1 June 1850, p. 385.
70. Vamplew, *op. cit.*, p. 23.
71. Robert Black, *Horse Racing in England. A Synoptical Review* (London: R. Bentley & Co., 1893), p. 86.

72. Richard Tattersall, speech at a dinner in honour of his firm (1865), cited in Curzon, *The Blue Ribbon of the Turf*, p. 112.
73. Pierce Egan, *Life in London* (London: 1821), pp. 189–90. The standard English definition of the verb 'levant' is to 'abscond, bolt, especially with betting or gaming losses unpaid', and it is presumed that it is derived from the term 'the Levant': the eastern part of the Mediterranean; Sykes, *op. cit.*, p. 577. Fairfax-Blakeborough gives a more plausible derivation, stating that the word comes from the Anglo-Saxon 'laefan', which meant 'to leave'; 'Memories of Old-Time Bookmakers', *Banyan*, June 1940, p. 26.
74. Curzon, *A Mirror on the Turf*, p. 206; Egan, *Life in London*, p. 190; Rice, *op. cit.*, vol. 2, p. 270. In a modern betting shop, a settler is the person who checks the bets for winners and who reckons up those which are successful.
75. 'Tattersall's', *Illustrated London News*, 25 March 1843, p. 214.
76. Nimrod, 'The Anatomy of Gaming, Dissection V', *Fraser's Magazine*, vol. 17, no. 101, May 1838, p. 543.
77. Black, *Horse Racing in England*, p. 87.
78. For an early use of the word 'leg' see Hellen, *The Greeks. Being the Jeremiad of an Exiled Greek; A Poem 'Venu de France d'une Mariere Inconnue'; Dedicated to All the Legs* (3rd edn, London: 1817). A Greek was a professional gambler. Partridge dated the term 'leg' to 1815, *op. cit.*, p. 530.
79. 'Tattersall's', *Illustrated London News*, 25 March 1843, p. 214.
80. Thormanby, *op. cit.*, pp. 25–6; see also The Druid, *op. cit.*, p. 47, who added to this list Highton, Holliday, Briscoe, Ridsdale, Frank Richardson and Bob Steward.
81. Thormanby, *op. cit.*, pp. 26–7; The Druid, *op. cit.*, p. 48; see also Sylvanus, *op. cit.*, pp. 325–48.
82. Rice, *op. cit.*, vol. 2, p. 269; see also S. Sidney, *op. cit.*, pp. 80–1 and Thormanby, *op. cit.*, p. 27.
83. Curzon, *A Mirror on the Turf*, p. 206.
84. 'Epsom Races', *Illustrated London News*, 1 June 1850, p. 385.
85. J. Fairfax-Blakeborough, 'Name of an Old-time Penciller', *Banyan*, October 1951, p. 29; Thormanby, *op. cit.*, p. 29.
86. The Druid, *op. cit.*, pp. 47–8; Rice, *op. cit.*, vol. 2, pp. 269–71; Thormanby, *op. cit.*, pp. 27–9.
87. Sylvanus, *op. cit.*, p. 127.
88. Disraeli, *op. cit.*, p. 6.
89. J. Fairfax-Blakeborough, 'Old-Time Bookmakers', *Banyan*, July 1949, p. 20.
90. The verb 'to fix it', meaning to arrange matters, is of American origin and it was anglicized around 1850; Partridge, *op. cit.*, p. 322. To crimp, meaning to play foul, dates to the late 1600s, *ibid.*, p. 224; and D'Urfey, 'Newmarket', in *Pills to Purge Melancholy* (4th edn, 1719), cited in Ashton, *op. cit.*, p. 178. For an example of ringing, see Nimrod, *The Chace, the Turf and the Road*, p. 135.
91. Cited in Cook, *op. cit.*, p. 142.
92. Thormanby, *op. cit.*, p. 21.
93. Longrigg, *op. cit.*, pp. 124 and 116.

94. Bogey is a term for the Devil; for a bookie, then, a bogey is a horse which will give him or her a bad result.
95. Partridge dates the term 'to nobble' to 1847, *op. cit.*, p. 627.
96. Longrigg, *op. cit.*, p. 116.
97. Rice, *op. cit.*, vol. 1, p. 114.
98. Longrigg, *op. cit.*, p. 116. The description of Dawson is taken from The Druid, *op. cit.*, pp. 166–7; Longrigg omitted that part in which it was stated that the tout 'had sunk into a low horse poisoner'.
99. Cook, *op. cit.*, p. 362 and Rice, *op. cit.*, vol. 1, p. 115.
100. Longrigg, *op. cit.*, p. 116.
101. Rice, *op. cit.*, vol. 1, p. 115.
102. 'Epsom Races', *Illustrated London News*, 1 June 1850, p. 385. See also Darwin, *op. cit.*, p. 62; and The Druid, *op. cit.*, p. 48.
103. Longrigg, *op. cit.*, pp. 99 and 116; see also Cook, *op. cit.*, pp. 362–4 and J. Fairfax-Blakeborough, 'Bookmakers and Nobblers', *Banyan*, February 1949, pp. 138–9.
104. The noun 'ramp' dates to about 1860, Partridge, *op. cit.*, pp. 752–3.
105. Cited in J. Fairfax-Blakeborough, 'Memories of Old-Time Bookmakers', *Banyan*, October 1940, p. 56.
106. The phrase 'dark horse' originated about 1830; Partridge, *op. cit.*, p. 243.
107. J. Fairfax-Blakeborough, 'Sixty Years of Bookmakers and Betting', *Banyan*, October 1948, pp. 102–3.
108. J. Fairfax-Blakeborough, 'Ring Associations with the Chester Cup and Lincoln Handicap', *Banyan*, December 1950, p. 184. For the Red Deer scandal, see also Emma Eadie, 'The Racing Career of Lord George Bentinck M.P. 1826–46', University of Birmingham, unpublished BA dissertation, 1987, *passim*; and Newmarket, *op. cit.*, pp. 126–43.
109. Partridge defined a leviathan as a heavy backer, *op. cit.*, p. 533; but it was used normally to describe the wealthiest bookmakers who laid the biggest bets, see 'Epsom Races', *Illustrated London News*, 1 June 1850, p. 385.
110. *Ibid.*
111. Ashton, *op. cit.*, pp. 122–3 and 128; see also Henry Blyth, *Hell or Hazard: or, William Crockford versus the Gentlemen of England*, (London: Weidenfeld and Nicolson, 1969), *passim.* The best contemporary description of Crockford's is by James Grant, *The Great Metropolis* (first published 1837. New York: Garland, 1985), vol. 1, pp. 159–91.
112. Sylvanus, *op. cit.*, p. 67.
113. Nimrod, 'The Anatomy of Gaming, Dissection V', *Fraser's Magazine*, vol. 17, no. 10, May 1838, p. 540.
114. Thormanby, *op. cit.*, p. 29.
115. Notice in *Bentley's Miscellany*, cited in Thormanby, *op. cit.*, p. 30, see also 'Epsom Races', *Illustrated London News*, 1 June 1850, p. 385.
116. Longrigg, *op. cit.*, p. 118.
117. 'Old Timers', *Banyan*, September 1934, p. 4.
118. 'Epsom Races', *Illustrated London News*, 1 June 1850, p. 385; Thormanby, *op. cit.*, pp. 31–2.
119. Grant, *op. cit.*, p. 190; Longrigg, *op. cit.*, p. 118 – the original description of Crockford's appearance is from Sylvanus, *op. cit.*, pp. 67–8; Darwin, *op. cit.*, p. 68. It is likely that 'Hump' Chippendale was a composite character based on Crockford as well as Crutch Robinson,

because Disraeli described him as the keeper of a second-rate gaming house, *op. cit.*, p. 6.

120. Thormanby, *Men of the Turf. Anecdotes of Their Careers and Notes on Many Famous Races* (London: Bateman & Co., 1887), p. 72; for Gully's career see pp. 72–8; Darwin, *op. cit.*, *passim*; Claud Golding, 'John Gully', *Evening Standard*, 21 August 1935; 'Old Timers', *Banyan*, September 1934, pp. 3–5.
121. William Day, *William Day's Reminiscences of the Turf* (London: Richard Bentley & Son, 1886), p. 63.
122. Longrigg, *op. cit.*, p. 118.
123. Thormanby, *Sporting Stories*, pp. 35–6; Day, *op. cit.*, pp. 68–70. Partridge dates this term to 1870, *op. cit.*, p. 247.
124. Samuel Chifney, *Genius Genuine* (London: 1784), p. 106. For Chifney's career see Cook, *op. cit.*, pp. 349–62.
125. Nimrod, *The Chace, the Turf and the Road*, p. 133.
126. Golding, *op. cit.*, p. 3 and J. Fairfax-Blakeborough, 'Bookmakers who Owned Derby Winners', *Banyan*, April 1951, p. 224.
127. Thormanby, *Sporting Stories*, pp. 34–6.
128. Darwin, *op. cit.*, p. 217.
129. Newmarket, *op. cit.*, p. 99.
130. Henry Reeve (ed.), *The Greville Memoirs* (4th edn, London: 1875), vol. 2, p. 335.
131. Day, *op. cit.*, p. 74.
132. *The Satirist*, cited in Bird, *op. cit.*, pp. 149–50.
133. Another Correspondent, 'Mr Davies, The Leviathan Betting Man', *Illustrated London News*, 1 June 1850, p. 386.
134. 'Epsom Races', *Illustrated London News*, 1 June 1850, p. 385. 'To take the knock' is a bookmaking term which Partridge dated to before 1890, *op. cit.*, p. 514. I believe that it originates from the practice of ignoring the debt collector's knock on the door, a tactic usual in working-class districts if a family could not pay their weekly instalments for goods bought on credit.
135. The Druid, *op. cit.*, p. 54.
136. Another Correspondent, 'Mr Davies, the Leviathan Betting Man', *Illustrated London News*, 1 June 1850, p. 386. Partridge dates the term 'crack' to about 1850, *op. cit.*, p. 218.
137. J. Fairfax-Blakeborough, 'Bookmakers and Race Executives and "Levanters"', *Banyan*, March 1951, p. 201.
138. 'Epsom Races', *Illustrated London News*, 1 June 1850, p. 385.
139. See J. Fairfax-Blakeborough, 'Origin and Evolution of "Tattersall's Ring"', *Banyan*, September 1951, p. 8; J. Fairfax-Blakeborough, 'Bookmakers and Race Executives and "Levanters"', *Banyan*, March 1951, p. 201; Disraeli, *op. cit.*, p. 5; and Harry Sargent, *Thoughts Upon Sport* (London: Photoprismatic Publishing Co., 1895), p. 334, who stated that on the morning of a meeting bettors would meet in the town where they would form a ring to back and lay ante-post.
140. For use of 'The Ring' see The Druid, *op. cit.*, p. 52.
141. *Sporting Magazine*, xv, n.s. 51/2, 1824 and xl, 70/1, 1812, cited in *The Oxford English Dictionary* (Oxford: Oxford University Press, 1989), vol. 2, p. 398; see also J. Fairfax-Blakeborough, 'Bookmakers of Today

and Yesterday', *Banyan*, November 1950, pp. 165–9; and Disraeli, *op. cit.*, pp. 1–9.

142. Nimrod, 'Anatomy of Gaming. Dissection V', *Fraser's Magazine*, vol. 17, no. 101, May 1838, p. 543; The Druid, *op. cit.*, p. 51.
143. *London Review*, 30 August 1862, p. 188, cited in *The Oxford English Dictionary* (1989), vol. 2, p. 398; 'Bookmakers', *Chambers's Journal*, 4th series, no. 221, 21 March 1868, pp. 177–80; and, 'Bookmaking', *All the Year Round*, 13 June 1868, p. 13. For the term 'penciller' see Rice, *op. cit.*, vol. 2, p. 271; Thormanby, *Sporting Stories*, pp. 34–43; and Partridge, who mentioned that the term was used in the *Daily News*, 24 October 1879, *op. cit.*, p. 678.

3 POPULAR RECREATION, LOTTERIES AND BETTING HOUSES

1. Vamplew, *op. cit.*, p. 23.
2. Henry Burstow, *Reminiscences of Horsham: being Recollections of Henry Burstow* (Horsham: Free Christian Book Society, 1911) p. 30 (thanks to West Sussex Institute of Higher Education); *Aberdeen Journal*, 5 April 1843 (thanks to Aberdeen Libraries).
3. Vamplew, *op. cit.*, p. 25. Until the mid-nineteenth century, any meeting was recognized so long as it was advertised in the *Racing Calendar*, but there were many other small fixtures – flappers – that supplemented the official number of racecourses.
4. Perkin, *op. cit.*, pp. 280–1.
5. Dorothy Thompson, *The Chartists. Popular Politics in the Industrial Revolution* (first published 1984. Aldershot: Wildwood House, 1986 edn), p. 123. The quote is from a letter written to *Notes to the People*, vol. 2, (1852), p. 709. I thank Dorothy Thompson and Rodney Hilton for their discussions with me on this point. See also David Vincent, *Bread, Knowledge and Freedom. A Study of Nineteenth-Century Working-Class Autobiography* (London: Europa, 1981), pp. 200–2.
6. Burstow, *op. cit.*, p. 33.
7. E. P. Thompson, 'Time, Work–Discipline and Industrial Capitalism', *Past and Present*, no. 38, December 1967, pp. 50–62.
8. For an example of a law against blood sports, see The Metropolitan Police Act, 1839 (2 & 3 Vic., cap. 47), in Shoolbred, *op. cit.*, pp. 204–5.
9. J. L. and B. Hammond, *The Skilled Labourer* (London: Longmans & Co., 1919), p. 7 and *The Age of the Chartists 1832–1854: A Study of Discontent* (London: Longmans & Co., 1930); Chapman, *op. cit.*, p. 103.
10. Malcolmson, *op. cit.*, pp. 274–5.
11. Peter Bailey, *Leisure and Class in Victorian England. Rational Recreation and the Contest for Control, 1830–1885* (first published 1978. London: Methuen, 1987), p. 5.
12. Hugh Cunningham, *Leisure in the Industrial Revolution c. 1780–1880* (London: Croom Helm, 1980), pp. 9–35.
13. *Ibid.*, p. 186.
14. Golby and Purdue, *op. cit.*, pp. 76–9.
15. Thomas Hawley, *Pottery Life and Characters, 1840–1850*, p. 15 (thanks to Stoke Libraries).

16. Henry Mayhew, *The Morning Chronicle Survey of Labour and the Poor in the Metropolitan District*, vol. 1 (first published 1851–2. Firle: Caliban Books, 1980), p. 452. For a good account of the sporting underworld see Chesney, *op. cit.*, pp. 314–62.
17. Hugh Shimmin, *Liverpool Life: Its Pleasures, Practices and Pastimes* (first published 1856. New York: Garland, 1985), p. 81 (thanks to Peter Bailey for this reference); see also John Hollingshead, *Ragged London in 1861* (first published 1861. London: J. M. Dent & Sons, 1986), pp. 41 and 79.
18. Rev. F. Close, *The Evil Consequences of Attending the Race Course Exposed* (Cheltenham: 1827), pp. 6–9 (thanks to Gloucestershire Libraries, Gloucester).
19. *Ibid.*, p. 9.
20. 'Review – Close's Sermon at Cheltenham', *Gentleman's Magazine*, vol. 97, part 2, August 1827, pp. 160–3 (thanks to Gloucestershire Libraries, Gloucester).
21. Robert John Rollason Poole, 'Wakes, Holidays and Pleasure Fairs in the Lancashire Cotton District, *c.* 1790–1890', University of Lancaster, unpublished PhD thesis, 1985, pp. 135–6.
22. Golby and Purdue, *op. cit.*, p. 87.
23. 'The Nudger Sports', *Spectator* (Rochdale), 1 October 1844. In the Potteries, too, the gentry were attacked for supporting the races at Etruria, Derek Ian Benning, 'The Development of Physical Recreation in the Staffordshire Potteries', University of Liverpool, unpublished MEd thesis, 1979, p. 16.
24. O Rochda Felley, 'O Lettur To Th' Worchin Classus, Oppo Nudgerin Un Sich Loik Wark etc.', *Spectator* (Rochdale), 1 September 1845.
25. *Ibid.*
26. Charlie O' Dick's, 'Heaw Bagslate Races Wur Stopped', in Rochdale *Observer*, 4 June 1927 and *ibid.*, 18 April 1885 (thanks to Rochdale Libraries for the references on nudging). For clerical opposition to North Staffordshire Races see Benning, *op. cit.*, pp. 17 and 179.
27. Burstow, *op. cit.*, p. 33; Anonymous, *The Races* (Paisley: 1836), p. 1 (thanks to Renfrew Libraries, Paisley). For Rotherham, see Anonymous, *A Correct Guide to the Frequenters of Races etc.*, (Rotherham: 1823).
28. An Observer, *Bolton Express*, 19 June 1824 (my researches have been helped by the indexing of the Bolton newspapers).
29. Bexley Vestry Minutes, 7 July 1826 (thanks to Bexley Libraries).
30. Letter, *Paisley Advertiser*, 12 June 1830; Abstract of statements brought before the Police Court, *Paisley Advertiser*, 19 August 1826 (thanks to Renfrew Libraries, Paisley).
31. Alfred Fellows, *The Laws as to Gaming, Betting and Lotteries* (London: The Solicitors' Law Stationery Society, 1935), p. 156. For Sundays see G. M. Trevelyan, *English Social History. A Survey of Six Centuries. Chaucer to Queen Victoria* (first published 1942. Harmondsworth: Penguin, 1986), pp. 246, 342–4 and 577–8. For the Society for the Reformation of Manners and its successor the Society for the Suppression of Vice, see E. J. Bristow, *Vice and Vigilance* (Dublin: Gill and Macmillan, 1977).
32. A. S. Frankland, *The Diary of Abraham Driver, Deputy Constable of Broughton 1834–1838*, pp. 1, 3 and 4 (thanks to Salford Libraries).
33. Warrington Police Commissioners, December 1838–July 1847,

meeting, 16 January 1840, p. 40 (thanks to Warrington Libraries); 'Gaming on Sundays', *Burnley Advertiser*, 1 August 1853 (thanks to Lancashire Libraries, Burnley).

34. Anonymous Letter, 1825, ref. Mayberry 4406 (thanks to the National Library of Wales); 'Sabbath Breaking', *Wakefield Journal*, 25 February 1842 (thanks to Wakefield Libraries). For knurr and spell see Chinn Interviews, Fred Prior, *passim*.
35. 'Pitch and Toss', *Lancaster Guardian*, 9 September 1854 (thanks to Lancashire Libraries, Lancaster); *Burnley Advertiser*, 1 August 1853. For London see Mr T. Baker, Superintendent of Police for St James's District, Evidence to Select Committee of the House of Lords appointed to inquire into the laws respecting Gaming (1844), *Minutes*, q. 438, p. 36; Hollingshead, *op. cit.*, p. 23; and Henry Mayhew, *London Labour and the London Poor* (first published 1851–2. Harmondsworth: Penguin, 1985), p. 19.
36. For working-class resistance to Sunday trading laws see Brian Harrison, 'The Sunday Trading Riots of 1865', *Historical Journal*, vol. 8, no. 2 (1965), pp. 219–45.
37. Sir Ernest Blackwell, 'Statement', Royal Commission on Lotteries and Betting (1932–3), *Minutes*, 30 June 1932; see also T. R. Gourvish, 'The Government and the Business of Gambling: State Lotteries in Britain, 1750–1826', paper given at the *Institute of Historical Research*, 23 February 1989. For advertisements of lotteries see 'First English State Lottery, 1803', John Goodhead MSS and M/58, Guildhall Library (thanks to); also Claud Golding, 'The First Lottery was Queen Elizabeth's Idea', *Evening Standard* (London), 11 January 1939.
38. Colquhoun, *op. cit.*, cited in Low, *op. cit.*, p. 10.
39. Select Committee on the Laws relating to Lotteries, *Second Report* (1808), pp. 11–12 and 31–67.
40. M'Elroy, *op. cit.*, p. 7.
41. Henry Fielding, *The Lottery* (a farce performed in 1731), cited in George Wallace, 'Lottery', *Freethinker*, 21 August 1938.
42. Samuel Roberts, *The State Lottery, A Dream* (London: 1817), p. 11.
43. James Montgomery, 'Thoughts on Wheels. A Poem', in Roberts, p. 25. See also Rev. William Symington (introduction), *Games of Chance Unlawful* (first published 1822. Reissued, Glasgow: 1891).
44. Blackwell, *op. cit.*, p. 23. Unofficial and illegal lotteries continued. They ranged from the Glasgow Lottery of 1834 – which was promoted by the city's street commissioners – to numerous smaller promotions which were run by landlords of public houses: see *Glasgow Evening Times*, 14 July 1937 (thanks to the Mitchell Library); and, for example, *Lancaster Gazette*, 27 January 1855 (thanks to Lancashire Libraries, Lancaster). Further laws were passed against lotteries in 1836 and 1845, Royal Commission on Lotteries and Betting, *Final Report* (Cmd. 4341, London: HMSO, 1932–3), p. 8.
45. Doncaster Association for the Suppression of Gambling Houses and Gaming Houses (Doncaster: 1829 – thanks to Doncaster Libraries); see also Robert Baxter, evidence to S. C., 1844, *Minutes*, q. 1019, p. 86.
46. *The Life of David Hoggart the Murderer* (1825).
47. See, for example, *Dreadful effects of Gambling. Being an Account of Mr*

John Wilkinson of Edinburgh etc. (1839 – thanks to Edinburgh Libraries); and *William Wells Who was Executed on 2nd April 1827, at Nottingham etc.* (1827; thanks to Roy Palmer).

48. The murder referred to by Close was probably that of Hoggart.
49. 'The Hells in London', *Fraser's Magazine*, vol. 8, no. 44, August 1833, pp. 191–206; Nimrod, 'The Anatomy of Gaming', Dissections 1–5, *Fraser's Magazine*, vols 16–18, nos 91, 93, 96, 99 and 101, July, September and December 1837, and March and May 1838. For a detailed description of the gaming houses of London, see Grant, *op. cit.*, vol. 1, pp. 159–220.
50. S. C., 1844, *Three Reports*; The Gaming Act, 1845 (8 & 9 Vic., cap. 109), Shoolbred, *op. cit.*, pp. 107–9 and 205–13.
51. Mark Clapson, 'Popular Gambling and English Culture, 1845–1961', unpublished PhD thesis, University of Warwick, 1989, pp. 30–1 – this study has since been published as *A Bit of a Flutter: Popular Gambling and English Society 1823–1961* (Manchester: Manchester University Press, 1991); E. C. Devereux, 'Gambling', *International Encyclopaedia of the Social Sciences*, vol. 6 (1968), p. 6. For more on the background to the Act see M'Elroy, *op. cit.*, p. 11.
52. S. C., 1844, *Three Reports*, p. v; for the belief that horse-racing was beneficial socially, see also Bailey, *op. cit.*, p. 35, and Hippolyte Taine, *Notes on England* (London: 1873), p. 42.
53. Hon. H. John Rous, evidence to S. C., 1844, *Minutes*, q. 3098, p. 204; Alphonse Esquiros, *The English at Home* (London: 1862), p. 320.
54. Miers, *op. cit.*, p. 108.
55. 'Betting Shops', *Household Words*, vol. 5, no. 118, 26 June 1852, p. 333.
56. David C. Itzkowitz, 'Victorian Bookmakers and Their Customers', *Victorian Studies*, vol. 32, no. 1, autumn 1988, p. 10. For an example of a sweepstake advertisement see 'Racing Office', Noble Collection (thanks to the Guildhall Library).
57. R. C., 1932–3, *Report*, p. 11; M'Elroy, *op. cit.*, p. 13; Itzkovitz, *op. cit.*, pp. 10–11. For a contemporary attack on sweepstake gambling as socially undesirable, see Sylvanus, *op. cit.*, pp. 203–8.
58. G. H. Stutfield, Evidence to the Select Committee of the House of Lords on Betting, 1901–2, *Minutes*, p. 387.
59. 'Horse Racing', *Quarterly Review*, vol. 161, no. 322, October 1885, p. 453.
60. 'Mr Davies, The Leviathan Betting Man', *Illustrated London News*, 1 June 1850, p. 386; see also *Truth*, 13 February 1876.
61. 'Horse Racing', *Quarterly Review*, vol. 161, no. 322, October 1885, p. 453; Thormanby, *Sporting Stories*, p. 36.
62. Rice, *op. cit.*, vol. 2, pp. 272–3.
63. The Druid, *op. cit.*, p. 60, see also Curzon, *A Mirror on the Turf*, p. 230; Itzkovitz, *op. cit.*, p. 11; Charles Sidney, *op. cit.*, p. 46.
64. R. C., 1932–3, *Report*, p. 11.
65. 'Betting Offices', *Chambers's Edinburgh Journal*, n.s., vol. 1, no. 446, 17 July 1852, p. 57.
66. Downes, *op. cit.*, p. 119.
67. George Cruikshank, *The Betting-Book* (London: W & F. G. Cash, 1852), p. 30.

68. Poole, *op. cit.*, p. 89; The Druid, *op. cit.*, p. 60.
69. *Hull Advertiser*, 15 August 1851 (thanks to Hull Libraries. The index to the *Hull Advertiser* has proven invaluable to my researches); R. C., 1932–3, *Report*, p. 11.
70. 'Paisley Races', *Paisley Advertiser*, 11 July 1840 (thanks to Renfrew Libraries, Paisley).
71. The Druid, *op. cit.*, pp. 62 and 174–5. For the effect of the railways on horse-racing see Vamplew, *op. cit.*, pp. 29–37.
72. J. Fairfax-Blakeborough, 'Bookmakers and Race Executives and "Levanters"', *Banyan*, March 1951, p. 202.
73. National Association of Bookmakers, Harold Hodgson, 'Some Notes on Early Bookmaking and Betting' (n.d.), p. 3. I am grateful to the National Association of Bookmakers for access to their archive; in particular, I thank its President, Alfie Bruce, and its secretary, Paul Massey. This archive has proven invaluable in my researches, and its existence owes much to the hard work of the former secretary of the NAB, Harold Hodgson.
74. Vincent George Dowling, evidence to S. C., 1844, *Minutes*, q. 236, p. 89; Dyke Wilkinson, *Rough Roads. Reminiscences of a Wasted Life* (London: Sampson Low & Co., 1912), pp. 11–12 (thanks to Val Hart). For *Bell's Life*, see also Grant, *op. cit.*, pp. 132–5, and Tony Mason, 'Sporting News, 1860–1914', in Michael Harris and Alan J. Lee (eds), *The Press in English Society from the Seventeenth to Nineteenth Centuries* (London: Press Group of the Acton Society Trust, 1986), pp. 168–70.
75. Cruikshank, *op. cit.*, p. 6.
76. Wilkinson, *op. cit.*, p. 12 and The Druid, *op. cit.*, p. 172.
77. Partridge dates the term 'tip' to about the 1840s, *op. cit.*, p. 971.
78. The Druid, *op. cit.*, pp. 169–77; 'The Modern Prophets', *Chambers's Journal*, vol. 18, no. 446, 19 July 1862, pp. 45–8.
79. *Hull Advertiser*, 15 August 1851; see also *Hull Advertiser*, 22 August 1851.
80. 'Betting Offices', *Chambers's Edinburgh Journal*, n.s., vol. 1, no. 446, 17 July 1852, p. 58.
81. Cruikshank, *op. cit.*, p. 5.
82. 'Betting Shops', *Household Words*, vol. 5, no. 118, 26 June 1852, pp. 334–5.
83. Ashton, *op. cit.*, pp. 219–20; see also Christopher Yorke, 'Betting Business in the Old List Houses', *Yorkshire Evening Post*, 18 January 1939.
84. Eddy and Loewe, *op. cit.*, pp. 3–4; R. C., 1932–3, *Report*, p. 12; 16–7 Vic., cap. 119, Shoolbred, *op. cit.*, pp. 213–17. Billiards and skittles were also seen as inducements to gambling and they were attacked as such, see 'Billiard Tables', *Spectator* (Rochdale), 1 February and 1 March 1846 (thanks to Rochdale Libraries); and Anonymous, *The Game of Skittles* (*c.* 1850 – thanks to Avon Libraries, Bath).
85. R. C., 1932–3, *Report*, p. 12; Shoolbred, *op. cit.*, pp. 4–5.
86. Cruikshank, *op. cit.*, p. 12.
87. Sylvanus, *op. cit.*, p. 206.
88. 'Scandalous Interference by the Police with the Amusements of the People', Walthamstow Libraries, *Pamphlets, Prints, etc.*, 1599 (1840 – thanks to Walthamstow Libraries).

89. Eddy and Loewe, *op. cit.*, p. 10; Vamplew, *op. cit.*, p. 205; Chesney, *op. cit.*, p. 339; Itzkovitz, *op. cit.*, p. 25.
90. Shimmin, *op. cit.*, pp. 98–105.
91. Itzkowitz, *op. cit.*, p. 16; Clapson, *op. cit.*, p. 35.
92. Thomas Archer, *The Pauper, the Thief and the Convict* (first published 1865. New York: Garland, 1985), p. 64.
93. George R. Sims, *My Life. Sixty Years' Recollections of Bohemian London* (London: Eveleigh Nash Company, 1917), pp. 36–7 (thanks to Islington Libraries, Finsbury); see also James Greenwood, *The Seven Curses of London* (first published 1869. New York: Garland, 1984), pp. 411–12.
94. Shimmin, *op. cit.*, pp. 117–22, and pp. 101–9.
95. Sims, *op. cit.*, p. 36; Archer, *op. cit.*, p. 64; see also Greenwood, *op. cit.*, pp. 405–7.
96. Shimmin, *op. cit.*, p. 103.
97. Sims, *op. cit.*, p. 36.
98. Downes, *op. cit.*, pp. 38–9.
99. See also Geoffrey Best, *Mid-Victorian Britain* (London: Fontana, 1971), pp. 282–90 and F. M. L. Thompson, *op. cit.*, pp. 307–61.
100. *Ibid.*
101. Greenwood, *op. cit.*, pp. 404–5; see also Archer, *op. cit.*, p. 64.
102. James Greenwood, 'Guides to the Turf', in *The Wilds of London* (first published 1874. New York: Garland, 1985), pp. 313–15 – this article was written in the later 1860s.
103. Rice, *op. cit.*, vol. 2, p. 274.
104. Greenwood, *The Wilds of London*, pp. 312–13, and *The Seven Curses*, p. 411.
105. 30 and 31 Vic., cap. 134, Shoolbred, *op. cit.*, p. 5.
106. Darwin, *op. cit.*, pp. 182–4; Anonymous, *The Gambler's Career, or the Progressive Course of Crime. An Address to Young Men. William Palmer* (Newcastle: 1856 – thanks to Newcastle Libraries). Thomas Houston, *The Races: The Evils Connected with Horse-Racing and the Steeple-Chase, and Their Demoralizing Effects* (Paisley: 1853); Rev. J. Thomson, *The Racecourse, the Theatre and the Ball-Room. A Warning for the Times Against Prevailing Vices and Amusements* (Paisley: 1854); Rev. J. Thomson, Letter, *Paisley Herald and Renfrewshire Advertiser*, 22 August 1857; and Memorial Against the Paisley Races, Miscellaneous File, 798.4, Ren 1 (thanks to Renfrew Libraries, Paisley).
107. 'Bookmaking', *op. cit.*, p. 13; 'Bookmakers', *op. cit.*, pp. 177 and 179–80.
108. *Ibid.*; 'The Turf: Its Frauds and Chicaneries', *Contemporary Review*, vol. 22, June 1873, pp. 43–5.
109. L. P. Curtis, *Apes and Angels. The Irishman in Victorian Caricature* (Newton Abbot: David & Charles, 1971).
110. 'The Turf: Its Frauds and Chicaneries', *op. cit.*, p. 34; Greenwood, *The Seven Curses*, p. 402.
111. Houston, *op. cit.*, pp. 113 and 118.
112. William Skerry, *A Few Words on Betting* (Newcastle: 1873), pp. 7–8 (thanks to Newcastle Libraries); see also 'Moral Courage, or, Temptation Resisted', *Young Men of Great Britain*, vol. 1, no. 7, 25 August 1868, p. 82.

113. See, for example, 'Derby Day', *The Times*, 30 May 1868; the broadsheet 'Flint Rural Sports. 1870' (thanks to Clywd County Record Office); 'The Turf: Its Frauds and Chicaneries', *op. cit.*, pp. 34–6. For mid-Victorian attacks on the immorality associated with racecourses see: James Inches Hillocks, *My Life and Labours in London, a Step Nearer the Mark* (London: William Freeman, 1865), pp. 67–71; and Rev. J. Martin, *Incidents in the Life of Robt. Henderson; or, Extracts from the Autobiography of 'Newcassel Bob' (A Tyneside Rake)* (Carlisle: Halstead and Beaty, 1869). For an assault on dog-racing see John Ashworth, *Strange Tales from Humble Life*, (Manchester: Tubbs and Brock, 1867), pp. 152–3.
114. 'Derby Day', *op. cit.*
115. Clapson, *op. cit.*, pp. 31–4. For stockmarket gambling, see Ashton, *op. cit.*, pp. 242–86.
116. 'Derby Day', *op. cit.*
117. Gustave Doré and Blanchard Jerrold, *London. A Pilgrimage* (first published 1872. New York: Arno Press, 1978), p. 73; 'Racing and Counter-Attractions', *Saturday Review*, vol. 28, no. 178, 31 July 1869, p. 152.
118. Itzkovitz, *op. cit.*, p. 16. For the story of Frederick Swindell, a highly successful and legitimate commission agent, see 'A Turf Notability', *Bailey's Monthly Magazine of Sport and Pastimes*, July 1885, pp. 258–66.
119. Convictions at Petty Sessions for betting offences, M117/1/7/1–27, Manchester Central Library (my thanks to). For the list houses of the Thomas Street area see 'The Betting Nuisance', *Free Lance*, 22 February 1868 (thanks to Mark Clapson).
120. For lotteries on horse-races, see Greenwood, *The Seven Curses of London*, pp. 381–6; and for gaming in public houses, see, for example, 'Gambling', *Derby Mercury*, 27 January 1864 (thanks to Derby Libraries), 'Can a Publican Play Cards in His Own House', *Lancaster Guardian*, 22 February 1873 (thanks to Lancashire Libraries, Lancaster), and Warrington, Chief Constable's Daily Report Book, 16 July 1867 (thanks to Warrington Libraries).
121. 35 & 36 Vic., cap. 94, Shoolbred, *op. cit.*, p. 222.
122. 36 & 37 Vic., cap. 38, *ibid.*
123. 'Horse Racing', *Quarterly Review*, vol. 16, no. 322, October 1885, p. 453.
124. 'The New Betting Bill', *Dublin University Magazine*, vol. 83, May 1874, pp. 636–7.
125. *Ibid.*, pp. 637–9.
126. Eddy and Loewe, *op. cit.*, pp. 6–7.
127. 37–8 Vic., cap 15, Shoolbred, *op. cit.*, p. 12.
128. 'Bookmaking', *op. cit.*, p. 13.

4 BETTING CLUBS AND STREET BETTING

1. J. G. B., 'Legislation on Betting, Practically Considered', *Fraser's Magazine*, n.s., vol. 10, no. 59, November 1874, pp. 611–12.
2. 'Conjugation' cited in, Otto Newman, *Gambling: Hazard and Reward* (London: The Athlone Press, 1972), p. 13.

3. Sargent, *op. cit.*, p. 342.
4. J. G. B., *op. cit.*, pp. 612–13 and 618–19. Curzon agreed about the benefits of cash betting; see *A Mirror on the Turf*, pp. 201–2.
5. J. G. B., *op. cit.*, p. 611; B, 'An Exposition of Betting and Bookmaking', *Fraser's Magazine*, vol. 96, July 1877, p. 84; Eddy and Loewe, *op. cit.*, p. 7; 'Horse Racing', *op. cit.*, p. 455. For a later bookmaker who established himself on the Continent – in Middleburg, Holland – see Thomas Henry Dey, *Leaves from a Bookmakers Book* (London: Hutchinson & Co., 1931), pp. 19–20.
6. Alan J. Lee, *The Origins of the Popular Press, 1855–1914* (first published 1976. London: Croom Helm, 1981), p. 127.
7. Tony Mason, *Association Football and English Society 1863–1915* (Brighton: Harvester, 1981), pp. 187–8; for the *Sporting Life*, see also Special Correspondent, '"The Sporting Life" Past, Present and Future', *Banyan*, April 1940, p. 16; and for the *Sporting Times*, see J. B. Booth, *Sporting Times. The 'Pink 'Un' World* (London: T. Werner Laurie, 1938).
8. 'The First Sporting Paper', *Irish Field*, February 1940; Edward (Teddy) Dawson, 'Some Memories of the Old Days', *Banyan*, October 1953, pp. 57–8.
9. J. G. B., *op. cit.*, p. 611.
10. See 'The Raid on the Manchester Betting Clubs', *Manchester Evening News*, 21 May 1885 (thanks to Mark Clapson); and 'Inside a Betting Club', *Chambers's Journal*, vol. 14, no. 682, 23 January 1897, p. 50.
11. George Cannon, *Betting Men* (Middleton: Jackson & Co., 1901), p. 17.
12. Rice, *op. cit.*, vol. 2, p. 275. For betting in a yard behind a 'social club' see 'The Nelson Betting Raid', *Leader*, 12 July 1901 (thanks to Lancashire Libraries, Nelson).
13. Cannon, *op. cit.*, p. 18.
14. Chinn Letters, E. J. G. Good, 1996, and for the Victoria Club see 'Bookmaking Then and Now', *op. cit.*, p. 78.
15. Rice, *op. cit.*, vol. 2, p. 275.
16. H. Denton, 'Fifty Years Ago', *Evening News* (London), 8 June 1936; for a raid on London's Albert Club in 1894, see J. M. Scott, *Exetel 100. The Centenary History of the Exchange Telegraph Company* (London: Benn, 1973), pp. 54–8.
17. *Mid-Week Gazette* (Burnley), 27 May 1885 (thanks to Lancashire Libraries, Burnley); 'The Raid on the Manchester Betting Clubs', *op. cit.*; see also Convictions at Petty Sessions for betting offences, M117/1/7/1–27, 3 and 4 June 1885.
18. For example, see 'The Raid on the Gambling-Clubs', *Spectator*, 18 May 1889, pp. 675–6.
19. Scott, *op. cit.*, pp. 30–2.
20. 'Inside a Betting Club', *op. cit.*, p. 50.
21. Rev. E. C. Chorley, *Gambling* (Abingdon: 1889), p. 5.
22. Curzon, *A Mirror on the Turf*, p. 192.
23. Charles Booth, *Life and Labour of the People in London, 1st series, 'Poverty (1) East, Central and South London* (London: Macmillan & Co., 1902), p. 94.
24. 'Club Betting', *Banyan*, May 1939, p. 77; Eddy and Loewe, *op. cit.*, p. 5. For clubs outside London, see: Birkenhead Vigilance Committee,

Sixth Annual Report, April 1906, *Twelfth Annual Report*, November 1912, and *Thirteenth Annual Report*, November 1913, *passim* (thanks to Wirral Libraries); Convocation of the Province of York, *Report of the Committee on Betting and Gambling with Appendix* (London: Society for Promoting Christian Knowledge, 1890) pp. 60–1.

25. *The Bulletin. The Quarterly Record of the National Anti-Gambling League*, vol. 5, no. 39, February 1910, p. 73.
26. R. C., 1932–3, *Report*, p. 101.
27. Chinn Interviews, Mr Cooper, pp. 20–2.
28. *Ibid.*, Mrs Ward (daughter of Walter King) pp. 1–5 and 13–17. For betting clubs in London, see 'Habitual Betting at City Club', *Morning Advertiser*, 30 December 1937.
29. For Grimsby, see Chinn Interviews, Mrs Ward, p. 27 and Ron Hanley, p. 4, and for the pre-war period, see Chinn Letters, Mrs Barass, no. 2, p. 2 and Mrs F. Cuthbert, no. 1, p. 1. For Hull, see Chinn Letters, L. E. Armitage, no. 2, *passim.*
30. *Ibid.*, Gordon Roper, p. 1.
31. 'False Club Evil: JPs to act', *Daily Mail* (Manchester edn), 16 October 1954.
32. 'Betting Sessions in Hull Clubs to End', *Hull Daily Mail*, 22 October 1954. For the survival of these clubs, see 'Grimsby Club Struck Off: £350 Fines', *Grimsby Evening Telegraph*, 16 August 1957.
33. Chinn Letters, Gordon Roper, pp. 1–2 and L. E. Armitage, no. 2, *passim.*
34. 'Grimsby Club Struck Off: £350 Fines', *Grimsby Evening Telegraph*, 16 August 1957.
35. 'Bets from Club were Sent up Pneumatic Tube', *Yorkshire Post*, 23 July 1957. For a betting club in Brighton see *Daily Telegraph*, 30 May 1958; in Derby, 'A Derby Club: Bookies, Officials to Pay £75', *Derby Evening Telegraph*, 20 December 1957; and in London, 'Poplar Club is Raided by the Police – for Fifth Time', *East London Advertiser*, 28 March 1952, 'Police "Raided" Social Club', *East End News*, 10 June 1960 (thanks to Tower Hamlets Libraries).
36. Since legalization, there have been periodic reports of illegal betting clubs, for example, 'Illegal Bets in Club', *Hackney Gazette*, 14 May 1968 (thanks to Tower Hamlets Libraries); 'Illegal Betting Club Raided by Police', *Sporting Life*, 22 December 1979; and Martyn Harris, 'The Illegal Gamblers', *New Society*, 24 November 1983, pp. 314–16.
37. Memorial to the Rt Hon. the Secretary of State for Home Dept, 30 August 1875 (thanks to Doncaster Libraries).
38. 'The Betting Pest. No. 1 – Skimmed Justice', *Porcupine*, 10 March 1877 (thanks to Mark Clapson).
39. Manchester Corporation Waterworks and Improvement Act 1875, no. 50, p. 28.
40. Convictions at Petty Sessions for betting offences, M117/1/7/1–27, 20 October and 26 October 1877.
41. David Jones, *Crime, Protest, Community and Police in Nineteenth-Century Britain* (London: Routledge & Kegan Paul, 1982) p. 22; see also David Woods, 'Community Violence', in John Benson (ed.), *The Working-Class in England 1875–1914* (London: Croom Helm, 1985), pp. 180–5.

42. J. T. Gent, *Banker's Secret or The Old Wardrobe* (Leicester: 1877 – thanks to Leicester Information Office); Charles Kingsley, 'On Betting and Gambling', in Kingsley, *Letters to Young Men* (London: 1877), pp. 4–5.
43. Kingsley, *op. cit.*, pp. 5–7 and 13. His comments were quoted later by anti-gamblers such as: Convocation of the Province of York, *op. cit.*, p. 17; Rev. W. Moore-Ede, 'Is Gambling Wrong?', *Sunday Magazine* (Gateshead: 1889 – thanks to Gateshead Libraries). Kingsley is best known for his novel *The Water Babies* (2nd edn, London: Macaullan & Co., 1864).
44. Cited in J. Fairfax-Blakeborough, 'Origin and Evolution of "Tattersall's Ring"', *Banyan*, September 1951, p. 9.
45. Frederick Gale, *Modern English Sports. Their Use and Abuse* (London: Sampson Low, Marston, Searle & Rivington, 1885), p. 46; and James Runciman, 'The Ethics of the Turf', *Contemporary Review*, vol. 60, April 1889, p. 606.
46. Anonymous racecourse bookmaker cited in J. Fairfax-Blakeborough, 'Memories of Old-Time Bookmakers', *Banyan*, December 1942, p. 60. Among the leviathans of the later nineteenth century were: Jacob Bayliss, once a jeweller in Coventry; Teddy Edwards, a former fish porter from Sheffield; Richard 'Red Hot' Fry, originally a draper in Liverpool, who was owed a reputed £200,000 at his death; and Joseph Pickersgill, who started life as a butcher's boy from Leeds and who left a fortune of £746,000 when he died in 1920. See J. Fairfax-Blakeborough, 'Memories of Old Time Bookmakers', *Banyan*, October 1942, p. 35; Dey, *op. cit.*, pp. 256–63.
47. Richard A. Proctor, 'Betting on Races', *Gentleman's Magazine*, vol. 243, no. 1774, October 1878, pp. 476–7.
48. Article in *Baily's Magazine*, cited in J. Fairfax-Blakeborough, 'Memories of Old-Time Bookmakers', *Banyan*, December 1942, p. 62; see also, 'The Horse as an Instrument of Gambling', *op. cit.*, p. 389. For Dey, see his autobiography, *op. cit.*, *passim*. Later 'gentlemen' bookies have included Archie Scott, whose mentor was Dey, Chinn Interviews Sam Dell, supplement, p. 1; Lord 'Tommy' Graves, *Evening Standard*, 21 December 1949; and Stephen Little, 'Ken Montgomery Talks to Stephen Little', *Sporting Life*, 25 April 1983. One of the most prominent 'blue-blooded' bookies was Helen Vernett; see *Daily Express*, 31 March 1955 and Richard Kaye with Ray Poskett, *The Ladbrokes' Story* (London: Pelham Books, 1969), pp. 45–6.
49. Curzon, *The Blue Ribbon of the Turf*, p. 171.
50. Gayle, *op. cit.*, p. 45. Partridge conjectured that the term 'welcher' was derived from the racist rhyme 'Taffy is a Welshman, Taffy is a thief', *op. cit.*, p. 1034; but Fairfax-Blakeborough argued that it was taken from David Welch, 'a pioneer bookmaker in London . . . of whom tradition says that he never paid', 'Memories of Old-Time Bookmakers', *Banyan*, December 1939, p. 160.
51. Dey, *op. cit.*, p. 275.
52. For the enclosure of racecourses see Vamplew, *op. cit.*, pp. 38–48. The term 'flapping' may be derived from the slang verb 'flap', which Partridge gave as meaning 'to swindle', *op. cit.*, p. 324. However, Fairfax-Blakeborough believed it came from the term 'leather-flapping',

which indicated either the careless saddling and bridling of the horses at an unauthorized fixture, or the wild antics of some of their jockeys; 'Memories of Old-Time Bookmakers', *Banyan*, March 1942, p. 3. For villainy at flappers, see J. Fairfax-Blakeborough, '"Flapping" and Old-Time Bookmakers', *Banyan*, September 1950, pp. 149–51; see also Dyke Wilkinson, 'By-Gone Birmingham', articles from *Birmingham Daily Mail* (1923 – thanks to Birmingham Libraries), p. 22. For a contemporary reaction to ill-supervised meetings, see 'The Suburban Race Nuisance', *Saturday Review*, vol. 47, no. 1,229, 17 May 1879, p. 617.

53. Greenwood, *The Seven Curses of London*, pp. 398–401. This incident is remarkably similar to one that occurred on an Australian racecourse and which was described by Keith Dunstan in *Wowsers. Being an Account of the Prudery Exhibited by Certain Outstanding Men and Women in Such Matters as Drinking, Smoking, Prostitution, Censorship and Gambling* (North Melbourne, Australia: Casell, 1968), pp. 234–41. For other attacks on welching bookies, see J. Fairfax-Blakeborough, 'Memories of Old-Time Bookmakers', *Banyan*, December 1939, pp. 160–1.
54. Cited in J. Fairfax-Blakeborough, 'More Memories of "The Ring"', *Banyan*, December 1949, pp. 89–90.
55. Wilkinson, *Rough Roads*, p. 242. Wilkinson himself had been a jewellery-maker whose heavy betting led him in to bookmaking. His memoirs emphasize the existence of middle-class betting and bring to the fore the need for more research into this phenomenon and that of middle-class bookmakers.
56. For example, in 1828 and 1831 there were battles between large gangs of thimbleriggers and the public at Lincoln and Doncaster racecourses, *Bell's Life in London*, 9 October 1831; 'Gambling', *Sheardown's Pamphlets* (Doncaster: 1861), vol. 1, pp. 41–2 (thanks to Doncaster Libraries); and Thormanby, *Sporting Stories*, pp. 141–7.
57. Partridge dates the verb 'to fleece' to about the sixteenth century, *op. cit.*, p. 328. It would seem to derive from the act of taking the coat from a sheep's back and as such would be connected to the bookmaking expression 'skinning the lamb'. This relates to a race in which the bookmaker lays hardly a winner and on which he or she makes a lot of money; hence the noun 'a skinner'. Partridge dated the former to 1864 and the latter to about 1870, *op. cit.*, pp. 850–1. For an interesting discussion of bookmaking terminology in the later nineteenth century, see 'Betting and Betting Men', *Chambers's Journal*, vol. 13, no. 658, 8 August 1896, pp. 497–9.
58. Wilkinson, *Rough Roads*, pp. 261–6.
59. Curzon, *The Blue Ribbon of the Turf*, p. 171; see also, J. Fairfax-Blakeborough, 'Memories of Old-Time Bookmakers', *Banyan*, June 1942, p. 1–2.
60. Anonymous, cited in J. Fairfax-Blakeborough, 'Memories of Old-Time Bookmakers', *Banyan*, November 1939, p. 147.
61. For a description of travel and overnight stops see Dick Philips, cited in J. Fairfax-Blakeborough, 'Memories of Old-Time Bookmakers', *Banyan*, December 1941, p. 62.
62. Curzon, *The Blue Ribbon of the Turf*, p. 171; J. Fairfax-Blakeborough,

'Part-Time Bookmakers of Yore', *Banyan*, June 1942, pp. 1–2; J. Fairfax-Blakeborough, 'The Ring in the Merry Past', *Banyan*, December 1948, pp. 119–2l.

63. Anonymous bookie cited in J. Fairfax-Blakeborough, 'Memories of Old-Time Bookmakers', *Banyan*, December 1941, p. 63; J. Fairfax-Blakeborough, 'Old-Time Clerks', *Banyan*, June 1942, p. 2; and Wilkinson, *Rough Roads*, p. 96. The noun 'gaffer' dates to about 1650, Partridge, *op. cit.*, p. 356.
64. Wilkinson, *Rough Roads*, pp. 95–8; and J. Fairfax-Blakeborough, 'More Memories of the Ring', *Banyan*, December 1949, p. 90.
65. J. Fairfax-Blakeborough, 'Origin and Evolution of "Tattersall's Ring"', *Banyan*, September 1951, pp. 8–9; Runciman, *op. cit.*, pp. 609–10.
66. Art., *op. cit.*, p. 467. For the Marquess of Hastings see Rice, *op. cit.*, vol. 1, pp. 355–90.
67. Runciman, *op. cit.*, p. 618; cited in 'The Horse as an Instrument of Gambling', *op. cit.*, p. 386. A member of the Jockey Club supported this observation, see J. Fairfax-Blakeborough, 'Past and Present Ring Notabilities', *Banyan*, July 1950, p. 130.
68. J. Fairfax-Blakeborough, 'Old-Time Bookmakers', *Banyan*, August 1946, p. 5.
69. Cited in J. Fairfax-Blakeborough, 'Betting and the Law', *Banyan*, July 1949, p. 29.
70. Reverend Alfred Rowland, *A Talk with Young Men on Betting and Gambling* (London: Sunday School Union, 1890), p. 11; Hawke, *op. cit.*, p. 32. See also 'The Great Turf Case', *Spectator*, no. 3183, 29 June 1889, pp. 886–8. Unabashedly, William Day joined in this attack on smaller bookmakers, calling them 'positively the curse of the turf', in 'The Evil of Betting and How to Eradicate It', *Fortnightly Review*, n.s., vol. 47, no. 279, March 1890, p. 345.
71. R. H. Gretton, *Modern History of the English People, 1880–1922* (London: Martin Secker, 1930), p. 278.
72. John Ruskin, 'Lecture III – War', in Ruskin, *The Crown of Wild Olive*, (Kent: Smith, Elder & Co., 1882 – the lecture itself was given in 1865 at the Royal Military Academy, Woolwich), p. 138; Reverend S. Reynolds Hole, *Gambling and Betting* (London: 1888), pp. 5 and 25, and for a comparison with Kingsley's arguments see pp. 5–17.
73. 'The Growth of Gambling', *Spectator*, 13 October 1888, p. 1386.
74. Convocation of the Province of York, *op. cit.*, p. 8. See also Henry Hart Chamberlain, *Gambling and Betting. Being the substance of a lecture* (Oxford: Society for the Promotion of Christian Knowledge, 1890) p. 2; Chorley, *op. cit.*, p. 3; Rev. J. Malet Lambert, *Gambling: Is It Wrong?* (London: Simpkin, Marshall & Co., 1890), p. 3.
75. Runciman, *op. cit.*, pp. 607–8; 'Is Gambling on the Increase?', *Spectator*, 14 February 1891, p. 236.
76. Rowland, *op. cit.*, p. 4.
77. Itzkowitz, *op. cit.*, p. 25; John Benson, *The Penny Capitalists. A Study of Nineteenth-century Working-Class Entrepreneurs* (Dublin: Gill and Macmillan, 1983), pp. 70–1; and Hugh Cunningham, 'Leisure', in Benson, *The Working Class in England*, p. 153.
78. McKibbin, *op. cit.*, p. 148.

79. For prosecutions of coin gamblers in the 1870s see, for example, 'The Pitch and Toss Nuisance – Caution to Gamblers', *Barnsley Chronicle*, 25 March 1871 (thanks to Barnsley Libraries).
80. Chinn Letters, John L. W., no. 3, p. 1; for pitch and toss in Salford in the 1920s and 1930s, see also Andrew Mark Davies, 'Leisure and Poverty in Salford and Manchester, 1900–1939', University of Cambridge, unpublished PhD thesis, 1989, pp. 203–9; and for Lancashire, North West Sound Archive, nos 257, 259 and 839 (*I Remember When*, BBC Radio Lancashire), and Bolton Oral History Survey, 108B. For these coin games in Birmingham, see Chinn Interviews, Steve Nicholls, pp. 5–6; for Liverpool, see Chinn Letters, Mr C. J. Morgan, no. 1, p. 7; and for a variant of Nudger in Bristol, Chinn Interviews, Mr Wheeler, pp. 2–3; and for the East End of London see Joe Jacobs, *Out of the Ghetto. My Youth in the East End, Communism and Fascism 1913–1939* (London: Janet Simpson, 1978), pp. 40–1. In Luton, Nearest the Mottie was played by costermongers who called it 'Pitchy up the Mot', Aubrey S. Darby, *A View from the Alley* (Luton: The Borough of Luton Museum and Art Gallery, 1974), p. 36. In Bermondsey, another variant was 'spansy'. In this game, the coins were tossed to a wall by two players, the second of whom became the winner if he could span with his hand the coins of his opponent, see Tom Ash, *Childhood Days. The Docks and Dock Slang* (London: the author, 1982), p. 1. For a Liverpudlian coin game called 'jinks' see Chinn Letters, M. Quinn, no. 2, p. 3.
81. Essex County Record Office, *Maldon Police Officers' Report Books*, D/B 3/3/653, 1 May 1887; and *Police Record Books*, Constable (later Sergeant) Jas Watson, 21 January 1900, 3 November 1901, 30 April 1911.
82. South Yorkshire Police Archival Material, *Sheffield Division of the West Riding, Magistrates' Courts Books*, MC/1/1–4 and MC/2/1–5, July 1882–March 1893, *passim* (thanks to the Chief Constable of South Yorkshire Police and Sheffield Libraries for access to this material). For pitch and toss in London, see Evidence of Horace Smith, a London magistrate, S. C. (1901–2) *Minutes*, q. 564, p. 490; and for Southampton, Chief Constable, 'Betting and Gambling', in *Annual Report* (1892 – thanks to Hampshire Libraries, Southampton).
83. 'Special Patrols to Stop Money Gambling', *Gateshead Post*, 24 August 1951 (thanks to Gateshead Libraries), Grace Foakes, *My Part of the River* (London: Shepheard & Walwyn, 1974) p. 22, and Bill Naughton, *Saintly Billy. A Catholic Boyhood* (first published 1989. Oxford: Oxford University Press, 1989), pp. 2–3; Chinn Interviews, Steve Nicholls, pp. 5–6; Chinn Letters, Mr E. McGuiness, no. 2, p. 5 and Ernie Benson, *To Struggle is to Live. (A working-class autobiography in Two Volumes*, vol. 1 (Newcastle-upon Tyne: People's Publications, 1979) p. 142; *The Dart* (a satirical journal in Birmingham), 8 September 1882, p. 5 and Chinn Interviews, Alf Spittle, pp. 37–8.
84. For two-up in Australia see John O'Hara's excellent study, *A Mug's Game. A History of Gaming and Betting in Australia* (Kensington: New South Wales University Press, 1988), *passim*, and Dunstan, *op. cit.*, pp. 207–13, who stated that the game began in Sydney 'some time around 1800'; the evidence would suggest that this is incorrect because the game was well-established in Britain before then, see Chapter 3. For two-up

in New Zealand see, 'The Illicit Pastime of "Heading 'Em"', *Dominion*, 23 October 1916 (thanks to the National Library of New Zealand).

85. Chinn Letters, Mr C. J. Morgan, no. 1, pp. 8–10.
86. This account is based on Chinn Interviews, Steve Nicholls, pp. 5–6 (Birmingham); *ibid.*, Jim Cooper, pp. 1–4 and Clarence Muff, *Unbelievable but True!* (Bradford: City of Bradford Metropolitan Council, 1984), pp. 5–6 (Bradford); Chinn Interviews, Mick Doyle, *passim* (Dublin); *ibid.*, Joe Stevens, pp. 1–3 (County Durham); Chinn Letters, Mr E. McGuinness, no. 2, pp. 5–6 and Chinn Interviews, Nicky Marshall, *passim* (Glasgow); *ibid.*, Sam Dunleavy, pp. 31–5 and Mr Lafferty, *passim* (Lanarkshire); Chinn Letters, John L. W., no. 3, p. 1 (Salford); Chinn Interviews, Frank Harris, pp. 1–3 (Sheffield); *ibid.*, Christy Rees, pp. 16–18 (Swansea); *ibid.*, Alf Spittle, pp. 37–8 (Wolverhampton); and *ibid.*, Jack Ingram, *passim* (West Yorkshire).
87. 'Smart Capture of Sunday Gamblers at Widdup', *Colne and Nelson Times*, 24 July 1891 (thanks to Lancashire Libraries, Nelson); Jack Lawson, *A Man's Life* (London: Hodder & Stoughton, 1932), p. 76.
88. 'The Raid Upon the Cold Well Gambling School', *Nelson Leader*, 20 October 1922 (thanks to Lancashire Libraries, Nelson). An excellent description of a Pennine moorland gambling school can be found in a novel by a Maurice Proctor, *Hell is a City* (London: Hutchinson, 1954), pp. 93–101. Proctor was a native of Nelson and he had been a policemen at Mixenden, a village near Halifax, 'Policeman Proctor Risked All at 40', *Yorkshire Evening Post*, 30 January 1956 (thanks to Calderdale Libraries, Halifax); see also T. W. Pateman (ed.), *Dunchurch. A Lancashire Background* (London: Museum Press, 1948), pp. 184–5. For a first-hand account of a small, local Pennine ring, see Chinn Interviews, Jack Ingram, *passim*.
89. 'A Raid on Gamblers', *Colne and Nelson Times*, 31 July 1880; see also 'Smart Capture of Sunday Gamblers at Widdup', *Colne and Nelson Times*, 24 July 1891 (thanks to Lancashire Libraries, Nelson).
90. 'A Public Gambling Resort', *Burnley Mid-Weekly Gazette*, 16 March 1887 (thanks to Lancashire Libraries, Burnley) and Chinn Interviews, Mr Hirst, p. 20; Chinn Interviews, Jim Farrar, p. 15 and Jim Cooper, pp. 1–3; *ibid.*, Frank Harris, p. 3; *ibid.*, Joe Stevens, pp. 1–3, and T. Dalkin, *Story of Fifty Years a Miner and Soldier*, (unpublished MS, *c.* 1975), p. 14 (thanks to Durham County Record Office); 'Sunday Gaming in Clydebank', *Glasgow Herald*, 11 September 1928 (the indexing of this newspaper has proven an invaluable help in my research), Chinn Interviews, Sam Dunleavy, p. 31, Mr Lafferty, *passim*; and *ibid.*, Christy Rees, pp. 16–17. For 'hoying' see Chinn Letters, Frederick C. Moffat, no. 1, p. 1 and Lawson, *op. cit.*, p. 83, and for 'burling', Chinn Interviews, Sam Dunleavy, p. 32 and Mr Lafferty, *passim*. For the ubiquity of gambling schools in the North of England, see also Convocation of the Province of York, *op. cit.*, p. 10; J. M. Hogge, *The Facts of Gambling* (London: Andrew Melrose, 1907), pp. 19–20 and 33; and 'How the Working Classes Gamble', *Tit Bits*, 17 July 1897, p. 296.
91. For example, in a raid in 1891, nine of those arrested were weavers, two were warp dressers, two were quarrymen, one was a tackler and one was a labourer, 'Smart Capture of Sunday Gamblers at Widdup', *Colne*

and Nelson Times, 24 July 1891. For prosperous gamblers see: Chinn Interviews, Sam Dunleavy, p. 31; Muff, *op. cit.*, p. 6; 'The Raid Upon the Cold Well Gambling School', *Nelson Leader*, 20 October 1922; Norman Smithson, 'Those Bygone Days of Pitch and Toss', *Yorkshire Life*, vol. 29, August 1975, p. 49, and Chinn Interviews, Joe Stevens, pp. 1–3.

92. For use of the word 'crow' see Chinn Interviews, Jim Cooper, p. 2 and Proctor, *op. cit.*, p. 96; 'The Raid Upon the Cold Well Gambling School', *Nelson Leader*, 20 October 1922.
93. 'Toller' is derived from the standard English meaning of 'toll' – tax or duty paid . . . for service rendered', J. B. Sykes (ed.), *op. cit.*, p. 1126. For tollers as hard men see Chinn Interviews, Sam Dunleavy, pp. 31–2 and Chinn Letters, J. Abbott, no. 2, pp. 10–11 and Peter Plunkett, no. 2, p. 4. For the commission of tollers see J. P. Bean, *The Sheffield Gang Wars* (Sheffield: D & D Publications, 1981), p. 7, Chinn Interviews, Frank Harris, p. 3, and Muff, *op. cit.*, p. 6.
94. Arthur Hopcraft, *The Great Apple Raid & Other Encounters of a Tin Chapel Tiro* (London: Heinemann, 1970), pp. 71–2.
95. For losses at tossing see: Foakes, *op. cit.*, p. 22; Ted Furniss, *The Walls of Jericho: Slum Life in Sheffield Between the Wars* (Sheffield: Rebel Press, 1979), p. 8; Chinn Letters, Bill Gleghorn, no. 2, p. 2; Máirín Johnston, *Around the Banks of Pimlico* (Dublin: 1985), p. 75.
96. Abe Moffat, *My Life with the Miners* (London: Lawrence & Wishart, 1965), p.20.
97. Lawson, *op. cit.*, p. 83, and Hopcraft, *op. cit.*, pp. 72–3.
98. For babbers see Chinn Interviews, Sam Dunleavy, pp. 31–2, and for an account by a babber see *ibid.*, John Lafferty, *passim*. For bebbers see Chinn Interviews, Mr Armstrong, *passim* (thanks to Mrs Armitage), and Joe Stevens, pp. 1–3.
99. As late as 1974, a bebber from Stanley explained that 'Queen Victoria coins were used because they were better balanced for spinning'; 'Police Swooped on Pitch-and-toss Game', *Newcastle Journal*, 1 March 1974 (thanks to Gateshead Libraries); see also Olive Fowler (ed.), *Innings and Outings. Voices from Barnsley*, (Yorkshire: Yorkshire Arts Circus, 1988), p. 48. Double-heading and flamming were age-old tricks: 'There are meritorious *professioners* who can always win at tossing up, either by a little *handicraft*, or by a piece of money with the same impression on each side, which may be seen by *every one* on the floor, but must be *picked up* by *one* bold friend, and ought not to appear too often, unless the *simples* see double'; Hellen, *op. cit.*, pp. 81–2. For these swindles in the twentieth century see Chinn Interviews, Nicky Marshall, *passim*, and Muff, *op. cit.*, pp. 5–6.
100. 'Police are after the Gamblers', Gateshead Libraries Newspaper Cuttings, 1949–53, p. 152 and Chinn Letters, Mr T. S., no. 2, p. 1.
101. Chinn Letters, Lilian Perry, p. 1, Chinn Interviews, Steve Nicholls, pp. 5–6, and 'It Always Happens on Sundays', *East End News*, 30 March 1951 (thanks to Tower Hamlet Libraries); Elizabeth Couchman (ed.), *Belgrave as I Remember It* (Leicester: Leicestershire Libraries and Information Service, 1984), p. 10, Chinn Interviews, the Ford and Kimberley families, *passim*, and Leicester Oral History Archive, *Crimes and Punishment*, *passim*; Chinn Letters, Jack Brodie, no. 3, p. 1; and

Chinn Interviews, Joe Stevens, pp. 1–3. In Belfast, a large tossing school was to be found on the Oval, by the football ground of Glentoran, see Chinn Interviews, Harry Gillan, p. 1.

102. *Ibid.*, C. J. Morgan, no. 2, p. 8.
103. *Ibid.*, M. Quinn, p. 3. It should be noted that a former member of the Liverpool City Police believed that, to his knowledge, tossing in the city was not organized, *ibid.*, G. Squires, no. 2, p. 2. In some parts of Britain, the belt man was known as the 'strap man', see Chinn Interviews, Frank Harris, p. 3.
104. Johnston, *op. cit.*, p. 74. Often, boxmen were called 'ball men', Chinn Interviews, Billy Hughes, p. 1. For Dublin, see also Chinn Interviews, Mick Doyle, *passim* and Joe Hegarty, p. 1.
105. 'The Raid upon the Cold Well Gambling School', *Nelson Leader*, 20 October 1922.
106. Johnston, *op. cit.*, p. 75.
107. For hyped-up versions of these 'wars' see local newspaper articles cited in Bean, *op. cit.*, *passim*; and for an excellent and undramatized description of life in poverty-stricken Sheffield during these years, see Alfred Green, *Growing up in Attercliffe. Honey with a Ladle . . . Vinegar with a Teaspoon* (Sheffield: New City, 1981).
108. This account is based on Chinn Interviews, Frank Harris, *passim* – a former member of the Alfed Road gang; and *ibid.*, William Lane – who was from the Park District and 'knew most of the principals', *passim*. The best written narrative is in Bean, *op. cit.*, which differs slightly from my oral evidence, see also, A. W. Cockerill, *Sir Percy Sillitoe*, (London: W. H. Allen, 1975), pp. 76–93; and Tony Fry, 'The Bad Old Days in Sheffield', *Sheffield Star*, 18, 19, 22 and 23 November 1976.
109. See Chinn Interviews, Sam Dunleavy, p. 35 and Chinn Letters, J. Abbott, no. 2, pp. 10–11. Mr Abbott was a member of the Lancashire Police Force, serving in Chadderton and then Darwen. A fictional account of violence at a Glaswegian school in the 1950s is found in Bill McGhee, *Cut and Run* (first published 1962. London: Corgi Books, 1986) pp. 117–29; and for children acting as watchers for a local ring in the city, see Jimmy Boyle, *A Sense of Freedom* (London: Pan, 1977), pp. 58–9.
110. The Royal Commission of 1932–3 reported that 'gambling schools, however, are less common than they used to be', *Report*, p. 49; but oral evidence would support their vitality into the 1950s and early 1960s, and for their survival into the 1970s, see 'Police Swooped on Pitch-and-toss Game', *Newcastle Journal*, 1 March 1974. In 1951, another Royal Commission noted that 'gaming in streets and like places is a public nuisance', Royal Commission on Betting, Lotteries and Gaming, (Cmd. 8190, London: HMSO, 1949–51), *Report*, p. 127.
111. Chinn Letters, E. McGuiness, no. 2, p. 5.
112. *Ibid.*, John L. W., no. 2, pp. 1–2.
113. *Ibid.*, Mr C. J. Morgan, no. 3, pp. 1–3.
114. Chinn Interviews, Steve Nicholls, p. 6; Chinn Letters, Bill Smith, no. 2, p. 2.
115. *Ibid.*; Chinn Letters, Mr C. J. Morgan, no. 2, pp. 4–5; *ibid.*, John L. W., no. 2, p. 2; Chinn Interviews, Christy Rees, pp. 16–17; Ash, *op. cit.*, p. 1; Darby, *op. cit.*, p. 36.

116. Essex County Record Office, *Police Record Books*, Constable (later Sergeant) Jas Watson, 24 June and 7 October 1900 – several men and youths from Braintree were fined for playing banker on the highway outside the town, 19 March 1911 – four men charged for playing nap on Heron Court Common; South Yorkshire Police Archival Material, *Upper Staniforth and Tickhill Division (Sheffield District) of the West Riding, Magistrates' Courts Books*, July 1882–December 1893, *passim* (thanks to the Chief Constable of South Yorkshire and Sheffield Libraries for access to this material).
117. Chinn Letters, Roy King, Kingswood History Project, p. 1, and Chinn Interviews, Donald Davies, p. 9.
118. *Dudley Herald*, 13 July 1889, see also M. B. D., 'Gambling on the Wren's Nest', *Dudley Herald*, 29 June 1889. In the same year, pigeon fancying was under attack, 'Pigeon Flying', *ibid.*, 3 August 1889 (thanks to Dudley Libraries).
119. 'Police Complimented on Smart Work', 'Hard Labour Sentence. Pentreach Gaming Charge', 'Gambling Must Stop. Youths Must be Taught Discipline', *Merthyr Express*, 13 April and 27 April 1940, and 2 August 1941 (thanks to Merthyr Libraries).
120. 'Police Surprise Sunday Gamers', *Lancaster Guardian*, 16 April 1943 (thanks to Lancashire Libraries, Lancaster).
121. Chinn Interviews, Mr Hirst, pp. 20–1, and Fred Prior, *passim* – in Birmingham, buck and stick was called 'tip cat' and it was played by boys, in Bolton it was known as 'piggy', Poole, *op. cit.*, p. 48, and in Brighton, it was termed as 'but and trap', Chinn Letters, Victor Baker, no. 2, p. 2; *ibid.*, Sam Dunleavy, p. 20, *ibid.*, Mr Armstrong, *passim*, *ibid.*, Christy Rees, pp. 18–19; *ibid.*, Ronald 'Mac' Davidson, *passim*, Michael D. Allen, 'The Gamblers', *Bedfordshire Magazine*, vol. 21, winter 1987, pp. 113–15 (thanks to Bedfordshire Libraries, Bedford and Luton), Chinn Letters, Donald Hyslop, Oral Historian Southampton, p. 1, Michael D. Conway, *Half-Timer. A Stockport Mill Boy Remembers* (Stockport: Stockport Metropolitan Borough Recreation and Culture Division, 1983), pp. 45–6, and Chinn Interviews, Jack Scotney, pp. 4–5. The best description of crown and anchor is in Allen, *op. cit.*, and it would seem that the game was brought back to the streets by soldiers and sailors who had picked it up during the First World War. See also Cleveland County Oral History Project, accession no. 260, pp. 16–17 (my thanks to).
122. Bill Naughton, *op. cit.*, pp. 2–3; in Bolton, 'nixers' was the name given to those who watched out for the police.
123. Chinn Letters, John L. W., no. 3, p. 2.
124. Chinn Interviews, Mr Hantman, pp. 5–6.
125. 'Chinamen and Puk-a-Pue', *East End News*, 15 July 1924, and for a description of the game see 'Puck-a-Poo', *East London Advertiser*, 10 March 1923. Fan Tan was another popular gambling activity among the Chinese, '£170 for a Shilling. New Gambling Game in East London', *East London Advertiser*, 26 April 1910 (thanks to Tower Hamlets Libraries). In Australia and New Zealand, the authorities were as concerned about the effects of Chinese gambling activities, see O'Hara, *passim*, and 'Police Strategy. The Trip to Chinatown', *Dominion*, 5 August 1913 (thanks to

the National Library of New Zealand). For later gambling among the Chinese see R. C., (1978), *Final Report*, pp. 374–80.

126. For working-class incomes, see Cunningham, 'Leisure', pp. 137–8; and McKibbin, *op. cit.*, pp. 163–4.
127. Stedman Jones, 'Working-class Culture and Working-class Politics', in Stedman Jones, *op. cit.*, p. 203–4.
128. McKibbin, *op. cit.*, pp. 151–3.
129. Convocation of the Province of York, *op. cit.*, p. 9.
130. For the fortunes of some leviathans see note 46.
131. 'The Street Betting Evil', *Chiswick Times*, 2 June 1905 (thanks to Hounslow Libraries).
132. Evidence of Samuel Chisolm, Lord Provost of Glasgow, S. C., (1901–2) *Minutes*, q. 1946, p. 554.
133. 'The Bookmakers "Pay, Pay, Pay"', 14 July 1900, newspaper cutting supplied by Smethwick Local History Society; Evidence of John Orr, Chief Constable of Glasgow, S. C., (1901–2) *Minutes*, q. 2093, p. 559.
134. B. Seebohm Rowntree, *Poverty. A Study of Town Life* (first published 1901. New York: Garland, 1980), p. 143.
135. W. C. Peterborough, 'Betting, Gambling and My Critics', *Fortnightly Review*, vol. 46, no. 276, December 1889, pp. 754–63.
136. Dunstan, *op. cit.*, pp. 205–94 and O'Hara, *op. cit.*, pp. 130–69. See also A. E. Fletcher, 'The Gambling Fever. Great Britain's Greatest Curse', *Temple Magazine*, 1896, pp. 826–7.
137. W. B. Curtis, 'The Increase in Gambling and Its Forms', *Forum* (1892), vol. 19, no. 279, pp. 24–30; and Newman Smyth, 'Suppression of the Lottery and Other Gambling', *Forum* (1895), vol. 20, no. 281, p. 282. For racecourse bookies in the USA, see Joseph Freeman Marsten, 'The Maelstrom of the Betting Ring', *Munsey's Magazine* (1903), vol. 29, pp. 705–11. A good historical survey of American gambling is in John M. Findlay, *The People of Chance. Gambling in American Society from Jamestown to Las Vegas* (New York: Oxford University Press, 1986).
138. 'Is Gambling on the Increase?', *Spectator*, 14 February 1891, p. 235.
139. Miller, *op. cit.*, p. i.
140. J. Gulland, 'The Psychology of Gambling', *The Sunday School Chronicle and Christian Outlook*, 15 December 1921; J. M. Hogge, *Betting and Gambling* (Edinburgh: R. W. Hunter, 1904), p. 4.
141. R. F. L. Blunt, *Betting and Gambling. A Paper Read at the York Diocesan Conference October 24, 1901* (London: Society for Promoting Christian Knowledge, 1902), p. 5. The definitive work on drink in this period is Brian Harrison, *Drink and the Victorians. The Temperance Question in England, 1815–72* (London: Faber and Faber, 1971); and for the later Victorian years see Lilian Lewis Shiman, *Crusade Against Drink in Victorian England* (Basingstoke: Macmillan Press, 1988).
142. O'Hara, *op. cit.*, p. 119.
143. Curtis, *op. cit.*, pp. 282–3.
144. Vamplew, *op. cit.*, p. 47; the most authorative account of football is by Mason, *op. cit.*
145. For example, see Chinn Interviews, Jack Scotney, p. 8.
146. *Musselburgh Sporting Chronicle*, 4 November 1889 (thanks to East Lothian Libraries); *Sporting Star* (Birmingham: 1889 – thanks to Mr

Yeoman, a descendant of George Pearce); Birmingham, *Racing Analysis* (1882). For a later period, see 'Racing Publications', *National Newsagent*, 19 March 1938 – which lists seventeen tipsters' sheets. See also: H. Bissell, *Modern Racing Tipsters. Some Facts, Criticisms and Exposures* (Tipton: 1899), and Rev. John William Horsley, *Sporting Prophets. A letter on the betting mania* (London: Christian Knowledge Society, 1902).

147. Mason, 'Sporting News', p. 183; Special Correspondent, '"The Sporting Life" Past, Present and Future', *Banyan*, April 1940, p. 16; and Edward 'Teddy' Dawson, 'Some Memories of the Old Days', *ibid.*, October 1953, pp. 57–8.
148. 'Fifty Years of Captain Coe', *Star*, 17 January 1938; for the memories of racing journalists see also A. Dick Luckman, *Sharps, Flats, Gamblers and Racehorses* (London: Grant Richards, 1914), formerly 'The Scout' of *Daily Express*; and Arthur J. Sarl, *Horses, Jockeys and Crooks. Reminiscences of Thirty Years' Racing* (London: Hutchinson & Co., 1935).
149. Mason, 'Sporting News', pp. 184–5.
150. Gretton, *op. cit.*, pp. 213–14 and 278.
151. McKibbin, *op. cit.*, p. 148.

5 STREET BOOKIES

1. Charles Sidney, *op. cit.*, p. 58. James Sutters was Secretary of the Commission Agents' Association; in 1901, he stated that the SP had been in existence for about twenty-five years, S. C. (1901–2), *Minutes*, q. 1144, p. 515.
2. Geoffrey Hamlyn, in Roger Mortimer (ed.), *The Encyclopaedia of Flat Racing* (London: Hale, 1971), p. 39; see also Lee, *op. cit.*, p. 127. The transmission of the SP was facilitated by the Press Association, which began its own service to newspapers in 1882, Harold Hodgson, 'Bookmakers and Betting', *Sporting Chronicle*, supplement, 29 May 1971.
3. *Bell's Life in London*, 9 April 1886, cited in Charles Sidney, *op. cit.*, p. 59.
4. Evidence of Henry Butly-Smith, S. C. (1901–2), *Minutes*, q. 268, p. 586; see also Cannon, *op. cit.*, p. 18.
5. Evidence of John Hawke, *ibid.*, q. 121 and 133, p. 364; for SPs taken from the *Sporting Chronicle*, see Bill Naughton, *A Roof Over Your Head* (London: The Pilot Press, 1945), p. 58. In Australia, illegal SP bookies took their odds from the Sydney *Morning Herald*, see 'S. A. Racecourses are "Clean" says Hedley Ward, Now Retiring', *Cape Times*, October 1956 – Mr Ward was an Australian who had been racing editor of the Sydney newspaper.
6. *Bulletin*, vol. 1, no. 8, May 1894, p. 77.
7. Evidence of John Hawke, S. C. (1901–2), *Minutes*, q. 119, p. 364.
8. For the differences in SPs, see Evidence of Colonel Fluder, Chairman of Tattersall's, S. C. (1901–2), *Minutes*, q. 117, p. 470; for the combined SP see Hamlyn, *op. cit.*, p. 39; Walter Meads, 'The Origin of Starting-Price Betting' (N. A. B. File, 'Starting Price', 1955); and Special Correspondent, *op. cit.*, p. 16. For the process of compiling the SP see Cope, *op. cit.*, pp. 125–7.
9. Gretton, *op. cit.*, p. 278.
10. Chinn Interviews, Mr Haworth, p. 4 and Jim Stock, pp. 47–8.

11. Chinn Letters, Thomas Buckley, no. 2, p. 1.
12. Chinn Interviews, Buck Chinn pp. 49–50. Jack Scotney took bets in the village of Farcet, near Peterborough, and he obtained his results from the *Evening Standard* (London); Chinn Interviews, p. 31.
13. W. B. Curtis, *op. cit.*, pp. 286–8 and Smith, *op. cit.*, pp. 242–3. In the United States, illegal bookmaking has been the subject of regular purges, see for example: *Sydney Referee*, 1 December 1938; 'Toppling a Gambling Empire', *Christian Science Monitor*, 2 December 1939; and 'Other Kennedy Causes Jitters Among Gambling Hoodlums', *Sunday Times*, 26 November 1961. The best descriptions of illegal bookmaking are: Chinn Interviews, Teddy D., supplement – in the early 1950s, Mr D. worked as an illegal bookie for the Mafia in Los Angeles; Robert Perrucci, 'The Neighbourhood "Bookmaker": Entrepreneur and Mobility Model', in Paul Meadows and Ephraim H. Mizruchi, *Urbanism, Urbanization, and Change: Comparative Perspectives* (Reading, Massachusetts: Addison-Wesley Publishing Co., 1969), pp. 302–11 (thanks to Mark Clapson); and Bill Surface, 'Big Action in a Phone Booth', *Sports Illustrated* (Chicago), 9 January 1967; see also the stories by Damon Runyon in *Damon Runyon on Broadway* (first published 1950. London: Picador, 1977) and *Damon Runyon from First to Last* (first published 1954. London: Picador, 1975). For a debate about the legalization of off-course betting see: Frank (Keystone) Harvey, 'American Scene', *Banyan*, July 1952, pp. 116–17; Thomas J. Gibbons, Philadelphia Commissioner of Police, 'Should Gambling be Legalized?', *Post* (Washington) 1958 (NAB File, 'America'); Henry D. Paley and John A. Glendinning, *Pattern for New York? A Report on Off-Track Betting in England* (New York: New York State Assembly, 1963 – thanks to Sam Dell); Samuel Roman and Henry D. Paley, *Off-Track Betting, 1966 Report* (New York: New York State Assembly, 1966). Discussions of legalized off-course betting in New York are in Richard Gilbert, 'Why Howie the Horse Feels a Million Dollars Every Day', *Observer*, 16 January 1972; for Las Vegas, see 'Betting Union Plaza Style . . .', *Licensed Bookmaker and Betting Office Proprietor*, February 1984, pp. 16–18.
14. Day, 'The Evil of Betting', *passim* and O'Hara, *op. cit.*, pp. 94–5.
15. Dunstan, *op. cit.*, p. 215, for a lively account of the Collingwood Tote and the controversy over its existence, see pp. 215–69; see also O'Hara, *op. cit.*, *passim*; and Frank Hardy's novel *Power without Glory* (East Malvern, Western Australia: Realist Printing and Publishing Co., 1950). Despite stringent laws against them, starting-price bookies have continued to operate in Australia, see O'Hara, *op. cit.*, pp. 238–41, Alfred W. McCoy, *Drug Traffic. Narcotics and Organised Crime in Australia* (Sydney: Harper & Row, 1980), pp. 176–82 and 244–53, and newspaper cuttings in the Archive of the NAB, file 'Australia'. For a modern account of on-course bookmaking there, see Chinn Interviews, Jim Hepburn, *passim*. Similarly, in New Zealand, illegal bookies survived in the face of especially fierce penalties. See, for example: 'Illegal Betting. Severe Fines in Auckland', *Dominion*, 8 April 1915 (thanks to the National Library of New Zealand); 'New Tactics to Avoid Detection. Bookmakers Go Still Further Underground', *Wellington Evening Post*, 14 May 1957. See also Royal Commission on Gaming and Racing, New

Zealand, *Report* (Wellington: 1948) and Len Scott, 'How New Zealand Came to Have Tote Monopoly. The Step-by-step Legislation', *Sporting Life*, 20 January 1966. For bookmaking in Canada see Select Committee on Betting Duty, *Proceedings* (Ottawa: 1924), pp. 50–2.

16. Longrigg, *op. cit.*, pp. 187–9 – these illegal operators survived at least until the later 1950s, see 'France Beating the Bookies', *Edinburgh Evening Dispatch*, 10 July 1956. Racecourse layers disappeared largely after 1891, when the *pari-mutuel* was introduced there, Neville, *op. cit.*, pp. 427–30. For bookmaking elsewhere on the Continent, see 'Belgian Boycott Worked', *Sporting Chronicle*, 7 November 1973; and 'Bookmaking in Germany', *Banyan*, September 1933, p. 26 and *ibid.*, October 1953, p. 68. As in France, it would seem that the introduction of the occupation was by British bookies, see Dey, *op. cit.*, pp. 217–19.
17. Circular Letter to bookmakers from P. O'Boyle, Secretary of the National Bookmakers' Protection Association Limited, 14 October 1932. For a full account of tote clubs, see Carl Chinn, 'Betting Shops and Race-by-Race Betting Before the Betting and Gaming Act, 1960', *Society for the Study of Gambling Newsletter*, no. 17, July 1990, pp. 10–20.
18. Convocation of the Province of York, *op. cit.*, p. 14.
19. Letter from Charles Winter, *Banyan*, August 1939, p. 123; Convocation of the Province of York, *op. cit.*, p. 9.
20. Cited in the *Bulletin*, May 1896, vol. 2, no. 5, pp. 159–60; see also Convocation of the Province of York, *op. cit.*, p. 9.
21. 'Remarkable Court Scenes. Film Shown of Betting Offences', *Derbyshire Times*, 17 May 1939 (thanks to Derbyshire Libraries); Chinn Letters, Samuel Watt, no. 1, pp. 1–5; Chinn Interviews, Mr Haworth, pp. 3–5, see also Chinn Letters, Margaret Aspin, no. 2, p. 4.
22. Evidence of Edward Hulton, proprietor of the *Sporting Chronicle*, S. C. (1901–2), *Minutes*, q. 2550, p. 58.
23. Herbert W. Rowsell and Clarence G. Morgan, *A Guide to the Law of Betting, Civil and Criminal* (London: Butterworth & Co., 1911), p. 63.
24. For example, see Birmingham Corporation (Consolidation) Act 1883 (46 and 47 Vict, cap. 52) no. 130 – in Leeds, the fine was £2 until 1905, 'Betting Laws for Leeds', *Leeds and Yorkshire Mercury*, 2 June 1905 (thanks to Leeds Libraries); Burgh Police (Scotland) Act (1892) section 393 (thanks to the Chief Constable of Strathclyde Police).
25. For example, see County Borough of Grimsby, *Byelaw with Reference to Betting* (1896 – thanks to Humberside Libraries); Borough of Leicester, *Byelaw for the Prevention of Betting in Streets* (1896 – thanks to Leicestershire Record Office); and Warrington Town Council Minutes, Meeting of the Watch Committee, 21 May 1896. Other places which adopted this byelaw included Wolverhampton (probably the first to do so in 1895), Accrington, Burslem and the counties of Stafford and Warwick; *Bulletin*, vol. 2, no. 5, May 1896, p. 166.
26. 'Return of Summary Convictions for Street Betting in the Metropolitan Police District During the Years 1903, 1904 and 1905' (London: House of Commons Papers, 179, xxcix, 747, 1906). This measure was followed rapidly by the councils of: Accrington, Aston Manor, Bradford, Bristol, Carlisle, East Ham, Halifax, Hyde, Kingston-upon-Hull, Leeds,

Manchester, Morley, Swindon and York. It annoyed moralists greatly that bookies paid their fines readily, for example, see Evidence of Horace Smith (a London JP) S. C. (1901–2), *Minutes*, q. 551, p. 490.

27. 'The Betting Crusade', *St Helens News*, 30 September 1902 (thanks to St Helens Libraries); see also Booth, *op. cit.*, final volume, p. 56.
28. Select Committee on the Betting Duty, *Report Together with the Proceedings of the Committee* (London: HMSO, 1924), p. xiv. The committee actually deliberated during 1923. See also Chinn Letters, Charles Noding, no. 1, p. 1.
29. For Cope's, see Cope (ed.), *op. cit.*, pp. 73–82 – on his death, David Cope left £127,000, 'Bookmaker Leaves £127,000', *Evening Standard*, 24 December 1936; Chinn Interviews, Joe Ward Hill, *passim*; *ibid.*, Charles Layfield, *passim.* For a café where bets where taken, see 'Poplar Betting Case', *East London Observer*, 21 December 1935 (thanks to Tower Hamlets Libraries).
30. For a prosecution against a hairdresser who used his premises to take bets, see 'Westhoughton Betting Cases', *Bolton Journal*, 20 November 1911; and for one against a barber, see 'The Betting Raid', *St Helens News*, 30 September 1902 (thanks to St Helens Libraries).
31. S. C. (1924), *Report*, p. xiv.
32. Chinn Letters, G. W. Cutts, no. 1, p. 1; *ibid.*, Albert Hardy, no. 2, p. 2; *ibid.*, Mr Riddall, p. 1; *ibid.*, Tony Wright, no. 1, p. 1. For a bookmaking baker in Long Melford (Suffolk), see *ibid.*, Audrey Copsey, nos 1 and 2, *passim.*
33. *Ibid.*, Mr A. McIntyre, no. 1, p. 1 and no. 2, p. 2; *ibid.*, Lew Reeves, no. 1, pp. 1–2.
34. Chinn Interviews, Albert Stanton, *passim*, Chinn Letters, Mr A. G. Ford, p. 1; *ibid.*, Charles Dearden, no. 1, p. 1; *ibid.*, Albert Hardy, no. 1, p. 1, pp. 2–5. For a greengrocer/bookie in Hove see *ibid.*, Mr Ford, p. 1 and for Rotherham see *ibid.*, John Shaw, no. 2, p. 2.
35. *Ibid.*, Samuel Fulwood, no. 1, p. 3; *ibid.*, Mrs N. Uscroft, no. 1, p. 1 (Hull) and *ibid.*, Dick Riley no. 1, pp. 1–2 (Tipton); *ibid.*, Mr J. Aslin, no. 1, p. 1 (Ross-on-Wye and Dawley); Tom Golding, *96 Years a Brummie* (Storton: Swinford Press, 1986), p. 13. For a second-hand furniture shop which doubled up as a bookie's, see Chinn Letters, Kathleen Latimer, no. 1, pp. 1–2.
36. Chinn Interviews, Mrs Packer (daughter of Rose Pickering), p. 1; see also *ibid.*, Richard Pickering, *passim.*
37. Chinn Letters, Reg Betts, no. 1, pp. 1–2 and no. 2, p. 3; see also *ibid.*, Tom W. Godwin, no. 2, pp. 1–2 (Ellesmere, Shropshire); and *ibid.*, Percy Preedy, no. 1, p. 1 and no. 2, p. 1 (Nottingham).
38. S. C. (1924), *Report*, p. xiv; for a business which became less important than the bookmaking 'sideline', see Chinn Letters, Tony Wright, no. 1, pp. 1–2.
39. Mass Observation, *The Pub and the People. A Worktown Study* (first published 1943. London: Cresset Library, 1987), p. 265. It is interesting to compare this description with that given in Chinn Letters, John Bootham, no. 1, pp. 3–4: 'Another bookmaker, a lady by the name of Bella Thomasson, she had a shop in the centre of Bolton. The police knew all about what was going on. She had dummy packets of cigarette

in the windows but if you went in the shop there was none for sale; it was full of men backing horses.'

40. 'The Betting Raid', *Bolton Journal*, 23 June 1905.
41. For the respect in which Bella Thomasson was held, see Chinn Letters, John Bootham, no. 2, p. 1 and Teddy Dean, no. 2, pp. 1–2; for the partnership with Albert Hampson, see Chinn Interviews, *passim*; and for the fame of the premises as an illegal betting shop, see Fred Shawcross, 'The Punter's Paradise', *Today*, 6 March 1986. In Bradford, there was a sweet shop/bookie's in which 'the sweets that were on display in the window were years old', Chinn Interviews, Jim Cooper, p. 6.
42. Convocation of the Province of York, *op. cit.*, pp. 14–15.
43. George Moore, *Esther Waters* (first published 1894. Oxford: Oxford University Press, 1983), pp. 249–60 and 290–339. For bookmaker/publicans see also Cannon, *op. cit.*, pp. 29–36.
44. For example, see Hall Caine, *The Christian. A Story* (first published 1892. London: Collier & Co., 1907); Alfred Colbeck, *The Fall of the Staincliffes* (London: The Sunday School Union, 1891) – written in the tradition of *The Banker* and published by the Council of the Sunday School Union after it had offered a prize of £100 for 'the best Tale illustrating the essential dishonesty of betting and setting forth its disastrous consequences'; and Hawley Smart, *'The Plunger'. A Turf Tragedy of Five and Twenty Years Ago* (London: White & Co., 1891).
45. 'What's in a Name?' (*c.* 1899 – thanks to Harvey Andrews for this leaflet); Moore provided an excellent description of racecourse bookies, *op. cit.*, pp. 260–90.
46. Convocation of the Province of York, *op. cit.*, p. 15.
47. *Ibid.*, pp. 21–2.
48. 'The Betting Raid', *Bolton Journal*, 6 June 1891.
49. 'The Raid on Racing Ticket Sellers and Betting Houses', *St Helens News*, 15 November 1884 (thanks to St Helens Libraries).
50. 'The Betting Crusade', *ibid.*, 30 September 1902.
51. Cecil C. H. Moriarty, *Police Law. An Arrangement of Law and Regulations for the Use of Police Officers* (London: Butterworth & Co., 1931), p. 324.
52. Chinn Letters, Jack Cooke, no. 1, p. 1 and no. 2, p. 2; Chinn Interviews, Jack Scotney, *passim.*
53. R. C. (1932–3), *Report*, p. 37. See also Memoranda of the National Consultative Council of the Retail Liquor Trade and the Licensed Victuallers' Central Protection Society of London, Limited, R. C. (1949–51) *Minutes*, 31 March 1951.
54. R. C. (1932–3), *Report*, p. 37; Evidence of John Hawke, S. C. (1901-2), *Minutes*, q. 122, p. 364.
55. Chinn Letters, Molly Bracegirdle, no. 2. pp. 1–2; see also *ibid.*, Kenneth A. Grant, no. 1, p. 1 (Edinburgh) and *ibid.*, Michael Hamilton, p. 1 (Essex).
56. Chinn Interviews, Charles Gleed, p. 2.
57. Chinn Letters, Jean Davies, no. 1, p. 1.
58. Mass Observation, *op. cit.*, p. 262.
59. Chinn Letters, Mr A. Griffiths, no. 1, p. 1; *ibid.*, Mr S. J. Ward, p. 1. See also *ibid.*, Veronica Banks, no. 1, p. 1 (Manchester).

60. *Mass Gambling* (unpublished report carried out for the National Anti-Gambling League, 1947), FR 2560, p. 138 (I am grateful to the Mass Observation Archive for access to this material); see also Chinn Letters, Gwen Cotton, no. 2, pp. 1–2 (Birmingham); *ibid.*, Frank Fellows, no. 1, p. 1 (Bilston); and *ibid.*, Mrs Pamela Smith, no. 1, p. 1 (Birmingham).
61. Chinn Interviews, Len Edwards, pp. 1–5 (South Yorkshire) and Chinn Letters, Winifred Austin, no. 1, p. 2 (Bradford); *ibid.*, Elizabeth Evans, no. 1, pp. 1–2; Mr T. Sainsbury, no. 1, pp. 1–2; *ibid.*, T. Horsfield, no. 1, p. 1; *ibid.*, Mr J. Abbott, no. 1, pp. 1–2; *ibid.*, Mr G. W. Yendell, no. 1, pp. 1–2; *ibid.*, Mr W. S. Davies, no. 1, p. 1; *ibid.*, John Shaw, no. 3, p. 1; *ibid.*, Ernest Wheeler, *passim*; and *ibid.*, Kenneth G. Blackburn, no. 1, p. 1; for billiard-hall betting in Glasgow, see *ibid.*, William McKerlie, p. 1. For pub betting elsewhere, see *ibid.*, Mary Downies, no. 1, pp. 1–3 (Washington), Meridian 'Under the Clock', *Jersey Evening Post*, 2 March 1988 (Jersey); Chinn Letters, Muriel Pryke, no. 1, p. 1 (Ipswich); *ibid.*, Shirley Ryan, no. 1, pp. 1–3 (Bristol); and *ibid.*, Mr J. D. Sabine, no. 1, p. 1. In 1960, it was claimed that '61,000 of the 76,000 public houses in the country have a regular street bookmaker or his agent doing business on their premises', Bill Munroe 'Facts behind Street Bookies', *Sporting Life*, 3 May 1960.
62. Chinn Letters, Syd Farrow, nos 1 and 2, *passim*; 'Case Against Bookmaker Fails', *Cheltenham Chronicle*, 19 October 1935; 'Lord Chief Justice Condemns Derby Police Betting "Trap"', *Derby Evening Telegraph*, 24 October 1947 (thanks to Derby Libraries); 'Police Raid on Victoria Bar' (Clydesdale Libraries, Scrapbooks of newspaper cuttings, 1924 – my thanks to); 'Police Raid at Patricroft', *Eccles and Patricroft Journal*, 11 May 1923 (thanks to Salford Libraries); 'Point in Betting Law', *Western Mail*, 17 August 1937; and for a policeman's account of a raid on a pub runner see, Chinn Letters, Terry Nattrass, no. 1, p. 1; *ibid.*, Shirley Ryan, no. 1, pp. 1–2; *ibid.*, Norman P. Chandler, no. 1, p. 1; *ibid.*, Muriel Pryke, no. 1, p. 1; Mr J. D. Sabine, p. 1; *ibid.*, Mr R. Bradley, no. 1, p. 2 and no. 2, p. 1; and *ibid.*, Fred Cross, no. 1, p. 1.
63. Evidence of John Hawke, S. C. (1901–2), *Minutes*, q. 88, p. 362; see also Convocation of the Province of York, *op. cit.*, p. 8.
64. Chinn Letters, Mr J. Stephens, no. 2, p. 3 (Cumbria); Chinn Interviews, Donald Davies, p. 14 (Shropshire); *ibid.*, John Lafferty, *passim* (Lanarkshire); *ibid.*, Jack Scotney, pp. 14–15 (Cambridgeshire). In 1947, the Mass Observation Gambling Survey focused on the people in eight areas, supposedly representative of differing and contrasting types of communities. One of these was a group of Exmoor villages. It was found that, compared to the industrial areas, more of their people claimed never to have put money on any of the six gambling items that were specified by the interviewers. However, of seventy young male factory workers in the district, 16 per cent stated that they betted every week, as against no agricultural workers who claimed this; *Mass Gambling*, pp. 7–8. In Orkney, the first betting shop was not opened until 1987, twenty-six years after legalization, Chinn Letters, James E. Miller, *Orcadian*, p. 1.
65. Chinn Interviews, Donald Davies, pp. 1–6; Chinn Letters, Tom Davies, no. 2, pp. 1–3; and *ibid.*, Kenneth G. Blackburn, no. 2, pp. 1–2.

66. *Ibid.*, Roy C. Whitehead, no. 1, p. 1.
67. Chinn Letters, Mrs G. Catten, no. 1, p. 1; S. C. (1924) *Report*, p. 37; see also Evidence of John Orr, S. C. (1901–2), *Minutes*, q. 2171, p. 561.
68. Chinn Letters, Samuel Draper, no. 1, p. 1, no. 2, p. 1.
69. *Ibid.*, Robert Hinds, no. 1, p. 1; *ibid.*, Jean B. Hall, no. 1, p. 1. For betting in mills in West Yorkshire, see also Chinn Interviews, Jim Cooper, *passim*, Muff, *op. cit.*, p. 4, Chinn Letters, Mr A. McIntyre, no. 1, pp. 1–2; *ibid.*, Mr G. Ritson, no. 1, p. 1.
70. *Ibid.*, John Rackham, no. 1, p. 1.
71. *Ibid.*, Nora Hog, no. 1, p. 1; *ibid.*, Norman Backhouse, no. 1, pp. 1–2.
72. *Ibid.*, Mrs Davis, pp. 1–2; see also Chinn Interviews, Sid Whitby, p. 2, and R. C. (1932–3) *Report*, p. 37.
73. *Mass Gambling*, p. 139.
74. *Ibid.*, Bolton Gambling, Factory Manager, 81, 3 May 1947.
75. Chinn Letters, G. Squires, no. 1, p. 2; for betting on Portsmouth Docks see *ibid.*, Kenneth Batt, no. 1, p. 1.
76. Chinn Interviews, Sid Whitby, *passim*; for 'The Austin' at Longbridge, see Chinn Letters, Thelma Hunter, pp. 1–3.
77. *Ibid.*, Iris Read, no. 1, p. 1. For betting in other Lancashire mills see: *ibid.*, John Bootham, no. 1, pp. 1–3; and Naughton, *A Roof Over Your Head*, pp. 58–9.
78. Chinn Interviews, Horace Foster (junior), p. 2.
79. *Ibid.*, Ken Overton, pp. 3–4; see also, 'The Late Mr Arthur Overton', *Banyan*, December 1954, p. 179. For Summer Lane, see Pauline and Bernard Mannion, *The Summer Lane and Newtown of the Years Between the Wars 1918–1938* (Birmingham: the authors, 1985).
80. Chinn Interviews, Jim Farrar, *passim*; *ibid.*, R. Elliot, pp. 1–5; for example, see Chinn Letters, *ibid.*, Sam Dunleavy, p. 1 (Bellshill) – whose employer paid between 2s and 2s 6d, after 1945; *ibid.*, Gerald Browne Leake, p. 1 (Shrewsbury) – who paid 1s 6d, after 1945; *ibid.*, Joseph Riley, no. 1, p. 1 (Bilston) – whose father and uncle paid 1s 6d; *ibid.*, Bernard Ryan, no. 1, p. 2 – whose father was a work's agent at Breedbury Steelworks, Stockport, receiving between 10d and 1s 3d, in the 1930s. For an apprentice joiner who received 'a drink', see *ibid.*, Roy Aspinall, no. 2, p. 1. Sometimes, works runners would receive 'a drink' off a punter if he or she had a 'good win', see, for example, *ibid.*, John Rackham, no. 1, p. 1.
81. *Ibid.*, Nora Hog, no. 1, p. 1; *ibid.*, Bernard Ryan, no. 1 p. 1 and no. 2, p. 3; *ibid.*, Mrs E. Baines, pp. 1–3.
82. Convocation of the Province of York, *op. cit.*, p. 59.
83. Chinn Letters, Kenneth G. Blackburn, no. 2, p. 1; *ibid.*, Mildred Jennings, pp. 1–2.
84. *Ibid.*, Lewis Marsden and Fred Norgate, pp. 1–2; Chinn Interviews, Cyril Beasley, *passim*. For a similar operation in Bradford, see *ibid.*, Jim Cooper, p. 13.
85. *Ibid.*, Rod Lester, *passim*.
86. *Ibid.*, Sid Brooks, pp. 4–5. For works betting elsewhere in Britain, see Chinn Letters, Charles Dearden, nos 1 and 2, *passim* (Vulcan Village, Merseyside); Chinn Interviews, Mr Haworth, pp. 19–20 (Blackburn); Chinn Letters, Lewis Marsden and Fred Norgate, pp. 1–2 (Nottingham); R. J. Meads, *Growing Up with Southall from 1904* (Southall: the author,

1979), p. 30; Chinn Letters, Mr T. E. Nattrass, no. 1, p. 1 (Yorkshire); *ibid.*, Beryl Norman, no. 1, pp. 1–2 and no. 2, p. 1 (Market Harborough); *ibid.*, Mrs M. Oliver, pp. 1–2 (Hampshire); *ibid.*, Mr R. Potts, no. 1, pp. 1–2 (County Durham); and *ibid.*, Tommy Tait, no. 1, p. 1 (Sheffield).

87. Chinn Letters, Bernard Ryan, no. 1, p. 1; for factory betting in Hyde, see also *ibid.*, W. H. Nevell, pp. 1–3. For a prosecution against the Kemps, see 'The Stalybridge Betting Raid' (newspaper cutting, NAB, Manchester File).
88. Chinn Letters, James Sefton, no. 1, p. 1 and no. 2, p. 2.
89. *Ibid.*, Doris Hall, p. 1; Chinn Interviews, Len Edwards, pp. 1–2.
90. Chinn Letters, Margaret Aspin, no. 1, pp. 1–2.
91. *Ibid.*, Mr L. Hawkes, no. 1, p. 1.
92. *Ibid.*, Mrs L. R. and Mr E. W. Kelley, no. 1, p. 1; *ibid.*, Mr W. S. Davies, no. 1, p. 1. For a prosecution against agents who put their bets through the letter-box of their commissioner see, 'Putting "Slips" into Letter Boxes', *Fairplay* (Northern Bookmakers' Association), June 1938.
93. Chinn Letters, Rita Coe, p. 1. For house betting in Wapping, see *ibid.*, Mr D. Aedo, pp. 1–6; in Dudley, *ibid.*, Evelyn Dobner, no. 1, pp. 1–2; and for Wem, Shropshire, Mr C. H. Lowe, no. 1, p. 1.
94. *Ibid.*, Ivy Day, no. 1, pp. 1–2; *ibid.*, June Bell, no. 1, pp. 1–2; and *ibid.*, Mrs G. Strachan, no. 1, p. 2 – from whom the quote is taken. For house betting in Coventry, see *ibid.*, Chinn Letters, Mr P. Bloomfield, no. 1, pp. 1–4.
95. '40 Summonses. Betting Offence at Eccles', *Eccles and Patricroft Journal*, 18 September 1936 (thanks to Salford Libraries). It seemed that if a bookie used a house for the collection of bets from agents, then he or she was not guilty of using the premises for the purpose of betting with persons resorting thereto (1853 Act) – but was guilty of using the premises for the purpose of ready-money betting (1853 Act); 'Bradford Magistrate and an Appeal', *Yorkshire Observer*, 4 June 1938.
96. 'Betting Raid. Nine Defendants at Eccles Court', *Eccles and Patricroft Journal*, 16 December 1932 (thanks to Salford Libraries).
97. Chinn Letters, Barbara Harsant, p. 1, see also Chinn Interviews, Barbara Harsant, *passim*.
98. Chinn Letters, Evelyn J. Gregory, no. 1, p. 4; for a woman who took bets in her house in Plymouth see *ibid.*, Gladys Northover, no. 1, pp. 1–3.
99. *Ibid.*, Maureen Newton, p. 1; *ibid.*, June Bailey, no. 1, pp. 1–2.
100. *Ibid.*, Mr P. H. Manning, no. 1, p. 2.
101. Chinn Interviews, Mr Haworth (junior), p. 1.
102. *Ibid.*, Joseph Hilton, pp. 1–4.
103. Chinn Letters, Fred Proctor, no. 2, p. 2.
104. *Ibid.*, Peter J. Collar, no. 1, p. 1; *ibid.*, W. J. Campbell, no. 1, pp. 1–2; *ibid.*, Fred Cross, no. 1, p. 1.
105. For examples see: 'Betting Raid. Woman Fined at the Southern Court', *Glasgow Citizen*, 19 November 1911; 'Police Raid Millwall Flat', *East London Advertiser*, 23 November 1951; 'Bookmaker's Appeal Withdrawn', *Dumfries Standard*, 1 May 1955.
106. R. C. (1932–3) *Report*, p. 37.
107. Dey, *op. cit.*, *passim.*
108. Dick Seymour, *Rule Book* (1905 – thanks to Andrew Seymour); for

another racecourse layer who doubled up as a credit bookmaker, see Chinn Interviews, Len Shaylor, pp. 5–7.

109. The best accounts of the workings of a credit business are: Chinn Interviews, Mr Guntrip, *passim*; Rhona Churchill, 'No Muddle at the Bookie's "HQ"', *Daily Mail*, 2 April 1949; and Alfred Cope, 'The Starting-Price Bookmaker', *Greyhound Express*, 11 July 1953. See also R. C. (1932–3) *Report*, pp. 33–5.
110. Joe Ward Hill, *The Betting Man. A Racing Biography of William Hill. The King of Bookies* (Marlborough, Wiltshire: Elcott Books, 1993), pp. 14–62; and Clive Graham, 'Bookies Like These were Also Broke Once', *Daily Express*, 28 March 1962. For Hill, see also: Chinn Interviews, Joe Ward Hill, *passim*; Geoff Hamlyn, 'William Hill – The Factory Bookie Who Became the Lord of the Ring', *Sporting Life*, 21 February 1963; Robert Jackson, 'Gambling Has Made His Fortune', *Illustrated*, 29 March 1952; John Morgan, 'The Biggest Bookie in the World', *New Statesman*, 3 April 1964.
111. For McLean see J. H. Park, ('Ajax'), '"New School" Bookmakers Who Livened up Betting', *Evening Standard*, 26 September 1938; and Gimcrack, 'Keep Your Shirt on!', *Daily Sketch*, 2 November 1954.
112. Chinn Interviews, Norman Miller, p. 20.
113. *Ibid., passim.*
114. *Ibid.*, Charlie Maskey, pp. 1–5; for the Chandlers later on, see John Santer, 'Survival of the Family Man', *Sporting Life*, 16 July 1984.
115. Chinn Interviews, Joe Coral, p. 1; see also Jack Wood, 'Beware! Never Chase Losses', *Daily Mail*, 23 March 1962.
116. For Guntrips see Chinn Interviews, Tom Guntrip, *passim*, 'The Brothers Guntrip', *Licensed Bookmaker*, November 1964; and John McCririck, 'Guntrips not Grousing After 100 Years in the Field', *Sporting Life*, 23 March 1982. For Moists, see Chinn Interviews, Mr Moist, pp. 1–3.
117. Dey, *op. cit.*, p. 60.
118. Chinn Interviews, Ken Overton, p. 40; see also *ibid.*, Geoff Gilbert, *passim*; 'Bad Debts', *Banyan*, November 1950, p. 165; ex-Commission Agent, 'Crooked Punters Smashed Me . . .', *Greyhound Express*, 11 December 1957; 'Barrister Pleads the Gaming Act', *Banyan*, June 1940, p. 30; 'Bookie Sues Vicar', *Daily Mirror*, 6 April 1940; 'Some Old Cases Reviewed (2) Rex v. Salamon Leon', *Banyan*, July 1949, pp. 23–4; 'The Problem of Bad Debts', *Banyan*, April 1952, p. 98; the records of the National Sporting League, *passim* – set up in 1902 with the purposes of providing members with lists of defaulters and adjudicating on betting disputes (thanks to the NSL); and for the Turf Guardian Society, 'He is Terror of Turf Crooks', *Daily Sketch*, 14 November 1937.
119. Chinn Interviews, Squadron Leader Blacklaw, p. 3.
120. The frauds against bookies were manifold. In letter betting, the date stamps could be interfered with: 'Bookmakers Duped', *Express and Star* (Wolverhampton), 21 January 1937; F. C. Cartwright (late chief investigator of the Post Office), 'Fighting Fraud at the G.P.O.', *Pearson's Monthly*, May 1938, pp. 428–32; 'Frauds by Postal Officials', *Banyan*, October 1938, p. 122; and there were other similar tricks – 'Gentle Arts of "Rooking"', *Morning Post*, 8 April 1936; and 'Alleged Fraud on Wallsend Bookmaker', *Shield Gazette*, 1 March 1938. Telegrams could be tinkered with also, see:

Galliard, 'Question of Timing Wired Commissions', *Sunday Chronicle*, 15 December 1936; 'Bookmakers are on the Warpath', *Evening News*, 3 February 1936. For the worry of tricks over the telephone see: 'Ironclad Protection Against Hidden Losses in Off-The-Course Betting', *Banyan*, July 1954, p. 14; and 'No Argument with Timeprint', *Banyan*, April 1955, p. 218. Street bookies could have their attention diverted so as to allow a bet to be placed after the result of a race was known: Chinn Letters, Tom W. Godwin, no. 1, pp. 1–3 and no. 2, p. 2; One of Them, 'How Bookmakers are Cheated', *Topical Times*, 8 February 1936; and for a ingenious swindle, see 'Alleged False Pretences', *Maidenhead Advertiser*, 25 August 1937 and 'Miners Defraud Bookmaker', *Daily Independent* (Sheffield), 13 October 1938. For clock-bag cheating see: 'Accused of Conspiring to Defraud Bookmaker', *Northern Echo* (Darlington) 6 July 1937; Chinn Letters and Chinn Interviews *passim*; Charles Frederick, 'Bookmakers Worry Too', *Newcastle Evening News*, 4 April 1950; 'Ingenious Fraud on Dumfries Bookmaker', *Daily Record and Mail*, 14 July 1937; 'Six-Race Carbon Dial Clock Bags', *Banyan*, October 1953, p. 71. See also Swaffer, *op. cit.*, pp. 251–60.

121. Chinn Letters, G. W. Yendell, no. 1, pp. 1–2.
122. For McLean's see 'Chaotic Betting Laws', *Manchester Evening News*, 4 August 1936; and for McLauchlan's see 'Bets that Made Bookies Suspicious', *Dundee Courier and Advertiser*, 6 January 1937 (thanks to North-East Fife Libraries). For cash betting by post see R. C. (1932–3), *Report*, pp. 35–6 and 89–94; and Statement of Roderick Ross, Chief Constable of Edinburgh, R. C. (1932–3), *Minutes*, 2 December 1932. He estimated that there were fifty-five postal bookies in his city, all of whom were fined regularly to the sum of £100; he explained that this was futile as a deterrent because 'in one particular case, a bookmaker's mail for a day consisted of 10,000 letters, involving a sum of £53,529 19s 6d'. William Harvey, George Rhind and Peter Shand spoke to this Royal Commission on behalf of the Convention of Royal Burghs, and they advocated legalization of this form of betting; see Statements (R. C. 1932–3), *Minutes*, 3 February 1933.
123. Chinn Letters, B. Bagley, pp. 1–2.
124. *Ibid.*, George Bailey, no. 1, p. 1.
125. Chinn Interviews, Squadron Leader Blacklaw, pp. 1–4.
126. For clock bags see: 'Betting Clocks: Appeals Allowed', *Sporting Life*, 12 July 1949; Chinn Interviews and Chinn Letters, *passim*; 'Six-Race Carbon Dial Clock Bags', NAB File, 'Clock Bags'. Clock bags were made by two firms: H. Love Time Recorders of Newport; and Richmond Time Recording Co. of Birmingham – who had started business in 1922.
127. Dick Seymour, *Rule Book* (1905).
128. Alf and Wal Chinn, *Rule Books* (1948 and 1959). For limits see also Chinn Letters, John G., no. 3, p. 1; and *ibid.*, Cyril Lofts, no. 2, pp. 2–3.
129. 'Getting Round the Law', *Leeds Mercury*, 2 May 1939.
130. 'The Richmond Time Recording Company', advert, *Banyan*, April 1939, p. 66.
131. 'Betting Clocks Appeal', *Sporting Life*, 21 January 1949; 'Betting Clocks: Appeals Allowed', *Sporting Life*, 12 July 1949; 'The Clock Bag Case. Rex v. Way and Sherman', *Banyan*, September 1949, p. 47; and Evidence

of the Police Federation of England and Wales and Lord Goddard, R. C. (1949–51), *Minutes*, 16 November 1949 and 16 June 1950.

132. When he died, Abe Sherman left £433,000 – although he had given hundreds of thousands of pounds to charities through the Sherman Foundation; see 'Abe Sherman leaves £433,660', *Sporting Life*, 15 January 1966.
133. Chinn Interviews, Mr Hantman, *passim*; for John Charles, see also Chinn Letters, Freda Watkins, *passim* – who worked as a clerk in his credit business but who noticed the arrival of runners in the office; *ibid.*, Elizabeth Evans, no. 1, pp. 1–2.
134. *Ibid.*, Barbara Gynne, nos 1 and 2, *passim*; *ibid.*, Iris Holden, nos 1 and 2, *passim.*
135. *Ibid.*, no. 2, p. 1.
136. For example see Chinn Letters, Barbara Gynne, no. 1, p. 1, and Iris Holden, p. 1, pp. 1–2.
137. Elizabeth Dawson, *Mother Made a Book* (London: Geoffrey Bles, 1962), pp. 6–7.
138. For greyhound-racing see Clapson, *op. cit.*, pp. 156–79. For opposition to its coming, see: Rt Hon. Winston Churchill, MP, Extract from Parliamentary Report, 16 March 1928, Cols 2355/6; 'Dog Racing to be Staged at Ynys Field', newspaper cutting, 25 November 1931 (thanks to Cynon Valley Libraries); 'The Greyhound Racing Track', *Town Clerk's Cuttings* (1926–9 – thanks to Trafford Libraries); 'Watch Committee Refuses Dog Track Application', *Burnley Express and News*, 23 March 1946 (thanks to Lancashire Libraries, Burnley).
139. Dog-racing was popular for bettors especially in: Birmingham, Chinn Interviews, Buck Chinn, *passim*; Glasgow, *ibid.*, Norman Miller, *passim*; and London, Chinn Letters, Cyril Lofts, no. 1, p. 5.
140. Chinn Letters, Cyril Lofts, no. 1, p. 10.
141. Chinn Interviews, Ray Fear and Bernard Nicklin, pp. 1 and 24–50; *ibid.*, the Ford and Kimberley Families, pp. 1–10; *ibid.*, Sid Brooks, *passim*; Chinn Letters, Syd Farrow, no. 1, pp. 1–2 and no. 2, pp. 1–2.
142. Convocation of the Province of York, *op. cit.*, p. 8.
143. Chinn Letters, Victor Baker, no. 1, p. 1.
144. *Ibid.*, Mr A. Williams, no. 1, p. 1.
145. R. C. (1932–3) *Report*, p. 37.
146. S. C. (1924) *Report*, p. xv.
147. 'Police and Dismissed Charge', *Daily Mail*, 13 January 1936.
148. Chinn Letters, J. Fisher, no. 1, p. 1; see also *ibid.*, Maurice Jacobs, no. 1, p. 1 (Brighton), and *ibid.*, Mr E. Leaver, no. 1, p. 1 (Blackburn).
149. *Ibid.*, Ellen V. Smith, no. 1, p. 1 – see also *ibid.*, Norman E. Bowyer, pp. 1–2 (Birmingham); R. C. (1932–3) *Report*, p. 37.
150. R. C. (1932–3) *Report*, p. 37.
151. Chinn Interviews, Jack Proudfoot, p. 4 (thanks to Marion Cunningham).
152. *Ibid.*, Peter Softley, p. 1; '22 Betting Slips Found at Stall', *East London Advertiser*, 6 July 1951 (thanks to Tower Hamlets Libraries).
153. Chinn Letters, Mrs K. S. Manley, no. 1, p. 1.
154. *Ibid.*, Alan Needham, no. 1, p. 1. For Stockton, see Cleveland County Oral History Project, accession no. 276, p. 12.

155. Liverpool Council of Voluntary Aid, *Report on Betting in Liverpool* (Liverpool: 1926), p. 2.
156. Chinn Letters, Raymond Addison, no. 1, pp. 1–2; *ibid.*, Mr J. Forbes, no. 2, p. 2, *ibid.*, Mr J. Gall, no. 1, p. 1, *ibid.*, Mrs M. T. Lane. p. 1 and *ibid.*, Mr T. McGunnigle, no. 2, p. 1. For Paddington, see *ibid.*, Mr A. W. Podd, p. 1.
157. *Ibid.*, Bill Gleghorn, no. 1, p. 1.
158. *Ibid.*, Mr J. H. Hobbs, p. 1. In Liverpool, these watchers were known as 'dowses', Liverpool Council of Voluntary Aid, *op. cit.*, p. 2.
159. Chinn Letters, Kit Brown, no. 1, p. 3.
160. For the variety and richness of *noms-de-plume*, see Chinn Interviews and Chinn Letters, *passim.*
161. Chinn Letters, C. J. Squires, no. 1.
162. Statement of Sir Trevor Bigham, R. C. (1932–3) *Minutes*, 1 July 1932, p. 33.
163. Chinn Letters, Mr L. Caket, no. 2, p. 1; Peter Sanders, *The Simple Annals. The History of an Essex and East End Family* (Gloucester: Alan Sutton, 1989), p. 110.
164. Robert Barltrop, 'The Bookies' Turning', *Terrier*, no. 11, summer 1988, p. 11 (thanks to Hackney Libraries).
165. Chinn Letters, Mr J. Clark, pp. 1–2. For Gateshead, see also *ibid.*, Rose McHugh, no. 1, p. 1 and *ibid.*, Mr T. S., no. 1, p. 2.
166. *Ibid.*, John Hodgson, no. 1, p. 1; *ibid.*, Lilian Crawford, no. 1, p. 1 – for Johnson Street, see also Patrick McLoughlin, *The Johnson Street Bullies* (Bognor Regis: New Horizon, 1980), pp. 131–3; Chinn Letters, Lorna Morton, no. 1, p. 1.
167. *Ibid.*, Alex Meldrum, no. 1, p. 1; for Sunderland, see also Chinn Interviews, Gordon Stokoe, *passim*, and Chinn Letters, Stan Tennet, nos 1 and 2, *passim.*
168. *Ibid.*, Jim Addison, no. 1, p. 1.
169. *Ibid.*, Allan Newman, no. 1, p. 1.
170. *Ibid.*, Patricia Bell, no. 2, p. 3 and no. 1, p. 1.
171. *Ibid.*, Bill Evans, no. 1, p. 1.
172. *Ibid.*, Mr Armstrong, pp. 1–2 and Chinn Interviews, *passim* (thanks to Mrs Armitage). For South Bank see Cleveland County Oral History Project, accession no. 204, pp. 4–5 and accession no. 151, pp. 19–20.
173. Chinn Letters, Anne Spence, no. 1, p. 1.
174. *Ibid.*, M. C. Percy, no. 1, p. 1; *ibid.*, Bill Whitely, no. 1, p. 3; *ibid.*, Mr D. Homer, no. 1, p. 2. For yards in the 'two cities', see also *ibid.*, Mr W. Flood, no. 1, pp. 1–3; Richard Heaton, *Salford. My Home Town* (Swinton: Neil Richardson, 1982), p. 10; Joe Kay, *Chronicles of a Harpurhey Lad* (Swinton: Neil Richardson, 1987), pp. 65–7; Chinn Letters, Jean Metcalfe, nos 1 and 2 *passim*; Robert Roberts, *The Classic Slum. Salford Life in the First Quarter of the Century* (first published 1971: Harmondsworth: Penguin, 1973), p. 164.
175. Chinn Letters, Bernard Ryan, no. 2, pp. 2–3; see also *ibid.*, D. Homer, no. 1, p. 1.
176. *Ibid.*, Eric Thornley Downs, no. 1, p. 1.
177. *Ibid.*, Bob Crewe, no. 1, pp. 1–2; *ibid.*, Ken Wadsworth, pp. 1–2 and 5–6 and Chinn Interviews, *passim*. For pub betting in Manchester, see

Chinn Letters, Les Kane, no. 1, pp. 1–2, and in nearby Swinton, see *ibid.*, Michael Ryan, no. 2, pp. 1–6.

178. Statement of Sir Charles Haughton Rafter, R. C. (1932–3) *Minutes*, 21 July 1932; statement of John Maxwell, Chief Constable of Manchester, R. C. (1932–3), *Minutes*, 21 July 1932.
179. Chinn Letters, Mrs M. Peake, p. 1; *ibid.*, Mr E. Evenson, no. 1, pp. 1–2; *ibid.*, Joseph Hillshead, p. 1.
180. Chinn Interviews, Buck Chinn, pp. 3–4.
181. Chinn Letters, Joseph Riley, no. 1, pp. 1–3.
182. *Ibid.*, Harry R. Vokes, p. 1. For Birmingham, see also *ibid.*, Geoffrey Brown, pp. 1–2; *ibid.*, F. Haycocks, p. 1; *ibid.*, A. Jones, p. 1; *ibid.*, Mrs J. K. Pearson, p. 1; *ibid.*, Mr J. F. Rose, p. 1; and *ibid.*, W. D., pp. 1–2.
183. *Ibid.*, Jean Burton, p. 2; for Smethwick, see *ibid.*, Mr G. T. Whitefoot, pp. 1–2.
184. For back-to-back housing in Birmingham, see Carl Chinn, *Homes for People. 100 Years of Council Housing in Birmingham* (Exeter: Birmingham Books, 1991), *passim.*
185. Chinn Letters, Miss E. Thexton, no. 1, pp. 1–2.
186. *Ibid.*, Mrs Hetty Bradbury, p. 1 (thanks to Joyce Gill).
187. Chinn Interviews, Jim Stock, p. 7.
188. *Ibid.*, Horace Foster, pp. 8–10; *ibid.*, Ken Overton, pp. 10–12.
189. *Ibid.*, Buck Chinn, p. 9.
190. A Legal Correspondent, 'Street Betting Law. Attempts at Evasion', *Glasgow Herald*, 4 June 1910; see also 'Kilmarnock Judgement Affirmed', *Glasgow Herald*, 12 December 1908.
191. Chinn Letters, Joe Gray, no. 1, p. 1.
192. *Ibid.*, Walter Littlejohn, no. 1, p. 1.
193. *Ibid.*, Robert Reid, no. 1, p. 1; see also *ibid.*, May Anderson, nos 1 and 2, *passim*, *ibid.*, M. G. 64, no. 1, p. 2, and *ibid.*, Catherine Wilson, no. 1, p. 1.
194. *Ibid.*, Norma Brodie, no. 1, p. 1.
195. *Ibid.*, E. McGuiness, no. 1, p. 4.
196. *Ibid.*, Henry McQuaid, no. 1, pp. 2–3.
197. *Ibid.*, Maurice McMahon, no. 1, p. 1; *ibid.*, Ernest Kyle, no. 1, p. 1.
198. 'Gambling Habits (Bookies)', *Mass Gambling*, p. 817.
199. Chinn Letters, Wilson Ditty, no. 1, p. 1. For East Kilbride see, 'Illegal Bookmaking. Early 1930s: Mr James Park', transcript supplied by East Kilbride Libraries.
200. 'The Story of the Three X Double', *Evening News*, 23 October 1937.
201. R. C. (1932–3), *Report*, p. 37; see also S. C. (1924) *Report*, p. lii.

6 BOOKMAKING: REACTIONS

1. Chorley, *op. cit.*, p. 11.
2. Convocation of the Province of York, *op. cit.*, p. 13.
3. R. F. L. Blunt, *op. cit.*, p. 5; S. C. (1923) *Report*, p. 41. See also 'Betting', *The Nineteenth Century*, vol. 99, no. 589, p. 39; Henry Durant, *The Problem of Leisure* (London: George Routledge & Sons, 1938), pp. 184–5; Constance Harris, *The Use of Leisure in Bethnal Green. A*

Survey of Conditions in the Borough 1925–6 (London: The Lindsey Press, 1927), p. 17; and R. C. (1932–3), *Report*, pp. 58–9.

4. Ferdynand Zweig, *The British Worker* (Harmondsworth: Penguin, 1952) p. 146: see also '"Commission's" Findings on Gambling. Cause: Drabness of Modern Life', *Harrow Observer*, 4 November 1948.
5. Walter A. Raleigh, 'Concerning Gambling', *National Review*, vol. 40, no. 240, February 1903, p. 928. See also C. E. B. Russell and E. T. Campagnac, 'Gambling and Aids to Gambling', *Economic Review*, vol. 10, October 1900, pp. 482–3
6. J. A. Hobson, *The Social Problem. Life and Work* (London: J. Nisbet & Co., 1901), pp. 258–9.
7. Friedrich Engels, *The Condition of the Working Class in England* (first published 1845. Harmondsworth: Penguin, 1987), pp. 68–110; John Edward Morgan, *The Danger of the Deterioration of Race from the Too Rapid Increase of the Great Cities* (first published 1866. New York: Garland, 1985).
8. J. Milner Fothergill, *The Town Dweller. His Needs and His Wants* (first published 1889. New York: Garland, 1985), p. 80. The best and most stimulating study of the 'town problem' is Gareth Stedman Jones, *Outcast London. A Study in the Relationship Between Classes in Victorian Society* (first published 1971. Harmondsworth: Penguin, 1984).
9. Clapson, *op. cit.*, p. 50.
10. Arthur Shadwell, *Industrial Efficiency. A Comparative Study of Industrial Life in England, Germany and America* (London: Longmans, Green & Co., 1920), p. 509.
11. Sir Leo Chiozza Money, 'Racing Versus Work', *Spectator*, 23 August 1924; Glass, *op. cit.*, p. 44; Isaac Foot, introduction, E. Benson Perkins, *Betting Facts: Being an Account of the Facts of Betting Given in Evidence Before the Select Committee on the House of Commons on a Betting Duty* (London: Student Christian Movement, 1925), p. 9; Rev. J. Glyn Davies, 'Gambling', *Y Dysfora*, no. 106, pp. 345–6 (thanks to the National Library of Wales and to Mr T. J. Henson for translation); and Rev. J. Clark Gibson, *Gambling and Citizenship* (London: Beckley Pamphlets, 1956), p. 7. See also Reverend Alfred E. Garvie, *Gambling and Character* (n.d., National Anti-Gambling League pamphlet, Friends' Library), pp. 5–6; and *Why not Make Money without Working?* (n.d., National Anti-Gambling League pamphlet, Friends' Library), p. 2. For the life of Perkins, see E. Benson Perkins, *So Appointed. An Autobiography* (London: Epworth Press, 1964); it should be noted that Perkins was a Fellow of the Royal Statistical Society.
12. Glass, *op. cit.*, p. 42; cited in R. C. (1932–3), *Report*, p. 57; 'Britain's Betting Industry – I', *The Economist*, 29 February 1936, see also Mary Stocks, 'Gambling. What Do We Pay and What Do We Get?', *Listener*, vol. 17, no. 419, 20 January 1937, p. 102. John Hilton put the pre-1939 'all-over expenditure' on betting and gambling as 'round about £500,000,000 a year', *Rich Man, Poor Man* (London: George Allen & Unwin, 1944), p. 123.
13. R. C. (1932–3), *Report*, p. 58.
14. McKibbin, *op. cit.*, p. 150.

15. R. C. (1932–3), *Report*, p. 58; for a further discussion on turnover, see McKibbin, *op. cit.*, pp. 150–3.
16. Rev. Ernest Benson Perkins, *The Problem of Gambling*, pp. 11–12; see also J. Martin, 'Gambling', in Sir H. Llewellyn Smith (ed.), *The New Survey of London Life and Labour, vol. IX, Life and Leisure* (London: P. S. King & Son, 1935), pp. 273–5.
17. An Ex-Serviceman, *Better Not Bet! A Straight Talk About the Folly of Gambling* (n.d., post 1915 – thanks to Gloucestershire Record Office), pp. 3–5; see also Perkins, *The Problem of Gambling*, p. 17.
18. Chinn Interviews, Steve Nicholls, pp. 1–2; Chinn Letters, Ellis McCormick, no. 2, pp. 1–2; see also Chinn Interviews, no. 1, Mr L., p. 1 (Cosham and Portsmouth).
19. Chinn Interviews, Jack Scotney, pp. 1–5; see also Walter Chinn, *From Victoria's Image* (unpublished MS, n.d., in author's possession), p. 96.
20. O' Hara, *op. cit.*, p. 119.
21. Chinn Letters, Mr G. W. Cutts, no. 1, p. 3.
22. Chinn Interviews, Steve Nicholls, pp. 1–2; Chinn Letters, Ellis McCormick, no. 2, pp. 1–2; see also Conway, *op. cit.*, p. 45.
23. *Ibid.*, Mr W. Duke, p. 1.
24. Chinn Interviews, Buck Chinn, pp. 1–6.
25. Walter Greenwood, *Love on the Dole* (first published 1933. Harmondsworth: Penguin, 1969), pp. 116–17. 'Tank' is an abbreviated form of 'Tommy Tank', rhyming slang for bank.
26. 'The game' is a term used regularly by working-class people to refer to their occupation; see also Partridge, *op. cit.*, p. 360.
27. 'Street Betting in Portsmouth', *Hampshire Times*, 11 August 1900 (thanks to Hampshire Libraries, Portsmouth).
28. Chinn Interviews, Mr Moist, pp. 1–3; *ibid.*, Harold Reynolds, pp. 1–5; V. W. Garratt, *A Man in the Street* (London: J. M. Dent, 1939), pp. 4–5.
29. Letter, *Birmingham Argus*, cited in the *Bulletin*, vol. 1, no. 8, May 1894, p. 84.
30. Chinn Interviews, Albert Shepherd, pp. 1–9; in Liverpool, Tom Davies's uncle used his position as a railway clerk to double up as a bookie in the 1930s, see Chinn Letters, Tom Davies, no. 2, pp. 3–4.
31. *Ibid.*, Harold Reynolds, pp. 1 and 17–18.
32. Chinn Letters, Hetty Bradbury, p. 1; Chinn Interviews, Mrs Packer, pp. 1–2; Chinn Letters, Rose Tunnah (Harry Hudson's daughter), p. 1; Chinn Interviews, Harold Reynolds, pp. 22–3 and Georgie Morgan, *passim*.
33. *Ibid.*, Buck Chinn, pp. 1–4 and 15–16; *ibid.*, Mrs N. Wright ('Nack' Carey's daughter), pp. 1–5. For another ex-Coldstream Guardsman who became a bookie in the city's Jewellery Quarter, see Chinn Letters, Albert Vincent, p. 1.
34. *Ibid.*, Horace Foster, pp. 1–3; *ibid.*, Buck Chinn, pp. 79–81.
35. *Ibid.*, Buck Chinn, p. 16. After the Second World War, the ranks of the established bookies were joined by the Bartletts in Queen Street; Whitaker in Brighton Road, a former postal worker; and Bates in Brunswick Road. See Chinn Interviews, Buck Chinn, *passim*; *ibid.*, Albert Whitaker, *passim*; and Chinn Letters, Robin Bates, p. 1–2.
36. *Ibid.*, Ernie Cashmore, pp. 1–5; *ibid.*, Ken Overton, pp. 1–4.

37. S. C. (1923), *Minutes*, q. 4603–12, pp. 273–4. However, it should be noted that in 1932 William Bowen stated that some of the pitches in Salford had been established for twenty-five years. Evidence on behalf of the Manchester and Salford Federation of Brotherhoods, R. C. (1932–3), *Minutes*. q. 4356, p. 312. At the same time, large numbers of runners were noted on the streets of Birmingham in 1904, but there is no evidence to suggest that they occupied pitches, as opposed to collecting bets in a peripatetic fashion, see letter in City of Birmingham, *Police Orders*, 28 July 1904 (thanks to the Chief Constable of the West Midlands for access to this material).
38. Chinn Interviews, Mr Moist, pp. 1–10; *ibid*., Buck Chinn, pp. 79–80.
39. *Ibid*., Matt O'Malley, p. 1.
40. For example, see *ibid*., Mr Moist, p. 11.
41. It should be noted that it was acceptable to start up in the same street as another bookie if that street was long enough to sustain the two (or more) of them.
42. Chinn Interviews, Buck Chinn, pp. 79–85. It should be stated that because of our family's long-standing connection with Oldfield Road, my Dad regarded the opening up of a pitch there as wrong.
43. *Ibid*., Frankie Goodwin, pp. 26–7.
44. *Ibid*., Ernie Cashmore, *passim*.
45. R. C. (1932–3), *Minutes*, p. 275.
46. S. C. (1923), *Report*, q. 8434–8719, pp. 484–98.
47. W. F. Kemsley and D. Ginsburg, *Betting in Britain* (London: The Social Survey, Consumer Expenditure Series, Central Office of Information, 1950) p. 3.
48. McKibbin, *op. cit*., p. 154.
49. 'Betting in Britain', *The Economist*, 26 May 1951.
50. Chinn Interviews, Horace Foster, p. 14.
51. 'Alleged Big Betting Business', *East End News*, 6 December 1912, for Pattman, see also 'Raid on East London Betting House', *East London Advertiser*, 3 December 1910 (thanks to Tower Hamlets Libraries). For the inter-war and post-war years, it is as problematical to work out stakes based on raids reported in the newspapers. For example see: 'Police Raid', *Journal*, 19 August 1938 (thanks to Salford Libraries); and, 'Poplar Betting House', *East End News*, 23 July 1948 (thanks to Tower Hamlets Libraries).
52. 'How the Working Classes Gamble', *Tit Bits*, 17 July 1897, p. 296; Convocation of the Province of York, *op. cit*., p. 12. For clubbing, see also Harry Payne, *op. cit*., pp. 372–3.
53. Shoolbred, *op. cit*., pp. 224–6.
54. E. Benson Perkins, *Gambling and Youth* (London: The National Sunday School Union, 1933), pp. 32–4; see also Statement of David C. Lamb, Commissioner of the Salvation Army, R. C. (1932–3), *Minutes*, 29 September 1932. For the bookmaking view against the betting of children, see *Fairplay*, February 1938.
55. Chinn Letters, Tom Davies, no. 1, pp. 3–4; *ibid*., Maurice McMahon, no. 1, p. 3. For youngsters betting outside greyhound tracks see *ibid*., pp. 3–4; *ibid*., Mr S. Murphy, no. 2, pp. 4–5; 'Police Story of Raid on Boys', *Manchester Evening News*, 28 November 1932; 'Boy Bookie

Caught Outside Track', *St Helens and District Reporter*, 1 December 1933.

56. *Ibid.*, Peter McCusker, no. 1, p. 1.
57. *Ibid.*, Mr A. T. Richardson, no. 1, p. 1.
58. *Ibid.*, L. S. Davis, pp. 1–5.
59. Birkenhead Vigilance Committee, *33rd Report* (1935); see also Alexander Paterson, *Across the Bridges. Life by the South London River-side* (first published 1911. New York: Garland, 1980), and R. C. (1932–3), *Minutes*, pp. 446, 451 and 458.
60. 'Children Carried Bets', *Gateshead Times*, 19 September 1947, and, 'Children Went With Bets', *ibid.*, 6 September 1946 (thanks to Gateshead Libraries). See also, 'Toddlers at the Bookie's', *Scottish Daily Express*, 24 July 1956.
61. 'A Glasgow Evil' and 'Gambling Evil', *Glasgow Herald*, 2 December 1923 and 8 February 1924.
62. Shoolbred, *op. cit.*, p. 230.
63. Chinn Letters, Brian McQuade, no. 1, p. 1; in contrast to my interpretation, the Edinburgh Voluntary Youth Welfare Association thought that the act was a success, see Memorandum, R. C. (1949–51), *Minutes*, 12 April 1950. For the continuing concern about the relationship of young people to betting see: *Gambling and Legislation* (London: The Churches' Committee on Gambling Annual Report, 1950), p. 8; *Gambling and the Welfare State* (London: The Churches' Committee on Gambling Annual Report, 1952), p. 21; Canon Peter Green, *This Gambling. The Wrong of It!* (n.d., Christian Social Council Committee on Gambling leaflet); Rev. J. Clark Gibson, 'Gambling and the Child', *Religion in Education*, vol. 18, no. 2, 1951, pp. 49–53; Vivian Loomes, 'Relegate Betting Shops to Side Streets', *North London Press* (cutting supplied by Islington Libraries).
64. Chinn Letters, Mr G. W. Langham, no. 1, p. 1; *ibid.*, Mary K. pp. 1–4; *ibid.*, Mrs P. Buckell, no. 1, p. 1; *ibid.*, John A. Bosworth, p. 2. See also, 'Bethnal Green Girl Takes "Slips"', *Eastern Post*, 1 June 1929 (thanks to Tower Hamlets Libraries).
65. Chinn Letters, Mrs L. Osborne, no. 1, p. 2.
66. Liverpool Council of Voluntary Aid, *op. cit.*, p. 17. Martin estimated that in 'four out of five of the families of poorer London some form of gambling goes on from time to time', *op. cit.*, p. 281; while the Ford family thought that at least 50 per cent of the people of Dundun Street betted with them. This was their core street, the one in which they lived, see Chinn Interviews, the Ford and Kimberley families, p. 14.
67. Convocation of the Province of York, *op. cit.*, p. 10.
68. 'How the Working Classes Gamble', *Tit Bits*, 17 July 1897; for Birmingham and female betting in works, see Edward Cadbury, M. Cecile Matheson and George Shann, *Women's Work and Wages. A Phase of Life in an Industrial City* (first published 1906. New York: Garland, 1980), p. 198.
69. Convocation of the Province of York, *op. cit.*, p. 10.
70. S. C. (1901–2), *Minutes*, q. 3636–3779, pp. 637–44; J. M. Hogge, 'Gambling Among Women', in Rowntree (ed.), *op. cit.*, pp. 74–8, C. E. B. Russel, *Social Problems of the North* (first published 1913. New

York: Garland, 1980), pp. 111–16; Isabel Parlane, 'Gambling Among Girls', *Glasgow Herald*, 6 December 1922.

71. Richard Pollock, 'Are Women the Worst Gamblers?', *Sunday Graphic*, 10 November 1957. For women and betting after legalization, see Linda Blandford, 'Women and Gambling', *Sunday Times*, 24 April 1966; Guy Daniel, 'The Betting Shop Wives', *Evening Post* (Bristol), 16 October 1968; 'Keep Women Out of the Bookies', *Sunday News* (Belfast), 10 July 1966; Peter Lewis, 'Feminine Flutter', *Daily Mail*, 25 March 1963; and Roy Turner, 'On Her Shopping List, A Bet', *Daily Herald*, 5 June 1962. The noun 'flutter', meaning to have a small gamble, dates to about the 1870s, Partridge, *op. cit.*, p. 334.
72. Chinn Letters, Dorothy Johnson, no. 1, p. 2.
73. Alice Linton, *Not Expecting Miracles* (London: Centreprise, 1982), p. 50; Chinn Letters, Evelyn Gregory, no. 1, p. 2; and *ibid.*, Nellie Stamer, p. 1.
74. *Ibid.*, Doris Magness, no. 1, pp. 1–2; *ibid.*, Mildred Kershaw, pp. 1–2.
75. *Ibid.*, Mr Riddall, p. 1.
76. *Ibid.*, Mr C. Brice, p. 1; *ibid.*, Mr J. Forbes, no. 1, p. 2.
77. For types of bets in this period see Cope (ed.), *op. cit.*, pp. 171–3.
78. Chinn Letters, Andrew Walls, no. 1, p. 1; *ibid.*, Mr J. M. Blevins, no. 1, p. 1 (actually, this bet adds up to 1s 3d, not 1s); *ibid.*, Mr J. W. Davies, no. 1, p. 1.
79. *Ibid.*, Mr J. Aslin, no. 1, p. 1.
80. *Ibid.*, Mr S. Murphy, no. 1, p. 3; see also *ibid.*, Jean B. Hall, no. 1, p. 1 (Clackheaton) and *ibid.*, Robert Reid, no. 1, p. 2 (Maryhill).
81. For example, see 'Police Raid', *Journal*, 6 November 1936 (thanks to Salford Libraries).
82. Chinn Letters, Joseph E. Riley, no. 1, p. 3.
83. McKibbin, *op. cit.*, pp. 155–6.
84. Wm H. Lovedee, 'The Gambling Menace', *Christian*, 15 July 1937.
85. Isaac Foot, 'Britain on Trial. A New Exposure of the Gambling Ramp', *Northern Daily Telegraph*, 24 April 1934; Rev. J. Clark Gibson, 'Gambling and the Child', p. 49. See also: Reverend Peter Green, 'The Moral Aspects of Gambling', *Expository Times*, vol. 41, February 1930, p. 215; Money, *op. cit.*, p. 250; Statement of Sir Josiah Stamp, R. C. (1932–3), *Minutes*, 12 January 1933, pp. 519–21; and Watchman, 'The Churches and Gambling', *Friend*, 30 July 1937 and for an earlier statement of this argument, W. J. K., 'Betting and Gambling', *Westminster Review*, vol. 143, no. 2, 1895, pp. 146–8.
86. 'Should Betting be Abolished? A Discussion between Brigadier A. C. Critchley and D. R. Grenfell', *Listener*, vol. 9, no. 218, 15 March 1933, p. 412.
87. Hopcraft, *op. cit.*, p. 69.
88. Garratt, *op. cit.*, pp. 4–8. See also Will Barnett, *The Life Story of Will Barnett: Better Known as the Ex-jockey. Written by Himself* (Congleton: Spurgeon Memorial Press, 1911), pp. 9–27.
89. Chinn Letters, Raymond A., no. 1, p. 1.
90. Alex Granger, *Life's a Gamble* (Bognor Regis: New Horizon, 1983), p. 1.
91. Chinn Letters, John Ward, no. 1, p. 3; *ibid.*, Mike M. and George M., p. 2. A compelling novel about a compulsive gambler in modern

Glasgow is by James Kelman, *A Chancer* (first published 1985. London: Picador, 1987).

92. Joseph H. Armitage, *The Twenty Three Years or the Late Way of Life and Living by 'The Exile'* (unpublished MS, n.d., in Brunel University Library), p. 92 (Hunslett). For Friendly Societies, see *Rules of Friendly Society of Operative Stone Masons* (1881), p. 37 (thanks to the Modern Records Centre, University of Warwick); and *Rules of the North Brewham Friendly Society*, no. 9 (Somerset Record Office – thanks to P. W. Randell).
93. Chinn Letters, Eva M., p. 2; *ibid.*, Maureen Marsh, no. 1, p. 1. See also Paul Thompson, *The Edwardians. The Remaking of British Society* (first published 1975. London: Paladin, 1979), p. 135.
94. Payne, *op. cit.*, pp. 372–3.
95. Article, *Manchester Guardian*, 9 January 1924, cited in Perkins, *Betting Facts*, pp. 14–5.
96. Ex-Serviceman, *op. cit.*, pp. 7–11.
97. 'Gambling Russia and Anti-Gambling Japan', *Bulletin*, vol. 3, no. 30, May 1905, p. 102. Influential on these attitudes was the novel by Fyodor Dostoyevsky, *The Gambler* (first published 1866. Harmondsworth: Penguin, 1966).
98. *Bulletin*, vol. 6, no. 62, November 1915, p. 9.
99. F. S. Preston and H. Crichton Miller, *The Gambling Spirit as a National Problem* (Address given at the Third Biennial Mental Health Conference, reprinted, London: National Anti-Gambling League, 1933), pp. 3–4 and 11; Professor John Murphy, *This Gambling. The Psychology of It* (London: Christian Social Council Committee on Gambling leaflet. n.d.). See also J. Gulland, 'The Psychology of Gambling', *Sunday School Chronicle and Christian Outlook*, 15 December 1921; and John Murphy, *Instinct, Adventure and Gambling* (London: Society for the Promotion of Christian Knowledge, 1934).
100. Martin, *op. cit.*, p. 273.
101. For psychological studies, see D. B. Cornish, Home Office Research Study No. 42, *Gambling: a Review of the Literature and its Implications for Policy and Research* (London: Her Majesty's Stationery Office, 1978); Jon Halliday and Peter Fuller (ed.), *The Psychology of Gambling* (London: Allen Lane, 1974). For sociological enquiries, see Downes, *op. cit.*; Michael P. Filby and Lee Harvey, 'Recreational Betting: Everyday Activities and Strategies', in *Leisure Studies*, vol. 7, 1988, pp. 159–72; and Newman, *op. cit.* See also E. C. Devereux, 'Gambling in Psychological and Sociological Perspective', in *International Encyclopaedia of the Social Sciences* (1968), pp. 53–62; W. R. Eadington (ed.), *Gambling and Society, Interdisciplinary Studies on the Subject of Gambling* (Springfield, Illinois: Charles C. Thomas, 1976); R. D. Herman (ed.), *Gambling* (New York: Harper and Row, 1967); T. Veblen, *The Theory of the Leisure Class* (New York: Macmillan, 1899); I. K. Zola, 'Observations on Gambling in a Lower-Class Setting', in Herman (ed.), *op. cit.*, pp. 19–31. Excellent resumés of current research in these fields can be read in the newsletters of the Society for the Study of Gambling.

102. William McIlvanney, *Docherty* (first published 1975. London: Sceptre, 1987), p. 243.
103. Victor Andrews, *Victor* (unpublished MS, n.d. – thanks to Harvey Andrews), pp. 24–32.
104. Walter Greenwood, *op. cit.*, pp. 110–21.
105. Chinn Interviews, Christy Rees, p. 5.
106. Chinn Letters, Jim Ross, no. 1, p. 1.
107. *Ibid.*, Jessica Martin, no. 2, p. 3.
108. Russell, *op. cit.*, pp. 109–11; Lady Bell, *At the Works. A Study of a Manufacturing Town* (first published 1907. London: Virago, 1985), pp. 256–7; E. Wight Bakke, *The Unemployed Man. A Social Study* (London: Nisbett & Co., 1933), pp. 199–200.
109. Pilgrim Trust, *Men Without Work* (first published 1938. New York: Garland, 1985), p. 99.
110. B. Seebohm Rowntree and G. R. Lavers, *English Life and Leisure. A Social Study* (London: Longmans, Green & Co., 1951), p. 147; J. A. Hobson, 'The Ethics of Gambling', in Rowntree (ed.), *op. cit.*, pp. 1–19.
111. McKibbin, *op. cit.*, p. 163; see also James Power, 'Aspects of Working-Class Leisure During the Depression Years: Bolton in the 1930s', University of Warwick, unpublished MA thesis, 1980, pp. 40–8.
112. Jerry White, *The Worst Street in North London. Campbell Bunk, Islington, Between the Wars* (London: Routledge & Kegan Paul, 1986), pp. 85 and 118.
113. Richard Hoggart, *The Uses of Literacy: Aspects of Working-class Life with Special Reference to Publications and Entertainments* (first published 1957. Harmondsworth: Penguin, 1977), p. 137; see also John Paton, *Proletarian Pilgrimage. An Autobiography* (London: George Routledge & Sons, 1935), pp. 91–4.
114. Roberts, *op. cit.*, p. 164; Kay, *op. cit.*, p. 59; see also McKibbin, *op. cit.*, pp. 166–71.
115. A. G. Markham, S. C. (1901–2), *Minutes*, q. 3196, p. 147; McKibbin, *op. cit.*, p. 171. See also 'The Intellectual Side of Horse Racing', *New Statesman*, 12 June 1920, pp. 274–5.
116. Chinn Letters, Mary Barras, no. 2, pp. 2–3.
117. John Blake, *Memories of Old Poplar* (London: Stepney Books, 1977), pp. 13–14.
118. Eric Fairclough, *In a Lancashire Street* (St Helens: the author, 1983), p. 67.
119. Chinn Letters, Betty Simonite, no. 1, p. 1; Ruth Johnson, *Old Road. A Lancashire Childhood 1912–1926* (Manchester: E. J. Morten, 1974), pp. 83–8.
120. Chinn Letters, Rose McHugh, no. 2, p. 1.
121. *Ibid.*, Anne Spence, no. 1, pp. 3–4.
122. McLoughlin, *op. cit.*, p. 130.
123. Elsie Elizabeth Goodhead, *The West End Story. Derby During the Depression. A Social and Personal History* (Matlock: Derbyshire Library Service, 1983), p. 23.
124. J. Ramsay MacDonald, 'Gambling and the Citizenship', in Rowntree (ed.), *op. cit.*, p. 127. Interestingly, Bismarck told Disraeli that 'so long as the English are devoted to racing Socialism has no chance with you', Newmarket, *op. cit.*, p. 114.

125. James D. Young, *Socialism and the English Working Class* (Hemel Hempstead: Harvester Wheatsheaf, 1989), pp. 26–7.
126. Will Crooks, *Working Men and Gambling* (London: Social Tracts of the Times, 1906); John Burns, *The Straight Tip to the Workers. Brains Better than Bets and Beer* (London: Clarion pamphlet no. 36, 1902); 'I.L.P. and Gambling', *Nelson Leader*, 28 March 1907 (thanks to Lancashire Libraries, Nelson).
127. Ross McKibbin, 'Arthur Henderson as Labour Leader', *International Review of Social History*, vol. 23, 1978, p. 81; see also Glass, *op. cit.*, pp. 45–6. For Barr and Boyle, see Jones, *op. cit.*, pp. 208–23, and Rev. James Barr, 'A Socialist View of Betting Report', *Forward* (Glasgow ILP), 24 June 1933. For Barr, see also Rev. James Barr, *Lang Syne* (Glasgow: William Maclellan, 1948).
128. Rev. Arthur Prince, *Gambling* (Radcliffe: 1909, an address given to the C.E.M.S. in St. John's Church Radcliffe, 28 November 1909), pp. 2–5 (thanks to Bury Libraries).
129. 'The Remedy for Gambling', *Commonwealth*, part 5, 1906, p. 25.
130. John Brown, *I was a Tramp* (London: Selwyn & Blount, 1934), pp. 211–12.
131. Kathleen Woodward, *Jipping Street* (first published 1928. London: Virago, 1983), p. 108.
132. Walter Greenwood, *op. cit.*, pp. 22–3, 113 and 239–56. See also Roger Webster, '*Love on the Dole* and the Aesthetic of Contradiction', in Jeremy Hawthorn (ed.), *The British Working Class Novel in the Twentieth Century* (London: Edward Arnold, 1984), p. 58.
133. Walter Greenwood, *op. cit.*, p. 113.
134. *Ibid.*, p. 24. The vilification of pawnbrokers has been countered in a penetrating book by Melanie Tebbutt, *Making Ends Meet. Pawnbroking and Working-Class Credit* (first published 1983. London: Methuen, 1984).
135. Walter Greenwood, *There was a Time* (London: Jonathan Cape, 1967), pp. 81–93 (thanks to Jim Thompson for this reference).
136. *Ibid.*, pp. 28–32 and 161.
137. Walter Greenwood, *Love on the Dole*, p. 114.
138. Chinn Letters, Maureen Fitzgibbon, 1996, including letter from Celia Brady, the wife of Billy Brady, the son of the famed Billy Brady; and James Cush, no. 1, p. 4. See also Andrew Davies, Interview with Mr Bill Brady (the nephew of Billy Brady), mid-1980s.
139. Robert Blatchford, *Merrie England* (London: Clarion Office, 1894).
140. Walter Greenwood, *There was a Time*, pp. 13 and 172. It is interesting to compare the thoughts of Mrs Greenwood with those of Billy Ashted, Walter Allen's fictitious character in *All in a Lifetime* (first published 1959. London: The Hogarth Press, 1986). Ashted was the son of a skilled worker, but he clung to his mother and he became a socialist and a member of the Labour Party; 'Nearly all craftsmen and artisans were Liberals; but labourers usually voted Tory. This puzzled me as a boy and it puzzles me still, but I see it now as a kind of universal law, for in the days when I was politically active, the early days of the ILP and the Labour Party, I soon learned that it was from the superior working man, the skilled man, one got a respectful hearing, whereas the

unskilled were reactionary almost to the last degree. I believe this is still true', p. 49.

The way in which Greenwood recognized Grundy's popularity – despite his disgust of illegal bookies – is reflected in the dilemma which was faced by Frank Hardy in his condemnation of John West, his fictitious representation of John Wren, the owner of the Collingwood Tote, *op. cit.*, pp. 162–3.

141. Chinn Letters, John W., no. 2, p. 1; see also Davies, *op. cit.*, p. 204.
142. The back cover to the Penguin edition of Water Greenwood, *Love on the Dole*; Andrew Davies, *Leisure, Gender and Poverty. Working-Class Culture in Salford and Manchester 1900–1939* (Milton Keynes: Open University Press, 1992); and Stephen Constantine, Eddie Frow and Andrew Davies, 'Walter Greenwood and "Love on the Dole" A Discussion', *History Workshop 23. Class, Community and Conflict* (3–5 November 1989).
143. Stephen Constantine, '*Love on the Dole* and Its Reception in the 1930s', *Literature and History*, vol. 8, no. 1, 1982, pp. 243–5, cited in Clapson, *op. cit.*, p. 160.
144. Shimmin, *op. cit.*, pp. 110–11 and 120.
145. James Greenwood, *The Wilds of London*, p. 311. Compare these descriptions to that in 'Bookmaking', *All the Year Round*, 13 June 1868, p. 13: 'their garments are nearly new, and, with the exception of a somewhat profuse quantity of watch-chain knick-knacks, they wear no more jewellery than well-dressed men should'.
146. 'Victoria Street, E. C. – Betting-Men Making Up Their Books for the St Leger' (1863 – thanks to Islington Libraries, Finsbury). Victoria Street later became Farringdon Street.
147. John F. Macdonald, 'Bill Burke, Bookmaker', *Bulletin*, vol. 3, no. 34, May 1907, p. 174. It is interesting to compare this and Walter Greenwood's portrayal with that of 'Nero', the street bookie mentioned in Mass Observation, *The Pub and the People*: 'He is a tall man, thick set, with thick gold chain very prominent, he also has the usual cigar and a very prominent display of gold rings on his hand. I personally have counted as many as six rings on both hands' (p. 262).
148. For an example from *Punch* see 'Chucked', 14 March 1891, p. 122 and for Tom Webster see his collection in the Centre for the Study of Cartoons and Caricature, University of Kent. Much of his work was published in the *Daily Mail*. For a later example of flashy, cartoon bookies, see Lee, *Evening News*, 23 March 1953.
149. 'The Public and the Bookmaking Profession', *Banyan*, March 1953, p. 34; see also Guardrail, 'Racing Ragout', *Tatler*, 14 June 1939.
150. J. Fairfax-Blakeborough, 'A Backward Glance at the Ring', *Banyan*, November 1949, pp. 61; see also J. Fairfax-Blakeborough, 'Memories of Old-Time Bookmakers', *Banyan*, July 1939, p. 105.
151. Chinn Interviews, Sam Dell, p. 7.
152. *Ibid.*, Horace Bottrell, pp. 11–12; see also Martin Cobbett, *Racing Life and Racing Characters* (London: Sands & Co., 1903), pp. 304–9.
153. Cannon, *op. cit.*, p. 37: 'all bookmakers are not rolling in wealth, but the exigencies of their position makes it imperative for this to appear so. Backers are not very ready to bet with a man who has a poverty-stricken

appearance'; 'Looks the Part', *Birmingham Gazette*, 26 January 1938: 'You might have seen Ted . . . dressed in loud checks, gaitered and fresh-complexioned, with hat at a jaunty angle and . . . a cigar emerging from a corner of his mouth. He inspires confidence by looking the part.' See also, Chinn Letters, Mr and Mrs A. West, p. 1.

154. Robert Perrucci, *op. cit.*, p. 307.
155. A. McArthur and H. Kingsley Long, *No Mean City* (first published 1956. London: Corgi, 1957), p. 11. This novel was set in Glasgow.
156. Chinn Letters, B. Bagley, p. 3; *ibid.*, Bill Caldow, p. 1.
157. John Hawke, S. C. (1901–2), *Minutes*, q. 5, p. 355.
158. Chinn Letters, Mr H. Dabbs, no. 2, p. 1.
159. Chinn Interviews, Mr Knowles, p. 33.
160. Chinn Letters, Eric Thornley Downs, no. 2, p. 1; see also *ibid.*, John Sharp, p. 1 (Birmingham). It ought to be noted that before 1914, the billycock was regarded as the headgear of the working man, see Roberts, *op. cit.*, photographs 8–10, and Letter in *Bradford Observer*, 2 August 1887, cited in Keith Laybourn and Jack Reynolds, *Liberalism and the Rise of Labour 1890–1918* (London: Croom Helm, 1984), pp. 32–3. For the etymology of billycock, see Partridge, *op. cit.*, p. 70.
161. Walter Greenwood, *Love on the Dole*, pp. 113 and 116.
162. Mass Observation, *op. cit.*, p. 255.
163. I have scoured every kind of source to find support for Greenwood's typification of Grundy as a pimp, to no avail.
164. Elizabeth Roberts, *A Woman's Place. An Oral History of Working-Class Women 1890–1914* (Oxford: Basil Blackwell, 1984), pp. 81–124; see also Carl Chinn, *They Worked All Their Lives. Women of The Urban Poor in England 1880–1939* (Manchester: Manchester University Press, 1988), pp. 141–54.
165. Chinn Interviews, Ken Overton, p. 22.
166. Chinn Letters, Wilson Ditty, no. 1, p. 2.
167. *Ibid.*, Jim Taylor, no. 1, pp. 3–4.
168. *Ibid.*, Patricia Bell, no. 1, p. 1.
169. Chinn Interviews, Buck Chinn, *passim.*
170. Chinn Letters, Rose Tunnah, no. 1, p. 1 and no. 2, p. 2; *ibid.*, Mrs Hetty Bradbury, no. 1, p. 1.
171. Chinn Interviews, Horace Foster, p. 4; *ibid.*, Ken Overton, pp. 32–3; *ibid.*, Ernie Cashmore, *passim*; *ibid.*, Mr Moist, p. 3; *ibid.*, p. 2; *ibid.*, Len Boden, pp. 26–32; *ibid.*, Horace Bottrell, p. 22.
172. Chinn Letters, James Cush, no. 1, pp. 1–2; *ibid.*, Mr C. Whitely, no. 1, p. 2; *ibid.*, Mr L. Caket, no. 1, p. 1.
173. Chinn Interviews, Horace Bottrell, p. 22.
174. *Ibid.*, Rosemary Whitaker, pp. 1–3.
175. Chinn Letters, Mr E. W. Burkinshaw, no. 1, pp. 4–6.
176. Chinn Interviews, Ken Overton, p. 34.
177. *Ibid.*, Horace Foster, p. 21.
178. Chinn Letters, Jean Davies, no. 1, p. 2.
179. Chinn Interviews, Buck Chinn, p. 6.
180. 'Britain's Betting Industry – II', *The Economist*, 7 March 1936, p. 517; 'Betting and the Public', *The Nineteenth Century*, July 1933, p. 60.
181. For example, see Chinn Letters, Iris Holden, no. 1, p. 2 (Plymouth). It

should be emphasized that 2s 6d was the upper limit of the range of commission and in most places the average paid was lower.

182. *Ibid.*, Peter McCusker, no. 2, p. 1.
183. *Ibid.*, Arthur Jones, no. 2, p. 1.
184. *Ibid.*, James Jepson, no. 1, p. 2; Chinn Interviews, Buck Chinn, p. 6; *ibid.*, Horace Foster, p. 2. See also *ibid.*, Harold Reynolds, p. 23 – who reckoned that his dad's Hick Street pitch took about £200 a week.
185. Fixed-odds betting relates to the combined results of a number of separate football matches. For an early coupon see that of F. Pattman (1910) in Globe Town Library, Tower Hamlets; and for a later one see 'Cashy' (Ernie Cashmore) in the Heslop Room, University of Birmingham Library. For its origins, see 'Coupon Betting: The Football Fungus', *Spectator*, 22 March 1913, pp. 482–3; 'Football Betting: The Coupon Craze, A Pernicious Practice and Effects of Coupons', *Glasgow Herald*, 3–5 March 1914; John Gulland, *Football Gambling. From 'Pontoon' to 'Pool'* (London: National Anti-Gambling League, n.d.); Ainslie J. Robertson, *Football . . . Betting* (Liverpool: Northern Publishing Co., 1907 – a paper read to the Liverpool Economic and Statistical Society); see also Nicholas Fishwick, *English Football and Society 1910–1950* (Manchester: Manchester University Press, 1989) pp. 117–35, and Mason, *Association Football* pp. 179–87. Fixed odds were offered also on cricket matches, see the *Bulletin*, vol. 5, no. 57, August 114, p. 103.

    Fixed odds should not be confused with the football pools which emerged in the 1920s, see 'Gambling. "God Help the Nation"', *News Review*, 19 August 1937; R. J. Russell (introduced), *The Peril of the Pools* (London: The Epworth Press, 1935); Shermans Pools Ltd, 'Memorandum', R. C. (1949–51), *Minutes*, 9 May 1950. For an account of a pools operator, see Chinn Interviews, Ray Fear, pp. 2–23.

    Like many street bookies, certain racecourse layers betted on events other than horse-racing. For local sports (athletics) meetings, see 'Bookmakers Change Their Pleas. Long Contest Avoided in Tweedmouth Feast Sports Betting Charges', *Berwickshire News*, 8 August 1939; Chinn Interviews, Mr Armstrong, *passim* (Hetton); and *ibid.*, Jack Pearse, p. 20 (Birmingham). For crown green bowling see: 'Bookies Can't Bet – on Bowling', *Sporting Life* (January 1967 – cutting in NAB File, 'Bowling'); Chinn Letters, Albert Hampson, no. 1, pp. 2–3 and Chinn Interviews, Albert Hampson, *passim*. For cycling, see John Hawke, S. C. (1901–2), *Minutes*, q. 146, pp. 365–6. For hound trails, see *ibid.*, q. 151, p. 366 and Chinn Letters, Mr J. Stephens, no. 2, pp. 1–3. For rabbit coursing, see Clapson, *op. cit.*, pp. 158–9.
186. Chinn Interviews, Ken Overton, p. 35.
187. Chinn Letters, Mr S. Murphy, no. 2, pp. 1–2.
188. 'The Story of the Three X Double', *Glasgow Evening News*, 23 October 1937.
189. R. C. (1949–51), *Report*, p. 159.
190. 'The Story of the Three X Double', *op. cit.*
191. John Stevenson and Chris Cook, *The Slump. Society and Politics During the Depression* (first published 1977. London: Quartet Books, 1979), p. 17.

192. Chinn Interviews, Ken Overton, p. 33; Chinn Letters, Iris Read, no. 2, pp. 1–2. In his autobiography, Steve Hamer wrote that his street bookie Dad had a £3,000 bet in 1920 and that he owned eighteen race-horses and five cars, *The Steamer. 60 Years On* (unpublished MS, n.d., in Bolton Reference Library), pp. 2–3. I do not dispute Mr Hamer's veracity, but his assertions are staggering.
193. Chinn Letters, W. J. Campbell, no. 1, p. 1.
194. *Ibid.*, Trevor Morris, no. 1, pp. 1–2; see also Chinn Interviews, Mr Alexander, *passim.*
195. W. J. Beesley, Memorandum, R. C. (1949–51), *Minutes*, 10 October 1949.
196. 'You'd Be Surprised Says Bill, Bookies' Runner', *Daily Mirror*, 11 October 1949.
197. John Bingham, 'The Unhappy Story of Big Bill Beesley', *Sunday Dispatch*, 19 May 1950.
198. Gus Dalrymple interview, *Sporting Life*, 31 October 1962.
199. Chinn Letters, Mr. W. Duke, pp. 3–4. Fixed-odds betting was notorious as causing losses among bookies, see Frank (Keystone) Harvey, 'Fixed-Odds Layers Will Suffer on a "Black Saturday"', *Banyan*, November 1949, pp. 66–7, and 'Racecourse B.P.A. (Birmingham)', *Banyan*, October 1953, p. 75. When I write of results that were bad for bookies, it must be remembered that they were good for punters.
200. Golding, *op. cit.*, p. 13.
201. Chinn Letters, Charles Gleed, no. 1, pp. 1–2; *ibid.*, Doris Wall, p. 1 (Bill Thomason's grandaughter).
202. *Ibid.*, Mr T. W. Allen, no. 2, p. 1.
203. *Ibid.*, James Jepson, no. 1, p. 1.
204. For example, see *ibid.*, Mr G. W. Cutts, no. 1, p. 3.
205. Jones, *op. cit.*, pp. 208–25.
206. 'Labour's Decision on Betting Bill. Free Vote for MPs', *The Times*, 13 November 1959.
207. A. G. Markham, S. C. (1901–2), q. 3190–3, p. 603.
208. Joe Gormley, *Battered Cherub. The Autobiography of Joe Gormley* (London: Hamish Hamilton, 1982), p. 8; Jack Ashley, MP, *Journey into Silence* (London: The Bodley Head, 1973), p. 29. For the Labour Party in the inter-war years, see McKibbin, 'Arthur Henderson', pp. 97–125.
209. Chinn Letters, Jim Farrar, no. 2, pp. 1–2; see also Chinn Interviews, Jim Farrar, *passim.*
210. Chinn Interviews, Ronald 'Mac' Davidson, *passim.* William Hill was also left-wing in politics, see Ward Hill, *op. cit.*, pp. 61–2.
211. *Ibid.*, the Ford and Kimberley families, pp. 11 and 22.
212. Chinn Letters, James Sefton, no. 2, p. 2 and no. 3, p. 3 – the *Daily Mirror* published an unflattering article on this occurrence; see also *ibid.*, Bernard Ryan, no. 2, p. 1.
213. For a credit layer who was a Liberal turned Tory, see Dey, *op. cit.*, pp. 315–19.
214. For popular Conservatism in Salford, see Robert Roberts, *op. cit.*, pp. 28–31 and 178–80; and for Birmingham, see Christopher Green, 'Birmingham's Politics, 1873–1891: The Local Basis of Change', *Midland History*, vol. 2, no. 2, autumn 1973, pp. 84–98, and Carl

Chinn, 'The Anatomy of a Working-Class Neighbourhood: West Sparkbrook, 1871–1914', University of Birmingham, unpublished PhD thesis, 1986, pp. 272–8.

215. Chinn Letters, Rose Tunnah, no. 1, p. 6 (Birmingham); Chinn Interviews, Mrs Packer, p. 12; Chinn Letters, Ellis McCormick, no. 2, pp. 1–2; Chinn Interviews, Walter Chinn, pp. 52–3. For Stockport, see Chinn Letters, Eric Thornley Downs, no. 2, p. 2.
216. Chinn Letters, Mrs J. Davies, no. 2, p. 3 (James Beasley's daughter).
217. Cook, *op. cit.*, vol. 2, Division 2, p. 687.
218. Colonel Fluder, S. C. (1901–2), q. 66, pp. 465–7; see also C. W. Tannet Walker (connected to a large engineering works in Leeds), S. C. (1901–2), q. 2839, p. 593.
219. Duke of Portland, cited in Cook, *op. cit.*, vol. 2, Division 1, pp. 688–9.
220. Durant, *op. cit.*, p. 167.
221. For example, see 'Tote or Bookie!', *Truth*, March 1937.
222. For example, see Donovan, 'Bookmakers or Tote?', *Evening Star* (Ipswich), 10 December 1937.
223. Day, 'Turf Reform', pp. 819–32; Ganian, 'Bookmakers and the Tote', *Banyan*, October 1956, p. 97.
224. Sir Clement Hindley, Chairman of the Racecourse Betting Control Board, 'The Tote – Democrat of the Turf', *Daily Herald*, 23 April 1930; 'Gimcrack Club Dinner', *The Times*, 24 November 1933.
225. 'Utilities & Futilities', *Banyan*, December 1933, p. 2.
226. 'The Aga Khan', *Banyan*, April 1935, p. 1; see also Tom Driberg, 'The Aga's Agony', *Reynold's News*, 6 January 1957, and Londoner at Large, 'The Aga Khan says: Ban the bookies', *News Chronicle*, 28 December 1956.
227. 'Sir Abe Bailey on Horse Racing in England', *African World*, 4 December 1937.
228. See *The Bookmakers and Backers Association* (London: *c.* 1922), and Ron Whytock, 'Southern Bookmakers Association: History File' (thanks to Ron Whytock, secretary of the Southern and to Jim Westwell, former president). The word Backers was dropped from the title in 1935.
229. 'News and Views', *Banyan*, June 1934, p. 1.
230. 'Outlook is Black for Bookmakers. The "Menace" of the Totalisator. A Call to Arms', report of speech by George Picken, *Sporting Chronicle*, 14 December 1932; see also 'W.P.B.', *Banyan*, October 1932, pp. 1–2. For Picken's untiring defence of bookmaking, see for example George Picken, 'Our Bettors. I – The "Bookie" Meets a Real Need', *Listener*, vol. 17, no. 421, pp. 197–8; 'Summary of Speech at Northern B.P.A. Dinner' (1935 – NAB File, 'Picken'). For a detailed account of the views of the NBPA, see NBPA, Memorandum, R. C. (1932–3), *Minutes*, 7 March 1950.
231. 'Fiat Lux', *Banyan*, February 1933, p. 3; 'Sweated Labour', *Banyan*, December 1935, p. 25.
232. 'Class Distinction', *Banyan*, July 1934, p. 2; 'Life and Death Legislation', *Banyan*, June 1934, p. 5.
233. Lieck, *op. cit.*, p. 68.
234. 'The Two Shilling Unit', *Banyan*, March 1934, p. 5.
235. 'Gate-Crashers Barred', *Sunday Dispatch*, 25 March 1934.

236. 'Our Betters', *Banyan*, April 1934, p. 1.
237. 'Hardships of the Bookmakers', *Yorkshire Evening Post*, 2 December 1938.
238. See extracts quoted in 'Lord Harewood at the Gimcrack Dinner', *Banyan*, January 1939, pp. 2–4. See also Donovan, 'Bookmakers or Tote?', *Evening Star* (Ipswich), 10 December 1937; and 'Pity the Bookie!', *Reynolds News*, 23 January 1938.
239. For later journalistic support of bookmaking, see for example, A. B. Clements (editor of *Sporting Life*), 'Turf Crisis Denied – A Reply, on the Issues of Betting and Ownership, to a Recent Article by the Field's Commentator', *Field*, 11 October 1956; J. L. Manning, *Daily Mail*, 7 April 1967; and 'Tote Monopoly. Not Bloody Likely!', *Sporting Life Guide*, 20 January 1967. For popular support for bookies, see Bob Rodney, 'Honest Joe Wins at 9–4', *Daily Mirror*, 27 January 1967; 'Who Wants a Tote Monopoly?', *Sporting Life*, 18 March 1967. Most punters were in favour of the continuance of bookmaking and the tote. A first-rate examination of the politics of the turf is in Christopher R. Hill, *op. cit.*; see also *Bookmaking and Racing Politics* (NAB file, 'Tote').
240. Ivor Herbert, 'Banish the Bookie?', *Evening News* (London) 7 October 1955; see also Ivor Herbert, 'Now It's the Bookies' Turn', *Evening News*, 14 December 1955.
241. 'Hotspur' (B. W. C. Curling) 'A Way to Make Racing Solvent', *Daily Telegraph*, 21 May 1954; Hotspur, 'Betting Laws that Would Work', *Daily Telegraph*, 4 February 1957; *Sporting Chronicle*, 25 October 1956.
242. 'Tote Monopoly – Sir Robin Says It Again', *Sporting Life*, 14 November 1969, and Jim Stanford, 'Now Owners Go into Battle Against the Bookies', *Daily Sketch*, 14 November 1969; The Scout (Clive Graham), 'Bookies Should Pay More Say Racing Owners', *Daily Express*, 18 November 1970.
243. NAB File, 'Racehorse Owners' Association Ltd' (extracted from the Companies Register, 25 May 1967).
244. Jack Waterman, 'Bookies Hit Back at Owners', 23 November 1967 – newspaper cutting in NAB File, 'Racehorse Owners' Association Ltd'); see also George Lodge, 'Beware this Betting Monopoly', *Liverpool Echo*, 4 August 1968.
245. William Keegan, 'Nationalise the Bookies', *New Statesman*, 24 February 1967; see also '130 MPs Urge', *Sunday Express*, 11 January 1948; The Editor, 'A Sign of the Times', *British Bookmaker*, no. 23, February 1966.
246. 'Nationalise Bets Shops, Says a Tory', *South London Press*, 25 June 1965.
247. Norman St John Stevas, 'Knock the "Bookies" and Bingo', *Catholic Herald*, 24 June 1966.
248. Speech of Viscount Astor, House of Lords, 27 June 1956, cited in *Bookmaking and Racing Politics* (NAB File, 'Tote'), pp. 3–4; see also Christopher R. Hill, *op. cit.*, pp. 6–8, and 'Nationalise the Tote, Tory Peer Suggests', *Daily Worker*, 28 June 1956. Astor's speech led to a syndicated article, 'Is the Old Firm (bookies) on the Way Out?', which

appeared in seven provincial newspapers, e.g, *Nottingham Guardian and Journal*, 20 July 1956.

249. For example, see the *Bulletin*, vol. 6, no. 72, May 1918, p. 96; see also Canon Horsley, 'Crime and Gambling', in Rowntree, *op. cit.*, pp. 85–91, and 'Gamblers and Suicides', *Spectator*, no. 2923, 5 July 1884, p. 879. For a denial of this view, see Mr J. F. Langmuir, Stipendiary Magistrate of Glasgow, Memorandum, R. C. (1949–51), *Minutes*, 14 April 1950, and for other more balanced assessments, see National Association of Probation Officers, Memorandum, R. C. (1949–51), *Minutes*, 15 June 1950, and Dr Roper, Principal Medical Officer, H. M. Prison, Wakefield, Memorandum, R. C. (1949–52), *Minutes*, 9 May 1950. For later views, see Cornish, *op. cit.*, pp. 66–9. For doping, see also the *Bulletin*, vol. 6, no. 68, May 1917, p. 58 and the Press Council, *The Press and the People. The 13th annual report of the Press Council* (London: The Press Council, 1966), pp. 39–41 – in which the protest of the NAB was upheld against an article in the *Daily Express* which alleged the involvement of bookmakers in a doping scandal.
250. Chinn Interviews, Horace Foster, p. 15; see also Mr J. F. Langmuir, Stipendiary Magistrate of Glasgow, Memorandum to R. C. (1949–51), *Minutes*, 14 April 1950, 'the street agent regards his employment as a justifiable means of getting a livelihood and sees no moral wrong in earning his living by breaking the law'.
251. Chinn Interviews, Matt O'Malley, p. 9.
252. John Maxwell, Chief Constable of Manchester, R. C. (1932–3), *Minutes*, 21 July 1932; Police Federation of England and Wales, Memorandum, R. C. (1949–51), *Minutes*, 16 November 1949.
253. Chinn Letters, Edmund King, no. 1, p. 3.
254. Chinn Interviews, Arthur Smith, p. 1 (thanks to Smethwick Local History Society); see also *ibid.*, Horace Foster, p. 15 – when Bill Heath, the former employer of Horace Foster's father, indicated the class bias of the betting laws when fining the bookie. For other magisterial discontent against the betting laws see: 'Attack by Mayor at Wednesbury. Discrimination Condemned', *Express and Star* (Wolverhampton) 25 March 1937; 'Betting Laws "Unsatisfactory", Says Bench Chairman', *Liverpool Evening Express*, 25 August 1937; 'Coatbridge Provost Attacks Betting Laws', *Glasgow Evening Citizen*, 6 April 1938.
255. Chief Constables' (Scotland) Association, Memorandum, R. C. (1949–51), *Minutes*, 12 April 1950.
256. Lord Chancellor, Parliamentary Debates (Hansard), 4 July 1960, col. 924. See also A. G. Markham, S. C. (1901–2), *Minutes*, q. 3212, p. 611; Chief Constable Peacock of Manchester, S. C. (1901–2), *Minutes*, q. 359, p. 479; and Sir Albert De Rutzer (London magistrate), S. C. (1901–2), *Minutes*, q. 523, p. 488.
257. Cobbett, *op. cit.*, pp. 136–7; see also, for example, 'A Result of Gambling', *Derry Standard*, 21 March 1949; and 'Luck in Betting Leads to Crime', *Lincolnshire Chronicle and Leader*, 3 December 1938.
258. 'District Notes – Northern B.P.A.', *Banyan*, December 1943, pp. 4–5; Secretary of the Joint Committee, Letter, *The Times*, 1 July 1956. In support of this assertion is the case of Fred Gilbert. On 25 March 1921, he attacked Charles (Derby) Sabini, at which time he described himself

as a fruiterer, but in another prosecution in 1922, he called himself a bookmaker. Actually he was a member of a race gang; 'Row at Race Meeting' and 'Blackmail Charge', *Glasgow Herald*, 25 March 1921 and 11 September 1922.

259. 'No Easy Year', *The Times*, 29 June 1956.
260. First Report of the Constabulary Commissioners, (1839) cited in Poole, *op. cit.*, p. 143.
261. Jerome Caminada, *Twenty-Five Years of Detective Life* (first published 1895. Warrington: Prism Books, 1983), vol. 1, pp. 1–17, and vol. 2, pp. 77–80.
262. Chinn Interviews, Sam Dell, p. 4. The Aldgate mob was known also as the 'Whizz Mob'.
263. *Ibid.*, Les Lewis and Mrs Lewis (mother), p. 12.
264. 'A Policeman's Losses with Three Card Tricksters', *Lancaster Guardian*, 25 June 1921 (thanks to Lancashire Libraries, Lancaster).
265. Chinn Interviews, Albert Henson, pp. 1–8 (thanks to Doncaster Libraries); see also Chinn Letters, Vinny Grant, *passim*.
266. Doncaster Police Records, *Race-week Minute Books of the Clerk of the Justices*, 1896–1910, *passim* (thanks to South Yorkshire Police for access to this material). For the three-card trick at Musselburgh, see 'Musselburgh Police Court', 11 October 1912 (newspaper cutting supplied by East Lothian Libraries); and for the spinning jenny at Chester, see 'Chester War on Racecourse Gang', *Liverpool Evening Express*, 5 May 1938.
267. Major F. S. James, Chief Constable of Sheffield and F. J. O. Callaghan, Barrister, 'The Racecourse. A Few Hints to Police Officers who May be Called Upon to Perform Duty at Race Meetings', *Police Review and Parade Gossip*, 20 October 1933.
268. Chinn Interviews, Jim Davis, *passim*; *ibid.*, Patsy Collins, *passim*; *ibid.*, Mr Price, pp. 1–8.
269. 'Serious Affray at Paisley Races', *Renfrewshire Advertiser*, 26 April 1848 (thanks to Renfrew Libraries, Paisley).
270. For the Redskins see Chinn Interviews, Sam Dell, p. 1; *ibid.*, Meg Goodwin and John Adair, *passim* (Scotstoun, Glasgow); and Bill Murray, *The Old Firm. Sectarianism, Sport and Society in Scotland* (Edinburgh: John Donald, 1984), p. 148.
271. Cited in J. Fairfax-Blakeborough, 'The Ring in the Merry Past', *Banyan*, December 1948, p. 19.
272. Ron Whytock, 'Southern History File', p. 4.
273. J. Fairfax-Blakeborough, 'Secrets of the Old Tyneside Race Gang', *Sunday Sun* (Newcastle), 20 January 1935; and for the later operations of this mob, see Chinn Interviews, Albert Donkin, *passim*.
274. C. R. Acton, *Silk and Spur* (London: Richards, 1935), p. 86. There is oral evidence to suggest that men did bite off the back legs of live rats, for example, Chinn Interviews, Georgie Wood, *passim*.
275. 'Roughs on the Turf', *Daily Telegraph*, 13 August 1898. See also, 'Roughs on the Turf', *Daily Telegraph*, 10, 15 and 22 August 1898, and 'Ruffianism on the Turf', *Field*, vol. 92, 20 August 1898. There was another outcry in 1913, see the *Bulletin*, vol. 5, no. 53, August 1913, p. 46.

276. J. Fairfax-Blakeborough, 'Menace of the "Birmingham Boys". Gigantic Attack on a Racecourse', *Sunday Mercury* (Birmingham), 13 January 1935; regarding metropolitan suburban racecourses, see Edward Spencer, *The Great Game and How It Is Played, etc.* (London: 1903), pp. 166–220, and 'Turf Ethics in 1868', *Broadway*, 1868, pp. 379–80.
277. J. Fairfax-Blakeborough, 'Menace of the "Birmingham Boys". Gigantic Attack on a Racecourse', *Sunday Mercury* (Birmingham), 13 January 1935; see also the memories of Tom Devereux, J. Fairfax-Blakeborough, 'Memories of Old-Time Bookmakers', *Banyan*, November 1938, p. 148. For the fear of a similar event at Salisbury races, see Dey, *op. cit.*, pp. 213–15; and for late-nineteenth-century worries about ruffianism at Northampton racecourse, see 'Moral Pollution', *Mercury and Herald*, 8 April 1938.
278. Spencer, *op. cit.*, p. 154, see also pp. 158–73.
279. Scott, *op. cit.*, pp. 287–8.
280. *Birmingham Mail*, cited in the *Bulletin*, vol. 3, no. 30, May 1905, p. 110.
281. For the boom in racing, see Tom Divall, *Scoundrels and Scallywags (and Some Honest Men)* (London: Ernest Benn, 1929), pp. 185 and 199; and Vamplew, *op. cit.*, p. 68.
282. Chinn Interviews, Dave Langham, *passim.*; see also *ibid.*, Jim Cooper, pp. 1–3.
283. For example, see 'Bookmakers' Accessories', *Sporting Life*, 17 January 1939; ex-Detective Chief Superintendent Edward Greeno, *War on the Underworld* (London: John Long, 1960), p. 17; and '1934 Betting and Lotteries Act', Banyan, 11 June 1935, p. 1.
284. Cited in Special Correspondent, 'Remember Race Gangs of 1920s', *News of the World*, 22 July 1956; Norman Lucas, *Britain's Gangland* (London: W. H. Allen, 1969) p. 19.
285. Chinn Interviews, Jim Cooper, p. 2.
286. *Ibid.*, Dave Langham, p. 3.
287. 'Blackmail Charge', *Glasgow Herald*, 11 September 1922; Chinn Interviews, Sam Dell, p. 5.
288. Chinn Interviews, Sam Dell, p. 11.
289. *Ibid.*, pp. 5 and 11.
290. *Ibid.*, Charlie Maskey, p. 9; *ibid.*, Horace Bottrell, supplement, p. 1. For Towie, see also *ibid.*, Jim Cooper, pp. 1–4.
291. Divall, *op. cit.*, p. 201.
292. *Ibid.*, p. 183.
293. Chinn Interviews, Simmy L., p. 3.
294. Raphael Samuel, *East End Underworld. Chapters in the Life of Arthur Harding* (London: Routledge & Kegan Paul, 1981), pp. 133–4 and 182. For the Italian community in Clerkenwell, see L. Sponza, 'The Italian Poor in Nineteenth-Century Britain', University of London, unpublished PhD thesis, 1984.
295. 'Row at Race Meeting', *Glasgow Herald*, 25 March 1921.
296. Norman Lucas and Bernard Scarlett, *The Flying Squad* (London: Arthur Barker, 1968), pp. 36–7; see also Divall, *op. cit.*
297. 'Rival Racecourse Gangs Feud', *Glasgow Herald*, 4 April 1921; see also Chinn Interviews, Lou Prince, p. 2.

298. Divall, *op. cit.*, p. 201.
299. 'Twenty-eight Men Charged with Assault', *Glasgow Herald*, 20 July 1921. Arthur Harding stated that most of the Brummagem Boys were Londoners from the Elephant and Castle, *op. cit.*, p. 181. It is likely that the gang was allied to the mob from South London, as is indicated by the address of Fred Gilbert, who was part of the crowd that attacked Derby Sabini at Greenford, 'Row at Race Meeting', *Glasgow Herald*, 25 March 1921. However, the twenty-eight men arrested at Kingston were all from Birmingham and their Brummie identity is confirmed by oral evidence from their city: Chinn Letters, Mrs H. Burnett, nos 1 and 2, *passim*; Chinn Interviews, Jackie Currigan, supplement, p. 1 – whose stepfather was slashed in the fighting; *ibid.*, Mr and Mrs Gilliver – Mrs Gilliver's dad was in the Brummagem Boys; *ibid.*, Charlie Greenhill, pp. 3–14 – whose uncle was a gang member; *ibid.*, Mrs Lewis and Les Lewis, pp. 6–13 and 26–30; *ibid.*, Steve Nicholls, p. 2 – his father was a member of the gang; and *ibid.*, Fred Sutton, *passim*.
300. Chief Inspector James Berrett, *When I was at Scotland Yard* (London: Sampson, Low & Co., 1932), pp. 116–20.
301. 'The Racing Feud Case Sentences', *Glasgow Herald*, 25 July 1921.
302. The Bookmakers and Backers Racecourse Protection Association, *What It Has Done and What It Can Do, with YOUR Help* (NAB File, 'History', 1921).
303. Whytock, *op. cit.*, p. 5.
304. Bookmakers and Backers Racecourse Protection Association, General Committee, *Minutes*, 12 September 1921.
305. Harding, *op. cit.*, p. 133.
306. *Ibid.*, p. 328; Southern BPA, Folio 47, 15 May 1933, 'Printing of Lists'.
307. BBRPA General Committee, *Minutes*, 15 May, 12 June and 4 September 1922.
308. Divall, *op. cit.*, pp. 205–6. At this time, the Sabinis were involved in a battle within Saffron Hill, see 'Harry Sabini Shot', *Daily Express*, 21 November 1922 (thanks to Islington Libraries, Finsbury).
309. Cited in Special Correspondent, *News of the World*, 22 July 1956; 'What has the B.P.A. Done?' (Southern File, 'History', 1939), p. 1.
310. Chinn Interviews, Sam Froggat, p. 4; *ibid.*, Teddy Sturmer, p. 1.
311. *Ibid.*, Sam Dell, p. 1; *ibid.*, Joe Martin, *passim*.
312. Warren Hill, 'With Rod of Iron Sabini Gang Ruled English Racecourses for More than 20 years', *Rhodesia Herald*, 5 August 1957; Chinn Interviews, Sam Dell, p. 9.
313. Divall, *op. cit.*, pp. 206–10.
314. Ex-Detective Superintendent David Thomas, with Roderick Grant, *Seek Out the Guilty* (London: John Long, 1969), p. 39, and Geoffrey Dart, 'The Cathay Park Law Courts', *Beak*, no. 9 (1986 – thanks to South Glamorgan Libraries).
315. Ex-Chief Inspector 'Nutty' Sharpe, 'Fade out of the Race Gangs', *Star*, 4 January 1938; Bean, *op. cit., passim.*; Murray, *op. cit.*, pp. 148–9.
316. Greeno, *op. cit.*, p. 26.
317. *Ibid.*; Sharpe, *op. cit.*
318. Chinn Interviews, Sam Dell, p. 4; Sharpe, *op. cit.*
319. Eric Rickman, *On and Off the Racecourse* (1937), pp. 26–45.

320. W. Bebbington, *Rogues Go Racing* (London: Goods and Betts, 1947), p. 26.
321. Whytock, *op. cit.*, p. 7.
322. 'What has the B.P.A. Done?' (Southern File, 'History', 1939), p. 1.
323. 'B.P.A. Badge', *Fairplay*, October 1938 and 'Misuse of "B.P.A." Earns Prison Sentence', *Banyan*, November 1939, p. 149. For mushroom bookies, see P. O'Boyle, Secretary BPA (Southern), letter, 'Derby Day Welching', *Sporting Life*, 10 June 1937; and Geoffrey Simpson, 'Clubhouse Chair', *Daily Mail*, 24 May 1937.
324. 'What has the B.P.A. Done?' (Southern File, 'History', 1939), p. 1.
325. Meeting Between the Stewards of the Jockey Club and the Representatives of the Three Branches of the BPA, *Report*, 16 October 1929, NAB File, 'Pitches'.
326. 'Alleged Monopoly of Bookmakers' Pitches', *Glasgow Herald*, 5 October 1955. For modifications to the original rules, see NAB General Committee, *Minutes*, 29 August 1938.
327. This changeover was known as the Ferguson Scheme, see Jockey Club letter, 2 June 1958 and 'Outline of the Scheme', NAB File, 'Ferguson Scheme'.
328. Address of Mr R. Yeadon, 'Southern B.P.A. Annual General Meeting', *Banyan*, February 1956, p. 44.
329. 'Gangs Active at Epsom', *Daily Telegraph*, 2 June 1937. Some gangsterism was evident on the free and unenclosed parts of Ascot, see 'Intimidation of Bookmakers at Ascot', *Banyan*, August 1938, p. 97; and 'Slasher Gang Raid Ascot', *Daily Express*, 15 June 1949. For intimidation at a flapper, see 'Caused by Racketeering', *Evening News* (Glasgow), 9 May 1938.
330. Norman Sherry, *The Life of Graham Greene, Vol. 1, 1904–1939* (London: Jonathan Cape, 1989), pp. 634–5; Graham Greene, *Brighton Rock* (first published 1938. Harmondsworth: Penguin, 1943).
331. Sharpe, *op. cit.*; Greeno, *op. cit.*, pp. 64–5; Lucas and Scarlett, *op. cit.*, pp. 38–9; Chinn Interviews, Mr Maskey, pp. 16–17 – Mr Maskey came from Hoxton.
332. '500 Gangsters Threaten Race Track War', *Daily Mirror*, 18 November 1936; 'Gang Terror in London', *Daily Express*, 7 May 1934. There was also a murder at a dog-track which heightened the imaginations of the press, 'Dog Track Trial: Accused Men', *Evening Standard* (London), 17 November 1936. For a dismissal of exaggerated newspaper reports, see 'Once Again', *Banyan*, 28 November 1936, p. 14.
333. 'The Gang Terror Here Now', *Daily Sketch*, 26 January 1938. For press reports of gangsterism and gambling in the USA, see for example: 'A Test for Tammany', *The Times*, 23 January 1939. Since the 1960s, casinos have replaced racecourses as the focus of attention for those fearful of the involvement of gangs in gambling, see for example Colin Bell, 'Why Legal Gambling Imperils Britain', *Weekend Telegraph*, 31 September 1966.
334. Chinn Letters, Graham Greene, p. 1.
335. Sherry, *op. cit.*, p. 636.
336. *Empire News* (1955 – newspaper cutting in NAB File, 'Gangs').
337. 'Race Gangs Again. Fight Over Pitches', *Daily Graphic*, 23 May 1947.

338. Sharpe, *op. cit.*
339. Article in *Manchester Guardian* (1913), cited in Rev. Peter Green, *Betting and Gambling* (London: Student Christian Movement, 1925), p. 41.
340. 'Attack on B.P.A.', *Banyan*, 26 October 1935, p. 3.
341. Letter from Northern BPA, 28 August 1940 and NAB File, 'Dots and Dashes'.
342. Edward Smithies, *Crime in Wartime. A Social History of Crime in World War II* (London: George Allen & Unwin, 1982), pp. 111–12.
343. *Sunday Pictorial*, 22 June 1956; see also Lucas, *op. cit.*, pp. 74–115 and 'A Day at the Races – with Billy Hill and Co', *Empire News*, 1 June 1956.
344. For example, see 'Jack Spot's Own Amazing Story', *Daily Sketch*, 30 September 1956; *Gambling and the Citizen of Tomorrow* (London: Churches' Committee on Gambling Annual Report, 1955), pp. 12–13.
345. 'Betting Pitch Questions in Stabbing Trial', *Daily Telegraph*, 20 September 1955; 'Jack Spot My Sworn Enemy', *Daily Mail*, 19 July 1956.
346. 'Bookmakers Reply to the Lords', *Sporting Life*, 29 June 1956.
347. Cited in Herbert Mannheim, *Social Aspects of Crime in England Between the Wars* (London: George Allen & Unwin, 1940), pp. 221–2.
348. Philip Jenkins and Gary W. Potter, *Criminal Justice History. An International Annual*, vol. 9 (1988), p. 221.
349. Harding, *op. cit.*, p. 183; see also Ralph Finn, *Grief Forgotten. The Tale of an East End Jewish Boyhood* (first published 1968. London: Macdonald & Co., 1985), p. 267; Frederick Porter Wensley, *Detective Days. The Record of Forty-Two Years' Service in the Criminal Investigation Department* (London: Cassell & Co., 1931), pp. 10–12.
350. See note 299.
351. 'Terrorised by a Gang', *Scottish Daily Express*, 5 June 1938.
352. McGhee, *op. cit.*, p. 8.
353. Chinn Interviews, Norman Miller, pp. 14–15.
354. Ken Coates and Richard Silburn, *Poverty: The Forgotten Englishmen* (first published 1970. Harmondsworth: Penguin, 1973), p. 71.
355. Chinn Interviews, Mr and Mrs Gilliver, p. 9.
356. *Ibid.*, Buck Chinn, p. 69.
357. *Ibid.*, Frankie Goodwin, pp. 3–4.
358. McGhee, *op. cit.*, p. 9. The activities of the Sabinis, the Brummagem Boys and others are covered in James Morton, *Gangland. London's Underworld* (London: Warner edition, 1993), pp. 1–32; and James Morton, *Gangland. Volume 2. The Underworld in Britain and Ireland* (London: Warner edition, 1995), pp. 1–16 and pp. 247–50.
359. Chinn Letters, Robert Reid, no. 2, pp. 3–4.
360. *Ibid.*, Ernest Kyle, no. 1, p. 2.
361. Chinn Interviews, Matt O'Malley, p. 9.
362. *Ibid.*, Jack McGhee, p. 41.
363. Rev. W. J. Spriggs, *Gambling an Enemy of Our Youth* (London: 1890), p. 4.
364. Rev. John Roberts, 'Gambling', a paper read at the Monthly Meeting in Bryncrug 13 and 14 October 1890, printed in *Y Drysorfa*, vol. 61,

1891, pp. 289–2 (thanks to the National Library of Wales and to Mr Henson for translation). For other exposures of the un-Christian nature of gambling, see A Student, *Betting and Gambling* (London: Society for Promoting Christian Knowledge, 1895); Rev. Hugh Bradley, 'The Ethics of Gambling', *Holborn Review*, July 1926, pp. 342–7; Glass, *op. cit.*, pp. 62–8; Chamberlain, *op. cit.*; Rev. Peter Green, *Is Gambling Morally Wrong? An Enquiry* (London: Friends' Book Centre, n.d.), pp. 2–14; Rev. Peter Green, 'The Moral Aspects of Gambling', *Expository Times*, vol. 41, February 1930, p. 213–17; Rev. T. Isfryn Hughes, 'What's Wrong with Gambling?', *Yr Eurgrawn*, November/December 1937, pp. 404–9 (thanks to the National Library of Wales and to Mr Henson for translation); Rev. H. S. Marshall, 'Gambling', *Expository Times*, vol. 46, March 1935, pp. 265–7; Rev. E. C. Newhall, *Gambling* (London: New Church Missionary and Tract Society, 1930), pp. 7–9; 'Notes of Recent Exposition', *Expository Times*, vol. 62, no. 3, December 1950, pp. 65–7. There were fears that gambling was invading business and as such it had to be rooted out, see Arthur T. Barnet, 'Why are Betting and Gambling Wrong?', *Economic Review*, vol. 7, April 1897, pp. 168–71; A. E. Fletcher, *op. cit.*, pp. 826–7; Glass, *op. cit.*, pp. 33–7. W. R. Sorley, 'Betting and Gambling', *International Journal of Ethics*, vol. 13, July 1903, p. 429; and for a defence of insurance against the charge that it was a form of betting, see, for example, Alan J. Dorward, 'Betting and Insurance', *International Journal of Ethics*, vol. 25, July 1915, pp. 494–7.

365. Hogge, *op. cit.*, p. 9; Rev. C. W. L. Christien, *Betting, Gambling and the Bible. An Appeal to Young People* (London, 1896), pp. 22–3; Lambert, *op. cit.*, p. 8.
366. E. J. S., 'Betting and Gambling', *Barnsley and District Sunday School Union Journal*, December 1890 (thanks to Barnsley Libraries).
367. Stedman Jones, *Outcast London*, p. 1. See also William J. Fishman, *East End 1888. A Year in a London Borough among the Labouring Poor* (London: Duckworth & Co., 1988); Peter J. Keating, *Into Unknown England, 1866–1913. Selections from the Social Explorers* (London: Fontana, 1976); Standish Meacham, *A Life Apart. The English Working Class 1890–1914* (London: Thames and Hudson, 1977); and James H. Treble, *Urban Poverty in Britain 1830–1914* (first published 1979. London: Methuen, 1983).
368. Jack London, *The People of the Abyss* (first published 1903. Journeyman, 1977), pp. 80–95; Arnold White, *The Problems of a Great City* (first published 1886. New York: Garland, 1985), pp. 11–63. See also G. R. Searle, *The Quest for National Efficiency: A Study in British Politics and Political Thought 1899–1914* (Oxford: Blackwell, 1971); and Bernard Semmel, *Imperialism and Social Reform: English Social Imperial Thought* (London: George Allen & Unwin, 1960).
369. William Booth, *In Darkest England and the Way Out* (London: International Headquarters, 1890).
370. Reuben Manton, 'Darkest Grimsby. Gambling', *Grimsby News*, 10 July 1896; see Mark Clapson, 'Gambling, "The Fancy", and Poverty in Charles Booth's "Life and Labour of the People in London"' (1989 – paper read to the Charles Booth Conference), pp. 4–7.

371. Perkins, *The Problem of Gambling*, p. 59.
372. Frank Lenwood, *Gambling – Why Not?* (London: Independent Press, 1934), p. 70.
373. Ven. Archdeacon Madden, *The Folly and Fallacy of Betting and Gambling*, (London: English Church Manuals, 1913) p. 19; see also 'Our Great Work', *Bulletin*, vol. 1, no. 7, November 1893, p. 61; and J. Lewis Paton, formerly High Master of Manchester Grammar School, *The Right or Wrong of Gambling* (London: National Anti-Gambling League, n.d.), p. 5.
374. E. Rosslyn Mitchell, 'Why I Do Not Bet', *Listener*, February 1937, p. 263.
375. Rowland, *op. cit.*, p. 1; see also Blunt, *op. cit.*, p. 6; and Rev. Peter Green, *The Fight Against the Betting Evil. A Trumpet Call to You* (Manchester: Manchester Council of Christian Congregations and National Anti-Gambling League, n.d.), pp. 3–4.
376. George Ridding, Bishop of Southwell, *Betting and Gambling: A Sermon Preached at St. Mary's Nottingham* (Nottingham: 1891), p. 15; see also Christien, *op. cit.*, pp. 31–2.
377. Seton Churchill, *Betting and Gambling* (1894), p. 55.
378. David Dixon, '"Class Law": The Street Betting Act of 1906', *International Journal of the Sociology of Law*, vol. 8 (1980), p. 117.
379. For example, see the *Bulletin*, vol. 5, no. 59, February 1915, p. 114; Prince, *op. cit.*, p. 5. For attacks on the patriotism of bookies during the Second World War, see William Ebor etc., Letter, 'Gambling in Time of War', *The Times*, 15 January 1940; for a rebuttal of this kind of attack on 'gambling profiteers', see Captain Coe, *Star*, 27 May 1940. Bookmakers took great exception to attacks on their patriotism – not surprisingly, given that many of them had fought and had been wounded in the First World War. *Banyan* included regular features on bookmakers who had volunteered to fight and on those who were killed in the battle against Hitler, see for example Mr Barker Bleasdale (of Blackpool), *Banyan*, December 1942, p. 3; and 'Killed in Action, Pte. Frank McManus', *Banyan*, March 1943, p. 5.
380. 'Last Week's Problem', *Luton News and Bedfordshire Advertiser*, 8 December 1938.
381. Nimrod, 'The Anatomy of Gaming. Dissection IV', *Fraser's Magazine*, vol. 17, no. 99, p. 272.
382. Chinn Interviews, Simmy L., p. 1.
383. *Ibid.*, Lulu Mendoza, p. 1; *ibid.*, Lennie Da Costa, *passim*, and *ibid.*, Ali Harris, *passim*; *ibid.*, Lou Prince, p. 1.
384. Finn, *op. cit.*, pp. 18–19.
385. Cathal Bellingham (ed.), *Confessions of a Turf Crook Told by Himself* (London: P. Allan, 1924), p. 1; Brian Thomas, Secretary London Workers' Protection Association, S. C. (1901–2), *Minutes*, q. 2275–6, p. 564.
386. Chinn Letters, Mr S. Moses, no. 2, p. 1; *ibid.*, Mr P. J. Ryan, no. 1, p. 1 – see also Chinn Interviews, Joe Coral, *passim*.
387. *Ibid.*, Mrs V. Connor, p. 1; *ibid.*, Mr C. J. Morgan, no. 2, p. 7; Dundee Oral History Project, O17/A/1, pp. 1 and 44.
388. Ralph Glasser, *Growing Up in the Gorbals* (London: Pan, 1986).

389. Chinn Interviews, Jack McGhee, pp. 2 and 7.
390. Jacobs, *op. cit.*, p. 40; 'The Jews Get Their Extra Flutter', *Daily Mail*, 2 April 1968 (thanks to Tower Hamlets Libraries). See also Harry Benjamin, *Adventure in Living. The Autobiography of a Myope* (London: Health for All Publishing, 1950), p. 20; Mark Benney, *Low Company: Describing the Evolution of a Burglar* (London: Peter Davies, 1936), pp. 24–79; Al Burnett, *Knave of Clubs* (London: Arthur Barker, 1963), pp. 23–5 and 199–212; S. J. M. Fernando, 'Alcoholism and Gambling: the Case of the Jews', *Society for the Study of Gambling Newsletter*, no. 1, May 1982, pp. 16–21; Alexander Hartog, *Born to Sing* (London: Dennis Dobson, 1978), pp. 110–22; *Bulletin*, vol. 5, no. 50, November 1910, p. 14; and Jerry White, *Rothschild Buildings. Life in a East End Tenement Block 1887–1920* (London: Routledge & Kegan Paul, 1980), pp. 181–2. For a controversy over this issue, see Gus Dalrymple, 'My Date at the Commons', *Sporting Life*, 29 May 1965; and Rabbi L. Jacobs, 'Jews and Gambling', *Jewish Chronicle*, 17 November 1950.
391. Chinn Interviews, Lou Rose, p. 1.
392. *Ibid.*, Jack McGhee, p. 20; *ibid.*, Sam Dunleavy, p. 18.
393. *Ibid.*, Sam Dunleavy, p. 22.
394. *Ibid.*, Mr Lafferty, *passim*.
395. *Ibid.*, Sam Dunleavy, p. 21; *ibid.*, Matt O'Malley, pp. 24–5.
396. *Ibid.*, Lou Rose, p. 3.
397. Chinn Letters, Vince McGlennan, no. 1, p. 2.
398. Chinn Interviews, Mr R. Elliot, p. 6.
399. Chinn Letters, Peter McCusker, no. 2, p. 2, and Chinn Interviews, Jimmy Crawford, p. 10.
400. Chinn Letters, Mr E. McGuinness, no. 2, pp. 1–2; *ibid.*, Henry McQuade, no. 2, p. 3 – see also *ibid.*, Brian McQuade, no. 2, p. 1.
401. *Ibid.*, Walter Littlejohn, no. 2, p. 2.
402. *Ibid.*, Ernest Kyle, no. 2, p. 3.
403. Perrucci, *op. cit.*, p. 307.
404. Chinn Letters, John Rourke, nos 1 and 2, *passim*.
405. *Ibid.*, Peter Plunkett, nos 1 and 2, *passim*.
406. *Ibid.*, Wilson Ditty, no. 2, p. 1; Chinn Interviews, Frankie Goodwin, *passim*, and Meg Goodwin and John Adair, *passim*.
407. Chinn Letters, Mr G. Squires, no. 2, pp. 1–2.
408. For Northern Ireland, see Geoffrey Beatie, 'Bookies, Cops and Robbers', *Guardian*, 27 September 1986 – regarding Barney Eastwood; Chinn Letters, Professor Tom Lovett and Mr Peter McNamee, Ulster People's College, p. 1, and Dr Seamas O Cathain, p. 1, University College, Dublin.
409. Chinn Letters, Tom Carroll, no. 2, pp. 1–2. See also 'Death of Mr Billy Brady', *Catholic Guardian*, September 1969, thanks to Maureen Fitzgibbon and Celia Brady.
410. Chinn Interviews, Ken Wadsworth, p. 13.
411. Nellie Nicholas, *Chimney Pot Park* (unpublished MS, n.d., Salford Libraries), p. 7; Chinn Interviews, George Tiano, *passim*.
412. R. C. (1978) *Report*, vol. 1, pp. 21–3. See also Rabbi L. Jacobs, 'Jews and Gambling', *Jewish Chronicle*, 17 November 1950; Rev. W. Lillie,

'Gambling – A Problem for Christian Ethics', *Expository Times*, vol. 61, September 1950, pp. 348–50; Roman Catholic Church in England and Wales, 'Memorandum', R. C. (1949–51), *Minutes*, 8 March 1950; Alex Rubner, *The Economics of Gambling* (London: Macmillan, 1966), pp. 102–6.

413. Irish Free State, *Report of the Joint Committee on the Betting Act, 1926 and the Law Relating to the Business of Bookmaking, Interim Report* (Dublin: 1929); Irish Correspondent, 'Gambling in Eire', *Sunday Times*, 2 April 1935. See also The Betting Laws Committee (Northern Ireland), *Report of the Inquiry into the Lottery, Betting and Gaming Laws and the Practices Thereunder* (Belfast: His Majesty's Stationery Office, 1947), pp. 39–48. The first sweepstake was held in 1930 and it was banned in Britain in 1932 – another ineffective piece of legislation.
414. 'Catholic Pools', *New Statesman*, 7 January 1950.
415. Chinn Letters, Doris Hall, pp. 1–2.
416. Roman Catholic Church in England and Wales, 'Memorandum', R. C. (1949–51), *Minutes*, 8 March 1950.
417. 'A Catholic Statement on Betting', *Clergy Review*, n.s., vol. 34, no. 2, August 1950, pp. 100–4.
418. Chinn Interviews, Matt O'Malley, pp. 25 and 60–1.
419. 'The Raid on Racing Ticket Sellers and Betting Houses', *St Helens News*, 22 November 1884 (thanks to St Helens Libraries).
420. Perkins, *Gambling in English Life* (revised edn, London: Epworth Press, 1958), p. 94.
421. *Church Times*, 31 August 1934.
422. 'Gambling', *Sunday Observer*, 25 April 1951; see also J. P. K. Byrnes, 'A Study of Differences Between the Anglican and Methodist Churches on Such Questions as Drink and Gambling', in W. S. F. Pickering (ed.), *Anglican–Methodist Relations. Some Institutional Factors* (London: Darton, Longman & Todd, 1961), pp. 170–3.
423. Chinn Letters, Ivor Edwards, no. 2, pp. 1–2.
424. Hopcraft, *op. cit.*, p. 69.
425. For example, see Rev. J. Hutchison Cockburn, Rev. A. Chisholm, and Rev. I. D. Nelson – on behalf of the Church and Nation Committee of the Church of Scotland, 'Statement', R. C. (1932–3) *Minutes*, 29 September 1932; Commissioner David Lamb – the Salvation Army, 'Statement', *ibid.*, 29 September 1932; The Most Reverend and Right Honourable William Temple, Rev. S. W. Hughes, Rev. E. Benson Perkins – Christian Social Council, 'Statement', *ibid.*, 19 October 1932.

7 STREET BOOKIES: REPRESSION AND RESISTANCE

1. 'Twenty-Four Years' Chronological Record', *Bulletin*, vol. 6, no. 72, May 1918, p. 96 (thanks to the Library of the Society of Friends for access to post-1912 material belonging to the National Anti-Gambling League). See also John Gulland – NAGL, 'Statement', R. C. (1932), *Minutes*, 30 September 1932, and for a scholarly study of this pressure group, see David Dixon, *From Prohibition to Regulation. Bookmaking, Anti-Gambling, and the Law* (Oxford: Oxford University Press, 1991).
2. 'The National Anti-Gambling League', back cover, J. Ramsay

Macdonald, *Gambling and Citizenship* (London: National Anti-Gambling League, n.d.).

3. For example, see 'Anti-Gambling Movement at Lancaster', *Lancaster Guardian*, 24 November 1906 (thanks to Lancashire Libraries, Lancaster); 'Anti-Gambling League', *Wigan Observer*, 12 October 1907 (thanks to Wigan Libraries); and *Bolton Journal and Guardian*, 10 October 1902. The pledge of the league read: 'By the help of Almighty God I hereby pledge myself to abstain from all forms of Betting and Gambling, and will do my utmost to discountenance the habit among my companions' (n.d., Library of Society of Friends, 059.7, Gamb 1/14).
4. 'Betting Crusade', *Yorkshire Gazette*, 26 May 1906 (thanks to North Yorkshire Libraries); 'Anti-Gambling Crusade', *Leader*, 28 March 1907, see also, 'Nelson and Gambling', *ibid.* (thanks to Lancashire Libraries, Nelson).
5. 'On Losin' m' Last 'Arf-Crown' (London: National Anti-Gambling League, n.d., Library of Society of Friends, 059.7, Gamb 1/9); for a leaflet in poem form, see 'Are You Betting?', *Bulletin*, vol. 5, no. 53, August 1913, p. 53. See also 'Betting. A Boy to a Bishop!' (London: National Anti-Gambling League, n.d.), and 'Shall I Bet?' (London: National Anti-Gambling League, n.d., Library of the Society of Friends, 059.7, Gamb 1/13 and 1/16); see also 'Great Anti-Gamblers', *Bulletin*, vol. 5, no. 50, November 1912, p. 20.
6. B. Seebohm Rowntree, 'The Repression of Gambling', in Rowntree (ed.), *op. cit.*, pp. 170–80.
7. John Hawke, 'Existing Legislation', in Rowntree (ed.), *op. cit.*, pp. 149–52. See also Dey, *op. cit.*, pp. 344–5; Gretton, *op. cit.*, pp. 422–3; Sarl, *op. cit.*, p. 25; and Shoolbred, *op. cit.*, pp. 114–1
8. John Hawke, S. C. (1901–2), *Minutes*, q. 133, p. 364. For a similar attempt to quash ready-money betting on racecourses in 1874, see J. Fairfax-Blakeborough, 'Betting and the Law', *Banyan*, July 1949, pp. 28–9.
9. 'Ten Million People in a City of No News', *Weekly News* (Dundee), 2 April 1955; see also 'Fleet Street without Newspapers', *Yorkshire Post*, 25 March 1955.
10. John Hawke, *A Blot on the Queen's Reign. Betting and Gambling. An Appeal to the Prince of Wales* (London: Elliot Stock, 1893), p. 27.
11. Perkins, *The Problem of Gambling*, p. 15; see also Glass, *op. cit.*, pp. 85–8.
12. *Bulletin*, vol. 1, no. 10, May 1895, p. 103. The rhyme was printed originally in 'All The Winners', *Punch*, 12 May 1894, p. 225.
13. Chinn Letters, Joe Savage, no. 2, p. 1; *ibid.*, Mr J. Smith, p. 1.
14. *Ibid.*, James Whelan, no. 1, p. 1; *ibid.*, James Bromley, no. 2, p. 2.
15. *Ibid.*, Mrs G. Strachan, no. 1, p. 1.
16. *Ibid.*, Mr A. McIntyre, no. 1, p. 4. See also Hogge, *The Facts of Gambling*, p. 26.
17. Russell Allen, S. C. (1901–2), *Minutes*, q. 1588–1608, pp. 536–7; see also Rev. Canon Atkinson, *Betting and Gambling. A Paper Read at the Lincoln Diocesan Conference* (Lincoln: 1897), pp. 6–7.
18. Canon Peter Green, R. C. (1932–3), *Minutes*, para 6800, p. 396. In 1953, BBC Television covered a dog-meeting – but gave no betting

information, 'Parliamentary Notes', *Banyan*, October 1953, p. 65. Four years later it was suggested that BBC Radio could regain 3,000,000 lost listeners 'if only it would report the starting prices of winners and placed horses', David Livingstone-Learnmouth, 'Gambling and the B.B.C.', *Field*, 29 August 1957.

19. Claud Cockburn, *I Claud* (Harmondsworth: Penguin, 1967), pp. 156–7.
20. Edward Fry, *Betting Newspapers and Quakerism. A Letter Addressed to Members of the Society of Friends* (Failand, near Bristol: 1911 – thanks to Somerset Libraries, Taunton).
21. Lord Sands, 'Gambling', in Professor W. Paterson and Dr David Watson (ed.), *Social Evils and Problems. The Church of Scotland Commission on the War* (Edinburgh: William Blackwood and Sons, 1918), p. 127; *A Reply (Addressed to Members of the Society of Friends) to a Pamphlet by Sir Edward Fry* (London: Headley Brothers, 1911 – thanks to Somerset Libraries, Taunton). See also 'The Ethics of Gambling', *Spectator*, 23 May 1914, pp. 858–60. For newspapers and betting in general see Rev. H. Allen Job and Mr G. Hunt, 'Statement', R. C. (1932–3), *Minutes*, 21 October 1932, and Mr R. M. Barrington Ward, editor of *The Times*, 'Statement', R. C. (1932–3), *Minutes*, 15 December 1932.
22. John Hawke, 'Existing Legislation', in Rowntree (ed.), *op. cit.*, p. 166.
23. *Bulletin*, vol. 1, no. 9, November 1894, p. 95; Borough of Leicester, *21st Annual Report of the Free Libraries Committee* (1891–2), pp. 6–7 (thanks to Leicestershire Libraries).
24. For example, see 'Blacking Out', *Weekly Sentinel*, 9 April 1898 (thanks to Stoke-on-Trent Libraries).
25. 'Obliterating Betting News', *Bolton Journal*, 20 April 1905; see also 'Librarians' Conference Glasgow. Publication of Betting News. Speech by Dr Carnegie', *Glasgow Herald*, 18 September 1907.
26. Wigan Public Library Committee, *Minutes*, 18 May 1905, p. 499; Wigan Public Library, *Suggested Blocking-Out of Racing News. Summary of Returns* (1905), p. 1 (thanks to Wigan Libraries).
27. Michael McLaverty, *The Three Brothers* (London: Jonathan Cape, 1948), p. 53 (thanks to the Belfast Library and Society for Promoting Knowledge).
28. 'Betting News', Huddersfield Library file VF203. For inter-war pressure by moralists, see Chinn Letters, Clackmannan Libraries; 'Newspapers and Betting', *Glasgow Herald*, 15 November 1922. See also Anthony Hugh Thompson, *Censorship in Public Libraries in the United Kingdom during the Twentieth Century* (Epping: Bowker, 1975), pp. 82–91.
29. Chinn Letters, Wolverhampton Libraries, p. 1. For the 1930s see: 'Blacking Out Racing News', *Edinburgh Evening News*, 2 December 1938 (thanks to Edinburgh Libraries); 'Gamblers and Derby Reading Room', *Derby Daily Telegraph*, 17 July 1931 (thanks to Derbyshire Libraries); Librarian – Amateur Policeman', *Northampton Independent*, 10 April 1936 (thanks to Northamptonshire Libraries); 'Library Ban', *Reporter*, 20 September 1930 (regarding Stalybridge – thanks to Tameside Libraries); 'News-Thirsty Public', *Grimsby Evening Telegraph*, 12 October 1933 (thanks to Humberside Libraries); Racing News Blacked Out at Rhyl Library', *Manchester Guardian*, 21 August 1936; 'Spotting the Winner', *Evening Star*, June 1939 (thanks to Ipswich

Libraries). Other libraries continued to obliterate racing information until a late date, among them: Chiswick (early 1950s); Lambeth (1950s); Liverpool (early 1970s); Newcastle-upon-Tyne (1950s); Nottingham (early 1950s – thanks to Ralph Gee); Rotherham (1958); South Shields (1950s); Sunderland (1961); Swansea (*c.* 1959); Walthamstow (early 1960s) – my thanks to the relevant librarians. As late as 1955, it was decided to black out the racing pages in Tonbridge, *Advertiser*, 19 October 1955 (thanks to Kent Libraries, Tonbridge).

30. Chinn Letters, Eric Jenkins, no. 1, p. 1.
31. *Ibid.*, Ronald Garnett, pp. 1–2.
32. *A Sketch of Worthing and Its Environs etc.* (Worthing: 1813), pp. 83–5 (thanks to West Sussex Libraries, Worthing).
33. Chinn Letters, Oxfordshire County Librarian, p. 1; Moriarty, *op. cit.*, p. 334.
34. John Hawke, 'Our Principles and Programme', *News Review*, vol. 10, no. 61, June 1894, 706; John Hawke, S. C. (1901–2), *Minutes*, q. 230, p. 373. As late as 1918, Lord Sands advocated that 'bookmaking, like fortune-telling, should be made an unlawful calling', *op. cit.*, p. 142. Even harsher measures were suggested by Atkinson – among them the sacking of employees who were found betting, *op. cit.*, p. 10. In the Isle of Man, an Act was passed later which banned betting by telephone or letter either on horse-racing or on football, M' Elroy, *op. cit.*, p. 19. Betting shops were not legalized there until 1970, 'Manxmen May Soon Have Betting Shops', *Sporting Life*, 5 March 1969.
35. Dixon, 'Class Law', pp. 104–9.
36. R. C. (1932–3), *Report*, pp. 13–14.
37. Shoolbred, *op. cit.*, pp. 227–8.
38. Huntley Jenkins, F. W. Morley and E. J. Purchase, *The Law Relating to Betting Offences* (London: Stevens & Son, 1912) p. 2; Dixon, 'Class Law', p. 109.
39. Cited in Dixon, 'Class Law', p. 109.
40. Chinn Letters, John Francis Givens, no. 2, p. 2; Chinn Interviews, Matt O'Malley, pp. 3–5.
41. 'State Lotteries', *Truth*, 13 October 1938. See also 'Working-class Gambling Hells', *Truth*, 13 January 1937; and 'The Everlasting "No"', *New Statesman*, 14 April 1923, pp. 9–10.
42. Samuel Hardman, *'In the Days of My Youth'. Some Early Reminiscences of Stand Lane, Radcliffe* (Radcliffe: Radcliffe Printing Co., 1921), p. 122.
43. Peter Donnelly, *The Yellow Rock* (London: Eyre & Spottiswoode, 1950), p. 113; see also Scottish Police Federation, 'Memorandum', R. C. (1949–51), *Minutes*, 12 April 1950.
44. David Dixon, 'Anti-Gambling and the State: Development in the Legal Control of Betting in England and Wales 1890–1929', University of Wales, unpublished PhD thesis, 1985, pp. 33–4.
45. W. H. Norris, *A Hint to the Clergy and Anti-Gambling Crusades from a Bookmaker and Backer* (London: 1894), pp. 1–14. Before the First World War, the National Sporting League was vigorous in the defence of bookmaking, betting and the publication of racing information, see William Allison, 'The Special Commissioner', *Memories of Men and*

Horses (London: Grant Richards, 1922), pp. 215–17; Dey, *op. cit.*, pp. 352–5.
46. Chinn Letters, John Francis Givens, no. 2, p. 1.
47. Robert Peacock, Chief Constable of Manchester, S. C. (1901–2), *Minutes*, q. 293–7, p. 13.
48. Cited in Dixon, 'Class Law', p. 120.
49. *Ibid.*
50. Bailey, *op. cit.*, p. 94.
51. John Monk, *The Memoirs of Chief Inspector John Monk (Metropolitan Police) 1859–1946* (unpublished MS, n.d. – I am grateful to Clive Emsley for access to this source), pp. 70 and 111.
52. David Dixon, 'Illegal Gambling and Histories of Policing', *Society for the Study of Gambling Newsletter*, no. 3, April 1983, p. 4.
53. Monk, *op. cit.*, p. 59.
54. Chinn Letters, John Solway, no. 1, p. 1; *ibid.*, Cliff French, no. 1, p. 2.
55. *Ibid.*, Edmund King, no. 1, p. 1.
56. *Bulletin*, vol. 2, no. 22, May 1901, p. 273.
57. Chinn Letters, Bob Sinclair, no. 2, p. 3; *ibid.*, Bill Smith, no. 1, p. 1.
58. *Ibid.*, Jos Harding, no. 1, p. 1.
59. *Ibid.*, Stan Tennet, no. 1, pp. 3–4; *ibid.*, James Lee, no. 1, p. 2.
60. *Ibid.*, Jimmy Addison, no. 1, p. 1. For similar recollections, see Commissioner of Police of the Metropolis, 'Memorandum', R. C. (1949–51), *Minutes*, 25 October 1949; Chinn Letters, James Lee, no. 2, pp. 1–2; *ibid.*, Jos Harding, no. 3, p. 2 (Sunderland); *ibid.*, Winifred Hughes, no. 1, p. 1 (Birmingham); *ibid.*, Terry Monaghan, no. 1, p. 2 (Newcastle); and *ibid.* Lorna Morton, no. 1, p. 2 (South Shields).
61. *Ibid.*, Anonymous, p. 1.
62. 'Hostile Crowd and Police', *Liverpool Daily Post*, 14 December 1937; 'Marylebone. Police Raid on Betting-house Ends in Fight', *Morning Advertiser*, 26 May 1937.
63. Chinn Letters, Terry Monaghan, no. 1, p. 1.
64. *Ibid.*, Wilson Ditty, no. 1, p. 1; *ibid.*, Jean Irwin, no. 2, p. 2. The cry 'Edge Up!' was famous in Glasgow, see 'The Story of the Three X Double', *op. cit.*
65. Chinn Letters, Catherine Wilson, no. 2, p. 2; *ibid.*, Mr H. McLennan, no. 2, p. 1.
66. *Ibid.*, May Anderson, no. 2, p. 1; *ibid.*, Tom Sprowell, p. 1. See also *ibid.*, Anne Spence, no. 2, p. 2.
67. *Bulletin*, vol. 5, no. 57, August 1914, p. 115; S. C. (1923), *Report*, p. xiii.
68. Mr John Maxwell, Chief Constable of Manchester, 'Statement', R. C. (1932–3), *Minutes*, 21 July 1932; Sir Charles Haughton Rafter, Chief Constable of Birmingham, 'Statement', *ibid.*
69. Chinn Letters, K. Wolfenden, no. 2, p. 2.
70. *Ibid.*, Mr J. Stephens, no. 1, pp. 4–5.
71. Robert Roberts, *op. cit.*, pp. 16 and 36–7.
72. Otto Newman, cited in Harris, *op. cit.*, p. 31 – see also Martin, *op. cit.*, p. 275; Davies, *op. cit.*, p. 201.
73. Chinn Letters, Robert Reid, nos 1 and 2, *passim*; *ibid.*, Anna Campbell, nos 1 and 2, *passim.*
74. *Ibid.*, Samuel Watts, no. 1, p. 6; *ibid.*, Alf Holdsworth, no. 1, p. 1.

75. *Ibid*., James Cowie, no. 1, pp. 1–2.
76. Ron Barnes, *Coronation Cups and Jam Jars. A Portrait of an East End Family Through Three Generations* (London: Centreprise, 1976), p. 55.
77. Chinn Letters, Gerry Beck, no. 1, pp. 1–3; *ibid*., Arthur Rollason, no. 1, p. 1; *ibid*., Mr S. Murphy, nos 1 and 2.
78. Foot, *op. cit*., p. 2.
79. 'Britain's Betting Industry – II', *The Economist*, 7 March 1936, p. 517.
80. R. C. (1949–51), *Report*, p. 47.
81. Chinn Letters, Mr L. Piper, no. 2, p. 1; see also letter of James Donachy, 19 October 1932 (NAB File, 'Donachy'), pp. 1–2.
82. Chinn Letters, Ernest Kyle, no. 2, p. 1.
83. *Ibid*., Anna Campbell, no. 1, p. 1; see also 'Glasgow Woman Bookmaker Fined', *Glasgow Herald*, 5 July 1923.
84. Chinn Letters, Mrs Smith, p. 4; *ibid*., F. Thompson, no. 2, p. 1.
85. *Ibid*., Paul Clavering, no. 2, p. 1; *ibid*., Frank Harrison, no. 1, p. 2.
86. *Ibid*., Nicky Marshall, p. 1.
87. *Ibid*., Mr A. Roseman, no. 2, p. 1.
88. *Ibid*., Mr A. Jones, no. 2, p. 1; Chinn Interviews, Cyril Beesley, p. 7.
89. Chinn Letters, John Bullivant, no. 1, pp. 1–4; see also *ibid*., Mr S. Murphy, no. 1, pp. 1–2.
90. *Ibid*., Mrs G. Shaw, no. 1, pp. 2–3.
91. Barnes, *op. cit*., p. 59.
92. Chinn Letters, Bill Smith, no. 1, pp. 1–2.
93. *Ibid*., Mr T. Carse, pp. 1–2.
94. *Ibid*., Ann Watt, no. 1, p. 3.
95. Chinn Interviews, Alfie Spittle, p. 10; for a man who owned his pitch and who did not receive commission, see *ibid*., Cyril Beesley, *passim*.
96. Chinn Letters, Josephine Bolam, no. 1, p. 1.
97. Chinn Interviews, Mr Brown, pp. 1–2.
98. Chinn Letters, Mary Brown, no. 1, p. 1.
99. *Ibid*., Bill Archibald, no. 1, pp. 3–6.
100. 'Street Bookie Pays £2,000 a Year in Fines', *South London Press*, 18 December 1959.
101. Chinn Interviews, Norman Miller, p. 20.
102. Chinn Letters, Albert Donkin, no. 1, p. 1.
103. *Ibid*., Jim Jordan, pp. 3–4.
104. *Ibid*., J. Forbes, no. 2, p. 1.
105. *Ibid*., T. McGunigle, no. 1, p. 1; *ibid*., Forbes B. Steel, no. 1, pp. 1–2; Chinn Interviews, Ned Cooper, *passim*.
106. *Ibid*., the Forbes family, p. 22; see also Chinn Letters, Robert Reid, no. 2, p. 1 (Maryhill).
107. Ashley, *op. cit*., p. 29; Chinn Interviews, John Dolman, p. 1 (thanks to Smethwick Local History Society); Chinn Letters, Jeanne Burton, no. 2, p. 2; *ibid*., R. Wallis-Clarke, no. 1, p. 1. See also Cleveland County Oral History Project, accession no. 102, p. 5 (Hartlepool).
108. Chinn Letters, Mrs M. Harvey, no. 2, p. 1.
109. For a discussion of the importance of the street to poorer working-class people, see Chinn, *They Worked All Their Lives*, pp. 23–4.
110. Chinn Letters, Mr J. Kelly, no. 1, p. 1.
111. *Ibid*., James Cowie, no. 2, pp. 3–4.

112. *Ibid.*, Walter Littlejohn, no. 1, p. 4.
113. A. J. Frain, 'Bets Shops Won't Kill Honest Joe', *Newcastle Journal*, 23 March 1955.
114. Chinn Letters, Teddy Dean, no. 1, pp. 1–2.
115. *Ibid.*, Lew Reeves, no. 2, p. 3.
116. Clapson, 'Popular Gambling and English Culture', p. 171.
117. Chinn Letters, S. H. Woodier, pp. 2–3.
118. Chinn Interviews, Trevor Newbold, pp. 18–19; see also Chinn Letters, Kenneth G. Blackburn, no. 2, p. 1.
119. Peter Keenan, *Glasgow Evening Times*, 6 February 1979; Chinn Letters, Charles Dearden, no. 1, p. 4; *ibid.*, John Shaw, no. 2, p. 3.
120. *Ibid.*, Mrs A. Dean, p. 5; *ibid.*, Joe Gray, no. 2, p. 1; *ibid.*, William Later, no. 2, p. 1.
121. *Ibid.*, Les Kane, no. 2, p. 4. For 'official' charity from bookmakers, see for example 'Disaster', *Fairplay*, May 1938 – regarding collections following the Gresford and Markham Colliery Disasters; 'Our "Bairns Effort"', *Fairplay*, July 1938 – regarding a day trip for 800 mothers and children, organized by the Northern BPA; and *Salford City Reporter*, 15 June 1938 – regarding the annual distribution to poor children of 10,000 pairs of boots and shoes.
122. Chinn Letters, Eva Somerset, no. 1, pp. 1–3. For other bookies from poor backgrounds, see Gus Dalrymple, 'Gus Dalrymple's Diary', *Sporting Life*, 26 August 1962 – regarding Jim Windsor; and Jack Overhill, *The Money Bug: A Novel* (unpublished MS, 1944, in Cambridge Library – this autobiographical novel was based on Mr Overhill's rise to bookmaking prosperity).
123. Chinn Letters, Mrs M. E. Heaton, no. 2, p. 2; Chinn Interviews, Trevor Newbold, pp. 19–20.
124. Chinn Letters, Henry McQuade, no. 1, pp. 6–7; see also *ibid.*, Maurice McMahon, no. 1, p. 3.
125. *Ibid.*, Joe Savage, nos 1 and 2, *passim*; *ibid.*, Peter Plunkett, no. 2, p. 2.
126. James D. Young, *Making Trouble. Autobiographical Explorations and Socialism* (Glasgow: Clydeside Press, 1989), p. 20 (thanks to Dorothy Thompson for this reference); see also May Hobbs, *Born to Struggle* (London: Quartet Books, 1973), pp. 109–26.
127. *Sunday Sun*, 15 June 1947, cited in *Mass Gambling*, p. 152.
128. See Robert Brown, Letter, *Daily Record* (1988 – cutting supplied by Wilson Ditty); Chinn Letters, Wilson Ditty, no. 1, p. 2; and *ibid.*, John Moir, no. 2, p. 5.
129. *Ibid.*, Jean Irwin, no. 1, p. 2; *ibid.*, Tommy Tait, no. 1, p. 1.
130. *Ibid.*, Anna Campbell, no. 2, p. 1.
131. *Ibid.*, James Bromley, no. 1, p. 3; Chinn Interviews, Matt O'Malley, p. 17; *ibid.*, Buck Chinn, *passim.*
132. *Ibid.*, Mr Knowles, p. 19.
133. *Ibid.*, Ernie Cashmore, *passim*; *ibid.*, Horace Foster, tape 3, pp. 1–8 – see also photograph of pensioners' outing paid for by bookie Tom Swift, *East London Advertiser*, 12 August 1962.
134. Chinn Letters, Michael Quinn, no. 1, p. 1.
135. *Ibid.*, Mrs J. Clarke, no. 2, p. 1; *ibid.*, Mrs Morphew, p. 1.
136. *Ibid.*, Peter J. Collar, no. 1, p. 1.

137. *Ibid.*, R. W. Jefferis, no. 1, p. 3; *ibid.*, Ivor Edwards, no. 1, p. 1; see also Clive Emsley Interviews, Nat Taylor, West Sussex Police, p. 7.
138. *Ibid.*, Frederick C. Moffatt, no. 1, p. 1.
139. *Ibid.*, Kenneth Batt, no. 2, p. 2.
140. *Ibid.*, Mr H. Hawkes, no. 1, p. 2.
141. Chinn Interviews, Ernest Wheeler, p. 2.
142. Samuel Chisolm, Lord Provost of Glasgow, S. C. (1901–2), *Minutes*, q. 1915, p. 553.
143. Chinn Letters, John Moir, no. 1, p. 2.
144. *Ibid.*, Frank Southall, no. 1, p. 1; *ibid.*, Mrs A. M. Zebrzyski, no. 1, p. 1; *ibid.*, Mr A. Burnett, no. 1, p. 4.
145. *Ibid.*, J. Abbott, no. 1, pp. 4–5. See also Arthur W. Battle, *This Job's not Like It Used to be* (unpublished MS, n.d. – thanks to Clive Emsley for access to this source, which relates to Hoxton), p. 35; Chinn Letters, Norman King, no. 1, pp. 4–5; Edward Lyscom, *London Policeman* (unpublished MS, n.d. – thanks to Clive Emsley for access to this source, which refers to Islington); and 'P.C. in Woman's Clothes', *St Pancras Chronicle*, 23 October 1938.
146. Chinn Letters, Mary Pearson, no. 1, p. 4; *ibid.*, Irene Rowe, no. 1, p. 1.
147. *Ibid.*, James Crawford, no. 1, pp. 1–2.
148. *Ibid.*, Lew Warren, p. 2.
149. *Ibid.*, A. W. Dance, no. 1, pp. 1–2.
150. See, for example, Evidence of Sir Charles Biron, Chief Magistrate of the Police Courts of the Metropolis, R. C. (1932–3), *Minutes*, 13 October 1932, q. 3001, p. 213.
151. Chinn Letters, Fred Calvert, no. 1, pp. 2–5.
152. *Ibid.*, Mr A. Morfitt, no. 1, pp. 2–3; *ibid.*, Jack Bullivant, no. 1, pp. 2–3; *ibid.*, Jack Brodie, no. 1, pp. 1–2.
153. *Ibid.*, C. Percy, no. 1, p. 2; *ibid.*, John W., no. 1, p. 1; *ibid.*, Mr W. Flood, pp. 2–5; *ibid.*, G. Steele, no. 1, pp. 1–2. See also *ibid.*, Mr W. Sutton, pp. 1–3.
154. *Ibid.*, C. Percy, no. 1, p. 1 – see also *ibid.*, G. Steele, no. 1, p. 1; *ibid.*, R. M. Gallagher, no. 1, p. 1.
155. City of Birmingham, *Police Orders*, 28 July 1904 – see also City of Birmingham, *Permanent Police Orders (Supplementary)*, no. 6, 17 October 1904 (thanks to the Chief Constable of the West Midlands for access to this material); Chinn Interviews, Fred Sutton, pp. 4–5.
156. Monk, *op. cit.*, p. 59; see also *Bulletin*, vol. 5, no. 49, August 1912, p. 5.
157. Chinn Letters, Edmund King, no. 1, pp. 1–2; see also Anthony Judge, *A Man Apart. The British Policeman and His Job* (London: Arthur Barker, 1972), pp. 158–60.
158. Chinn Letters, Hetty Bradbury, p. 1; see also *ibid.*, Rose Tunnah, no. 1, pp. 1–4; and Chinn Interviews, Horace Foster, p. 9. For Dundee, see 'Gave 10/– to Policeman. Cripple Woman Fined', *Dundee Courier and Advertiser*, 28 January 1937 (thanks to North East Fife Libraries). See also Harry Daley, *This Small Cloud. A Personal Memoir* (London: Weidenfeld and Nicolson, 1986), pp. 92–135.
159. George Fancourt, *The Police Service of George Frederick Fancourt: Birmingham City Police 1929–1960* (unpublished MS, n.d. – I am grateful to Clive Emsley for access to this source).

160. Chinn Letters, Cliff French, no. 1, pp. 3–5.
161. *Ibid.*, Terry Nattrass, no. 2, p. 1.
162. Chinn Interviews, Terry Saunders, p. 11.
163. Chinn Letters, John Solway, no. 1, p. 2. See also Sir Trevor Bigham, Deputy Commissioner of Police of the Metropolis, 'Statement', R. C. (1932–3), *Minutes*, 1 July 1932; Lysom, *op. cit.*, p. 184; Chinn Interviews, Ted Schuck, *passim* (formerly a member of the West Midlands Police Force).
164. Chinn Letters, John Sands, p. 1.
165. Chinn Interviews, Buck Chinn, p. 20.
166. For Brighton, see Robert Traini, 'Drama as Town Learns of Bribery Suspect', *Daily Herald*, 3 October 1957, and Chinn Letters, Mr T. E. Murphy, no. 1, p. 1; for Leeds, see for example 'Police Chief Reports on Complaints by Bookies', *Daily Mail*, 6 June 1953, 'Leeds Move on Police Probe Reply', *Yorkshire Evening Post*, 14 September 1954 (thanks to Leeds Libraries); Gilbert Kelland, *Crime in London* (first published 1987. London: Grafton Books, 1987), pp. 31–49; see also Battle, *op. cit.*, pp. 35–6; and Smithies, *op. cit.*, pp. 127–9.
167. Chinn Interviews, Gilbert Kelland, p. 1.

8 BETTING SHOPS

1. Dixon, 'Anti-Gambling and the State', p. 75.
2. 'Betting Evil. New Scottish League Formed', *Glasgow Herald*, 22 November 1927.
3. 'Movie Evidence', *Birmingham Post*, 12 August 1933; 'Bookies Who Soak the Poor', *South London Observer*, 25 March 1937.
4. 'Bookmakers Sent to Prison', *Fairplay*, July 1938, 'Justiciary Appeal Court', *Scotsman*, 2 February 1938, *South London Observer*, 19 March 1937; 'Silent Witness', *Cinema*, 26 May 1937, 'Masked Police Witnesses', *Banyan*, May 1939, p. 83. See also 'Determined to Try and Stamp This Thing Out', *Western Daily Press and Bristol Mirror*, 21 July 1933; 'Edinburgh's "Army" of 1,000 Street Bookies', *Noon Record*, 16 June 1938; 'Last Warning on Street Betting', *Daily Herald*, 29 May 1937.
5. 'Hopeless War on Betting in Bristol', *Evening World and Evening Times*; S. C. (1923), *Report*, xiv. This report concluded that 'the imposition of a betting duty was practicable', but in 1926, the Finance Act imposed an excise duty in Great Britain on every bet made with a bookmaker on an event of any kind, R. C. (1932–3), *Report*, pp. 14–15. The measure was aimed chiefly at legal bookies, but it was a disaster and it was repealed in 1929; see Christopher C. Hood, *The Limits of Administration* (London: John Wiley & Sons, 1976), pp. 171–81; Collingwood Hughes, *Bets and the Betting Tax* (London: Henry J. Drane, 1927). A few illegal bookies took out a licence under the act , but this did not legalize their operations; it merely registered them for payment, see Chinn Interviews, Albert Stanton, *passim*, and Chinn Letters, Ernest Wheeler, p. 1.
6. Sir Charles Haughton Rafter, Chief Constable of Birmingham, 'Statement', R. C. (1932–3), *Minutes*, 21 July 1932.
7. R. C. (1932–3), *Report*, pp. 101–6.

8. Chinn Letters, Wilf Murphy, no. 1, p. 1.
9. 'Bookmakers Fined Out of Business', *Daily Dispatch*, 25 November 1933.
10. See Davies, *op. cit.*, pp. 193–7; and Andrew Davies, 'The Police and the People: Gambling in Salford, 1900–1939', *Historical Journal*, 34, 1 (1991), pp. 87–115. Bowen was a member of the Manchester and Salford Brotherhood Federation, and on their behalf he had made a detailed statement to the R. C. (1932–3), *Minutes*, 20 October 1932.
11. 'Street Betting', *Manchester Guardian*, 7 January 1936.
12. 'Legalise Cash Betting', *Daily Express*, 6 February 1936.
13. 'Legalising Ready Money Betting', *News of the World*, 12 January 1936; see also 'Bookmakers' Opposition. Move to Legalise Street Betting', *Leeds Mercury*, 8 January 1936; *Sporting Life*, 7 January 1936.
14. 'Ready-Money Bets. Home Office Reply to Salford's Proposal', *Manchester Guardian*, 7 March 1936.
15. In 1938, A. P. Herbert failed to have enacted a Bill to legalize cash betting by post, A. P. Herbert, 'The Case of the Missing Letter Box', *Spectator*, 15 February 1963.
16. James Christie, Chief Constable of Greenock, 'Statement', R. C. (1932–3), *Minutes*, 22 July 1932.
17. Chinn Letters, Mr Lafferty, p. 1.
18. 'Gambling by Telephone', *Glasgow Herald*, 27 November 1907.
19. Chinn Letters, Gerald Lucas, no. 1, p. 2; *ibid.*, James Condron, no. 2, p. 1. See also *ibid.*, John Francis Givens, no. 1, p. 1.
20. For Glasgow, see Alastair Borthwick, 'You Bet', *Glasgow Evening Citizen*, 9 and 12 March 1956. See also Chinn Interviews, Frankie Goodwin, Norman Miller, Matt O'Malley, *passim*; Chinn Letters, Mr S. Murphy, no. 2, p. 1.
21. *Ibid.*, Ernest Kyle, no. 1, *passim*; see also Alastair Borthwick, 'But Still They Pull in the Bookies', *News Chronicle*, 27 April 1956.
22. Chinn Interviews, Ron Hanley, pp. 1–4; see also 'Betting Sessions in Hull Clubs to End', *Hull Daily Mail*, 22 October 1954.
23. Chinn Letters, Bill Gleghorn, no. 2, pp. 2–3.
24. *Ibid.*, G. Squires, no. 1, pp. 2–4.
25. Chinn Interviews, Mrs Rylance, pp. 1–5.
26. Chinn Letters, J. K. Green, no. 2, pp. 3–4. For Blackburn see *ibid.*, Margaret Aspin, no. 1, pp. 3–4, and no. 2, pp. 1–2; and for Stockport see *ibid.*, Eric Thornley Downs, no. 1, pp. 1–3. See also 'Betting Shops in England', *News of the World*, 13 December 1949.
27. Chinn Interviews, Albert Hampson, p. 15; see also, Fred Shawcross, 'The Punter's Paradise', *Today*, 6 March 1986.
28. R. C. (1949–51), *Report*, *passim.*
29. Chinn Letters, Barbara Gardiner, no. 1, p. 1; see also Fred Redman, 'Farce of the Betting Shops. The Danger of a Laughed-At Law', *Sunday Pictorial*, 3 June 1956.
30. Jack Stoneley, 'You Bet It's Very Easy . . . in Punters' Paradise', *Daily Mirror*, 23 May 1958; '"Betting Shops" in York', *Yorkshire Evening Post*, 10 December 1959 – see also 'Betting Shop Business: The "Inside" Story', *Yorkshire Evening Post*, 11 February 1960; Fred Redman, 'Farce of the Betting Shops. The Danger of a Laughed-at Law', *Sunday*

Pictorial, 3 June 1956 – see also 'Betting Shops Openly Defy the Police', *Daily Sketch*, 25 November 1955, 'And Why *NOT* Betting Shops?', *Daily Sketch*, 26 November 1955.

31. Chinn Letters, G. Ritson, no. 1, p. 1; *ibid.*, T. E. Nattrass, no. 1, p. 1; *ibid.*, John Atkinson, no. 1, pp. 1–2.
32. Chinn Letters, Joe Jordan, *passim*; Mrs Hazel Horsley, nos 1 and 2, *passim*; Chinn Interviews, Bert Jenkins, *passim*. See also Norman Dennis, Fernando Henriques, Clifford Slaughter, *Coal is Our Life. An Analysis of a Yorkshire Mining Community* (London: Tavistock Publications, 1956), pp. 148–9.
33. The Scout, 'North Likes Bets Clubs', *Daily Express*, 30 December 1959.
34. 'Betting Shops in York', *Yorkshire Evening Post*, 10 December 1959.
35. Chinn Letters, Mrs Murrel, no. 1, p. 1 – see also 'Not Criminal, Says Betting Shop Man', *Evening News* (London), 10 October 1957, and 'Police Found Ascot TV on in Gambling Houses', *Evening News*, 21 June 1956; Fred Redman, 'Farce of the Betting Shops. The Danger of a Laughed-At Law', *Sunday Pictorial*, 3 June 1956; Chinn Interviews, Gilbert Kelland, p. 1 – see also 'Betting Shop Run Openly in London', *Sunday Pictorial*, 27 May 1956.
36. Chinn Interviews, Buck Chinn, pp. 18–20 and 41; see also 'They Go Racing at Betting Dens', *Sunday Mercury* (Birmingham), 5 November 1950.
37. *Ibid.*, Jackie Currigan, pp. 3–5; *ibid.*, John Williams, pp. 1–4; *ibid.*, Bill Gallie, pp. 1–9. For Dorking, see Chinn Letters, Mrs Booker, p. 1. For Leicester see Chinn Interviews, Jack Lippit, *passim*, and for Derby see *ibid.*, Trevor Morris, *passim*.
38. Chinn Interviews, Norman Miller, pp. 2–5; see also Alastair Borthwick, 'The Ever Open Door', *Glasgow Evening Citizen*, 13 March 1956; Christopher Hall, 'Inside a Betting Shop', *Daily Express*, 13 September 1956.
39. Peter Donnelly, 'Why the Gamblingest City is No More', *Glasgow Evening Citizen*, 27 September 1966; M. J. Nicholson, 'Las Vegas Fun on Clydeside Sheds Its Glitter', *Bulletin*, 13 December 1955. See also Alastair Borthwick, 'You Bet', *Glasgow Evening Citizen*, 8 March 1956; Cliff Hanley, 'Gambling Hell', *Glasgow Record*, 9 September 1955; Clifford Hanley, *Dancing in the Streets* (first published 1958. London: Corgi, 1983 edn), pp. 193–7.
40. '"Shovel Shops" Lowering Dog Track Attendances', *Scotsman*, 12 July 1957; see also Alistair Cameron, 'The Ready Money Business Gets Curiouser and Curiouser. Bet Shops Mushroom All Over the Town', *Scottish Daily Express*, 13 September 1956.
41. 'Dundee Commission Agent Wins Appeal', *Evening Telegraph* (Dundee), 8 October 1957; 'Sheriff Attacks Use of TV By Bookmakers', *Glasgow Citizen*, 4 October 1956; 'Bailie Condemns Betting Laws', *Kilmarnock Standard*, 14 September 1957; Chinn Interviews, Mac Davidson, *passim*. For Edinburgh, see 'A Blow for "Punters"', *Edinburgh Evening News*, 13 October 1954.
42. Chinn Letters, Ernest Kyle, no. 1, p. 3.
43. *Ibid.*, Norma Brodie, no. 1, p. 2; see also Merrick Winn, 'Yesterday in Glasgow . . . Today in Britain', *Daily Express*, 27 October 1959.

44. Chinn Interviews, Buck Chinn, pp. 45–6; see also 'Birmingham Police Deny that Gambling Laws are Neglected', *Birmingham Post*, 27 March 1954.
45. 'Scarborough and Betting', *Yorkshire Post*, 8 August 1955; Chinn Interviews, Mr Hantman, *passim*, 'Cardiff's Betting Shops', *South Wales Echo*, 11 March 1954; Chinn Interviews, Jim Stock, pp. 8–20; *ibid.*, John Sands, pp. 3–6.
46. See, for example, Douglas Howell, 'These Evil Betting Shops', *Daily Mirror*, 26 February 1953.
47. '"Big-store betting" Not Likely Under New Bill', *Birmingham Gazette*, 10 March 1956; Warren Hill, 'Cash Betting a Little Nearer', *Sporting Life*, 15 September 1954; '"Fantastic Growth of Gambling" is His Main Concern', *Bradford Evening Telegraph and Argus*, 1 February 1957; Herbert, *op. cit.*

9 LEGALIZATION AND COMMERCIALIZATION

1. John Bourne, 'The British Working Man in Arms', in Hugh Cecil and Peter Liddle (eds), *Facing Armageddon* (Barnsley: Leo Cooper, Pen & Sword, 1996, 2003), pp. 336–52.
2. R. C. (1949–51), *Minutes*, 157 and 373–4.
3. See, for example, B. Seebohm Rowntree and G. R. Lavers, *English Life and Leisure. A Social Study* (London: Longmans, Green and Co., 1951).
4. Howard Hodgson, 'Bookmakers and Racing Politics', (unpublished MS, no date), pp. 2–3.
5. *Ibid.* p. 3.
6. *Ibid.*, pp. 4–5.
7. Ward Hill, *op. cit.*, pp. 66–7.
8. *Ibid.*, pp. 13 and 68–9.
9. House of Commons Debates, 11 November 1959, cols 934–5.
10. *Sporting Life*, 16 November 1959.
11. House of Commons Debates, 16 November 1959, cols 807–12.
12. The National Bookmakers' and Associated Bodies' Joint Protection Association, *Notes on the Betting and Gaming Act, 1960* (London: The National Bookmakers' and Associated Bodies' Joint Protection Association: 1960), *passim*; and Betting and Gaming Act, 1960, 8 & 9 Eliz. 2. CH. 60 (London: Her Majesty's Stationery Office, 1960).
13. *Ibid.*
14. *Ibid.*
15. Sid Chaplin, 'Bet you anything', newspaper cutting, no date.
16. 'Betting shop bookies have backed a winner', *Post*, 10 May 1961. Thanks to Celia Harris.
17. Chinn Interviews, Buck Chinn, pp. 33–4.
18. Paley and Glendenning, *op. cit.*, pp. 7 and 21–2.
19. Chinn Interviews, Buck Chinn, p. 27; and Paley and Glendenning, *op. cit.*, pp. 24–5.
20. Chinn Interviews, Buck Chinn, pp. 26–7.
21. Paley and Glendenning, *op. cit.*, pp. 22–3.
22. Chinn Interviews, Buck Chinn, pp. 1–2.
23. Chinn Interviews, Ali Harris, pp. 8–9.

24. Hodgson, 'Bookmakers and Racing Politics', p. 9.
25. Paley and Glendenning, *op. cit.*, p. 13. See also Ward Hill, *op. cit.*, pp. 67–9.
26. John Morgan, 'The biggest bookie in the world', *New Statesman*, April 1964.
27. Paley and Glendenning, *op. cit.*, p. 13.
28. *Ibid.*, pp. 15–16.
29. *Ibid.*, p. 17. See also Ward Hill, *op. cit.*, p. 111.
30. Ron Pollard, *Odds and Sods. My Life in the Betting Business* (first published 1991. Sevenoaks, Kent: Coronet Books, 1992), p. 185.
31. Richard Kaye, *The Ladbrokes Story* (London: Pelham Books, 1969), pp. 43–4.
32. Ken Lawrence, 'Profile. Cyril Stein. Tough bookie the City can always bet on', *Sunday Express*, 6 September 1987.
33. Jamie Reid, *A Licence to Print Money. A Journey through the Gambling and Bookmaking World* (London: Macmillan, 1992), pp. 60–1.
34. *Ibid.*
35. Kaye, *op. cit.*, pp. 146–7.
36. Lawrence, *op. cit.*
37. Ward Hill, *op. cit.*, p. 74.
38. *Ibid*, pp. 78–9.
39. Kaye, *op. cit.*, pp. 155–6.
40. *Ibid.*, pp. 173–5.
41. Munting, *op. cit.*, p. 99.
42. *Ibid.*, p. 98.
43. Graham Rock, 'The good gambler', *Observer*, 1 May 2001.
44. *Ibid.*
45. National Association of Bookmakers, *Into the 1970s with the N.A.B.* (London: National Association of Bookmakers, no date), p. 13.
46. Pollard, *op. cit.*, p. 215.
47. Fred Shawcross, 'The punter's paradise', *Today*, 6 March 1986.
48. Rock, *op. cit.*
49. David Brierley, 'Shake-up threat to bookies', *Sunday Times* cutting, 1986.
50. Munting, *op. cit.*, p. 101–3.
51. *Ibid.*, pp. 99–100.
52. *Ibid*, pp. 100–1.
53. Rock, *op. cit.*
54. Victor Chandler website: www.victorchandler.co.uk.
55. BBC Sports website, 7 March 2001, 17:21 GMT.
56. Mike Brunker, MSNBC website: www.msnbc.com, 7 March 2001.
57. *Ibid.*
58. *Ibid.*
59. *Ibid.*
60. Rock, *op. cit.*
61. Jacques Black, *Spread Betting to Win. The definitive guide to index betting on the sporting and financial markets* (Harpenden: Old Castle Books, 1998), pp. 13–17.
62. 'British online betting exchange upsets world of sports betting', *Malaysian Star*, 21 October 2003.
63. *Ibid.*

64. 'System that empowers the punters', *Express and Star*, 17 March 2004.
65. Rob Davies, 'Gambling on the electronic bookie', *Express and Star*, 17 March 2004.
66. 'British Horseracing Board chairman calls for inquiry into betting exchanges', *Thoroughbred Times*, 10 October 2003.
67. Jamie Doward, 'Betting watchdog to tackle race-fixing', *Observer*, 14 March 2004.
68. John Sexton, 'Police arrest 16 over horse race fix claims', *Express and Star*, 1 September 2004.
69. Joint Committee on the Draft Gambling Bill, Minutes of Evidence, 20 January 2004, Q637.
70. Reid, *op. cit.*, pp. 50–2.
71. *Ibid.*, p. 53.
72. *Ibid.*, p. 91.
73. *Ibid.*, pp. 102–7.
74. 'Memorandum from the National Joint Pitch Council', JC Draft Gambling Bill, December 2003.
75. Reid, *op. cit.*, pp. 93–5.
76. Chinn Interviews, Micky Fletcher, 27 April 2004, pp. 1 and 5.
77. JC Draft Gambling Bill, 20 January 2004, Q650.
78. Jamie Doward, 'Betting watchdog to tackle race-fixing', *Observer*, 14 March 2004.
79. JC Draft Gambling Bill, 20 January 2004, Q636.
80. The Horserace Betting Levy Board's website: www.hblb.org.uk.
81. JC Draft Gambling Bill, 20 January 2004, Q634.
82. 'Internet betting a winner for Hill', *Express and Star*, 6 September 2004.

INDEX